Blackstone's Police Manual

Evidence and Procedure

Blackstone's Police Manual

Volume 2

Evidence and Procedure

2008

David Johnston

LLB, LLM, Barrister

and

Glenn Hutton

BA, MPhil, FCIPD

OXFORD

UNIVERSITY PRESS

Great Clarendon Street, Oxford OX2 6DP

Oxford University Press is a department of the University of Oxford.
It furthers the University's objective of excellence in research, scholarship,
and education by publishing worldwide in

Oxford New York

Auckland Bangkok Buenos Aires Cape Town Chennai
Dar es Salaam Delhi Hong Kong Istanbul Karachi Kolkata
Kuala Lumpur Madrid Melbourne Mexico City Mumbai Nairobi
São Paulo Shanghai Taipei Tokyo Toronto

With offices in

Argentina Austria Brazil Chile Czech Republic France Greece
Guatemala Hungary Italy Japan Poland Portugal Singapore
South Korea Switzerland Thailand Turkey Ukraine Vietnam

Published in the United States
by Oxford University Press Inc., New York

British Library Cataloguing in Publication Data

Data available

Library of Congress Cataloging in Publication Data

Data available

Typeset by Laserwords Private Limited, Chennai, India
Printed and bound in Great Britain by
William Clowes Ltd, Beccles, Suffolk

ISBN 978-0-19-922924-6

10 9 8 7 6 5 4 3 2 1

Foreword for 2008
Blackstone's Police Manuals

The role of a police officer has become more technical and more demanding over the last decades. To be properly qualified as a frontline officer, particularly a frontline supervisor and manager, there is a huge quantity of law, legal precedent and its interpretation that is required. Unlike a barrister, solicitor or judge, who has the books to hand or a website one click away with their mouse, a police officer frequently has to make crucial legal decisions with partial knowledge of all the facts, the pressure of time and events, and the presence of a none-too-cooperative citizen. It is a testimony to the training that officers receive that they get the decisions right most of the time.

However, the training is crucially dependent on the quality of the training materials. These manuals are the product of a partnership between the National Policing Improvement Agency (NPIA) and Blackstone's. The NPIA has a key role in promoting learning and the development of leadership in policing. It is building on more than two decades of national expertise in supporting learning for police officers, and now has responsibility for improving every aspect of learning in the policing profession from recruit training to the most senior ranks. Alongside Blackstone's we are committed to ensuring that the public is served by qualified, well trained and well led officers and police staff. These manuals are a key part of that mission.

Peter Neyroud QPM
Chief Constable and Chief Executive of the
National Policing Improvement Agency

Preface

The Blackstone's Police Manuals are the only official study guides for OSPRE® Part I Police Promotion Examinations—if the law is not in the Manuals, it will not be in the exams.

All the Manuals include explanatory keynotes and case law examples, providing clear and incisive analysis of important areas. As well as covering basic law and procedure they take full account of the PACE Codes of Practice and human rights implications. They can also be used as a training resource for police probationers, special constables and police community support officers, or as an invaluable reference tool for police staff of all ranks and positions. In relation to being used as a reference tool, this is particularly relevant to officers and others involved in the procedures connected with the custody, identification and interviews of offenders, all of which are detailed in Part III of the Manual.

The *Evidence and Procedure* Manual contains a wide range of activities to cover the complex and demanding legislative framework governing the increasing depth and breadth of policing delivery. In an attempt to present this shifting and growing body of national and European law the Manual has been structured in three distinct parts: Part I—The Criminal Justice System; Part II—The Law of Evidence; and Part III—Police Station Procedure.

The majority of the outstanding provisions of the Criminal Justice Act 2003, Domestic Violence, Crime and Victims Act 2004, and Constitutional Reform Act 2005 have now been brought into force and have been included in the Manual. Recent legislation contained within the Manual includes provisions of the Police and Justice Act 2006 and the Violent Crime Reduction Act 2006. The revised PACE Codes of Practice are also included.

An in-depth review of the OSPRE® examination syllabus conducted by National Police Improvement Agency, Examinations and Assessment, feedback from users of the Manual, and a review by the authors, has resulted in a significant reduction in the content, with three chapters being excluded, two other chapters being combined and the remaining chapters amended where required. The result of this rationalisation has been the retention of the law of evidence relevant to policing requirements, whilst affording examination candidates a less onerous task when undertaking their studies.

All recent relevant UK and European case law has been provided together with consideration of the effect of the Human Rights Act 1998.

Although every care is taken to ensure the accuracy of the contents of the Manual, neither the authors nor the publisher can accept any responsibility for any actions taken, or not taken, on the basis of the information contained within it.

Oxford University Press are always happy to receive any useful written feedback from any reader on the content and style of the Manual, especially from those involved in or with the criminal justice system. Please email this address with any comments or queries: police.uk@oup.com.

The law is stated as at 1 June 2007.

Acknowledgements

This is the tenth edition of the *Evidence and Procedure* Manual and each edition has been greatly influenced by the support it receives from across the police service and other parts of the criminal justice system. In particular we would like to express our thanks to the staff of the Legal Services Department of the National Policing Improvement Agency (NPIA) and Examinations and Assessment. The monthly Digest produced by Legal Services Department is an invaluable reference and the informative syllabus review conducted by Examinations and Assessment has helped to shape the content and style of the Manual.

Thanks to George Cooper (Northamptonshire Police), Stuart K. Fairclough (Metropolitan Police), Paul Murphy (Greater Manchester Police), and Kevin Whitehouse (West Midlands Police).

It would be remiss not to acknowledge the contribution made to the series of Manuals by Fraser Sampson since their inception 10 years ago. Last year Fraser became an Executive Director of the Civil Nuclear Police Authority and decided it was time to hand over his authorship of three of the Manuals to others. In addition to being an author, Fraser was also the series editor and retains an editorial consultancy role. We thank him for his support over the years and give him, Claire, and the family, our very best wishes for the future.

Our thanks, as always, to all the staff involved in the production of the Manual in the Academic and Professional Law Department at Oxford University Press, especially Peter Daniell, Lindsey Davis, Rowena Lennon, Janice Sayer, Geraldine Mangley, Paul Hawksworth and Ashley Mackie. Special thanks also to Rosalie for her continued support and forbearance and thanks to Bertie and Hilda.

Contents

Contents

Table of Cases

This table is a compilation of cases referred to in the *Evidence and Procedure* volume of Blackstone's Police Manuals. Case law, containing the decisions of the courts, is one of the primary sources of law in England and Wales.

Cases are referred to by the names of parties. A full citation includes the abbreviation of the law report (of which there are many different series), the volume number and page numbers as follows:

Atkins *v* DPP [2000] 1 WLR 1427

[Names of parties, year case reported, volume no., publication name (Weekly Law Reports), page no.]

In criminal actions the single letter *R* (meaning Rex or Regina) comes first, indicating the state's role as prosecutor, followed by the name of the accused person (the defendant).

In some family cases the report may be headed '*In re Brown*' or in more modern cases, *Re Brown* meaning 'in the matter of'. *Ex parte Brown* may also be used, meaning '*Brown*' is the name of the applicant for whom the case is heard. Where a single letter is used for one of the parties, eg T *v* DPP this means that one of the parties to the case cannot be named for legal reasons.

Cases in the table of cases below are listed alphabetically with references to the relevant paragraph number in this Manual.

Tables of Primary Legislation

These tables are a compilation of all references to Statutes (also known as Acts of Parliament) found in the *Evidence and Procedure* volume of Blackstone's Police Manuals.

Statutes are usually referred to by their short title and date, eg Abortion Act 1967, and in many cases this Manual may refer to just one Part, section (s.) or Schedule (sch.) of an Act. This Manual states the current law as at 1 June 2007 (unless stated otherwise).

The Statutes below are listed alphabetically with references to the relevant paragraph number in this Manual.

International Legislation

EC Legislation

Tables of Secondary Legislation

Secondary, subordinate or delegated legislation is legislation made by a body other than Parliament with powers conferred by Parliament through a specific Act. Secondary legislation is published in the Statutory Instruments (SI) series, and SIs are cited in the following ways:

The Misuse of Drugs Regulations 2001 (SI 2001/2066)
[Title, year, number]

SIs deal with the detail of how legislation is to work in practice and they can be speedily amended or revoked as necessary. They may also be used to bring legislation into force. This Manual states the current law as at 1 June 2007 (unless stated otherwise).

The tables also contain Codes of Practice, which are not legislation but should be regarded as legally binding on the relevant parties unless exceptional circumstances prevail.

The legislation below is listed alphabetically with references to the relevant paragraph number in this Manual.

For further information on sources of law, please see Chapter 1 Sources of Law in this Manual, pages 3–7.

Codes of Practice

Home Office Circulars

How to use this Manual

Volume numbers for the Manuals

The 2008 Blackstone's Police Manuals each have a volume number as follows:

Volume 1: *Crime*

Volume 2: *Evidence and Procedure*

Volume 3: *Road Policing*

Volume 4: *General Police Duties*

The first digit of each paragraph number in the text of the Manuals denotes the Manual number. For example, paragraph 2.3 is Chapter 3 of the *Evidence and Procedure* Manual and 4.3 is Chapter 3 of the *General Police Duties* Manual.

All index entries and references in the Tables of Legislation and the Table of Cases, etc. refer to paragraph numbers instead of page numbers, making information easier to find.

Length of sentence for an offence

Where a length of sentence for an offence is stated in this Manual, please note that the number of months or years stated is the maximum number and will not be exceeded.

OSPRE® Rules & Syllabus Information

The rules and syllabus for the OSPRE® system are defined within the OSPRE® Rules & Syllabus document published by the National Policing Improvement Agency (NPIA) Examinations and Assessment on behalf of the Police Promotions Examination Board (PPEB). The Rules & Syllabus document is published annually each September, and applies to all OSPRE® assessments scheduled for the calendar year following its publication. For example, the September 2007 Rules & Syllabus document would apply to all OSPRE® Part I and Part II assessments held during 2008.

The document provides details of the law and procedure to be tested within the OSPRE® Part I examinations, information on the Part II assessment centre, and also outlines the rules underpinning the OSPRE® system.

All candidates who are taking an OSPRE® Part I examination or Part II assessment centre are strongly encouraged to familiarise themselves with the Rules & Syllabus document during their preparation. The OSPRE® Part I rules also apply to candidates who take the Part I and then go on to apply for their force's work-based assessment promotion trials.

The document can be downloaded from the Recruitment, Assessment and Selection section of the NPIA website, which can be found at www.npia.police.uk. Electronic versions are also supplied to all force OSPRE® contacts.

If you have any problems obtaining the Rules & Syllabus document from the above source, please e-mail the OSPRE® Candidate Administration Team at:
exams.ospre@npia.pnn.police.uk

Usually, no further updates to the Rules & Syllabus document will be issued during its year-long lifespan. However, in exceptional circumstances, the NPIA (on behalf of the PPEB) reserves the right to issue an amended syllabus prior to the next scheduled annual publication date.

For example, a major change to a key area of legislation or procedure (e.g. the Codes of Practice) during the lifespan of the current Rules & Syllabus document would render a significant part of the current syllabus content obsolete. In such circumstances, it may be necessary for an update to the syllabus to be issued, which would provide guidance to candidates on any additional material which would be examinable within their Part I.

In such circumstances, an update to the Rules & Syllabus document would be made available through the NPIA website, and would be distributed to all force OSPRE® contacts. The NPIA will ensure that any syllabus update is distributed well in advance of the examination date, to ensure that candidates have sufficient time to familiarise themselves with any additional examinable material. Where possible, any additional study materials would be provided to candidates free of charge.

Please note that syllabus updates will only be made in *exceptional* circumstances, an update will not be made for every change to legislation included within the syllabus. For further guidance on this issue, candidates are advised to regularly check the NPIA website, or consult their force OSPRE® contact, during their preparation period.

PART ONE

The Criminal Justice System

2.1 | Sources of Law

2.1.1 Introduction

As with most branches of the law in England and Wales, the sources of criminal law are found partly in common law and partly in statute law. However, these sources are impacted on by decisions made by the courts and the rights protected by the European Convention for the Protection of Human Rights. These are all subject of this chapter.

2.1.2 Common Law

Common law originated from the customs of the early communities, which were unified and developed in the Royal Courts during the three centuries following the Norman Conquest.

There is no authoritative text of the common law (although *Stephen's Digest* is one of the most often cited) and, as a whole, its sources lie in the principles of the law declared by the judges in the course of deciding particular cases. It should be noted that the common law can only be declared authoritatively by the judge(s) of the superior courts (i.e. from the High Court) and then only to the extent that it is necessary to do so for the purpose of deciding a particular case. For this reason, the development of the common law has always been dependent upon the incidence of cases arising for decision, and the particular facts of those cases.

Those decisions are the *authoritative sources* of certain offences and powers, in exactly the same way as an Act (such as the Theft Act 1968) and will be relevant irrespective of how ancient the case is—if anything, the older a case authority is, the more persuasive it is, having stood the test of time. A good example of this would be the decision in *Doodeward* v *Spence* (1907) 6 CLR 406 where it was held that a human body could not be 'property' for the purposes of theft (**see Crime, chapter 1.11**). Reviewing this decision in 1998, Lord Justice Rose said that he was reluctant to interfere with a decision which had stood the test of time for so long and left the issue for Parliament.

In relation to certain offences which originate in the common law, e.g. murder, theft, rape, robbery and arson, precise definitions were evolved because the severity of the punishment rendered this necessary. As most were punishable by death, the burden of proof on the prosecution (as to which, **see chapter 2.7**) was also very high—and has remained so ever since. Other offences of similar origin, however, e.g. conspiracy and attempts to commit crime, are notable for the lack of precision in their formulation (**see Crime, chapter 1.3**), and are still being used to bring new sets of facts within the ambit of the criminal law, as in the decisions of *Shaw* v *DPP* [1962] AC 220 and *Knuller (Publishing, Printing and Promotions) Ltd* v *DPP* [1973] AC 435 on conspiracy to corrupt public morals.

2.1.3 **Legislation**

Statutes, in the form of Acts of Parliament, have always been regarded as supplementary to the common law. It is true that the major part of criminal law and procedure is now in statutory form, but it is equally true that the principles of common law, notably in relation to criminal liability generally, homicide and the rules of evidence and procedure at a criminal trial, have not lessened in importance.

Statutes are enacted by Parliament and it is the duty of the court, as and when the occasion arises, to interpret and give effect to the intention of Parliament as expressed in the words of the statute. The courts have the same task in relation to delegated legislation, i.e. in the form of Orders in Council, statutory instruments and bye-laws made by Ministers, heads of Government Departments, local authorities and other bodies under powers delegated to them by Parliament. In looking at the intentions of Parliament, the courts may now consider the content of any debates within either House as reported in *Hansard* (*Pepper* v *Hart* [1993] AC 593).

The only distinction, for practical purposes, between statutes and delegated legislation is that, while the validity of the former cannot be questioned in a court, the latter are valid only within the limits of the powers conferred by the enabling statute, and in the case of bye-laws they must also be reasonable. Consequently, the courts have the power, most notably in the context of judicial review applications (**see para. 2.2.5.7**), to hold that delegated legislation is invalid because the terms of the statute under which it is made have not been complied with.

A statute is construed so far as possible in conformity with the common law, because of the presumption against the alteration of general common law principles. Where the two cannot be reconciled, the statute prevails.

The Interpretation Act 1978 (which is the main authority for interpreting the effect of statutes), s. 18 states:

> Where an act or omission constitutes an offence under two or more Acts, or both under an Act and at common law, the offender shall, unless the contrary intention appears, be liable to be prosecuted and punished under either or any of those Acts or at common law, but shall not be liable to be punished more than once for the same offence.

2.1.4 **Judicial Precedents**

The decision in a criminal trial as to the guilt or innocence of the defendant is a matter for the jury (or the magistrate(s); **see chapter 2.2**) although this decision will only be left to a jury when the trial judge is satisfied that a verdict of guilty would be proper in law on the facts, and that there is evidence which, if believed, would justify such a verdict.

Juries decide questions of *fact*; judges decide questions of *law* (and, confusingly, magistrates decide both *fact and law*), (**see para. 2.2.5.5**), although in relation to the latter, they are advised by the court clerk (**see para. 2.2.6.2**).

Matters of law are solely for the judge who frequently has to rule on these during the course of a trial. Ultimately, the judge directs the jury on the law in summing up. In a trial by jury these rulings and directions alone are important in the development and illustration of the law.

2.1.4.1 The Courts and Decided Cases

The system of courts in England and Wales is a hierarchy, the various courts being related to one another as superior and inferior. An inferior court is generally bound by the decision and directions of a superior court. For example, judges of the Divisional Court and Crown Courts are bound by the decisions of the Court of Appeal. The Appeal Court is in turn bound by the decisions of the House of Lords, which is also bound—to an extent—by decisions of the European Court of Justice. It should be noted that, although the Crown Court is superior to a magistrates' court and enjoys wider powers (**see para. 2.2.8**), it is still a 'lower' court and its decisions are not generally binding on other courts.

When it is said that a decision is binding, or more fully, a binding and authoritative precedent, what is meant is that the *principle of law* on which the decision was based, or the reason for the decision, is binding. This principle of the law is known as the *ratio decidendi* of the case. An example of this would be the decision that, once the prosecution have proved that a defendant was carrying a weapon that is 'offensive' *per se*, there is no need to prove any intention to use that weapon offensively (*Ohlson v Hylton* [1975] 1 WLR 724). (For the law on weapons generally, **see General Police Duties, chapter 4.8.**)

The *ratio decidendi* consists only of the principle(s) of law essential to a decision. A judge, or court as a whole, may sometimes go beyond the facts of a particular case and give an *opinion* on some connected matter, which is intended to be of guidance in future cases. Such an opinion is known as an *obiter dictum*, and may be persuasive, but not binding, on other courts in a future case. Such *obiter dicta* are often made where an important point has arisen from the arguments in an appeal case but that point has not been directly raised by either party to the case.

In some cases, particularly those which go to the House of Lords, the *dissenting* judgment—that is, the speech of a judge who does not agree with his/her fellow judges on the bench—can also be very instructive and it is not uncommon for those judgments to become law through Acts of Parliament at a later date (see, for example, Lord Mustill's speech in the 'Spanner trial' involving sado-masochism (*R v Brown* [1993] 2 All ER 75, at 101)).

Where a case decision becomes authoritative or binding, it is a 'reported' (**see para. 2.1.4.3**) or 'decided' case. Such cases are often referred to as *stated cases*, a description which is inaccurate and also misleading as stated cases are a very specific form of appeal to the Queen's Bench Divisional Court (**see chapter 2.2**).

2.1.4.2 Human Rights Act 1998

Introduction

The Human Rights Act 1998 introduced into English law most of the rights protected by the European Convention for the Protection of Human Rights and Fundamental Freedoms.

The 1998 Act created a statutory general requirement that all past and future legislation be read and given effect in a way that is compatible with the Convention (s. 3).

Briefly, in relation to evidence and procedure, the 1998 Act has the following effects. The courts must:

- decide cases having regard to the compatibility of their decision with Convention rights (s. 6(1));
- interpret existing and future legislation in conformity with the Convention (s. 3); and
- take account of Strasbourg case law where relevant (s. 2(1)).

If a statute or statutory instrument is clear in its terms and not compatible with the Convention, the courts will not give effect to the Convention even though this may result in a breach of a Convention right. This in effect preserves Parliamentary sovereignty (s. 3(2)(b) and (c)) and is different from the position with *EU* law where any incompatible domestic legislation will be 'superseded' by EU legislation. However, the higher courts have the power to issue 'declarations of incompatibility', and a fast-track procedure has been put in place so that the government can legislate to remedy any incompatibility (ss. 4 and 10 and sch. 2).

In relation to taking account of Strasbourg case law the obligation on UK courts is considered less than an obligation to adopt or apply it (*R* v *Davis* [2001] 1 Cr App R 115). In *Tyrer* v *United Kingdom* (1978) 2 EHRR 1 it was recognised that the Convention was a 'living instrument which must be interpreted in the light of present day conditions'. Therefore it may well be that the decision of an earlier case may not be relevant where factors have changed over time. See also *R (on the application of Anderson)* v *Secretary of State for the Home Department* [2002] UKHL 446.

Convention Rights

As indicated in the introduction above, the 1998 Act will have considerable effect on the police but more especially on the courts and their procedures.

This Manual is concerned with those rights that impact directly on 'evidence and procedure'. The Convention rights are contained within sch. 1, part I of the Human Rights Act 1998 (**see General Police Duties, chapter 4.3**).

2.1.4.3 Law Reports

The authority of judicial precedents dates from the beginning of modern law reporting in the eighteenth century. Until 1865, there were numerous private reports, each series published under the name of the reporter, and which are still occasionally referred to today. Since 1865, the Incorporated Council of Law Reporting in England and Wales has published the series known as 'The Law Reports'. These are cited according to the court (e.g. Appeal Court; Queen's Bench Divisional Court) in which the case was heard and the year in which the case is reported (e.g. *R* v *Brown* [1994] 1 AC 212; *R* v *Bryant* [1979] QB 108).

These reports are now supplemented by various commercial series, of which the best known are:

- Criminal Appeal Reports (e.g. *R* v *Bray* (1988) 88 Cr App R 354);
- Justice of the Peace Reports (e.g. *R* v *Britzman* (1983) 147 JP 531);
- All England Law Reports (e.g. *R* v *Bryce* [1992] 4 All ER 567);
- Weekly Law Reports (e.g. *R* v *Khan* [1996] 3 WLR 162);
- Criminal Law Review (e.g. *R* v *Deakin* [1972] Crim LR 781).

The examples shown in parentheses are how cases are usually referenced (cited) in law texts. The numbers which follow the date in a reported case are simply the *volume*, and then the *page* where the report begins, or the page where the relevant speech of the judge can be found. Many important cases can be found in a number of different reports, though decisions of the House of Lords are usually to be found in the Appeal Cases (AC).

Since January 2001 all cases from the Court of Appeal and all the divisions of the High Court have been assigned what are known as neutral citations. This was extended in 2002 to cover cases from the House of Lords. Each case is given a unique number to identify the case which is not tied to any law report series, and which may be cited in court. These include:

- England and Wales Court of Appeal (e.g. *R* v *Ashton* [2006] EWCA Crim 794);

- England and Wales High Court (e.g. *R (on the application of Malik)* v *Central Criminal Court* [2006] EWHC 1539 (Admin));
- United Kingdom House of Lords (e.g. *Jones* v *Whalley* [2006] UKHL 41).

In the examples given 'EWCA Crim' refers to cases heard in the Criminal Division of the Court of Appeal, and 'EWHC (Admin)' to cases heard in the Administrative Division of the High Court. Wherever possible, references to neutral citations are used throughout the Manual.

When researching a legal reference it is worth remembering that many authors in criminal law texts refer simply to the surname or family name of the defendant (e.g. *Deakin* and not '*R* v *Deakin*').

In relation to the European Court of Human Rights, cases are cited in relation to the appellant and country concerned, e.g. *Campbell and Fell* v *United Kingdom* (1984) 7 EHRR 165.

Individual judgments and decisions are published by the Council of Europe under the title *Publications of the European Court of Human Rights*. In the United Kingdom, the best source available is the *European Human Rights Reports* (EHRR) which publishes all the Court judgments and the important decisions of the Commission.

Current decisions and judgments can be found on the Internet at the Court's website: www.echr.coe.int/

(Note that the European Commission of Human Rights ceased to exist in November 1998 and all cases are now dealt with by the European Court of Human Rights.)

In addition to the above reports, notes of cases are also published in some newspapers, e.g. *The Times* and the *Independent*.

Other reports of cases which may appear in newspapers for their general news value are *not* 'reported' cases and this often causes frustration when trying to look up a particular case that has appeared in the press.

2.2 | The Courts

2.2.1 Introduction

The nature of an offence will determine in which court a case is heard. In England and Wales offences can be tried in either the magistrates' court or the Crown Court. Cases tried in the magistrates' court are tried by either a district judge (magistrates' courts), who is a qualified lawyer, or a panel of lay magistrates (**see para. 2.2.6**). Offences committed by a child or young person are generally heard in the youth court (**see para. 2.2.7**). In the magistrates' court the magistrates decide on questions of law and fact. Cases tried in the Crown Court are presided over by a judge, who is a qualified lawyer; he/she decides on any points of law while questions of fact are decided by a jury (**see para. 2.2.8**). All cases will start with the defendant appearing at the magistrates' court who will either deal with the matter themselves or commit the case to the Crown Court for trial or, on occasions, for sentence.

The purpose of this chapter is to provide an overview of the categories of offences and the criminal courts where these are dealt with, appeals, juries, tribunals and inquiries, and information on the European Court of Justice and European Court of Human Rights.

2.2.2 Categories of Trial

Offences are categorised in three groups:

- summary offences—which can only be tried in the magistrates' courts.
- indictable offences—which can only be tried in the Crown Court
- either way offences—which are capable of being tried in either court.

2.2.2.1 Summary Offences

Where statutes create offences and provide for a maximum penalty imposable on summary conviction, but do not provide for a penalty on conviction on indictment, the offences are summary offences.

Summary offences tend to be considered as less 'serious' in the eyes of the law and can only be tried in the magistrates' court (s. 2 of the Magistrates' Courts Act 1980—**see para. 2.2.6**). The Powers of Criminal Courts (Sentencing) Act 2000, s. 78 provides that the maximum sentence of imprisonment for a summary offence is six months or the sentence prescribed in the statute creating the offence. When the provisions of the Criminal Justice Act 2003 are in force the maximum sentence of imprisonment will be 12 months (s. 154) or 51 weeks for a number of summary offences (sch. 26). The maximum fine for a summary offence is prescribed in the offence-creating provision where any fine is fixed to a level on the standard scale of fines; the current maximum is £5,000.

When an offender is charged with either way or indictable offences, which go to the Crown Court, any linked or connected summary offences may also go to the Crown Court, though these may not necessarily be pursued (Criminal Justice Act 1988, ss. 40 and 41).

2.2.2.2 Indictable Offences

Where statutes create offences and provide only for a penalty on conviction on indictment, the offences are indictable offences. All common law offences are indictable offences.

These offences are considered to be the more serious offences and must be dealt with in the Crown Court whether the person pleads guilty or not. There are no committal proceedings for indictable-only offences (ss. 51, 51A–51E and 52 and sch. 3 to the Crime and Disorder Act 1998); a much quicker and simple procedure is followed called 'sending for trial' (ss. 51A–51E inserted by the Criminal Justice Act 2003 are not yet in force).

2.2.2.3 Either Way Offences

Where statutes create offences and provide for both a maximum penalty imposable on summary conviction and for a penalty on conviction on indictment, the offences are known as triable either way offences.

The procedure to determine whether an either way offence is dealt with summarily (in the magistrates' court), or on indictment (in the Crown Court), is provided by ss. 17A–21 of the Magistrates' Courts Act 1980. This applies only to a person who has attained the age of 18 when they first appear before the court (for persons under 18 **see para. 2.2.3**).

If an either way offence is dealt with in the magistrates' court the maximum term of imprisonment that can be imposed is six months and a fine of £5,000. However, when the provisions of the Criminal Justice Act 2003 are in force the maximum term of imprisonment will be 12 months (s. 282).

2.2.2.4 Either Way Offences: Mode of Trial Hearing

The magistrates' court will convene a mode of trial hearing, the first part of which is known as the 'plea before venue'. The defendant will be asked to indicate a plea of guilty or not guilty to the either way offence with which they have been charged. If the indication is a *guilty plea* the case can be dealt with by the magistrates' court and it would then proceed to sentence. However, the court may commit the defendant to the Crown Court if they consider the offence itself is so serious, and/or where the defendant's previous convictions are such, that they consider their powers of punishment to be inadequate. When in force, a further reason for a magistrates' court to commit a defendant to the Crown Court is where the summary or either way offence is related to an offence for which the defendant or another defendant has been sent for trial to the Crown Court. (New s. 51(3)–(5) of the Crime and Disorder Act 1998 substituted by the Criminal Justice Act 2003.)

Where the defendant indicates a *not guilty plea* the magistrates will initially determine the mode of trial, by considering the seriousness of the offence, the defendant's previous convictions, and assessing whether their powers of punishment are sufficient (s. 17A(4)).

The court will hear representations from both the prosecution and the defence. If they decide not to deal with the case it will be committed to the Crown Court for trial (**see para. 2.2.8**). However, even where the magistrates accept jurisdiction, the defendant retains the right to choose between being dealt with by the magistrates' court or the Crown Court (s. 20(2)(b)).

In cases where the accused is charged with a specified violent or sexual offence (s. 224 of the Criminal Justice Act 2003) the magistrates may still hear the case summarily, with the accused's consent, but if convicted may commit him/her for sentence to the Crown Court (s. 20(2)(c)).

The accused may require the magistrates to indicate the type of sentence they would consider appropriate if he/she pleaded guilty to the offence(s) charged. The magistrates have a broad discretion as to whether or not to provide such an indication. The court is only bound by this indication where the accused has entered a guilty plea (s. 20(3)–(9)).

Where the magistrates' court determine to hear the case summarily, even where the accused has pleaded not guilty or not entered any plea at the plea before venue hearing, and they find the accused guilty, they cannot commit him/her for sentence to the Crown Court (Powers of Criminal Courts (Sentencing) Act 2000, s. 3). As discussed above, this does not apply to specified violent or sexual offences.

KEYNOTE

Practice Direction (Criminal Proceedings: Consolidation) [2002] 1 WLR 2870, para. V51, Mode of Trial, provides magistrates' courts with guidance, not direction, in relation to where either way offences should be tried. Generally the guidelines recommend that such offences should be tried summarily unless certain conditions apply, or where the magistrates consider their sentencing powers are insufficient.

2.2.3 Offences Committed by Juveniles

The general principle is that persons under the age of 18 years should be tried and sentenced in the youth court for both summary and indictable offences. However, the Magistrates' Courts Act 1980, s. 24, provides three exceptions where the trial of a juvenile can take place in the Crown Court for offences:

- of homicide (murder, manslaughter or causing or allowing the death of a child or vulnerable adult (Domestic Violence, Crime and Victims Act 2004, s. 5)), or a firearms offence under the Firearms Act 1968, s. 51A, or where s. 29(3) of the Violent Crime Reduction Act 2006 (minimum sentences in certain cases of using someone to mind a weapon) would apply if the juvenile were convicted of the offence
- mentioned within the terms of s. 91 of the Powers of Criminal Courts (Sentencing) Act 2000 (offenders under 18 convicted of certain serious offences: powers to detain for specified periods); namely offences carrying a sentence of 14 years or more imprisonment in the case of an adult and specified sexual offences
- jointly charged with an adult who has been sent for trial for the same or related offence.

In determining whether a juvenile jointly charged with an adult should be sent to the Crown Court for trial, the magistrates' court must decide whether or not it is in the interests of justice to do so (s. 24(1)(b)). The younger the juvenile, the less serious the charge(s), and the lesser degree of involvement of the juvenile in the offence(s) may determine whether or not they should be sent for trial to the Crown Court. In *R (on the application of the Director of Public Prosecutions) v South East Surrey Youth Court* [2005] EWHC 2929 (Admin) it was held that even where a juvenile is jointly charged with an adult the case is better dealt with in the youth court.

Where a youth court deal with a juvenile for indictable offences they may still commit the juvenile for sentence to the Crown Court. These provisions are contained within:

- s. 91(1) of the Powers of Criminal Courts (Sentencing) Act 2000, where the youth court considers its powers of sentencing insufficient or the juvenile has pleaded guilty and been convicted of an offence but for other related offences has been committed to the Crown Court for trial
- s. 226 of the Criminal Justice Act 2003, life sentences for dangerous offenders
- s. 228 of the 2003 Act, extended sentences.

In relation to s. 24 of the Magistrates' Courts Act 1980 and s. 91 of the Powers of Criminal Courts (Sentencing) Act 2000, it has been held that these sections only apply to offences of such gravity that a court is likely to consider a sentence of at least two years' detention (*R (On the Application of D)* v *Manchester City Youth Court* [2001] EWHC 860 (Admin)).

The trial of juveniles in the Crown Court has proved a contentious area particularly regarding breaches of a juvenile's right to a fair trial when considered by the European Court of Human Rights. In the Jamie Bulger case, the two year old abducted and murdered by two boys both aged 10, the European Court held that the boys had been denied a fair trial under Article 6(1) (*V* v *UK* (2000) 30 EHRR 121). Similarly, in *S.C.* v *UK* (2005) 40 EHRR 226, it was held that an 11 year old boy did not receive a fair trial because his intellectual level was unusually low. However, in *R (on the application of P)* v *West London Youth Court* [2005] EWHC 2583 (Admin) where the accused was aged 15 with an intellect of 8, it was held that there was no breach of Article 6 where the youth court adapted its procedures so that the defendant could effectively participate in the proceedings. Special measure directions available to witnesses (**see para. 2.5.10**) are not available to juvenile defendants, and although counter to the decision of *V* v *United Kingdom* (2000) 30 EHRR 121, in *R* v *H (Special Measures)* [2003] EWCA Crim 1208 it was held that other types of assistance can be provided by the trial judge, in this case by helping an accused with learning difficulties. These issues have been addressed by the Consolidated Criminal Practice Direction, para. IV. 39, *Trial of children and young persons* (*see Blackstone's Criminal Practice, 2008*), which contains detailed guidance on the trial procedure for juveniles in the Crown Court).

There are also two instances where a juvenile can be tried in the adult magistrates' court. Generally, these are where a juvenile is jointly charged with an adult (s. 46(1) of the Children and Young Persons Act 1933), and where a juvenile is charged with aiding, abetting, causing, procuring, allowing or permitting an adult to commit an offence (s. 18 of the Children and Young Persons Act 1963).

2.2.4 Limitation on Proceedings

In the law of England and Wales the general rule is that there is no restriction on the time which may elapse between the commission of an offence and the commencement of a prosecution for it. However, there are a number of statutory provisions prohibiting proceedings once a certain time has elapsed. The relevant provisions are outlined below.

2.2.4.1 Summary Offences

Section 127 of the Magistrates' Courts Act 1980 states:

(1) Except as otherwise expressly provided by any enactment and subject to subsection (2) below, a magistrates' court shall not try an information or hear a complaint unless the information was

laid, or the complaint made, within 6 months from the time when the offence was committed, or the matter of complaint arose.

KEYNOTE

Where there is uncertainty as to whether an information has been laid in time, the magistrates should use the ordinary criminal standard of proof (*Atkinson* v *DPP* [2004] EWHC 1457 (Admin)). In *R* v *Clerk to the Medway Justices, ex parte DHSS* (1986) 150 JP 4012, the clerk refused to issue a summons because four months had been allowed to elapse between the interview of the suspect and the laying of an information.

The day on which the offence etc. arose is not to be included when determining the time limit. A 'month' means a calendar month and a month ends at midnight on the day of the next month which has the same number as the day on which the offence was committed. For example, X commits a driving licence offence at 10am on 24 September; the information should be laid before midnight on 24 March the following year, i.e. within six months.

2.2.4.2 Indictable Offences (Either Way and Indictable Only)

Section 127 of the Magistrates' Courts Act 1980 states:

(2) Nothing in—
  (a) subsection (1) above; or
  (b) subject to subsection (4) below, any other enactment (however framed or worded) which, as regards any offence to which it applies, would but for this section impose a time-limit on the power of a magistrates' court to try an information summarily or impose a limitation on the time for taking summary proceedings,
  shall apply in relation to any indictable offence.
(3) Without prejudice to the generality of paragraph (b) of subsection (2) above, that paragraph includes enactments which impose a time-limit that applies only in certain circumstances (for example where the proceedings are not instituted by or with the consent of the Director of Public Prosecutions or some other specified authority).
(4) Where, as regards any indictable offence, there is imposed by any enactment (however framed or worded, and whether falling within subsection (2)(b) above or not) a limitation on the time for taking proceedings on indictment for that offence no summary proceedings for that offence shall be taken after the latest time for taking proceedings on indictment.

In the case of an offence triable either way, where there is no time limit for taking proceedings on indictment, there is no time limit for summary proceedings. Where there is a time limit on indictment, summary proceedings cannot be taken once the time limit bars proceedings on indictment.

The definition of 'indictable offence' under s. 64(1)(a) of the Criminal Law Act 1977 includes offences triable either way. Section 127 excludes purely indictable offences and offences triable either way from the operation of s. 127(1) of the Magistrates' Courts Act 1980 (which prohibits summary trial where the information is not laid within six months of the offence being committed). Consequently, an offence triable either way such as theft, contrary to ss. 1 to 7 of the Theft Act 1968 (**see Crime, chapter 1.11**) can still be tried summarily after the six-month limitation has expired.

Although there is no time limit on instituting proceedings for indictable (and either way) offences, unless specifically stated within statute, consideration needs to be given to the European Convention on Human Rights. In *Attorney-General's Reference (No. 2 of 2001)* [2004] 2 AC 72, the right to a fair trial under Article 6, which includes the right to have a trial in a reasonable time, was considered. It was held that if a breach of a reasonable time requirement occurred it could not be cured and would be in breach of the Convention right.

2.2.5 Appeals

A person has a right of appeal from the magistrates' court to the Crown Court, following a plea of not guilty, against either conviction and/or sentence and, following a guilty plea, against sentence (s. 108(1) of the Magistrates' Courts Act 1980). In certain circumstances both the defence and prosecution have a right to appeal to the Crown Court or Divisional Court of the Queen's Bench Division, by way of 'case stated'; this challenges whether the process was correctly followed in the case and examines whether the magistrates' court either incorrectly applied the law or exceeded their powers (s. 111(1) of the Magistrates' Courts Act 1980).

2.2.5.1 Leave to Appeal

Appeals from the Crown Court to the Court of Appeal (Criminal Division) normally require leave to be heard unless it is purely an appeal on a point of law. Leave is also required for appeals to the House of Lords which will usually be granted where the appeal raises a question of law of general public importance.

2.2.5.2 Appeals Against Conviction and Sentence

Appeals Against Conviction

The determination of appeals is provided by s. 2 of the Criminal Appeal Act 1968, which states:

> (1) Subject to the provisions of this Act, the Court of Appeal—
>   (a) shall allow an appeal against conviction if they think that the conviction is unsafe; and
>   (b) shall dismiss such an appeal in any other case.

This does not mean that every time a mistake has been made during a trial that a conviction must be overturned. The ultimate question is whether the conviction is *unsafe* (*Stafford* v *DPP* [1974] AC 878). If the court take the view that it is, and that there has been a 'miscarriage of justice', the conviction will not stand. The approach taken by the Court of Appeal is shown in the judgment of *R* v *Cohen* (1909) 2 Cr App R 197, where the court explained:

> There is such a miscarriage of justice not only where the court comes to the conclusion that the verdict of guilty was wrong, but also when it is of opinion that the mistake of fact or omission on the part of the judge may reasonably be considered to have brought about that verdict, and when, on the whole facts and with a correct direction, the jury might fairly and reasonably have found the appellant not guilty. Then there has been not only a miscarriage of justice but a substantial one, because the appellant has lost the chance which was fairly open to him of being acquitted. ... If, however, the court in such a case comes to the conclusion that, on the whole of the facts and with a correct direction, the only reasonable and proper verdict would be one of guilty, there is no miscarriage of justice, or at all events no substantial miscarriage of justice ...

The effect of this approach is that, on occasions, even if it concludes that certain evidence was wrongly admitted or that a judge failed to do something relevant to the defendant's trial, the Court of Appeal may still refuse to overturn the conviction.

In addition to allowing or dismissing an appeal, where a defendant is found guilty by a jury the Court of Appeal may substitute a conviction of an alternative offence on the same facts (s. 3).

Appeals Against Sentence

Appeals against sentence, where the defendant has pleaded guilty to an offence, are provided by ss. 9 to 11 of the Criminal Appeal Act 1968. The occasions when such appeals will be allowed are usually where the sentence was wrong in law, in principle or manifestly excessive. Normally, where an appeal is allowed, the sentence is reduced, or the Court of Appeal may substitute a conviction of an alternative offence where the facts admitted justify a conviction of that other offence (s. 3A).

The Criminal Justice Act 2003, sch. 22, para. 14(1) introduced a new transitional appeal which provides a right of appeal to the Court of Appeal and the House of Lords, if appropriate, to prisoners who have had their minimum term of a mandatory life sentence either reviewed or determined by the High Court (Criminal Justice Act 2003 (Mandatory Life Sentences: Appeals in Transitional Cases) Order 2005 (SI 2798/2005)).

Criminal Cases Review Commission

The Criminal Cases Review Commission was set up by the Criminal Appeal Act 1995 to investigate allegations of miscarriages of justice. The Commission may refer cases to the Court of Appeal for both conviction and sentence of an offence on indictment (s. 9(1)). It may also refer cases to the Crown Court in relation to conviction and sentence imposed in the magistrates' court (s. 11).

2.2.5.3 Appeals to the House of Lords

Appeals to the House of Lords, from a decision of the Criminal Division of the Court of Appeal, can be by the prosecution and defence. Before an appeal can be heard in the House of Lords the Court of Appeal must certify that the decision which is sought to appeal involves a point of law of general public importance. In addition either the Court of Appeal or the House of Lords believes the point of law is one that ought to be considered by the House of Lords (s. 33 of the Criminal Appeal Act 1968).

2.2.5.4 Appeals and Human Rights Considerations

In relation to appeal proceedings, Article 6 of the European Convention on Human Rights (right to a fair trial) applies. For the purpose of satisfying the requirements of Article 6 it is sufficient, after hearing the evidence and submissions, for the court to determine whether the applicant's convictions were safe and satisfactory. It has also been held that the 'presumption of innocence' does not apply in appeal proceedings (*Callaghan* v *United Kingdom* (1989) 60 DR 296). An appeal can be heard in the absence of the defendant and again this is not in breach of Article 6 (*Prinz* v *Austria* (2001) 31 EHRR 12).

2.2.5.5 The Appeals Process

Cases can be appealed for a number of reasons:

- questions of fact
- questions of law
- mixed questions of fact and law.

Questions of Fact

This is an appeal on the basis that the facts do not support the decision that has been reached. These appeals are unlikely to succeed as an appellate court will not change a decision of fact unless it feels that no reasonable tribunal could have reached the decision made by the trial court.

The Crown Court is not bound by the findings of fact by the magistrates' court and so where the defendant appeals against sentence to the Crown Court, the Crown Court may determine the appeal on a different factual basis to that accepted by the magistrates. Where the Crown Court is minded to reflect the view taken by the magistrates, and that view was unfavourable to the defendant, the Crown Court should warn the defendant that this is so and give him/her the opportunity to challenge the factual basis the Crown Court wishes to adopt (*Bussey* v *Chief Constable of Suffolk* [1999] 1 Cr App R (S) 125).

Questions of Law

Unlike questions of fact (which are decided by the jury), questions of law are determined by the trial judge or judges. Of course, in a magistrates' court, the magistrate(s) decides on both questions and therefore, to understand an appeal proceeding from a magistrates' court, it is first necessary to understand whether that appeal is based on a question of fact or law. An appeal on a question of law is one where a party to the proceedings wishes a higher court to give a ruling on the *interpretation* or *application* of the law, for instance, what 'recklessness' means in relation to criminal damage (**see Crime, para. 1.1.4.2**).

Having considered the question of law, the higher court will then give a judgment on the point. This will either allow the original court hearing the case to continue with it or, in some circumstances, allow the appeal court to decide the outcome of the case.

Mixed Questions of Fact and Law

As the heading suggests, this is where a party to the proceedings appeals on an issue which requires the appeal court to consider both a question of fact and a point of law. This often involves the court being asked to make a finding, first on the facts and then to interpret them in relation to the law. This allows parties to take a case to the appeal court on occasions where, if it were just a question of fact, an appeal would not be allowed.

2.2.5.6 Appeals by Prosecution

Appeals Against Acquittal

The rule against 'double jeopardy' has been part of common law for centuries. In the leading case, *Connelly* v *DPP* [1964] AC 1254 it was held that, 'A man may not be tried for a crime in respect of which he has previously been acquitted or convicted.' However, the following statutory provisions provide for occasions where a person may be tried again even though they have been acquitted.

The Criminal Procedure and Investigations Act 1996, ss. 54 to 57 deals with what is referred to as 'tainted acquittals' where an accused has been wrongly acquitted of an offence due to the interference with or intimidation of a juror or witness.

The High Court is required to grant an order quashing the acquittal.

The Criminal Justice Act 2003, ss. 75 to 97 provide that a prosecutor, with the written consent of the Director of Public Prosecutions, can apply to the Court of Appeal to quash a person's acquittal for a qualifying or lesser qualifying offence (s. 76). A 'qualifying offence' means an offence listed in part 1 of sch. 5 (s. 75(8)). The measures may also apply to some acquittals under foreign jurisdiction for equivalent offences to those specified in the 2003 Act. A retrial must be ordered if there is new and compelling evidence in the case and it is in the interests of justice for an order to be made. Evidence is new if it was not adduced in previous proceedings, either at trial or on appeal, and is compelling if it is reliable, substantial and appears highly probative of the case against the acquitted person (s. 78).

Appeals Against Rulings

The Criminal Justice Act 2003 provides that the prosecution can appeal to the Court of Appeal against certain rulings by a judge in a trial on indictment (ss. 57 to 74). The prosecution may appeal against a ruling made, at any time up to the start of the judge's summing-up to the jury (or at any time up to when the judge would have started his summing-up to the jury in a trial without a jury), that in the absence of a right of appeal, would necessitate the prosecution offering no further evidence (s. 58). The Court of Appeal may confirm, reverse or vary any ruling that is appealed against. Section 62 (not yet in force) provides the prosecution with an additional right to appeal against one or more evidentiary rulings made by a judge in a trial on indictment before the opening of the case for the defence. The ruling must relate to a qualifying offence, most of which carry a maximum sentence of life imprisonment (sch. 4). The Court of Appeal may not reverse a ruling unless it was wrong in law, involved an error of law or principle, or it was not reasonable for the judge to have made.

Appeals by the Attorney-General

The prosecution can appeal to the Court of Appeal to test the correctness of a ruling of law which occurred during the course of a trial in the Crown Court (Criminal Justice Act 1972, s. 36). The importance of this is to ensure that a potentially false decision of law does not affect future decisions of other courts (*Attorney-General's Reference (No. 1 of 1975)* [1975] 1 QB 773). The accused remains acquitted whatever the outcome of the appeal and the procedure to be adopted on making a reference is contained in the Criminal Appeal (Reference of Points of Law) Rules 1973 (SI 1973/1114).

Sections 35 and 36 of the Criminal Justice Act 1988 provide that where the Attorney-General considers an offender was sentenced unduly leniently by the Crown Court he may refer the case to the Court of Appeal for a review of the sentence (see *Attorney-General's Reference (No. 104 of 2004) sub nom. R v Garvey* [2005] Crim LR 150). The cases that can be referred are contained in Schedule 1 to the 1988 Act and include:

- offences which are triable only on indictment (para. 1);
- listed miscellaneous offences (para. 2);
- listed offences under the Sexual Offences Act 2003 (para. 3);
- attempting to commit or inciting the commission of most offences listed in paragraphs 2 and 3 (para. 4).

In each case, leave of the Court of Appeal is required before a referral can be made. Additionally, it must appear to the Attorney-General that the judge erred in law as to his powers of sentencing, or failed to impose a sentence required by s. 51A(2) of the Firearms Act 1968, by ss. 110(2) or 111(2) of the Powers of Criminal Courts (Sentencing) Act 2000, or by any of ss. 225 to 228 of the Criminal Justice Act 2003.

Where sentence is passed following a period of deferral it is wrong to allow the Attorney-General leave to refer the sentence as being unduly lenient (*Attorney-General's Reference (No. 118 of 2004) sub nom. R v Barrett* (2004) *The Times*, 29 November).

2.2.5.7 Judicial Review

Judicial review is a method of challenging decisions made by administrative bodies and office holders such as the police service. Cases can range from policy decisions made by the organisation—such as the decision not to prosecute someone—to decisions made by individual supervisors (e.g. the cautioning of a juvenile). The circumstances under which a matter can go before the High Court for judicial review are quite limited. Generally, applications for judicial review can only proceed if there is no other method by which to appeal the decision. An application for judicial review must be made as soon as reasonably practicable and generally within three months of the decision. In reviewing the decision the High Court can look at whether the administrative body or individual was acting within the law when making that decision; it will also consider whether the decision was a reasonable one and whether the common law rules of natural justice were applied.

The procedure for applying for judicial review is provided by s. 31 of the Supreme Court Act 1981 and part 54 of the Civil Procedure Rules 1998.

Whether a decision was made within the law will be determined by a number of features surrounding the decision-making process. These would include:

- whether the organisation or individual actually had the authority or power to make the decision;
- what procedure was followed and whether that procedure observed the requirements of 'natural justice';
- whether the decision-maker exercised his/her own discretion or whether he/she delegated or fettered that discretion in a way which was not permitted in law.

This is one reason why the documentation and recording of any significant decision-making procedure is important.

In reviewing whether or not a decision is 'reasonable' the court will consider whether the decision is one that any reasonable person in the position of the decision-maker could have made, applying the *Wednesbury* principles (from the case of *Associated Provincial Picture Houses Ltd* v *Wednesbury Corporation* [1948] 1KB 223). The court is not asking whether *it* would have made that decision itself; it is asking whether the decision was lawfully and reasonably made in the circumstances. Therefore it would be possible for conflicting decisions made under similar circumstances to be upheld provided both were lawful and reasonable. If the court considers that a decision is unreasonable or unlawful it can make a declaration to that effect.

The declaration can be made in one of three ways: a mandatory order instructing the administrative body to perform a function that it is required to perform (i.e., a chief officer must consider each case involving officers convicted of drink-driving on its merits and not have a blanket policy requiring them to resign); a quashing order where the court quashes the earlier decision (e.g. a caution given to a juvenile where there was insufficient evidence to obtain a conviction); a prohibiting order directing the administrative body *not* to perform an act which the court has found to be unlawful or outside the body's power (*Practice Direction (Administrative Court: Establishment)* [2000] 1 WLR 1654).

The key points to remember are that applications for judicial review are made to the High Court, they will only be heard if there are no other avenues of appeal available and that the application has been made as soon as reasonably practicable.

Following the case of *Smith and Grady* v *United Kingdom* (2000) 29 EHRR 493 where the Court noted that judicial review did not allow the applicants to challenge the armed forces ban as being contrary to the European Convention on Human Rights and the requirement for the courts to apply the Convention, the *Wednesbury* principles will be replaced by more stringent tests under human rights law.

2.2.6 Magistrates' Courts

The Magistrates' Courts Act 1980 provides that a magistrates' court has the jurisdiction:

- to try any summary offence (**see para. 2.2.2.1**)
- to try summarily certain either way offences (**see para. 2.2.2.3**)
- to try summarily an indictable offence (**see para. 2.2.2.2**)
- over offences conferred on the court by any other enactment
- as examining justices over any offence committed by a person who is brought before the court.

Section 1(1) of the 1980 Act provides that a justice of the peace may issue a summons or warrant where a person has or is suspected of having committed an offence (**see para. 2.3.4**).

2.2.6.1 Justices of the Peace

Magistrates' courts consist of justices of the peace (otherwise known as 'lay justices'), the majority of whom are unpaid lay men and women. A minority of justices are paid and are known as District Judges (Magistrates' Courts) and Deputy District Judges (Magistrates' Courts) (**see para. 2.2.6.3**).

2.2.6.2 Justices' Clerks and Assistant Clerks

Section 27 of the Courts Act 2003 provides that a justices' clerk may be appointed by the Lord Chancellor (the Lord Chief Justice will undertake this role when the provisions of the Constitutional Reform Act 2005 are in force) only if he/she has a five-year magistrates' court qualification, is a barrister or solicitor who has served for not less than five years as an assistant to a justices' clerk or has previously been a justices' clerk. A justices' clerk is assigned to one or more local justice areas.

An assistant clerk may be employed as a clerk in court only if he/she is a barrister or solicitor of the Supreme Court or has passed the necessary examinations for either of those professions, or has been granted an exemption in relation to any examination by the appropriate examining body (The Assistants to Justices' Clerks Regulations 2006, reg. 3 (SI 2006/3405)).

The functions of a justices' clerk include giving advice to any or all of the justices of the peace to whom he/she is clerk about matters of law (including procedure and practice) on questions arising in connection with the discharge of their functions (s. 28(4)).

The Justices' Clerks Rules 2005 (SI 2005/545), rr. 2 and 3, make provisions enabling things to be done by a single justice of the peace also to be done by a justices' clerk or an assistant clerk.

2.2.6.3 District and Deputy District Judges (Magistrates' Courts)

District and Deputy District Judges (Magistrates' Courts) are both paid and legally qualified barristers or solicitors of at least seven years' standing who are appointed by Her Majesty on the recommendation of the Lord Chancellor. They may be removed from office by the Lord Chancellor on the grounds of incapacity or misbehaviour (ss. 22 and 24 of the Courts Act 2003).

These judges, by virtue of their office, are justices of the peace for England and Wales and may act as such in accordance with arrangements made by or on behalf of the Lord

Chancellor (s. 25). District Judges (Magistrates' Courts) are able to sit alone in court apart from granting or transferring a licence (s. 26).

2.2.7 Youth Courts

The constitution of youth courts is governed by s. 45 of the Children and Young Persons Act 1933, which states:

(1) Magistrates' courts—
 (a) constituted in accordance with this section or section 66 of the Courts Act 2003 (judges having powers of District Judges (Magistrates' Courts)), and
 (b) sitting for the purpose of—
  (i) hearing any charge against a child or young person, or
  (ii) exercising any other jurisdiction conferred on youth courts by or under this or any other Act,
 are to be known as youth courts.
(2) A justice of the peace is not qualified to sit as a member of a youth court for the purpose of dealing with any proceedings unless he has an authorisation extending to the proceedings.

KEYNOTE

The Lord Chancellor may make rules about the qualifications required before a justice of the peace may be authorised to sit as a member of a youth court. These personal authorisations will be valid throughout England and Wales. These rules may also include the provisions for the appointment of chairmen of youth courts and the composition of such courts (Courts Act 2003, s. 50(4)).

Although District Judges (Magistrates' Courts) may sit alone in a youth court, where lay justices are sitting there should be no more than three and wherever possible one should be a man and one a woman. Where no man or woman is available to sit as a properly constituted court a decision to proceed with the case must be made in open court after hearing submissions from all the parties (*R* v *Birmingham Youth Court, ex parte F (a minor)* [2000] Crim LR 588).

2.2.7.1 Restrictions on Persons Present and Reporting

Restrictions are placed on those persons who may be present during proceedings in the youth court and this is contained in s. 47(2) of the 1933 Act which states:

(2) No person shall be present at any sitting of a youth court except—
 (a) members and officers of the court;
 (b) parties to the case before the court, their solicitors and counsel, and witnesses and other persons directly concerned in that case;
 (c) bona fide representatives of newspapers or news agencies;
 (d) such other persons as the court may specially authorise to be present.

Although the press are permitted to attend proceedings in the youth court they are not permitted to report the name, address or any other detail which may lead to the identity of the juvenile concerned (s. 49(1)). Exceptions to this rule include where the youth court consider it necessary to avoid injustice to the juvenile, or where it is necessary to secure the juvenile's apprehension to either appear before the court or to be returned to custody (s. 49(5)). The restrictions on reporting can also apply to juveniles who may be witnesses in the proceedings (s. 49(4)). However, where during the course of proceedings a defendant attains the age of 18 the provisions of s. 49 no longer apply (*T v DPP; North East Press Ltd* (2004) 168 JP 194).

2.2.7.2 Attendance of Parent or Guardian

The youth court has the power to order the juvenile's parent or guardian to attend the proceedings (s. 34A of the 1933 Act). This power equally applies to the attendance of the parent or guardian in the adult magistrates' court and Crown Court.

2.2.8 Crown Court

The Crown Court is part of the Supreme Court and was created by the Courts Act 1971. It derives its jurisdiction from s. 1 of the Supreme Court Act 1981 which states:

> (1) The Supreme Court of England and Wales shall consist of the Court of Appeal, the High Court of Justice and the Crown Court, each having such jurisdiction as is conferred on it by or under this or any other Act.

The reference to 'Supreme Court' is to be changed to 'Senior Court' under the Constitutional Reform Act 2005 (not yet in force).

The Crown Court is a single court though it sits in many locations across England and Wales. The court has exclusive jurisdiction over trials on indictment and will normally hear cases which involve offences committed within its geographical area but there are no territorial restrictions on the cases it can hear. Section 46 of the Supreme Court Act 1981 states:

> (2) The jurisdiction of the Crown Court with respect to proceedings on indictment shall include jurisdiction in proceedings on indictment for offences wherever committed, and in particular on indictment for offences within the jurisdiction of the Admiralty of England

2.2.8.1 Judges

Section 8 of the Supreme Court Act 1981 states:

> (1) The jurisdiction of the Crown Court shall be exercisable by—
> (a) any judge of the High Court; or
> (b) any Circuit Judge Recorder, or District Judge (Magistrates' Courts); or
> (c) subject to and in accordance with the provisions of sections 74 and 75(2), a judge of the High Court, circuit judge or recorder sitting with not more than four justices of the peace, and any such persons when exercising the jurisdiction of the Crown Court shall be judges of the Crown Court.

All proceedings in the Crown Court must be heard and disposed of by a single judge except where a justice is permitted to sit with such a judge (s. 73(1) of the 1981 Act).

2.2.8.2 Modes of Address

The following guidelines relate to the address of judges in open court. Other conventions may apply when meeting a judge in chambers.

High Court judges should be addressed as 'My Lord' or 'My Lady'.

Circuit judges, recorders and deputy circuit judges should be addressed as 'Your Honour'. Exceptions to this are:

- a judge is sitting at the Central Criminal Court

- any circuit judge who holds the office of honorary Recorder of Liverpool or honorary Recorder of Manchester

who should be addressed as 'My Lord' or 'My Lady' (*Consolidated Criminal Practice Direction: Practice Direction* (*Criminal Proceedings: Consolidation*) [2002] 1 WLR 2870, [2002] 3 All ER 904, [2002] 2 Cr App R 533).

Ordinary judges of the Court of Appeal are addressed as either 'Lord Justice of Appeal' or 'Lady Justice of Appeal' (s. 2(3) of the 1981 Act).

However, the Lord Chancellor may by order alter the name and styling of a number of judicial offices (s. 64(1)(b) of the Courts Act 2003).

2.2.8.3 Right of Audience in the Crown Court

Until the enactment of the Courts and Legal Services Act 1990 only practising barristers had a right of audience in the Crown Court. The 1990 Act introduced a statutory scheme for the definition and regulation of the rights of audience before the courts, preserving all existing rights (ss. 31 and 32) and setting up a framework for the granting of new rights (s. 27). Advocates who are not barristers can now obtain rights of audience in the Crown Court. This includes solicitors, whether employed or in private practice, provided they meet the requirements of s. 27 of the 1990 Act as amended by the Access to Justice Act 1999.

2.2.8.4 Juries

Qualification for jury service is provided by s. 1 of the Juries Act 1974 as amended by the Criminal Justice Act 2003, which states:

(1) Subject to the provisions of this Act, every person shall be qualified to serve as a juror in the Crown Court, the High Court and county courts and be liable accordingly to attend for jury service when summoned under this Act if—
  (a) he is for the time being registered as a parliamentary or local government elector and is not less that eighteen nor more than seventy years of age;
  (b) he has been ordinarily resident in the United Kingdom, the Channel Islands or the Isle of Man for any period of at least five years since attaining the age of thirteen;
  (c) he is not a mentally disordered person; and
  (d) he is not disqualified for jury service.

Persons disqualified under subsection (d) include: persons on bail in criminal proceedings; those having served, or who are serving, prison sentences or community orders of varying degrees of seriousness (sch. 1, part 2, paras 6 and 7); and full-time serving members of the armed forces if their commanding officer certifies their absence to be prejudicial to the efficiency of the service (s. 9(2A)). There is also a provision in the Act for discretionary deferral and excusal (ss. 9A and 9 respectively). If a person who has been summoned to do jury service can show that there is a 'good reason' that their summons should be deferred or excused, then discretion exists to defer or excuse. This discretion is the responsibility of the Jury Central Summoning Bureau, part of the Lord Chancellor's Department, which administers the jury summoning system for the Crown Court in England and Wales. Serving police officers, and staff of the Crown Prosecution Service, can serve on juries as this does not offend against principles of fairness where there are no circumstances which would give rise to concerns of bias (*R* v *Abdroikov, Green and Williamson* [2005] EWCA Crim 1986).

A jury generally consists of 12 jurors whose role is to determine the guilt or innocence of an accused where he/she has pleaded not guilty in relation to the offence(s) charged. The 12 jurors are selected by ballot in open court from the panel of jurors summoned to attend on a particular date (s. 11).

2.2.9 Tribunals and Inquiries

Tribunals and inquiries were originally created to cope with the increasing volume of grievances within central and local government. In more recent years there has been a marked overlap with the criminal justice system.

2.2.9.1 Tribunals

Tribunals are alternative mechanisms to the courts which provide remedies for decision making in the public sector and grievances in both central and local government. They are supervised by the courts and directly supervised by the Council on Tribunals which was created by the Tribunals and Inquiries Act 1958 (now 1992). Tribunals cover a wide area of subject matter: those that deal with the issues of the ordinary citizen (e.g. benefits, education of children, fair rents); those that perform a licensing role (e.g. Civil Aviation Authority); and those that deal with a variety of other functions.

The role of the Council of Tribunals is:

- to keep under review the constitution and working of tribunals specified in sch. 1 to the 1992 Act and from time to time report on their constitution and working;
- to consider and report in matters referred to the Council under the 1992 Act with respect to tribunals other than ordinary courts of law, whether or not specified in sch. 1 to the Act; and
- to consider and report on these matters, or matters the Council may consider to be of special importance, with respect to administrative procedures which involve or may involve the holding of a statutory inquiry by or on behalf of a Minister (s. 1(1) of the Tribunals and Inquiries Act 1992).

This role extends to the Police Appeals Tribunal (as to which, **see General Police Duties, chapter 4.1**).

Tribunals are subject to the supervisory jurisdiction of the High Court under the application for judicial review procedure (**see para. 2.2.5.7**). They must act within their powers and are under a duty to act fairly.

If enacted the Tribunals, Courts and Enforcement Bill will create a new statutory Framework for tribunals.

2.2.9.2 Inquiries

The use of statutory and non-statutory inquiries has increased considerably during the past few decades, from inquiries into building nuclear power stations, airport terminals and extending motorways, to the Bichard Inquiry (2005) on child protection methods and the Hutton Inquiry (2004) surrounding the death of Dr David Kelly. This considerable increase, together with public concern as to the nature and structure of inquiries, has resulted in the Inquiries Act 2005. The Act is designed to provide a comprehensive framework under which future inquiries can operate effectively.

The Inquiries Act consolidates and codifies past practice in relation to statutory inquiries that are set up by Ministers. Future inquiries will not determine any civil or criminal liability but will be used to restore public confidence and focus on preventing re-occurrence of the events which led to the inquiry being set up. Included within the Act is the setting up of inquiries, the appointment of people to conduct them, and their procedures and powers. It also provides for the submission and publication of reports together with the control and regulation of the inquiries' costs. The Inquiries Rules 2006 (SI 2006/1838) provide the procedure for conducting proceedings of an inquiry held under the 2005 Act.

2.2.10 European Court of Justice and European Court of Human Rights

The impact on English criminal law of our membership of the European Union has been considerable over the past decade and this section examines the two European courts that are principally involved.

2.2.10.1 European Court of Justice

Article 177 of the European Economic Community Treaty (the Treaty of Rome) provides the powers for the European Court of Justice to give rulings concerning the interpretation of the Treaty. Any civil or criminal English court may request a preliminary ruling on a point of European law which arises in its proceedings.

The procedure for obtaining rulings from the European Court of Justice are dealt with by r. 29 of the Crown Court Rules 1982 for the Crown Court, and in the Appeal Court by the Criminal Appeal (References to the European Court) Rules 1972 (SI 1972/1786).

2.2.10.2 European Court of Human Rights

The Court was established by the European Convention for the Protection of Human Rights and Fundamental Freedoms. It is located in Strasbourg, France, and judges sitting at the court are representatives of those countries who are contracted to the Convention. As the name implies, the Court deals with matters related to human rights referred to it from any of its signatories.

As a matter of international law, the Convention creates rights against States, not against private individuals. Those rights are discussed elsewhere in this series (**see General Police Duties**). Decisions of the court are binding on the country concerned but are not necessarily followed where similar facts arise again.

2.3 Summonses and Warrants

2.3.1 Introduction

In order to secure the attendance of parties to criminal and civil cases, it is important that courts and tribunals have the relevant powers to bring people—and evidence—before them. Many of those powers are exercised through the issuing of summonses and warrants.

Before examining in detail aspects of summonses and warrants, it is useful to identify the meaning of the terms information, summons and complaint.

2.3.1.1 Information

Generally, an information means a written or verbal allegation made to a magistrate (known as laying an information) that a person has committed an offence or is suspected of having committed such an offence. This has to be done before a summons or warrant can be issued.

2.3.1.2 Summons

A summons means a written order issued by a magistrate or a magistrates' clerk, on behalf of the magistrate. It orders the person named therein to appear at a named court at a given time and date to answer an allegation of an offence which is set out in the summons or, in the case of a witness summons, to give evidence and/or produce exhibits.

2.3.1.3 Complaint

A complaint is a verbal allegation made before a magistrate to the effect that a person has committed a breach of the law not being a criminal offence (such as breach of the peace, resulting in a common law binding-over to keep the peace). Acts of Parliament sometimes enact that proceedings are to be taken by way of complaint (e.g. under s. 2 of the Dogs Act 1871 where proceedings instituted by 'information' are invalid).

2.3.2 The Process

The appearance of a defendant before a magistrates' court is secured by:

- his/her arrest without warrant, followed by his/her being charged with an offence at a police station and being bailed to attend at court on a specified day to answer the charge; or
- as above except, instead of being bailed, the person is brought before the court in police custody; or

- the laying of an information by the prosecutor before a magistrate (or a magistrates' clerk) resulting in the issue of a summons requiring the accused to attend at court on a specified day to answer the allegation in the information; or
- as above except that the magistrate issues a warrant for the defendant to be arrested and brought before the court. Alternatively, the warrant may be backed for bail where the defendant is arrested and then released on bail to attend court on a specified day.

For the law relating to powers and procedures for arrest, entry, search and seizure (with and without warrant), **see General Police Duties, chapter 4.4**; for the law relating to questioning, detention, charge and bail, **see chapters 2.4 and 2.11**.

KEYNOTE

When in force, s. 29 of the Criminal Justice Act 2003 will introduce a new method of instituting proceedings in the magistrates' court. A public prosecutor will not have the power to lay an information for the purpose of obtaining a summons but may institute criminal proceedings by issuing a document (a 'written charge'), which charges the person with an offence (s. 29(1)). At the same time as a written charge is issued the public prosecutor will also be required to issue a document known as a 'requisition' which will require the person to appear before a magistrates' court to answer the written charge (s. 29(2)). A copy of both documents must be served on the person and the court named in the requisition (s. 29(3)). This new procedure will not affect the power of a public prosecutor to lay an information to obtain a warrant, the power of some other person to lay an information for the issue of a summons, or the power to charge a person while they are in custody.

2.3.3 Laying an Information

Rule 7.1 of the Criminal Procedure Rules 2005 (SI 2005/384) provides that an information (i.e. an allegation that a person has committed an offence), may be laid orally or in writing. It may be laid either by the prosecutor in person, or by counsel or a solicitor on his/her behalf, or by any other authorised person.

Under s. 1(1) of the Magistrates' Courts Act 1980, on an information being laid before him/her, a magistrate may issue either:

- a summons requiring the person named in the information to appear before a magistrates' court to answer thereto; or
- a warrant to arrest that person and bring him/her before a magistrates' court.

An information should provide the following details:

- the name of the informant and his/her address;
- brief particulars of the offence suspected; and
- the law which has been contravened.

A written information is laid when it is received in the office of the clerk of the justices (*R v Manchester Stipendiary Magistrate, ex parte Hill* [1983] 1 AC 328). An oral information is laid by the informant going before a magistrate or clerk to make his/her allegation for the issue of a summons. However, in order to obtain the issue of a warrant for arrest, an information must be in writing (s. 1(3) of the Magistrates' Courts Act 1980).

The information must be laid by a named, actual person and must disclose the identity of that person. In *Rubin v DPP* [1990] 2 QB 80 it was held that a police force was *not* a named, actual person. Some police forces now have a policy of laying all informations in the name of the Chief Constable or other senior officer.

2.3.4 Issue of Summons

Section 1 of the Magistrates' Courts Act 1980 provides:

(1) On an information being laid before a justice of the peace that a person has, or is suspected of having, committed an offence, the justice may issue—
   (a) a summons directed to that person requiring him to appear before a magistrates' court to answer the information, or
   (b) a warrant to arrest that person and bring him before a magistrates' court.

KEYNOTE

For a justice of the peace to issue a summons or warrant it is irrelevant where the offence was committed.

2.3.4.1 Criteria for Issue of a Summons

The decision to issue the summons is judicial, not merely administrative (*R* v *Gateshead Justices, ex parte Tesco Stores Ltd* [1981] QB 470). Consequently, the justice or clerk must be satisfied that:

- the information alleges an offence known to the law;
- it was laid within any time limit applicable to commencing a prosecution for the offence in question;
- any consent necessary for the bringing of the prosecution has been obtained; and
- there is jurisdiction to issue a summons having regard to the provisions of s. 1(2) of the 1980 Act.

Where the above criteria are met it is normal that a summons would be issued. In *R* v *Clerk to the Bradford Justices, ex parte Sykes* (1999) 163 JP 224, it was held that the magistrate and clerk has no obligation to make inquiries before issuing a summons. It would only be in exceptional circumstances where the justice or clerk made use of their residual discretion to refuse a summons. Such refusal applies in applications which appear frivolous or vexatious or to be an abuse of the process of the court. For example, in *R* v *Bros* (1901) 66 JP 54, a summons was not issued against a Jewish baker for Sunday trading in a predominantly Jewish area. In *R* v *Clerk to the Medway Justices, ex parte DHSS* (1986) 150 JP 401, the clerk refused to issue a summons because of the failure of the prosecutor to lay an information within a reasonable time. Four months had been allowed to elapse between the interview of the suspect and the laying of the information.

2.3.5 Service of the Summons

The Criminal Procedure Rules 2005, r. 7.7(1), require that a summons must be signed by the justice or clerk issuing it or (in the case of a summons issued by a justice) must state his/her name and be authenticated by the clerk's signature. It is now common practice for the necessary signature to be affixed by means of a rubber stamp, and r. 7.7(4) permits the use of an electronic signature.

2.3.5.1 Contents of the Summons

Under r. 7.7(2) of the 2005 Rules, a summons should state:

- the substance of the information which has been laid against the person summoned; and
- the time and place at which he/she is required to appear to answer the charge.

One summons may be issued in relation to several informations against a person but it is usual for a separate summons to be issued for each information (r. 7.7(3)).

2.3.5.2 Delivery of the Summons

Under r. 4.7(1)(a) of the 2005 Rules (as amended by the Criminal Procedure (Amendment) Rules 2007), a summons may be served on a person by:

(a) handing it to him/her; or
(b) by leaving it at an address where it is reasonably believed that he/she will receive it; or
(c) by sending it to that address by first class post or by the equivalent of first class post.

A court can proceed in the accused's absence where a person proves service of the summons by signing a certificate explaining how and when it was served (r. 4.11).

A summons for service on a corporation may be undertaken by handing it to a person holding a senior position in that corporation, or by leaving it at, or sending it by first class post to, its principal office in England and Wales, and if there is no readily identifiable principal office then any place in England and Wales where it carries on its activities or business (r. 4.7(1)(b)).

Generally, the service of a summons on a member of the armed forces is effected by its being served on the commanding officer in the case of army and RAF personnel, and the commanding officer of a ship or other establishment in the case of Royal Navy or Royal Marines personnel, as well as on the individual concerned.

KEYNOTE

There are occasions where the prosecutor may wish to delay the issue of a summons when laying an information, for example, where the defendant is known to be out of the country. However, an information should be laid with the intention of having the consequent summons served as soon as reasonably possible. Where a prosecutor has not decided to proceed and an information is laid for the purpose of ensuring the prosecution should not be out of time, this amounts to an abuse of the process of the court and the magistrates should stay the proceedings if ultimately he/she does decide to proceed (*R* v *Brentford Justices, ex parte Wong* [1981] QB 445).

2.3.5.3 Service Elsewhere in the United Kingdom

The Criminal Law Act 1977 deals with the service of summonses issued throughout the United Kingdom. Section 39 of the 1977 Act states:

(1) A summons requiring a person charged with an offence to appear before a court in England and Wales may, in such manner as may be prescribed by rules of court, be served on him in Scotland or Northern Ireland.

(2) A summons requiring a person charged with an offence to appear before a court in Northern Ireland may, in such a manner as may be prescribed by rules of court, be served on him in England, Wales or Scotland.

(3) Citation of a person charged with a crime or offence to appear before a court in Scotland may be effected in any part of the United Kingdom in like manner as may be done in Scotland, and for this purpose the persons authorised to effect such citation shall include, in England and Wales and Northern Ireland, constables and prison officers serving in those parts of the United Kingdom.

These provisions will be amended by the Criminal Justice Act 2003, when in force.

The Scottish term for a summons is a 'citation'. A 'summons' is said to be 'served' in England or Wales and a 'citation' is said to be 'effected' in Scotland.

Postal service of summonses issued in England and Wales is permitted throughout Great Britain, although postal service of a summons is not acceptable to courts in Northern Ireland. Therefore, all service of Northern Ireland summonses in England and Wales must be served in person. The service of a Scottish citation in England and Wales by post is permitted.

2.3.6 Issue of Warrants

There are several different types of warrants which may be issued by justices, some of which are detailed below. For search warrants, **see General Police Duties, chapter 4.4.**

2.3.6.1 Warrant to Arrest an Offender

Section 1(1)(b) of the Magistrates' Court Act 1980 provides that, whenever a justice before whom an information is laid has power to issue a summons, he/she may alternatively issue a warrant for the arrest of the person named in the information, save that:

- the information must be in writing (s. 1(3)); and
- either the offence alleged must be indictable or punishable with imprisonment, or the accused's address must be insufficiently established for a summons to be served (s. 1(4)).

Warrants for arrest under s. 1 of the 1980 Act are not commonly issued as many offences will carry a power of arrest without warrant.

Unlike the issue of a summons (**see para. 2.3.4**), the justices' clerk is not allowed to issue a warrant; the information has to be on oath and made to a justice.

2.3.6.2 Warrant to Arrest a Witness

The Magistrates' Courts Act 1980 provides that a justice of the peace may issue a warrant where they are satisfied that it is in the interests of justice to secure the attendance of a person who could give material evidence. However, a warrant may only be issued where the justice of the peace is satisfied, by evidence on oath, that a summons would not procure the attendance of the person (s. 97(2)). In addition, a warrant may also be issued where a person fails to attend the court in answer to a summons where there is proof of its service (**see para. 2.3.5.2**) if it appears to the court that there is no just excuse for the failure (s. 97(3)).

Similar powers exist for witness warrants (and summonses) for the High Court and the Crown Court.

2.3.6.3 Warrant to Arrest in Default

This warrant is issued where a person defaults in payment of a fine or other sum and is a type of commitment warrant.

2.3.6.4 Warrant to Commit to Prison

This is a warrant of arrest directing that the person be taken to a specified place. On arrest the constable should take the person to the place specified and obtain a receipt. This is one of the very rare occasions where a person need not be taken to a police station after arrest.

2.3.6.5 Warrant to Distrain Property

This warrant is issued in an effect to collect money. It allows certain goods to be seized and sold as prescribed by the Criminal Procedure Rules 2005.

2.3.7 Execution of Warrants

A warrant of arrest, commitment or detention may be executed by:

(a) the persons to whom it is directed; or
(b) by any of the following persons, whether or not it was directed to them—
   (i) a constable for any police area in England and Wales, acting in his own police area, and
   (ii) any person authorised under section 125A (civilian enforcement officers) or section 125B (approved enforcement agencies) of the Magistrates' Courts Act 1980.

(Rule 18.3(3) of the Criminal Procedure Rules 2005)

2.3.7.1 Warrants Executed by a Constable

There are other types of warrants that may be executed by a constable even where it is not in their possession at the time. Section 125D(3) of the 1980 Act provides a list of such warrants as follows:

(a) a warrant to arrest a person in connection with an offence;
(b) a warrant under section 186(3) of the Army Act 1955, section 186(3) of the Air Force Act 1955, section 105(3) of the Naval Discipline Act 1957 or schedule 2 to the Reserve Forces Act 1996 (desertion etc.);
(c) a warrant under section 102 or 104 of the General Rate Act 1967 (insufficiency of distress);
(d) a warrant under section 47(8) of the Family Law Act 1996 (failure to comply with occupation order or non-molestation order);
(e) a warrant under paragraph 4 of schedule 3 to the Crime and Disorder Act 1988 (unwilling witnesses);
(f) a warrant under paragraph 3(2) of schedule 1 to the Powers of Criminal Courts (Sentencing) Act 2000 (offenders referred to court by youth offender panel); and
(g) a warrant under section 55, 76, 93, 97 or 97A above [warrants relating to the non-appearance of a defendant, warrants of commitment, warrants of distress and warrants to arrest a witness].

Rule 18.11(1) of the Criminal Procedure Rules 2005 provides that where a constable executes a warrant of arrest, commitment or detention he/she must, when arresting the relevant person:

- show the warrant (if he/she has it with him/her) to the relevant person, or tell the relevant person where the warrant is and what arrangements can be made to let that person inspect it;
- explain, in ordinary language, the charge and the reason for the arrest; and
- (unless a constable in uniform) show documentary proof of his/her identity.

If the person executing the warrant is one of the persons referred to in r. 18.3(b) or (c) (civilian enforcement officers or approved enforcement agencies), he/she must also show the relevant person a written statement under s. 125A(4) or s. 125B(4) of the Magistrates' Courts Act 1980, as appropriate. The written statement must include: the officer's name; the authority by which he/she is employed; and the fact that he/she is authorised to execute warrants (**see para. 2.3.7.3**).

In order to execute a warrant of arrest issued in connection with, or arising out of criminal proceedings, or a warrant of commitment issued under s. 76 of the Magistrates' Courts Act 1980, a constable may enter and search any premises when he/she has reasonable grounds for believing the person sought is on the premises.

The search may only be to the extent required and is restricted to the parts of the premises where the constable reasonably believes the person may be. Reasonable force may be used when necessary.

These powers are derived from ss. 17(1)(a) and 117 of the Police and Criminal Evidence Act 1984 and the Codes of Practice—Codes A and B (**see General Police Duties, Appendices 4.1 and 4.2**). For the law regulating powers of entry, search and seizure, **see General Police Duties, chapter 4.4**.

For court orders in relation to harassment and domestic violence, **see General Police Duties, chapter 4.5**.

2.3.7.2 Warrants Executed by Other Persons

The Magistrates' Courts Act 1980 provides that certain warrants may be executed in England and Wales by civilian enforcement officers (s. 125A), and approved enforcement agencies (s. 125B). Warrants that may be executed by such authorised officers or agencies under these sections are any warrant of arrest, commitment, detention, distress or in connection with the enforcement of a fine or other order imposed or made on conviction. Authorised officers have the power to enter and search any premises for the purpose of executing a warrant (for or in connection with any criminal offence), only to the extent reasonably required, and where they have reasonable grounds for believing the person is on the premises (sch. 4A to the 1980 Act).

For the types of warrants described in ss. 125A and 125B above, a magistrates' court may make a disclosure order requiring the person to whom it is directed to supply the following information about the person to whom the warrant relates: their name, date of birth or national insurance number; address or addresses (s. 125CA). This information may be required from a 'relevant public authority', including government departments, local authorities and chief officers of police.

It is an offence for a person who has information supplied to them under a disclosure order to intentionally or recklessly disclose that information otherwise than as permitted, or to use such information otherwise than for the purpose of facilitating the execution of the warrant (s. 125C(4)).

2.3.7.3 Execution of Warrants throughout the United Kingdom

Section 136 of the Criminal Justice and Public Order Act 1994 states:

(1) A warrant issued in England, Wales or Northern Ireland for the arrest of a person charged with an offence may (without any endorsement) be executed in Scotland by any constable of any police force of the country of issue or of the country of execution, or by a constable appointed under section 53 of the British Transport Commission Act 1949, as well as by any other persons within the directions of the warrant.

(2) A warrant issued in—
(a) Scotland; or
(b) Northern Ireland,
for the arrest of a person charged with an offence may (without any endorsement) be executed in England and Wales by any constable of any police force of the country of issue or of the country of execution, or by a constable appointed under section 53 of the British Transport Commission Act 1949, as well as by any other persons within the directions of the warrant.

KEYNOTE

In addition to a warrant for the arrest of a person charged with an offence, this section also relates to: (a) a warrant of commitment and a warrant to arrest a witness issued in England, Wales or Northern Ireland, and (b) a warrant for committal, a warrant to imprison (or apprehend and imprison) and a warrant to arrest a witness issued in Scotland. In addition, the section also applies to a warrant for the arrest of an offender referred back to court by a youth offender panel (sch. 1, para. 3(2) to the Powers of Criminal Courts (Sentencing) Act 2000), issued in England and Wales.

Section 38A of the Criminal Law Act 1977 provides for the cross-border execution of Scottish commitment warrants for non-payment of fines, and s. 38B contains similar provisions for such warrant being executed between England, Wales and Northern Ireland.

The Indictable Offences Act 1848, s. 13 provides that warrants from the Isle of Man and the Channel Islands may be executed in England and Wales where they have been endorsed by a justice of the peace.

The execution of warrants from other countries is dealt with by the Extradition Act 2003. This provides a fast-track extradition arrangement with Member States of the European Union and Gibraltar. Such warrants must state that the person in question is accused in the territory issuing the warrant of the commission of a specified offence and that the warrant has been issued for the purposes of arrest and prosecution.

2.4 | Bail

2.4.1 Introduction

The Bail Act 1976 is the primary source of legislation in relation to bail in criminal proceedings granted by the police and courts. Important amendments to the 1976 Act, in relation to police bail, have recently been made by the Police and Justice Act 2006. Other legislation also impacts upon bail, in particular the Police and Criminal Evidence Act 1984 and the Criminal Justice and Public Order Act 1994.

The meaning of 'bail in criminal proceedings' is contained in s. 1 of the Bail Act 1976 which states:

(1) In this Act 'bail in criminal proceedings' means—
   (a) bail grantable in or in connection with proceedings for an offence to a person who is accused or convicted of the offence, or
   (b) bail grantable in connection with an offence to a person who is under arrest for the offence or for whose arrest for the offence a warrant (endorsed for bail) is being issued, or
   (c) bail grantable in connection with extradition proceedings in respect of an offence.

KEYNOTE

This section provides that bail can be granted immaterial of whether the offence was committed in 'England or Wales or elsewhere', and immaterial as to which country's law the offence relates (s. 1(5)).

2.4.2 Police Bail

Bail can either be granted by a custody officer at a police station or by a constable elsewhere than at a police station (known as 'street bail').

2.4.2.1 Street Bail

The Police and Criminal Evidence Act 1984, s. 30A provides for persons arrested elsewhere than at a police station to be released on bail without being required to attend a police station.

The Police and Justice Act 2006 has amended s. 30A of the 1984 Act to provide that bail provisions already available in relation to people at the charging stage of the process are now available to officers granting bail elsewhere than at a police station.

2.4.2.2 Release on Bail

Section 30A(1)   A constable may release on bail a person who is arrested or taken into custody in the circumstances mentioned in s. 30(1).

Section 30A(2)	A person may be released on bail under subs. (1) at any time before he arrives at a police station.
Section 30A(3)	A person released on bail under subs. (1) must be required to attend a police station.
Section 30A(3A)	Where a constable releases a person on bail under subs. (1)— (a) no recognisance for the person's surrender to custody shall be taken from the person, (b) no security for the person's surrender to custody shall be taken from the person or from anyone else on the person's behalf, (c) the person shall not be required to provide a surety or sureties for his surrender to custody, and (d) no requirement to reside in a bail hostel may be imposed as a condition of bail.
Section 30A(3B)	Subject to subs. (3A), where a constable releases a person on bail under subs. (1) the constable may impose, as conditions of the bail, such requirements as appear to the constable to be necessary— (a) to secure that the person surrenders to custody, (b) to secure that the person does not commit an offence while on bail, (c) to secure that the person does not interfere with witnesses or otherwise obstruct the course of justice, whether in relation to himself or any other person, or (d) for the person's own protection or, if the person is under the age of 17, for the person's own welfare or in the person's own interests.
Section 30A(4)	Where a person is released on bail under subs. (1), a requirement may be imposed on the person as a condition of bail only under the preceding provisions of this section.
Section 30A(5)	The police station which the person is required to attend may be any police station.

KEYNOTE

The new s. 30A(3B) enables the officer granting bail to consider attaching conditions relevant and proportionate to the suspect and the offence. The conditions that may be considered are the same as those available to a custody officer as contained in s. 3A(5) of the 1976 Act (**see para. 2.4.7.2**), except for those specified in s. 30A(3A) above.

2.4.2.3 Notice in Writing

Section 30B(1)	Where a constable grants bail to a person under s. 30A, he must give that person a notice in writing before he is released.
Section 30B(2)	The notice must state: (a) the offence for which he was arrested, and (b) the grounds on which he was arrested.
Section 30B(3)	The notice must inform him that he is required to attend a police station.
Section 30B(4)	It may also specify the police station which he is required to attend and the time when he is required to attend.

Section 30B(4A)   If the person is granted bail subject to conditions under s. 30A(3B), the notice also—
(a) must specify the requirements imposed by those conditions,
(b) must explain the opportunities under ss. 30CA(1) and 30CB(1) for variation of those conditions, and
(c) if it does not specify the police station at which the person is required to attend, must specify a police station at which the person may make a request under s. 30CA(1)(b),

Section 30B(5)   If the notice does not include the information mentioned in subs. (4), the person must subsequently be given a further notice in writing which contains that information.

Section 30B(6)   The person may be required to attend a different police station from that specified in the notice under subs. (1) or (5) or to attend at a different time.

Section 30B(7)   He must be given notice in writing of any such change as is mentioned in subs. (6) but more than one such notice may be given to him.

KEYNOTE

This section requires that the person bailed be given a written notice identifying the offence and grounds for arrest, informing him/her that he/she is required to attend a police station. It may also specify the police station which he/she is required to attend and the time when he/she is required to attend or a further notice containing this information must be sent. Section 30B(4A), inserted by the Police and Justice Act 2006, requires the notice to include how the bailed person may apply for variation to any bail conditions. It also states that the notice must (a) specify the requirements imposed by those conditions and (b) if it does not specify the police station at which the person is required to attend, must specify a police station at which the person may make a request under s. 30CA(1)(b).

2.4.2.4 Release, Attendance and Re-arrest

Section 30C(1)   A person who has been required to attend a police station is not required to do so if he is given notice in writing that his attendance is no longer required.

Section 30C(2)   If a person is required to attend a police station which is not a designated police station he must be:
(a) released, or
(b) taken to a designated police station, not more than six hours after his arrival.

Section 30C(3)   Nothing in the Bail Act 1976 applies in relation to bail under s. 30A.

Section 30C(4)   Nothing in s. 30A or 30B or in this section prevents the re-arrest without warrant of a person released on bail under s. 30A if new evidence justifying a further arrest has come to light since his release.

2.4.2.5 Variation of Bail Conditions: Police

Section 30CA(1)   Where a person released on bail under s. 30A(1) is on bail subject to conditions—

(a) a relevant officer at the police station at which the person is required to attend, or

(b) where no notice under s. 30B specifying that police station has been given to the person, a relevant officer at the police station specified under s. 30B(4A)(c),

may, at the request of the person but subject to subs. (2), vary the conditions.

Section 30CA(2) On any subsequent request made in respect of the same grant of bail, subs. (1) confers power to vary the conditions of the bail only if the request is based on information that, in the case of the previous request or each previous request, was not available to the relevant officer considering that previous request when he/she was considering it.

Section 30CA(3) Where conditions of bail granted to a person under s. 30A(1) are varied under subs. (1)—

(a) paragraphs (a) to (d) of s. 30A(3A) apply,

(b) requirements imposed by the conditions as so varied must be requirements that appear to the relevant officer varying the conditions to be necessary for any of the purposes mentioned in paragraphs (a) to (d) of s. 30A(3B), and

(c) the relevant officer who varies the conditions must give the person notice in writing of the variation.

Section 30CA(4) Power under subs. (1) to vary conditions is, subject to subs. (3)(a) and (b), power—

(a) to vary or rescind any of the conditions, and

(b) to impose further conditions.

KEYNOTE

This section was inserted by the Police and Justice Act 2006. The 'relevant officer' (s. 30CA(3)(c)) means a custody officer in relation to a designated police station, or a constable or person designated as a staff custody officer in any other police station. A constable involved in the investigation should not deal with the request unless no other constable or officer is available (s. 30CA(5)).

2.4.2.6 Variation of Bail Conditions: Court

Section 30CB(1) Where a person released on bail under s. 30A(1) is on bail subject to conditions, a magistrates' court may, on an application by or on behalf of the person, vary the conditions if—

(a) the conditions have been varied under s. 30CA(1) since being imposed under s. 30A(3B),

(b) a request for variation under s. 30CA(1) of the conditions has been made and refused, or

(c) a request for variation under s. 30CA(1) of the conditions has been made and the period of 48 hours beginning with the day when the request was made has expired without the request having been withdrawn or the conditions having been varied in response to the request.

2.4.2.7 Power of Arrest for Non-attendance and Breach of Bail Conditions

Section 30D(1)   A constable may arrest without warrant a person who:
  (a) has been released on bail under s. 30A subject to a requirement to attend a specified police station, but
  (c) fails to attend the police station at the specified time.

Section 30D(2)   A person arrested under subs. (1) must be taken to a police station (which may be the specified police station or any other police station) as soon as practicable after the arrest.

Section 30D(2A)   A person who has been released on bail under s. 30A may be arrested without a warrant by a constable if the constable has reasonable grounds for suspecting that the person has broken any of the conditions of bail.

Section 30D(2B)   A person arrested under subs. (2A) must be taken to a police station (which may be the specified police station mentioned in subs. (1) or any other police station) as soon as practicable after the arrest.

Section 30D(3)   In subs. (1), 'specified' means specified in a notice under subs. (1) or (5) of s. 30B or, if notice of change has been given under subs. (7) of that section, in that notice.

2.4.3 Police Bail Without Charge

The Police and Criminal Evidence Act 1984 provides that where one of the following conditions applies then the custody officer must release a detained person either unconditionally or on bail:

- there is insufficient evidence to charge and the officer is not willing to authorise detention for questioning, etc. (s. 37(2)).
- there is sufficient evidence to charge for the purpose of enabling the Director of Public Prosecutions to make a decision under s. 37B (s. 37(7)(a));
- there is sufficient evidence to charge but not for the purpose outlined in s. 37(7)(a) above (this would usually be where further inquiries are to be made) (s. 37(7)(b));

- the officer conducting the review concludes the detention without charge can no longer be justified (s. 40(8));
- at the end of 24 hours' detention without charge unless the detained person is suspected of an indictable offence and continued detention up to 36 hours is authorised by a superintendent (s. 41(7)).

Section 37B above relates to the decision by the Crown Prosecution Service as to whether the person will be charged, cautioned or informed in writing that they are not to be prosecuted. The Police and Justice Act 2006 has amended s. 37(7)(a) to allow the custody officer to either release the person without charge and on bail, or keep them in police detention pending the prosecutor's decision as to whether or not to bring a charge. It is a matter for the custody officer to determine on an individual basis whether the person should be detained or granted bail whilst awaiting the outcome of the statutory charging process. Where a person is released under this section their bail conditions may be varied by the custody officer by notice in writing (s. 37D(1) and (2)). (**See para. 2.11.9** for a full discussion on charging and bail.)

In relation to s. 41(7) above, where continued detention is authorised for up to 36 hours, the detained person must be released with or without bail at or before the expiry of this time. Alternatively, for indictable offences an application can be made to a magistrates' court for a warrant of further detention (s. 42(10) of the 1984 Act).

2.4.4 Police Bail After Charge

Where a person is charged at the police station (otherwise than on a warrant backed for bail), the custody officer must make a decision:

- to keep the person in custody until he/she can be brought before a magistrates' court, or to release the person; and
- to release the person either unconditionally or on bail (s. 38(1) of the 1984 Act).

This is a review of the person's detention and therefore the person and his/her legal representative should be given an opportunity to make representations to the custody officer. The review should be conducted with regard to PACE Code of Practice, Code C, paras 15.1 to 15.16. Where the detained person is a juvenile, an opportunity to make representations should also be given to the 'appropriate adult'.

Where the decision is made to release a person who has been charged, it would be usual for the person to be released on bail being required to attend at the magistrates' court on a specified day and time.

With the exception of the circumstances set out below in s. 25 of the Criminal Justice and Public Order Act 1994, a person charged with an offence will be given bail unless certain conditions (contained in s. 38 of the 1984 Act) exist allowing the custody officer to refuse bail.

2.4.5 Police Bail Restrictions

The decision to deny any unconvicted person bail is a significant one, both personally and constitutionally. Every person has a general right not to be subject to unnecessarily onerous bail conditions, a right which has existed since the Magna Carta in the thirteenth century.

However, the Criminal Justice and Public Order Act 1994 provides for those occasions when bail may only be granted in exceptional circumstances where a person is charged with certain specified offences. Section 25 of the 1994 Act states:

(1) A person who in any proceedings has been charged with or convicted of an offence to which this section applies in circumstances to which it applies shall be granted bail in those proceedings only if the court or, as the case may be, the constable considering the grant of bail is satisfied that there are exceptional circumstances which justify it.

(2) This section applies, subject to subsection (3) below, to the following offences, that is to say—
   (a) murder;
   (b) attempted murder;
   (c) manslaughter;
   (d) rape under the law of Scotland or Northern Ireland;
   (e) an offence under section 1 of the Sexual Offences Act 1956 (rape);
   (f) an offence under section 1 of the Sexual Offences Act 2003 (rape);
   (g) an offence under section 2 of that Act (assault by penetration);
   (h) an offence under section 4 of that Act (causing a person to engage in sexual activity without consent) where the activity caused involved penetration within subsection (4)(a) to (d) of that section;
   (i) an offence under section 5 of that Act (rape of a child under 13);
   (j) an offence under section 6 of that Act (assault of a child under 13 by penetration);
   (k) an offence under section 8 of that Act (causing or inciting a child under 13 to engage in sexual activity), where an activity involving penetration within subsection (3)(a) to (d) of that section was caused;
   (l) an offence under section 30 of that Act (sexual activity with a person with a mental disorder impeding choice), where the touching involved penetration within subsection (3)(a) to (d) of that section;
   (m) an offence under section 31 of that Act (causing or inciting a person, with a mental disorder impeding choice, to engage in sexual activity), where an activity involving penetration within subsection (3)(a) to (d) of that section was caused;
   (n) an attempt to commit an offence within any of paragraphs (d) to (m).

(3) This section applies to a person charged with or convicted of any such offence only if he has been previously convicted by or before a court in any part of the United Kingdom of any such offence or of culpable homicide and, in the case of a previous conviction of manslaughter or of culpable homicide, if he was then sentenced to imprisonment or, if he was then a child or young person, to long-term detention under any of the relevant enactments.

(4) This section applies whether or not an appeal is pending against conviction or sentence.

(5) In this section—
   'conviction' includes—
      (a) a finding that a person is not guilty by reason of insanity;
      (b) a finding under section 4A(3) of the Criminal Procedure (Insanity) Act 1964 (cases of unfitness to plead) that a person did the act or made the omission charged against him; and
      (c) a conviction of an offence for which an order is made discharging the offender absolutely or conditionally;
   and 'convicted' shall be construed accordingly; and
   'the relevant enactments' means—
      (a) as respects England and Wales, section 91 of the Powers of Criminal Courts (Sentencing) Act 2000;
      (b) as respects Scotland, sections 205(1) to (3) and 208 of the Criminal Procedure (Scotland) Act 1995;
      (c) as respects Northern Ireland, section 73(2) of the Children and Young Persons Act (Northern Ireland) 1968.

KEYNOTE

Section 25 provides that bail may not be granted where a person is charged with murder, attempted murder, manslaughter, rape or attempted rape if they have been convicted of any of these offences *unless* there are exceptional circumstances.

In *R (on the application of O)* v *Crown Court at Harrow* [2006] UKHL 42 it was held that s. 25 was compatible with the European Convention on Human Rights 1950, Art. 5(3)—presumption of an individual's right to liberty. Even where a person's custody time limit (**see para. 2.5.7.3**) had expired s. 25 could still be applied and the evidential burden was on the defence to demonstrate that exceptional circumstances existed. Also, in the case of *Hurnam* v *State of Mauritius* [2005] UKPC 49, the Privy Council stated that the seriousness of the offence is not a conclusive reason for refusing bail and the court must consider whether or not the accused is likely to abscond if released on bail.

In all other cases the custody officer must consider the issue of bail and s. 38(1) of the 1984 Act sets out the occasions where bail can be refused (**see para. 2.4.6**). Where bail is refused, the custody officer must inform the detained person of the reasons why and make an entry as to these reasons in the custody record (s. 38(3) and (4)).

2.4.5.1 Condition of Detained Person and Communication of Refused Bail

A detained person should be informed of the bail decision as soon as it is made. This can be delayed if the conditions set out in Code C, para. 1.8 apply, in which case the detainee should be informed as soon as practicable. The conditions are that the detained person:

- is incapable of understanding what is said;
- is violent, or likely to become violent; or
- is in urgent need of medical attention.

In reaching a decision as to whether a person should be refused bail the custody officer should consider whether the same objective can be achieved by imposing conditions to the bail, that is, for the person to appear at an appointed place at an appointed time. If conditions attached to a person's bail are likely to achieve the same objective as keeping the person in detention, bail must be given.

In *Gizzonio* v *Chief Constable of Derbyshire* (1998) *The Times*, 29 April, Gizzonio had been remanded in custody in respect of certain charges which had not ultimately been pursued. Damages (for the wrongful exercise of lawful authority) were sought on the basis that the police had wrongly opposed the grant of bail. It was held that the decision regarding bail is part of the process of investigation of crime with a view to prosecution and so the police enjoyed immunity in that respect.

2.4.6 Grounds for Refusing Police Bail

Section 38(1) of the Police and Criminal Evidence Act 1984 provides that a custody officer need not grant bail to an unconvicted accused who is charged with an offence if one or more of the following grounds apply.

2.4.6.1 Name and Address cannot be Ascertained

If there are reasonable grounds for doubting whether the accused's name and address is correct, these doubts would have to be recorded, along with the decision to refuse bail, on the custody record. If the person refuses to give his/her name, this does not automatically satisfy the requirements of s. 38. The actual wording of the section is that the name *or* address *cannot be ascertained* or that which is given is doubted.

2.4.6.2 Risk of Absconding

If there are reasonable grounds for believing that the accused will fail to appear at court if bailed, there are certain factors which the custody officer should consider when taking a decision to refuse bail under this section. These factors include:

- the nature and seriousness of the offence;
- the character, antecedents, associations and community ties of the accused;
- the accused's 'record' for having answered bail in the past;
- the strength of the evidence against the accused.

2.4.6.3 Interference with Administration of Justice

There may be reasonable grounds for believing that detention is necessary to prevent the detained person from interfering with the administration of justice or with the investigation of offences or a particular offence.

This ground would not apply for the purpose of the police making further inquiries or where other suspects are still to be arrested. It is generally intended to protect witnesses, keeping them free from fear of intimidation or bribery and enabling other evidence to be properly obtained. For the offences of interfering with witnesses, **see Crime, chapter 1.14**.

2.4.6.4 Commission of Further Offences (Imprisonable Offences Only)

If there are reasonable grounds for believing that bail should be refused to prevent the accused committing other offence(s) the custody officer should give due weight to whether the accused had committed offences when previously on bail and also the 'factors' outlined under **para. 2.4.6.2** above.

2.4.6.5 Risk of Injury to Another, etc. (Non-imprisonable Offences Only)

There may be reasonable grounds for believing that detention is necessary to prevent the accused causing physical injury to another or causing loss or damage to property.

2.4.6.6 Own Protection

There may also be reasonable grounds for believing that detention is necessary for the accused's own protection. 'Own protection' can relate to protection from themselves, such as people who are suicidal, alcoholic, drug addicted or mentally unstable, or protection from others, such as in child abuse cases where there is a lot of public anger directed at the suspect.

2.4.6.7 Juvenile: Welfare

Reasonable grounds for believing that detention is necessary for the juvenile's own welfare provide another reason whereby bail may be denied.

The expression 'welfare' has a wider meaning than just 'protection' and could apply to juveniles who, if released, might be homeless or become involved in prostitution or vagrancy.

In respect of the above conditions, the custody officer must have regard to the same considerations that a court has to consider in taking the corresponding decisions under sch. 1, part I, para. 2 to the Bail Act 1976 (s. 38(2A) of the Police and Criminal Evidence Act 1984). This relates to imprisonable offences where a court need not grant bail if it is satisfied there are *substantial* grounds for believing the accused would:

- fail to surrender to custody;
- commit an offence; or
- interfere with witnesses or otherwise obstruct the course of justice, whether in relation to him/herself or any other person.

2.4.7 Custody Officer: Granting Bail

The granting of bail in criminal proceedings is provided by s. 3 of the Bail Act 1976 and this section examines the general provisions in relation to bail granted by a custody officer, the conditions that may be attached and applications to vary or remove those conditions.

2.4.7.1 General Provisions

The general provisions as to bail in criminal proceedings are provided by s. 3 of the 1976 Act, but this is modified by s. 3A which relates specifically to a custody officer. Section 3 states:

(1) A person granted bail in criminal proceedings shall be under a duty to surrender to custody, and that duty is enforceable in accordance with section 6 of this Act.

(2) No recognisance for his surrender to custody shall be taken from him.

(3) Except as provided by this section—
   (a) no security for his surrender to custody shall be taken from him,
   (b) he shall not be required to provide a surety or sureties for his surrender to custody, and
   (c) no other requirement shall be imposed on him as a condition of bail.

(4) He may be required, before release on bail, to provide a surety or sureties to secure his surrender to custody.

(5) He may be required, before release on bail, to give security for his surrender to custody. The security may be given by him or on his behalf.

(6) He may be required to comply, before release on bail or later, with such requirements as appear to the court to be necessary—
   (a) to secure that he surrenders to custody,
   (b) to secure that he does not commit an offence while on bail,
   (c) to secure that he does not interfere with witnesses or otherwise obstruct the course of justice whether in relation to himself or any other person,
   (ca) for his own protection or, if he is a child or young person, for his own welfare or in his own interests,

(7) If a parent or guardian of a child or young person consents to be surety for the child or young person for the purposes of this subsection, the parent or guardian may be required to secure that the child or young person complies with any requirement imposed on him by virtue of subsection (6), (6ZAA) or (6A) above but—
   (a) no requirement shall be imposed on the parent or the guardian of a young person by virtue of this subsection where it appears that the young person will attain the age of 17 before the time to be appointed for him to surrender to custody; and
   (b) the parent or guardian shall not be required to secure compliance with any requirement to which his consent does not extend and shall not, in respect of those requirements to which his consent does extend, be bound in a sum greater than £50.

KEYNOTE

Guidance to courts, applicable also to a custody officer, when approaching the decision to grant bail was given in *R* v *Mansfield Justices, ex parte Sharkey* [1985] 1 All ER 193, where it was held that any relevant risk, for example, absconding, must be a 'real' risk, not just a fanciful one.

Where a custody officer grants bail there is a requirement for a record to be made of the decision in the prescribed manner and containing the prescribed particulars. If requested, a copy of the record of the decision must, as soon as practicable, be given to the person in relation to whom the decision was taken (s. 5(1)).

Further details on sureties and security are provided in **paras 2.4.7.5 and 2.4.7.6**, respectively.

2.4.7.2 Custody Officer: Conditions of Bail

The power of a custody officer to impose bail conditions is provided by s. 3A of the 1976 Act, which states:

(5) Where a constable grants bail to a person no conditions shall be imposed under subsections (4), (5), (6) or (7) of section 3 of this Act unless it appears to the constable that it is necessary to do so—

    (a) for the purpose of preventing that person from failing to surrender to custody, or

    (b) for the purpose of preventing that person from committing an offence while on bail, or

    (c) for the purpose of preventing that person from interfering with witnesses or otherwise obstructing the course of justice, whether in relation to himself or any other person, or

    (d) for that person's own protection, or if he is a child or young person, for his own welfare or in his own interests.

Where a custody officer decides to grant bail and considers one or more of the requirements in s. 3A(5)(a) to (d) apply, one or more of the following conditions can be imposed:

- the accused is to live and sleep at a specified address;
- the accused is to notify any changes of address;
- the accused is to report periodically (daily, weekly or at other intervals) to his/her local police station;
- the accused is restricted from entering a certain area or building or to go within a specified distance of a specified address;
- the accused is not to contact (whether directly or indirectly) the victim of the alleged offence and/or any other probable prosecution witness;
- the accused is to surrender his/her passport;
- the accused's movements are restricted by an imposed curfew between set times (i.e. when it is thought the accused might commit offences or come into contact with witnesses);
- the accused is required to provide a surety or security.

In *McDonald* v *Procurator Fiscal, Elgin* (2003) *The Times*, 17 April, it was held that a condition for an accused to remain in his dwelling at all times except between 10am and 12 noon did not amount to detention or deprivation of his liberty and did not constitute an infringement of his right to liberty under the European Convention on Human Rights, Article 5.

In relation to non-imprisonable offences it has been held that a hunt protester who was arrested for an offence under s. 5 of the Public Order Act 1986 was rightly required as a condition of his bail not to attend another hunt meeting before his next court appearance (*R* v *Bournemouth Magistrates' Court, ex parte Cross* [1989] Crim LR 207).

KEYNOTE

The conditions outlined in this section can also be imposed by a constable granting bail elsewhere than at a police station under s. 30A(3B) of the Police and Criminal Evidence Act 1984 (see para. 2.4.2.2).

2.4.7.3   Applications to Vary or Remove Bail Conditions

The power to vary or remove conditions is provided by s. 3A of the Bail Act 1976. Section 3A(4) substitutes s. 3(8) and states:

> Where a custody officer has granted bail in criminal proceedings he or another custody officer serving at the same police station may, at the request of the person to whom it was granted, vary the conditions of bail and in doing so he may impose conditions or more onerous conditions.

KEYNOTE

Section 3A(5) above also applies on any request to a custody officer to vary or remove conditions of bail (see para. 2.4.7.2).

There is a requirement that a custody officer either imposing or varying the conditions of bail must include a note of the reasons in the custody record and give a copy of that note to the person in relation to whom the decision was taken (s. 5A(3)).

An accused may also apply to the magistrates' court under s. 43B(1) of the Magistrates' Courts Act 1980, to vary conditions of police bail. Details of the procedure to be followed are contained in r. 19(1) of the Criminal Procedure Rules 2005 (see **Blackstone's Criminal Practice 2008, Appendix 1**).

2.4.7.4   Sureties

Section 3(4) of the Bail Act 1976 provides that before a person is granted bail he/she may be required to provide one or more sureties to secure his/her surrender to custody. A custody officer is entitled (as a court) to require such sureties.

The question of whether or not sureties are necessary is at the discretion of the custody officer (or court) but this condition can be applied only where it is believed the accused may abscond, commit further offences, interfere with witnesses, etc. (sch. 1, part I). It should be noted that sureties have no responsibilities (liability) in relation to an accused committing further offences or interfering with witnesses etc. while on bail.

The suitability of sureties is provided by s. 8 of the 1976 Act and provides for the following considerations as to a surety's suitability:

- financial resources
- character and previous convictions
- relationship to the accused.

The decision as to the suitability of individual sureties is a matter for the custody officer.

The normal consequence for a surety if the accused does not answer bail is that the surety is required to forfeit the entire sum in which he/she stood surety. The power to forfeit recognisances is a matter for the court and is contained in s. 120(1) to (3) of the Magistrates' Courts Act 1980 and rr. 21 and 21A of the Crown Court Rules 1982.

It is not necessary to prove that the surety had any involvement in the accused's non-appearance (*R* v *Warwick Crown Court, ex parte Smalley* [1987] 1 WLR 237). However, where a surety has taken all reasonable steps to ensure the appearance of an accused it was held that the recognisance ought not to be forfeited (*R* v *York Crown Court, ex parte Coleman* (1987) 86 Cr App R 151). In *R* v *Stipendiary Magistrate for Leicester, ex parte Kaur* (2000) 164 JP 127, it was held that the means of the surety *at the time of enforcement* must be taken into account when the court decides whether or not to remit the whole or part of the forfeited recognisance. Section 7(3)(c) of the Bail Act 1976 provides for a surety to notify a constable *in writing* that the accused is unlikely to surrender to custody and that for that reason the surety wishes to be relieved of his/her obligations as a surety. Such an action may well be determined to be 'reasonable steps'.

2.4.7.5 Security

Section 3(5) of the Bail Act 1976 provides that, before a person is granted bail, he/she may be required to give security for his/her surrender to custody. As with sureties, a custody officer is entitled (as a court) to require such security, as far as s. 3(6)(a) to (c) (surrender to custody, not commit an offence on bail, interfere with witnesses, etc.) applies. The security required may be a sum of money or other valuable item and may be given either by the accused or someone on his/her behalf. A third party may make an asset available to an accused for the purpose of providing a security and where the security is forfeited there is no requirement for the third party to be informed (*R (Stevens)* v *Truro Magistrates' Court* [2002] 1 WLR 144).

As with sureties, where an accused absconds this would result in forfeiture of the security. This would not be the case if there appears reasonable cause for the (accused's) failure to surrender to custody (s. 5(7) to (9) of the 1976 Act).

2.4.7.6 The Human Rights Act 1998

Generally, the approach of European Court and Commission is that an accused person should be released unconditionally unless factors that would otherwise lead to a refusal of bail can be met by imposing bail conditions.

Against this background the Court has accepted:

- use of sureties (*Schertenlieb* v *Switzerland* (1980) 23 DR 137)
- surrender of a passport (*Stögmüller* v *Austria* (1969) 1 EHRR 155)
- restrictions on movement (*Schmid* v *Austria* (1985) 44 DR 195).

In the case of *Neumeister* v *Austria* (1968) 1 EHRR 91, the Court considered that it would be a violation of the Convention where the amount of a surety was set by reference to the losses allegedly caused by the person charged.

2.4.8 Appointment of Court Date

There is a statutory requirement on a custody officer in relation to when a person must appear before a magistrates' court when he/she is being released on bail.

Section 47 of the Police and Criminal Evidence Act 1984 states:

(3A) Where a custody officer grants bail to a person subject to a duty to appear before a magistrates' court, he shall appoint for the appearance—

    (a) a date which is not later than the first sitting of the court after the person is charged with the offence; or

    (b) where he is informed by the designated officer for the relevant local justice area that the appearance cannot be accommodated until a later date, that later date.

2.4.9 Juveniles Refused Police Bail

Under s. 38(6) of the Police and Criminal Evidence Act 1984, where a juvenile has been refused bail, the custody officer must try and make arrangements for the detained juvenile to be taken into the care of a local authority in order that he/she can be detained pending appearance in court.

Two exceptions are provided:

- where the custody officer certifies that it is impracticable to do so, or
- in the case of a juvenile of at least 12 years of age, where no secure accommodation is available and there is a risk to the public of serious harm from that juvenile which cannot be adequately protected by placing the juvenile in other local authority accommodation.

The certificate signed by the custody officer must be produced when the juvenile first appears at court (s. 38(7)).

PACE Code C, Note 16D makes it clear that the availability of secure accommodation is only a factor in relation to a juvenile aged 12 or over, when the local authority accommodation would not be adequate to protect the public from serious harm from the juvenile.

The obligation to transfer a juvenile to local authority accommodation applies equally to a juvenile charged during the daytime as it does to a juvenile to be held overnight, subject to a requirement to bring the juvenile before a court in accordance with s. 46 of the 1984 Act (see below).

2.4.10 Treatment of People Refused Police Bail

The custody officer must continue to comply with the PACE Codes of Practice in relation to the treatment of the person while detained pending his/her appearance at court or any latter decision to give bail. Even though a decision to refuse bail may have been taken properly at the time, the circumstances may change and bail may become appropriate. It may be that bail has been refused because of the fear that the person may interfere with a witness. If that witness then informs the police that he/she is going to stay with friends abroad, it may be sufficient to protect the witness by granting bail on the condition that the accused surrenders his/her passport.

2.4.10.1 Review of Detention

Section 40 of the 1984 Act requires that a person who has been refused bail must have his/her detention reviewed by the custody officer *within nine hours of the last decision to refuse bail*. This can only be delayed if the custody officer is not available to carry out the review and then it must be carried out as soon as practicable. Any reason for the delay must be recorded in the custody record along with the decision. If detention can no longer be justified, the person should be bailed with or without conditions as appropriate.

2.4.10.2 Bringing Person Charged before Magistrates' Court

A person charged with an offence and refused bail must be brought before a magistrates' court in accordance with s. 46 of the 1984 Act. Section 46 states:

> (1) Where a person—
>   (a) is charged with an offence; and
>   (b) after being charged—
>   (i) is kept in police detention; or
>   (ii) is detained by a local authority in pursuance of arrangements made under section 38(6) above,
>   he shall be brought before a magistrates' court in accordance with the provisions of this section.

KEYNOTE

The person must be brought before the next available court (it is for the clerk of the court to decide when the next available court is sitting (*R* v *Avon Magistrates, ex parte Broome* [1988] Crim LR 618)). If no court is sitting on the next day after charging, (other than Sundays, Christmas Day or Good Friday), the custody officer must inform the clerk of the court. If the court in which the person is to appear is in another area, the person must be taken to the area as soon as practicable and then be taken to that court at the next available sitting. Section 46(9) provides an exception to this requirement if the person is in hospital and is not fit to appear.

Schedule 1, part I, para. 2 of the Bail Act 1976 and s. 38(2A) of the Police and Criminal Evidence Act 1984 provide that the custody officer need not grant bail if he/she is satisfied there are 'reasonable grounds' for believing the defendant, if released on bail (whether subject to conditions or not), would:

- fail to surrender; or
- commit an offence while on bail; or
- interfere with witnesses or otherwise obstruct the course of justice, whether in relation to him/herself or any other person.

These factors are the same as those considered by the courts except that a court needs to be satisfied that there are 'substantial grounds' in their belief as opposed to the custody officer's 'reasonable grounds'.

The detained person may also be refused bail for his/her own protection. Where the accused is a juvenile, bail may also be refused if he/she should be kept in custody for his/her own welfare.

2.4.11 Offence of Absconding

Section 6 of the Bail Act 1976 Act creates an offence of absconding and states:

> (1) If a person who has been released on bail in criminal proceedings fails without reasonable cause to surrender to custody he shall be guilty of an offence.
> (2) If a person who—
>   (a) has been released on bail in criminal proceedings, and
>   (b) having reasonable cause therefor, has failed to surrender to custody,
>   fails to surrender to custody at the appointed place as soon after the appointed time as is reasonably practicable he shall be guilty of an offence.

KEYNOTE

The burden of proof in relation to showing ' reasonable cause' (s. 6(1)) is a matter for the accused (s. 6(3)).

A person who has 'reasonable cause' still commits the offence if he/she fails to surrender 'as soon after the appointed time as is reasonably practicable'. In *Laidlaw* v *Atkinson* (1986) *The Times*, 2 August, it was held that being mistaken about the day on which one should have appeared was not a reasonable excuse. Also, there is no requirement on the court to inquire as to whether a person arrested for failing to comply with bail conditions had any reasonable excuse for breaching bail (*R* (*On the Application of Vickers*) v *West London Magistrates' Court* (2003) 167 JP 473).

However, in *R* v *Ashley* [2004] 1 WLR 2057 the accused had been bailed on condition that he surrender his passport and not leave the country. He both failed to surrender his passport and left the country but in fact returned for the trial on the appointed day. He was convicted of contempt of court but on appeal this was overturned as although he had breached bail conditions he had returned for his trial and s. 7 of the Bail Act 1976 does not itself create any offence.

Section 6(4) also states:

A failure to give to a person granted bail in criminal proceedings a copy of the record of the decision shall not constitute reasonable cause for that person's failure to surrender to custody.

The procedure for prosecuting offences under s. 6 is provided by *Practice Direction (Bail: Failure to Surrender and Trials in Absence)* [2004] 1 Cr App R 402. In relation to a person who has been bailed by the police to attend at a magistrates' court or a police station and fails to attend, proceedings should be initiated by charging the accused or by the laying of an information. For a person granted bail by a magistrates' court, the court initiates proceedings for failure to appear by its own motion where there has been an express invitation to do so by the prosecutor.

A magistrates' court may only try an offence of absconding, where a person was bailed by a constable, if an information is laid for the relevant offence within six months from the time of the commission of the relevant offence and/or if an information is laid for the relevant offence no later than three months from the time of the occurrence of the first of the events to occur after the commission of the relevant offence. Those events are:

- the person surrenders to custody at the appointed place;
- the person is arrested, or attends at a police station, in connection with the relevant offence or the offence for which he was granted bail;
- the person appears or is brought before a court in connection with the relevant offence or the offence for which he was granted bail (s. 6(10)–(14)).

The Crown Court can deal with a breach of bail as a criminal contempt of court but is required to decide whether an offence under s. 6(1) (failure to surrender without reasonable cause), has been committed (*R* v *Hourigan* [2003] EWCA Crim 2306). The Court of Appeal has held that any custodial sentence imposed for failure to surrender to custody should normally be served consecutively to any other sentence of imprisonment (*R* v *White* [2003] 2 Cr App R (S) 133).

2.4.11.1 Failure to Comply with Police Bail

There are occasions where a person who has been bailed to return to a police station at a later date or to appear at court may be arrested without warrant. These occasions are dealt with by s. 46A of the Police and Criminal Evidence Act 1984 and s. 7 of the Bail Act 1976.

Section 46A of the Police and Criminal Evidence Act 1984 states:

(1) A constable may arrest without a warrant any person who, having been released on bail under this Part of this Act subject to a duty to attend at a police station, fails to attend at that police station at the time appointed for him to do so.

(1A) A person who has been released on bail under section 37, 37C(2)(b) or 37CA(2)(b) above may be arrested without warrant by a constable if the constable has reasonable grounds for suspecting that the person has broken any of the conditions of bail.

(2) A person who is arrested under this section shall be taken to the police station appointed as the place at which he is to surrender to custody as soon as practicable after the arrest.

(3) For the purposes of—
   (a) section 30 above (subject to the obligation in subsection (2) above), and
   (b) section 31 above,
   an arrest under this section shall be treated as an arrest for an offence.

KEYNOTE

The offence for which the person is arrested under subsection (1) above is the offence for which he/she was originally arrested (s. 34(7) of the 1984 Act). This power of arrest applies only where the person *has failed* to attend the police station at the appointed time; it does not extend to situations where there is a 'reasonable suspicion' that the person has failed to attend.

This should be contrasted with s. 46A(1A) where the arresting officer only has to have reasonable grounds for suspecting that the person has broken any of the conditions of bail.

2.4.11.2 Failure to Appear at Court (or Expected Not to Appear)

Section 7 of the Bail Act 1976 states:

(1) If a person who has been released on bail in criminal proceedings and is under a duty to surrender into the custody of a court fails to surrender to custody at the time appointed for him to do so the court may issue a warrant for his arrest.

(1A) Subsection (1B) applies if—
   (a) a person has been released on bail in connection with extradition proceedings,
   (b) the person is under a duty to surrender into the custody of a constable, and
   (c) the person fails to surrender to custody at the time appointed for him to do so.

(1B) A magistrates' court may issue a warrant for the person's arrest.

(2) If a person who has been released on bail in criminal proceedings absents himself from the court at any time after he has surrendered into the custody of the court and before the court is ready to begin or to resume the hearing of the proceedings, the court may issue a warrant for his arrest but no warrant shall be issued under this subsection where that person is absent in accordance with leave given to him by or on behalf of the court.

(3) A person who has been released on bail in criminal proceedings and is under a duty to surrender into the custody of a court may be arrested without warrant by a constable—
   (a) if the constable has reasonable grounds for believing that person is not likely to surrender to custody;
   (b) if the constable has reasonable grounds for believing that person is likely to break any of the conditions of his bail or has reasonable grounds for suspecting that that person has broken any of those conditions; or
   (c) in a case where that person was released on bail with one or more surety or sureties, if a surety notifies a constable in writing that that person is unlikely to surrender to custody and that for that reason the surety wishes to be relieved of his obligations as a surety.

KEYNOTE

Section 7 therefore provides a power of arrest without warrant if the constable:

- has reasonable grounds for believing that the person is not likely to surrender to custody;
- has reasonable grounds for believing that the person is likely to break, or reasonable grounds for suspecting that the person has broken, any conditions of bail; or
- is notified by a surety in writing that the person is unlikely to surrender to custody and for that reason the surety wishes to be relieved of his/her obligations as a surety.

Where a person is arrested under s. 7 he/she shall be brought before a magistrate as soon as practicable and in any event within 24 hours (s. 7(4)(a)).

This section requires that a detainee be brought not merely to the court precincts or cells but actually before a justice of the peace within 24 hours of being arrested. This requirement is absolute and since the justice's jurisdiction under s. 7(5) to remand a detainee in custody only arises once s. 7(4) has been complied with; a detainee who is brought before the justices out of time cannot be remanded in custody (*R* v *Governor of Glen Parva Young Offender Institution, ex parte G (a minor)* [1998] QB 887).

Where a person is arrested within 24 hours of the time appointed for him/her to surrender to custody he/she must be brought before the court at which he/she was to have so surrendered (s. 7(4)(b)). In reckoning the 24-hour period no account is to be taken of Christmas Day, Good Friday or any Sunday (s. 7(4)).

In dealing with a person brought before the court under subsection (4), if the magistrate is of the opinion that the person is not likely to surrender to custody or has broken or is likely to break any bail conditions he/she may:

- remand or commit the person to custody;
- grant bail subject to the same or different conditions.

Where the justice is not of such an opinion, he/she shall grant bail with the same conditions (if any) as were originally imposed (s. 7(5)).

Where the person being dealt with is a child or young person and the justice does not grant bail, he/she should remand such person to the care of the local authority (s. 7(6)).

2.4.12 Courts and Bail

Where a person is accused of an offence and appears before a magistrates' court or Crown Court and applies to the court for bail there is a presumption (under s. 4(1) of the Bail Act 1976) in favour of granting bail:

> A person to whom this section applies shall be granted bail except as provided in Schedule 1 to this Act.

(**See para. 2.4.13** for sch. 1.)

This presumption is also reinforced by Article 5(1) of the European Convention on Human Rights which states:

1. Everyone has the right to liberty and security of person. No one shall be deprived of his liberty save in the following cases and in accordance with a procedure prescribed by law:
   (a) the lawful detention of a person after conviction by a competent court;
   (b) the lawful arrest or detention of a person for non-compliance with the lawful order of a court or in order to secure the fulfilment of any obligation prescribed by law;

(c) the lawful arrest or detention of a person effected for the purpose of bringing him before the competent legal authority on reasonable suspicion of having committed an offence or when it is reasonably considered necessary to prevent his committing an offence or fleeing after having done so . . .

In addition to a person appearing before the court in connection with proceedings for an offence, s. 4(1) of the 1976 Act also applies to adjournments for reports before sentencing and persons being dealt with for an alleged breach of a requirement in a community rehabilitation, community punishment, community punishment and rehabilitation or curfew order.

2.4.12.1 Bail by Magistrates' Courts

A magistrates' court may remand an accused person in custody or on bail (ss. 5(1), 10(4) and 18(4) of the Magistrates' Courts Act 1980). In exercising their powers of remand or bail the magistrates must do so in accordance with the Bail Act 1976 (s. 128(1) of the 1980 Act). These provisions relate to the magistrates' jurisdiction to adjourn and remand a case. Such jurisdiction applies when the court is:

- inquiring into an offence as examining justices;
- trying an information summarily; or
- determining mode of trial for an offence triable either way.

Section 51(1) of the Crime and Disorder Act 1998 provides that, subject to s. 4 of the Bail Act 1976, a magistrates' court must send an adult defendant charged with an indictable offence to the Crown Court for trial. The defendant can be sent to the Crown Court for that offence, and for any either way or summary offence with which he/she is charged which appears to the court to be related to the indictable-only offence. In the case of a summary offence it must be punishable with imprisonment or involve obligatory or discretionary disqualification from driving. The defendant may be committed to custody or released on bail to appear before the Crown Court for trial.

The provisions of s. 25 of the Criminal Justice and Public Order Act 1994 (right to bail only in exceptional circumstances) apply to bail in the magistrates' court (see para. 2.4.5).

When in force, the Criminal Justice Act 2003 will repeal s. 5(1) of the 1980 Act and amend s. 51 of the 1998 Act.

2.4.12.2 Appeals Against Granting of Bail by Magistrates' Courts

The Bail (Amendment) Act 1993 provides that where a magistrates' court has granted bail, the prosecution may appeal to a judge of the Crown Court against that decision. For this to apply the accused must have been charged with or convicted of an offence which is (or would be in the case of an adult) punishable by a term of imprisonment (s. 1(1)). The prosecution must have opposed bail before it was granted and the conduct of the case must have been by the Crown Prosecution Service, or other prescribed person.

The procedure on appeal against the grant of bail by a magistrates' court is contained in r. 19.17 of the Criminal Procedure Rules 2005 (see Blackstone's Criminal Practice 2008, Appendix 1).

In extradition proceedings the prosecution appeal is to a judge of the High Court and not the Crown Court (s. 1(1A)).

2.4.12.3 Appeals Against Conditions of Bail Granted by Magistrates' Courts

Section 16 of the Criminal Justice Act 2003 provides that a person granted bail by the magistrates' court may appeal to the Crown Court against particular conditions of bail if the adjournment of the case relates to: a trial; an intention as to plea; initial procedure on information against adult for offence triable either way; intention as to plea by child or young person; a preliminary hearing; remand for medical examination.

An appeal under this section may only be brought if an application under s. 3(8)(a) of the 1976 Act (by or on behalf of the person granted bail), s. 3(8)(b) of the 1976 Act (application by constable or prosecutor), or s. 5B(1) of that Act (application by prosecutor) was made and determined before the appeal was brought. On an appeal the Crown Court may vary the conditions of bail.

2.4.12.4 Bail by the Crown Court

The Crown Court may grant bail to those persons listed in s. 81(1)(a) to (g) of the Supreme Court Act 1981 which includes all those appearing before that court for trial, sentence or other types of disposal.

Bail applications in the Crown Court are frequently held in judges' chambers but any application to sit in public must start from the 'fundamental presumption in favour of open justice' (*R (on the application of Malik)* v *Central Criminal Court and another* [2006] EWHC 1539 (Admin)).

Where the Crown Court grants conditional bail after a magistrates' court has refused it, an accused subsequently arrested under s. 7 of the Bail Act 1976 for a breach of conditions will be dealt with for that offence in the magistrates' court (*R (On the application of Ellison)* v *Teesside Magistrates' Court* [2001] EWCA Admin 11).

2.4.12.5 Bail by the High Court

The High Court can only hear bail applications where the accused is appealing by way of case stated against conviction or sentence and these occasions are likely to be rare.

The Court may also consider applications for judicial review of a decision to refuse bail in the Crown Court under s. 29(3) of the Supreme Court Act 1981, but this again would be only in exceptional cases (*R (On the Application of Shergill)* v *Harrow Crown Court* [2005] EWHC 648).

Section 37 of the Criminal Justice Act 1948 provides three further occasions where the High Court may grant bail to:

- persons who have applied to the Crown Court to state a case for opinion or seeking an order to quash that court's decision;
- persons appealing from the Crown Court by way of judicial review, seeking an order quashing the decision of the Crown Court;
- persons convicted or sentenced by the magistrates' court and appealing by way of judicial review seeking an order to quash that decision.

2.4.12.6 Bail by Court of Appeal

The Court of Appeal may grant bail to a person who has served notice of appeal or notice of application for leave to appeal against conviction and sentence in the Crown Court (s. 19 of the Criminal Appeal Act 1968). People appealing from the Court of Appeal to the House of Lords can also be granted bail (s. 36 of the 1968 Act).

Where the Court of Appeal has quashed a conviction and ordered a re-trial, and a fresh indictment has been laid in the Crown Court, bail is solely a matter for the Crown Court (*R v X* [2004] All ER (D) 400 (Feb)).

2.4.13 Courts Refusing Bail

The considerations of the court in relation to granting bail are similar but not identical to those of the custody officer (**see para. 2.4.6**) and can be divided into the same two groups, namely:

- those offences that are imprisonable; and
- those offences that do not carry a sentence of imprisonment.

2.4.13.1 Imprisonable Offences

Schedule 1, part I of the Bail Act 1976 provides those occasions where a court need not grant bail to an unconvicted accused charged with an imprisonable offence. These occasions include where the court is satisfied the accused:

- would fail to surrender to custody (para. 2(1)(a));
- would commit an offence while on bail (para. 2(1)(b));
- would interfere with witnesses or otherwise obstruct the course of justice, whether in relation to himself or any other person (para. 2(1)(c));
- is aged 18 or over and it appears to the court that he was on bail in criminal proceedings on the date of the offence (unless the court is satisfied that there is no significant risk of his committing an offence while on bail (whether subject to conditions or not)) (para. 2A);
- (in connection with extradition proceedings) was on bail on the date of the offence and the conduct constituting the offence would, if carried out by the defendant in England and Wales, constitute an indictable offence or an offence triable either way (para. 2B);
- should be kept in custody for his own protection or, if he is a child or young person, for his own welfare (para. 3);
- is in custody in pursuance of the sentence of a court or of any authority acting under any of the Services Acts (para. 4);
- should be kept in custody as it has not been practicable to obtain sufficient information for the purpose of taking the decisions required by this part of this schedule for want of time since the institution of the proceedings against him (para. 5);
- is aged 18 or over and it appears to the court that, having been released on bail in or in connection with the proceedings for the offence, he failed to surrender to custody, unless the court is satisfied that there is no significant risk that, if released on bail (whether subject to conditions or not), he would fail to surrender to custody (para. 6);
- has a specified Class A drug in his body (identified by way of a lawful test); either the offence is a drugs offence associated with a specified Class A drug or the court is satisfied that there are substantial grounds for believing that the misuse of a specified Class A drug caused or contributed to that offence or provided its motivation; and the person does not agree to undergo an assessment as to his dependency upon or propensity to misuse specified Class A drugs or, has undergone such an assessment but does not agree to participate in any relevant follow-up offered (paras 6A–6C).

KEYNOTE

Schedule 1, part I, para. 9 requires that in taking the decisions required by para. 2(1), or in deciding whether it is satisfied as mentioned in para. 2A(1), 6(1) or 6A, of this part of this schedule, the court shall have regard to such of the following considerations as appear to it to be relevant:

- the nature and seriousness of the offence or default (and the probable method of dealing with the defendant for it);
- the character, antecedents, associations and community ties of the defendant; the defendant's record as respects the fulfilment of his obligations under previous grants of bail in criminal proceedings;
- except in the case of a defendant whose case is adjourned for inquiries or a report, the strength of the evidence of his having committed the offence or having defaulted;

as well as to any others which appear to be relevant.

The Criminal Justice Act 2003 has inserted two new paragraphs within this part of the schedule relating to offenders aged under 18. Paragraph 9AA provides that where a defendant is on bail in criminal pro-ceedings on the date an offence was committed, particular weight can be given to this fact when the court is deciding whether or not the defendant would be likely to re-offend if released on bail. Paragraph 9AB requires the court to give particular weight to the fact that a defendant has failed to surrender to bail in assessing the risk of future absconding.

2.4.13.2 Non-imprisonable Offences

Schedule 1, part II of the Bail Act 1976 provides those occasions where a court need not grant bail to an unconvicted accused charged with a non-imprisonable offence. These oc-casions include where:

- it appears to the court that, having been previously granted bail in criminal proceedings, the accused has failed to surrender to custody in accordance with his obligations under the grant of bail and the court believes, in view of that failure, that the accused, if re-leased on bail (whether subject to conditions or not) would fail to surrender to custody (para. 2);
- the court is satisfied that the accused should be kept in custody for his own protection or, if he is a child or young person, for his own welfare (para. 3);
- the accused is in custody in pursuance of the sentence of a court or of any authority acting under any of the Services Acts (para. 4);
- the court is satisfied that there are substantial grounds for believing that the defendant, if released on bail (whether subject to conditions or not) would fail to surrender to custody, commit an offence on bail or interfere with witnesses or otherwise obstruct the course of justice (whether in relation to himself or any other person) (para. 5).

In addition to the above, s. 4(9) of the 1976 Act provides that in taking any decisions the court should also have regard to any misuse of controlled drugs by the defendant.

2.4.13.3 Court Bail and Human Rights Considerations

When considering bail, the courts also need to take account of the provisions of Article 5 of the European Convention on Human Rights (right to liberty and security) as already outlined in relation to bail by the police.

In *Letellier* v *France* (1991) 14 EHRR 83, it was held that the task of any court in considering bail is to:

> ... examine all the facts arguing for or against the existence of a genuine requirement of public interest justifying, with due regard to the principle of the presumption of innocence, a departure from the rule of respect for individual liberty and set them out in their decisions on applications for release.

The European Court has also held that where a person is subject to pre-trial detention, this should be reviewed at reasonable intervals. An interval of one month was considered reasonable (*Bezicheri* v *Italy* (1989) 12 EHRR 210).

2.4.14 Detention of Adults and Juveniles

Where an accused is aged 21 or over and a court refuses bail, that person is detained in prison until the next hearing.

In relation to an accused under 17 years old, where a court remands, sends or commits them for trial or sentence without bail, that person must be remanded to local authority accommodation unless the criteria laid down in s. 23(5) of the Children and Young Persons Act 1969 are satisfied (s. 23(1)).

Before a child or young person can be placed and kept by a local authority in 'secure accommodation' the conditions set out in s. 23(5) of the 1969 Act must be satisfied. These conditions are:

- the person must have attained the age of 12;
- the person is charged with or has been convicted of a violent or sexual offence, or an offence punishable in the case of an adult with imprisonment for a term of 14 years or more; or is charged with or has been convicted of one or more imprisonable offences which, together with any other imprisonable offences of which he has been convicted in any proceedings amount, or would, if he were convicted of the offences with which he is charged, amount to a recent history of repeatedly committing imprisonable offences while remanded on bail or to local authority accommodation;
- the court is of the opinion, after considering all the options for the remand of the person, that only remanding him to local authority accommodation with a security requirement would be adequate to protect the public from serious harm from him; or to prevent the commission by him of imprisonable offences.

KEYNOTE

Section 23(5) applies to boys and girls aged 12 to 16 (Secure Remands and Committals Prescribed Description of Children and Young Persons) Order 1999 (SI 1999/1265). In addition to this power, s. 60(3) of the Criminal Justice Act 1991 enables the youth court to remand young persons aged 15 to 18 in secure accommodation for a period of 28 days at a time (Children (Secure Accommodation) Regulations 1991 (SI 1991/1505)).

In *R* v *Croydon Crown Court, ex parte G* (1995) *The Times*, 3 May, 'serious harm' was held to be assessed by reference to the nature of the offences charged and the surrounding circumstances.

Section 23A of the Children and Young Persons Act 1969 provides the police with a power of arrest where a constable has reasonable grounds for suspecting that a person is breaking his/her conditions (i.e. remanded or committed to local authority accommodation). Where the arrested person cannot be brought before the court, before which he/she was to have appeared, within 24 hours then he/she must 'be brought as soon as practicable and in any event within 24 hours after his arrest before a justice of the peace (s. 23A(2)).

Section 23AA provides the conditions where electronic monitoring can be imposed on a person aged 12 or over where they are charged or convicted of a violent or sexual offence or repeatedly commit imprisonable offences.

2.4.15 Remands in Police Custody

As outlined in **para. 2.4.14** above, where a person is remanded in custody it normally means detention in prison. However, s. 128 of the Magistrates' Courts Act 1980 provides that a magistrates' court may remand a person to police custody:

- for a period not exceeding three days (24 hours for persons under 17) (s. 128(7));
- for the purpose of inquiries into offences (other than the offence for which he/she appears before the court) (s. 128(8)(a));
- as soon as the need ceases he/she must be brought back before the magistrates (s. 128 (8)(b));
- the conditions of detention and periodic review apply as if the person was arrested without warrant on suspicion of having committed an offence (s. 128(8)(c) and (d)).

This option is colloquially referred to as a 'three day lie down'.

2.4.16 Human Rights Act 1998

Custody officers need to be aware and give consideration to the rights and freedoms guaranteed under the European Convention on Human Rights when reaching a decision as to bail.

Article 5 of the Convention relates to the right to liberty and security. Article 5(3) provides that a person arrested under Article 5(1)(c) is entitled to 'trial within a reasonable time or to release pending trial'. Article 5(1)(c) states:

> ... the lawful arrest or detention of a person effected for the purpose of bringing him before the competent legal authority on reasonable suspicion of having committed an offence or when it is reasonably considered necessary to prevent his committing an offence or fleeing after having done so ...

It should be noted that 'trial within a reasonable time' and 'release pending trial' have been held not to be alternatives (*Wemhoff* v *Germany* (1968) 1 EHRR 55).

The Convention requires that every arrested person be brought 'promptly' before a judge or other judicial officer. The meaning of 'promptly' is not specified but in *Brincat* v *Italy* (1992) 16 EHRR 591, the European Court held that a person who had been detained for four days on blackmail charges before being brought before a court was not treated in accordance with the Article. However it is likely that the periods of detention provided by the Police and Criminal Evidence Act 1984 would be acceptable for most purposes of the Convention.

Article 5(3) provides the right to be released pending trial where a person's continuing detention ceases to be reasonable (*Neumeister* v *Austria* (1968) 1 EHRR 91). Bail should only be refused where there are 'relevant' and 'sufficient' reasons and in all cases these reasons should be provided (*Wemhoff* v *Germany*, above; *Tomasi* v *France* (1992) 15 EHRR 1). In *Yagci and Sargin* v *Turkey* (1995) 20 EHRR 505, the European Court were sceptical about what it referred to as 'stereotyped' reasons for refusing bail and it is likely that our domestic courts will take a similar view to anything other than a genuine consideration of each person's individual circumstances.

In *R (On the Application of DPP)* v *Havering Magistrates' Court* [2001] 1 WLR 805, no oral evidence was available to prove the breach of bail conditions. It was held that such a hearing does not equate to facing a criminal charge and therefore Article 6 (right to a fair trial) does not apply. Also Article 5 would not necessarily be breached as evidence could be considered which was not admissible in the strict sense and the case did not need to be proved beyond reasonable doubt.

The European Court has identified four grounds where the refusal of bail may be justified under the Convention:

- fear of absconding
- interference with the course of justice
- the prevention of crime
- the preservation of public order.

These will be considered in turn.

2.4.16.1 Fear of Absconding

The seriousness of the offence alone has been deemed not to be a sufficient reason to suppose a person will necessarily abscond (*Yagci and Sargin* v *Turkey* (1995) 20 EHRR 505). Regard must be taken of other factors including the character of the detained person, their background, financial status, etc. (*W* v *Switzerland* (1993) 17 EHRR 60).

2.4.16.2 Interference with the Course of Justice

As with s. 38(1) of the Police and Criminal Evidence Act 1984 (**see para. 2.4.6**), this would apply where there are reasonable grounds for believing that detention is necessary to prevent the interference with the administration of justice or with the investigation of offences or a particular offence.

The approach in some European cases has been that where further evidence is obtained and statements taken, the risk of interference diminishes and further detention under this ground is difficult to justify (*W* v *Switzerland*, above). Also, if the detained person has previously been bailed and there was no evidence of interference with the course of justice, using this ground would be very difficult to justify (*Ringeisen* v *Austria* (1971) 1 EHRR 455).

2.4.16.3 The Prevention of Crime

Again, this is similar to the condition contained in s. 38(1) of the Police and Criminal Evidence Act 1984, where the custody officer has reasonable grounds for believing that the detained person will commit other offence(s) if bailed. It was held in *Matznetter* v *Austria* (1979–80) 1 EHRR 198 and *Toth* v *Austria* (1991) 14 EHRR 551 that a reasonable risk of the person committing further offences whilst on bail was a valid reason for refusal.

In considering a person's previous convictions, the European Court has held that, where these were not comparable either in nature or seriousness with the offence(s) charged, their use as grounds for refusing bail would not be acceptable for the purposes of Article 5 (*Clooth* v *Belgium* (1991) 14 EHRR 717).

2.4.16.4 **The Preservation of Public Order**

This provides for the temporary detention of a person where the particular gravity of the offence(s) and the likely public reaction is that the release may give rise to public disorder (*Letellier* v *France* (1991) 14 EHRR 83). This may be difficult to reconcile with the recent approach of the Court in *Redmond-Bate* v *DPP* (1999) 163 JP 789, where the predicted unlawful acts of others were held not to be a reason for arresting and detaining the individual whose lawful behaviour was antagonising them (**see General Police Duties, chapter 4.6**).

2.4.17 International Criminal Court

Sections 16 to 18 of the International Criminal Court Act 2001 provides the requirements for people arrested at the request of the International Criminal Court (ICC). These sections incorporate Article 59 of the ICC Statute that deals with the question of interim release pending surrender (i.e. bail).

Section 16 provides that a court may grant bail if an application is made. However, s. 18(1) and (2) provide for compulsory consultation with the ICC.

Section 18(3) requires the court to consider the matters specified in Article 59(4), that is whether, given the gravity of the alleged crime, there are urgent and exceptional circumstances to justify bail and whether necessary safeguards exist to ensure that the State can fulfil its duty to surrender the person to the ICC.

2.4.18 Release of Short-term Prisoners on Licence and Subject to Home Curfew

2.4.18.1 **Release of Short-term Prisoners on Licence**

Section 246 of the Criminal Justice Act 2003 provides the Secretary of State with the power to release a prisoner on licence where the prisoner has served the 'requisite period' for the term of his/her sentence. The 'requisite period' for prisoners with terms of imprisonment of four months or more but less than 18 months is one quarter of their term, and for those with terms of imprisonment of 18 months or more is a period that is 135 days less than one half of their term.

There is no age restriction for early release so that short-term prisoners under the age of 18 are eligible for release on licence (Release of Short-term Prisoners on Licence (Repeal of Age Restriction) Order 2003 (SI 2003/1691)).

Release may be subject to conditions that may include conditions for either securing the electronic monitoring of his/her compliance with any other conditions of his/her release or securing the electronic monitoring of his/her whereabouts (s. 62(1) and (2) of the Criminal Justice and Court Services Act 2000). Electronic monitoring does not include monitoring a curfew condition imposed under s. 253 of the Criminal Justice Act 2003 (s. 62(3) of the 2000 Act). A further licence condition could be an exclusion requirement under s. 250(2) of the 2003 Act. Where such a requirement is included, the power of a constable to direct a person to leave a place from which they are excluded under s. 112 of the Serious Organised Crime and Police Act 2005 applies (**see General Police Duties, para. 4.5.5.4**).

Even where a prisoner is categorised as eligible for early release, they may not be eligible for home curfew where it is determined their release would undermine public confidence.

2.4.18.2   Release of Short-term Prisoners Subject to Home Curfew

The release of short-term prisoners subject to home curfews is provided by s. 253 of the Criminal Justice Act 2003.

The home detention curfew is set up for a prisoner to complete their sentence and runs for a minimum period of 14 days and a maximum period of 60 days. The prisoner is required to agree to the curfew conditions. The governor at the relevant prison determines the details of the curfew. This will normally be from 7pm to 7am and may be varied. The minimum period of curfew is nine hours but there is no maximum. HM Prison Service Parole Unit is responsible for the management and monitoring of home detention curfews. The curfew equipment is operated and monitored by an approved private contractor. The contractor installs a home monitoring unit at the approved address and fits the prisoner with the personal identification device at this address on the day of release. Although there is no involvement in the release process, the police are notified of all prisoners subject to home detention curfew 14 days prior to release. The police may request information from the monitoring contractor as to the offender's compliance, or otherwise, with the curfew, including any short-term 'unexplained' absences. Such requests for information are authorised by an officer of the rank of superintendent or above. Electronic monitoring contractors are obliged to provide such information within 24 hours of the request being made.

2.4.18.3   Recall of Prisoners Released Early

Where a person released on licence under s. 246 fails to comply with any conditions of the licence, or his/her whereabouts can no longer be electronically monitored at the place specified in the curfew condition, the Secretary of State may revoke the licence and recall the person to prison (s. 255).

2.4.18.4   Police Arrests

The guidance provided to police forces in relation to persons who are subject of a home detention curfew is as follows:
Where arrested:

- custody officer to notify the monitoring contractor immediately of:
  - ♦ details of the prisoner
  - ♦ details of the offence
  - ♦ whether the prisoner is to be bailed or retained in custody
  - ♦ whether the prisoner continues to wear the electronic tag;
- custody officer to notify the monitoring contractor when the prisoner is released.

Where charged:

- custody officer to immediately inform HM Prison Service Parole Unit;
- custody officer to inform contractor *if* the prisoner is to be returned to prison to remove and collect the monitoring unit.

Where a person is charged with an offence while subject to a home detention curfew the PACE Code C in relation to detention following charge continues to apply.

Where a prisoner has been charged with an offence, the decision to revoke the prisoner's licence is a matter for HM Prison Service Parole Unit and not the police.

2.4.18.5 **Police Requests for Revocation**

Where the police consider that a prisoner subject to a home detention curfew represents a serious risk to the public they may make a request for it to be revoked. Any such request should be authorised by an officer of the rank of superintendent or above and made to HM Prison Service Parole Unit at the Home Office.

'Serious risk' means:

- Offenders convicted of a sexual or violent offence: death or serious injury (physical or psychological) occasioned by further offences committed by the offender. Sexual and violent offences are considered the same in that a prisoner convicted of an offence of violence may be recalled following concerns about offences of a sexual nature.
- Offenders convicted of a non-sexual or violent offence: death or serious injury, etc. The offence which may cause that risk need not be the same as the original offence.
- It is only necessary to demonstrate that the prisoner has acted in such a way as to give *reasonable cause for belief* that recall is necessary to protect the public.

The chief of police and local parole board for an area also have a statutory duty to make suitable arrangements for managing dangerous offenders (**see Crime**).

2.5 | Court Procedure and Witnesses

2.5.1 Introduction

This chapter deals with the conditions where an adult defendant can plead guilty by post for certain summary offences, the procedure in dealing with offenders for summary, either way and indictable offences, and the law in relation to witnesses.

2.5.2 'Statement of Facts' Procedure

The procedure for a defendant to plead guilty by post is provided by s. 12 of the Magistrates' Courts Act 1980 and applies to proceedings by way of summons in the adult magistrates' court for summary offences. This procedure also applies to a summons in the youth court for persons aged 16 or 17 (s. 12(2)). The summons is served on the defendant together with a 'statement of facts' and a prescribed form of explanation. This enables the defendant an opportunity to plead guilty and put forward any mitigation in his/her absence. The magistrates' designated officer informs the prosecution of any written guilty plea.

Where service of the summons and 'statement of facts' is proved, and a guilty plea has been received from the defendant, the 'statement of facts' and any mitigation are read out by the magistrates' clerk in open court. Failure to read out any mitigation submitted by the defendant will nullify the proceedings (*R* v *Epping and Ongar Justices, ex parte Breach* [1987] RTR 233). No further facts or evidence can be given by the prosecution. Where the defendant is present in court at this time, he/she must be given an opportunity of giving any mitigation in person (s. 12A).

The magistrates have the discretion to decide that a case is not appropriate to be dealt with under the 'statement of facts' procedure and may adjourn the case for the defendant to appear in court. In these circumstances the guilty plea entered by the defendant is disregarded (s. 12(9)).

At any time before the hearing, a defendant may withdraw his/her guilty plea by notifying the magistrates' clerk in writing. Also the court may allow a defendant to change his/her plea at the hearing and contest the case (*R* v *Bristol Justices, ex parte Sawyers* [1988] Crim LR 754).

2.5.3 Mode of Trial

Trials are either trials on indictment, which take place in the Crown Court, or summary trials that take place in the magistrates' court. As outlined in **chapter 2.2 (paras 2.2.2.1 to 2.2.2.3)** the classification of the offence determines in which court the trial takes place; generally, summary offences in the magistrates' court and indictable offences in the Crown

Court. Either way offences can be tried in both courts and the determination as to which court is outlined in **para. 2.2.2.4**.

Where an offence is triable on indictment only, the defendant is sent immediately to the Crown Court from a preliminary hearing in the magistrates' court (s. 51 of the Crime and Disorder Act 1998). In the case of an either way offence which the magistrates' court have determined will be tried on indictment in the Crown Court, committal proceedings are held in accordance with s. 2(2) of the Administration of Justice (Miscellaneous Provisions) Act 1933.

There are two types of committal: those where the magistrates consider the evidence and those where they do not. In the former case, no witnesses are called and the prosecutor outlines the case. The evidence, which is tendered in written form, is either read out or summarised. Following this the accused may make a submission of 'no case to answer' though the defence cannot tender any evidence. The court then decides if there is sufficient evidence to commit the accused for trial or to discharge him/her (s. 6(1) of the Magistrates' Courts Act 1980). In committal proceedings where magistrates do not consider the evidence, all the evidence must consist of written statements, the accused must be legally represented and the accused's counsel or solicitor must not have requested the justices to consider a submission of there being insufficient evidence to justify trial by jury. The court do not have to consider the contents of any statements, depositions, other documents or any exhibits before committing the accused for trial (s. 6(2) of the 1980 Act). The provisions of s. 6 will be repealed by the Criminal Justice Act 2003, when in force.

2.5.3.1 Pre-trial Hearings

In the magistrates' court there is a system of pre-trial hearings. These are known as an 'Early First Hearing' where a guilty plea is anticipated or an 'Early Administrative Hearing' where a not guilty plea is expected. Section 8A of the Magistrates' Courts Act 1980 provides that at a pre-trial hearing, once a not guilty plea has been entered, the court may make rulings on any question as to the admissibility of evidence and any other question of law relating to criminal cases to be tried in the magistrates' court. However, such rulings can only be made if the accused is legally represented or he/she has been offered and granted or otherwise the right to representation by the Legal Services Commission as part of the Criminal Defence Service.

These rulings are binding and will continue to be so until the case is disposed of by the accused being acquitted, the prosecutor deciding not to proceed with the case, or the information is dismissed (s. 8B).

2.5.4 Summary Trial

Summary trials take place in the magistrates' court before at least two lay justices or a single District or Deputy District Judge (Magistrates' Courts).

The prosecution and defence may conduct their own case in person or be represented by counsel or solicitor (s. 122(1) of the Magistrates' Courts Act 1980). In the Crown Court the prosecution must appear by legal representative but the accused may still conduct his/her own case. An accused conducting his/her own case may be allowed a friend to accompany them as an advisor though such an advisor may not question witnesses or address the court (*McKenzie* v *McKenzie* [1970] 3 All ER 1034).

Where there is a 'guilty plea' in the magistrates' court, the hearing starts with the prosecution stating the facts of the case and introducing the offender's previous convictions, if there are any that are relevant. The defence then puts any mitigation to the court before sentence is passed.

A 'not guilty' plea in the magistrates' court allows the prosecution to call its evidence. The prosecution will begin proceedings by addressing the court in an opening speech. If the prosecution have established that there is a case to answer, the defendant can then call evidence. Very occasionally this may be followed by rebuttal evidence being called by the prosecution which is confined to unexpected matters raised by the defence. At the end of the evidence for the defence (and the rebuttal evidence, if any), the defence will usually address the court, if they have not already done so, in a closing speech. If the defence considers that the prosecution has not established a case to answer, they may make a submission of 'no case to answer'. There is no clear direction as to what would constitute 'no case to answer' in the magistrates' court, and if the prosecution have provided the necessary minimum amount of evidence on which a reasonable court could convict, the trial should continue. In *Moran* v *DPP* (2002) 166 JP 467 it was held that the justices are not required to give reasons in rejecting a submission of 'no case to answer'.

The Criminal Justice Act 2003 provides that, following a summary trial where the offender either pleads guilty or is convicted, the magistrates' court are under a duty to give reasons for, and explain the effect of, any sentence they might impose (s. 174(1)). In cases where they pass a custodial sentence or a community sentence they must explain why they regard the offence as being sufficiently serious to warrant such a sentence and mention any important aggravating or mitigating factors (s. 174(2)). The same duties are imposed on the Crown Court.

2.5.5 Trial on Indictment

Trials on indictment take place in the Crown Court, generally before a judge of the High Court, circuit judge or a recorder (**see para. 2.2.8**).

Where there is a 'guilty plea', which must be entered personally by the accused (*R* v *Ellis* (1973) 57 Cr App R 571), the only evidence which the prosecution needs to call are details of the accused's antecedents and criminal record. Occasionally, where there is disagreement about the precise facts of the offence, the prosecution may be required to call evidence to support their version of the facts; known as *Newton* hearings (*R* v *Newton* (1982) 77 Cr App R 13).

Where there is a 'not guilty plea', the prosecution are required to satisfy the jury beyond reasonable doubt that the accused committed the offence. Where the prosecution fails to provide sufficient evidence as to *any* element of the offence, the accused is entitled to be acquitted. This acquittal would take place on the direction of the judge, at the end of the prosecution case, following a defence submission of 'no case to answer'.

There are occasions where an accused may plead not guilty to the offence charged but guilty to a lesser offence (s. 6(1)(b) of the Criminal Law Act 1967). If the prosecution accepts the plea of guilty to the lesser offence, the court proceeds to sentence the accused for that lesser offence and treats him/her as being acquitted of the original offence charged (s. 6(5) of the 1967 Act). However, if the prosecution refuses to accept the plea of guilty to the lesser offence, the case proceeds as if the accused had pleaded not guilty (*R* v *Hazeltine* [1967] 2 QB 857).

An accused may be allowed to change his/her plea from not guilty to guilty as long as this occurs before the jury return their verdict. The judge then directs the jury to return a formal verdict of guilty (*R* v *Heyes* [1951] 1KB 29). Similarly, an accused may be allowed to change his/her plea from guilty to not guilty and the judge has the discretion to allow this at any stage before sentence is passed (*R v Plummer* [1902] 2 KB 339).

Although trial by jury has always been seen as the cornerstone of English law, this will be changed for limited occasions when the provisions of the Criminal Justice Act 2003 are in force. The Act provides that the prosecution may apply for a serious or complex fraud trial on indictment in the Crown Court to proceed in the absence of a jury (s. 43). Additionally, a trial on indictment in the Crown Court may be conducted without a jury where there is a danger of jury tampering, or continued without a jury where the jury has been discharged because of jury tampering.

2.5.6 Defendant's Non-appearance

Where the defendant fails to appear in the magistrates' court in answer to bail, the court can issue a warrant for his/her arrest under s. 7 of the Bail Act 1976 (**see para. 2.4.11.2**) or s. 1 of the Magistrates' Courts Act 1980 (**see para. 2.3.6.1**).

Section 11 of the Magistrates' Courts Act 1980 provides that where at the place and time appointed for the trial or adjourned trial of an information the prosecutor appears but the accused does not, the court may proceed in the accused's absence (s. 11(1)). However, where the accused's appearance was by way of summons, the court must be satisfied that the summons was served in a prescribed manner before commencing in the accused's absence (s. 11(2)).

The Magistrates' Courts (Procedure) Act 1998 also provides a procedure where the police serve witness statements on the defendant at the same time as the summons, rather than just a statement of facts (**see para. 2.5.2**). Where the defendant fails to appear, issue a plea or object to the witness statements, the case may be heard in his/her absence and the statements are admissible as evidence.

Where the court proceeds in the defendant's absence, a not guilty plea is entered and the prosecution is required to prove the case to the normal criminal standard. If the prosecution evidence is insufficient to reach the standard, the defendant should be acquitted. Where the case is proved the court may pass sentence or adjourn for the defendant to be present, either giving the defendant notice that he/she should attend or issuing a warrant for his/her arrest (ss. 10(3) and (4), 11(3) and (4), and 13(5)).

The Crown Court does have the discretion to conduct a trial in the absence, from its commencement, of the defendant and the seriousness of the offence is not a matter which is relevant to the exercise of this discretion. It is generally desirable that the defendant is represented by counsel during the trial, even where he/she had voluntarily absconded. In *R v Jones* [2002] 1 AC 1, the House of Lords held that in conducting a trial in the defendant's absence, where the defendant was represented by counsel, the defendant had enjoyed his convention right to a fair trial.

Practice Direction (Bail: Failure to Surrender and Trials in Absence) [2004] Cr App R 402 provides further guidance on conducting a trial in the defendant's absence. Due regard must be taken of the judgment in *R v Jones*, above, and the overriding concern is that the trial is as fair as circumstances permit and leads to a just outcome. The direction includes five circumstances which should be taken into account before proceeding in the defendant's absence: (a) the conduct of the defendant; (b) the disadvantages to the defendant; (c) public interest; (d) the effect of any delay; and (e) whether the attendance of the defendant could be secured at a later hearing. Other considerations include the seriousness of the offence and the likely outcome if the defendant is found guilty.

The European Court has held that it is for the authorities to satisfy the court that the accused was aware of the proceedings and adequate steps had been taken to trace the accused (*Colozza* v *Italy* (1985) 7 EHRR 516). In *Re X* [2001] Dalloz Jur 1899, the European Court held that where a judgment was made in the absence of the accused the court must hear the defence counsel and any written plea from the accused.

2.5.7 Adjournments and Remands

A magistrates' court may need to adjourn proceedings for a variety of reasons: where an accused wishes to obtain legal advice; the preparation of advance information for the defence; where an accused pleads not guilty and more time is required for the hearing; for reports, etc. Where an adjournment is necessary the court may have the power to remand an accused in custody. This section examines the powers of the magistrates' court in relation to adjournments and remands.

2.5.7.1 Adjournments

Adjournment of Inquiry into Offence

A magistrates' court may, before beginning to inquire into an offence which may be tried 'either way' as examining justices, or at any time during the inquiry, adjourn the hearing, and if it does so shall remand the accused (s. 5 of the Magistrates' Courts Act 1980 (to be repealed by the Criminal Justice Act 2003, when in force)).

Adjournment of Trial

A magistrates' court may adjourn a summary trial at any time before or after beginning to try an information. It need not remand the defendant unless one of the following conditions apply:

- the defendant has attained the age of 18 years; and
- the offence is triable 'either way'; and
- the accused has been in custody when first appearing or having been released on bail was surrendering to the custody of the court; or
- the accused has been remanded at any time during the proceedings (s. 10 of the Magistrates' Courts Act 1980).

Initial Procedure on Information for Offence Triable Either Way

Where a magistrates' court is hearing an information for an offence, triable either way, against a person who has attained the age of 18 years and they or their representative indicates a not guilty plea they may adjourn the proceedings and may remand that person. However, they shall remand that person if:

- the accused has been in custody when first appearing or having been released on bail was surrendering to the custody of the court; or
- the accused has been remanded at any time during the proceedings (s. 18 of the Magistrates' Courts Act 1980).

Where a person aged over 18 years is charged with an offence which may only be tried on indictment, the magistrates' court may adjourn the proceedings but must remand the defendant (s. 52(5) of the Crime and Disorder Act 1998).

'Remands' can be either by committing the defendant to custody or to remand on bail in accordance with the provisions of the Bail Act 1976 (**see chapter 2.4**).

References in ss. 10 and 18 to the trial of an information, or a defendant appearing in answer to an information, extend to cases where the proceedings are brought by way of a police charge. The charge sheet prepared at the police station is conventionally treated as the equivalent of an information laid before a magistrate.

2.5.7.2 Remands

The Magistrates' Courts Act, s. 128(6) provides that a magistrates' court shall not remand a person for a period exceeding eight clear days except where the person is:

- remanded on bail and the prosecution and defendant consent;
- remanded for inquiries to be made or of determining the most suitable method of dealing with the case; but, if the person is remanded, the remand can be no longer than four weeks on bail or three weeks in custody (s. 10(3) of the 1980 Act);
- remanded for a medical report (s. 11 of the Powers of Criminal Courts (Sentencing) Act 2000); or
- remanded where the court is to try an either way offence summarily and needs to be constituted for that purpose even where the remand is for a period exceeding eight clear days.

A magistrates' court may also remand a person in custody by committing him/her to detention at a police station for a period not exceeding three clear days. This may only occur where there is a need for the person to be so detained for the purpose of inquiries into other offences for which the person has not been charged (s. 128(7) of the Magistrates' Courts Act 1980). Where a person is eliminated from an inquiry he/she must be taken back to the magistrates' court even though the permitted period of detention has not expired. While in detention, the requirements of s. 39 of the Police and Criminal Evidence Act 1984 apply (responsibilities in relation to person detained) as do the requirements of s. 40 (review of police detention) (s. 128(8) of the Magistrates' Courts Act 1980).

A court may further remand a person where they are unable to appear because of illness or injury (s. 129 of the 1980 Act).

'Eight clear days' in s. 128(6) means, for example, from Monday (when the court remanded a person) to Wednesday of the following week.

Section 128A provides that, in certain circumstances, a magistrates' court may remand a person in custody before conviction for longer than eight days, which in any event cannot exceed 28 days, but the period of time must be stipulated. Failure to stipulate the period of time will result in a person being set free without any conditions being imposed (*Re Szakal* [2000] 1 Cr App R 248). Section 128(3A) to (3E) provides conditions where a person can be remanded in his/her absence for a period up to 32 days though he/she must be brought back before the court at least every fourth application for a remand. These provisions apply to both adults and persons under the age of 17 years.

2.5.7.3 Time Limits

Youth Courts

The Prosecution of Offences (Youth Court Time Limits) Regulations 2003 (SI 2003/917) provide that there are no maximum periods in proceedings in youth courts.

Magistrates' Courts

The Prosecution of Offences (Custody Time Limits) (Amendment) Regulations 1999 (SI 1999/2744) provides for a maximum magistrates' court custody time limit (from first appearance to start of trial) of 56 days in relation to those charged with summary offences.

Crown Courts

The Prosecution of Offences (Custody Time Limits) (Amendment) Regulations 2000 (SI 2000/3284) provides a maximum Crown Court custody time limit of 182 days less any period previously spent in custody of a magistrates' court for the relevant offence.

2.5.8 Witnesses

At the heart of a criminal trial will be the oral testimony provided by witnesses. A witness is a person called by a party in court proceedings with a view to proving a particular matter material to the case. This section examines the following key issues in relation to witnesses:

- attendance of witnesses at court
- competence and compellability
- issues of age
- witnesses with impaired intellect
- hostile witnesses.

The European Court and Commission have considered that specific rules concerning the admissibility, relevance and probity of evidence should be matters for regulation under domestic law (*Schenk* v *Switzerland* (1988) 13 EHRR 242).

The interference with witnesses or potential witnesses is included in the common law offence of perverting the course of public justice (as to which, **see Crime, chapter 1.14**).

2.5.8.1 Attendance of Witnesses at Court

The prosecution or defence can apply for a summons, warrant or order requiring a witness to attend a magistrates' court (s. 97 or 97A of the Magistrates' Courts Act 1980, or para. 4 of schedule 3 to the Crime and Disorder Act 1998), or the Crown Court (s. 2 of the Criminal Procedure (Attendance of Witnesses) Act 1965). The procedure to be followed is contained in r. 28 of the Criminal Procedure Rules 2005 (as amended by the Criminal Procedure (Amendment) Rules 2007). Where appropriate, such an application can be used as a pre-emptive measure to secure the attendance of witnesses.

The conditions that must be satisfied before a court issues a summons, warrant or order are:

- what evidence the proposed witness can give or produce
- why it is likely to be material evidence
- why it would be in the interests of justice to issue a summons.

There are two conditions that must be satisfied before a court issues a summons:

- that the person is likely to be able to give evidence which is likely to be material evidence, or produce any document or thing likely to be material evidence for the purpose of any criminal proceedings, and

• that it is in the interests of justice.

Where a witness is summoned but refuses to give evidence or to answer some question asked of them, they may be dealt with for contempt of court. The court has a range of powers to deal with contempt and these include imprisonment (*R* v *Haselden* [2000] All ER (D) 56).

The European Court has taken the view that where repeated and unsuccessful attempts have been made to bring a witness before the court—and in this case where he was forcibly brought before the court but absconded before giving evidence—it is open to domestic courts to have regard to any statement the witness made to the police, particularly where it is corroborated by other evidence (*Doorson* v *Netherlands* (1996) 22 EHRR 330).

2.5.8.2 Competence and Compellability

In looking at witnesses, it is crucial to consider two related questions:

• Whether there are any restrictions to a witness being called to provide testimony. This question is frequently one of whether a witness is *competent*.
• Whether a witness may be compelled or made to provide testimony. This is a question of whether a witness is *compellable*.

Competence in its simplest interpretation is whether in law a witness is allowed to be a witness. For a witness to be compellable two aspects must be considered:

• the witness must be competent; *and*
• the law requires the witness to give evidence even if the witness would rather not do so.

2.5.8.3 General Rule of Competence and Compellability

There is a general rule in English law that 'All people are competent and all competent witnesses are compellable.' The rule was sanctioned by the provisions of s. 53 of the Youth Justice and Criminal Evidence Act 1999. Section 53 states:

> (1) At every stage in criminal proceedings all persons are (whatever their age) competent to give evidence.

2.5.8.4 Exceptions to the Rule of Competence and Compellability

The exceptions to the general rule of competence and compellability are set out in various statutes and these exceptions can be listed as follows:

• the accused
• spouses and civil partners
• children
• those of defective intelligence
• other special groups.

The European Court of Human Rights has accepted that some categories of witness may not be compellable under a country's domestic law to give evidence, for example, spouses, cohabitees and family members. In *Unterpertinger* v *Austria* (1986) 13 EHRR 175, the Court held that the Convention:

> ... makes allowance for the special problems that may be entailed in a confrontation between someone 'charged with a criminal offence' and a witness from his own family and is calculated to protect such a witness by avoiding his being put in a moral dilemma ...

2.5.8.5   **The Accused**

Evidence on Behalf of the Prosecution

The competence of the accused to give evidence on behalf of the prosecution is dealt with under s. 53 of the Youth Justice and Criminal Evidence Act 1999, which states:

> (4) A person charged in criminal proceedings is not competent to give evidence in the proceedings for the prosecution (whether he is the only person, or is one of two or more persons, charged in the proceedings).

However, a person charged in criminal proceedings will be competent to give evidence for the prosecution at such time as:

- they plead guilty
- are convicted
- the charges against them are dropped (referred to as entering a *nolle prosequi*—a promise not to prosecute) (s. 53(5)).

It follows from the application of s. 53(4) and (5) of the 1999 Act, that should the prosecution wish to use the testimony of an accused against a co-accused, they must first make that person competent to be able to give that evidence. The person can only give evidence if that person pleads guilty, or they are convicted of the offence or the charges are dropped against them.

The European Commission of Human Rights held that the admission of the guilty plea of a co-defendant did not violate the accused's rights to a fair trial under Article 6 (*MH* v *United Kingdom* [1997] EHRLR 279).

However, the Commission has directed domestic courts to adopt a 'critical approach' in their assessment of 'accomplice' evidence where the accomplice stood to lose the benefit of sentence reductions if he/she retracted previous statements or confessions. In such cases it was considered crucial that the accomplice evidence could be challenged and that such evidence was not the sole basis for a conviction (*Baragiola* v *Switzerland* (1993) 75 DR 76).

Evidence on Behalf of the Defence

The Criminal Evidence Act 1898 sets out the position of whether an accused person is competent and compellable for the defence. Section 1 of the 1898 Act states:

> (1) A person charged in criminal proceedings shall not be called as a witness in the proceedings except upon his own application.
> . . .
> (4) Every person charged in criminal proceedings who is called as a witness in the proceedings shall, unless otherwise ordered by the court, give his evidence from the witness-box or other place from which the other witnesses give their evidence.

KEYNOTE

When an accused elects to give evidence, s. 72 of the Criminal Justice Act 1982 requires that such evidence be given on oath and that the accused is liable to cross-examination.

In being cross-examined, an accused may also be questioned by the prosecution about a co-accused (*R* v *Paul* [1920] 2KB 183).

2.5.8.6 Spouses and Civil Partners

A wife, husband or civil partner (other than when the wife, husband or civil partner are jointly charged) is competent to give evidence on behalf of the prosecution against their spouse, or partner.

A wife, husband or civil partner is only compellable to give evidence on behalf of the prosecution against their spouse or partner (unless jointly charged) in certain circumstances. These circumstances are provided by s. 80 of the Police and Criminal Evidence Act 1984 as amended by sch. 4 to the Youth Justice and Criminal Evidence Act 1999. The circumstances are:

- the offence charged involves an assault on, or injury or a threat of injury to, the wife, husband or civil partner of the accused; or
- the offence charged involves an assault on, or injury or a threat of injury to, a person who at the material time is under the age of 16; or
- the offence charged is a sexual offence alleged to have been committed in respect of a person who was at the material time under 16; or
- in the case of attempting or conspiring to commit, or of aiding, abetting, counselling, procuring or inciting the commission of any of the above offences.

A wife, husband or civil partner is competent and compellable to give evidence on behalf of the *accused*, unless jointly charged.

A wife, husband or civil partner is competent to give evidence on behalf of any *co-accused*. Section 80A of the 1984 Act also states:

The failure of a wife, husband or civil partner of a person charged in any proceedings to give evidence in the proceedings shall not be made the subject of any comment by the prosecution.

KEYNOTE

The Civil Partnership Act 2004 made ss. 80 and 80A of PACE 1984 applicable to 'civil partners' as well as wives and husbands. Legal civil partners are same sex couples who have registered their partnership in accordance with the 2004 Act.

Cohabitees are not afforded the same concessions as a wife, husband or civil partner in giving evidence against each other (that of being competent but not compellable). In *R* v *Pearce* [2002] 1 WLR 1553 it was held that the position with cohabitees was not in breach of Article 8 of the European Convention on Human Rights (the right to respect for family life).

In *Bellinger* v *Bellinger* [2002] 1 All ER 311 it was held that a marriage is void if the parties involved are not male and female. Gender is fixed immutably at birth for the purpose of marriage (s. 11 of the Matrimonial Causes Act 1973) and this even applies to a male who has undergone a sex change operation.

2.5.8.7 Children

The Youth Justice and Criminal Evidence Act 1999 deals with the position of children to act as witnesses in criminal proceedings.

Section 55 of the 1999 Act states:

(1) Any question whether a witness in criminal proceedings may be sworn for the purpose of giving evidence on oath, whether raised—
   (a) by a party to the proceedings, or
   (b) by the court of its own motion,

shall be determined by the court in accordance with this section.

(2) The witness may not be sworn for that purpose unless—

    (a) he has attained the age of 14, and

    (b) he has a sufficient appreciation of the solemnity of the occasion and of the particular responsibility to tell the truth which is involved in taking an oath.

(3) The witness shall, if he is able to give intelligible testimony, be presumed to have sufficient appreciation of those matters if no evidence tending to show the contrary is adduced (by any party).

(4) If any such evidence is adduced, it is for the party seeking to have the witness sworn to satisfy the court that, on a balance of probabilities, the witness has attained the age of 14 and has a sufficient appreciation of the matters mentioned in subsection (2)(b).

KEYNOTE

The statutory provisions require that no witness under the age of 14 is to be sworn. This sets up a presumption that witnesses are to be sworn if they are 14 or over.

Witnesses of 14 or over are only eligible to be sworn if they understand the solemnity of a criminal trial and that by taking the oath they are responsible for telling the truth.

The 1999 Act provides that a person *of any* age who is competent to give evidence, but by virtue of s. 55(2) is not permitted to be sworn, may give unsworn evidence (s. 56(1) and (2)).

In *G* v *DPP* [1997] 2 All ER 755, 'intelligible testimony' was defined as evidence which is capable of being understood. In this case it was also determined that whether a child was capable of giving evidence was within the capacity of the judge and did not require expert evidence. A child under the age of four years could still be a competent witness as long as they display such competency throughout the whole of their evidence (*R* v *P* [2006] EWCA Crim 3). See also *R* v *MacPherson* [2006] 1 Cr App R 30 and *R* v *Powell* [2006] 1 Cr App R 31 (competence of child witnesses).

Witnesses who are under the age of 17 might be allowed 'special measures' to help them with giving evidence in criminal proceedings (s. 16(2) of the 1999 Act) (see para. 2.5.10).

2.5.8.8 Issues of Age

The time when a person is deemed to have reached a particular age is covered by s. 9(1) of the Family Law Reform Act 1969.

The time at which a person attains a particular age expressed in years shall be the commencement of the relevant anniversary of the date of his/her birth.

Section 150 of the Magistrates' Courts Act 1980 states:

(4) Where the age of any person at any time is material for the purposes of any provision of this Act regulating the powers of a magistrates' court, his age at the material time shall be deemed to be or to have been that which appears to the court after considering any available evidence to be or to have been his age at that time.

KEYNOTE

Similar provisions appear in the following Acts:

- s. 1(6) of the Criminal Justice Act 1982 (for the purposes of sentencing young offenders (young offenders institution));
- s. 99 of the Children and Young Persons Act 1933 (parent or guardian assisting in the conduct of the defence).

A birth certificate is usually accepted as evidence of age. A statement from a person present at the birth may be useful in difficult cases. If a certificate of birth is produced to prove age, evidence must also be provided to positively identify the person as the person named in the certificate (*R* v *Rogers* (1914) 10 Cr App R 276).

In *R* v *Viazani* (1867) 31 JP 260, it was held that where the statement of an accused as to his/her age is in conflict with his/her appearance the statement of the accused may be disregarded.

2.5.8.9 People with Impaired Intellect

Under the Youth Justice and Criminal Evidence Act 1999 in determining whether a witness is competent to give evidence, proceedings take place in the absence of any jury (s. 55(5)). Expert evidence can be received as to the witness's competence (s. 55(6)), and the questioning of the witness is conducted by the court in the presence of the prosecution and defence (s. 55(7)).

In considering whether a witness is able to give 'intelligible testimony', s. 55(8) defines this as testimony where the witness is able to:

- understand questions put to him as a witness, and
- give answers to them which can be understood.

The decision in *R* v *Hayes* [1977] 1 WLR 234 may still apply to a witness's competence, where the courts are likely to take the view that the ability to understand and tell the truth is more important than an understanding of the religious meaning attached to the oath. Where such a person gives evidence, it is for the jury to determine how much weight to attach to the testimony.

Clearly, there is no inherent reason why a person suffering from a mental condition would not make a reliable witness. In *R* v *Barratt* [1996] Crim LR 495, a witness was suffering from a psychiatric condition and the court considered that her evidence was as reliable as that of any other witness save for certain aspects affected by her condition. The video-taped interview of a witness suffering from Alzheimer's Disease was admitted in evidence where she was deemed unfit to attend trial (*R* v *Ali Sed* [2004] EWCA Crim 1294).

Witnesses suffering from a mental disorder, mental impairment or a learning disability might be allowed 'special measures' to help them with giving evidence in criminal proceedings (s. 16(2) of the 1999 Act) (**see para. 2.5.10**).

2.5.8.10 Other Groups

In addition to the main exceptions outlined above, other people and groups may be incompetent or not compellable as witnesses. These situations are likely to be less frequent than the earlier exceptions:

- The Sovereign and Heads of State are competent but not compellable.
- Diplomats and consular officers may have total or partial immunity from being compelled.
- Restrictions also apply in respect of bankers and judges.

2.5.8.11 Hostile Witnesses

A party calling a witness, whether it be the defence or prosecution, would ordinarily do so in the expectation that the witness will be providing testimony that supports a point being advanced by that party. A witness may, however, provide unfavourable testimony to the side calling him/her. In such circumstances, it is said that the witness has failed to come up to proof. In other words, their oral testimony has not been consistent with their original witness statement, e.g. by not proving the matter intended or by proving the opposite. It is a general rule that a party calling a witness does not impeach the credit of his/her witness by asking leading questions and cross-examining the witness on his/her earlier previous inconsistent statement.

However, should a witness not give his/her evidence fairly and show no regard for the truth as against the party calling him/her, the judge may deem that witness to be a hostile witness. In this instance, the party calling the witness may contradict him/her with other evidence or, with the leave of the judge, prove that on an earlier occasion he/she made a statement inconsistent with the present testimony.

Where such cross-examination occurs as a result of a witness being treated as hostile, the jury should be reminded in clear terms what weight should be attached to it, namely that the previous inconsistent statement is not evidence as such, but simply goes to undermine the credibility of the witness's oral testimony. This is the case even where the 'hostile witness' gives evidence that is consistent with his/her previous statement. The rationale for this is that the witness would not otherwise have given evidence if he/she had not been treated as hostile (*R v Ugorji* (1999) *The Independent*, 5 July). (**See para. 2.7.17.3** concerning previous inconsistent statements.)

It is important to distinguish between an unfavourable witness and one who is hostile. Simply because a witness does not provide testimony to prove a matter does not make them hostile. A hostile witness deliberately goes beyond this.

....

EXAMPLE

Consider the situation where the defence calls witness A to provide evidence of a particular issue, e.g. that A saw a particular car at a particular place. However, in giving testimony A, in good faith or as a result of an earlier misunderstanding, believes he was mistaken. In this instance A is an unfavourable witness. If, however, A in fact decides to lie and say he did not in fact see the car when he really did then A may be deemed by the judge to be a hostile witness.

....

2.5.9 Live Television Links for Witnesses

Witnesses will ordinarily give their evidence from the witness box. However, there has been an increasing trend towards allowing some witnesses (particularly vulnerable ones) to give their testimony by other means, e.g., through a live television link. These statutory developments in this area are summarised below.

2.5.9.1 Criminal Justice Act 1988

Section 32(1) of the Criminal Justice Act 1988 provides that a witness outside the United Kingdom (other than the accused) may give evidence through a live television link. This provision relates to trials on indictment, appeals to the criminal division of the Court of Appeal or the hearing of a reference under s. 9 of the Criminal Appeal Act 1968.

Requests for assistance to hear witnesses outside their jurisdiction can be made by judicial authorities and designated prosecuting authorities under s. 7 of the Crime (International Co-operation) Act 2003. Where such requests are made' the normal procedure adopted is contained in the Crown Court Rules 1982 (SI 1982/1109).

KEYNOTE

There is no presumption in favour of using a television link, under any of the legislative provisions, and its use has to be justified for displacing the general rule that a witness should give evidence in the presence of the defendant (*R (On the Application of DPP)* v *Redbridge Youth Court* [2001] 4 All ER 411).

2.5.9.2 Crime and Disorder Act 1998

Section 57 of the Crime and Disorder Act 1998 provides for the use of live television links at preliminary court hearings where an accused is being detained in custody in prison or any other institution. The purpose of this provision is to reduce both delays in proceedings and the number of escapees from custody during transportation to and from courts.

Section 57 states:

(1) In any proceedings for an offence, a court may, after hearing representations from the parties, direct that the accused shall be treated as being present in the court for any particular hearing before the start of the trial if, during that hearing—

    (a) he is held in custody in a prison or other institution; and

    (b) whether by means of a live television link or otherwise, he is able to see and hear the court and to be seen and heard by it.

(2) A court shall not give a direction under subsection (1) above unless—

    (a) it has been notified by the Secretary of State that facilities are available for enabling persons held in custody in the institution in which the accused is or is to be so held to see and hear the court and to be seen and heard by it; and

    (b) the notice has not been withdrawn.

(3) If in a case where it has power to do so a magistrates' court decides not to give a direction under subsection (1) above, it shall give its reasons for not doing so.

(4) In this section 'the start of the trial' has the meaning given by subsection (11A) or (11B) of section 22 of the 1985 Act.

KEYNOTE

For the purposes of s. 57 no consent is required from either the accused or his/her legal adviser; it is a matter for the discretion of the court.

The phrase 'start of trial' (s. 57(4)) means:

- for cases being tried summarily, at the point where the prosecution start to present their evidence or when a guilty plea is accepted;
- for cases being tried on indictment, when a jury is sworn to consider the issue of guilt or fitness to plead, or, before a jury is sworn, at the time a plea of guilty is accepted by the court.

2.5.9.3 Youth Justice and Criminal Evidence Act 1999

Section 24 of the Youth Justice and Criminal Evidence Act 1999 provides for the use of a television link as part of a series of special measures designed to help young, disabled or intimidated witnesses give evidence in criminal proceedings. This section relates to witnesses in the Crown Court but only vulnerable witnesses (s. 16) in the magistrates' court. (**See para. 2.5.10** for the details of vulnerable (s. 16) and intimidated (s. 17) witnesses and other 'special measures'.)

Section 24 of the 1999 Act states:

(1) A special measures direction may provide for the witness to give evidence by means of a live link.
(2) Where a direction provides for the witness to give evidence by means of a live link, the witness may not give evidence in any other way without the permission of the court.
(3) The court may give permission for the purposes of subsection (2) if it appears to the court to be in the interests of justice to do so, and may do so either—
    (a) on an application by a party to the proceedings, if there has been a material change of circumstances since the relevant time, or
    (b) of its own motion.
(4) In subsection (3) 'the relevant time' means—
    (a) the time when the direction was given, or
    (b) if a previous application has been made under that subsection, the time when the application (or last application) was made.

KEYNOTE

'Live link' means a live television link where the witness is able to see and hear the proceedings and to be seen and heard by the judge or justices, legal representatives, and any interpreter appointed to assist the witness (s. 24(8)).

The House of Lords has held that the use of live television links is compatible with the right to a fair trial under Article 6 of the European Convention on Human Rights (*R (On the Application of D)* v *Camberwell Green Youth Court* [2005] 1 WLR 393).

When in force, s. 51 of the Criminal Justice Act 2003 will provide for witnesses to give evidence through a live link in criminal proceedings where the court is satisfied that it is in the interests of the efficient or effective administration of justice for the witness to give evidence by this means. The Police and Justice Act 2006 inserted a new s. 33A into the 1999 Act whereby vulnerable accused may give evidence over a live video link.

2.5.10 Special Measures for Vulnerable or Intimidated Witnesses

The Youth Justice and Criminal Evidence Act 1999 contains a range of measures designed to help young, disabled, vulnerable or intimidated witnesses to give evidence in criminal proceedings. In applying for a special measure direction the procedure to be followed is contained in r. 29 of the Criminal Procedure Rules 2005.

2.5.10.1 Eligible Witnesses

There are three categories of witness eligible for assistance and it is for the court to determine whether a witness falls into one of these categories:

- a witness who is under the age of 17 at the time of the hearing (s. 16(1));
- a witness who suffers from a mental or physical disorder or otherwise has a significant impairment of intelligence (s. 16(2));
- a witness whose evidence is likely to be affected on grounds of fear or distress about testifying (s. 17(1)).

The prosecution or defence may apply to the court for a special measure direction to be made or the court may make such a direction of its own motion (s. 19).

There are also special provisions relating to a 'child witness' (i.e. under the age of 17). Section 21 provides that a child witness will be deemed to be 'in need of special protection' if the offence to which the proceedings relate is a proscribed sexual offence or one of kidnapping, assault, etc. In such instances, the court must give a special measures direction for the witness's evidence to be obtained by means of a video recording. Where this is not possible, subject to availability, the evidence must be given by means of a live link. The provision that child witnesses can give evidence in a room where the accused is not present is not in breach of the European Convention of Human Rights, Article 6 (right to a fair trial), (*R (On the Application of D)* v *Camberwell Green Youth Court* [2003] 2 Cr App R 257). In *TS* v *Germany* (2005) 36 EHRR 1139 it was held that organising criminal proceedings in such a way as to protect the interests of a child witness are legitimate, particularly where sexual offences are concerned, but clear and precise reasons are needed if the evidence of a child witness is to be admitted without any opportunity of challenge by the defence.

KEYNOTE

Witnesses who fall outside the three categories may still be assisted by use of the court's inherent powers preserved under s. 19(6)(a) of the 1999 Act, for example, use could be made of screens or modification of court dress. Courts may also use their common law powers to ensure that witnesses remain anonymous. This is a particularly difficult area where the defendant may be seriously disadvantaged and it is essential that the court is satisfied that a fair trial can take place (*R* v *Davis* [2006] EWCA Crim 1155). This ruling was upheld by the European Court of Human Rights (*Krasniki* v *The Czech Republic* [2006] ECHR 176).

2.5.10.2 Screening Witnesses

The court can direct to provide a witness, while giving testimony or being sworn, to be prevented by means of a screen or other arrangement from seeing the accused. However, the witness must be able to be seen by the judge or justices (or both), the jury (if there is one), legal representatives and any interpreter or other person appointed to assist the witness (s. 23).

2.5.10.3 Evidence given in Private

A special measures direction may provide for the exclusion of any persons from the court whilst the witness is giving evidence (s. 25(1)). This does not include the exclusion of the accused, legal representatives and any interpreter acting for the witness (s. 25(2)).

This direction may only be used where the proceedings relate to a sexual offence or there are reasonable grounds to believe that the witness has or will be intimidated by any person other than the accused (s. 25(4)).

2.5.10.4 Removal of Wigs and Gowns

A direction may be provided for the wearing of wigs and gowns to be dispensed with while a witness gives his/her evidence in the Crown Court (s. 26).

2.5.10.5 Video Recorded Evidence

Section 27 of the Youth Justice and Criminal Evidence Act 1999 provides for video recorded evidence-in-chief and states:

(1) A special measures direction may provide for a video recording of an interview of the witness to be admitted as evidence in chief of the witness.

(2) A special measures direction may, however, not provide for a video recording, or part of such a recording, to be admitted under this section if the court is of the opinion, having regard to all the circumstances of the case, that in the interests of justice the recording, or that part of it, should not be so admitted.

(3) In considering for the purposes of subsection (2) whether any part of a recording should not be admitted under this section, the court must consider whether any prejudice to the accused which might result from that part being so admitted is outweighed by the desirability of showing the whole, or substantially the whole, of the recorded interview.

KEYNOTE

It was held in *R (On the Application of DPP)* v *Redbridge Youth Court* [2001] 4 All ER 411 that an accused could successfully oppose an order under this section if it could be established that the appearance of a witness in court was not likely to impact on the quality of the evidence.

When in force, s. 137 of the Criminal Justice Act 2003 will provide for further occasions where evidence by video recording can be admitted. This will be where a witness's account of an event has been video recorded at a time when the event was fresh in the witness's memory. On such occasions the court may accept the recording as evidence-in-chief from that witness.

Where a video recording is admitted as a witness's evidence-in-chief, the direction can provide for any cross-examination or re-examination of the witness before trial to be recorded by means of a video recording (s. 28(1) of the 1999 Act). The judge or justices and legal representatives, in the absence of the accused, must be able to see and hear the examination of the witness. The accused must also be able to see and hear the examination of the witness probably by use of a live link (s. 28(2) of the 1999 Act).

2.5.10.6 Examination through an Intermediary

This special measures direction may provide for any examination of the witness to be conducted through an interpreter or other person approved by the court (s. 29(1)).

The intermediary's function is to communicate questions to the witness, answers to any person asking such questions and provide an understanding of the questions and answers to the witness or person in question (s. 29(2)).

This special measure does not apply to witnesses affected on the grounds of intimidation, fear or distress (s. 17).

2.5.10.7 Aids to Communication

This special measures direction provides for any device which will enable questions or answers to be communicated to or by the witness despite any disability or disorder or other impairment which the witness has or suffers from (s. 30).

In relation to all the special measures directions, where such a direction has been used to provide evidence, in a trial on indictment with a jury, the judge must warn the jury that the use of such a direction does not prejudice the accused (s. 32).

This special measure does not apply to witnesses affected on the grounds of intimidation, fear or distress (s. 17).

2.5.11   Refreshing Memory

The Criminal Justice Act 2003 provides for the use of documents and transcripts by witnesses to refresh their memory.

Section 139 of the 2003 Act states:

(1) A person giving oral evidence in criminal proceedings about any matter may, at any stage in the course of doing so, refresh his memory of it from a document made or verified by him at an earlier time if—

    (a) he states in his oral evidence that the document records his recollection of the matter at that earlier time, and

    (b) his recollection of the matter is likely to have been significantly better at that time than it is at the time of his oral evidence.

(2) Where—

    (a) a person giving oral evidence in criminal proceedings about any matter has previously given an oral account, of which a sound recording was made, and he states in that evidence that the account represented his recollection of the matter at that time,

    (b) his recollection of the matter is likely to have been significantly better at the time of the previous account than it is at the time of his oral evidence, and

    (c) a transcript has been made of the sound recording,

he may, at any stage in the course of giving his evidence, refresh his memory of the matter from that transcript.

KEYNOTE

For the purposes of s. 139 a 'document' means anything in which information of any description is recorded, but not including any recording of sounds or moving images (s. 140). However, under common law a document includes a tape recording (*R* v *Bailey* [2001] All ER (D) 185 (Mar)).

The fact that the witness refreshed their memory from a document or transcript before going into the witness box does not affect the presumption contained within s. 139.

The Court of Appeal made clear that training or coaching witnesses in relation to a forthcoming criminal trial is prohibited (*R* v *Momodou*: *R* v *Limani* [2005] EWCA Crim 177).

2.5.12   Evidence of Oral Statement made through an Interpreter

It is inadmissible for a police officer to give evidence of a conversation held through the use of an interpreter. The only valid witness would be the interpreter (*R* v *Attard* (1958) 43 Cr App R 90) **(see para. 2.11.14).**

2.5.13   Victims' Personal Statements, Code and Advisory Panel

Guidance on the relevance of victims' personal statements is provided by the Consolidated Criminal Practice Direction, para. III.28 (**see** *Blackstone's Criminal Practice 2008*, Appendix 8, and the decision of the Court of Appeal in *R* v *Perks* [2000] Crim LR 606).

Paragraph III.28.1 of the Consolidated Criminal Practice Direction outlines the purpose of the scheme whereby a victim is given:

- a more formal opportunity to say how a crime has affected them;

- help to identify whether they have a particular need for information, support and protection.

It will also enable the court the opportunity to take the victim's statement into account when determining sentence.

When a police officer takes a statement from a victim, the victim will be told about the scheme and given the chance to make a victim personal statement. A victim personal statement may be made or updated at any time prior to the disposal of the case. The decision about whether or not to make a victim personal statement is entirely for the victim (para. III.28.2).

The Domestic Violence, Crime and Victims Act 2004 introduced a Victim's Code setting out the services to be provided to victims of criminal conduct (s. 32(1)). 'Victims' for the purposes of the Code are not specifically defined, though this could be one or more persons, such as where the actual victim is under the age of 17 or deceased. A person can be a 'victim' even where no person has been charged with or convicted of an offence in respect of criminal conduct (s. 32(6)).

Where a person is convicted of a sexual or violent offence, and a relevant sentence has been imposed, victims may make representations through the local probation board as to any licence conditions or supervision requirements in the event of an offender's release from custody. The local probation board is also required to keep victims informed of any such conditions or requirements (s. 35).

The 2004 Act has also created a Victims' Advisory Panel appointed by the Secretary of State who can consult with the Panel on matters relating to victims and witnesses of crime and anti-social behaviour (s. 55). The Panel comprises ten voluntary lay members, who have direct experience of victimisation, three co-opted members representing wider victims' interests, representatives of voluntary organisations to which the government provides core funding to provide direct services to victims and witnesses, and senior officials from criminal justice agencies. When in force, s. 48 of the 2004 Act will enable the Secretary of State to appoint a Commissioner for Victims and Witnesses. The Commissioner's primary functions will be to promote the interests of victims and witnesses of crime and anti-social behaviour, take steps to encourage good practice in their treatment, and keep the Victim's Code under review.

In relation to the protection of witnesses, the Serious Organised Crime and Police Act 2005 provides for the arrangements of protecting witnesses and other persons who are involved in the investigations or proceedings, where the risk to their safety is so serious and life threatening that a change of identity and/or relocation is necessary. The provisions contained in the 2005 Act relating to the protection of witnesses are explained in detail in *HOC 9/2006: New Provisions on Witness Protection in the Serious Organised Crime and Police Act 2005*.

2.5.14 Oaths and Affirmations

It is the general rule that every witness who gives evidence must be sworn, that is, take the oath or make an affirmation.

The manner in which the oath is administered is provided by s. 1 of the Oaths Act 1978. This requires the witness to hold the New Testament (Old Testament in the case of a Jew) in his uplifted hand and repeat, after the person administering the oath, the words 'I swear by Almighty God that . . .', followed by the oath prescribed by law.

Where the witness is neither a Christian nor a Jew they can object to taking the oath in the prescribed manner. Alternatively, they may affirm or take an oath upon a holy book appropriate to their religious belief. For example, Hindus are sworn on the Vedas and Muslims are sworn on the Koran (*R* v *Morgan* (1764) 1 Leach 54).

An affirmation may be made by a witness who objects to being sworn or where his/her request for an alternative form of oath is not reasonably practicable and would delay or inconvenience the proceedings (s. 5 of the 1978 Act). The witness repeats after the person administering the affirmation, the words 'I [name] do solemnly, sincerely and truly declare and affirm', followed by the words of the oath prescribed by law (s. 6 of the 1978 Act).

There are two exceptions to the general rule:

- children may give unsworn evidence (s. 55 of the Youth Justice and Criminal Evidence Act 1999);
- witnesses merely producing a document need not be sworn (*Perry* v *Gibson* (1834) 1 A & E 48).

Where a compellable witness refuses to take an oath or make an affirmation in the Crown Court, he/she can be held in contempt of court and where appropriate face a penalty of imprisonment (s. 45(4) of the Supreme Court Act 1981, to be amended by the Constitutional Reform Act 2005 to 'Senior Court Act 1981', when in force).

Where a witness refuses, without just excuse, to be sworn or give evidence in the magistrates' court, he/she can be committed to custody for a period not exceeding one month and/or be fined to an amount not exceeding £2,500 (s. 97(4) of the Magistrates' Courts Act 1980).

2.5.15 Examination-in-Chief

The party who calls a witness (prosecution or defence) is entitled to examine the witness by asking questions with a view to providing evidence which is favourable to that party's case. This is known as 'examination-in-chief'.

All witnesses are examined in chief with one exception; where the prosecution determine not to examine its witness in chief but allow the witness to be cross-examined by the defence. This is common in the case of police officers whose evidence-in-chief will be identical. Consequently, one police officer can give the evidence-in-chief but other officers involved may be required for cross-examination by the defence.

Cross-examination and re-examination are discussed in more detail below (**see paras 2.5.16** and **2.5.17**).

2.5.15.1 Leading Questions

The general rule is that leading questions, i.e. those which suggest the desired answer, may not be asked of a party's own witness. However, it is quite common practice for a party to lead a witness through certain parts of his/her evidence which are not in dispute.

There are two forms of leading questions: those which indicate to a witness the answer required and those which assume something to be true when it has not been established.

The first form is where a question puts words into the witness's mouth. For example, if evidence is given that A assaulted B and the question for the court is whether the defendant did in fact assault B, a prosecution witness should not be asked 'Did you see the defendant assault B?', but should be asked 'What did you see A do?

Exceptions to the Leading Questions Rule

Where leading questions are asked of a witness, these do not nullify proceedings but the judge will stop a party asking questions in the prohibited form. Evidence obtained from leading questions is not *inadmissible* but may affect the *weight* placed on it by the judge or jury.

Leading questions are admissible in the following circumstances:

- To refresh a witness's memory (**see para. 2.5.11**).
- Where the witness is deemed 'hostile' (**see para. 2.5.8.11**).
- For identification purposes (**see chapter 2.12**).
- Usually in matters accepted as being uncontroversial.
- In cross-examination.

2.5.16 Cross-examination

Under Article 6(3)(d) of the European Convention on Human Rights everyone charged with a criminal offence shall be entitled:

> to examine or have examined witnesses against him and to obtain the attendance and examination of witnesses on his behalf under the same conditions as witnesses against him ...

Cross-examination is the process by which one party may ask questions of the other party's witnesses. This examination is usually focused on either undermining their evidence or supporting that of the party's own witnesses.

Cross-examination, like any other form of questioning, is subject to the rules of evidence. The answers elicited from witnesses must be directly relevant to an issue in the case, or indirectly so, concerning evidence of collateral issues which means that although all witnesses (except generally the defendant) may be asked credit questions, as a general rule, their answers to such questions will be final. A collateral issue is one which is only relevant to the credibility of the witness. In *Attorney-General* v *Hitchcock* (1847) 1 Exch 91, the court determined the general rule preventing a party from calling evidence on collateral issues. However, there are five exceptions to this general rule. These relate to where a witness:

- is biased;
- has previous convictions;
- has a reputation for untruthfulness;
- is unreliable because of some physical or mental disability or illness;
- has made a statement inconsistent with what he/she has said in the witness box.

If any of these exceptions apply, then further questions can be asked of the witness to disprove his/her answer to the credit question.

The rules in relation to cross-examination do not prevent a party from asking the other party's witnesses about any matter which, if accepted by the witness, will undermine the witness's evidence.

Where a party decides not to cross-examine an opponent's witness, this is held to be an *acceptance* of the witness's evidence-in-chief. Consequently, it is not open to the party that failed to cross-examine to criticise, in a closing speech, the unchallenged evidence of the witness (*R* v *Bircham* [1972] Crim LR 430).

In *R* v *Bingham* [1999] 1 WLR 598, it was held that a defendant who goes into the witness box and is sworn thereby exposes him/herself to cross-examination by the prosecution and any co-accused, even if he/she does not give any evidence-in-chief. The prosecution is entitled to cross-examine the defendant even where no questions have been put to him/her by the defence counsel and adverse inferences can be drawn if the defendant does not answer those questions (**see chapter 2.7**). It was held that in a summary trial, where the prosecution fail to cross-examine an accused, the trial is not to be considered unfair as the magistrates are entitled to reject the accused's evidence (*Wilkinson* v *DPP* (2003) 167 JP 229).

2.5.16.1 Protection of Witnesses from Cross-examination

The Youth Justice and Criminal Evidence Act 1999 prohibits defendants from personally cross-examining complainants and particular witnesses in certain circumstances. The Act also creates a new statutory framework in relation to questioning witnesses about their previous sexual behaviour.

2.5.16.2 Protection of Complainants from Cross-examination

Section 34 of the 1999 Act states:

> No person charged with a sexual offence may in any criminal proceedings cross-examine in person a witness who is the complainant, either—
> (a) in connection with that offence, or
> (b) in connection with any other offence (of whatever nature) with which that person is charged in the proceedings.

Section 35 of the 1999 Act states:

> (1) No person charged with an offence to which this section applies may in any criminal proceedings cross-examine in person a protected witness, either—
> (a) in connection with that offence, or
> (b) in connection with any other offence (of whatever nature) with which that person is charged in the proceedings.

KEYNOTE

A 'protected witness' for the purposes of s. 35(1) is the complainant, a witness to the commission of the offence or a child, i.e. a person under the age of 17 (s. 35(2)).

The offences to which s. 35 apply are part 1 offences under the Sexual Offences Act 2003.

The following offences are also included in s. 35(3):

- kidnapping, false imprisonment or an offence under s. 1 or 2 of the Child Abduction Act 1984
- any offence under s. 1 of the Children and Young Persons Act 1933
- any offence which involves an assault on, or injury or a threat of injury to, any person.

2.5.16.3 Protection of Particular Witnesses from Cross-examination

Section 36 of the 1999 Act states:

> (1) This section applies where, in a case neither of sections 34 and 35 operates to prevent an accused in any criminal proceedings from cross-examining a witness in person—
> (a) the prosecutor makes an application for the court to give a direction under this section in relation to the witness, or
> (b) the court of its own motion raises the issue whether such a direction should be given.

(2) If it appears to the court—

    (a) that the quality of evidence given by the witness on cross-examination—

        (i) is likely to be diminished if the cross-examination (or further cross-examination) is conducted by the accused in person, and

        (ii) would be likely to be improved if a direction were given under this section, and

    (b) that it would not be contrary to the interests of justice to give such a direction, the court may give a direction prohibiting the accused from cross-examining (or further cross- examining) the witness in person.

KEYNOTE

Where an accused is prohibited from cross-examining the complainant or a witness, he/she must appoint a legal representative to conduct the cross-examination on his/her behalf. If the accused refuses or fails to appoint a legal representative, the court must consider appointing one on his/her behalf in order to test the witness's evidence.

2.5.16.4   Cross-examination of Witnesses about Previous Sexual Behaviour

Section 41 of the 1999 Act states:

    (1) If at a trial a person is charged with a sexual offence, then, except with the leave of the court—

        (a) no evidence may be adduced, and

        (b) no question may be asked in cross-examination,

    by or on behalf of the accused at the trial, about any sexual behaviour of the complainant.

KEYNOTE

It is for the defence to apply to the court if it wishes to introduce evidence or ask questions about the complainant's previous sexual behaviour (s. 41(2)). The procedure to be followed is contained in r. 36 of the Criminal Procedure Rules 2005 which have been revised and simplified in relation to applications under this section (Criminal Procedure (Amendment No 2) Rules 2006 (SI 2006/2636)).

Evidence will only be allowed if it is relevant to an issue in the case or is necessary to rebut prosecution evidence. It will also be allowed if it is an issue of consent and relates to sexual behaviour alleged to have taken place at or about the same time as the event which is the subject matter of the charge (s. 41(3)).

No evidence or question will be regarded as relating to a relevant issue where it is designed to impugn the credibility of the complainant as a witness (s. 41(4)).

Where the defence makes application under s. 41, the application is heard in private and in the absence of the complainant (s. 43(1)).

Following the hearing in private, the court must state in open court the reasons for giving or refusing the application (s. 43(2)).

In *R* v *Y* [2001] 2 WLR 1546, it was held that the complainant could be questioned about her sexual history with the defendant as otherwise s. 41 was in danger of being found to be in breach of Article 6 of the Convention (right to a fair trial). The House of Lords considered that it is common sense that a prior sexual relationship between a complainant and defendant could be relevant to the defence of consent.

The defence may still cross-examine a complainant as to allegedly false complaints made on other occasions, but in allowing this a court must consider s. 100 of the Criminal Justice Act 2003 (see para. 2.7.18.1) as such an allegation may amount to evidence of bad character (*R* v *V* [2006] EWCA Crim 1901).

In *S* [2003] All ER (D) 408 (Feb) it was held that s. 41(1) applies in relation to a complainant's false assertion that she was a virgin at the time of the offence, whereas she had sexual intercourse with another on the same day as the alleged offence.

2.5.17 Re-examination

Following cross-examination, the party calling the witness is entitled to re-examine. The questions put to the witness at this time may only relate to those matters upon which there was a cross-examination. No leading questions are allowed within the re-examination of a witness.

After the defendant has been re-examined it is open to the judge to ask questions to clear up uncertainties, to fill gaps, or to answer queries which might be lurking in the jury's mind. It is not appropriate for the judge to cross-examine the witness (*R* v *Wiggan* (1999) *The Times*, 22 March).

2.5.18 Further Evidence

It is the general rule that the prosecution must call the whole of their evidence before closing their case (*R* v *Francis* [1991] 1 All ER 225).

However, there are three well established exceptions to the general rule:

- evidence in rebuttal of defence evidence, that is, matters arising *ex improviso* (i.e. evidence which becomes relevant in circumstances which the prosecution could not have foreseen at the time when they presented their case) (*R* v *Owen* [1952] 2 QB 362);
- evidence not called by reason of oversight or inadvertence (*Royal* v *Prescott-Clarke* [1966] 2 All ER 366 and *Hammond* v *Wilkinson* [2001] Crim LR 323);
- evidence not previously available (*R* v *Pilcher* (1974) 60 Cr App R 1).

New evidence may be admitted in appeals for criminal cases as provided by s. 23(1) of the Criminal Appeal Act 1968. Section 23 allows the Court of Appeal, 'if they think it necessary or expedient in the interests of justice' *inter alia* to receive the evidence, if tendered, of any competent but not compellable witness or to order any compellable witness to attend for examination, whether or not that witness was called at the trial. In *R* v *Ahluwalia* [1992] 4 All ER 889, s. 23 was used to admit fresh evidence of the accused's alleged endogenous depression which, if put forward at the trial, may have provided an arguable defence to the charge of murder. Similarly, in *R* v *O'Brien* [2000] Crim LR 676, expert psychiatric evidence was admitted as fresh evidence to show that a defendant's abnormal disorder might render a confession or evidence unreliable. However, in *R* v *Horsman* (2001) *The Times*, 14 December, the Court of Appeal held that generally, at a re-trial, a defendant could not adduce as fresh evidence a statement which he/she had withheld for tactical reasons during his/her first trial.

2.5.19 Contempt of Court

This section is not intended to provide full details of criminal contempt of court but to consider occasions where police officers may be involved or required to take action.

Section 12 of the Contempt of Court Act 1981 deals with criminal contempt in the magistrates' court and states:

(1) A magistrates' court has jurisdiction under this section to deal with any person who—
    (a) wilfully insults the justice or justices, any witness before an officer of the court or any solicitor or counsel having business in the court, during his or their sitting or attendance in court or in going to or returning from the court; or

(b) wilfully interrupts the proceedings of the court or otherwise misbehaves in court.

(2) In any such case the court may order any officer of the court, or any constable, to take the offender into custody and detain him until the rising of the court; and the court may, if it thinks fit, commit the offender to custody for a specified period not exceeding one month or impose on him a fine not exceeding £2,500, or both.

Practice Direction (*Criminal Proceedings: Consolidation*) [2002] 1 WLR 2870, para. 54, *Contempt in the face of the magistrates' court*, describes the principles to be applied in exercising jurisdiction for the 1981 Act.

KEYNOTE

Contempt of court in the High Court and Crown Court is dealt with under Order 52 of the Civil Procedure Rules 1998. The 1981 Act provides for an offender to be committed to custody for a fixed term not exceeding two years in the case of committal by a superior court and one month by an inferior court.

<table>
<tr><td>

2.6

</td><td>

Youth Justice, Crime and Disorder

</td></tr>
</table>

2.6.1 Introduction

The Crime and Disorder Act 1998, apart from creating a framework of partnership between agencies for the reduction of crime and fear of insecurity, was also enacted to address the causes of youth crime.

The first part of this chapter examines the 1998 Act's introduction of the youth justice scheme which includes youth offending teams, youth justice plans, Youth Justice Board, and reprimands and final warnings for those under 17 years of age; and youth offender panels introduced by the Powers of Criminal Courts (Sentencing) Act 2000. The second part of the chapter looks at those provisions of the Act that take account of a parent's responsibility for their child's behaviour and other elements concerned with anti-social behaviour. This part includes parenting orders, child safety orders, anti-social behaviour orders, child curfew schemes, parental compensation orders and the removal of truants to designated premises.

2.6.2 Youth Justice Scheme

The Crime and Disorder Act 1998 states that the principal aim of the youth justice scheme is to prevent offending by children and young persons and that it shall be the duty of all persons and bodies carrying out functions in relation to the youth justice scheme to have regard to that aim (s. 37(1) and (2)). The persons and bodies prescribed as working within the youth justice scheme include local authorities, probation services, voluntary agencies, the police and the courts.

> **KEYNOTE**
>
> Local authorities have a duty, acting in co-operation with these persons and bodies, to provide all youth justice services (s. 38(1)). These services are determined by national standards drawn up by the Youth Justice Board (see para. 2.6.5). The duty is performed in co-operation with every chief officer of police or police authority and every local probation board or health authority (s. 38(2)).

2.6.3 Youth Offending Teams

The multi-agency approach to the reduction of crime and disorder is formalised by s. 39 of the 1998 Act which states:

(1) Subject to subsection (2) below, it shall be the duty of each local authority, acting in co-operation with the persons and bodies mentioned in subsection (3) below, to establish for their area one or more youth offending teams.

(2) Two (or more) local authorities acting together may establish one or more youth offending teams for both (or all) their areas; . . .

(3) It shall be the duty of—

    (a) every chief officer of police any part of whose police area lies within the local authority's area; and

    (b) every local probation board, Strategic Health Authority, Health Authority or Primary Care Trust, any part of whose area lies within that area,

to co-operate in the discharge by the local authority of their duty under subsection (1) above.

KEYNOTE

Youth offending teams carry out those functions which are required of the team within the local authority's youth justice plan (**see para. 2.6.4**).

The primary work of the youth offending teams include:

- a 'responsible officer' role in relation to parenting and child safety orders;
- assessment and intervention work;
- supervision of community sentences;
- an 'appropriate adult' service for police interviews;
- bail information, supervision and support;
- placement of young offenders;
- court work and preparation of reports.

In addition, the Powers of Criminal Courts (Sentencing) Act 2000 also requires youth offending teams to establish youth offender panels to deal with referral orders (s. 21)). (For further details about 'referral orders' see *Blackstone's Criminal Practice 2008*, **para. E12.1**).

2.6.3.1 Youth Offender Panels

Section 21 of the Powers of Criminal Courts (Sentencing) Act 2000 states:

(1) Where a referral order has been made in respect of an offender (or two or more associated referral orders have been so made), it is the duty of the youth offending team specified in the order (or orders)—

    (a) to establish a youth offender panel for the offender;

    (b) to arrange for the first meeting of the panel to be held for the purposes of section 23 below; and

    (c) subsequently to arrange for the holding of any further meetings of the panel required by virtue of section 25 below (in addition to those required by virtue of any other provision of this Part).

KEYNOTE

Each meeting of the panel will be made up of a member of the youth offending team and two members who are not from the youth offending team (s. 21(3)). The other two members are volunteers from the local community.

Panel members will have such qualifications or satisfy such criteria as determined by the Secretary of State (s. 21(4)).

Section 23 of the 2000 Act relates to a youth offender contract and the first meeting of the panel where a programme of behaviour to prevent re-offending will be agreed with the offender. The terms of the programme may include a number of provisions such as: financial or other reparation to the victim; attendance at mediation sessions; unpaid work or service; curfew requirements; educational attendance; rehabilitation for drugs and alcohol misuse; etc.

2.6.4 Youth Justice Plans

Youth justice plans are designed to prevent re-offending by children and young persons. A duty to produce these plans is provided by s. 40 of the Crime and Disorder Act 1998 which requires local authorities to annually formulate and implement plans setting out how youth justice services are to be provided and funded. There is also a requirement in relation to the establishment of youth offending teams, including their composition, operation, functions and funding.

2.6.5 Youth Justice Board

The Youth Justice Board consists of up to 12 members who have extensive recent experience of the youth justice system and are appointed by the Secretary of State (s. 41(1), (2) and (4) of the 1998 Act).

The functions of the Board include: monitoring the operations of the youth justice system and provision of youth justice services; the content of any national standards and promotion of good practice; the accommodation in which children and young persons are kept in custody; and steps that might be taken to prevent offending by children and young persons (s. 41(5)).

2.6.6 Reprimands and Final Warnings

Reprimands and final warnings are a statutory disposal, created by ss. 65 and 66 of the Crime and Disorder Act 1998 to replace cautions for offenders aged 17 and under. Guidance on the scheme is available through joint Home Office/Youth Justice Board guidance published in November 2002 (*Final Warning Scheme: Further Guidance for the Police and Youth Offending Teams*), and *HOC 14/2006: The Final Warning Scheme*. Reprimands are for those not previously convicted of an offence and final warnings for those who have received a reprimand or have committed an offence not considered serious enough to warrant a charge.

When offending behaviour occurs the presumption should be that the provisions of the Final Warning Scheme would be the first response when dealing with a young person (HOC 14/2006).

2.6.6.1 Reprimand

Section 65(1) of the 1998 Act provides a constable with a power to reprimand an offender where:

(a) a constable has evidence that a child or young person ('the offender') has committed an offence;

(b) the constable considers that the evidence is such that, if the offender were prosecuted for the offence, there would be a realistic prospect of his being convicted;

(c) the offender admits to the constable that he committed the offence;

(d) the offender has not previously been convicted of an offence; and

(e) the constable is satisfied that it would not be in the public interest for the offender to be prosecuted.

KEYNOTE

An offender may only be reprimanded where he/she has not previously been reprimanded or warned (s. 65(2)). The admission under s. 65(1)(c) should be 'clear and reliable' and be an admission 'to all the elements of the offence' (HOC 14/2006).

2.6.6.2 Warning

Section 65(3) of the 1998 Act provides a constable with a power to warn an offender where:

(a) the offender has not previously been warned; or

(b) where the offender has previously been warned, the offence was committed more than two years after the date of the previous warning and the constable considers the offence to be not so serious as to require a charge to be brought;

but no person may be warned under paragraph (b) above more than once.

2.6.6.3 Reprimand and Warning: Police Powers

In relation to the giving of a reprimand or warning s. 65(5) of the 1998 Act provides that a police officer must:

(a) where the offender is under the age of 17, give any reprimand or warning in the presence of an appropriate adult; and

(b) explain to the offender and, where he is under that age, the appropriate adult in ordinary language—

    (i) in the case of a reprimand, the effect of subsection 5(a) of section 66 below;

    (ii) in the case of a warning, the effect of subsections (1), (2), (4) and (5)(b) and (c) of that section, and any guidance issued under subsection (3) of that section.

KEYNOTE

In relation to s. 65(5)(b)(i) above, s. 66(5)(a) provides that a reprimand may be cited in criminal proceedings in the same way as a conviction.

In relation to s. 65(5)(b)(ii) above, explanations of each of the subsections referred to are provided in brackets:

- s. 66(1) (referral to youth offending team);
- s. 66(2) (participation in a rehabilitation programme);
- s. 66(4) (restrictions on a court to impose a conditional discharge);
- s. 66(5)(b) and (c) (citation as a criminal conviction).

In *R (On the Application of U)* v *Metropolitan Police Commissioner* (2002) *The Times*, 29 November, it was held that where the full and informed consent from the offender and the appropriate adult were not obtained, the administration of a reprimand or warning could be considered a breach of Article 6 of the European Convention on Human Rights (the right to a fair trial). However, this decision was contradicted in

---

R (On the Application of R) v *Durham Constabulary* [2005] UKHL 21, where it was held that as a warning did not involve the determination of a criminal charge, the rights of the offender under Article 6 were not engaged.

2.6.7 Parenting Orders

These orders are about influencing parental responsibility and control and the importance placed upon this by the government. The orders were introduced to give parents more help and support to change the criminal and/or anti-social behaviour of their children in providing a framework where parents participate in their child's supervision. The strategy here is one of prevention in attempting to dissuade a recurrence of criminality or truancy.

Parenting orders are defined by s. 8 of the Crime and Disorder Act 1998:

(4) A parenting order is an order which requires the parent—
  (a) to comply, for a period not exceeding twelve months, with such requirements as are specified in the order, and
  (b) subject to subsection (5) below, to attend, for a concurrent period not exceeding three months, such counselling or guidance programme as may be specified in directions given by the responsible officer.

(5) A parenting order may, but need not, include such a requirement as is mentioned in subsection 4(b) above in any case where a parenting order under this section or any other enactment has been made in respect of the parent on a previous occasion.

In considering the requirements of an order s. 9 of the 1998 Act states:

(4) Requirements specified in, and directions given under, a parenting order shall, as far as practicable, be such as to avoid—
  (a) any conflict with the parent's religious beliefs; and
  (b) any interference with the times, if any, at which he normally works or attends an educational establishment.

KEYNOTE

For the purpose of the 1998 Act, 'child' is someone under the age of 14 and 'young person' is someone of 14 years or over but under 18 (s. 117).

'Parenting order' should not be confused with 'parental responsibility order' (Children Act 1989) and 'parental order' (Human Embryology and Fertilisation Act 1990) which are available for other purposes.

2.6.7.1 Counselling and Guidance

Counselling and guidance sessions referred to in s. 8(4)(b) of the 1998 Act are intended to educate parents in how to respond more effectively to the demands of their child. These sessions could include the setting and enforcement of consistent standards of behaviour or a requirement that the child be escorted to school by a responsible adult.

Where a parent has attended counselling and guidance sessions under an earlier parenting order the court may waive this requirement (s. 8(5)).

The requirements provided by s. 8(4)(a) above are not specified but in drafting the legislation certain examples were given. These included a parent escorting their child to school and a child being supervised by a responsible adult during the evenings.

2.6.7.2   Responsible Officer

The definition of 'responsible officer' is provided in s. 8(8) of the 1998 Act which states:

> In this section and section 9 below 'responsible officer', in relation to a parenting order, means one of the following who is specified in the order, namely—
> (a)   an officer of a local probation board;
> (b)   a social worker of a local authority; and
> (bb) a person nominated by a person appointed as director of children's services under section 18 of the Children Act 2004, or by a person appointed as chief education officer under section 532 of the Education Act 1996;
> (c)   a member of a youth offending team

2.6.7.3   The Parenting Order

Section 8 of the 1998 Act states:

> (1)   This section applies where, in any court proceedings—
>   (a)   a child safety order is made in respect of a child, or the court determines on an application under section 12(6) below that a child has failed to comply with any requirement included in such an order;
>   (aa) a parental compensation order is made in relation to a child's behaviour;
>   (b)   an anti-social behaviour order or sexual offences prevention order is made in respect of a child or young person;
>   (c)   a child or young person is convicted of an offence; or
>   (d)   a person is convicted of an offence under section 443 (failure to comply with a school attendance order) or section 444 (failure to secure regular attendance at a school of registered pupil) of the Education Act 1996.
> (2)   Subject to subsection (3) and section 9(1) below, if in the proceedings the court is satisfied that the relevant condition is fulfilled, it may make a parenting order in respect of a person who is a parent or guardian of the child or young person or, as the case may be, the person convicted of the offence under section 443 or 444 ('the parent').

KEYNOTE

A parenting order may be made against:

- One or both biological parents (this could include an order against a father who may not be married to the mother).
- A person who is a guardian.

Guardians are defined as any person who, in the opinion of the court, has for the time being the care of a child or young person (s. 117(1)).

The court will be required to establish whether or not the making of an order is 'desirable' in the circumstances of a particular case. This is seen as an entirely subjective test (except for the requirement in s. 9(1)(a) below), following on from s. 8(2) above which states that the court *may* make an order. Consequently, the court generally retains a discretion not to impose an order.

Sections 20 and 26 of the Anti-social Behaviour Act 2003 and s. 324 of the Criminal Justice Act 2003 extend the situations in which parenting orders can be made. These include applications by local education authorities where a child has been excluded from school, and applications in respect of criminal conduct or anti-social behaviour. The Police and Justice Act 2006, when in force, will insert new ss. 26A and 26B into the Anti-social Behaviour Act 2003 whereby local authorities and registered social landlords can apply for parenting orders in respect of anti-social behaviour. The Magistrates' Courts (Parenting Orders) Rules 2004

(SI 2004/247) set out the procedure for applying for and varying or discharging parenting orders under the Crime and Disorder Act 1998, Anti-social Behaviour Act 2003 and Criminal Justice Act 2003.

Child safety orders and anti-social behaviour orders are discussed in **paras 2.6.8 and 2.6.9** respectively. For the law in relation to sex offenders, **see Crime, chapter 1.9.**

2.6.7.4 **Parenting Order: Statutory Requirement**

Section 9 of the 1998 Act states:

(1) Where a person under the age of 16 is convicted of an offence, the court by or before which he is so convicted—
   (a) if it is satisfied that the relevant condition is fulfilled, shall make a parenting order; and
   (b) if it is not so satisfied, shall state in open court that it is not and why not.

(1A) The requirements of subsection (1) do not apply where the court makes a referral order in respect of the offence.

(1B) If an anti-social behaviour order is made in respect of a person under the age of 16 the court which makes the order—
   (a) must make a parenting order if it is satisfied that the relevant condition is fulfilled;
   (b) if it is not so satisfied, must state in open court that it is not and why it is not.

(2) Before making a parenting order—
   (a) in a case falling within paragraph (a) of subsection (1) of section 8 below;
   (b) in a case falling within paragraph (b) or (c) of that subsection, where the person concerned is under 16; or
   (c) in a case falling within paragraph (d) of that subsection, where the person to whom the offence related is under that age,
   a court shall obtain and consider information about the person's family circumstances and the likely effect of the order on those circumstances.

(2A) In a case where a court proposes to make both a referral order in respect of a child or young person convicted of an offence and a parenting order, before making the parenting order the court shall obtain and consider a report by an appropriate officer—
   (a) indicating the requirements proposed by that officer to be included in the parenting order;
   (b) indicating the reasons why he considers those requirements would be desirable in the interests of preventing the commission of any further offence by the child or young person; and
   (c) if the child or young person is aged under 16, containing the information required by subsection (2) above.

(2B) In subsection (2A) above 'an appropriate officer' means—
   (a) an officer of a local probation board;
   (b) a social worker of a local authority; or
   (c) a member of a youth offending team.

KEYNOTE

Section 9(1) provides a statutory requirement in favour of making an order where the relevant condition relates to where a child or young person (under 16) is convicted of an offence (s. 8(1)(c)). Where a court is proposing to make both a referral order and parenting order they are required to consider a report by an officer of the local probation board, social worker or member of the youth offending team (s. 8(2A) and (2B)).

In determining the legislation the government decided to provide a distinction between offenders under 16 and those of 16 and 17. The decision appears to have been made on advice concerning the differences in emotional, intellectual and physical development between juveniles aged 16 and 17 and younger children. It was considered that parents of those under 16 who are subject to criminal proceedings must be involved in preventing a further commission of an offence. For 16 and 17 year olds the court should determine any parental involvement.

2.6.7.5 Procedure

Apart from considering information about the family circumstances of each case, whatever the age of the child or young person, s. 9 of the 1998 Act places the following requirement on the court:

> (3) Before making a parenting order, a court shall explain to the parent in ordinary language—
> (a) the effect of the order and of the requirements proposed to be included in it;
> (b) the consequences which may follow (under subsection (7) below) if he fails to comply with any of those requirements; and
> (c) that the court has power (under subsection (5) below) to review the order on the application either of the parent or of the responsible officer.

KEYNOTE

The parent or responsible officer can apply for the discharge or variation of an order and the court can agree to cancel, add or substitute any of its provisions. This can only be done by the court making the original order.

2.6.7.6 Breach of a Parenting Order

Section 9 of the 1998 Act states:

> (7) If while a parenting order is in force the parent without reasonable excuse fails to comply with any requirement included in the order, or specified in directions given by the responsible officer, he shall be liable on summary conviction to a fine not exceeding level 3 on the standard scale.
> (7A) In this section 'referral order' means an order under section 16(2) or (3) of the Powers of Criminal Courts (Sentencing) Act 2000 (referral of offender to youth offender panel).

KEYNOTE

The section does not specify who would be responsible for instituting proceedings but it is assumed this will be the 'responsible officer' and that the normal processes will be followed whereby the Crown Prosecution Service will make decisions as to a prosecution applying the usual test of public interest.

2.6.7.7 Binding Over of Parent or Guardian

Section 150 of the Powers of Criminal Courts (Sentencing) Act 2000 provides for the binding over of a parent or guardian and states:

> (1) Where a child or young person (that is to say, any person aged under 18) is convicted of an offence, the powers conferred by this section shall be exercisable by the court by which he is sentenced for that offence, and where the offender is aged under 16 when sentenced it shall be the duty of the court—
> (a) to exercise those powers if it is satisfied, having regard to the circumstances of the case, that their exercise would be desirable in the interests of preventing the commission by him of further offences; and

(b) if it does not exercise them, to state in open court that it is not satisfied as mentioned in paragraph (a) above and why it is not so satisfied;

but this subsection has effect subject to section 19(5) above and paragraph 13(5) of schedule 1 to this Act (cases where referral orders made or extended).

(2) The powers conferred by this section are as follows—

(a) with the consent of the offender's parent or guardian, to order the parent or guardian to enter into a recognizance to take proper care of him and exercise proper control over him; and

(b) if the parent or guardian refuses consent and the court considers the refusal unreasonable, to order the parent or guardian to pay a fine not exceeding £1,000;

and where the court has passed a community sentence on the offender, it may include in the recognizance provision that the offender's parent or guardian ensure that the offender complies with the requirements of that sentence.

KEYNOTE

The recognisance can be imposed on the parent or guardian for up to three years or until the offender is aged 18, whichever is the shorter (s. 150(4)).

For the purposes of s. 150, taking 'care' of a person includes giving him/her protection and guidance, and 'control' includes discipline (s. 150(11)).

2.6.8 Child Safety Orders

These orders were introduced to help prevent children under 10 from turning to crime. Such orders are concerned with the child's potential offending behaviour and in practice are likely to be used in conjunction with parenting orders under s. 8 of the Crime and Disorder Act 1998.

Section 11 of the 1998 Act states:

(1) Subject to subsection (2) below, if a magistrates' court, on the application of a local authority, is satisfied that one or more of the conditions specified in subsection (3) below are fulfilled with respect to a child under the age of 10, it may make an order (a 'child safety order') which—

(a) places the child, for a period (not exceeding the permitted maximum) specified in the order, under the supervision of the responsible officer; and

(b) requires the child to comply with such requirements as are so specified.

KEYNOTE

In order to ensure any such proceedings are not viewed as 'criminal', jurisdiction for making the order rests with the magistrates' family proceedings court.

The section provides evidence of the government's determination to deliver crime prevention through a partnership approach. A local authority with social services responsibilities must make the application for such an order. However, it would probably be the police who first become aware of the misconduct which triggers such an application.

There is a right of appeal to the High Court against a magistrates' court making a child safety order (s. 13(1)).

2.6.8.1 Child Safety Order: Conditions

The court must be satisfied that one or more of four conditions are fulfilled before making an order. These are provided by s. 11(3) of the 1998 Act:

(a) that the child has committed an act which, if he had been aged 10 or over, would have constituted an offence;

(b) that a child safety order is necessary for the purpose of preventing the commission by the child of such an act as is mentioned in paragraph (a) above;

(c) that the child has contravened a ban imposed by a curfew notice; and

(d) that the child has acted in a manner that caused or was likely to cause harassment, alarm or distress to one or more persons not of the same household as himself.

KEYNOTE

The civil standard of evidence (the 'balance of probabilities') is the standard of proof in determining whether a condition is fulfilled. There is no minimum age for an order. The permitted maximum period of supervision of such an order is 12 months (s. 11(4)).

2.6.8.2 Breach of Child Safety Order

Section 12 of the 1998 Act states:

(6) Where a child safety order is in force and it is proved to the satisfaction of the court which made it or another magistrates' court acting for the same local justice area, on the application of the responsible officer, that the child has failed to comply with any requirement included in the order, the court may make an order varying the order—

(i) by cancelling any provision included in it; or

(ii) by inserting in it (either in addition to or in substitution for any of its provisions) any provision that could have been included in the order if the court had then had power to make it and were exercising the power.

KEYNOTE

'Section 31 of the 1989 Act' relates to the Children Act 1989. Although the section does not provide the court with the power to make a supervision order in response to a breach, there is nothing to stop an application being made for such an order by a local authority or other authorised person in the ordinary way.

2.6.9 Anti-social Behaviour Orders

Anti-social behaviour orders (ASBO), which can be made against a child or young person aged 10 to 17 years, are provided by the Crime and Disorder Act 1998, s. 1 which states:

(1) An application for an order under this section may be made by a relevant authority if it appears to the authority that the following conditions are fulfilled with respect to any person aged 10 or over, namely—

(a) that the person has acted, since the commencement date, in an anti-social manner, that is to say, in a manner that caused or was likely to cause harassment, alarm or distress to one or more persons not of the same household as himself; and

(b) that such an order is necessary to protect relevant persons from anti-social acts by him.

KEYNOTE

An application for an ASBO can be made by way of complaint to a magistrates' court (s. 1(3)), or an order can be issued on conviction in criminal proceedings, either on an application or by a court's own initiative (s. 1C). Where an order is made, it may prohibit the defendant from doing anything for the purpose of protecting others from further anti-social acts (s. 1(4)).

When in force, the Police and Justice Act 2006 will also amend s. 153A of the Housing Act 1996 to provide for anti-social behaviour injunctions on the application of a landlord. Where the landlord is a local authority a power of arrest condition may be attached to the injunction and a constable may arrest without warrant a person whom he has reasonable cause for suspecting to be in breach of the provision.

For a full discussion of anti-social behaviour orders and individual support orders, **see General Police Duties, chapter 4.5.**

2.6.10 Child Curfew Schemes

Child curfew schemes are designed to tackle the problem of unsupervised young children committing crime, anti-social activities and causing real harm and misery to local communities. The age of the young child was raised by the Criminal Justice and Police Act 2001 from under 10 to under 16. The 2001 Act also gives the police the power to initiate a local child curfew scheme in addition to local authorities.

Section 14 of the Crime and Disorder Act 1998 states:

(1) A local authority or a chief officer of police may make a scheme (a 'local child curfew scheme') for enabling the authority or (as the case may be) the officer—
   (a) subject to and in accordance with the provisions of the scheme; and
   (b) if, after such consultation as is required by the scheme, the authority or (as the case may be) the officer considers it necessary to do so for the purpose of maintaining order,
   to give a notice imposing, for a specified period (not exceeding 90 days), a ban to which subsection (2) below applies.
(2) This subsection applies to a ban on children of specified ages (under 16) being in a public place within a specified area—
   (a) during specified hours (between 9 pm and 6 am); and
   (b) otherwise than under the effective control of a parent or a responsible person aged 18 or over.

KEYNOTE

The local authority or chief officer of police are required to consult with each other and such people or other bodies as are considered appropriate (s. 14(3)). The extent of the consultation with other people or bodies is totally discretionary but if appropriate community groups are not consulted the Home Secretary may decide not to confirm the scheme (see below).

Most schemes should come into force one month after confirmation of their introduction by the Home Secretary (s. 14(5)).

'Public place' for the purpose of the section has the same meaning as in part II of the Public Order Act 1986 (s. 14(8)) (see General Police Duties, chapter 4.6).

2.6.10.1 Contravention of Curfew Notices

Section 15 of the 1998 Act states:

(1) Subsections (2) and (3) below apply where a constable has reasonable cause to believe that a child is in contravention of a ban imposed by a curfew notice.
(2) The constable shall, as soon as practicable, inform the local authority for the area that the child has contravened the ban.
(3) The constable may remove the child to the child's place of residence unless he has reasonable cause to believe that the child would, if removed to that place, be likely to suffer significant harm.

KEYNOTE

This provision does not give the constable a power to use force. However, in applying common law principles, a constable may use reasonable force in exercising a lawful power (see **General Police Duties, chapter 4.4**).

Section 15(3) does not state what a constable should do with a child if he/she does not remove the child to its home. However, it would seem appropriate to use the power under s. 46 of the Children Act 1989 in removing the child to suitable accommodation, i.e. a police station or care of social services (see **Crime, chapter 1.10**).

Where a constable has informed the local authority about a contravention of the curfew notice s. 15(4) places a duty on the local authority to enquire into the circumstances of the child and to initiate the investigation within 48 hours of receiving such notification.

2.6.11 Parental Compensation Orders

The Crime and Disorder Act 1998 provides for parental compensation orders. Section 13A states:

(1) A magistrates' court may make an order under this section (a 'parental compensation order') if on the application of a local authority it is satisfied, on the civil standard of proof—
   (a) that the condition mentioned in subsection (2) below is fulfilled with respect to a child under the age of 10; and
   (b) that it would be desirable to make the order in the interests of preventing a repetition of the behaviour in question.
(2) The condition is that the child has taken, or caused loss of or damage to, property in the course of—
   (a) committing an act which, if he had been aged 10 or over, would have constituted an offence; or
   (b) acting in a manner that caused or was likely to cause harassment, alarm or distress to one or more persons not of the same household as himself.

KEYNOTE

To satisfy an application under this section only the 'civil standard of proof' is required, that is 'on the balance of probability', and not 'beyond all reasonable doubt' as required by the 'criminal standard'.

The amount of compensation specified cannot exceed £5,000 in all (s. 13A(4)). Collection and enforcement conditions are the same as if the parent had been convicted of an offence (s. 13A(6)).

2.6.12 Removal of Truants to Designated Premises, etc.

Section 16 of the Crime and Disorder Act 1998 states:

(1) This section applies where a local authority—
    (a) designates premises in a police area ('designated premises') as premises to which children and young persons of compulsory school age may be removed under this section; and
    (b) notifies the chief officer of police for that area of the designation.

(2) A police officer of or above the rank of superintendent may direct that the powers conferred on a constable by subsection (3) below—
    (a) shall be exercisable as respects any area falling within the police area and specified in the direction; and
    (b) shall be so exercisable during a period specified;
    and references in that subsection to a specified area and a specified period shall be construed accordingly.

KEYNOTE

'Designated premises' are not defined in the 1998 Act and are a matter for the local authority. In drafting the legislation it was considered that in many cases children would ultimately be removed to their own schools.

2.6.12.1 Police Powers

Section 16 provides the police powers in relation to dealing with truants.

(3) If a constable has reasonable cause to believe that a child or young person found by him in a public place in a specified area during a specified period—
    (a) is of compulsory school age; and
    (b) is absent from school without lawful authority,
    the constable may remove the child or young person to designated premises, or to the school from which he is so absent.

KEYNOTE

Again 'public place' has the same meaning as in part II of the Public Order Act 1986.

'Without lawful authority' is qualified by subs. (4) in that lawful authority will be that which falls within s. 444 of the Education Act 1996—leave, sickness, unavoidable cause or day set apart for religious observation.

The power of a constable to remove a child or young person to 'designated premises' is not an arrest in the traditional sense of detention and statutory powers relating to arrests will not apply. However, the duty to explain the reason for a persons 'seizure' may well apply in such cases (as to which, **see General Police Duties, chapter 4.4**).

As with the powers conferred in relation to curfew notices (**see para. 2.6.10**), it appears probable that the common law rule entitling a constable to use reasonable force would apply. However, legal commentators are not convinced this is the case as the use of force could be seen as having a damaging effect on relations between the police and young persons and the possibility of criminal or civil action against individual officers. The requirement for the officer to have 'reasonable cause to believe' that the person meets the criteria at (a) and (b) is more stringent than mere suspicion (**see General Police Duties, chapter 4.4**).

2.6.12 Removal of Truants to Designated Premises, etc.

Section 444A of the Education Act 1996 (inserted by the Anti-social Behaviour Act 2003) provides a penalty notice scheme for parents or guardians of children failing to attend school regularly. The notices will normally be issued by a constable, teacher (head, deputy or assistant head teacher, or authorised staff member) or authorised officer of a local education authority, and the amount of the penalty to be paid will be £50 (if paid within 28 days) or £100 (if paid after 28 days but within 42 days) (Education (Penalty Notices) (England) Regulations 2004 (SI 2004/181)).

PART TWO

The Law of Evidence

2.7 | Evidence

2.7.1 Introduction

Evidence can be described as information that may be presented to a court so that it may decide on the probability of some facts asserted before it, that is information by which facts in issue tend to be proved or disproved. There are several types of evidence by which facts are open to proof—or disproof—and these are discussed later in the chapter.

2.7.2 Weight and Admissibility of Evidence

The two questions that need to be applied to any evidence are:

- admissibility; and
- weight.

The question of admissibility, to be decided by the judge in all cases, is whether the evidence is relevant to a fact in issue. All evidence of facts in issue and all evidence which is sufficiently relevant to prove (or disprove) facts in issue are potentially admissible.

The admissibility of evidence is very important to the outcome of any trial as it is from this that a person's guilt is decided. When collecting evidence in a case it should always be a consideration whether the evidence being collected is the best available (although, **see para. 2.7.8**) and whether it will be admissible.

Once it is established that the evidence is admissible, it is put before the court to determine what weight it will attach to the evidence; that is, how much effect does it have on proving or disproving the case.

2.7.2.1 Evidence Gathering

The word evidence must not be confused with information. In relation to preparing an offence file, the investigation of the offence will result in the collection of information. What is and what is not evidence can be decided at a later stage with the help of the Crown Prosecution Service. The importance of this distinction is that rules of evidence should not restrict the initial collection of information, otherwise a fact vital to the outcome of the case may be disregarded as irrelevant and/or inadmissible.

2.7.2.2 Reasons for Excluding Admissible Evidence

Even though evidence may be admissible in criminal cases, at common law, the trial judge has a general discretion to exclude legally admissible evidence tendered by the prosecution. This can be seen in *R v Sang* [1980] AC 402, where it was held that:

- A trial judge, as part of his/her duty to ensure that an accused receives a fair trial, always has a discretion to exclude evidence tendered by the prosecution if in his/her opinion its prejudicial effect outweighs its probative value. In deciding if the evidence should be admitted, the question the judge asks himself/herself is whether it is fair to allow the evidence not whether it is obtained fairly or by unfair means.
- With the exception of admissions and confessions (here s. 76 of the Police and Criminal Evidence Act 1984 applies) and generally with regard to evidence obtained from the accused after the commission of the offence, the judge generally has no discretion whether to exclude relevant admissible evidence on the ground that this was obtained by improper or unfair means.

If the evidence is relevant to the matters in issue then it is admissible and the court is not concerned with how the evidence was obtained (*Kuruma, Son of Kaniu* v *The Queen* [1955] AC 197). This proposition was upheld in *Jeffrey* v *Black* [1978] QB 490 where evidence was admissible concerning the unlawful search of premises.

Evidence may also be excluded for the following reasons:

- the incompetence of the witness;
- it relates to previous convictions, the character or disposition of the accused;
- it falls under hearsay;
- it is non-expert opinion evidence;
- it is privileged information;
- it is withheld as a matter of public policy.

There are also powers to exclude evidence under ss. 76 and 78 of the Police and Criminal Evidence Act 1984 (**see chapter 2.9**).

2.7.3 Facts in Issue

In a criminal case, facts in issue are those facts which must be proved by the prosecution in order to establish the defendant's guilt, or in exceptional cases those facts which are the essential elements of a defence, where the burden of proof is on the defendant to prove the defence.

Such facts will include:

- the identity of the defendant;
- the *actus reus* (**see Crime, chapter 1.2**);
- the *mens rea* (**see Crime, chapter 1.1**).

The relevant criminal conduct (*actus reus*) and state of mind (*mens rea*) will always be facts in issue, and it is therefore essential that these features are understood, both as general concepts and also in relation to the particular offence being investigated.

2.7.4 Burden of Proof

The facts in issue fall into two distinct categories:

- the facts that the *prosecution* bear the burden of proving or disproving in order to establish the defendant's guilt;

- the facts which, in exceptional circumstances, the *defence* need to prove to show that the defendant is not guilty.

2.7.4.1 Duty of the Prosecution

'Throughout the web of the English criminal law one golden thread is always to be seen; that is the duty of the prosecution to prove the prisoner's guilt.' This famous passage is taken from the House of Lords' decision in *Woolmington* v *DPP* [1935] AC 462. The underlying principle was perhaps best explained by Geoffrey Lawrence QC in an address to the jury in a murder trial:

> The possibility of guilt is not enough, suspicion is not enough, probability is not enough, likelihood is not. A criminal matter is not a question of balancing probabilities and deciding in favour of probability.
>
> If the accusation is not proved beyond reasonable doubt against the man accused in the dock, then by the law he is entitled to be acquitted, because that is the way our rules work. It is no concession to give him the benefit of the doubt. He is entitled by law to a verdict of not guilty.

(See Brian Harris, *The Literature of the Law*, Blackstone Press, 1998.)

Therefore the general rule is that the prosecution have the legal (or persuasive) burden of proving all the elements of the offence in order to prove guilt.

In *Evans* v *DPP* (2001) *The Times*, 9 July, it was held that the justices had wrongly applied *the balance of probabilities* in finding the defendant guilty rather than the full criminal standard of proof.

Where the defendant enters a plea of not guilty to the charge, the onus is on the prosecution to prove the whole of their case. This includes 'the identity of the accused, the nature of the act and the existence of any necessary knowledge or intent' (*R* v *Sims* [1946] KB 531).

Generally the onus is on the prosecution in the first instance to establish particular facts to prove the accused's guilt beyond all reasonable doubt. However, once a prima facie case is made out, the defence has to establish particular facts in order to rebut the prosecution evidence. Here there is a shift of the onus to establish particular facts.

2.7.4.2 Duty on the Defence

Exceptionally, the defence may have the burden of proof. In such circumstances the standard of proof for the defence is less rigorous than for the prosecution when establishing guilt (beyond all reasonable doubt). The defence will succeed if the court or jury are satisfied that the defence evidence is more probably true than false. This standard of proof is referred to as *the balance of probabilities*, the same standard of proof that operates in a civil trial.

Generally the prosecution bear the duty of proving or disproving certain facts and, if they fail to do so, the defence need say nothing; the prosecution fails and the defendant is acquitted.

Exceptionally, the common law (e.g. the defence of insanity), or a statute (e.g. diminished responsibility (s. 2 of the Homicide Act 1957)), may impose a burden on the defence to prove the defence.

The law relating to the carrying of weapons is a good illustration of where the defence may have a burden of proof. Once the prosecution have proved (beyond a reasonable doubt) that a defendant was carrying an offensive weapon, the burden then shifts to the defence to prove (on the balance of probabilities) that the defendant had lawful authority or reasonable excuse (**see General Police Duties, para. 4.8.2**).

There will also be occasions where the defence has what is called an *evidential burden* in relation to certain specific defences they intend to rely on. Common examples of defences that only place an evidential burden on the defence are defences relating to alibis, self-defence, accident and provocation. In contrast to the evidential burden borne by the prosecution (to show that there is a case to answer by the end of the prosecution evidence), the defence's evidential burden arises somewhat differently. Unlike those defences that place a full legal burden of proof on the defence, the defence does not have to satisfy the judge of anything as such. All that the defence has to do is to ensure that there is enough evidence relating to the defence that is to be raised to enable the judge to direct the jury upon that defence as a live issue. In other words, the defence cannot invite the jury merely to speculate what there might have been, e.g. provocation or self-defence, or accident. There has to be some firm evidence about a defence before the judge will direct the jury in relation to it. This does not in any sense mean that the judge has to believe the evidence. Very little evidence in fact will do because if a judge does wrongly withdraw a defence from the jury any resulting conviction is likely to be quashed. All that the judge has to find is that there has been some evidence, however flimsy, of a given defence so that he/she can direct the jury about it. Of course, once the defence has satisfied this evidential burden, the legal burden of proof is with the prosecution to disprove the defence beyond a reasonable doubt.

With the incorporation of the European Convention of Human Rights into UK law, there was some argument that placing a full legal burden of proof on the defence violated the defendant's right to a fair trial under Article 6(2), which deals with the presumption of innocence. There has now been some clear guidance given by the House of Lords on this issue in *R v Lambert* [2001] 3 WLR 206 (which has been followed in *Sheldrake v DPP* [2004] UKHL 43).

The *Lambert* case involved an allegation of possession with intent to supply cocaine contrary to s. 5 of the Misuse of Drugs Act 1971. Section 28(2) of the Act provides an accused with a defence where they can prove they neither new nor suspected nor had reason to suspect the existence of some fact alleged by the prosecution. The House of Lords held that s. 28(2) needed to be read in light of s. 3 of the Human Rights Act 1988. Section 3(1) provides that:

> So far as it is possible to do so, primary legislation and subordinate legislation must be read and given effect in a way which is compatible with the Convention rights.

On this basis the House of Lords were prepared to read the wording of the section as imposing an evidential, as opposed to a persuasive, burden of proof. This ruling was followed in *Attorney-General's Reference (No. 4 of 2002)* [2003] HRLR 15, in relation to the burden of proof contained in s. 11(2) of the Terrorism Act 2000 (belonging to a proscribed organisation).

In *L v DPP* [2002] QB 137 it was held that the reverse onus provision, where the defence were required to give good reason why the defendant had with him in a public place a blade or sharp point, did not conflict with Article 6 of the Convention.

Section 101 of the Magistrates' Courts Act 1980 places a legal burden of proof on the accused either expressly or by implication. Section 101 of the 1980 Act states:

> Where the defendant to an information or complaint relies for his defence on any exception, exemption, proviso, excuse or qualification, whether or not it accompanies the description of the offence or matter of complaint in the enactment creating the offence or on which the complaint is founded, the burden of proving the exception, exemption, proviso, excuse or qualification shall

be on him; and this notwithstanding that the information or complaint contains an allegation negativing the exception, exemption, proviso, excuse or qualification.

KEYNOTE

Although s. 101 applies to summary trials, it has now been established that where the burden of proof is placed on an accused then that burden relates whether the offence is being tried summarily or on indictment (*R* v *Hunt* [1987] AC 352).

An example of a summary offence where the burden of proof is on the defence is driving without insurance where the accused is required to prove he/she is insured (*Williams* v *Russell* (1933) 149 LT 190). An example of an indictable offence is where the accused was convicted on indictment of selling intoxicating liquor without a licence and the Court of Appeal held that it was for the accused to prove that he was the holder of a licence (*R* v *Edwards* [1975] QB 27).

2.7.5 Formal Admissions

Where a fact is accepted by the defence, there is a process by which this can be formally admitted under s. 10 of the Criminal Justice Act 1967. In such formal admissions the fact ceases to be an issue.

Section 10 states:

(1) Subject to the provisions of this section, any fact of which oral evidence may be given in any criminal proceedings may be admitted for the purpose of those proceedings by or on behalf of the prosecutor or defendant, and the admission by any party of any such fact under this section shall as against that party be conclusive evidence in those proceedings of the fact admitted.

(2) An admission under this section—
   (a) may be made before or at the proceedings;
   (b) if made otherwise than in court, shall be in writing;
   (c) if made in writing by an individual, shall purport to be signed by the person making it and, if so made by a body corporate, shall purport to be signed by a director or manager, or the secretary or clerk, or some other similar officer of the body corporate;
   (d) if made on behalf of a defendant who is an individual, shall be made by his counsel or solicitor;
   (e) if made at any stage before the trial by a defendant who is an individual, must be approved by his counsel or solicitor (whether at the time it was made or subsequently) before or at the proceedings in question.

(3) An admission under this section for the purpose of proceedings relating to any matter shall be treated as an admission for the purpose of any subsequent criminal proceedings relating to that matter (including any appeal or retrial).

(4) An admission under this section may with the leave of the court be withdrawn in the proceedings for the purpose of which it is made or any subsequent criminal proceedings relating to the same matter.

KEYNOTE

Where the accused enters a not guilty plea at a plea and directions hearing in the Crown Court, both the prosecution and defence are expected to inform the court of facts which are to be admitted and which are then accepted in written form in accordance with s. 10(2)(b) of the 1967 Act (see *Practice Direction (Criminal Proceedings: Consolidation)* [2002] 1 WLR 2870, para. 44.13(f)).

Formal admission may be made by counsel or a solicitor during court proceedings. In such cases the admission is written down and signed by or on behalf of the party making the admission. This procedure applies for the purpose of summary trial or proceedings before magistrates acting as examining justices (r. 37.4 of the Criminal Procedure Rules 2005).

2.7.6 Inferences from Silence

At common law, when being questioned about involvement in a criminal offence, a suspect is under no obligation to answer any of the questions. This is another key feature of the criminal justice system in England and Wales and is the reason behind the cautioning of suspects required by the Police and Criminal Evidence Act 1984 (**see General Police Duties, chapter 4.4**). However, ss. 34 to 38 of the Criminal Justice and Public Order Act 1994 have a potentially important impact on the law in relation to the accused's silence.

Sections 34 to 37 permit the court to draw 'such inferences as appear proper' against the accused in the circumstances contained within the sections.

2.7.6.1 Inferences from Silence when Questioned or Charged

Section 34 of the Criminal Justice and Public Order Act 1994 provides that inferences can be drawn if, when questioned by the police under caution, charged or officially informed that he/she may be prosecuted, the accused fails to mention a fact on which he/she later relies in his/her defence, and which he/she could reasonably have been expected to mention at the time.

Section 34 states:

(1) Where, in any proceedings against a person for an offence, evidence is given that the accused—
  (a) at any time before he was charged with the offence, on being questioned under caution by a constable trying to discover whether or by whom the offence had been committed, failed to mention any fact relied on in his defence in those proceedings; or
  (b) on being charged with the offence or officially informed that he might be prosecuted for it, failed to mention any such fact,
  being a fact which in the circumstances existing at the time the accused could reasonably have been expected to mention when so questioned, charged or informed, as the case may be, subsection (2) below applies.
(2) Where this subsection applies—
  (a) a magistrates' court, in deciding whether to grant an application for dismissal made by the accused under section 6 of the Magistrates' Courts Act 1980 (application for dismissal of charge in course of proceedings with a view to transfer for trial);
  (b) a judge, in deciding whether to grant an application made by the accused under—
    (i) section 6 of the Criminal Justice Act 1987 (application for dismissal of charge of serious fraud in respect of which notice of transfer has been given under section 4 of that Act); or
    (ii) paragraph 5 of schedule 6 to the Criminal Justice Act 1991 (application for dismissal of charge of violent or sexual offence involving child in respect of which notice of transfer has been given under section 53 of that Act);
  (c) the court, in determining whether there is a case to answer; and
  (d) the court or jury, in determining whether the accused is guilty of the offence charged,
  may draw such inferences from the failure as appear proper.
(2A) Where the accused was at an authorised place of detention at the time of the failure, subsections (1) and (2) above do not apply if he had not been allowed an opportunity to consult a solicitor prior to being questioned, charged or informed as mentioned in subsection (1) above.

(3) Subject to any directions by the court, evidence tending to establish the failure may be given before or after evidence tending to establish the fact which the accused is alleged to have failed to mention.

(4) This section applies in relation to questioning by persons (other than constables) charged with the duty of investigating offences or charging offenders as it applies in relation to questioning by constables; and in subsection (1) above 'officially informed' means informed by a constable or any such person.

(5) This section does not—

   (a) prejudice the admissibility in evidence of the silence or other reaction of the accused in the face of anything said in his presence relating to the conduct in respect of which he is charged, in so far as evidence thereof would be admissible apart from this section; or

   (b) preclude the drawing of any inference from any such silence or other reaction of the accused which could properly be drawn apart from this section.

(6) This section does not apply in relation to a failure to mention a fact if the failure occurred before the commencement of this section.

KEYNOTE

Although judges have discretion in individual cases it has been recommended that in relation to s. 34 they should closely follow the Judicial Studies Board specimen direction. This direction was followed in *Beckles* v *United Kingdom (Chenia)* [2003] 2 Cr App R 83 and accepted by the European Court of Human Rights. However, failure to give proper direction does not necessarily involve a breach of Article 6 (right to a fair trial).

Section 34 deals with the 'failure to mention any fact' and the word 'fact' is given its normal dictionary definition of 'something that is actually the case' (*R* v *Milford* [2001] Crim LR 330). Where an accused alleges that they did mention the relevant fact when being questioned it is for the prosecution to prove the contrary before any adverse inference can be drawn.

There have been numerous domestic and European case decisions about failure to advance facts following legal advice to remain silent, and more recent cases have attempted to unravel the difficulties experienced in this area. These cases have accepted that a genuine reliance by a defendant on his/her solicitor's advice to remain silent is not in itself enough to preclude adverse comment. The real question to be answered is whether the defendant remained silent, not because of legal advice, but because there was no satisfactory explanation to give (*R* v *Beckles* [2005] EWCA Crim 2766, *R* v *Bresa* [2005] EWCA Crim 1414, and *R* v *Loizou* [2006] EWCA Crim 1719).

In relation to s. 34, the accused cannot be convicted solely on an inference drawn from silence. In *Condron* v *United Kingdom* (2001) 31 EHRR 1, the European Court of Human Rights, although accepting that there are cases which clearly call for an accused to provide an explanation, the court are required to apply 'particular caution' before invoking the accused's silence against him.

In *R* v *Argent* [1997] 2 Cr App R 27, the court stated that personal factors which might be relevant to an assessment of what an individual could reasonably have been expected to mention were age, experience, mental capacity, state of health, sobriety, tiredness and personality.

In *R* v *Flynn* [2001] EWCA Crim 1633, the court held that the police are entitled to conduct a second interview with a suspect, having obtained evidence from their witnesses which was not available in the first interview, and adverse inference could be drawn from the suspect's silence.

Where an accused, following legal advice, fails to answer questions during interview but presents a prepared statement, no adverse inference can be drawn where the accused's defence does not rely on any facts not mentioned in the interview (*R* v *Campbell* [2005] EWCA Crim 1249). However, this would not be the case when evidence of facts relied on during the trial was not contained within the pre-prepared statement (*R* v *Turner* [2003] EWCA Crim 3108).

Section 34 differs from the other 'inference' sections in that the questioning need not occur at a police station and therefore the presence of a legal representative is not required. However, it appears clear that, should the prosecution seek to draw any inferences of an accused's silence where such questioning has occurred, the questions would need to be asked of the suspect again once he/she had access to legal advice.

A requirement to caution the person is contained in s. 34(1)(a) to make it clear of the risks connected with a failure to mention facts which later form part of the defence (see **General Police Duties, chapter 4.4**).

The National Centre for Policing Excellence produces a practice advice document on the 'Right to Silence' that outlines the legislation, provides practical advice for investigators and considers the special warnings under the provisions of ss. 34, 16 and 37.

When the provisions of the Criminal Justice Act 2003 are in force s. 34(2)(a) and (2)(b)(i) and (ii) will be repealed and replaced by 'sch. 3, para. 2 to the Crime and Disorder Act 1998'. In relation to cases sent for trial under s. 51 or 51A(3)(d), this is in force, but for all other purposes the date in force is yet to be appointed. Section 6 of the Magistrates' Courts Act 1980 will also be repealed by the 2003 Act.

2.7.6.2 Where Access to Legal Advice is Delayed

Guidance has been provided by the government (Home Office Circular 53/1998). This requires that where access to legal advice has been delayed in accordance with Annex B of PACE Code C, the procedures for conducting the interview at the police station should be as follows:

- the interviewing officer should conduct any interview with the suspect at the police station in accordance with PACE Code C.
- the interviewing officer should make a written note of those questions which the suspect has failed or refused to answer;
- once the suspect has had the opportunity of access to legal advice, the interviewing officer should put these questions to the suspect again; and ask the suspect whether he/she wishes to say/add anything further.

(For a full discussion on delaying access to legal advice, **see para. 2.11.6.7**).

2.7.6.3 Inferences from Silence: Failure to Account for Objects, Substances and Marks

Section 36 of the Criminal Justice and Public Order Act 1994 provides that inferences can be drawn from an accused's failure to give evidence or refusal to answer any question about any object, substance or mark which may be attributable to the accused in the commission of an offence.

Section 36 states:

(1) Where—
  (a) a person is arrested by a constable, and there is—
      (i) on his person; or
     (ii) in or on his clothing or footwear; or
    (iii) otherwise in his possession; or
     (iv) in any place in which he is at the time of his arrest,
    any object, substance or mark, or there is any mark on any such object; and
  (b) that or another constable investigating the case reasonably believes that the presence of the object, substance or mark may be attributable to the participation of the person arrested in the commission of an offence specified by the constable; and

(c) the constable informs the person arrested that he so believes, and requests him to account for the presence of the object, substance or mark; and

(d) the person fails or refuses to do so,

then if, in any proceedings against the person for the offence so specified, evidence of those matters is given, subsection (2) below applies.

(2) Where this subsection applies—

(a) a magistrates' court, in deciding whether to grant an application for dismissal made by the accused under section 6 of the Magistrates' Courts Act 1980 (application for dismissal of charge in course of proceedings with a view to transfer for trial);

(b) a judge, in deciding whether to grant an application made by the accused under—

(i) section 6 of the Criminal Justice Act 1987 (application for dismissal of charge of serious fraud in respect of which notice of transfer has been given under section 4 of that Act); or

(ii) paragraph 5 of schedule 6 to the Criminal Justice Act 1991 (application for dismissal of charge of violent or sexual offence involving child in respect of which notice of transfer has been given under section 53 of that Act);

(c) the court, in determining whether there is a case to answer; and

(d) the court or jury, in determining whether the accused is guilty of the offence charged, may draw such inferences from the failure or refusal as appear proper.

(3) Subsections (1) and (2) above apply to the condition of clothing or footwear as they apply to a substance or mark thereon.

(4) Subsections (1) and (2) above do not apply unless the accused was told in ordinary language by the constable when making the request mentioned in subsection (1)(c) above what the effect of this section would be if he failed or refused to comply with the request.

(4A) Where the accused was at an authorised place of detention at the time of the failure or refusal, subsections (1) and (2) do not apply if he had not been allowed an opportunity to consult a solicitor prior to the request being made.

(5) This section applies in relation to officers of customs and excise as it applies in relation to constables.

(6) This section does not preclude the drawing of any inference from a failure or refusal of the accused to account for the presence of an object, substance or mark or from the condition of clothing or footwear which could properly be drawn apart from this section.

(7) This section does not apply in relation to a failure or refusal which occurred before the commencement of this section.

KEYNOTE

As with s. 37 below, an inference may only be drawn where four conditions are satisfied:

- the accused has been arrested;
- a constable reasonably believes that the object, substance or mark (or the presence of the accused (s. 37)) may be attributable to the accused's participation in a crime (s. 36 (an offence 'specified by the constable') or s. 37 (the offence for which he/she was arrested));
- the constable informs the accused of his/her belief and requests an explanation (by giving a special warning (see below));
- the constable tells the suspect (in ordinary language) the effect of a failure or refusal to comply with the request.

It is considered that the request for information under both s. 36 and s. 37 are a form of questioning and should be undertaken during the interview at the police station. The request for such information prior to this would be an exception to the rule.

> The interviewing officer is required to give the accused a 'special warning' for an inference to be drawn from a suspect's failure or refusal to answer a question about one of these matters or to answer it satisfactorily. This 'special warning' is provided by PACE Code C, para. 10.11 which states that the interviewing officer must first tell the suspect *in ordinary language*:
>
> - what offence is being investigated;
> - what fact the suspect is being asked to account for;
> - that the interviewing officer believes this fact may be due to the suspect's taking part in the commission of the offence in question;
> - that a court may draw a proper inference if the suspect fails or refuses to account for the fact about which he/she is being questioned;
> - that a record is being made of the interview and that it may be given in evidence at any subsequent trial.
>
> As with s. 34, in relation to s. 36 the accused cannot be convicted solely on an inference drawn from a failure or refusal (s. 38(3)) **(see para. 2.7.6.6)**.
>
> When the provisions of the Criminal Justice Act 2003 are in force s. 36(2)(a) and (2)(b)(i) and(ii) will be repealed and replaced by sch. 3, para. 2 to the Crime and Disorder Act 1998.

2.7.6.4   Inferences from Silence: Failure to Account for Presence

Section 37 of the Criminal Justice and Public Order Act 1994 provides that inferences can be drawn from an accused's failure to give evidence or refusal to answer any question about his/her presence at a place or time when the offence for which he/she was arrested was committed.

Section 37 states:

(1) Where—
   (a) a person arrested by a constable was found by him at a place at or about the time the offence for which he was arrested is alleged to have been committed; and
   (b) that or another constable investigating the offence reasonably believes that the presence of the person at that place and at that time may be attributable to his participation in the commission of the offence; and
   (c) the constable informs the person that he so believes, and requests him to account for that presence; and
   (d) the person fails or refuses to do so,
   then if, in any proceedings against the person for the offence, evidence of those matters is given, subsection (2) below applies.
(2) Where this subsection applies—
   (a) a magistrates' court, in deciding whether to grant an application for dismissal made by the accused under section 6 of the Magistrates' Courts Act 1980 (application for dismissal of charge in course of proceedings with a view to transfer for trial);
   (b) a judge, in deciding whether to grant an application made by the accused under—
      (i) section 6 of the Criminal Justice Act 1987 (application for dismissal of charge of serious fraud in respect of which notice of transfer has been given under section 4 of that Act); or
      (ii) paragraph 5 of schedule 6 to the Criminal Justice Act 1991 (application for dismissal of charge of violent or sexual offence involving child in respect of which notice of transfer has been given under section 53 of that Act);
   (c) the court, in determining whether there is a case to answer; and
   (d) the court or jury, in determining whether the accused is guilty of the offence charged,
   may draw such inferences from the failure or refusal as appear proper.

(3) Subsections (1) and (2) do not apply unless the accused was told in ordinary language by the constable when making the request mentioned in subsection (1)(c) above what the effect of this section would be if he failed or refused to comply with the request.

(3A) Where the accused was at an authorised place of detention at the time of the failure or refusal, subsections (1) and (2) do not apply if he had not been allowed an opportunity to consult a solicitor prior to the request being made.

(4) This section applies in relation to officers of customs and excise as it applies in relation to constables.

(5) This section does not preclude the drawing of any inference from a failure or refusal of the accused to account for his presence at a place which could properly be drawn apart from this section.

(6) This section does not apply in relation to a failure or refusal which occurred before the commencement of this section.

KEYNOTE

Section 37 appears somewhat restrictive in that it is only concerned with the suspect's location at the time of arrest and applies only when he/she was found at that location at or about the time of the offence.

PACE Code C also applies to s. 37 in relation to the 'special warning' required to be given by the interviewing officer.

Unlike s. 36, here the officer that sees the person at or near the scene of the alleged offence must be the arresting officer.

As with ss. 34 and 36, in relation to s. 37 the accused cannot be convicted solely on an inference drawn from a failure or refusal (s. 38(3)) **(see para. 2.7.6.6)**.

When the provisions of the Criminal Justice Act 2003 are in force s. 37(2)(a) and (2)(b)(i) and (ii) will be repealed and replaced by sch. 3, para. 2 to the Crime and Disorder Act 1998.

2.7.6.5 Inferences from Silence at Trial

Section 35 of the Criminal Justice and Public Order Act 1994 provides that inferences can be drawn from an accused's failure to give evidence or refusal to answer any question, without good cause, where the person has been sworn. Section 35 states:

(1) At the trial of any person for an offence, subsections (2) and (3) below apply unless—
   (a) the accused's guilt is not in issue; or
   (b) it appears to the court that the physical or mental condition of the accused makes it undesirable for him to give evidence;
   but subsection (2) below does not apply if, at the conclusion of the evidence for the prosecution, his legal representative informs the court that the accused will give evidence or, where he is unrepresented, the court ascertains from him that he will give evidence.

(2) Where this subsection applies, the court shall, at the conclusion of the evidence for the prosecution, satisfy itself (in the case of proceedings on indictment with a jury, in the presence of the jury) that the accused is aware that the stage has been reached at which evidence can be given for the defence and that he can, if he wishes, give evidence and that, if he chooses not to give evidence, or having been sworn, without good cause refuses to answer any question, it will be permissible for the court or jury to draw such inferences as appear proper from his failure to give evidence or his refusal, without good cause, to answer any question.

(3) Where this subsection applies, the court or jury, in determining whether the accused is guilty of the offence charged, may draw such inferences as appear proper from the failure of the accused to give evidence or his refusal, without good cause, to answer any question.

(4) This section does not render the accused compellable to give evidence on his own behalf, and he shall accordingly not be guilty of contempt of court by reason of a failure to do so.

(5) For the purposes of this section a person who, having been sworn, refuses to answer any question shall be taken to do so without good cause unless—

(a) he is entitled to refuse to answer the question by virtue of any enactment, whenever passed or made, or on the ground of privilege; or

(b) the court in the exercise of its general discretion excuses him from answering it.

(6) [repealed]

(7) This section applies—

(a) in relation to proceedings on indictment for an offence, only if the person charged with the offence is arraigned on or after the commencement of this section;

(b) in relation to proceedings in a magistrates' court, only if the time when the court begins to receive evidence in the proceedings falls after the commencement of this section.

KEYNOTE

In *R* v *Friend* [1997] 1 WLR 1433 (in considering s. 35(1)(b) of the Act), the accused was aged 15 with a mental age of nine and an IQ of 63. It was held that the accused's mental condition did not make it 'undesirable' for him to give evidence and it was right that inferences be drawn under s. 35(3).

As with s. 34, in relation to s. 35 the accused cannot be convicted solely on an inference drawn from a failure or refusal (s. 38(3)) (see para. 2.7.6.6).

It must be made clear to the accused that when the prosecution case has finished he/she may give evidence if he/she so wishes. The court must inform the accused that if he/she fails to give evidence or, being sworn, refuses to answer any question without good cause, then the jury may infer such inferences that appear proper from such a failure to give evidence or a refusal to answer any question (*Practice Direction (Criminal Proceedings: Consolidation)* [2002] 1 WLR 2870, para. 44, defendant's right to give or not to give evidence). In *R* v *Gough* [2002] 2 Cr App R 121, it was held that it is mandatory for the court to inform the accused of his/her right to give or not to give evidence even where the accused has absconded.

2.7.6.6 Inferences from Silence: No Conviction on Silence Alone

Section 38 of the Criminal Justice and Public Order Act 1994 applies to all of the four provisions relating to inferences from silence (ss. 34, 35, 36 and 37) and provides that an inference cannot be the sole basis for a finding of a case to answer, issue or dismissal of a notice to transfer, or for a finding of guilt. Nothing in s. 38 prejudices the court's general powers to exclude evidence (**see chapter 2.9**).

In *R* v *Gowland-Wynn* [2002] 1 Cr App R 569, the Court of Appeal held that in cases involving directions under s. 34, the burden of proof remained on the Crown despite the fact that a defendant chose to make no comment. Where a case is weak it has been held to be crucial that a clear direction be given to the jury of the limited function of an accused's failure to mention something in interview (*R* v *Parchment* [2003] All ER (D) 43 (Sep), [2003] EWCA (Crim) 2428).

2.7.7 Relevant Facts

The cardinal rule of the law of evidence is that, subject to the exclusionary rules, all evidence which is sufficiently relevant to the facts in issue is admissible, and all evidence which is irrelevant or insufficiently relevant to the facts in issue should be excluded.

In *DPP* v *Kilbourne* [1973] AC 729, Lord Simon of Glaisdale stated that: 'relevant ... evidence is evidence which makes the matter which requires proof more or less probable'.

Evidence of the *facts in issue* (**see para. 2.7.3**) might include a statement that the witness saw the accused hit the victim over the head with a bottle. This is directly relevant to the charge of assault. Other *relevant facts*, on the other hand, might require the court to put together pieces of evidence in order to come to the conclusion that some other relevant incidents occurred. For instance, that the witness saw the accused walk past the victim, heard a scream, looked round to see blood coming from a cut on the victim's head and the accused running away. In these circumstances, the witness does not actually see the assault but there may be sufficient circumstantial evidence from that witness for the court to draw the conclusion that the accused assaulted the victim.

2.7.8 The Best Evidence Rule

This rule of evidence covers the best evidence that the nature of the case will allow. The rule was propounded in 1745 and generally required that only the people having immediate personal knowledge of a fact in issue (**see para. 2.7.3**) could give evidence as to that fact. With the social and technological changes since the rule was introduced this rule is all but defunct.

Nevertheless, for the purpose of evidence gathering, the general principle to produce evidence from the best practicable source still holds good.

2.7.9 Sources of Evidence

For the purpose of this chapter evidence is categorised into the following two groups: the ways in which evidence can be proved and the main evidential rules.

Evidence can be proved in the following ways:

- original (primary) evidence
- real evidence
- secondary evidence
- documentary evidence.

The main evidential rules are:

- hearsay evidence
- circumstantial evidence
- presumptions
- character
- opinion
- corroboration
- judicial notice.

Each of these categories is considered in detail below.

2.7.10 Original Evidence

This is where a witness gives evidence to the court directly from the witness box. The evidence is presented to the court *as evidence of the truth of what he/she states* (contrast this with the exceptions to hearsay; **see para. 2.7.14**). Here the witness is giving direct testimony about a fact of which he/she has personal or first-hand knowledge and therefore can be challenged on the truth of that fact in cross-examination (**see chapter 2.5**).

2.7.11 Real Evidence

Real evidence usually takes the form of a material object for inspection by the court. This evidence is to prove, either that the material object in question exists, or to enable the court to draw an inference from its own observation as to the object's value and physical condition (an example would be pornographic material to determine whether it is 'obscene'). Such material objects, referred to as exhibits, produced to the court would normally be accompanied by written testimony and identified by a witness. This testimony usually includes an explanation of the connection between the exhibit and the facts in issue or the relevance to an issue.

Little if any weight can attach to real evidence in the absence of accompanying testimony identifying the object and connecting it with the facts in issue. So, in the example of the assault (**see para. 2.7.7**) simply producing a bottle without an accompanying statement identifying it as the one actually used would prove nothing.

There is no rule of law that an object must be produced, or its non-production excused, before oral evidence may be given about it. For example, it is not necessary for the police to produce the very breath test device used by them on a particular occasion (see *Castle* v *Cross* [1984] 1 WLR 1372). However, the weight of the oral evidence may be adversely affected by the non-production of the object in question (*Armory* v *Delamirie* (1722) 1 Str 505).

In addition to material objects, behaviour, appearance and demeanour may be regarded as real evidence. Examples would be:

- Behaviour (e.g. a person's misconduct in a court of law for the purposes of contempt of court).
- Appearance (e.g. a person's physical appearance in relation to evidence of identification or on the question of the existence or causation of personal injuries).
- Demeanour (e.g. a person's attitude may be relevant to the weight to be attached to his/her evidence, or whether he/she is to be treated as a hostile witness (**see chapter 2.5**).

The court has the responsibility to preserve and retain exhibits until the conclusion of the trial. It is usual for the court to entrust the exhibits to the police or Crown Prosecution Service and this places a duty on them to:

- take all proper care to preserve the exhibits safe from loss or danger;
- co-operate with the defence in order to allow them reasonable access to the exhibits for the purpose of inspection and examination; and
- produce the exhibits at the trial (*R* v *Lambeth Metropolitan Stipendiary Magistrate, ex parte McComb* [1983] QB 551). (**See chapter 2.10** for the general rules on disclosure.)

2.7.12 Secondary Evidence

Secondary evidence is evidence of an inferior kind, e.g. a copy of a document or a copy of such a copy. Such evidence can be admissible, e.g. in *Butler* v *Board of Trade* [1971] Ch 680 where a copy of a letter from the claimant's solicitor to the claimant had been accidentally included in papers handed over to the Official Receiver. It was held that, although the original letter was privileged, a copy was admissible in the criminal proceedings. (See also *Calcraft* v *Guest* [1898] 1 QB 759.)

Secondary documentary evidence is admissible by way of exception in the following cases (although the list is not exhaustive):

- Where the other party fails to produce a document at court after being served with a notice to do so.
- Where a stranger to the case lawfully refuses to produce a document, e.g. where he/she could claim privilege.
- Where a document has been lost and after due search cannot be found or has been destroyed.
- Where the production of the original document is impossible, such as, writing on a wall or where the law requires the document to remain where it is for reasons of security.
- Where a public document is concerned, on the grounds that its production would be illegal or inconvenient.

Nowadays the court is not confined to the best evidence rule but can admit all relevant evidence (*Kajala* v *Noble* (1982) 75 Cr App R 149).

2.7.13 Documentary Evidence

Documentary evidence consists of documents produced for inspection by the court, either as items of real evidence or as hearsay or original evidence. Here 'document' includes maps, plans, graphs, drawings, photographs, discs, tapes, video tapes and films, including CCTV recordings and tapes from police control rooms. The contents of a document may be admissible *as evidence of their truth* or *for some other purpose*. Documents produced to the court are usually accompanied by some testimony and identified by a witness.

2.7.13.1 Evidence by Certificate of Plan or Drawing

Section 41 of the Criminal Justice Act 1948 states:

(1) In any criminal proceedings, a certificate purporting to be signed by a constable, or by a person have the prescribed qualifications, and certifying that a plan or drawing exhibited thereto is a plan or drawing made by him of the place or object specified in the certificate, and that the plan or drawing is correctly drawn to a scale so specified, shall be evidence of the relative position of the things shown on the plan or drawing.

...

(4) Nothing in this section shall be deemed to make a certificate admissible as evidence in proceedings for an offence except in a case where and to the extent to which oral evidence to the like effect would have been admissible in those proceedings.

(5) Nothing in this section shall be deemed to make a certificate admissible as evidence in proceedings for any offence unless a copy thereof has, not less than seven days before the hearing or trial, been served in the prescribed manner on the person charged with the offence; or if that person, not later than three days before the hearing or trial or within such further time as the court may in special circumstances allow, serves notice in the prescribed form and manner on the prosecutor requiring the attendance at the trial of the person who signed the certificate.

(6) In this section the expression prescribed means prescribed by rules made by the Secretary of State.

KEYNOTE

Police officers are quite often required to produce plans or drawings, the most common example of this being the road layout and positions of vehicles following a road traffic accident.

Prescribed qualification as mentioned in s. 41(1) refers to registered architects, chartered surveyors, civil engineers, municipal engineers and members of the Land Agents Society.

Where a witness makes a statement to the police and video footage of the events subsequently becomes available, it is acceptable for the witness to be permitted to see the video and to be allowed to correct or modify his/her statement in the light of the video evidence (*R* v *Rebuts* (1998) *The Times*, 2 May).

2.7.13.2 Computer Records

Computer printouts containing records produced without human intervention, for example, printout of an Intoximeter that has performed an analysis of specimens of breath, are generally admissible in evidence (*R* v *Minors* [1989] 1 WLR 441). However, printouts containing information implanted by a human will be considered as hearsay and be inadmissible (*R* v *Coventry Justices, ex parte Bullard* (1992) 95 Cr App R 175).

2.7.13.3 Proof of Public Documents and Bye-laws

Where necessary the proof of a public document can be made as follows. A certified copy of an entry under the hand of the deputy superintendent registrar of births, deaths and marriages, is admissible evidence provided he/she also certifies the register was in his/her lawful custody (s. 14 of the Evidence Act 1851).

2.7.14 Hearsay Evidence

The Criminal Justice Act 2003 placed hearsay evidence on a more statutory footing though preserving certain common law categories of admissibility.

2.7.14.1 Admissibility of Hearsay Evidence

Section 114 of the 2003 Act concerns the admissibility of hearsay evidence and states:

(1) In criminal proceedings a statement not made in oral evidence in the proceedings is admissible as evidence of any matter stated if, but only if—
  (a) any provision of this Chapter or any other statutory provision makes it admissible,
  (b) any rule of law preserved by section 118 makes it admissible,
  (c) all parties to the proceedings agree to it being admissible, or
  (d) the court is satisfied that it is in the interests of justice for it to be admissible.
(2) In deciding whether a statement not made in oral evidence should be admitted under subsection 1(d), the court must have regard to the following factors (and to any others it considers relevant)—
  (a) how much probative value the statement has (assuming it to be true) in relation to a matter in issue in the proceedings or how valuable it is for the understanding of other evidence in the case;
  (b) what other evidence has been, or can be, given on the matter or evidence mentioned in paragraph (a);

(c) how important the matter or evidence mentioned in paragraph (a) is in the context of the case as a whole;

(d) the circumstances in which the statement was made;

(e) how reliable the maker of the statement appears to be;

(f) how reliable the evidence of the making of the statement appears to be;

(g) whether oral evidence of the matter stated can be given and, if not, why it cannot;

(h) the amount of difficulty involved in challenging the statement;

(i) the extent to which that difficulty would be likely to prejudice the party facing it.

(3) Nothing in this Chapter affects the exclusion of evidence of a statement on grounds other than the fact that it is a statement not made in oral evidence in the proceedings.

KEYNOTE

In relation to this section what is important is the quality of the evidence that has not been verified on oath or tested by cross-examination. The court should be mindful of reminding the jury of these facts (*Grant* v *The Queen* [2006] UKPC 2). In *R* v *Xhabri* [2005] EWCA Crim 3135 it was held that Article 6 of the European Convention on Human Rights (right to a fair trial), does not give an accused an absolute right to examine every witness whose testimony was adduced against them.

All references to a 'statement' mean any representation of fact or opinion made by a person by whatever means and include a representation made in a sketch, photo-fit or other pictorial form. References to a 'matter stated' mean where the purpose, or one of the purposes, of the person making the statement appears to the court to have been to cause another person to believe the matter, or to cause another person to act or a machine to operate on the basis that the matter is as stated (s. 115).

In relation to s. 114(1)(b) the following rules of law were preserved by s. 118 of the 2003 Act: public information; reputation as to character; and reputation or family tradition; *res gestae*; admissions by agents etc.; common enterprise; reputation as to character; and confessions. All these exceptions are described within this chapter apart from confessions, for which see chapter 2.9.

2.7.14.2 Public Information

This common law exception is retained by the Criminal Justice Act 2003 no doubt as of necessity. Such public information is admissible provided statements and entries in records have been made by authorised agents of the public in the course of their official duties and that the facts recorded are of public interest or notoriety, or required to be recorded for the benefit of the public (*Sturla* v *Freccia* (1880) 5 App Cas 623). Examples of public information would include: registers of baptisms, marriages and funerals; surveys of Crown Lands; university records.

This common law exception has been largely superseded by the effects of various statutes which are discussed later in this chapter.

2.7.14.3 Reputation or Family Tradition

This relates to any rule of law under which in criminal proceedings evidence of reputation or family tradition is admissible for the purpose of providing pedigree or the existence of a marriage, the existence of any public or general right, or the identity of any person or thing.

2.7.14.4 *Res Gestae*

Section 118(1) of the Criminal Justice Act 2003 which preserves this rule of law, states:

(4) Any rule of law under which in criminal proceedings a statement is admissible as evidence of any matter stated if—

(a) the statement was made by a person so emotionally overpowered by an event that the possibility of concoction or distortion can be disregarded,

(b) the statement accompanied an act which can be properly evaluated as evidence only if considered in conjunction with the statement, or

(c) the statement relates to a physical sensation or a mental state (such as intention or emotion).

Res gestae relates to statements which are so closely associated with an action or state of affairs which is relevant to a fact in issue that they become part of that action or state of affairs. These statements may be admissible as evidence *of the truth of their contents* if they concern contemporaneous actions, physical sensations or state of mind, or they are closely associated with a dramatic event.

These statements fall into four main categories, i.e. statements relating to:

- a specific event;
- the maker's physical state;
- the maker's state of mind;
- the maker's performance of an act.

A specific event This principle can best be explained by use of the case of *R v Andrews* [1987] 2 WLR 413. Two men entered M's flat and attacked him with knives and stole some property. Shortly afterwards M, grievously wounded, made his way to the flat below his own to get help. Two police officers arrived within minutes and M told them that O and the defendant had been the assailants. Two months later M died as a result of his injuries. The defendant was jointly charged with O with aggravated burglary and the murder of M.

The prosecution sought to have the deceased's statement admitted, not as a dying declaration (see below), but *as evidence of the truth of the facts that he had asserted*, namely that he had been attacked by O and the defendant. Ordinarily the rule against hearsay would exclude such a statement from being used for that purpose. The prosecution argued that the statement made by the deceased was *so closely connected with the specific event (the stabbing) that it ought to be admitted in evidence under the res gestae exception.*

The case went to the House of Lords who held that, where the victim of an attack informed a witness of what had occurred, such a statement may be admitted in evidence if the circumstances in which it was made satisfy the trial judge that:

- the event was so unusual or startling or dramatic as to dominate the thoughts of the victim; and
- that very effect on the thoughts of the victim excluded the possibility of their lying or being mistaken; and
- the statement was made at approximately (although not *exactly*) the same time as the event.

Under these conditions evidence of what the victim said would be admissible as to the truth of the facts recounted. It has since been held that *Andrews* is not an authority on this *res gestae* exception if better evidence is available (*Attorney-General's Reference (No. 1 of 2003)* [2003] Crim LR 547).

In *R v Ward* [2001] Crim LR 316 it was held that evidence tending to confirm a suspect's presence at a scene might be admissible, despite its being *prima facie* hearsay, provided a clear direction is given to the jury.

The maker's physical state A statement concerning its maker's physical sensations, made at the time when he/she felt them is admissible to prove that he/she did in fact experience that sensation.

If, for example, a person states 'my hand hurts' or 'my hand really hurt yesterday', both statements would be admissible to show that the person's hand had hurt.

Similarly, 'I feel really embarrassed', might be admissible to show that the person felt embarrassed at the time.

Such statements are only admissible to prove that *the sensation* existed; they may not be used to show what *caused* the sensation and must, as with all evidence, be relevant to a fact in issue in the case.

The maker's state of mind   Statements concerning the maker's state of mind at the time when he/she made it are admissible to prove what the maker *intended* or *believed* at that time. Such statements *are not admissible as evidence of the truth of the maker's beliefs.*

In *Ratten* v *The Queen* [1972] AC 378, the defendant's wife had been shot dead in her home. The defendant, in his defence to the charge of murder, claimed that the shooting was an accident. He also denied that any telephone call had been made from his house, where only he and his wife and small children were present, before the shooting. In these circumstances evidence of a telephone call made by the wife to an emergency operator was held to be admissible.

In deciding that the telephone call was admissible, Lord Wilberforce said:

> ... [the operator's statement] can be analysed into the following elements. (1) At about 1.15pm the number Echuca 1494 rang. I plugged into that number. (2) I opened the speak key and said 'number please'. (3) A female voice answered. (4) The voice was hysterical and sobbed. (5) The voice said 'Get me the police please.'
>
> The factual items numbered (1)–(3) were relevant in order to show that, contrary to the evidence of the appellant, a call was made, by a woman only some 3–5 minutes before the fatal shooting. It not being suggested that there was anybody in the house other than the appellant, his wife and small children, this woman, the caller, could only have been the deceased. Items (4) and (5) were relevant as possibly showing ... that the deceased woman was at this time in a state of emotion or fear. They were relevant and necessary evidence in order to explain and complete the fact of the call being made. ...

The longer the time gap between the making of the statement and the performance of the act, the lower the probative value of the statement and the likelihood of its being admissible.

The maker's performance of an act   Where an act carried out by a person needs to be proved, the statement of the person undertaking the act is likely to be the best evidence of why that act was completed. In order to amount to an exemption under the *res gestae* rule, the statement must be reasonably contemporaneous with the act; it must also be *related to* the act. For example, a person (X) boarding a plane saying 'I'm leaving the country to avoid being arrested' may be admissible as evidence of the reason why X got on the plane or why X left the country.

An example of this principle in practice is the case of *R* v *McCay* [1990] 1 WLR 645. Here a witness was asked to attend an identification parade to see if he could identify the defendant who was suspected of an attack on another man. The witness, a police inspector, and the appellant's solicitor watched the parade from behind a screen. The witness identified the defendant and said, 'It is number 8'. The defendant was charged with the assault and, at the trial, the witness gave evidence that he had attended the parade, made an identification but that he was unable to recall the number of the person whom he identified. The inspector was then called and gave evidence that the appellant had occupied position number 8 on the parade and that the witness had said 'It is number 8'. The defence argued that what the inspector said should be inadmissible hearsay. It was held that, although the words spoken by the witness at the parade were said in the absence of the appellant, they accompanied the relevant act of identification and therefore were contemporaneous with, and necessary to explain, the act of identification.

2.7.14.5 Admissions by Agents

Normally in criminal matters an agent of an accused person will be their legal adviser and an admission by such an agent may be admissible against the accused. For example, where a barrister made an admission in court on behalf of and in the presence of his client it could be inferred that the barrister was authorised to make the admission (*R* v *Turner* (1975) 61 Cr App R 67).

In *R* v *Mallory* (1884) 13 QBD 33, an accused's wife, at his request and in his presence, supplied a list of where certain items which were suspected of being stolen had been purchased. It was held that the list was admissible against the accused.

2.7.14.6 Common Enterprise

Generally, the acts and statements of one party to a common purpose, which may be evidence against another, are associated with offences of conspiracy. However, the rule has been applied to a joint enterprise to evade the prohibition on the importation of drugs even where there was no charge of conspiracy (*R* v *Jones* [1997] 2 Cr App R 119).

2.7.14.7 Cases where a Witness is Unavailable

The Criminal Justice Act 2003 includes the now abolished common law exceptions to hearsay in respect of dying declarations and statements that have been made by persons before their death.

Section 116 states:

(1) In criminal proceedings a statement not made in oral evidence in the proceedings is admissible as evidence of any matter stated if—
    (a) oral evidence given in the proceedings by the person who made the statement would be admissible as evidence of that matter,
    (b) the person who made the statement (the relevant person) is identified to the court's satisfaction, and
    (c) Any of the five conditions mentioned in subsection (2) is satisfied.
(2) The conditions are—
    (a) that the relevant person is dead;
    (b) that the relevant person is unfit to be a witness because of his bodily or mental condition;
    (c) that the relevant person is outside the United Kingdom and it is not reasonably practicable to secure his attendance;
    (d) that the relevant person cannot be found although such steps as it is reasonably practicable to take to find him have been taken;
    (e) that through fear the relevant person does not give (or does not continue to give) oral evidence in the proceedings either at all or in connection with the subject matter of the statement, and the court gives leave for the statement to be given in evidence.

In relation to s. 116(2)(e), 'fear' is to be widely construed and can include fear of the death or injury of another person or of financial loss (s. 116(3)). A statement may only be admitted under this subsection where the court considers it ought to be in the interests of justice having regard to the following:

- the statement's contents;
- any risk that its admission or exclusion may be unfair to any party and particularly any difficulty in challenging the statement where no oral evidence is given;

- the fact that a special measures direction under s. 19 of the Youth Justice and Criminal Evidence Act 1999 could be made for a witness to testify;
- any other relevant circumstances (s. 116(4)).

In *R v Sellick and Sellick* [2005] EWCA Crim 651, a witness statement had been read out in court because the witness was well known to the defendant and had been kept away through fear. The evidence was decisive evidence and it was held that there was no absolute rule that its admission would automatically lead to an infringement of the defendant's rights under European Convention on Human Rights, Article 6 (right to a fair trial).

Where a condition in s. 116(2) is satisfied it is not to be treated as such if the circumstances described in the condition are caused by any person in support of whose case it is sought to give the statement in evidence, or by a person acting on their behalf, in order to prevent the witness giving oral evidence (s. 116(5)).

Nothing in s. 116 makes a statement admissible if it was made by a person who did not have the required capability at the time when the statement was made. A person has the required capability if they are capable of understanding questions put to them about matters stated and give answers to such questions that can be understood. In relation to statements the court may determine the capability of the maker, in the absence of the jury, by receiving expert evidence and evidence from any person to whom the statement was made. The burden of proof is on the party seeking to adduce the statement and the standard of proof is the balance of probabilities (s. 123).

Section 124 deals with the credibility of witnesses who do not give oral evidence but whose statements are admitted. In such cases the following will be admissible: evidence as to the credibility of a witness; matters which could have been put in cross-examination relevant to their credibility as a witness; evidence of any previous inconsistent statement for the purpose of showing the witness contradicted him/herself.

The Act also provides the following safeguards in relation to statements made otherwise than in oral evidence. Where a trial before a judge and jury is based wholly or partly on a statement not made in oral evidence, following the prosecution case the court may direct the jury to acquit the offender if the evidence provided by the statement is so unconvincing that, considering the importance of the case against the defendant, a conviction would be unsafe (s. 125). Also a court may refuse to admit a statement not made in oral evidence where it is satisfied that the case for excluding the statement, taking account of the danger that to admit it would result in undue waste of time, substantially outweighs the case for admitting it, taking account of the value of the evidence (s. 126). In addition the court may exclude evidence under s. 78 of the Police and Criminal Evidence Act 1984 or any other power of a court (**see para. 2.9.3**).

2.7.14.8 Admissibility of Written Statements in Summary Proceedings

Section 9 of the Criminal Justice Act 1967 states:

(1) In any criminal proceedings, other than committal proceedings, a written statement by any person shall, if such of the conditions mentioned in the next following subsection as are applicable are satisfied, be admissible as evidence to the like extent as oral evidence to the like effect by that person.

(2) The said conditions are—
    (a) the statement purports to be signed by the person who made it;
    (b) the statement contains a declaration by the person to the effect that it is true to the best of his knowledge and belief and that he made the statement knowing that, if it were tendered

in evidence, he would be liable to prosecution if he wilfully stated in it anything which he knew to be false or did not believe to be true;

(c) before the hearing at which the statement is tendered in evidence, a copy of the statement is served, by or on behalf of the party proposing to tender it, on each of the other parties to the proceedings; and

(d) none of the other parties or their solicitors, within seven days from the service of the copy of the statement, serves a notice on the party so proposing objecting to the statement being tendered in evidence under this section:

Provided that the conditions mentioned in paragraphs (c) and (d) of this subsection shall not apply if the parties agree before or during the hearing that the statement shall be so tendered.

KEYNOTE

The statement must be signed by the person making it but the declaration outlined at s. 9(2)(b) need not be separately signed.

The procedure for serving a statement under s. 9 is set out in Rule 27.1 of the Criminal Procedure Rules 2005 (SI 2005/384) which provides for a notice to be sent to the defendant, or if legally represented, their solicitor. The notice informs the defendant of the effect of the procedure and requires them, within seven days, to inform the prosecutor if they wish the witness to attend court. Failure to inform the prosecutor will deprive the defendant of his/her right to insist on the witness's attendance.

Statements that are admitted under s. 9 are either read out in full to the court or parts of it may be summarised at the court's discretion.

The court may still require a witness to attend and give oral evidence even where there has been no objection from the other parties (s. 9(4)(b)).

Although under s. 9(1) the statement is 'admissible as evidence' the statement itself does not have to be accepted as the truth. Even where the defence have failed to serve notice of a witness being required to give oral evidence they may still present evidence in court which might be inconsistent with a witness's written statement (*Lister* v *Quaife* [1983] 1 WLR 48). In these circumstances the prosecution may seek an adjournment of the case for the witness to attend court and give evidence.

When in force, the words in s. 9(1) 'other than committal proceedings' will be repealed by the Criminal Justice Act 2003.

Section 9 goes on to state:

(3) The following provisions shall also have effect in relation to any written statement tendered in evidence under this section, that is to say—

(a) if the statement is made by a person under the age of 18, it shall give his age;

(b) if it is made by a person who cannot read it, it shall be read to him before he signs it and shall be accompanied by a declaration by the person who so read the statement to the effect that it was so read; and

(c) if it refers to any other document as an exhibit, the copy served on any other party to the proceedings under paragraph (c) of the last foregoing subsection shall be accompanied by a copy of that document or by such information as may be necessary in order to enable the party on whom it is served to inspect that document or a copy thereof.

(4) Notwithstanding that a written statement made by any person may be admissible as evidence by virtue of this section—

(a) the party by whom or on whose behalf a copy of the statement was served may call that person to give evidence; and

(b) the court may, of its own motion or on the application of any party to the proceedings, require that person to attend before the court and give evidence.

(5) ...

(6) So much of any statement as is admitted in evidence by virtue of this section shall, unless the court otherwise directs, be read aloud at the hearing and where the court so directs an account shall be given orally of so much of any statement as is not read aloud.

(7) Any document or object referred to as an exhibit and identified in a written statement tendered in evidence under this section shall be treated as if it had been produced as an exhibit and identified in court by the maker of the statement.

(8) A document required by this section to be served on any person may be served—
   (a) by delivering it to him or to his solicitor; or
   (b) by addressing it to him or leaving it at his usual or last known place of abode or place of business or by addressing it to his solicitor and leaving it at his office; or
   (c) by sending it in a registered letter or by recorded delivery service or by first class post addressed to him at his usual or last known place of abode or place of business or addressed to his solicitor at his office; or
   (d) in the case of a body corporate, by delivering it to the secretary or clerk of the body at its registered or principal office or sending it in a registered letter or by the recorded delivery service or by first class post addressed to the secretary or clerk of that body at that office; and in paragraph (d) of this subsection references to the secretary, in relation to a limited liability partnership, are to any designated member of the limited liability partnership.

KEYNOTE

The provisions of s. 9 of the Criminal Justice Act 1967 had a major impact on both witness's time (particularly the police) and the cost of court cases. The section allows for evidence to be admitted without the necessity of physically calling the witness who gave the statement.

2.7.14.9 Business and Other Documents

The Criminal Justice Act 2003 contains the provisions for the admissibility of business and other documents and s. 117 states:

(1) In criminal proceedings a statement contained in a document is admissible as evidence of any matter stated if—
   (a) oral evidence given in the proceedings would be admissible as evidence of that matter,
   (b) the requirements of subsection (2) are satisfied, and
   (c) the requirements of subsection (5) are satisfied, in a case where subsection (4) requires them to be.

(2) The requirements of this subsection are satisfied if—
   (a) the document or the part containing the statement was created or received by a person in the course of a trade, business, profession or other occupation, or as the holder of a paid or unpaid office,
   (b) the person who supplied the information contained in the statement (the relevant person) had or may reasonable be supposed to have had personal knowledge of the matters dealt with, and
   (c) each person (if any) through whom the information was supplied from the relevant person to the person mentioned in paragraph (a) received the information in the course of a trade, business, profession or other occupation, or as the holder of a paid or unpaid office.

(3) The persons mentioned in paragraphs (a) and (b) of subsection (2) may be the same person.

(4) The additional requirements of subsection (5) must be satisfied if the statement—
   (a) was prepared for the purpose of pending or contemplated criminal proceedings, or for criminal investigation, but
   (b) was not obtained pursuant to a request under section 7 of the Crime (International Co-operation) Act 2003 (c. 32) or an order under paragraph 6 of Schedule 13 of the Criminal Justice Act 1988 (c. 33) (which relates to overseas evidence).

(5) The requirements of this subsection are satisfied if—
    (a) any of the five conditions mentioned in section 116(2) is satisfied (absence of relevant person etc), or
    (b) the relevant person cannot reasonably be expected to have any recollection of the matters dealt with in the statement (having regard to the length of time since he supplied the information and all other circumstances).

KEYNOTE

If the court is doubtful about the statement's reliability in view of its contents, the source of the information contained in it, or the way in which or the circumstances in which it was created or received, they may direct that the statement is not admissible under this section (s. 117(6) and (7)).

2.7.15 Circumstantial Evidence

In contrast to direct evidence which is evidence of facts in issue, circumstantial evidence is evidence of relevant facts *from which the facts in issue may be presumed with more or less certainty*.

An example would be where a bank robbery has occurred and a witness sees the defendant hurriedly climbing into a vehicle near to the bank at the relevant time and carrying bank cash bags. The witness has not actually *seen* the defendant inside the bank committing the offence, but can still provide circumstantial evidence from which it can be proved that the witness saw the bank robber.

Pollack CB in *R* v *Exall* (1866) 4 F & F 922 described circumstantial evidence as:

> . . . a combination of circumstances, no one of which would raise a reasonable conviction, or more than a mere suspicion; but the whole, taken together, may create a strong conclusion of guilt. . . .

Circumstantial evidence may be admissible if it is relevant to a fact in issue and examples of circumstantial evidence include:

- evidence of facts which supply a motive;
- facts which tend to suggest that a person made plans or preparations relevant to a subsequent action performed;
- evidence of a person's mental or physical capacity to do a particular act;
- evidence of opportunity—or lack of opportunity to act in a certain way;
- evidence of identity, e.g. fingerprints (**see chapter 2.12**);
- inferences from silence (**see para. 2.7.6**);
- presumptions of fact (**see para. 2.7.16**).

Circumstantial evidence is not necessarily a weakness where there are a number of strands of evidence which collectively give rise to a powerful case (*R* v *Dove, Davies and Chesterman* [2005] EWCA Crim 1982).

2.7.16 Presumptions

Facts in issue and relevant facts must generally be proved before a court by admissible evidence before they can be accepted by the court as being true. There are occasions, however, when the courts will allow the proof of a fact or number of facts which lead it to presume the existence of a further fact, without any evidence of that fact being given in evidence. That is, from the facts that have been given in evidence, the court will then presume another fact for which no direct evidence has been given. A presumption is normally a conclusion which can be drawn until, where permissible, the contrary is proved.

There are three types of these 'presumptions':

- irrebuttable presumptions of law;
- rebuttable presumptions of law;
- presumptions of fact.

2.7.16.1 Irrebuttable Presumptions of Law

This is also known as a conclusive presumption. In these cases, where the courts accept the existence of certain basic fact(s) then they must also assume the existence of another fact and the other party to the proceedings cannot produce evidence questioning its existence.

For instance, s. 50 of the Children and Young Persons Act 1933 states:

It shall be conclusively presumed that no child under the age of ten years can be guilty of any offence.

Where the defence produce a birth certificate for the accused showing he/she is only nine then, from that basic fact, the courts *must* presume that the child is not guilty of the offence charged. It is an irrebuttable presumption that a child under ten can never be guilty of an offence and matters not what other evidence the prosecution call. Once the birth certificate is accepted as being that of the child, the court will find him/her not guilty.

2.7.16.2 Rebuttable Presumptions of Law

In these cases, once one party has satisfied the court of the basic fact from which a presumption about other facts must be made, it is for the other party to prove that the presumed fact does not exist. That is, the other party can *rebut* the presumption but, if he/she is unable to do so, the court will draw the appropriate inference from it.

Where the prosecution have to disprove an assumption they must do so beyond reasonable doubt but the defence only have to show on a balance of probabilities that the fact (the presumption) exists (**see para. 2.7.4**).

There are a number of rebuttable presumptions but the most likely to apply to criminal cases are 'presumptions of regularity'.

Presumption of regularity

It is presumed that where evidence shows that a person acted in a public or official capacity, in the absence of contrary evidence, that person was regularly and properly appointed and the act was regularly and properly performed. A typical example is on a charge of assaulting a police officer in the course of his/her duty (**see Crime, chapter 1.7**). Evidence that the police officer acted in that capacity is sufficient proof of his/her due appointment (*R v Gordon* (1789) 1 Leach 515; and see *Cooper v Rowlands* [1971] RTR 291).

There is also a presumption that mechanical and other instruments were in working order at the time of their use. For example, automatic traffic signals are presumed to be in proper working order unless the contrary is proved (*Tingle Jacobs & Co. v Kennedy* [1964] 1 WLR 638) and in the case of a public weighbridge (*Kelly Communications Ltd v DPP* (2003) 167 JP 73). However, there must be evidence of usually correct operation, for example, in relation to the admissibility of evidence of the results of a breath test in excess alcohol cases, where the reliability of the testing device is in question (*Cracknell v Willis* [1988] AC 450 and *Newton v Woods* [1987] RTR 41).

The Criminal Justice Act 2003 preserves the common law presumption that a mechanical device has been properly set or calibrated (s. 129(2)). However, where a statement generated by a machine is based on information implanted into the machine by a human, the output of the device is not admissible in criminal proceedings unless it is proved that the information was accurate (s. 129(1)).

2.7.16.3 Presumptions of Fact

The court may, after evidence is given about certain facts, presume (in the absence of sufficient evidence to the contrary), that another fact exists. This differs from rebuttable presumptions of law in that here the court *may* presume the fact exists from other facts presented to the court. With rebuttable presumptions of fact the court *must* presume the fact exists unless it is proved to the contrary. In reality this is just another way of showing that the courts use circumstantial evidence to infer that a fact is true.

Cases where the courts regularly infer the existence of facts from other circumstantial evidence are labelled 'presumptions of fact'. The following are examples of presumptions of fact.

Presumption of intention
Section 8 of the Criminal Justice Act 1967 states:

A court or jury in determining whether a person has committed an offence—
(a) shall not be bound in law to infer that he intended or foresaw a result of his actions by reason only of its being a natural and probable consequence of those actions; but
(b) shall decide whether he did intend or foresee that result by reference to all the evidence, drawing such inferences from the evidence as appear proper in the circumstances.

(For further discussion on this area, **see Crime, chapter 1.1**.)

Presumption of life
Where evidence that a person was alive on a certain date is given to the court, it may be presumed that he/she was still alive on some subsequent date (*Mac Darmaid* v *Attorney-General* [1950] P 218; *Re Peete* [1952] 2 All ER 599). Of course, where additional evidence is provided showing that the person was in good health and spirits, the chances of such an inference being made will be greater.

2.7.17 Character Evidence

Where a witness is being cross-examined they may be asked questions about matters which were not raised during the examination-in-chief. Such questions may relate to any fact in issue or to the credibility of the witness.

2.7.17.1 Credit Questions

During cross-examination, witnesses may be asked leading questions even where they appear to be more favourable to the cross-examining party than to the party which called them (*Parkin* v *Moon* (1836) 7 C & P 408).

Judges have the power to restrain unnecessary, improper or oppressive questions in cross-examination and the exclusionary rules of evidence relating to hearsay, opinion and privilege etc. all apply to cross-examination as they apply to examination-in-chief.

What is known as 'cross-examination as to credit' is where the credibility of a witness is questioned under cross-examination. These questions may relate to the witness's previous convictions, bias, mental or physical disability affecting his/her reliability, reputation for untruthfulness, and previous inconsistent statements relative to the subject matter of the indictment. Where a witness denies any of these matters the cross-examining party is entitled to prove them (**see para. 2.7.17.3**).

Any cross-examination of a witness designed to impugn his/her credibility should comply with the rules contained in the Code of Conduct of the Bar of England and Wales but although the rules have a strong persuasive force they are not binding on the courts (*R v McFaden* (1975) 62 Cr App R 187).

The extent to which police officers may be cross-examined about their behaviour was considered in the case of *R v Edwards* [1991] 1 WLR 207. The evidence against the accused consisted of a witness, who was an accomplice, and of certain police officers, who produced interview notes and spoke about interviews with the accused. At these interviews the accused had made admissions but had refused to sign the interview notes, two of which had been certified by senior officers. The accused denied making the admissions and claimed that the interview was a charade, that the interrogating officers had written down what suited them, that it was unrelated to what he had said and that he had been 'fitted up' with false evidence.

The prosecution had been asked to supply the names of any police officers subject to investigation for fabricating evidence. They failed to provide the details of one of the certifying officers who had recently been disciplined internally in relation to another case. In this case the officer had certified interview notes which, to his knowledge, had been wrongly re-written, resulting in the case against the defendants failing.

The Court of Appeal held that a police officer giving evidence, who had allegedly fabricated an admission, could properly be cross-examined to make the jury aware of the fact that his evidence of an admission in a previous case was demonstrably disbelieved; it would have been relevant and admissible to put to the officers concerned that they had given evidence in the earlier trials involving an issue whether alleged confessions had been fabricated and that the trials had ended as they had; that the cross-examination would have been as to credit alone. (See also **para. 2.7.20** with regard to uncorroborated police evidence.)

Where the defence introduce evidence alleging misconduct on the part of the prosecution witnesses, it is not open to the Crown to introduce evidence of good character to boost the testimony of these witnesses (*R v Hamilton* (1998) *The Independent*, 6 July).

2.7.17.2 Rule of Finality

The general rule is that evidence is not admissible to contradict answers given by a witness to questions put in cross-examination that concern collateral matters. These are matters which merely go to credit but which are otherwise irrelevant to the issues in the case (*Harris v Tippett* (1811) 2 Camp 637; *Palmer v Trower* (1852) 8 Exch 247).

The test whether a matter is collateral or not is that if the answer of a witness is a matter which the cross-examining party would be allowed to prove in evidence, that is, if it has such a connection with the issues that it would be allowed to be given in evidence, then it is a matter on which the witness may be contradicted (*Attorney-General v Hitchcock* (1847) 1 Exch 91). In *R v Bisby* (1981) 75 Cr App R 79 police officers were cross-examined to the effect that they had fabricated statements attributed to the accused and threatened a potential defence witness to stop them testifying. The judge ruled that the defence could not call the witness who had been allegedly threatened because this would solely go to the credit of the defence. The Court of Appeal held that the evidence of the potential defence witness was relevant to an issue that had to be tried because, if true, the statements attributed to the accused had been fabricated.

2.7.17.3 Previous Inconsistent Statements

Sections 3 to 5 of the Criminal Procedure Act 1865 provide that the party calling a witness is not entitled to impeach the credit of that witness by evidence of bad character. However, where the witness becomes 'hostile' or 'unfavourable' to the party calling them that party may call other witnesses to contradict them. Where the witness can be shown to have made a previous oral or written statement inconsistent with their present testimony they may be asked about these earlier statements. If it can be proved that they made the previous statement, even where they deny it, the statement can become admissible in evidence.

Section 119 of the Criminal Justice Act 2003 provides that:

(1) If in criminal proceedings a person gives oral evidence and—
    (a) he admits making a previous inconsistent statement, or
    (b) a previous inconsistent statement made by him is proved by virtue of section 3, 4 or 5 of the Criminal Procedure Act 1865 (c. 18),
    the statement is admissible as evidence of any matter stated of which oral evidence by him would be admissible.
(2) If in criminal proceedings evidence of an inconsistent statement by any person is given under section 124(2)(c), the statement is admissible as evidence of any matter stated in it of which oral evidence by that person would be admissible.

KEYNOTE

This section clarifies the relationship between hearsay evidence and previous inconsistent statements in that if a witnesses admits making a previous inconsistent statement, or it is proved they made one, then it is not only evidence which undermines their credibility but is also evidence of the truth of its contents.

2.7.17.4 Other Previous Statements by Witnesses

Section 120 of the Criminal Justice Act 2003 provides further circumstances when other previous statements of witnesses are admissible as evidence of the truth of their contents. This includes:

- statements which are admitted to rebut a suggestion that the witness's oral evidence is untrue (subs. (2));
- where a witness is refreshing their memory from a written document, if they are being cross-examined on the document and it is received in evidence, the statement will be evidence of any matter contained within it (subs. (3));
- where a witness states that they made the statement and believe it to be true and one of the following conditions is met:
    - the statement describes or identifies a person, place or thing (which includes objects such as a car registration number); or
    - the statement was made when the incident was fresh in the witness's memory and he/she cannot reasonably be expected to remember the matters stated; or
    - the statement consists of a complaint by a victim of the alleged offence which was made as soon as could reasonably be expected after the conduct in question, and the

witness gives oral evidence in relation to the matter. The complaint must not have been made as a result of a threat or promise (subss. (4)–(7)).

2.7.17.5 Admissibility of Multiple Hearsay

Section 121 of the Criminal Justice Act 2003 states:

(1) A hearsay statement is not admissible to prove the fact that an earlier hearsay statement was made unless—
   (a) either of the statements is admissible under section 117, 119 or 120,
   (b) all parties to the proceedings so agree, or
   (c) the court is satisfied that the value of the evidence in question, taking into account how reliable the statements appear to be, is so high that the interests of justice require the later statement to be admissible for that purpose.

KEYNOTE

For the purpose of s. 121, 'hearsay statement' means a statement not made in oral evidence, that is relied on as evidence of a matter stated in it (subs. (2)).

The discretion provided by this section is intended to cover exceptional circumstances.

Where the maker of a hearsay statement does not give oral evidence in person in the proceedings, the person against whom the evidence is admitted may challenge the credibility of the maker. They may produce evidence to discredit the maker of the statement or show that they have contradicted themselves.

In *R v Xhabri* [2006] EWCA Crim 3135, s. 121(1)(a) and (c) was satisfied in relation to a complaint of false imprisonment which was relayed by two friends of the victim to a police officer and where the complainant and police officer were available for cross-examination.

2.7.18 Evidence of Bad Character

The Criminal Justice Act 2003 abolished the common law rules governing the admissibility of evidence of bad character (s. 99(1)), though it preserves the rule under which a person's reputation is admissible for proving his/her bad character (s. 99(2)).

'Bad character' for both non-defendants and defendants is defined by s. 98 of the 2003 Act which states:

References in this Chapter to evidence of a person's 'bad character' are to evidence of, or of a disposition towards, misconduct on his part, other than evidence which—
(a) has to do with the alleged facts of the offence with which the defendant is charged, or
(b) is evidence of misconduct in connection with the investigation or prosecution of that offence.

2.7.18.1 Non-defendant's Bad Character

Section 100 sets out three conditions where evidence can be given of the previous misconduct of a person other than a defendant in the proceedings:

(1) In criminal proceedings evidence of the bad character of a person other than the defendant is admissible if and only if—
   (a) it is important explanatory evidence,
   (b) it has substantial probative value in relation to a matter which—
      (i) is a matter in issue in the proceedings, and

(ii) is of substantial importance in the context of the case as a whole, or

(c) all parties to the proceedings agree to the evidence being admissible.

Important Explanatory Evidence

For the purposes of s. 100(1)(a) this is evidence without which the court or jury would find it impossible or difficult to understand other evidence in the case and its value for understanding the case as a whole is substantial (s. 100(2)).

Substantial Probative Value

The matter in issue in the proceedings covers both issues of disputed fact and issues of credibility and must be of substantial importance in the context of the case (*R v Weir* [2005] EWCA Crim 2866). Evidence only marginally relevant or trivial would not be admissible. The court, for the purposes of s. 100(1)(b), is required to take into account a number of factors when assessing the probative value of evidence. These include:

- the nature and number of events to which the evidence relates;
- when those events or things are alleged to have occurred;
- the nature and extent of the similarities and dissimilarities between alleged instances of misconduct;
- the extent to which the evidence shows or tends to show that the same person was responsible each time (s. 100(3)).

Agreement to Admissibility of Evidence

Evidence of the bad character of another person may be admitted with the agreement of all the parties in the case (s. 100(1)(c)), and in such instances the leave of the court to admit the evidence is not required (s. 100(4)).

KEYNOTE

In *R v Weir* [2005] EWCA Crim 2866, in a case of sexual assault, it was held that the judge had erred in concluding that the evidence of a caution had substantial probative value in relation to a witness's credibility, and the evidence of a caution (for possession of cocaine) was inadmissible under s. 100. However, in the light of the very strong warning given in summing up, the convictions were not unsafe. Convictions that are old, and criminal allegations which have been withdrawn, were not considered to have substantial probative value (*R v Bovell* (2005) *The Times*, 13 May). The Court of Appeal, in *R v Edwards* [2005] EWCA Crim 3244, examined whether allegations and not convictions could be admitted under this section and held that this may be possible dependent on the context of the allegations, for example, allegations which might form the basis of an inference of propensity.

Where evidence is relied upon under s. 100, the defence may argue that it should be excluded under the provisions of s. 78 of the Police and Criminal Evidence Act 1984, in that its inclusion would have an adverse effect on the fairness of the proceedings (see chapter 2.9).

Convictions of Witnesses

Section 6 of the Criminal Procedure Act 1865 provides that:

> If, upon a witness being lawfully questioned as to whether he has been convicted of any felony or misdemeanour, he either denies or does not admit the fact, or refuses to answer, it shall be lawful for the cross-examining party to prove such conviction.

KEYNOTE

Previous convictions may be proved by the production of a certificate of the court of conviction, which will include the substance of the charge and conviction recorded, coupled with the identity of the witness as the person convicted (s. 73 of the Police and Criminal Evidence Act 1984). The admissibility of a witness's convictions are a matter for the court in accordance with the conditions set out in s. 100 of the Criminal Justice Act 2003 (s. 74 of the 1984 Act).

The Rehabilitation of Offenders Act 1974 governs those convictions that may properly be put to a witness in accordance with s. 6 of the 1865 Act.

Where an accomplice is giving evidence on behalf of the prosecution it is usual for any convictions to be disclosed to the jury at the outset unless the defence indicates otherwise (*R* v *Taylor* [1999] Cr App R 163).

2.7.18.2 Defendant's Bad Character

Section 1(2) of the Criminal Evidence Act 1898 provides that, subject to s. 101 of the 2003 Act below, a defendant who gives evidence in the proceedings may be asked any questions in cross-examination which tend directly to incriminate him or her.

Sections 101 to 108 of the Criminal Justice Act 2003 provide an inclusionary approach to a defendant's previous convictions and other misconduct or disposition, under which relevant evidence is admissible but can be excluded in certain circumstances where the court considers it would have an adverse affect on the fairness of the proceedings.

The admissibility of a defendant's bad character is provided by s. 101 of the 2003 Act which states:

(1) In criminal proceedings evidence of the defendant's bad character is admissible if, but only if,—
  (a) all parties to the proceedings agree to the evidence being admissible,
  (b) the evidence is adduced by the defendant himself or is given in answer to a question asked by him in cross-examination and intended to elicit it,
  (c) it is important explanatory evidence,
  (d) it is relevant to an important matter in issue between the defendant and the prosecution,
  (e) it has substantial probative value in relation to an important matter in issue between the defendant and a co-defendant,
  (f) it is evidence to correct a false impression given by the defendant, or
  (g) the defendant has made an attack on another person's character.

Important Explanatory Evidence

In relation to s. 101(1)(c), this mirrors that used in the context of non-defendants, that is evidence without which the court or jury would find it impossible or difficult properly to understand other evidence in the case, and its value for understanding the case as a whole is invaluable (s. 102).

Matters in Issue between Defendant and Prosecution

For the purposes of s. 101(1)(d) the matters in issue include whether the defendant has a propensity to commit offences similar to the kind with which he/she is charged, except where such a propensity makes it no more likely that he/she is guilty of the offence. This can be established by evidence that he/she has been convicted of an offence either of the same description or of the same category as the one charged. However, by reason of the length of time since the conviction or, for any other reason, the court may consider it unjust for the conviction to be considered. The matters in issue also include whether the defendant has a propensity to be untruthful except where it is not suggested that the defendant's case is untruthful. Only prosecution evidence is admissible under this section (s. 103(1) to (3) and (6)).

Matters in Issue between Defendant and Co-defendant

Evidence as to whether the defendant has a propensity to be untruthful is admissible under s. 101(e) only if the nature or conduct of his/her defence is such as to undermine the co-defendant's defence. Only evidence which is to be adduced (or has been) by the co-defendant, or which a witness is to be invited to give (or has given) in cross-examination by the co-defendant, is admissible under this section (s. 104(1) and (2)).

Evidence to Correct False Impression

For the purposes of s. 101(1)(f) the defendant gives a false impression if he/she is responsible for the making of an express or implied assertion that may give a false or misleading impression about him/herself. Evidence to correct such an impression is evidence that has probative value in correcting it.

A defendant is treated as being responsible for the making of an assertion if the assertion:

- is made by the defendant in the proceedings (whether or not in evidence given by him/her);
- was made by the defendant on being questioned under caution, before charge, about the offence with which he/she is charged, or on being charged with the offence or officially informed that he/she might be prosecuted for it, and evidence of the assertion is given in the proceedings;
- is made by a witness called by the defendant;
- is made by any witness in cross-examination in response to a question asked by the defendant that it is intended to elicit it, or is likely to do so; or
- was made by any person out of court, and the defendant adduces evidence of it in the proceedings.

However, if a defendant withdraws or disassociates him/herself from making an assertion then he/she will not be treated as being responsible for making it (s. 105(3)).

Where it appears to the court that a defendant, by means of his/her conduct (other than the giving of evidence) is seeking to give an impression about him/herself that is false or misleading, the court may treat the defendant as being responsible for making an assertion that is apt to give that impression. Conduct can also include appearance and dress (s. 105(4) and (5)).

Evidence to correct a false impression is admissible only if it goes no further than is necessary to correct the false impression and, similarly with s. 101(1)(d), only prosecution evidence is admissible under s. 101(1)(f) (s. 105(6) and (7)).

Attack on Another Person's Character

For the purpose of s. 101(1)(g) an attack on another person's character can include:

- adducing evidence attacking the other person's character;
- asking questions in cross-examination that are intended, or likely, to elicit such evidence (either by the defendant or any legal representative appointed under s. 38(4) of the Youth Justice and Criminal Evidence Act 1999);

- evidence is given of an imputation about the other person when the defendant was questioned under caution, before charge, about the offence charged, or on being charged with the offence or officially informed that he/she might be prosecuted for it (s. 106(1)).

Evidence attacking another person's character means evidence that the person has committed an offence, or behaves or has behaved in a reprehensible way. In *R v Brima* [2006] EWCA Crim 408 the accused alleged that a friend who was with him at the time was responsible for the knife attack on the victim and the judge correctly allowed evidence of his previous convictions to be admitted. Section 101(1)(g) provides that only prosecution evidence is admissible (s. 106(2) and (3)).

Under s. 101(1)(d) or (g) the defendant may apply to exclude evidence where it is relevant to an issue in the case or has become admissible because of the defendant's attack on another person. The court must not admit the evidence if it appears that its admission would have an adverse effect on the fairness of the proceedings (s. 101(3)).

Where evidence of bad character has been admitted under s. 101(1)(c) to (g) and the court is satisfied that following the prosecution case the evidence is contaminated to the extent that any conviction would be unsafe, the court must direct the jury to acquit the defendant or order a re-trial (s. 107). This could include collusion between witnesses and any such contamination should be examined during the trial (*R v Card* [2006] EWCA Crim 1079).

KEYNOTE

In *R v Highton, Nguyen and Carp* [2005] 1 WLR 3472, it was held that, once evidence of bad character has been admitted through one of the statutory 'gateways' in s. 101(1), the use to which that evidence is put depends on the matters to which it is relevant and not the 'gateway' through which it has been admitted.

Where evidence is admitted under s. 101(1)(g) which might be relevant to any propensity to dishonesty, in summing up the judge must give a clear warning to the jury not to place undue reliance on previous convictions as these could not prove guilt by themselves. There is no rigid formula in summing up as long as the judge gives a clear warning (see *R v Hanson* [2005] 1 WLR 3169, and *R v Edwards, Fysh, Duggan and Chohan* [2006] 1 Cr App R 3).

Convictions of Defendants

Previous convictions may be proved by the production of a certificate of the court of conviction identical to the procedure described above for witnesses.

In *Barley v DPP* (1998) *The Times*, 30 July, the defendant contended that a memorandum of conviction bearing his name and address did not relate to him. Evidence had to be adduced to disprove the suggestion that some other person had given the defendant's details to the police and court in respect of the earlier offence.

Previous convictions of an offender aged over 21, of offences which were committed when they were under 14, are admissible if both the previous conviction(s) and offence(s) charged are indictable, and the court is satisfied that they should be admitted in the interests of justice (s. 108).

In relation to police cautions, as it is a prerequisite of a caution that the offender admits the offence, the court is entitled to have regard to them when character is in issue (*R v Maikin* [1999] All ER (D) 1482).

Exclusions

Nothing in the Criminal Justice Act 2003 affects the exclusion of evidence on certain other grounds:

- the rule in s. 3 of the Criminal Procedure Act 1865 against a party impeaching the credit of his own witness by general evidence of bad character (**see para. 2.7.17.3**);
- s. 41 of the Youth Justice and Criminal Evidence Act 1999 which places restrictions on evidence or questions about a complainant's sexual history (**see para. 2.5.16.4**);
- any other power to exclude the evidence, on grounds other than it is evidence of a person's bad character, for example under s. 78 of the Police and Criminal Evidence Act 1984 which provides for the exclusion of unfair evidence (**see chapter 2.9**), or under the provisions of ss. 114 to 136 of the 2003 Act relating to hearsay (**see para. 2.7.14**).

Section 7(2)(a) of the Rehabilitation of Offenders Act 1974 provides that spent convictions may be used in criminal proceedings. However, the *Consolidated Criminal Practice Direction*, para. I.6 (**see** *Blackstone's Criminal Practice 2008*, Appendix 8) requires that courts only allow spent convictions to be mentioned where it is in the interests of justice to do so. There is also an absolute prohibition on allowing previous convictions, spent or not, to be admitted for offences committed by the accused as a child, unless both of the offences are triable only on indictment, and the court is satisfied that the interests of justice require the evidence to be admissible (s. 108(2) of the Criminal Justice Act 2003).

KEYNOTE

The National Centre for Policing Excellence, on behalf of ACPO, publish a practice advice document on evidence of bad character. This document explains the admissibility of such evidence, gives advice on dealing with it during interview, and contains a legal guidance paper prepared for Crown Prosecutors.

2.7.18.3 Defendant's Good Character

The accused is entitled to adduce evidence of his good character. In *R v Aziz* [1996] AC 41 Lord Steyn said: 'It has long been recognised that the good character of a defendant is logically relevant to his credibility and to the likelihood that he would commit the offence in question'. In this case the accused's claim to a good character rested on his assertion that he had no previous convictions. However, this would not be accepted where an accused had been recently cautioned (*R v Martin* [2000] 2 Cr App R 42) or where they had been found guilty by a foreign court (*R v El Delbi* [2003] All ER (D) 281).

A claim to a good character may also be made where an accused can adduce positive evidence to that effect. In *R v Young* [2004] Crim LR 234, it was held that the trial judge must give a direction to the jury where there is evidence of the accused's good character.

There are also specific statutory powers that may permit the prosecution to adduce evidence of the accused's bad character. Examples of this would include proof of an earlier disqualification in a trial on driving while disqualified and guilty knowledge in cases of handling and theft.

2.7.18.4 Guilty Knowledge in Cases of Handling and Theft

Section 27 of the Theft Act 1968 allows for the admissibility of previous misconduct and states:

> (3) Where a person is being proceeded against for handling stolen goods (but not for any offence other than handling stolen goods), then at any stage of the proceedings, if evidence has been given of his having or arranging to have in his possession the goods the subject of the charge, or of his undertaking or assisting in, or arranging to undertake or assist in, their retention, removal, disposal or realisation, the following evidence shall be admissible for the purpose of proving that he knew or believed the goods to be stolen goods—
>
> (a) evidence that he has had in his possession, or has undertaken or assisted in the retention, removal, disposal or realisation of, stolen goods from any theft taking place not earlier than 12 months before the offence charged; and
>
> (b) (provided that seven days' notice in writing has been given to him of the intention to prove the conviction) evidence that he has within the five years preceding the date of the offence charged been convicted of theft or of handling stolen goods.

KEYNOTE

This provision applies to all forms of handling (*R* v *Ball* [1983] 1 WLR 801) and can be used where handling is the only offence involved in the proceedings.

The question as to what constitutes recent possession is a matter of fact and degree dependent on the circumstances of each case. This presumption can be rebutted by the person offering a true explanation for the possession (*R* v *Schama* (1914) 84 LJ KB 396, *R* v *Garth* [1949] 1 All ER 773, *R* v *Aves* [1950] 2 All ER 330 and *R* v *Williams* [1962] Crim LR 54).

The term 'recent possession' is not defined and so is a question of fact in each case. In *R* v *Smythe* (1980) 72 Cr App R 8, the Court of Appeal held that property found in the possession of an accused, stolen two or three months earlier during some robberies and burglaries, did not amount to recent possession for the offence of handling stolen goods generally (For a full discussion on handling stolen goods **see Crime, para. 1.11.10**).

2.7.19 Opinion

The general rule is that the opinion of a witness is inadmissible. However, where it is admissible it can be divided into two groups:

- non-expert evidence;
- expert evidence.

2.7.19.1 Non-expert Evidence

The courts have allowed the following non-expert opinion evidence from a witness:

- identification of a person or object;
- the speed of a moving vehicle;
- evidence as to temperature or time;
- the value of an item (provided it does not require specialist knowledge to estimate the price).

Two examples of non-expert evidence that are likely to be given by police officers are provided by the following two cases:

- *R* v *Davies* [1962] 1 WLR 1111: any competent witness may give evidence that in his/her opinion a person is drunk provided that he/she describes the facts on which his/her opinion is based.
- *R* v *Hill* (1993) 96 Cr App R 456: police officers could identify substances as prohibited drugs (as to which, **see Crime, chapter 1.6**).

2.7.19.2 Expert Evidence

There will be instances in which the issues that the court will need to decide on are beyond its knowledge. In such instances it may be necessary to call on witnesses who, through their own experience or training or both, have the necessary expertise. It is for the judge to decide whether a witness is competent to give expert opinion. The expert witness is only there to assist the court in deciding the facts of the case.

Where more than one expert witness is called and their opinions differ, it will be for the tribunal of fact to decide which evidence they prefer. It must be remembered that expert evidence is not admissible where the issue before the court is one that should fall within the experiences of those deciding the case.

Where the parties have instructed a single joint expert it is not permissible for one party to have a conference with the expert in the absence of the other party without the latter's prior written consent (*Peet* v *Mid-Kent Area Healthcare NHS Trust* [2002] 3 All ER 688).

Expert evidence has been held appropriate in the following areas:

- medical issues and science;
- determining mental illness and the effects of a mental condition on mental processes;
- handwriting samples and facial mapping.

The Criminal Procedure Rules 2005 require any party intending to produce expert evidence to furnish to the other parties in the proceedings a statement in writing of the expert finding. This allows the other parties to review the statement and, if necessary, call a countering expert witness. (Note that this applies equally to the defence as it does to the prosecution.)

Where an expert gives evidence of work undertaken by an assistant, the court may give a direction that the assistant is required to give evidence but only if it is satisfied that it is in the interests of justice (Criminal Justice Act 2003, s. 127). In the case of an assistant not being called to give evidence the expert witness will be able to base their evidence on the information supplied by the assistant.

Guidance in respect of expert evidence is provided by *R* v *Harris and Others* [2005] EWCA Crim 1980 where it was emphasised that the duties of an expert witness in a criminal trial are owed to the court and override any obligation to the person from whom the expert has received instructions or by whom the expert is paid. Experts are required to maintain professional objectivity and impartiality at all times.

Even where the evidence given is considered to be hearsay, a court is entitled to deem a police officer an expert witness where the officer has a considerable wealth of experience and knowledge on a specific topic (*R* v *Hodges* [2003] 2 Cr App R 247).

2.7.20 Corroboration

The classic definition of corroboration is to be found in *R* v *Baskerville* [1916] 2KB 658 (per Lord Reid):

> ... evidence in corroboration must be independent testimony which affects the accused by connecting or tending to connect him with the crime. In other words, it must be evidence which implicates him, that is, which confirms in some material particular not only the evidence that the crime has been committed, but also that the prisoner committed it.

In order to satisfy the full technical meaning of the term corroboration, evidence must be:

- admissible in itself;
- from a source independent of the evidence required to be corroborated; and
- such as to tend to show, by confirmation of some material particular, not only that the offence charged was committed, *but also that it was committed by the accused.*

Although a conviction may be based on the testimony of a single prosecution witness who swears that he/she saw the accused commit the crime, it was recognised by Lord Morris in *DPP* v *Hester* [1973] AC 296 that:

> Any risk of the conviction of an innocent person is lessened if conviction is upon the testimony of more than one acceptable witness.

Where possible, supporting evidence should be collected while offences are being investigated to strengthen the prosecution case (or, where appropriate, to support the case the suspect has put forward).

The corroborating evidence does not have to confirm *all* the evidence already given by the witness requiring corroboration. In *R* v *Hill* (1988) 86 Cr App R 337, Lord Lane said:

> For example, in a rape case where the defendant denies he ever had sexual intercourse with the complainant, it may be possible to prove (1) by medical evidence that she had had sexual intercourse within an hour or so prior to the medical examination, (2) by other independent evidence that the defendant and no other man had been with her during that time, (3) that her underclothing was torn and that she had injuries to her private parts. None of these items of evidence on their own would be sufficient to provide the necessary corroboration, but the judge would be entitled to direct the jury that if they were satisfied so as to feel sure that each of those three items had been proved the combined effect of the three items would be capable of corroborating the girl's evidence.

The general rule is that a court's decision can be based on the evidence of one witness but there are occasions when corroboration or other supporting evidence is needed. These occasions include:

- where corroboration is required as a matter of law;
- obligatory care warnings;
- discretionary care warnings;
- in relation to identification evidence.

2.7.20.1 Corroboration Required as a Matter of Law

A conviction in the following cases can only be successful if the evidence is corroborated. There are three offences that fall into this category:

- treason;
- perjury;
- speeding (corroboration as to the speed the vehicle was travelling);
- attempts to commit any such offences.

2.7.20.2   Obligatory Care Warnings

There used to be a number of cases that fell into this group but with recent legislation it now only applies to cases involving persons who are mentally handicapped where they have made a confession which was not witnessed by an independent person. This is now covered by s. 77 of the Police and Criminal Evidence Act 1984, which states:

(1) Without prejudice to the general duty of the court at a trial on indictment to direct the jury on any matter on which it appears to the court appropriate to do so, where at such a trial—
    (a) the case against the accused depends wholly or substantially on a confession by him;
    (b) and the court is satisfied—
        (i) that he is mentally handicapped; and
        (ii) that the confession was not made in the presence of an independent person,
the court shall warn the jury that there is special need for caution before convicting the accused in reliance on the confession, and shall explain that the need arises because of the circumstances mentioned in paragraphs (a) and (b) above.
(2) In any case where at the summary trial of a person for an offence it appears to the court that a warning under subsection (1) above would be required if the trial were on indictment, the court shall treat the case as one in which there is a special need for caution before convicting the accused on his confession.
(3) In this section—
    (a) 'independent person' does not include a police officer or a person employed for, or engaged on, police purposes;
    (b) 'mentally handicapped' in relation to a person, means that he is in a state of arrested or incomplete development of mind which includes significant impairment of intelligence and social functioning ...

KEYNOTE

When in force, the Criminal Justice Act 2003 will amend subss. (1) and (2) to include the words 'with a jury' and also insert a new subs. (2A) relating to trials on indictment without a jury.

2.7.20.3   Discretionary Care Warnings

Sections 32 and 33 of the Criminal Justice and Public Order Act 1994 abolished the rule requiring a corroboration warning be given in relation to the evidence of accomplices and the evidence of complainants in sexual offences.

As a direct result of the provisions of ss. 32 and 33 of the 1994 Act it was recognised by the Court of Appeal that there was still a need to retain a discretion to warn the jury about convicting on the evidence of an unreliable witness (*R* v *Makanjuola* [1995] 1 WLR 1348). Although there is no set form of warning, it is seen as good practice for a judge to warn the jury of any reason(s) why a witness's testimony should be treated with caution (*R* v *R* [1996] Crim LR 815), and to point out to the jury any evidence that potentially corroborates the witness's evidence.

In relation to the evidence of accomplices and giving a warning to the jury, it was held in *R* v *Jones* [2004] 1 Cr App R 60 that a trial judge might consider four separate issues: the case for and against each accused separately; the evidence given by each co-accused; the fact that each co-accused may have an interest to serve or axe to grind; and the evidence of each co-accused should be assessed as that for any other witness.

In *R* v *Isham* (1998) 162 JP 391 it was held that in cases involving sexual offences, where the prosecution adduces evidence of complaints made by the complainant after the alleged assault, the jury must be directed that the evidence of the complaint is only of limited relevance and, since it does not come from a source which is independent of the complainant, does not amount to independent confirmation of the complainant's evidence.

In complaints involving sexual offences, a requirement at common law is that the complaint was not only made on the first occasion that reasonably offered itself but also that it was recent. The principle relating to recent complaints in sexual cases has been extended by the Criminal Justice Act 2003 which requires that for a previous statement to be admissible, the complaint should have been made as soon as could reasonably be expected after the alleged conduct (s. 120(7)(d)—**see para. 2.7.17.4**). In *R v O* [2006] EWCA Crim 556 it was held that the common law rules and the provisions of the 2003 Act were freestanding, provided their own criteria, and were not limited to sexual cases. Section 120(7)(d) does not contain a 'recency' requirement and a statement of complaint could be admissible whether it was made days, weeks or even months after the offence.

2.7.20.4 Identification Evidence

R v Turnbull [1976] 3 WLR 445 is the leading case on how the court should approach disputed visual identification evidence. In this case the Court of Appeal outlined those factors that should be considered when identification evidence is presented to the court and therefore those factors that should be considered by police when investigating offences.

In the *Turnbull* case the Court of Appeal laid down important guidelines, reproduced below, for judges in trials where identification evidence was disputed:

First, whenever the case against an accused depends wholly or substantially on the correctness of one or more identifications of the accused which the defence alleges to be mistaken, the judge should warn the jury of the special need for caution before convicting the accused in reliance on the correctness of the identification or identifications. In addition he should instruct them as to the reason for the need for such a warning and should make some reference to the possibility that a mistaken witness can be a convincing one and that a number of such witnesses can all be mistaken. Provided this is done in clear terms the judge need not use any particular form of words.

Secondly, the judge should direct the jury to examine closely the circumstances in which the identification by each witness came to be made. How long did the witness have the accused under observation? At what distance? In what light? Was the observation impeded in any way, as for example, by passing traffic or a press of people? Had the witness ever seen the accused before? How often? If only occasionally, had he any special reason for remembering the accused? How long elapsed between the original observation and the subsequent identification to the police? Was there any material discrepancy between the description of the accused given to the police by the witness when first seen by them and his actual appearance? If in any case, whether it is being dealt with summarily or on indictment, the prosecution have reason to believe that there is such a material discrepancy they should supply the accused or his legal advisors with particulars of the description the police were first given. In all cases if the accused asks to be given particulars of such descriptions, the prosecution should supply them. Finally, he should remind the jury of any specific weaknesses which had appeared in the identification evidence.

Recognition may be more reliable than identification of a stranger; but even when the witness is purporting to recognise someone whom he knows, the jury should be reminded that mistakes in recognition of close relatives and friends are sometimes made.

All these matters go to the quality of the identification evidence. If the quality is good and remains good at the close of the accused's case, the danger of a mistaken identification is lessened; but the poorer the quality, the greater the danger.

In our judgment when the quality is good, as for example when the identification is made after a long period of observation, or in satisfactory conditions by a relative, a neighbour, a close friend, a workmate and the like, the jury can safely be left to assess the value of the identifying evidence even though there is no other evidence to support it; provided always, however, that an adequate warning has been given about the special need for caution....

> When, in the judgment of the trial judge, the quality of the identifying evidence is poor, as for example when it depends solely on a fleeting glance or on a longer observation made in difficult conditions, the situation is very different. The judge should then withdraw the case from the jury and direct an acquittal unless there is other evidence which goes to support the correctness of the identification. . . .
>
> The trial judge should identify to the jury the evidence which he adjudges is capable of supporting the evidence of identification. If there is any evidence or circumstances which the jury might think was supporting when it did not have this quality, the judge should say so.

In relation to corroboration of identification evidence, the court made it clear that this is wider than corroboration in the strict legal sense. The court held:

> This may be corroboration in the sense lawyers use that word; but it need not be so if its effect is to make the jury sure that there has been no mistaken identification: for example, X sees the accused snatch a woman's handbag; he gets only a fleeting glance of the thief's face as he runs off but he does see him entering a nearby house. Later he picks out the accused on an identity parade. If there was no more evidence than this, the poor quality of the identification would require the judge to withdraw the case from the jury; but this would not be so if there was evidence that the house into which the accused was alleged by X to have run was his father's.

An example of supporting identification evidence is *R v Long* (1973) 57 Cr App R 871. Here the defendant was charged with robbery. He had been identified by three witnesses in different places on different occasions but each had only a momentary opportunity for observation. Immediately after the robbery the accused had left his home and could not be found by the police. When he was later seen by the police he claimed to know who had done the robbery and offered to help to find the robbers. At his trial he put forward an alibi which the jury rejected. The court considered that it was an odd coincidence that the eye-witnesses should have identified a man who had behaved in this way and without some explanation by the defence this was admissible as supporting the identification.

The *Turnbull* guidelines should always be followed by judges where the possible mistaken identification of an accused is in issue. Even where an accused has admitted being present at the scene of an offence, there will still be occasions where a judge should give such a direction as required by the guidelines (*R v Thornton* [1995] 1 Cr App R 578).

It has been held that in cases where voice identification evidence is an issue the *Turnbull* guidelines should be used to direct the jury as to the 'quality' of the evidence (*R v Hersey* [1998] Crim LR 281).

Within the PEACE model used to train police officers, in relation to the taking of both witness statements and suspect statements, the mnemonic **ADVOKATE** is used as an *aide-memoire*:

A—Amount of time under observation
D—Distance between suspect and witness
V—Visibility at time
O—Any Obstructions
K—Known or seen before
A—Any reason to remember
T—Time lapse since witness saw suspect
E—Error or material discrepancy.

For an examination of the law relating to identification, **see chapter 2.12.**

2.7.21 Judicial Notice

The courts may take judicial notice of various matters that are so well known or clearly established that proof thereof is not required. Judicial notice is another way of saying that a court accepts a fact or facts without formal proof.

Examples of the operation of the exception to the burden of proof include matters which are common knowledge, Acts of Parliament, and custom such as the Home Secretary's approval of certain breath test devices (**see Road Policing, chapter 3.5**).

2.8 Similar Fact Evidence

2.8.1 Introduction

This chapter looks at similar fact evidence. This can be a complex area of the law of evidence and the aim of this chapter is to give the reader an understanding of the subject. The chapter also considers what evidence should be collected against a suspect where the similar fact rule may apply.

As discussed earlier, evidence is admissible if it is relevant to a fact in issue necessary to prove or disprove the case against the accused. Normally such evidence will be directly related to the offence in question, for instance the defendant was seen hitting the victim using a bottle. But what if the victim described the bottle as being a green lager bottle with a German name on it? What relevance would this have if a suspect has been convicted of previous assaults using a green lager bottle from a German brewer or where there are several victims all of whom have been assaulted in the same way? Should this evidence be admissible at the defendant's trial or is there too big a risk that such evidence will be prejudicial to his/her case? Throughout this particular aspect of the law of evidence there is a common theme: balancing the usefulness of the evidence in proving the case in question (its 'probative value') against the possible detrimental effects of that evidence on the defendant (its prejudicial effect').

Thus this chapter is concerned with when evidence of the defendant's previous convictions or conduct on other occasions may be admissible as evidence of his/her guilt in relation to the present offence.

2.8.2 The Similar Fact Principle

This principle was recognised as far back as 1894 in *Makin* v *Attorney-General for New South Wales* [1894] AC 57, where Lord Herschell LC said that:

> It is undoubtedly not competent for the prosecution to adduce evidence tending to show that the accused has been guilty of criminal acts other than those covered by the indictment, for the purpose of leading to the conclusion that the accused is a person likely from his criminal conduct or character to have committed the offence for which he is being tried. On the other hand, the mere fact that the evidence adduced tends to show the commission of other crimes [or similar actions of the accused] does not render it inadmissible if it be relevant to an issue before the jury, and it may be so relevant if it bears upon the question whether the acts alleged to constitute the crime charged in the indictment were designed or accidental, or to rebut a defence which would otherwise be open to the accused.

This passage sets out the two key propositions surrounding the similar fact doctrine. The first proposition is that evidence which shows that the accused has a *particular disposition* to commit crimes in general, or to commit the kind of crime with which he/she has been charged, is *not* admissible. This is because, although it may appear to be relevant to a case, there is no direct link between the crime committed and the past actions of the accused. Such evidence is excluded, not because it does not support the fact that the accused might have committed the offence, but because of the danger that the jury might attach a disproportionate importance to this evidence compared with other evidence directly concerning the commission of the offence charged.

The second proposition really takes us back to the question of what facts are admissible in court. The answer is those facts which are relevant to prove or disprove the offence(s) charged. Evidence is likely to be admissible if it goes beyond mere evidence of a propensity to commit crime and has a crucial bearing upon the question whether the offence charged was committed by this defendant. In these cases the evidence of previous offences or actions of the accused *may be* admissible because they *connect* the defendant with the offence charged. If so, the evidence that he/she has a disposition to commit that kind of offence or act in a particular way *is* relevant because it makes it more likely that he/she committed the offence charged. Therefore the probative value of that evidence may outweigh any prejudicial effect it might have on the defendant's case.

....

EXAMPLE

An example of such a case is the infamous one of *R* v *Smith* (1915) 11 Cr App R 229 where a man was charged with the murder of his wife who was found dead in the bath. There was evidence of two further marriages where his former wives had been found dead in a bath, along with other similarities including the defendant's profiting financially from the death on each occasion. Lord Reading approved the direction given by the trial judge to the jury:

> If you find an accident which benefits a person and you find that the person has been fortunate to have that accident happen to him a number of times, benefiting each time, you draw a very strong, frequently irresistible inference that the occurrence of so many accidents benefiting him is such a coincidence that it cannot have happened unless it was designed.

Generally, evidence of prior incidents in respect of which a defendant has been acquitted are not admissible in evidence (*R* v *X* [1999] All ER (D) 1373). However, in *R* v *Z* [2000] 3 WLR 117 similar fact evidence in relation to previous sexual conduct was held to be admissible to help disprove the accused's claim that he believed that the victim was consenting to sexual intercourse on this occasion (see para. 2.8.4.7).

....

2.8.3 Evidence of Similar Facts

As the cases above illustrate, it is a common law rule that evidence which merely shows a similarity to the fact in issue is irrelevant and just because a person has acted in a particular way previously, does not make it probable that he/she so acted on a given occasion. This is one of the reasons why, generally, a person's previous convictions may not be put before a court because its prejudicial effect will generally outweigh any probative value of such evidence. The Criminal Justice Act 2003 has now put the issue of a person's previous convictions on a statutory footing. Evidence of an accused's propensity to commit offences of the kind with which he/she is charged is admissible where certain conditions provided by s. 101(1) of the Act are met (**see para. 2.7.18.2**).

An exception to this exclusionary rule is when such evidence is positively probative (helpful or evidential) of the offence before the court. Similar fact evidence is not just evidence of previous crimes; it can include evidence of non-criminal misconduct and evidence of a disposition to behave in a particular way. The categories falling within the doctrine of similar fact evidence could be relevant to any case where the courts feel that the evidence has probative value which outweighs any potential prejudicial effect in deciding an issue before them.

2.8.4 Admissibility of Similar Fact Evidence

Similar fact evidence is admissible in a number of ways:

- striking similarity;
- non-criminal behaviour;
- probative value without striking similarity;
- multiple offence cases;
- possession of objects by the accused;
- association with an event;
- previous sexual conduct and the 'same transaction' rule;
- use of similar fact evidence by a co-accused.

Each of these is examined in detail below.

2.8.4.1 Striking Similarity

Here the court will look for something more than some feature which is common place. Offences may be identical without being 'striking', e.g. where the *modus operandi* of a burglary is common to thousands of other offences of burglary. However, if a burglar has used a blow torch to crack the window of a building before entering in the past, that feature may be admissible against him/her if charged with similar burglaries in the future (*R v Mullen* [1992] Crim LR 735). So it may be better to think in terms of similarities which are really peculiarities to the accused. Lord Hailsham gave a very extreme but memorable example in *DPP v Boardman* [1975] AC 421. This example was of a man who commits repeated homosexual offences and whose victims all state that he was attired in 'ceremonial head-dress ... or other eccentric garb'. If a victim of an offence of gross indecency described the assailant as being dressed in a North American native 'war bonnet', that fact may be so similar to previous offences committed by the defendant that the courts would accept evidence of those earlier offences as 'similar fact' evidence. Whether or not evidence of similar facts will be accepted under this head will depend on the likelihood or otherwise of repetition being attributable to mere coincidence.

In assessing similar fact evidence the question is one of relevance; it does not matter whether similar fact evidence displays its relevance by revealing features of a striking similarity with the offence itself, or simply with its surrounding circumstances.

Probably the best example of such evidence is the case against Rosemarie West. Here, Mrs West was accused of assisting her husband who had been convicted of ten murders before killing himself in prison. In seven of the murders the bodies had been naked, bound and mutilated and had been found under the defendant's house. Evidence from witnesses that the defendant actively engaged in violent sexual assaults with her husband at that address was admitted under the striking similarity rule (*R v West* [1996] 2 Cr App R 374).

In relation to public misfeasance and similar fact evidence in *O'Brien v Chief Constable of South Wales* (2003) *The Times*, 22 August, it was held that where a claimant's murder conviction was quashed and they wished to bring a claim for police malpractice it was on occasions permissible to adduce similar fact evidence of incidence of similar malpractice by the same police officers.

Dissimilarities in the evidence, which detract from its probative value, must be taken into account and should be presented to the prosecutor along with the other evidence (**see chapter 2.10**).

In determining the admissibility of similar fact evidence the question, as always, is whether the probative value outweighs the prejudicial effect the evidence could have on the accused.

2.8.4.2 Non-criminal Behaviour

Evidence of non-criminal behaviour of the accused is admissible if such behaviour has a sufficient degree of probative force linking that behaviour and the circumstances surrounding the commission of the offence charged.

In *R v Barrington* [1981] 1 WLR 419, the accused was charged with indecently assaulting three girls. The prosecution alleged that the girls had been lured to the house of a co-accused as baby-sitters, had been shown pornographic photographs, had been asked to pose for photographs in the nude and had then been indecently assaulted. Evidence was also admitted from three other girls concerning another incident. They had not been indecently assaulted, but they had been lured to the house on the same pretext, had been shown the photographs and had been asked to pose in the nude. The Court of Appeal held that the evidence had been properly admitted on the grounds that, although it included no evidence of the commission of offences, it was logically probative of guilt because it was *inexplicable on the basis of coincidence*. Consequently, while the actions were not part of the offence itself, the evidence went to link all the cases together and would assist the jury in deciding the case.

2.8.4.3 Probative Value without Striking Similarity

In *DPP* v *P* [1991] 2 AC 447 it was held that where the court is dealing with the issue of an offender's identity similar fact evidence must always provide something in the nature of a 'signature or other special feature'. However, in addition to a signature or special feature which identifies the accused, similar fact evidence can also be used to link an offence to an accused by a chain of reasoning which does not include this feature. In *R v W (John)* [1998] 2 Cr App R 289 two offences took place within two weeks where, in both cases, the female victim was detained for a short time by the offender. One of the females was indecently assaulted but the other scared the offender away by screaming. The descriptions of the attacker fitted the accused, he was shown to be in the vicinity at the time of both incidents, and his clothing was torn in a way consistent with an injury suffered by the attacker when escaping. The Court of Appeal deduced that a 'relationship in time and circumstances' sufficient to satisfy the required degree of probative value was present and rejected an argument that striking similarity had to be present.

2.8.4.4 Multiple Offence Cases

Where a defendant faces more than one charge of a similar nature or where evidence of similar allegations is tendered in support of one charge, the evidence of one accuser may be admissible to support the evidence of another. Often this point becomes an issue before a trial starts, when the defence apply to the court to have counts which are of a similar nature tried separately to avoid the overall evidence being heard at one time. This type of evidence has also been used where corroboration used to be in issue.

The underlying principle here is that the probative value of multiple accusations may depend in part on their similarity, but also on the unlikely probability that the same person would find him/herself falsely accused on different occasions by different and independent individuals. The making of multiple accusations may be a coincidence in itself, which has to be taken into account in deciding admissibility.

Having regard to s. 101(1)(d) of the Criminal Justice Act 2003 (**see para. 2.7.18.2**) it is for the accused to persuade the court that it would be unfair to admit evidence of accusations of another offence where it is relevant to an important issue between the prosecution and defence. It is unlikely courts will not admit such evidence given that it will be heard in any event.

The use of similar fact evidence in this area was considered in *R v Sims* [1946] KB 531, where it was observed that the evidence of a number of accusations taken together is much greater than one alone, for:

> whereas the jury might think one man might be telling an untruth, three or four are hardly likely to tell the same untruth unless they were conspiring together.

In *R v Venn* [2003] All ER (D) 207 (Feb), [2003] EWCA Crim 236, the evidence of one complainant to indecent assault was confirmed by an independent witness who had been similarly assaulted by the defendant some years previously.

In cases of multiple complainants/witnesses there is always a chance of collusion and this should be borne in mind when taking witness statements.

2.8.4.5 Possession of Objects by the Accused

There may be occasions where a suspect is arrested and during subsequent searches articles are found which could be used in the type of offence suspected. Such items may be admitted as similar fact evidence *provided the evidence goes beyond mere criminal disposition*. In the assault case referred to above (**see para. 2.8.1**), if the bottle used was a distinctive or unusual one, the defendant's previous possession of a similar bottle might be used to identify him/her as the offender.

In *Thompson v The King* [1918] AC 221 the accused, a homosexual pederast, assaulted two young boys and their identification of him was confirmed by his possession of powder puffs and indecent photographs. Although these items were not used in the offence, or constituted the accused's 'signature', they were admitted as evidence in the light of the probative value they possessed to rebut the accused's claims of mistaken identity.

2.8.4.6 Association with an Event

Another function which similar fact evidence may be called upon to perform is to show an event involving an accused person in its true light. For instance, it may be relevant in deciding whether an event occurred by accident or innocently or intentionally. It may also be relevant against an alibi, i.e. to show that the accused committed another crime in the vicinity shortly before or after the offence charged. In such cases the evidence may not relate to the actual offence but to the background leading up to the incident.

Makin v Attorney-General for New South Wales [1894] AC 57 (**see para. 2.8.2**) is a good example of 'association with an event'. A husband and wife were accused of murdering a small child whom they were looking after for payment. The child's body was found buried at their home along with the bodies of other children. Evidence of the bodies of the other children was admitted as similar fact evidence as this was relevant to the issue of how the child had died.

2.8.4.7 Previous Sexual Conduct and the 'Same Transaction' Rule

Evidence of sexual or other behaviour which is not the subject of the charge may also be admissible to show the true nature of the relationship between the relevant parties (i.e. the defendant and the victim). In *DPP v Boardman* [1975] AC 421, evidence of the accused's previous approaches to a boy with whom he was alleged to have committed buggery was admitted, including evidence of an indecent assault taking place several months before. Similar evidence was given by another complainant of indecent conduct leading over a period of time to incitement to buggery. However, the House of Lords stressed that in such cases, and sexual cases generally, similar fact evidence is only received on the same principle as in other cases.

There is also a general rule which allows evidence of continuing behaviour to be adduced as part of the 'same transaction', for instance, where a nine-year-old girl gave evidence of indecent assaults, rapes and threats by the defendant, leading up to a final offence of rape which was the subject of the charge against him. The court held that the preliminary behaviour was all part of the 'same transaction' and therefore admissible (*R v Rearden* (1864) 4 F & F 76).

Similarly, in *R v M* [2000] 1 All ER 148, evidence that M had been taught from a young age to abuse his sisters sexually was admitted where the prosecution contended that this would assist the jury in understanding S's evidence by explaining why she had not sought help and why M had felt able to carry out the alleged offences without fear.

In *R v Z* [2000] 3 WLR 117, the accused was charged with rape and there were four similar previous incidents involving the accused and four different women. He had been found guilty on one occasion, but had been acquitted on the other three. It was held that the evidence would be allowed as the evidence of the earlier complaints was relevant to the issue of the accused's belief in consent and such evidence was not inadmissible simply because the accused had been previously acquitted.

In relation to previous sexual conduct and the 'same transaction' rule, the Criminal Justice Act 2003 provides only one standard of admissibility, that is, that all such evidence must be relevant to an important matter at issue between the prosecution and the accused (s. 101(1)(d)) (**see para. 2.7.18.2**).

2.8.4.8 Use of Similar Fact Evidence by Co-accused

A co-accused can also rely on similar fact evidence if it is relevant to an issue before the court. This will normally be to support the accused's defence or damage his/her co-accused's case.

In *R v Randall* [2004] 1 All ER 467, the defendant and co-accused raised a cut-throat defence in that each gave evidence against the other as being the perpetrator of violence against the deceased. Evidence of bad character was raised where it was shown that the defendant had only minor convictions as opposed to the co-accused who had numerous convictions for burglary and was on remand for armed robbery. It was held that evidence of bad character, including previous convictions, was admissible as evidence of propensity. Similarly, in *R v Rafiq* [2005] Crim LR 963 it was held that even where the evidence of propensity related to an offence for which the co-accused had not been convicted, it was admissible.

2.8.5   **Discretionary Exclusion of Similar Fact Evidence**

It will always be for the judge to decide whether in a particular case similar fact evidence should be admissible. It is for the prosecution, based on the evidence provided by the police, if it feels that the evidence is relevant to the case, to raise the issue of admissibility for the judge to rule on. The discretion to exclude similar fact evidence may be used where its prejudicial effect may be so disproportionate to its probative value (i.e. it will do more harm than good) that it ought not to be admitted (*R* v *Straffen* [1952] 2 QB 911).

As already described above, s. 101(1)(d) of the Criminal Justice Act 2003 places a statutory discretion as to the admissibility of evidence. It is for the prosecution to establish that the evidence is relevant to an important issue and for the defence to persuade the court to use its discretion (**see para. 2.7.18**).

2.8.6   **Handling Stolen Goods**

The handling stolen goods provision under s. 27 of the Theft Act 1968 (outlined in full within **para. 2.7.18.4**) can also be construed as being admissible as 'similar fact evidence'.

KEYNOTE

This section can only be relied on where handling stolen goods is the only offence in the proceedings and to prove guilty knowledge or belief. It cannot be used to prove any issues of dishonesty or possession of the goods in question (*R* v *Duffas* (1994) 158 JP 224).

The previous conviction of a defendant can be proved by the production of a certificate of the court of conviction in accordance with s. 73(2) of the Police and Criminal Evidence Act 1984. It was held in *R* v *Hacker* [1994] 1 WLR 1659 that the substance of the previous conviction contained within the certificate could be read out, in this instance the fact that the accused, charged with handling the bodyshell of a car, had previously been convicted of receiving stolen cars, was relevant to help prove guilty knowledge or belief. (For offences in relation to handling stolen goods, **see Crime, para. 1.11.10.**)

2.9 | Exclusion of Admissible Evidence

2.9.1 Introduction

Under the law, every person is presumed innocent until proved guilty. The duty of the courts is not only to decide on the guilt or innocence of a person, but also to ensure that the person has a fair hearing. When considering the second question, the courts will consider the evidence that the prosecution intend to use in the case and how that evidence was obtained.

In ensuring that a person has a fair trial the court may exclude evidence, *even though the evidence itself is admissible*. The court may exclude any evidence in certain circumstances and has additional powers in relation to evidence obtained by confession. The courts' powers to exclude evidence comes generally from s. 78 of the Police and Criminal Evidence Act 1984 (and specifically in relation to confession evidence from s. 76(2) of that Act), although the courts also have common law powers to exclude evidence. The exclusion of confession evidence is the most common and occupies the bulk of this chapter. However, the exclusion of evidence generally will also be discussed here.

The courts bear a substantial responsibility in deciding what evidence should be admitted. Clearly this can have a huge impact on the fairness of the trial. The Human Rights Act 1998 introduced the European Convention for the Protection of Human Rights and Fundamental Freedoms into domestic law in October 2000. When determining an issue which has arisen in connection with a Convention right, courts must consider Convention law which includes judgments, declarations and opinions of the European Court of Human Rights (and previously the European Commission of Human Rights) and all domestic legislation, as far as possible must be interpreted in a way which is compatible with the Convention rights (**see General Police Duties, chapter 4.3**).

2.9.2 Confessions

There are three general ways in which you can prove a person's involvement in an offence:

- confessions (or admissions)
- witnesses
- forensic science.

In some cases where the suspect initially confesses to the offence, he/she may still plead not guilty alleging that the confession was obtained by oppression and/or in circumstances that would render it unreliable or that it should be excluded as having been unfairly obtained. The courts are concerned with the reliability of evidence and often regard confessions as the least reliable way to prove a person's involvement in an offence.

A confession, which is defined by s. 82 of the Police and Criminal Evidence Act 1984 (see below), is an out of court statement made by a person and therefore falls into the category of evidence known as 'hearsay' evidence. Hearsay evidence is inadmissible unless it falls within one of the statutory or common law exceptions which are considered in **chapter 2.7**.

Confessions are such an exceptional category and are admissible in evidence as outlined in s. 76(1) of the 1984 Act. However, evidence of confession may be excluded by a court under either s. 76(2) or 78 of the 1984 Act.

Section 76 of the Police and Criminal Evidence Act 1984 states:

(1) In any proceedings a confession made by an accused person may be given in evidence against him insofar as it is relevant to any matter in issue in the proceedings and is not excluded by the court in pursuance of this section.

A 'confession' is defined by s. 82 of the 1984 Act, which states:

(1) In this Part of this Act—
   'confession' includes any statement wholly or partly adverse to the person who made it, whether made to a person in authority or not and whether made in words or otherwise;...

KEYNOTE

A confession, therefore, is a positive action by the person making it. The person must use words or some other method of communication (e.g. nodding his/her head to a question, or a video tape of the suspect taking police to a murder weapon). Therefore confessions do not include silence by a person (although this may be relevant to special warnings, **see chapter 2.13**). It could include a filmed re-enactment of the crime (*Li Shu-Ling* v *The Queen* [1989] AC 270).

The confession does not have to be a pure statement of guilt and can include the answers to questions asked in interview which are *adverse to the defendant*. In *R* v *Z* [2003] 1 WLR 1489 the Court of Appeal considered the meaning of 'confession' for the purposes of PACE in light of the Human Rights Act 1998. The court held that the decision as to whether or not a statement was a confession was to be made at the time it was sought to give the statement in evidence as opposed to at the time the statement was made by the person.

With the introduction of the Human Rights Act 1998 and the inclusion of the European Convention on Human Rights directly into domestic legislation, this area is becoming very important, particularly in relation to the way a detained person is treated, the length of his/her detention and the manner in which a confession is obtained. Not only may it lead to the exclusion of evidence, but also to a stay of proceedings or a claim for damages or compensation. For the effects of the 1998 Act generally, **see General Police Duties**.

A confession by one defendant can be indirectly used in evidence against another defendant. In *R* v *Hayter* [2005] 1 WLR 605 the House of Lords held that there was no reason why one defendant's guilt established by that defendant's own out of court confession could not be taken into account by a jury when considering the guilt of another defendant.

2.9.2.1 The Exclusion of Confession Evidence

Section 76(2) of the Police and Criminal Evidence Act 1984 gives the courts a responsibility to exclude confessions where they have been obtained by oppression (s. 76(2)(a)), or where the court considers they are unreliable (s. 76(2)(b)). There is also a general power (under s. 78 of the 1984 Act and at common law) to exclude any evidence that the court considers would be detrimental to the fairness of the trial if allowed, which can also be applicable to the exclusion of confessions. These powers are dealt with at **para. 2.9.3.1**. In relation to s. 76(2), the court is more concerned about the circumstances in which the confession was obtained than the truthfulness of what was said. Once the defence raise the issue of oppression and/or unreliability it is for the prosecution to prove the confession was not obtained in such circumstances (*R v Allen*, 10 July 2001, (CA), unreported).

The European Court of Human Rights has held that the admission of confession evidence is a matter for domestic courts where procedures and safeguards exist for examining such evidence (*Austria v Italy* (1963) 6 YB 740). It was considered that in the United Kingdom there were sufficient procedures and safeguards with the *voir dire* procedure and the fact that the burden of proof that any statement had been obtained voluntarily was on the prosecution.

2.9.2.2 Oppression

Section 76 of the Police and Criminal Evidence Act 1984 states:

> (2) If, in any proceedings where the prosecution proposes to give in evidence a confession made by an accused person, it is represented to the court that the confession was or may have been obtained—
> (a) by oppression of the person who made it; or
> ...
> the court shall not allow the confession to be given in evidence against him except in so far as the prosecution proves to the court beyond reasonable doubt that the confession (notwithstanding that it may be true) was not obtained as aforesaid.

KEYNOTE

A court is under a duty to exclude a confession where it has been, or may have been, obtained by the oppression of the person making the confession. This means that there must be some link between the oppressive behaviour and the confession. So for instance, if the confession was made *before* the oppressive behaviour, this would not justify exclusion *under this subsection* (it may, however, justify exclusion under the general power of the courts; **see chapter 2.7**). Where a confession has been obtained by oppression, any later confession obtained properly may also be excluded from evidence (*R v Ismail* [1990] Crim LR 109). It does not matter whether the confession is true or not; the issue under s. 76(2)(a) is *how* the person has been treated and whether any mistreatment led, or might have led, the person to make the confession. This issue is of particular importance in the interviewing of suspects (**see chapter 2.13**). In looking at this the courts seem to take into account the nature of the person being interviewed. It was said in *R v Gowan* [1982] Crim LR 821, that hardened criminals must expect vigorous police interrogation.

2.9.2.3 What is Oppression?

In s. 76(8) of the Police and Criminal Evidence Act 1984, 'oppression' includes torture, inhuman or degrading treatment, and the use or threat of violence (whether or not amounting to torture).

KEYNOTE

In *R v Fulling* [1987] QB 426, the Court of Appeal held that oppression is:

> [The] exercise of authority or power in a burdensome, harsh or wrongful manner; unjust or cruel treatment of subjects, inferiors etc., the imposition of unreasonable or unjust burdens.

It is suggested by some commentators that oppression involves some kind of impropriety on the part of the police, which might be suggested by a deliberate failure to follow the PACE Codes of Practice, although a failure to follow the Codes is not of itself an automatic reason for excluding evidence. Given that the courts have occasionally excluded evidence even where the relevant Code of Practice *has* been followed, the converse does not appear to be true and it is possible that a court might conclude that treatment had been 'oppressive' under all the circumstances even though the Codes of Practice had been followed.

The oppression must have been against the person who makes the confession.

As already mentioned, when the defence raise the issue of oppression it will be for the prosecution to show beyond reasonable doubt (*R* v *Miller* (1992) *The Times*, December) that this was not the case. For these reasons (as well as those of professional ethics) it is of great importance to comply with the PACE Codes of Practice. It is also important to keep records of how a case is investigated, together with the reasons for taking decisions during the course of the investigation so that the prosecution can present a case which demonstrates that there was no oppressive or improper conduct in obtaining the confession.

It is a question of fact on each occasion whether a person's treatment was oppressive and whether there was any link between that person's treatment and his/her decision to make the confession. It might be possible for the defence to use evidence against officers involved in the case who have allegedly 'mistreated' suspects in other cases (*R* v *Twitchwell* [2000] 1 CR App R 373).

The legislation itself gives little guidance as to what will amount to oppression. For this reason it is necessary to look at the case law. Below are examples where the courts have held that the treatment of a person was 'oppressive'. Where:

- A person who was on the border of being mentally impaired admitted the offence after denying it over 300 times because of the bullying manner of the questioning (*R* v *Paris* (1993) 97 Cr App R 99). This case does not mean that interviewers cannot go over the same point several times or even suggest to the interviewee that he/she is lying. However, *Paris* does suggest that this should be done in moderation and not to the point where it becomes oppressive.
- A person confessed but had been kept in custody longer than the court felt was justified and therefore lawful (*R* v *Davison* [1988] Crim LR 442).
- The suspect was wrongly informed that he/she had been recognised when this was not true (*R* v *Heron* (1993), unreported).
- There was a failure to have an appropriate adult present (*R* v *Silcott* (1991) *The Times*, 9 December).
- The defendant was a choir master and the police had told him that if he did not make a statement they would have to interview all the members of the choir and this could disclose other offences on his part (*R* v *Howden-Simpson* [1991] Crim LR 49).
- A confession was obtained where the person was being held without access to a solicitor (*Barbera* v *Spain* (1988) 11 EHRR 360).
- Where interviews had extended over a three-hour period and were conducted in a manner that was persistent, aggressive and calculated to get a conviction as opposed to necessarily getting to the truth (*R* v *Ridley*, 17 December 1999, unreported). The court went on to comment that the manner in which the interviews were conducted was to be deplored and was an exploitation of a naïve man by methods which were unacceptable and had prejudiced the fair conduct of the trial.

2.9.2.4   **Unreliability**

Section 76(2) of the Police and Criminal Evidence Act 1984 states:

> (2) If, in any proceedings where the prosecution proposes to give in evidence a confession made by an accused person, it is represented to the court that the confession was or may have been obtained—
>
> ...
>
> (b) in consequence of anything said or done which was likely, in the circumstances existing at the time, to render unreliable any confession which might be made by him in consequence thereof,
>
> the court shall not allow the confession to be given in evidence against him except in so far as the prosecution proves to the court beyond reasonable doubt that the confession (notwithstanding that it may be true) was not obtained as aforesaid.

KEYNOTE

A court is under a duty to exclude a confession where it is, has been or may have been obtained in consequence of anything which was likely, in the circumstances that existed at the time, to render it *unreliable*.

When looking at whether a confession is reliable, the court will consider the circumstances as they actually were at the time and not as they were believed to be. For instance, if it was believed that a suspect was in a fit state to be interviewed but it later transpires that he/she was medically unfit, there is likely to be some doubt as to whether a confession made at that time is reliable. (The belief of the officers at the time of acting, however, may be relevant to any disciplinary matters.)

For instance in *R* v *Walker* [1998] Crim LR 211 the court held that the defendant's mental state may be taken into account when considering the surrounding circumstances, regardless of whether it was known to the police. The prosecution bore the burden of proof to show that the confession was *admissible*. The court went further and said that s. 76(2)(b) was not restricted in its application to use by the police of oppression. It was not necessary to show that the confession was unreliable by reference to the old common law test of 'threat or inducement'. A successful submission under s. 76(2)(b) does not require a breach of a Code of Practice.

It is not for the defendant to prove that his/her confession is unreliable; it is for the prosecution to show (beyond reasonable doubt) that the confession is reliable once the question of unreliability has been raised by the defence.

In *R* v *Fulling* [1987] QB 426 it was suggested that:

... questioning which by its nature, duration, or other attendant circumstances (including the fact of custody) excites hopes (such as the hope of release) or fears, or so affects the mind of the subject that his will crumbles and he speaks when otherwise he would have stayed silent.

Thus the circumstances of a case can affect the reliability of the accused's statement.

2.9.2.5   **What is Unreliable?**

It is a question of fact on each occasion whether the reliability of a person's confession is in question as a result of something said or done. Below are examples where the courts have held that a confession was unreliable. Where:

- No caution was given to the suspect, the suspect was not asked if he wanted his solicitor present and was not shown the note of the interview (*R* v *Trussler* [1998] Crim LR 446).
- The PACE Codes of Practice were flagrantly breached (*R* v *Delaney* (1988) 88 Cr App R 338).

- A suspect who had just vomited was interviewed (any medical condition could affect the reliability of a confession; if in doubt have the person examined by a doctor) (*R v McGovern* (1991) 92 Cr App R 228).
- The appropriate adult had a low IQ and was unable to assist the detained person (*R v Silcott*).
- It was suggested to a suspect of a sexual assault that it would be better for them to receive treatment than go to prison (*R v Delaney*).
- A person had been kept in custody for 14 hours, had been interviewed four times before confessing and had been refused any visits from family (*R v Silcott*).
- The officers had a 'warm up chat' with the suspect before the interview, and the 'chat' lasted over two hours (*R v Trussler*).
- An offer of bail is made subject to the suspect admitting the offence or conversely, telling the suspect that he/she will be kept in custody until he/she admits the offence (*R v Barry* (1992) 95 Cr App R 384).
- Psychiatric evidence suggested that the suspect suffered from a severe personality disorder and that her admissions in her interview were unreliable (*R v Walker* [1998] Crim LR 211).
- A suspect had been forcibly overcome, and a confession was obtained in response to a question designed to elicit details of the offence from him without any prior caution having been administered (*R v Allen*, 10 July 2001, unreported).

2.9.2.6 Effect of Excluding Confessions

The exclusion of a confession may have implications for the value of other evidence.

Often further evidence is obtained after a person makes a confession. If a court excludes all or any part of a confession, then this may impact on the value of the additional evidence obtained by the prosecution.

While the additional evidence obtained after a confession may be admissible, much of the value of the evidence may be lost because s. 76(5) of the 1984 Act prevents the prosecution from linking the discovery of the additional evidence to any confession which has been excluded.

If the additional evidence cannot be linked to the confession then it might not be possible to link the evidence to the suspect (and the evidence may also be excluded under s. 78 of the 1984 Act or at common law).

....

EXAMPLE

For instance, in the case of a murder, if a suspect confesses to the murder and tells the investigators where he/she has hidden the murder weapon, this would be good evidence that the person committed the offence. If the confession is excluded then, although evidence can be given that the weapon found is in fact the murder weapon, it will not be possible to show any connection between the suspect and the weapon. Therefore, unless there is some other evidence to link the weapon to the suspect (e.g. fingerprint evidence), the case may fail. The reason is that it would not be possible to say that the police went to the location where the weapon was hidden without at least implying that the suspect had indicated that it was there when interviewed. All that can be said is that the weapon was found at the particular location, which could be accessible to any number of people.

Section 76(4) of the Police and Criminal Evidence Act 1984 provides that the exclusion of such additional evidence is not affected by the exclusion of the confession. Even where a confession is excluded, it may still be admissible for other matters such as the fact that the accused speaks in a certain way or writes or expresses him/herself in a particular fashion. In such a case it would only be that part of the confession which is necessary to prove the point that will be admissible. Once again, this illustrates the point that evidence is often only admissible for a specific purpose.

2.9.3 Exclusion of Evidence Generally

Although there is no equivalent of the American doctrine of 'due process' whereby any evidence which is not obtained by proper procedures is rendered inadmissible, the courts in England and Wales can exclude any evidence under certain circumstances.

Those circumstances will usually be concerned with the way in which the evidence has been obtained (as with confessions above) or with the potential effect of allowing it to be adduced at trial.

Again, the European Convention does influence the courts' approach in applying ss. 76 and 78, in particular Article 6(1) which deals with the right to a fair trial.

2.9.3.1 Exclusion of Unfair Evidence

Section 78 of the Police and Criminal Evidence Act 1984 states:

(1) In any proceedings the court may refuse to allow evidence on which the prosecution proposes to rely to be given if it appears to the court that, having regard to all the circumstances, including the circumstances in which the evidence was obtained, the admission of the evidence would have such an adverse effect on the fairness of the proceedings that the court ought not to admit it.

(2) Nothing in this section shall prejudice any rule of law requiring a court to exclude evidence.

KEYNOTE

Section 78 is wider than s. 76 and applies to *all evidence that the prosecution intend to produce in court.*

When applying s. 78, the courts will look at the fairness of allowing the evidence to be admitted against the defendant.

Compliance with the Codes of Practice is vital. In *Batley* v *DPP* (1998) *The Times*, 5 March, the court said that where steps required by the Codes were not observed and where material was entered as evidence, without those checks which formed an important aspect of the case, there was a real risk to the fairness of the proceedings against the defendant. This must be balanced against *R* v *Parris* (1988) 89 Cr App R 68 where the court held that a breach of the Codes is not an automatic exclusion of evidence. It is important to note that the court may take account of any changes to the Codes of Practice (even when changed after the person was in police detention) on the basis that the new Code reflects what is considered to be fair (*R* v *Word* (1994) 98 Cr App R 337).

This point is also made in *R* v *Hassan* [2004] EWCA Crim 1478 where the Court of Appeal agreed with the judge's decision to allow the evidence of a witness even though no identification procedure had been held.

In *R* v *Allen*, 10 July 2001, unreported, the Court of Appeal held that where significant and substantial breaches of the Act were likely to lead to the exercise of the court's discretion to exclude evidence under s. 78 of the Act, in particular where that evidence was an admission or confession obtained following such breaches.

> In *R* v *Samuel* [1988] QB 615 the court stated that it is undesirable to attempt any general guidance as to the way in which a judge's discretion under s. 78 should be exercised. It is a question of fact in each case and, while s. 76 requires links with the treatment of the person spoken to, the only issue under s. 78 is whether it would be unfair to admit the evidence in court. It is therefore difficult to give specific guidance but the following are examples of evidence that has been excluded.

2.9.3.2 Evidence which will be Excluded

- Evidence of a driver being over the prescribed limit where the officer did not suspect the driver had alcohol in his/her body (**see Road Policing, chapter 3.5**).
- Some cases of 'entrapment' where the court are not satisfied that the person would have committed such an offence had it not been for the action of the police/customs officers. The court may look to see whether the person was pressurised into committing the offence/providing information or whether by some ruse, the person was given an opportunity of so doing (**see para. 2.9.3.4**).
- Informing the suspect and his/her solicitor that the suspect's fingerprints had been found on items at the scene of the offence when this was not true.
- Undercover operations where the officers failed to record conversations in accordance with the PACE Codes of Practice.
- Failure by custody officers to inform a detained person of his/her rights.
- Interviewing a suspect without informing the person of his/her rights.
- Failing to provide the detained person with adequate meals.
- 'Off the record' interviews that were not recorded as required by the PACE Codes of Practice.
- Failing to make a contemporaneous note of a conversation.
- Failing to get an interpreter or appropriate adult.
- Interviewing a person suffering from schizophrenia without an appropriate adult being present (*R* v *Aspinall* [1999] 2 Cr App R 115).
- Identification of a suspect by police officers who had seen the person after he had been arrested and in handcuffs (*R* v *Bazil*, 6 April 1996, unreported).
- Failing to inform a suspect arrested in respect of one offence that it is proposed to question him/her in respect of another more serious offence or ensure they are aware of the true nature of the investigation (*R* v *Kirk* [1999] 4 All ER 698).

2.9.3.3 Exclusion at Common Law

Section 82(3) of the Police and Criminal Evidence Act 1984 retained the courts' common law power to exclude evidence at its discretion (as to which, see *R* v *Sang* [1980] AC 402). For evidence to be excluded at common law the court will not so much concern itself with *how* evidence is obtained, but rather the *effect* that the evidence will have at trial. The court can exclude evidence at common law where the prejudicial effect of the evidence on the defendant greatly outweighs its probative value.

In these cases the courts are looking at the trial process itself, as opposed to the investigation, and therefore this power has less impact on how investigations should be conducted.

2.9.3.4 Entrapment

The issue of entrapment falls into two categories: that is to say, trying to obtain evidence relating to offences that have already been committed; and those cases where evidence is obtained of offences yet to be committed.

In relation to investigations concerning offences already committed, the House of Lords in *R v Sang* [1980] AC 402 held that:

> Save with regard to admissions and confessions and generally with regard to evidence obtained from the accused after commission of the offence, [the judge] has no discretion to refuse to admit relevant admissible evidence on the ground that it was obtained by improper or unfair means. The court is not concerned with how it was obtained. It is no ground for the exercise of discretion to exclude that the evidence was obtained as the result of the activities of an *agent provocateur*.

(This is now subject to s. 78 of the 1984 Act but the principle still applies.)

The issues surrounding entrapment are considered by some to be an infringement of a person's human rights. In *Teixeira de Castro* v *Portugal* (1998) 28 EHRR 101, the European Court of Human Rights (subject to the following two qualifications) held that the use of undercover agents is not incompatible with Article 6 of the European Convention (right to a fair trial). Those qualifications were that:

- their use must be restricted and safeguards observed to prevent abuse;
- their actions must not exceed passive surveillance.

This is an area where the substantive criminal law overlaps with evidence and procedure. For the relevant considerations on police operations, **see Crime, chapter 1.3**.

Evidential factors to consider in running an operation that involves forms of entrapment include:

- The nature of the offence, as some offences are difficult to detect otherwise. Therefore, the more difficult the offence is to detect without intrusive inducement from the police, the more such intrusion will be justifiable.
- What suspicion officers have that an offence of that kind would be committed in the locality. For example, the setting up of a van containing cigarettes to see if someone takes the opportunity to steal them (*Williams and O'Hare* v *DPP* (1994) 98 Cr App R 209). 'If the trick had been the individual enterprise of a policeman in an area where such crime was not suspected to be prevalent, it would have been an abuse of State power.' (Lord Hoffmann in *Attorney-General's Reference (No. 3 of 2000)* [2001] 1 WLR 2060.)

The key question is whether the suspects voluntarily applied themselves to 'the trick' and that they were not enticed or provoked into committing a crime which they would otherwise have not committed.

An example of a case where evidence was not excluded is *R v Breen* [2001] EWCA Crim 1213. In this case police officers had attended the suspect's address unannounced and asked for 'blow'. The suspect gave the police his mobile telephone number and they returned the following day and were supplied with £20 worth of cannabis resin. The officers were invited to return at any time and they were supplied with drugs on subsequent visits. The Court of Appeal held that the judge had been entitled to find that the undercover officers had done no more than give the appellants an opportunity to break the law, of which each of them freely took advantage.

2.10.1 Introduction

The need for the prosecution to provide the defence with material relating to the charge(s) in a case has been recognised by the courts and the government to be crucial in ensuring that defendants get a fair trial. This point is further enforced with the introduction of the Human Rights Act 1998 which incorporates the European Convention on Human Rights and in this area brings in Article 6.

Article 6(3):

Everyone charged with a criminal offence has the following minimum rights:
(a) to be informed promptly, in a language which he understands and in detail, of the nature and cause of the accusation against him;
(b) to have adequate time and facilities for the preparation of his defence;
(c) to defend himself in person or through legal assistance of his own choosing or, if he has no sufficient means to pay for legal assistance, to be given it free when the interests of justice so require;
(d) to examine or have examined witnesses against him and to obtain the attendance and examination of witnesses on his behalf under the same conditions as witnesses against him. . .

In *Rowe and Davis* v *United Kingdom* (2000) 30 EHRR 1, the European Court of Human Rights emphasised that the right to a fair trial means that the prosecution authorities should disclose to the defence all material evidence in their possession for and against the accused. Only such measures restricting the rights of the defence to disclosure as are strictly necessary are permissible under Article 6(1). *Rowe and Davis* is an important decision in relation to the disclosure of material in criminal cases and the principles that apply. This can be summarised as follows:

- It is a fundamental aspect of the right to a fair trial that criminal proceedings, including the elements of such proceedings which relate to procedure, should be adversarial and that there should be equality of arms between the prosecution and defence.
- The right to an adversarial trial means, in a criminal case, that both the prosecution and defence must be given the opportunity to have knowledge of and comment on the observations filed and the evidence adduced by the other party.
- Article 6(1), in common with English law, requires that the prosecution authority should disclose to the defence all material evidence in their possession for or against the accused.
- The entitlement of disclosure of relevant evidence is not an absolute right.
- Only such measures restricting the right of the defence which are strictly necessary are permissible under Article 6(1).
- Moreover, to ensure that the accused receives a fair trial, any difficulties caused to the defence by limitation on its rights must be sufficiently counter balanced by the procedures followed by the judicial authorities.

- Decision-making procedure must, so far as is possible, comply with the requirements to provide adversarial proceedings and equality of arms, and incorporate adequate safeguards to protect the interests of the accused.

The requirement to provide the defence with material can be divided between that required prior to the person pleading, which is known as advanced information and that which is required once the defendant has pleaded not guilty in the magistrates' court or is committed/transferred to the Crown Court. The second stage assumes that the defence has been provided with the prosecution case and therefore any evidence that is left is unused material and that it will remain unused by the prosecution. This is usually referred to as 'disclosure'. These two stages are considered below.

Within this chapter reference will be made to the Criminal Procedure and Investigations Act 1996 (as amended by the Criminal Justice Act 2003), the Code of Practice for the 1996 Act (the Code), the 2005 Attorney-General's Guidelines: Disclosure of Information in Criminal Proceedings (which provides further guidance/interpretation to the Act and Codes) and the Prosecution Team Disclosure Manual, that replace the Joint CPS/Police Project JOPI Guidelines which set out in detail actions required to meet the disclosure requirements of the 1996 Act. The Criminal Justice Act 2003 made changes to the 1996 Act, some of which came into force on 4 April 2005 and therefore applies to cases from that date. These changes are discussed against the existing legislation contained in earlier editions of this book. It will be important to note when an investigation started as this will determine whether the changes introduced on 4 April 2005 apply or the previous disclosure rules. Further guidance has also been given by the Court of Appeal in Disclosure: A protocol for the Control and Management of Unused Material in the Crown Court. In this document the Court of Appeal stated that, for the Criminal Procedure and Investigations Act 1996 to work properly, investigators and disclosure officers responsible for the gathering, inspection, retention and recording of relevant unused prosecution material must perform their tasks thoroughly, scrupulously and fairly. In this, they must adhere to the appropriate provisions of the CPIA Code of Practice.

2.10.2 Advanced Information

Advance information refers to the material that the defence are entitled to have in order to consider whether to plead guilty or not guilty. In some cases it is not a question of whether the defendant committed the crime but whether the prosecution are in a position to prove the offence and, in order to consider this, the defence are unlikely to agree to plead or decide on the mode of trial without knowing the strength of the prosecution case. It is clearly in the public interest that guilty pleas are entered or indicated as soon as possible (*R v Calderdale Magistrates' Court, ex parte Donahue* [2001] Crim LR 141) and often this cannot be achieved unless advanced information has been provided. The need to know as early as possible whether a defendant is going to plead not guilty can be particularly important as there are time limits by which the courts have to set trials and committals. Often these can be delayed because the prosecution have not complied with their disclosure duties.

Ensuring that all defendants receive copies of any advanced information (or any later disclosure) is also important. In *R v Tompkins* [2005] EWCA Crim 3035 the court held that where there has been non-disclosure at the time a plea had been entered, a defendant who had pleaded guilty should not in any way be in a worse position than those who had pleaded not guilty.

2.10.2.1 Obligations on Prosecution Regarding Advanced Information

The prosecution is required, on request, to supply the defence with a summary of the prosecution case and/or copies of the statements of the proposed prosecution witnesses. In indictable and either way offences this is covered by parts 21 to 26 of the Criminal Procedure Rules 2005 and in summary only cases by the Attorney-General's Guidelines: Disclosure of Information in Criminal Proceedings. In *R v K & others* [2006] EWCA Crim 724, the court held that criminal trials are dependent on and subject to the Criminal Procedure Rules 2005 which imposed duties and burdens on all the participants in a criminal trial. Whereas the rules state that advanced information is only required when requested by the defence, in practice this should, where possible, be made available to the CPS at the first hearing.

It is suggested that Article 6 of the European Convention supports the need to provide advanced information to the defence and that this should be done as soon as possible:

Article 6(3)(a) states that a person is:

... to be informed promptly ... and in detail, of the nature and cause of the accusation against him;

Article 6(3)(b), states that an accused is entitled to:

... have adequate time ... for the preparation of his defence.

The point concerning advanced information in summary cases was considered in *R v Stratford Justices, ex parte Imbert* [1999] 2 Cr App R 276 where the court gave their opinion that Article 6 does not give an absolute right to pre-trial disclosure, it will be a question of whether the defendant can have a fair trial. Clearly it will be easier to satisfy this test where advanced information as been provided to the defence.

Rule 21.3 of the 2005 Rules provides that the prosecutor, when requested, must provide the accused or a person representing the accused who requests the prosecutor to furnish him/her with advance information.

- a copy of those parts of every written statement which contain information as to the facts and matters of which the prosecutor proposes to adduce evidence in the proceedings; or
- a summary of the facts and matters of which the prosecutor proposes to adduce evidence in the proceedings.

Advanced information might also include the following and so consideration should be had to providing this material to the prosecutor so that he/she can forward it to the defence where appropriate (ensuring the addresses and other details of witnesses and victims are protected):

- copy of the custody record;
- copies of any interview tape(s);
- copy of any first descriptions where relevant;
- significant information that might affect a bail decision or that might enable the defence to contest the committal proceedings (A-G's Guidelines, para. 55);
- any material which is relevant to sentence (e.g. information which might mitigate the seriousness of the offence or assist the accused to lay blame in whole or in part upon a co-accused or another person) (A-G's Guidelines, para. 58);
- statements and/or a summary of the prosecution cases;
- copy of any video evidence.

Where a person has made several statements but all the relevant evidence for the prosecution case is contained in one statement, it is only that one statement which needs to be disclosed. In order to comply with advanced information the defence needs to be either given a copy of the document or allowed to inspect the document (or a copy of it).

However, where the OIC considers that providing advanced information might lead to a witness being intimidated or some other interference with the course of justice he/she should consult with the CPS as the rules allow the prosecutor to limit disclosure of some or all the prosecution case (2005 Rules, r. 21.4).

2.10.3 Disclosure and the Criminal Procedure and Investigations Act 1996

As stated above this stage assumes that the defence has already been informed of the details of the prosecution case. In most investigations there will be material that has come to the attention of the police which will not be used as evidence to prove the prosecution case but which might be useful to the defence. It is through the disclosure rules that this information will be provided to the defendant. The rules of disclosure are governed by the Criminal Procedure and Investigations Act 1996. The 1996 Act puts the prosecution duty to disclose information to the defence on a statutory footing, and also introduced a new concept in criminal law where the defence have a duty to advise the prosecution of certain matters relating to their case. This is also supported by the 1996 Act Code of Practice, the Attorney-General's Guidelines on Disclosure and the Disclosure Manual.

The 1996 Act is further recognition of the need to disclose material to each side to allow the case to be dealt with fairly. This point as well as the need for timely disclosure of material, is further reinforced by Article 6(3) of the European Convention on Human Rights.

In *Jasper* v *United Kingdom* (2000) 30 EHRR 441 the Court expressed the importance of equality of arms being a fundamental aspect of a fair trial; both the defence and the prosecution must be given the opportunity to have knowledge of and comment on filed observations and evidence adduced by the other party. The Court did recognise that the entitlement to disclosure of relevant evidence was not an absolute right but could be restricted as was strictly necessary (**see para. 2.10.6.6**).

2.10.3.1 The Criminal Procedure and Investigations Act 1996

The Criminal Procedure and Investigations Act 1996 is made up of seven parts. It is the first two parts which are of interest to the police:

- Part I sets out the procedures for disclosure and the effects of failing to comply with the Act; and
- Part II sets out the duties of police officers in relation to the disclosure provisions.

2.10.3.2 Aims of the 1996 Act

The aim of the disclosure rules within the Criminal Procedure and Investigations Act 1996 is to make sure that a defendant gets a fair trial and speeds up the whole trial process. This was confirmed by *R* v *Stratford Justices, ex parte Imbert* [1999] 2 Cr App R 276, where the court said that the legislation was to try to ensure that nothing which might assist the defence was kept from the accused.

Paragraph 3 of A-G's Guidelines states that:

> The scheme set out in the Criminal Procedure and Investigations Act 1996 (as amended by the Criminal Justice Act 2003) (the Act) is designed to ensure that there is fair disclosure of material which may be relevant to an investigation and which does not form part of the prosecution case. Disclosure under the Act should assist the accused in the timely preparation and presentation of their case and assist the court to focus on all the relevant issues in the trial. Disclosure which does not meet these objectives risks preventing a fair trial taking place.

The Act originally placed a responsibility on the prosecution to make *primary* disclosure of material to the defence; a responsibility for the defence—under certain conditions—to disclose their case to the prosecution with a further responsibility on the prosecution to make a *secondary* disclosure to the defence. As a 'catch all' the prosecution also have a continuing duty to review the material they have disclosed.

From 4 April 2005, this distinction between primary and secondary disclosure has now changed. The changes introduced by the Criminal Justice Act 2003 provide for an initial duty to disclose with a continuing duty to disclose until the accused is acquitted or convicted or the prosecutor decides not to proceed with the case. One of the effects of this change is that under the pre April 2005 position the prosecution only had to provide disclosure of material that was relevant to the prosecution case. Now disclosure from the start has to consider any material that might undermine the prosecution case or assist the defence. It is submitted that this requires the prosecution to consider in more detail the types of defence that might be used at trial.

This now places a duty on the prosecutor to disclose to the defence material which may prove helpful to the defendant's case. This has to be balanced against the risk of disclosing so much material under their duty to disclose that the defence collapses under the sheer volume of paperwork. Alternatively, allowing the defence relentless requests for material which may be of no real value ('fishing expeditions') could lead to situations where a guilty person is acquitted.

While the duty of disclosure is placed on the prosecutor, the police have a responsibility to assist in this process. It is therefore vital that police officers understand, not only the statutory requirements made of them, but also the extent of their role within the whole disclosure process. This view is supported by the 2005 A-G's Guidelines. Paragraph 23 states:

> Investigators and disclosure officers must be fair and objective and must work together with prosecutors to ensure that disclosure obligations are met. . . .

2.10.3.3 Jurisdiction of the 1996 Act

The Criminal Procedure and Investigations Act 1996 is primarily concerned with the disclosure of material which does not form part of the prosecution case resulting from a criminal investigation (i.e. 'unused material'). A criminal investigation is defined by s. 1(4) of the 1996 Act and para. 2.1 of the Code of Practice. In order to satisfy the disclosure requirements police officers should consider recording and retaining material in the early stages of an investigation. This will include:

- investigations into crimes that have been committed;
- investigations whose purpose is to ascertain whether a crime has been committed, with a view to the possible institution of criminal proceedings; and
- investigations which begin in the belief that a crime may be committed,

for example when the police keep premises or individuals under observation for a period of time, with a view to the possible institution of criminal proceedings.

In these cases the investigation may well have started some time before the defendant became a suspect. In such cases all the material from the investigation/operation would have to be considered to see if it was relevant to the defence case. In cases where there is a surveillance operation or observation point, it may be that the details of the observation point and the surveillance techniques would not be revealed but it would be necessary to retain material generating from it (**see para. 2.10.6.6**).

It will be important to know when an investigation commenced as to whether the changes introduced on 4 April 2005 or the earlier rules should still be used, the MG6 must state when the investigation started (Disclosure Manual, para. 6.7).

2.10.3.4   Failure to Comply

Compliance with the rules of disclosure, by both the defence and prosecution, is essential if the 1996 Act is to have any real value. First, in cases where the defence are obliged to make disclosure to the prosecution, failure to do so may lead to the court or jury drawing such inferences as appear proper in deciding the guilt or innocence of the accused (s. 11(5)). Should the prosecution fail to comply with their obligations then an accused does not have to make defence disclosure and no such inference can be made. Secondly, failure by the prosecution to comply with the rules could lead to the court staying the proceedings on the grounds that there has been an abuse of process (s. 10). It could also lead to an action for damages or such other relief as the court sees fit under the Human Rights Act 1998, particularly in relation to Article 6 of the European Convention and the right to a fair trial.

Additionally, where the prosecution have not made disclosure on time or fully, a stay on the proceedings or a further adjournment is possible. It is suggested that the more adjournments in a case, the more likely that witnesses will get fed up with the delays and will fail to attend on the next occasion and the case could therefore be lost!

Even if there has been a failure to comply with disclosure the case will not automatically be stayed and therefore any failings should be brought to the attention of the CPS so that the matter can be considered. In *R (On the Application of Ebrahim)* v *Feltham Magistrates' Court* [2001] 1 WLR 1293 the court stated that:

> It must be remembered that it is a commonplace in criminal trial for the defendant to rely on holes in the prosecution case. If in such a case, there is sufficient credible evidence, apart from the missing evidence, which, if believed, would justify safe conviction then the trial should proceed, leaving the defendant to seek to persuade the jury or magistrates not to convict because evidence might otherwise have been available was not before the court through no fault of the defendant.

Further guidance was provided in *R* v *Brooks* (2004) 13 August, CA, unreported, a case where the prosecution failed to comply with the disclosure requirements. The Court of Appeal held that if the court was satisfied that the prosecution had deliberately withheld evidence from the court or frustrated the defence, the court did have the power to stay the prosecution. If the court was not so satisfied it would consider whether, despite all that had gone wrong, a fair trial was possible.

Failure to disclose may result in convictions being overturned, for instance in *R* v *Poole* (2003) *The Times*, 26 June, the Court of Appeal allowed appeals against convictions for murder because the non-disclosure of prosecution evidence influenced the jury's assessment of the reliability of the evidence of a key eye-witness. In this case the witness gave an account that was false in a material particular. However, the police did not follow up those inconsistencies and they failed to inform the CPS that his evidence was unreliable. The level of disclosure that is required will be a question of fact in each case. In *Filmer* v

DPP [2006] EWHC 3450 (Admin) the court held that the extent of disclosure required from the prosecution depends on the evidence and issue in a particular case. The prosecution are required to provide sufficient disclosure to enable a defendant to present their case. The court went on to say that this has to be the approach otherwise the prosecution would have to second guess every question the defence may want to ask (this is where the defence disclosure becomes relevant, **see para. 2.10.4.4**).

2.10.4 Part I of the 1996 Act: Rules of Disclosure

2.10.4.1 Application of the Disclosure Provisions

Section 1 of the Criminal Procedure and Investigations Act 1996 defines in which type of cases the disclosure provisions apply. In reality this applies to all cases other than those where the defendant pleads guilty at the magistrates' court. These rules only apply where no criminal investigation into the alleged offence took place before 1 April 1997. If an investigation began before 1 April 1997, then it will be necessary to refer to the common law rules, however ACPO have stated that the 1996 Act should be followed in all cases when considering disclosure. For those investigations that started after 4 April 2005, the amendments introduced by the Criminal Justice Act 2003 will apply.

Some guidance is given by the case of *R v Uxbridge Magistrates' Court, ex parte Patel* (2000) 164 JP 209, as to the time an investigation begins. There it was said that the phrase 'criminal investigation' in s. 1(3) of the 1996 Act means that a criminal investigation could begin into an offence before it was committed. This could be so in a surveillance case or where a series of cases was committed, some before and some after the appointed day. Whether in any given case that was the correct view would be a question of fact for the court to determine.

Section 1 also defines a criminal investigation and states:

> (4) For the purposes of this section a criminal investigation is an investigation which police officers or other persons have a duty to conduct with a view to it being ascertained—
> (a) whether a person should be charged with an offence, or
> (b) whether a person charged with an offence is guilty of it.

Consequently, this part of the Act also applies to other people, besides the police, who carry out investigations where they have a duty to ascertain whether criminal offences have been committed (e.g. HM Revenue and Customs; Benefits Agency investigators). It does not apply to those whose primary responsibility does not relate to criminal offences (e.g. local authorities and schools). It also includes the situation where an investigation is started before any offence has been committed, for instance where a surveillance operation is being conducted with a view to gathering prosecution evidence. In this case it is only the information obtained and not the surveillance operation that is disclosable.

2.10.4.2 Primary or Initial Disclosure by Prosecutor

This is covered by s. 3 of the Criminal Procedure and Investigations Act 1996. This section talks about material which '*might undermine the prosecution case against the accused*'. The courts are likely to consider this to include material which has an adverse affect on the strength of the prosecution case. Section 3 was amended by the Criminal Justice Act 2003, so for cases where the investigation commenced after 4 April 2005 the requirement is wider in that it covers material that might reasonably be considered capable of undermining the case for the prosecution against the accused, or of assisting the case for the accused. This introduces a more objective test and in effect incorporates the previous secondary disclosure test at this earlier stage. Clearly there is a need to guess what the defence case may be in considering what should be disclosed but this can be further reviewed after the defence disclosure.

Under the 1996 Act, while a schedule of all relevant material must be provided, only material that undermines the prosecution case must be disclosed at the primary or initial disclosure stage. There is only limited case law in this area but it is likely that such material will consist mainly of material which raises question marks over the strength of the prosecution case, the value of evidence given by witnesses and issues relating to identification. If officers feel that the material is not relevant to the prosecution case but may be useful to the defence in cross-examination, it may well come within the category of material which undermines the prosecution case. Disclosure of previous convictions and other matters that might affect the credibility of a witness may 'undermine the prosecution case' as it may limit the value of the witness's testimony. This factor may not be apparent at the time but may come to light after the initial disclosure, such as where it becomes known that the witness has a grudge against the defendant. This is one reason why the 1996 Act requires the decision as to whether material undermines the prosecution case to be continuously monitored throughout the case.

The Code of Practice at para. 3.4 states that:

> In conducting an investigation, the investigator should pursue all reasonable lines of inquiry, whether these point towards or away from the suspect. What is reasonable in each case will depend on the particular circumstances.

In *R (On the Application of Ebrahim)* v *Feltham Magistrates' Court* [2001] 1 WLR 1293 the court stated that the extent of the investigation should be proportionate to the seriousness of the matter being investigated. What is reasonable in a case may well depend on such factors as the staff and resources available, the seriousness of the case, the strength of evidence against the suspect and the nature of the line of inquiry to be pursued. If in doubt it is suggested the CPS are contacted for guidance.

Paragraph 5.16 of the Disclosure Manual makes important observations concerning negative results when making enquiries 'negative results can sometimes be as significant to an investigation as positive ones'. It is impossible to define precisely when a negative result may be significant, as every case is different. However it will include the result of any inquiry that differs from what might be expected, given the prevailing circumstances. Not only must material or information which points towards a fact or an individual be retained, but also that which casts doubt on the suspect's guilt, or implicates another person. Examples of negative information include:

- a CCTV camera that did not record the crime/location/suspect in a manner which is consistent with the prosecution case. (The fact that a CCTV camera did not function or have videotape loaded will not usually be considered relevant negative information);
- where a number of people present at a particular location at the particular time that an offence is alleged to have taken place state they saw nothing unusual;
- where a finger-mark from a crime scene cannot be identified as belonging to a known suspect;
- any other failure to match a crime scene sample with one taken from the accused.

The prosecution only have to disclose material relevant to the prosecution in question. For instance, surveillance logs concerning another matter would not need to be disclosed (*R v Dennis*, 13 April 2000, unreported). It is up to the prosecutor to decide on the format in which material is disclosed to the accused. If material is to be copied, s. 3(3) leaves the question of whether this should be done by the prosecutor or the police open. The prosecutor must also provide the defence with a schedule of all non-sensitive material (s. 4(2)). This includes all other information in police possession, or material that has been examined by the police other than 'sensitive material' (this is disclosed to the prosecutor separately). 'Sensitive material' is material which it is not in the public interest to disclose. At this stage the defence is not entitled to inspect items on the schedule that have not been disclosed (s. 3(6) and (7)).

Material must not be disclosed to the extent that the court concludes it is not in the public interest to disclose it and orders accordingly or it is material whose disclosure is prohibited by s. 17 of the Regulation of Investigatory Powers Act 2000 unless it falls within the exception provided by s. 18 of the Act.

2.10.4.3 Time Period for Primary/Initial Disclosure

While there are provisions to set specific time periods by which primary initial disclosure must be met, none currently exist. Until such times primary initial disclosure must be made as soon as practicable after the duty arises. Where disclosure is not made within a reasonable period it could lead to the case being lost. In *R v Bourimech* [2002] EWCA Crim 2089 the defendant sought disclosure following the service of his defence statement of a previous crime report made by the victim. One day before the trial was scheduled to begin the crime report relating to that incident was served amongst other papers on the defence. This report escaped the notice of the defence until the final day of the trial. The court held that the defect in disclosure amounted to unfairness in the proceedings and the court could not be confident that if the victim had been cross-examined in relation to the previous allegation the jury might have been influenced by the credit and credibility of the witness.

The 1996 Act in effect only applies once the defendant has been committed/transferred to the Crown Court or is proceeding to trial in the magistrates'/youth court. In most cases prosecution disclosure can wait until after this time without jeopardising the defendant's right to a fair trial. However, the prosecutor must always be alive to the need to make advance disclosure of material that should be disclosed at an earlier stage (*R v DPP, ex parte Lee* [1999] 2 All ER 737). Examples include:

- previous convictions of a complainant or a deceased if that information could reasonably be expected to assist the defence when applying for bail;
- material that might enable a defendant to make a pre-committal application to stay the proceedings as an abuse of process;
- material that might enable a defendant to submit that he/she should only be committed for trial on a lesser charge, or perhaps that he/she should not be committed for trial at all;
- depending on what the defendant chooses to reveal about his/her case at this early stage, material that would enable the defendant and his/her legal advisers to make preparations for trial that would be significantly less effective if disclosure were delayed; for example, names of eye-witnesses whom the prosecution did not intend to use.

It should be noted that any disclosure by the prosecution prior to committal would not normally exceed the initial disclosure which, after committal, would be required by s. 3 of the 1996 Act.

2.10.4.4 Disclosure by the Defence

The duty on the defence to make disclosure only arises *after* the prosecution has made the initial disclosure (s. 5(1)). This duty falls into two categories:

- compulsory
- voluntary.

The disclosure required by the defence is limited to material that they intend to use at trial.

There may be occasions where the defence statement is allowed to be used in cross-examination when it is alleged that the defendant has changed his defence or in re-examination to rebut a suggestion of recent invention (*R v Lowe* [2003] EWCA Crim 3182).

2.10.4.5 Compulsory Disclosure by Defence (s. 5)

The duty for the defence to make disclosure does not apply to cases being tried summarily. The duty on the defence, whether the accused is represented or not, is to provide a defence statement to the court and the prosecutor within 14 days of the prosecution making primary disclosure (this period can be extended by the courts). From 4 April 2005, where there are other accused in the proceedings and the court so orders, the accused must also give a defence statement to each of the other accused specified by the court, and a request for a copy of the defence statement may be made by any co-accused. The court will set the time for disclosure to be given where a defence statement is to be given to a co-accused (s. 5(5A) to (5D)).

The defence statement should outline the defence case in general terms, including any particular defences on which he/she intends to rely. In addition, those issues, relevant to the case, which the accused disputes with the prosecution must be set out with reasons. Additionally, from 4 April 2005 the defence statement must indicate any point of law (including any point as to the admissibility of evidence or an abuse of process) which he/she wishes to take, and any authority on which he/she intends to rely for that purpose (s. 6A of the 1996 Act). This requirement to give reasons is intended to stop the defence going on a 'fishing expedition' to speculatively look at material in order to find some kind of defence.

Where the defence case involves an alibi, the statement must give details of the alibi, including the name and address of any alibi witness. In cases where there are co-accused, there is no duty to disclose this information to the other defendants, although this could be done voluntarily.

It should be noted that the changes added since 4 April 2005 define an alibi for the purposes of the defence statement as evidence tending to show that by reason of the presence of the accused at a particular place or in a particular area at a particular time, he/she was not, or was unlikely to have been, at the place where the offence is alleged to have been committed at the time of its alleged commission. Where this applies, the defence must provide details including the name, address and date of birth of any witness the accused believes is able to give evidence in support of the alibi, or as many of those details as are known to the accused when the statement is given. Where such details are not known, the statement must include any information in the accused's possession which might be of material assistance in identifying or finding any such witness (s. 6A(2) of the 1996 Act).

2.10.4.6 Voluntary Disclosure by Defence (s. 6)

The purpose of s. 6 of the 1996 Act is to allow the defence, in cases where the case is being tried summarily as a not guilty plea, to obtain further disclosure from the prosecution after the primary disclosure. This is only likely to happen where:

- the defence is not satisfied with the material disclosed at the primary disclosure stage or where they wish to examine items listed in the schedule of non-sensitive material;

- the defence wish to show the strength of their case in order to persuade the prosecution not to proceed.

If the defence decide to make a defence statement they must comply with the same conditions imposed on compulsory defence disclosure.

2.10.4.7 Effect of Failure in Defence Disclosure

If the defence fails to give a defence statement under s. 5 or where a defence statement is provided it is:

- outside the time limits;
- sets out inconsistent defences in a defence statement or at trial puts forward a different defence; or
- at trial adduces evidence in support of an alibi without having given particulars of the alibi in a defence statement, or calls a witness in support of an alibi without providing details of the witness or information that might help trace the witness;

then following sanctions may apply:

- the court or, with the leave of the court, any other party may make such comment as appears appropriate;
- the court or jury may draw such inferences as appear proper in deciding whether the accused is guilty of the offence concerned (but there must also be other evidence to convict the defendant).
- Even if the defence serve the defence statement outside the 14 days the prosecution must still consider the impact of the statement in terms of the need for any further disclosure (*Murphy* v *DPP* [2006] EWHC 1753 (Admin)).

2.10.4.8 Secondary Disclosure by Prosecutor (s. 7)/Further Disclosure

For investigations commencing after 4 April 2005, s. 7 is repealed. Once a defence statement has been provided, the prosecutor must disclose to the accused any prosecution material which has not previously been disclosed to the accused and which might be reasonably expected to assist the accused's defence as disclosed by the defence statement. However, if after reviewing the defence material he/she considers that there is no further material to disclose, he/she must give the accused a written statement that there is no such material. The discussion below still applies.

Once a defence statement has been provided (whether compulsorily or voluntarily), the prosecution must disclose any prosecution material that:

- might be reasonably expected to assist the accused's defence; and
- has not already been disclosed.

It will be a question of fact whether material in police possession might be reasonably expected to assist the defence case. If the court feels that material that was not disclosed would to any reasonable person have been expected to help the defence case, the case may fail. The test for secondary disclosure (i.e. pre 4 April 2005 investigations) is wider than primary disclosure in that this test is objective in that it requires disclosure where any reasonable person would expect the material to assist the defence whereas primary disclosure talks of 'the prosecutor's opinion'.

If there is no additional material to be disclosed then the prosecutor must give a written statement to this effect. It is not the responsibility of the prosecutor or the police to examine material held by third parties which the defence have stated they wish to examine (the defence can request this from the third party or apply for a witness summons). However, there may be occasions where matters disclosed in the defence statement lead investigators to look at material held by third parties as it might impact on the prosecution case. This stage of the disclosure process may require further inquiries prompted by the defence statement. The result of those inquiries may then have to be disclosed because it either undermines the prosecution case or it assists the accused's defence.

Material must not be disclosed to the extent that the court concludes it is not in the public interest to disclose it and orders accordingly or it is material whose disclosure is prohibited by s. 17 of the Regulation of Investigatory Powers Act 2000.

2.10.4.9 Continuing Duty of Prosecutor to Disclose (s. 9)

For investigations commencing after 4 April 2005, s. 9 is repealed and replaced by s. 7A, which places a continuing duty on the prosecutor at any time between the initial disclosure and the accused being acquitted or convicted or the prosecutor deciding not to proceed with the case concerned, to keep under review the question of further disclosure. In considering the need for further disclosure the prosecutor must consider whether material might reasonably be considered capable of undermining the case for the prosecution against the accused or of assisting the case for the accused. If there is any such material it must be disclosed to the accused as soon as is reasonably practicable. Consideration of what might need to be disclosed could change depending on the state of affairs at that time (including the case for the prosecution as it then stands) and so should be reviewed on a continuing basis (s. 7A(4)).

There is a duty on the prosecution to continue to review the disclosure of prosecution material right up until the case is completed (acquittal, conviction or discontinuance of the case).

For investigations that commenced before 4 April 2005, this duty to review is in two stages:

- after primary disclosure the prosecutor must review material not disclosed in terms of whether it might undermine the prosecution case (s. 9); and
- after secondary prosecution disclosure (s. 7).

The review of the material must also be in terms of whether material might be reasonably expected to assist the accused's defence as disclosed by the defence statement. This responsibility is mirrored in the Code of Practice. This is a continuous duty even after secondary disclosure has been made, failure to review could lead to an acquittal, abuse of process or even acquittal at a later appeal.

If the defence is not satisfied that the prosecution have disclosed all they should have, s. 8 of the 1996 Act allows for the defence to apply to the court for further disclosure.

2.10.5 Roles and Responsibilities under the 1996 Act

The Code of Practice identifies certain roles within the disclosure process:

- prosecutor
- officer in charge of the case (OIC)
- disclosure officer

- investigator
- supervisor of OIC and disclosure officer.

In addition, it is the responsibility of the chief officer of police of each force to put arrangements in place to ensure that the identity of the OIC and disclosure officer is recorded for each criminal investigation (Code of Practice, para. 3.2). Force policy should be followed in recording this information.

The MG6 series should be used when complying with disclosure to the CPS.

The roles described within the 1996 Act are independent of each other but all must be completed for the disclosure provisions to work (para. 3.1). All police officers involved in an investigation are likely to have to comply with the role of investigator.

Some investigations may involve a large quantity of material, both used and unused. Examples of cases where this may occur include substantial frauds; large-scale conspiracies; drug related offences involving manufacture, importation or supply; homicide or other major inquiries. These are often large or complex cases and additional guidance for these cases is provided in the CPS/Police Joint Operational Instructions (JOPI) Guidelines (2003), paras 2.113 to 2.117.

Although the police roles are independent they may be combined, the OIC may also be an investigator and, depending on the complexity of the case, may also be the disclosure officer. Whether there is one officer involved in the case or several, each role can be considered separately and must be completed fully in order that the right information can be given to the prosecutor who, ultimately, is responsible for the disclosure of material to the defence. It is important that all officers consult fully in order that the disclosure officer can complete his/her task properly. Each role is considered below as if undertaken by a different person.

2.10.5.1 Prosecutor

This role is defined by s. 2(3) of the 1996 Act as being 'any person acting as prosecutor whether an individual or a body'. In other words, the person who will be taking the case to court. On most occasions this will be the Crown Prosecution Service. It would also apply to the Serious Fraud Office or the Data Protection Registrar. In the case of private prosecutions, the prosecutor is obliged to comply with the disclosure provisions of the 1996 Act but does not have to comply with the Code of Practice. The prosecutor is responsible for ensuring that primary initial disclosure is made to the defence and, where appropriate, secondary disclosure. The prosecutor should also be available to advise the OIC, disclosure officer and investigators on matters relating to the relevance of material recorded and retained by police, sensitive material and on any other disclosure issues that might arise.

Should there need to be an application to the court to withhold material because of public interest (**see para. 2.10.6.6**), this will be done through the prosecutor.

A more detailed explanation of the roles and responsibilities of the prosecutor are set out in the CPS/Police Joint Operational Instructions (JOPI) Guidelines (2003).

2.10.5.2 Officer in Charge of the Case (OIC)

This role may be performed by a person directly involved in the investigation or by person who has been given the role of overseeing the investigation (Disclosure Code, paras 3.1 and 3.4). Whoever has this role is both responsible and accountable for the investigation (para. 3.4). (See also Disclosure Manual, para. 3.5.)

The Attorney-General's Guidelines state that an individual must not be appointed as disclosure officer, or continue in that role, if that is likely to result in a conflict of interest, for instance, if the disclosure officer is the victim of the alleged crime which is the subject of criminal proceedings. It is suggested that the same approach should also be taken when identifying the OIC. This is an important consideration as it should be remembered that the officer is a victim and may be in need of support.

The OIC is responsible for ensuring that proper procedures are in place for the recording of information and that records and materials are retained for the required period (**see para. 2.10.6.3**). Paragraph 4.1 of the Code requires that the material is recorded in a durable and retrievable form and that, where possible, the record is made contemporaneously. If not, the record must be made as soon as practicable. These requirements to record information should be paramount in the mind of all investigators, as well as the OIC.

The need for contemporaneous records is also required under the Police and Criminal Evidence Act 1984 and if not complied with could affect the admissibility of important evidence (see s. 78 of the 1984 Act). Note that, under para. 4.3, relevant material to be recorded includes *negative* material. Such material might include the fact that several people at the scene of a crime were spoken to and claimed to have seen nothing, or that they saw several other people at the scene as well. This last point reiterates the position at common law; that police officers have a duty to get to the truth and allow a suspect a fair trial, a duty which includes recording and retaining material which helps the defence (this also assists in complying with Article 6 of the European Convention).

Having made sure that material is recorded and retained by the investigators in the case, the OIC must make the material available to the disclosure officer (Code, para. 3.4). Where the function of disclosure officer is carried out by the OIC, there is little problem as the OIC should have a full understanding of the case and the implication of all the material collected, in terms of it being adverse to the case or being of a sensitive nature. In cases where the roles are performed by different people, it is important that the OIC and the disclosure officer consult fully about the material in order that the disclosure officer has as full an understanding of the case as he/she can in order to carry out his/her functions properly (para. 3.1 of the Disclosure Manual). This must be done in order that the disclosure officer can complete the certification stage (paras 3.1 and 9.1). These responsibilities can be delegated to other police officers or non-police staff but it remains the responsibility of the OIC to ensure that the tasks are completed (para. 3.4). It may be necessary to demonstrate to the court that these powers have been carried out.

As with all people involved in the disclosure process, s. 9 of the 1996 Act (from 4 April 2005 s. 9 was replaced by s. 7A) places a duty on the OIC to review material in the case. This duty is emphasised by para. 5.3 of the Code so that, where the OIC becomes aware that previously examined material which has not been disclosed has since become relevant to the case, he/she must take steps to ensure that the material is retained and inform the prosecutor so that disclosure can be made to the defence. At this stage it will be for the OIC to decide in which format that material should be retained (para. 4.1) considering the need to be able to produce it for inspection by the court.

2.10.5.3 Disclosure Officer

The disclosure officer creates the link between the investigation team and the prosecutor (Crown Prosecution Service) and is therefore very important to the disclosure process. For investigations carried out by the police, generally speaking there is no restriction on who performs this role however they must be suitably trained and experienced. It could be the OIC or, equally, it could be performed by police support staff (Code, paras 2.1 and 3.4), or the disclosure officer who is responsible for providing information and material to the prosecutor at the primary disclosure stage (para. 7.1) and, where necessary, carrying out any additional work requested by the prosecutor before the primary disclosure is made (para. 7.4). The role and responsibility of the disclosure officer is set out in the Disclosure Manual at para. 3.9. It is important that the disclosure officer does not have a conflict of interest, this is set out in the A-G's Guidelines at para. 25:

> An individual must not be appointed as disclosure officer, or continue in that role, if that is likely to result in a conflict of interest, for instance, if the disclosure officer is the victim of the alleged crime which is the subject of criminal proceedings. The advice of a more senior officer must always be sought if there is doubt as to whether a conflict of interest precludes an individual acting as the disclosure officer. If thereafter the doubt remains, the advice of a prosecutor should be sought.

In some cases it will be desirable to appoint a disclosure officer at the outset of the investigation. In making this decision, the OIC should have regard to the nature and seriousness of the case, the volume of material which may be obtained or created, and the likelihood of a committal or a not guilty plea. If not appointed at the start of an investigation, a disclosure officer must be appointed in sufficient time to be able to prepare the unused material schedules for inclusion in the full file submitted to CPS (Disclosure Manual, para. 3.11).

The disclosure officer is responsible for examining all material retained by the police during the investigation (Code, para. 2.1). The first step is to establish that all material which has been retained in relation to the case has been recorded and made available for examination. The disclosure officer should verify with the OIC that all material has been made available to him/her.

There is now a recognition that the disclosure officer may need to have deputy disclosure officers, this is particularly so in investigations where there is material of a sensitive nature. There may be a number of disclosure officers, especially in large and complex cases. However, there must be a lead disclosure officer who is the focus for inquiries and whose responsibility it is to ensure that the investigator's disclosure obligations are compiled with.

Disclosure officers, or their deputies, must inspect, view or listen to all relevant material that has been retained by the investigator, and the disclosure officer must provide a personal declaration to the effect that this task has been done.

There will occasionally be cases where the police investigation has been intelligence led, there may be a deputy disclosure officer appointed just to deal with intelligence material which, by its very nature, is likely to be sensitive (**see para. 2.10.6.6**). In cases where more than one disclosure officer has been appointed to deal with different aspects of the case, a lead disclosure officer should be identified as the single point of contact for the prosecutor. Where an officer other than the lead disclosure officer submits a disclosure schedule to the prosecutor, that officer should inform the lead disclosure officer (2005 A-G's Guidelines, para. 26).

Should the disclosure officer fail to provide information to the prosecutor within a reasonable time or to comply with any requests made by the prosecutor for additional material, this could lead to the defence not having to provide a defence statement or adverse remarks being made in court. At worse it could lead to a stay of proceedings for an abuse of process (s. 10 of the 1996 Act).

2.10.5.4 Duties of the Disclosure Officer: Initial Disclosure

Under s. 3 of the 1996 Act all previously undisclosed material that might undermine the prosecution case must be disclosed to the defence (for the position of cases since 4 April 2005, **see para. 2.10.5.3**). If there is no such material, then the accused must be given a written statement to that effect. This applies to all material in possession of the police or that has been inspected under the provisions of the Disclosure Code of Practice. This therefore requires the disclosure officer to know what material exists and what material has already been made available to the defence.

Where disclosure is required, the first task is to create a schedule of all *non-sensitive material*, which has been retained by the police and which does not form part of the prosecution case, which may be relevant to the investigation (Code, para. 6.3). If in doubt, the prosecutor should be consulted so that he/she can advise on the relevance of material (para. 6.1). This schedule must be endorsed by the disclosure officer to the effect that, to his/her best ability, it does not contain any sensitive material.

Initially, these schedules only have to be produced where the person is charged with an indictable offence, where the offence is triable either way or where the defendant will be tried summarily and is likely to plead not guilty. If the offence is witnessed by a police officer, or the person has admitted an either way or summary offence, then a schedule is not required unless the person then pleads not guilty. This provision has been added to avoid preparing material which will never be needed. If the person then pleads not guilty the schedule must be prepared as soon as practicable (Code, para. 6.8). However, some forces may require the schedule to be prepared in all cases.

The next step is to create a separate schedule of all sensitive material, which must include the reasons why the disclosure officer believes the material is of a sensitive nature (para. 6.4). Paragraph 6.12 gives examples of the type of material that would be classed as sensitive. If all material has been disclosed and there is no sensitive material, then a statement to that effect should be included on a schedule of sensitive material. The schedule(s) should include all material, excluding that which forms part of the prosecution case (para. 6.2).

There may be cases where material is so sensitive that the disclosure officer or other investigators consider that it should not even appear on the schedule (**see para. 2.10.6.6**). In these cases the prosecutor should be informed of these separately (para. 6.4). It is the responsibility of the investigator who knows the details of the sensitive material to inform the prosecutor.

Once the schedules have been completed, the disclosure officer must decide what material, if any (whether listed on the schedules or not), might undermine the prosecution case. There will be a great reliance placed on the opinion of the disclosure officer as to what material might undermine the prosecution case, and for those investigations that started after the 4 April 2005, material that might be capable of assisting the case for the accused. It is only material that falls into this category that the defence can inspect at this stage. The disclosure officer should draw the attention of the prosecutor to any material an investigator has retained which may satisfy the test for prosecution disclosure in the Act, and should explain why he/she has come to this view (para. 7.2) (depending on when the investigation stated this may or may not include material that assists the prosecution case). This creates a catch all provision and presumably requires the disclosure officer to make inquires of the other officers in the case to ensure all material is included.

The A-G's Guidelines give guidance as to what material might potentially undermine the prosecution case. Paragraph 10 states that:

> Generally, material which can reasonably be considered capable of undermining the prosecution case against the accused or assisting the defence case will include anything that tends to show a fact inconsistent with the elements of the case that must be proved by the prosecution. Material can fulfil the disclosure test:
> (a) by the use to be made of it in cross-examination; or
> (b) by its capacity to support submissions that could lead to
>   (i) the exclusion of evidence; or
>   (ii) a stay of proceedings; or

(iii) a court or tribunal finding that any public authority had acted incompatibly with the accused's rights under the ECHR, or

(c) by its capacity to suggest an explanation or partial explanation of the accused's actions.

This would include any material individually or when viewed with other factors. Examples are material which:

- casts doubt upon the accuracy of any prosecution evidence;
- may point to another person, whether charged or not (including a co-accused) having involvement in the commission of the offence;
- casts doubt upon the reliability of a confession;
- might go to the credibility of a prosecution witness;
- might support a defence that is either raised by the defence or apparent from the prosecution papers;
- which may have a bearing on the admissibility of any prosecution evidence;
- relates to the defendant's mental or physical health, his/her intellectual capacity;
- relates to any ill-treatment which the defendant may have suffered when in the investigator's custody (A-G's Guidelines, paras 12 and 14).

However, what needs to be disclosed should be balanced by A-G's Guidelines, para. 3.

The case of *R* v *Hadley and others* [2006] EWCA Crim 2544, it is suggested, shows that the courts will err on the side of caution when deciding if material should be disclosed as possibly undermining the prosecution case and that this approach should be considered prior to trial to avoid later appeals. In this case the court held that, given the importance of disclosure in ensuring a fair trial, the court is likely to be slow to accept that the safety of a conviction is unaffected if it was satisfied that a substantial volume of disclosable material is wrongly withheld from the acccused, unless the court could be satisfied that the evidence tending to establish guilt is so strong that the undisclosed material could have made no difference to the outcome of the case.

2.10.5.5 Completing the Schedules

It is important that the schedules themselves are completed fully. Guidance is given by paras 6.9 to 6.11 of the Code and in detail in the Disclosure Manual, chs 6 to 8. The schedule should have each item numbered consecutively with a description of the item in sufficient detail to allow the prosecutor, when examining the schedule to make an informed decision about the importance of the item, and whether it needs to be disclosed to the defence, in addition to the items suggested by the disclosure officer, as undermining the prosecution case or assisting the defence (A-G's Guidelines, para. 29). While items should be listed separately, there may be occasions where items are similar or the same, in which case these may be listed together (Disclosure Manual, para. 7.4). This also applies to sensitive schedules, in so far as is possible without compromising the confidentiality of the information (see also the Disclosure Manual, para. 7.4). Paragraph 9 of the A-G's Guidelines also allow in some circumstances, because of the large volumes of material, not to examine all the material. If such material is not examined by the investigator or disclosure officer, and it is not intended to examine it, its existence should be made known to the accused in general terms.

The schedules and copies of any material which is considered to undermine the prosecution case should be given to the prosecutor (Code, paras 7.1 to 7.3). The disclosure officer should include an explanation as to why they consider that the material should be disclosed (para. 7.2). As it is unlikely that the prosecutor will have a chance to examine all the material, it is important that the disclosure officer gives clear reasons in his/her report. For the type of material which might undermine the prosecution case, **see para. 2.10.6.2**.

In addition to the schedules and copies of material which undermine the prosecution case or, where appropriate, assists the accused, para. 7.3 requires the disclosure officer to provide a copy of any material which falls into the following categories:

- information provided by an accused person which indicates an explanation for the offence with which he/she has been charged;
- any material casting doubt on the reliability of a confession;
- any material casting doubt on the reliability of a prosecution witness;
- any other material which the investigator believes may satisfy the test for prosecution disclosure in the Act.

The following items should also be considered when deciding on initial disclosure in cases where the disclosure is in the public interest (that is where they are not '*sensitive material*'). The material is (A-G's Guidelines, para. 12) (see also Disclosure Manual, para. 10.1):

- Any material casting doubt upon the accuracy of any prosecution evidence.
- Any material which may point to another person, whether charged or not (including a co-accused) having involvement in the commission of the offence.
- Any material which may cast doubt upon the reliability of a confession.
- Any material that might go to the credibility of a prosecution witness.
- Any material that might support a defence that is either raised by the defence or apparent from the prosecution papers.
- Any material which may have a bearing on the admissibility of any prosecution evidence.

The disclosure officer must certify that, to the best of his/her knowledge, all material which has been retained by police and made available to them has been revealed to the prosecutor in accordance with the para. 9.1 of the Code. While the disclosure officer may not always be able to know if all material has been made available to him/her, he/she should consult with the OIC to verify as far as possible that it has been (para. 3.1). The disclosure officer should be mindful of the need to demonstrate that he/she has taken all reasonable steps should it transpire that full disclosure had not been made.

Often the police may not possess all the material that could become relevant in a case. It may be that this material has been inspected and a decision made that the material is not relevant to the case at this stage, or that it was not necessary to inspect the material. To cover the risk of material being lost, the disclosure officer should inform third parties of the investigation and invite them to retain material. The disclosure officer should inform the prosecutor that third parties may have such material (para. 3.1). (**See para. 2.10.6.9** for third party material.)

Under para. 8.1 of the Code, information provided by the disclosure officer may be accepted by the prosecutor or might be returned with requests for additional information or for amendments to be made to the schedule or items to be disclosed to the defence. The disclosure officer should comply with any instructions given by the prosecutor and any request for the inspection or copying of material should be met (para. 7.4). If the disclosure officer and OIC consider that material is so sensitive it should not be copied, the disclosure officer should inform the prosecutor and make arrangements for the prosecutor to inspect the material instead (para. 7.4). If copies of materials which are not in writing are requested, the disclosure officer and prosecutor must agree on the format of how it will be provided to the prosecutor (para. 7.5).

It should be remembered that the prosecutor is required to advise the disclosure officer of any omissions or amendments or where there are insufficient or unclear descriptions, or where there has been a failure to provide schedules at all. The disclosure officer must then take all necessary remedial action and provide properly completed schedules to the prosecutor. Failure to do so may result in the matter being raised with a senior officer. There may also be occasions where schedules need to be edited, this is covered in the Disclosure Manual at paras 7.7 and 7.8.

Once this stage is complete, the prosecutor is able to make initial disclosure to the defence. It will be the responsibility of the disclosure officer to disclose material to the defence if requested to do so by the prosecutor (Code, para. 10.1).

The defence do not have to provide a defence statement until such times as initial disclosure has been made, they then (subject to an extension from the court) have 14 days in which to serve their defence statement. Clearly the sooner initial disclosure is made the more time, in theory, the disclosure officer will have to complete his/her responsibilities under secondary disclosure before the next effective court date.

2.10.5.6 Duties of the Disclosure Officer: Secondary Disclosure/Ongoing Disclosure

For investigations that commenced before 4 April 2005 this stage of the disclosure process involved a review of the unused material to see whether it undermined the prosecution case or assisted the defence case. Since 4 April 2005, consideration of the unused material in terms of its assisting the accused is made from the start of the disclosure process and therefore this will be just a review which is further informed by knowing what the defence statement contains.

Once initial disclosure has been made, the defence may provide a defence statement setting out their case, together with reasons why they wish to inspect additional items on the schedule which have not been disclosed. Under para. 8.3 of the Code, once the defence statement has been provided, the disclosure officer must:

- review the material which is contained on the schedules; and
- inform the prosecutor of any material which might reasonably be expected to assist the defence case.

This role will often be performed in conjunction with the prosecutor and, at times, may even be undertaken by the prosecutor. However, the Code of Practice does require the disclosure officer to carry out this function and as such there is a duty to review this material even if it is also done by the prosecutor. This responsibility remains with the disclosure officer and must be complied with. It should be remembered that the review of disclosure is based on the defence statement, not a full investigation.

After the material has been reviewed, further disclosure can be made to the defence. As with the initial disclosure stage, the disclosure officer must certify that, to the best of his/her knowledge, all material which has been retained by the police and made available to them has been revealed to the prosecutor in accordance with para. 9.1 of the Code. Again, while the disclosure officer may not always know if all material has been made available to him/her, he/she should consult with the OIC to verify as far as possible that it has been (Code, para. 3.1). Guidance on continuing duty to review is provided in chapter 14 of the Disclosure Manual.

Where the defence statement points the prosecution to other lines of inquiry, e.g. the investigation of an alibi, or where forensic expert evidence is involved, the disclosure officer should inform the officer in charge of the investigation and copy the defence statement to him/her, together with any CPS advice provided if appropriate (Disclosure Manual, para. 15.17).

2.10.5.7 Continuing Duty of Disclosure Officer

The disclosure officer has a continuing duty to review material for items that should be disclosed to the defence as undermining the prosecution case or which might assist the defence case (Code, para. 8.3).

In *R* v *Tyrell* [2004] EWCA Crim 3279 this responsibility was clearly outlined. The court held that there was an obligation to consider whether there was any material in the hands of the prosecution which might undermine the case against the applicants or might reasonably be expected to assist the disclosed defences. In addition, the Crown had to consider whether there was any material which might be relevant to an issue which might feature in the trial; this clearly required a continuing duty. In this case the court found that disclosure had been considered many times as the case progressed in relation to a variety of issues as they arose and ensured a fair trial.

2.10.5.8 Disclosing Material to the Defence

The disclosure officer may also be involved in the actual disclosure of material to the defence which is covered in para. 10 of the Code of Practice.

The court can also order disclosure of material which the prosecution contend is sensitive. In such cases it may be appropriate to seek guidance on whether to disclose the material or offer no evidence thereby protecting the sensitive material or the source of that material (e.g. where informants or surveillance techniques are involved).

The disclosure officer can make disclosure to the defence by either:

- providing copies of the material; or
- allowing the defence to inspect the material (para. 10.3 of the Codes).

Where a request is made for copies, the material must be provided unless it is not practicable or desirable to do so. Examples of such occasions are given in para. 10.3 of the Code. In cases where the material is not recorded in a written format (for instance an audio or video tape) then the disclosure officer has a discretion whether to provide a copy of the item or transcript of what is contained on the tape. This must be certified as a true copy of the tape (para. 10.4). For further guidance, see the Disclosure Manual, paras 10.16, 10.17 and 12.25. Forces may have instructions as to providing further copies when requested by the defence in relation to procedures and costs. It is suggested that where copies are provided, some proof of delivery should be obtained.

2.10.5.9 Duties of Investigators

The roles of investigator may involve just one officer or several officers. An 'investigation' may be completed in a very short time, e.g. from stopping a car, discovering it was stolen, arresting the suspect, obtaining a victim statement and charging the suspect. Alternatively, the case may involve a long, protracted inquiry with several officers, various witnesses and numerous suspects, arrests and interviews.

An officer who is classed as an investigator must pursue all reasonable lines of inquiry (Code, para. 3.5) and having done so retain all material which is relevant to the case (**see para. 2.10.6.3**), whether or not it is helpful to the prosecution (Code, para. 5.1). Failure to do so could lead to a miscarriage of justice. In *R v Poole* (2003) 1 WLR 2931 Y provided a statement to police in a murder case. It transpired that N had been with Y at the relevant time and this cast doubt over Y's evidence. The police did not follow up the inconsistencies. The Court of Appeal held that the failure to disclose N's evidence was a material irregularity which in part led to a successful appeal by the defendant. The investigator also has a responsibility to identify material that could be sensitive and bring this to the attention of the CPS (**see para. 2.10.6.6**). Where material is identified steps must be taken to record and retain the material. For information recorded on computers, see the JOPI Guidelines from para. 2.29 onwards.

The issue of sensitive material is discussed below (**see para. 2.10.6.6**). Often it is only the investigator who obtained the evidence who will be fully aware of the sensitive nature of the material. In order to balance the need to protect sensitive material yet give the prosecutor full details of why the material is sensitive, para. 6.14 of the Code places the responsibility of informing the prosecutor of details of sensitive material on the investigator. The investigator must take steps to ensure the prosecutor can inspect the material. This does not mean that the disclosure officer or any other officer cannot carry out this function; simply that the investigator must ensure that it is carried out.

When completing the disclosure schedules the investigating officer must be mindful that there may be cases where material is so sensitive that he/she or other investigators consider that it should not even appear on the schedule (such as where disclosure would be likely to lead directly to the loss of life or directly threaten national security (para. 6.13)). It is the responsibility of the investigator who knows the details of the sensitive material to inform the prosecutor.

2.10.5.10 Continuing Duty of Investigators

The continuing duty of disclosure imposed by ss. 7 and 9 of the 1996 Act (for cases since 1 April 2005, both s. 7 and s. 9 have been replaced by s. 7A of the 1996 Act) means that investigators have a corresponding duty to keep under review the revelation of material which meets the test for disclosure. It is therefore important that investigators are aware of which material might undermine the prosecution case and which might assist the defence case. It is also important therefore that investigators are aware of the content of defence statements provided after primary disclosure. This will therefore require consultation between OICs, disclosure officers and investigators. If investigators do not carry out their function properly, this has an impact on all the others involved in the disclosure process and may lead to disclosure on the defence being defective, which in turn could lead to a miscarriage of justice or stay of proceedings.

2.10.5.11 Supervisor of OIC and Disclosure Officer

In all cases there must be an OIC and a disclosure officer. If for any reason, either the OIC or the disclosure officer can no longer perform their respective tasks, para. 3.7 of the Code places a responsibility on that person's supervisor or the police officer in charge of the investigation to assign another person to take over that role. It is suggested, that this requires a supervisor to know what cases their staff are involved in and who the OIC and disclosure officer is in each of those cases.

2.10.6 **Definitions**

Paragraph 2.1 of the Code provides definitions to be used when considering the Code and some additional guidance is provided below.

2.10.6.1 **Relevant Material**

The 1996 Act is concerned with the disclosure of material which is obtained during the course of a criminal investigation and which may be relevant to the investigation. Material can be in any form and should be widely interpreted. This applies to any material coming to the knowledge of officers involved in the case at any stage of the investigation or even after a suspect has been charged. This is material which the investigator, OIC or disclosure officer consider has some bearing on any offence being investigated or any people being investigated for those offences or any of the surrounding circumstances.

The material will be *relevant* whether it is beneficial to the prosecution case, weakens the prosecution case or assists the defence case. It is not only material that will become 'evidence' in the case that should be considered, any information, record or thing which may have a bearing on the case can be material for the purposes of disclosure. The way in which evidence has been obtained in itself may be relevant.

What is relevant to the offence is once again a question of fact and will not include everything. In *DPP* v *Metten*, 22 January 1999, unreported, it was claimed that the constables who had arrested the defendant had known the identities of potential witnesses to the arrest and these had not been disclosed. The court said that this was not relevant to the case as it did not fall within the definition of an investigation in s. 2(1) of the Criminal Proceedings and Investigations Act 1996 in that it concerned the time of arrest not what happened at the time the *offence* was committed. Paragraphs 5.4 and 5.5 of the Code gives guidance on items that might be considered to be relevant material in a case, they include:

- crime reports (including crime report forms, relevant parts of incident report books or police officer's notebooks);
- custody records;
- records which are derived from tapes of telephone messages (for example, 999 calls) containing descriptions of an alleged offence or offender;
- final versions of witness statements (and draft versions where their content differs from the final version), including any exhibits mentioned (unless these have been returned to their owner on the understanding that they will be produced in court if required);
- interview records (written records, or audio or video tapes, of interviews with actual or potential witnesses or suspects);
- communications between the police and experts such as forensic scientists, reports of work carried out by experts, and schedules of scientific material prepared by the expert for the investigator, for the purposes of criminal proceedings;
- records of the first description of a suspect by each potential witness who purports to identify or describe the suspect, whether or not the description differs from that of subsequent descriptions by that or other witnesses;
- any material casting doubt on the reliability of a witness;
- information provided by an accused person which indicates an explanation for the offence with which he/she has been charged;

- any material casting doubt on the reliability of a confession;
- any material casting doubt on the reliability of a prosecution witness.

Relevant material may relate to the credibility of witnesses such as previous convictions, the fact that they have a grudge against the defendant or even the weather conditions for the day if relevant to the issue of identification. It may include information that house to house inquiries were made and that no one witnessed anything.

It should be noted that where material is available to police from a particular source, e.g. local authority records, a decision that some of the material is relevant does not mean that it all has to be disclosed. This point is reinforced by the case of *R* v *Abbott* where the Court of Appeal held that the defendant was not entitled to blanket disclosure of all the files. He was certainly not entitled to documents which were not relevant to the case.

2.10.6.2 Material that Undermines the Prosecution Case

There is only limited case law in this area but it is likely that such material will consist mainly of material which raises question marks over the strength of the prosecution case, the value of evidence given by witnesses and issues relating to identification. If officers feel that the material is not relevant to the prosecution case but may be useful to the defence in cross-examination, it may well come within the category of material which undermines the prosecution case.

Disclosure of previous convictions and other matters that might affect the credibility of a witness may 'undermine the prosecution case' as it may limit the value of the witness's testimony. This factor may not be apparent at the time but may come to light after primary disclosure, such as where it becomes known that the witness has a grudge against the defendant. This is one reason why the 1996 Act requires the decision as to whether material undermines the prosecution case to be continually monitored throughout the case. If in doubt advice should be sought from the CPS.

The amendment to s. 3 of the 1996 Act which adds **might reasonably be considered capable** of undermining the case for the prosecution against the accused, introduces a more of objective test to what needs to be disclosed.

2.10.6.3 Retention of Material

Clearly in order to disclose material to the defence there is a need first to find it and secondly retain it. Retention of material applies to documents and other evidence including videos. Failure to retain material could lead to the prosecution losing the case, particularly where the court feel its absence will lead to the defendant not being able to receive a fair trial (Article 6 of the European Convention). In *Mouat* v *DPP* [2001] 1 WLR 1293 the defendant had been charged with speeding. Police officers had recorded a video of the defendant driving at speed and had showed the video to the defendant prior to charge but had later recorded over it. The defendant contended that he had been intimidated by the unmarked police car being driven only inches from his rear bumper. The policy of the force was to keep videos for 28 days, unless they recorded an offence, in which case they were kept for 12 months. The court held that the police were under a duty to retain the video tapes at least until the end of the suspended enforcement period, during which time the defendant was entitled to consider whether he wished to contest his liability in court.

In considering what material should be retained in an investigation consideration should be given to any force orders, what powers there are to seize and retain the said material, as well as the Disclosure Code and the A-G's Guidelines. Where an investigator discovers material that is relevant to the case, he/she must record that information or retain the material

(Code, para. 4.1). Once again, this duty to record and retain material relevant to the case includes material that would be regarded as negative to the prosecution case (Code, para. 4.3). This does not just mean witness statements and evidence from inquiries but would include arrest notes, custody records, forensic reports, records of interview and all other material the investigator is aware of that might be relevant to the investigation. To this end, para. 5.1 of the Code places a duty on the investigator to retain all relevant material. Paragraph 5.1 of the Code states that:

> The investigator must retain material obtained in a criminal investigation which may be relevant to the investigation. Material may be photographed, video-recorded, captured digitally or otherwise retained in the form of a copy rather than the original at any time, if the original is perishable; the original was supplied to the investigator rather than generated by him and is to be returned to its owner; or the retention of a copy rather than the original is reasonable in all the circumstances.

Often, particularly at the early stages of an investigation (sometimes not until the defence statement is provided outlining the defence case), it will not be possible to know whether material is relevant. If in doubt it should be recorded and placed on the schedule of un-disclosed material. Throughout the case, investigators and all others involved should continually review the material in the light of the investigation. Any material which becomes relevant and which has not been disclosed should be disclosed and, where it has not been retained, the OIC should be informed in order that he/she can decide what action to take (Code, para. 5.3).

When deciding if the material should be retained the A-G's Guidelines provide that: 'investigators should always err on the side of recording and retaining material where they have any doubt as to whether it may be relevant' (A-G's Guidelines, para. 24).

It is important to note that the material itself does not have to be admissible in court for it to undermine the prosecution case. This point was made in *R v Preston* (1994) 98 Cr App R 405, where it was said that:

> In the first place, the fact that an item of information cannot be put in evidence by a party does not mean that it is worthless. Often, the train of inquiry which leads to the discovery of evidence which is admissible at a trial may include an item which is not admissible, and this may apply, although less frequently, to the defence as well as the prosecution.

In cases where officers are in doubt as to whether material should be recorded and retained, the prosecutor should be consulted. If this cannot be done, the material should be retained and recorded. If the material is not in a format that it can be retained (for instance because it was said orally), it should be recorded in a durable and retrievable form (Code, paras 4.1 and 4.2).

If during the lifetime of a case, the OIC becomes aware that material which has been examined during the course of an investigation, but not retained, becomes relevant as a result of new developments, para. 5.3 of the Code will apply. That officer should take steps to recover the material wherever practicable, or ensure that it is preserved by the person in possession of it (Disclosure Manual, para. 5.25).

2.10.6.4 CCTV

CCTV is becoming more prevalent in towns and cities, both from 'in store' cameras and those run through local authorities. The likelihood of an incident being caught on CCTV can be quite strong, which raises the question as to the responsibility of the police to investigate the possibility of there being a tape and retaining the tape. This point was considered in *R (On the Application of Ebrahim)* v *Feltham Magistrates' Court* [2001] 1 WLR 1293. These cases related to the obliteration of video evidence. In coming to their judgment, the court considered a number of previous decisions where the police were not required to retain CCTV evidence. The general question for the court was whether the prosecution had been under a duty to obtain or retain video evidence. If there was no such duty, the prosecution could not have abused the process of the court simply because the material was no longer available, i.e. it was a reasonable line of inquiry (as to whether they were under a duty to obtain the evidence, **see para. 2.10.5.9**). *Ebrahim* shows that CCTV does not necessarily have to be retained in all cases. *R v Dobson* [2001] All ER (D) 109 (Jul) followed *Ebrahim*. Dobson had been convicted of arson with intent to endanger life, his defence being that he was elsewhere at the time. There had been a strong possibility that the route that Dobson claimed to have taken would have been covered by CCTV but it would have depended on which side of the road he had been using and which way the cameras were pointing at the time. Dobson's solicitors had not asked for the tapes to be preserved at interview and the police confirmed that the possibility of investigating the tapes had been overlooked. The tapes had been overwritten after 31 days. In following the principles set down in *Ebrahim*, the police, by their own admissions, had failed in their duty to obtain and retain the relevant footage. While there was plainly a degree of prejudice in Dobson being deprived of the opportunity of checking the footage in the hope that it supported his case, that prejudice was held not to have seriously prejudiced his case given the uncertainty of the likelihood that it would assist and the fact that Dobson had equally been in a position to appreciate the possible existence and significance of the tapes. The fact that there was no suggestion of malice or intentional omission by the police was also an important consideration for the court.

2.10.6.5 Complaints Against Police Officers Involved in a Case

Not only might the credibility of witnesses undermine the prosecution case, but so too might complaints against officers involved in the case, together with any occasions where officers have not been believed in court in the past. In these cases, it will be necessary to decide whether this information should be disclosed to the defence and, if disclosed, in how much detail. This question is probably best answered by the following extract from advice given to prosecutors by the Director of Public Prosecutions:

> It is, of course, necessary in the first instance for the police to bring such matters to the notice of the prosecutor, but it is submitted that the prosecutor should have a greater element of discretion than with the disclosure of previous convictions. With convictions against prosecution witnesses, disclosure normally follows, whereas in relation to disciplinary findings regard should be had to the nature of the finding and its likely relevance to the matters in issue. Findings which involve some element of dishonesty should invariably be disclosed, while matters such as disobedience to orders, neglect of duty and discreditable conduct will often have no relevance to the officer's veracity or the guilt or otherwise of a defendant. Certainly, there should be no duty on the prosecution to disclose details of unsubstantiated complaints even though this is a popular type of inquiry from some defence representatives. The imposition of such a duty would only encourage the making of false complaints in the hope that they might be used to discredit an officer in the future.

Detailed guidance is provided in chapter 18 of the Disclosure Manual.

The prosecutor should be informed if officers involved in a case have discipline matters on their record. This may well appear on the schedule in order that the prosecutor can consider the matter and amend the schedule if necessary. It is suggested that advice should be sought from the prosecutor as to what information is included on the schedule and if disclosure is to be made, advice on what information to be included should also be sought.

Some guidance is given by the courts. In *R v Edwards* [1991] 2 All ER 266 the court held that a disciplinary finding and reprimand of a DCI for countersigning interview notes which had been wrongly re-written in another case should have been disclosed to the defence. *R v Guney* [1998] Cr App R 242 followed *Edwards*, in *Guney* six police officers went to the defendant's home with a warrant to search for drugs. Three of the officers had formerly been members of a squad which had been subject to 'considerable internal police interest'. The court held that the defence was not entitled to be informed of every occasion when any officer had given evidence 'unsuccessfully' or whenever allegations were made against him/her. In this case the information should have been disclosed. The court went on to say that the records available to the CPS should include transcripts of any decisions of the Court of Appeal Criminal Division where convictions were quashed because of the misconduct or lack of veracity of identified police officers as well as cases stopped by the trial judge or discontinued on the same basis. The systematic collection of such material was preferable to the existing haphazard arrangement.

Once again, if in doubt advice should be sought from the Crown Prosecution Service.

Disclosure of Statements in Cases of Complaints against the Police

Statements made by witnesses during an investigation of a complaint against a police officer are disclosable, however the timing of the disclosure may be controlled. In *R v Police Complaints Authority, ex parte Green* (2002) *The Times*, 6 May, the Court of Appeal stated that there is no requirement to disclose witness statements to eyewitness complainants during the course of an investigation. The evidence of such complainants could be contaminated and, therefore, disclosure would risk hindering or frustrating the very purpose of the investigation. A complainant's legitimate interests were appropriately and adequately safeguarded by his/her right to a thorough and independent investigation, to contribute to the evidence, to be kept informed of the progress of the investigation and to be given reasoned conclusions on completion of the investigation. However, a complainant had no right to participate in the investigation as though he/she were supervising it. The general rule was that complainants, whether victims or next of kin, were not entitled to the disclosure of witness statements used in the course of a police investigation until its conclusion at the earliest.

Police complaints and disciplinary files may also fall within sensitive material that does not have to be disclosed (*Halford* v *Sharples* [1992] 1 WLR 736). However this would not apply to written complaints against the police prompting investigations or the actual statements obtained during the investigations, although immunity may be claimed in the case of a particular document by reason of its contents (*Chief Constable of the West Midlands Police, ex parte Wiley* [1995] 1 AC 274). However, the working papers and reports prepared by the investigating officers do form a class which is entitled to immunity, and therefore production of such material should be ordered only where the public interest in disclosure of their contents outweighs the public interest in preserving confidentiality (*Taylor* v *Anderton* [1995] 1 WLR 447).

2.10.6.6   **Sensitive Material**

This is material which the investigator believes is not in the public interest to disclose. While the general principle that governs the 1996 Act and Article 6 of the European Convention is that material should not be withheld from the defence, sensitive material is an exception to this. In *Van Mechden v Netherlands* (1997) 25 EHRR 647, the court stated that in some cases it may be necessary to withhold certain evidence from the defence so as to preserve the fundamental rights of another individual or to safeguard an important public interest. However, only such measures restricting the rights of the defence which are strictly necessary are permissible under Article 6. It should be noted that the court did recognise that the entitlement of disclosure of relevant evidence was not an absolute right but could only be restricted as was strictly necessary. In *R v Keane* [1994] WLR 746 Lord Taylor CJ stated that 'the judge should carry out a balancing exercise, having regard both to the weight of the public interest in non-disclosure and to the importance of the documents to the issues of interest, present and potential, to the defence, and if the disputed material might prove a defendant's innocence or avoid a miscarriage of justice, the balance came down resoundingly in favour of disclosure'.

Decisions as to what should be withheld from the defence are a matter for the court and where necessary an application to withhold the material must be made to the court (*R v Ward* [1993] 1 WLR 619). The application of public interest immunity was considered by the House of Lords in *R v H* [2004] 2 AC 134. In this case the defendants were charged with conspiracy to supply a class A drug following a covert police investigation, and sought disclosure of material held by the prosecution relating to the investigation. The prosecution resisted the disclosure on grounds of public interest immunity. The court held that if the material did not weaken the prosecution case or strengthen the defence, there would be no requirement to disclose it. Only in truly borderline cases should the prosecution seek a judicial ruling on the disclosability of material in its hands. In considering any disclosure issue the trial judge had constantly to bear in mind the overriding principle that deorgation from the principle of full disclosure had always to be the minimum necessary to protect the public interest in question and must never imperil the overall fairness of the trial. Such applications will usually be made at the primary or secondary disclosure stages. Once material is considered to be sensitive then it should be disclosed only if the pubic interest application fails (unless abandoning the case is considered more appropriate) or with the express written approval of the Treasury Solicitor. Such material is not as wide as it seems, for instance it does not mean evidence which might harm the prosecution case. This category is quite limited and the Code of Practice, at para. 6.12, gives a number of examples of such material. It will be for the disclosure officer to decide what material, if any, falls into this category. Guidance is provided in chapters 13 and 18 of the Disclosure Manual.

Paragraph 6.12 states that depending on the circumstances, examples of such material may include the following among others:

- material relating to national security;
- material received from the intelligence and security agencies;
- material relating to intelligence from foreign sources which reveals sensitive intelligence gathering methods;
- material given in confidence;
- material relating to the identity or activities of informants, or undercover police officers, or witnesses, or other persons supplying information to the police who may be in danger if their identities are revealed;
- material revealing the location of any premises or other place used for police surveillance, or the identity of any person allowing a police officer to use them for surveillance;
- material revealing, either directly or indirectly, techniques and methods relied upon by a police officer in the course of a criminal investigation, for example covert surveillance techniques, or other methods of detecting crime;
- material whose disclosure might facilitate the commission of other offences or hinder the prevention and detection of crime;
- material upon the strength of which search warrants were obtained;

- material containing details of persons taking part in identification parades;
- material supplied to an investigator during a criminal investigation which has been generated by an official of a body concerned with the regulation or supervision of bodies corporate or of persons engaged in financial activities, or which has been generated by a person retained by such a body;
- material supplied to an investigator during a criminal investigation which relates to a child or young person and which has been generated by a local authority social services department, an Area Child Protection Committee or other party contacted by an investigator during the investigation;
- material relating to the private life of a witness.

Many of these items are included within the common law principles of public interest immunity. The case law in this area will still apply to decisions regarding the disclosure of such material. These groups are not exclusive and the areas most likely to apply will be those concerning the protection of intelligence and intelligence methods. In any consideration as to what should be withheld the provisions of part II of the Regulation of Investigatory Powers Act 2000 should be referred to. Part II of the Act will make provision, not only for the gathering and recording of intelligence, but also disclosure of any material gained and methods used. Claims to withhold material may be made by parties other than the prosecutor (who would do so on behalf of the police). In some cases, the relevant minister or the Attorney-General may intervene to claim immunity. Alternatively, the claim to immunity may be made by the party seeking to withhold the evidence, either on its own initiative or at the request of the relevant government department.

Guidance is also provided in paras 20 to 22 of the A-G's Guidelines, even where an application is made to the court to withhold material a prosecutor should aim to disclose as much of the material as he/she properly can (by giving the defence redacted or edited copies of summaries). *R* v *Davis* (1993), unreported, sets out further guidance when applying for immunity from disclosure. The court said that the procedure to be adopted in such cases depended upon the sensitivity of the material for which public interest immunity was claimed. In most cases where the prosecution sought to avoid disclosure the matter could be resolved by an *inter partes* hearing but in ultra sensitive cases the prosecution should notify the defence of an *ex parte* application which it would make. Where, however, disclosure of the category of material for which immunity was to be claimed would 'let the cat out of the bag' the prosecution might apply to the court without putting the defence on notice. Where the court ruled for non-disclosure before the hearing, the decision was not necessarily final as the situation might change and issues might emerge so that the public interest in non-disclosure was eclipsed by the need to secure fairness for the defendant. The court would therefore have to continually monitor the issue and it was desirable that the same judge who made the ruling should hear the whole case or, if that was impossible, the court must continually keep in mind the ruling which had been made. If there was such a change the prosecution must be told so that it could decide whether to disclose or offer no further evidence.

In deciding whether material attracts public interest immunity the court will have to be satisfied that the material in no way helps the defence or undermines the prosecution case. Where the material related to secret or confidential systems they should not be revealed as this would aid serious criminal enterprise in the future (*R* v *Templair* (2003) unreported).

Where police consider that material should not be disclosed due to their sensitive nature the Disclosure Manual should be followed. These are covered at paras 8.5 to 8.27. Some of the key points from these paragraphs include:

- Consultation should take place at a senior level, and a senior officer (who may be independent of the investigation) should be involved.
- The consultation should cover:
  - ◆ the reasons why the material is said to be sensitive;
  - ◆ the degree of sensitivity said to attach to the material, i.e. why it is considered that disclosure will create a real risk of serious prejudice to an important public interest;
  - ◆ the consequences of revealing to the defence:
    - the material itself,
    - the category of the material,
    - the fact that an application is being made;
  - ◆ the apparent significance of the material to the issues in the trial;
  - ◆ the involvement of any third parties in bringing the material to the attention of the police;
  - ◆ where the material is likely to be the subject of an order for disclosure, what police views are regarding continuance of the prosecution.
- Any submission that is to be made to the court will be signed by the prosecutor, and by the senior officer, who will state that to the best of his/her knowledge and belief the assertions of fact on which the submission is based are correct. In applications for public interest immunity the CPS has an obligation to ensure that all such material is in their possession and the police have a duty to pass the material on (*R v Menga* [1998] Crim LR 58).
- whether it is possible to disclose the material without compromising its sensitivity.

Care must be taken to safeguard material that is sensitive and keep it separate from other material because if the material subject to a public interest immunity order for non-disclosure is inadvertently disclosed by the prosecution to lawyers for the defendants, those lawyers cannot be ordered not to further disseminate that material to any third party, including their own clients (*R v G* [2004] 1 WLR 2932).

2.10.6.7 Informants

The courts recognise the need to protect the identity of informants to ensure that the supply of information about criminal activities does not dry up and for their own safety. However, there may be occasions where if the case is to continue the identity of the informant will have to be disclosed.

> ... if the judge should be of opinion that the disclosure of the name of the informant is necessary or right in order to show the prisoner's innocence, then one public policy is in conflict with another public policy, and that which says that an innocent man is not to be condemned when his innocence can be proved is the policy that must prevail.
>
> (*Marks v Beyfus* (1890) 25 QBD 494, per Lord Esher MR at p. 498)

This is particularly so where there is a suggestion that an informant has participated in the events constituting, surrounding or following the crime, the judge must consider whether this role so impinges on an issue of interest to the defence, present or potential, as to make disclosure necessary (*R v Turner* [1995] 1 WLR 264).

In *R v Agar* [1990] 2 All ER 442 the court held that if a defence was manifestly frivolous and doomed to failure, a trial judge might conclude that it must be sacrificed to the general public interest in the protection of informers. But if there was a tenable defence the rule of public policy protecting informants was outweighed by the stronger public interest in allowing a defendant to put forward a case. In this case the defendant alleged that the police had arranged with an informer to ask the accused to go to the informer's house, where drugs allegedly found on him had been planted by the police and the court ruled that the disclosure of the informant should have been made.

The need to disclose details of informants has been considered by the Court of Appeal in two recent cases. The first case, *R v Denton* [2002] EWCA Crim 72, concerned a defendant who was a police informer. The defendant was charged with murder and alleged that he had been told by his police handlers not to tell his lawyers about his status. The Court held that there was no duty for the Crown to disclose to the defence, nor to seek a ruling from the judge, as to any information regarding an accused being a police informer. On any common sense view the material had already been disclosed to the defendant and the Crown had no duty to supply the defendant with information with which he was already familiar. This last point may also be relevant to other situations. The second case, *R v Dervish* [2002] 2 Cr App R 105 concerned an undercover operation that was commenced after an informant gave information. The court held in this case that the public interest in protecting the identification of an informant had to be balanced against the right of the defendant to a fair trial, if there was material that might assist the defence, the necessity for the defendant to have a fair trial would outweigh the other interests in the case and the material would have to be disclosed or the prosecution discontinued. There had been no such material in this case.

Where an informant who has participated in the crime is called to give evidence at the trial there would have to be very strong reasons for this fact not to be disclosed (*R v Patel* [2002] Crim LR 304).

2.10.6.8 Observation Points and the *Johnson* Ruling

R v Rankine [1986] 2 WLR 1075 considering previous cases stated that it was the rule that police officers should not be required to disclose sources of their information, whether those sources were paid informers or public spirited citizens, subject to a discretion to admit to avoid a miscarriage of justice and that observation posts were in this rule.

In *R v Johnson* [1988] 1 WLR 1377, the appellant was convicted of supplying drugs. The only evidence against him was given by police officers, who testified that, while stationed in private premises in a known drug-dealing locality, they had observed him selling drugs. The defence applied to cross-examine the officers on the exact location of the observation posts, in order to test what they could see, having regard to the layout of the street and the objects in it. In the jury's absence the prosecution called evidence as to the difficulty of obtaining assistance from the public, and the desire of the occupiers, who were also occupiers at the time of the offence, that their names and addresses should not be disclosed because they feared for their safety.

The judge ruled that the exact location of the premises need not be revealed. The appeal was dismissed; although the conduct of the defence was to some extent affected by the restraints placed on it, this led to no injustice. The jury were well aware of the restraints, and were most carefully directed about the very special care they had to give to any disadvantage they may have brought to the defence. *Johnson* was applied and approved in *R v Hewitt* (1992) 95 Cr App R 81 (see also *R v Grimes* [1994] Crim LR 213).

In *Johnson*, Watkins LJ at pp. 1385–6 gave the following guidance as to the minimum evidential requirements needed if disclosure is to be protected:

(a) The police officer in charge of the observations to be conducted, no one of lower rank than a sergeant should usually be acceptable for this purpose, must be able to testify that beforehand he visited all observation places to be used and ascertained the attitude of occupiers of premises, not only to the use to be made of them, but to the possible disclosure thereafter of the use made and facts which could lead to the identification of the premises thereafter and of the occupiers. He may of course in addition inform the court of difficulties, if any, usually encountered in the particular locality of obtaining assistance from the public.

(b) A police officer of no lower rank than a chief inspector must be able to testify that immediately prior to the trial he visited the places used for observations, the results of which it is proposed to give in evidence, and ascertained whether the occupiers are the same as when the observations took place and whether they are or are not, what the attitude of those occupiers is to the possible disclosure of the use previously made of the premises and of facts which could lead at the trial to identification of premises and occupiers.

Such evidence will of course be given in the absence of the jury when the application to exclude the material evidence is made. The judge should explain to the jury, as this judge did, when summing up or at some appropriate time before that, the effect of his ruling to exclude, if he so rules.

The guidelines in *Johnson* do not require a threat of violence before protection can be afforded to the occupier of an observation post; it suffices if the occupier is in fear of harassment (*Blake* v *DPP* (1993) 97 Cr App R 169).

This extended the rules established in *R* v *Rankine* [1986] QB 861 and is based on the protection of the owner or occupier of the premises, and not on the identity of the observation post. Thus, where officers have witnessed the commission of an offence as part of a surveillance operation conducted from an unmarked police vehicle, information relating to the surveillance and the colour, make and model of the vehicle should not be withheld (*R* v *Brown and Daley* (1987) 87 Cr App R 52). Hodgson J said in *Brown*:

We do not rule out the possibility that with the advent of sophisticated methods of criminal investigation, there may be cases where the public interest immunity may be successfully invoked in criminal proceedings to justify the exclusion of evidence as to police techniques and methods. But if and when such an argument is to be raised, it must, in the judgment of this court, be done properly. … It would seem clear that if such a contention is put forward the judge must be given as much information as possible and the application will have to be supported, not by the instructions of the junior officer in charge of the case, but by the independent evidence of senior officers.

2.10.6.9 Third Party Material

Third party material can be considered in two categories:

(a) that which is or has been in the possession of the police or which has been inspected by the police;
(b) all other material not falling under (a).

Material that which falls into the first category is covered by the same rules of disclosure as any other material the police have. Where police do not have material that they believe may be relevant to the case, para. 3.6 of the Code provides that:

If the officer in charge of an investigation believes that other persons may be in possession of material that may be relevant to the investigation, and if this has not been obtained under paragraph 3.5 above, he should ask the disclosure officer to inform them of the existence of the investigation and to invite them to retain the material in case they receive a request for its disclosure. The disclosure officer should inform the prosecutor that they may have such material. However, the officer in charge of an investigation is not required to make speculative enquiries of other persons: there must be some reason to believe that they may have relevant material. That reason may come from information provided to the police by the accused or from other inquiries made or from some other source.

In the vast majority of cases the third party will make the material available to the investigating officer. However there may be occasions where the third party refuses to hand over the material and/or allow it to be examined.

If the OIC, the investigator or the disclosure officer believes that a third party holds material that may be relevant to the investigation, that person or body should be told of the investigation. They should be alerted to the need to preserve relevant material. Consideration should be given as to whether it is appropriate to seek access to the material, and if so, steps should be taken to obtain such material. It will be important to do so if the material or information is likely to undermine the prosecution case, or to assist a known defence. A letter should be sent to the third party together with the explanatory leaflet, specimens of which are provided in the Disclosure Manual at Annex B.

Where access to the material is declined or refused by the third party and it is believed that it is reasonable to seek production of the material before a suspect is charged, the investigator should consider making an application under sch. 1 to the Police and Criminal Evidence Act 1984 (special procedure material).

Where the suspect has been charged and the third party refuses to produce the material, application will have to be made to the court for a witness summons. In the magistrates' court this is covered by s. 97 of the Magistrates' Courts Act 1980 and in the Crown Court it is covered by ss. 2(2) and 2A–2D of the Criminal Procedure (Attendance of Witnesses) Act 1965. The third party may still wish to resist the requirement to produce the material and the point was considered in *R* v *Brushett* [2001] Crim LR 471 (this was a case that concerned Social Services Department files relating to a children's home). The court considered a number of earlier cases and established some central principles as follows:

- To be material evidence documents must be not only relevant to the issues arising in the criminal proceedings, but also documents admissible as such in evidence.
- Documents which are desired merely for the purpose of possible cross-examination are not admissible in evidence and, thus, are not material for the purposes of s. 97.
- Whoever seeks production of documents must satisfy the justices with some material that the documents are 'likely to be material' in the sense indicated, likelihood for this purpose involving a real possibility, although not necessarily a probability.
- It is not sufficient that the applicant merely wants to find out whether or not the third party has such material documents. This procedure must not be used as a disguised attempt to obtain discovery.
- Where social services documents are supplied to the prosecution, the prosecution should retain control of such material as part of the disclosure regime. That is envisaged by the rules. It cannot be acceptable to return material to social services to avoid the obligations arising under the rules. In any event, the obligation would arise in relation to the notes taken and retained.
- The obligation laid on the prosecution by statute and rules cannot be avoided by a third party making an agreement with the prosecution that the prosecution will abrogate any duties laid upon it by either common law or statute.
- If circumstances arise where it would be unjust not to allow disclosure of certain other material, so a defendant would not receive a fair trial, in the sense that he/she could not establish his innocence where he/she might otherwise do so, then that material must be disclosed.
- The fact that the prosecution have knowledge of the third party material may be a relevant factor to allow the defence access.
- Material concerning false allegations in the past may be relevant material (*R* v *Bourimech* [2002] EWCA Crim 2089).

- If the disputed material might prove the defendant's innocence or avoid a miscarriage of justice, the weight came down resoundingly in favour of disclosing it (*R v Reading Justices, ex parte Berkshire County Council* (1996) 1 Cr App R 239).

In *R v Alibhai* [2004] EWCA Crim 681 the Court of Appeal held that under the Criminal Procedure and Investigations Act 1996 the prosecutor was only under a duty to disclose material in the hands of third parties if that material had come into the prosecutor's hands and the prosecutor was of the opinion that such material undermined the case. However, the A-G's Guidelines went further by requiring a prosecutor to take steps pursuing third party disclosure if there was a suspicion that documents would be detrimental to the prosecution or of assistance to the defence. However, in such circumstances, the prosecutor enjoyed a margin of consideration as to what steps were appropriate. The provisions for disclosure are not intended to create duties for third parties to follow. The disclosure duties under the 1996 Act were created in respect of material that the prosecution or the police had and which the prosecution had inspected. Material was not prosecution material unless it was held by the investigator or by the disclosure officer (*DPP v Wood and McGillicuddy* [2006] EWHC 32).

The A-G's Guidelines also deal with materials held by third parties (including government agencies) in paras 47 to 54. Paragraphs 47 to 50 deals with material held by government departments or other Crown bodies and suggests that reasonable steps should be taken to identify and consider material that may be relevant to an issue in the case. Paragraph 51 examines the circumstances in which the prosecution should take steps to obtain access to material or information in the possession of other third parties. In such cases consideration should be given to take steps to obtain such material or information. It will be important to do so if the material or information is likely to undermine the prosecution case, or assist a known defence. Paragraph 52 deals with the situation where the police or prosecutor meet with a refusal by the third party to supply such material or information. It, despite the reasons put forward for refusal by the third party, it still appears reasonable to seek its production, a witness summons requiring the third party to produce the material should be applied for (such an application can also be made by the defence). The third party can then argue at court that it is not material, or that it should not be disclosed on grounds of public interest immunity.

2.10.6.10 Confidentiality

The defence may only use material disclosed to them under the 1996 Act for purposes related to the defence case; any other use will be a contempt of court. Once evidence has been given in open court, however, the material is available for other purposes.

2.10.6.11 Retention Periods

Material must be retained in all cases until a decision is taken whether to institute proceedings against a person for an offence. Where a decision is taken to institute proceedings material must then be retained until the case has been dealt with. The Code gives specific guidance in cases where a person is convicted as to how long material must be retained for. Paragraphs 5.7 to 5.10 set out the retention periods where a person has been convicted. All material which may be relevant must be retained at least until:

- the person is released from custody or discharged from hospital in cases where the court imposes a custodial sentence or hospital order;
- in all other cases, for six months from the date of conviction.

If the person is released from the custodial sentence or discharged from hospital earlier than six months from the date of conviction, the material must be retained for at least six months from the date of conviction. If an appeal is in progress at the end of one of these periods, or an application is being considered by the Criminal Cases Review Commission, the period is extended until:

- the appeal is determined; or
- the Commission decide not to refer the application to the Court of Appeal; or
- the Court of Appeal determines the appeal resulting from the reference.

Where material has been seized under the powers provided by the Police and Criminal Evidence Act 1984, para. 5.2 confirms that retention of the material should reflect the provisions of s. 22 of the 1984 Act.

PART THREE

Police Station Procedure

2.11 | Custody Officer's Duties

2.11.1 Introduction

The powers to detain people who have been arrested and the manner in which they must be dealt with are primarily contained in the Police and Criminal Evidence Act 1984 and the PACE Codes of Practice whose creation and status come from s. 66 of the Act. The Codes were revised in 2005 to take into account the changes made to PACE by the Serious Organised Crime and Police Act 2005 (SOCPA) and the Drugs Act 2005. The Codes were further amended on 24 July 2006 creating a new Code H to deal with the treatment of terrorist suspects. As a result of this a small number of revisions were made to Code C to remove references to detention under sch. 41 and sch. 8 of the Terrorism Act 2000. A brief summary of the new Code H can be found at **appendix 2.5**. The 1984 Act provides directions to police officers in how detained persons should be treated. The main responsibility for detained persons lies with the custody officer, however it is important that *all* officers, including supervisors involved in investigations or those dealing with detained persons, are aware of the provisions of the Act and the Codes. Failure to follow the requirements of the law could lead to prosecutions failing because evidence is excluded (**see chapter 2.9**), civil claims against forces, bad publicity and the possibility of disciplinary action or even criminal proceedings against officers.

2.11.1.1 The Human Rights Act 1998

The Human Rights Act 1998 makes it even more important to comply with the 1984 Act and its associated Codes of Practice. This can be seen from the case of *R v Chief Constable of Kent Constabulary, ex parte Kent Police Federation Joint Branch Board* [2000] 2 Cr App R 196, where it was held that while Article 5 of the European Convention on Human Rights was not then part of the domestic law of England and Wales, the Article embodied important and basic rights which English law recognised and protected, and any deprivation of liberty must be in accordance with the law. The court went on to say that the 1984 Act and the Codes of Practice represented the balance between the important duty of the police to investigate crime and apprehend criminals and the rights of the private citizen. A breach of Code C is fundamental in affecting the fairness of the evidence (*R v Aspinall* [1999] 2 Cr App R 115).

The Human Rights Act 1998 incorporates the European Convention into UK legislation and as such domestic legislation still applies, but will be interpreted so as to incorporate the Articles of the Convention and the relevant case law. Where there is a conflict between domestic law and the Convention, it will be for Parliament to change domestic legislation to come into line with the Convention. The main Articles which need to be considered for the custody officer and others involved in the detention of a person include Articles 3, 5, 6 and 8, **see General Police Duties, chapter 4.3.**

2.11.2 General Requirements

The custody officer carries the main responsibility towards prisoners who are brought to the police station. Initially it must be decided whether the person should be detained as a prisoner at the police station. If there are grounds to detain him/her, the detention period must be *for those reasons only*. Once a decision to detain a person has been made, the manner in which he/she must be treated while in detention is set out in the PACE Codes (**see appendices 2.1 to 2.5**). These Codes are intended to protect the basic rights of detained people. If these Codes are followed it is more likely that evidence obtained while people are in custody will be admissible. The provisions of the 1984 Act give guidance in numerous areas including:

- length of time in detention;
- information about the detained person's arrest;
- searching;
- taking of samples;
- interviewing of suspects;
- identification methods;
- charging; and
- bail.

The PACE Codes set out the minimum standard of treatment that a detained person can expect. These requirements may be extended with the incorporation of the European Convention on Human Rights and its associated case law. The maximum length of detention is also prescribed by the 1984 Act, as are the requirements for charging, bailing and appearances at court.

The following chapter outlines some of the requirements of the legislation and the powers police have in relation to detained people. The chapter is aimed at providing guidance when using the legislation and it is intended to point the reader to the correct sections of the 1984 Act and the PACE Codes of Practice when dealing with detained people and investigations.

Whilst it is common practice for custody officers to have gaolers to assist in managing detained people, it is still the custody officer's responsibility to ensure that PACE is complied with. However, the Police Reform Act 2002 allows the role of support staff to be expanded in this regard (see below).

2.11.3 Designated Support Staff

Sections 38 and 39 of the Police Reform Act 2002 allow persons employed by the police authority or persons employed by a contractor of the police authority (in relation to detention and escort officers) to be designated as investigating officers, detention officers and escort officers.

Designated officers are given powers to carry out certain functions that would up to this time have been carried out by police officers only. Before a person can be given the powers of a designated officer, the chief officer of police must be satisfied that the person is a suitable person to carry out the functions for which he/she is designated, is capable of effectively carrying out those functions, and has received adequate training in the carrying out of those functions and in the exercise and performance of the powers and duties of a designated officer. It should be noted that not all designated officers will be designated with the same range of powers and it will be important to know what powers a particular designated officer has been given and therefore what their role will be. Schedule 4 to the Police Reform Act 2002 outlines these powers, some of which are set out below.

2.11.3.1 Investigating Officers

- To act as the supervisor of any access to seized material to which a person is entitled, to supervise the taking of a photograph of seized material, or to photograph it him/herself.
- To arrest a detainee for a further offence if it appears to him/her that the detainee would be liable to arrest for that further offence if released from their initial arrest.
- Power for the custody officer to transfer to a designated civilian investigating officer responsibility for a detainee. This power includes a duty for the person investigating the offence, once the detainee is returned to the custody of the custody officer, to report back to the custody officer on how the Codes were complied with.
- To question an arrested person under ss. 36 and 37 of the Criminal Justice and Public Order Act 1994 about facts which may be attributable to the person's participation in an offence. The designated person may also give the suspect the necessary warning about the capacity of a court to draw inferences from a failure to give a satisfactory account in response to questioning.

2.11.3.2 Detention Officers

- Powers to search detained persons, to take fingerprints and certain samples without consent and to take photographs.
- To require certain defined categories of persons who have been convicted, cautioned, reprimanded or warned in relation to recordable offences to attend a police station to have their fingerprints taken.
- To carry out non-intimate searches of persons detained at police stations or elsewhere and to seize items found during such searches.
- To carry out searches and examinations in order to determine the identity of persons detained at police stations. Identifying marks found during such processes may be photographed.
- To carry out intimate searches in the same very limited circumstances that are applicable to constables.
- To take fingerprints without consent in the same circumstances that a constable can.
- To take non-intimate samples without consent and to inform the person from whom the sample is to be taken of any necessary authorisation by a senior officer and of the grounds for that authorisation.
- To require certain defined categories of persons who have been charged with or convicted of recordable offences to attend a police station to have a sample taken.
- To inform a person that intimate samples taken from him/her may be the subject of a speculative search (i.e. this will satisfy the requirement that the person must be informed that the sample will be the subject of a speculative search).
- To photograph detained persons in the same way that constables can.

2.11.3.3   **Escort Officers**

- To transport arrested persons to police stations and escort detained persons from one police station to another or between police stations and other locations specified by the custody officer.
- To carry out the duty of taking a person arrested by a constable to a police station as soon as practicable.
- With the authority of the custody officer, to escort detainees between police stations or between police stations and other specified locations.
- To conduct non-intimate searches of the detainee; and to seize or retain, or cause to be seized or retained, anything found on such a search (restrictions on power to seize personal effects are the same as for police officers, as is the requirement that the search be carried out by a member of the same sex).

Where any of the powers allow for the use of reasonable force when exercised by a police constable, a designated person has the same entitlement to use reasonable force as a constable.

The Police Reform Act 2002 creates offences of assaulting, obstructing or impersonating designated persons which mirror offences in ss. 89 and 90 of the Police Act 1996 for such offences against police officers.

Guidance is provided within the various PACE Codes of Practice and in detail in Code C, paras 1.13 to 1.17. It should be noted that the guidance makes it clear that any reference to a police officer includes a designated person acting in the exercise or performance of the powers and duties conferred or imposed on them by their designation.

It is important to note that not all support staff will be designated for the purposes of the Police Reform Act 2002 and non-designated staff will not have the additional powers as outlined above. Code C, para. 1.15 provides that nothing in the Code prevents the custody officer, or other officer given custody of the detainee, from allowing police staff who are not designated persons to carry out individual procedures or tasks at the police station if the law allows. Where staff are used in this way to support the custody officer, the officer remains responsible for making sure that the procedures and tasks are carried out correctly in accordance with the Codes of Practice. Designated persons and other police staff must have regard to any relevant provisions of the Codes (Code C, para. 1.16).

2.11.4   **Designated Police Stations**

Section 30 of the Police and Criminal Evidence Act 1984 requires that a person who has been arrested must be taken to a police station *as soon as practicable* after arrest, unless the arrested person has been bailed prior to arrival at the police station. Section 30A of the 1984 Act allows a constable to release on bail a person who is under arrest. However, not all police stations have charge rooms or facilities for dealing with prisoners, so the 1984 Act requires that prisoners who will be detained (or who are likely to be detained) for more than six hours must go to a 'designated' police station. A designated police station is one that has enough facilities for the purpose of detaining arrested people. Section 35 requires the Chief Officer of Police to designate sufficient police stations to deal with prisoners. It is for the Chief Officer to decide which stations are to be designated stations and these details are then published. Police stations can be designated permanently or for any specified periods provided that they are not designated for part of a day.

2.11.5   **Custody Officers**

Custody officers are responsible for the reception and treatment of prisoners detained at the police station.

The role of the custody officer is to act independently of those conducting the investigation, thereby ensuring the welfare and rights of the detained person. This requirement is contained in s. 36(5) of the 1984 Act. PACE Code C, para. 3.4 also supports this point in that it makes it clear that the custody officer must not ask a detained person any questions regarding his/her involvement in any offence. The custody officer should not make any comment which may be seen as placing a value judgement on what the person is alleged to have done, nor should he/she make any other comment which in any way casts doubt on his/her impartiality.

Section 36 requires that one or more custody officers must be appointed for each designated police station. However, in *Vince v Chief Constable of Dorset* [1993] 1 WLR 415, it was held that a chief constable was under a duty to appoint one custody officer for each designated police station and had a discretionary power to appoint more than one but this duty did not go so far as to require a sufficient number to ensure that the functions of custody officer were always performed by them. The provision of the facility of a custody officer must be reasonable. Section 36(3) states that a custody officer must be an officer of at least the rank of sergeant. However, s. 36(4) allows officers of any rank to perform the functions of custody officer at a designated police station if a sergeant is not readily available to perform them. The effect of s. 36(3) and (4) is that the practice of allowing officers of any other rank to perform the role of custody officer where a sergeant (*who has no other role to perform*) is in the police station must therefore be unlawful. Should a decision be made to use acting sergeants or untrained custody officers, this may lead to a claim in negligence by the officer or the detained person where there is a breach of the Codes or someone is injured as a result of the failure to manage the custody suite effectively.

For cases where arrested people are taken to a non-designated police station, s. 36(7) states that an officer of any rank not involved in the investigation should perform the role of custody officer. If no such person is at the station, the arresting officer (or any other officer involved in the investigation) or the officer that granted him/her bail under s. 30A of the 1984 Act (bail prior to being taken to a police station) should perform the role. In these cases, an officer of at least the rank of inspector at a designated police station must be informed. It is suggested that once informed, that officer should consider the circumstances of the detained person. Code C, para. 2.1A requires a person under arrest or attending the police station to be brought before a custody officer as soon as is practicable after their arrival at the police station. 'At a police station' is now defined as within the boundary of any building or enclosed yard that forms part of that police station.

The role of the custody officer is crucial to the effective and fair operation of the criminal justice system. In addition to protecting the rights of detained people the role, if performed properly, should also prevent evidence being declared inadmissible because of a violation of the rules. In order to provide as full a record as possible about the detention of a person, the custody officer is required to open a custody record for each detained person (Code C, para. 2.1) and entries should be recorded *as soon as practicable*. Guidance on the completion of custody records is given in Code C, paras 2.1 to 2.7. Custody officers must become very familiar with this guidance, as they are responsible for the accuracy and completeness of the custody record (Code C, para. 2.3). It is important that all entries (subject to Code C, para. 2.6A) in the custody record are timed and signed by the maker (Code C, para. 2.6). If a person is requested to sign an entry in accordance with the Codes and refuses, this too should be recorded as should the time the detained person refused (Code C, para. 2.7).

It is also recognised that the role of custody officer is very demanding and, on occasions, the time restraints created by the legislation can become unrealistic. For this reason Code C, para. 1.1A states that a custody officer will not be in breach of the Codes if delay in taking some action was justifiable and reasonable steps had been taken to prevent the unnecessary delay.

However, if that delay was not 'justified', it could lead to actions for unlawful detention and false imprisonment and any evidence obtained as a result may be held to be inadmissible (*Roberts* v *Chief Constable of Cheshire Constabulary* [1999] 1 WLR 662).

Where a custody officer feels that he/she is unable to comply with the minimum standards of detention as required by PACE, it is suggested that he/she should draw this to the attention of the line manager and/or the superintendent responsible for the custody suite. Custody officers should be mindful of Article 5 of the European Convention on Human Rights in considering whether they are able to manage the number of detained persons in their custody to ensure that their detention is not any longer than needed.

2.11.6 Police Detention and the Treatment of Detained Persons

Depriving a person of his/her liberty is a serious step (**see General Police Duties, chapter 4.4**). The legislation and the PACE Codes of Practice are intended to ensure that where a person's liberty is taken it is for no longer than is necessary. There is a growing trend towards civil claims against the police for unlawful detention and false imprisonment, some of which is as a result of a failure to follow the guidelines. There are strict limits on a person's detention period and the best defence to such cases is to ensure that the 1984 Act and its Codes of Practice are followed.

2.11.6.1 Meaning of Police Detention

Police detention is defined by s. 118 of the Police and Criminal Evidence Act 1984 which states:

> (2) Subject to subsection (2A) a person is in police detention for the purposes of this Act if—
>   (a) he has been taken to a police station after being arrested for an offence or after being arrested under section 41 of the Terrorism Act 2000, or
>   (b) he is arrested at a police station after attending voluntarily at the station or accompanying a constable to it,
>   and is detained there or is detained elsewhere in the charge of a constable, except that a person who is at a court after being charged is not in police detention for those purposes.
> (2A) Where a person is in another's lawful custody by virtue of paragraph 22, 34(1) or 35(3) of Schedule 4 to the Police Reform Act 2002, he shall be treated as in police detention.

Paragraph 22 of sch. 4 to the Police Reform Act 2002 refers to the power to transfer persons into the custody of investigating officers, para. 34(1) relates to designated escort officers taking an arrested person to a police station, and para. 35(3) deals with a designated escort officer transferring a detainee from one police station to another.

PACE Code of Practice C also states:

> 1.10 ... Section 15 applies solely to people in police detention, e.g. those brought to a police station under arrest or arrested at a police station for an offence after going there voluntarily.

1.11 People in police custody include anyone detained under the Terrorism Act 2000, schedule 8 and section 41, having been taken to a police station after being arrested under the Terrorism Act 2000, section 41. In these cases, reference to an offence in this Code includes the commission, preparation and instigation of acts of terrorism.

1.12 This Code's provisions do not apply to people in custody:

   (i) arrested on warrants issued in Scotland by officers under the Criminal Justice and Public Order Act 1994, section 136(2), or arrested or detained without warrant by officers from a police force in Scotland under section 137(2). In these cases, police powers and duties and the person's rights and entitlements whilst at a police station in England or Wales are the same as those in Scotland;

   (ii) arrested under the Immigration and Asylum Act 1999, section 142(3) in order to have their fingerprints taken;

   (iii) whose detention is authorised by an immigration officer under the Immigration Act 1971;

   (iv) who are convicted or remanded prisoners held in police cells on behalf of the Prison Service under the Imprisonment (Temporary Provisions) Act 1980;

   (v) detained for examination under the Terrorism Act 2000, Schedule 7 and to whom the Code of Practice issued under that Act, Schedule 14, paragraph 6 applies;

   (vi) detained for searches under stop and search powers except as required by Code A. The provisions on conditions of detention and treatment in sections 8 and 9 must be considered as the minimum standards of treatment for such detainees.

KEYNOTE

The last two lines of Code C, para. 1.12 above, make it clear that the way such prisoners are treated should be of no lower standard than that for other detained people. If in doubt as to whether a person falls within the definition of a detained person, it is suggested that he/she should be afforded all the rights and privileges outlined in the Codes of Practice. A similar approach should be adopted when it comes to reviewing a detainee's detention (see para. 2.11.7.6).

With the exception of those groups listed in Code C, para. 1.12, Code C applies to people in custody at police stations in England and Wales, whether or not they have been arrested, and to those removed to a police station as a place of safety under the Mental Health Act 1983, ss. 135 and 136.

2.11.6.2 Right to Have Someone Informed

Section 56 of the Police and Criminal Evidence Act 1984 provides that a person arrested and held in custody at a police station or other premises may, on request, have one friend or relative or person known to him/her or who is likely to take an interest in his/her welfare, informed at public expense of his/her whereabouts as soon as practicable (Code C, para. 5.1). (If the detainee's first choice cannot be contacted, see Code C, para. 5.1 and Notes 5C and 5D.) This fundamental human right is known as the right not to be held *incommunicado* and guidance on this right is contained in Code C, paras 5.1 to 5.8. If a person transfers to another police station, the same right applies at the next police station (Code C, para. 5.3), even if they have already had someone informed at the previous places of detention.

This right can only be delayed if the offence is 'an indictable offence' (**see General Police Duties, chapter 4.4**) and an officer of the rank of inspector or above (whether or not connected to the investigation) authorises the delay (see Code C, Annex B) (**see para. 2.11.6.7**). Where a person has to be given information under the Code but is not in a fit state to understand it, it is to be given to him/her as soon as practicable but only when he/she is in a fit state to understand it (see Code C, para. 1.8 for what might amount to not being in a fit state). The delay can only be for a maximum of 36 hours (48 hours in cases involving terrorism), and the 36-hour period is calculated from the 'relevant time' (**see para. 2.11.6.8**). In the case of a juvenile, the power to authorise the delay does not apply to the person responsible for their welfare, but only to any other person the juvenile wishes to have informed (Code C, para. 3.13).

There may be occasions where officers wish to conduct a search under s. 18 of the 1984 Act (**see General Police Duties, chapter 4.4**) and the detained person has requested to have someone informed. Clearly if such a person is informed before the search is conducted, vital evidence or property may be lost. Often the custody officer has two methods by which he/she can inform the person requested about the detained person's detention; either in person or on the phone. Contacting the person by telephone is likely to be the quickest, however, there is no requirement to use the quickest method in order to pass on this information. While there is no case law on this point, Code C, Note 5D, supports the view that, where the s. 18 search is to be conducted relatively quickly after the request is made by the detained person, it would be permissible to inform that person at the time the s. 18 search is conducted. Where the search is not to be conducted straight away, it is suggested that consideration would have to be given to obtaining the authority of an officer of at least the rank of inspector to delay the notification as outlined in **para. 2.11.6.7**. A lengthy delay may be seen as a breach of this right which may lead to a stay of proceedings or a claim for damages as a breach of the detained person's human rights.

Detained people may also be allowed to speak to one person on the telephone for a reasonable time or send letters. If a person has an interpreter, he/she can do this on the detained person's behalf. This right can be denied or delayed in the case of indictable offences or where a person is detained under s. 41 or sch. 7 to the Terrorism Act 2000 by an officer of the rank of inspector or above (Code C, para. 5.6 and for terrorism cases Code H, para. 5.6). The grounds are the same as those regulating the holding of people *incommunicado* (**see para. 2.11.6.7**). Where a person is allowed to make a telephone call or send a letter, the procedure in Code C, para. 5.7 should be followed. Should there be any delay in complying with a request by a detained person to have someone informed of his/her detention or to communicate with someone, the detained person should be informed of this and told the reason for it and a record kept (s. 56(6) of the 1984 Act). The custody officer also has a discretion to allow visits to the detained person at the police station (Code C, para. 5.4 and Note 5B). It is suggested that with the Codes of Practice outlining the limited rights for the detained person to make telephone calls and the right to restrict these calls, that if the person has a mobile telephone it can be seized for the period of their detention. There is no case law on this point and any force policy should be followed.

There are, in addition, also special requirements for juveniles and detained people from other countries.

2.11.6.3 Right to Have Someone Informed: Juveniles

In the case of juveniles, where practicable, a person who is responsible for a juvenile's welfare must be informed of his/her arrest. This person may be the appropriate adult (see Code C, para. 1.7(a)) but if not, arrangements must be made for an adult to attend the police station to look after the interests of the juvenile. This action must be undertaken regardless of whether the juvenile wishes to have someone informed or has requested that some other person other than the appropriate adult be informed.

Code C, para. 3.13 states:

If the detainee is a juvenile, the custody officer must, if it is practicable, ascertain the identity of a person responsible for their welfare. That person:
- may be:
  - the parent or guardian;
  - if the juvenile is in local authority or voluntary organisation care, or is otherwise being looked after under the Children Act 1989, a person appointed by that authority or organisation to have responsibility for the juvenile's welfare;
  - any other person who has, for the time being, assumed responsibility for the juvenile's welfare.
- must be informed as soon as practicable that the juvenile has been arrested, why they have been arrested and where they are detained. This right is in addition to the juvenile's right in s. 5 not to be held incommunicado. See Code C, Note 3C.

If a juvenile is known to be subject to a court order under which a person or organisation is given any degree of statutory responsibility to supervise or otherwise monitor them, reasonable steps must also be taken to notify that person or organisation (the 'responsible officer'). The responsible officer will normally be a member of a Youth Offending Team, except for a curfew order which involves electronic monitoring when the contractor providing the monitoring will normally be the responsible officer (Code C, para. 3.14).

2.11.6.4 Right to Have Someone Informed: Special Groups

If the detainee appears to be deaf or there is doubt about his/her hearing or speaking ability or ability to understand English, and the custody officer cannot establish effective communication, the custody officer must, as soon as practicable, call an interpreter for assistance to go through the detainee's rights under Code C, paras 3.1 to 3.5 (Code C, para. 3.12).

If the detainee is a mentally disordered or otherwise mentally vulnerable, the custody officer must, as soon as practicable, inform the appropriate adult of the grounds for their detention and their whereabouts. The appropriate adult should also be asked to come to the police station to see the detainee (Code C, para. 3.15). In managing mentally disordered or otherwise mentally vulnerable persons detained under the Mental Health Act 1983, s. 136, the custody officer must be mindful that it is imperative that the detainee is assessed as soon as possible (Code C, para. 3.16).

Code C, para. 13.1 requires chief officers to make arrangements for suitably qualified interpreters for the deaf and those who do not understand English. The interpreters should be registered with the National Register of Public Service Interpreters or the Council for the Advancement of Communication with Deaf People (CADCP) Directory of British Sign Language/English Interpreters.

2.11.6.5 Right to Have Someone Informed: Detained People from Other Countries

Citizens of independent commonwealth countries or foreign nationals may communicate with their High Commission, Embassy or Consulate as soon as practicable (Code C, para. 7.1). If the country is included on the list at Annex F to Code C, the High Commission, Embassy or Consulate must be informed of their arrest and detention as soon as practicable unless the detained person is a political refugee or is seeking political asylum (para. 7.4).

Where a person who is a friend, relative or a person with an interest in the detained person's welfare, makes enquires about that person, the detained person should be asked whether he/she agrees to the person being informed prior to any information being given (Code C, para. 5.5). The information must not be given if a delay has been authorised.

Right to Legal Advice

Section 58 of the Police and Criminal Evidence Act 1984 provides an almost inalienable right for a person arrested and held in custody at a police station or other premises to consult privately with a solicitor free of charge at any time if he/she requests it (or the appropriate adult makes the request (Code C, para. 3.19)). This provision is very similar to that of s. 56 of the 1984 Act: the right to have a person informed of the arrest. This right to consult a solicitor is considered to be so important that a detained person must be informed of the right when he/she first arrives at the police station and asked for reasons if he/she declines to exercise this right. Detainees are also reminded of this right at other times, e.g. prior to interview and when detention is being reviewed. In *R* v *Alladice* (1988) 87 Cr App R 380 the Court of Appeal made it clear that:

> no matter how strongly and however justifiably the police may feel that their investigation and detection of crime is being hindered by the presence of a solicitor ... they are nevertheless confined to the narrow limits imposed by section 58.

In *R* v *Aspinall* [1999] 2 Cr App R 115 the court stated that the right to access to legal advice was a fundamental right under Article 6 of the European Convention on Human Rights and even greater importance had to be attached to advice for a vulnerable person. While the appropriate adult of a juvenile can request legal advice from a solicitor, the detained juvenile cannot be forced to see the solicitor (Code C, para. 6.5A).

Once a person has requested a solicitor this must be provided without delay; what will be considered to be without delay will be a question of fact in each case (*Whitley* v *DPP* [2004] Crim LR 585). It will be important to justify any delay as even short delays in calling a solicitor might be considered to be a breach of the Codes and be challaenged by the defence. This was the case in *Kirkup* v *DPP* [2004] Crim LR 230, which involved a seven minute delay from requesting to calling a solicitor. The court held that the delay only just gave rise to a breach of s. 58 of the 1984 Act and the Codes of Practice but that it was so short a period that it did not lead to the exclusion of any evidence under s. 78.

Code C, Annex B provides an exception to this right to legal advice: cases where an officer of the rank of superintendent or above (whether or not connected to the investigation) authorises the exercise of the right to be delayed. This only applies if the offence is an indictable offence (**see General Police Duties, chapter 4.4**) and Code C, Annex B applies.

The same exception also apples where the person is held under the prevention of terrorism legislation (Terrorism Act 2000, s. 41 or sch. 8) and the conditions in Code H, Annex B apply. Here a uniformed officer of at least the rank of inspector not connected with the case may be present if authorised by an Assistant Chief Constable of Commander (Terrorism Act 2000, sch. 8, para. 9 and Code H paras 6.4, 6.5).

The delay can only be for a maximum of 36 hours (48 hours from the time of arrest in terrorism cases) or until the time the person will first appear at court, which ever is the sooner (see below). The 36-hour period is calculated from the 'relevant time' (**see para. 2.11.6.8**). The authorisation can initially be made orally either in person or by telephone but must be recorded in writing as soon as practicable. Where a delay is authorised then this restricts the drawing of adverse inferences from silence (see Code C, para. 6.6).

The consultation with a solicitor can be either on the telephone, in person or in writing and it must be in private (Code C, para. 6.1). This right to have a private consultation is a good example of where a person's rights under the European Convention need to be considered. In many custody suites this is difficult to comply with (see Code C, Note 6J) but could lead to adverse comment, particularly if officers act on what they heard the detained person say while consulting with their legal representative. Code C, Note 6J gives clear indication that the normal expectation should be that facilities will be available for the detainee to speak in private to a solicitor. This right to have a private consultation also apples to juveniles who, should they wish to have a private consultation without the appropriate adult being present, must be permitted to do so (Code C, Note 1E). This point was considered in *R (On the Application of M (A Child))* v *Commissioner of the Police of the Metropolis* [2002] Crim LR 215, where the court said that ideally there ought be a consultation room at every police station and facilities for private telephone calls to be made for legal consultations. However, there was no breach of Article 6(3) of the European Convention where it could not be shown that a detainee had been denied adequate facilities for the preparation of his defence.

Once a person has indicated a wish to have a solicitor, and has not yet been advised by a solicitor, he/she can only be interviewed in limited circumstances as set out in Code C, para. 6.6, but it is not necessary to delay taking breath, blood or urine samples from a motorist until a solicitor arrives or to delay searching the detainee or the taking of non-intimate samples, fingerprints or footwear impressions without consent for evidential purposes (Code C, Note 3D and **Road Policing, chapter 3.5**). Of particular note is Code C, para. 6.6(b). This allows an officer of the rank of superintendent or above to allow an interview to take place or continue without a solicitor being present, if he/she has reasonable grounds for believing that:

(i) the consequent delay might:
- lead to interference with, or harm to, evidence connected with an offence;
- lead to interference with, or physical harm to, other people;
- lead to serious loss of, or damage to, property;
- lead to alerting other people suspected of having committed an offence but not yet arrested for it;
- hinder the recovery of property obtained in consequence of the commission of an offence.
(ii) when a solicitor, including a duty solicitor, has been contacted and has agreed to attend, awaiting their arrival would cause unreasonable delay to the process of investigation.

Another exception is in relation to the drink drive procedure for s. 7 of the Road Traffic Act 1988. In *DPP* v *Noe* [2000] RTR 351 a request to see a solicitor or alternatively to consult a law book to verify the legality of the police request for a specimen of breath was not a reasonable excuse under s. 7. This decision has not been affected by the enactment of the Human Rights Act 1998. This is confirmed by *Campbell* v *DPP* [2003] Crim LR 118 who held that it was entirely proportionate to allow a police officer to require a member of the community to provide a specimen albeit that legal advice had not been obtained.

Where Code C, para. 6.6 is used it will have to be justified at court if the interview is to be admissible. This power might prove useful in circumstances where there are 'delaying tactics' by legal representatives, particularly where they are aware that the detained person's relevant time is due to expire within a short period.

Code C, para. 6.6 provides two further occasions where the interview may go ahead without a solicitor being present provided the consent of an officer of inspector rank or above has been obtained. Paragraph 6.6(c) deals with the situation where the solicitor the detainee has nominated or selected from a list cannot be contacted, has previously indicated they do not wish to be contacted, or having been contacted, has declined to attend; and the detainee has been advised of the Duty Solicitor Scheme but has declined to ask for the duty solicitor. Paragraph 6.6(d) deals with the situation where the detainee changes his/her mind, about wanting legal advice. In these circumstances the interview may be started or continued provided that the detainee agrees to do so, in writing or on tape. In this case the officer of inspector rank or above must inquire about the detainee's reasons for their change of mind and must give authority for the interview to proceed. Paragraph 6.6(d) outlines what information must be recorded in the written interview record or the audio or visual interview record.

Where an interview has started without the solicitor being present and access has not been refused under Code C, Annex B, the solicitor must be allowed to be present when he/she arrives at the station unless Code C, para. 6.6(b) applies or he/she has been excluded because of his/her conduct (Code C, para. 6.10).

In considering whether to conduct an interview in these circumstances, guidance is given Code C, Note 6A.

A solicitor for these purposes means a solicitor who holds a current practising certificate, or an accredited or probationary representative included on the register of representatives maintained by the Legal Services Commission (Code C, para. 6.12). An accredited or probationary representative may also attend and give advice unless an officer of the rank of inspector or above considers that such a visit will hinder the investigation of crime and directs otherwise and once admitted he/she should be treated as any other legal adviser (Code C, para. 6.12A).

In deciding whether to admit an accredited or probationary representative, the officer should take into account in particular whether the identity and status of the accredited or probationary representative have been satisfactorily established; whether he/she is of suitable character to provide legal advice (a person with a criminal record is unlikely to be suitable unless the conviction was for a minor offence and is not of recent date); and any other matters in any written letter of authorisation provided by the solicitor on whose behalf the person is attending the police station (Code C, para. 6.13). The Law Society has advised solicitors that if an accredited or probationary representative is refused admission, a written reason for the decision should be requested. If access is refused or a decision is taken that such a person should not be permitted to remain at an interview, the inspector must forthwith notify a solicitor on whose behalf the accredited or probationary representative was to have acted or was acting, and give him/her an opportunity to make alternative arrangements. The detained person must also be informed and the custody record noted (Code C, para. 6.14 and Note 6F).

2.11.6.7 Authority to Delay Rights under s. 56 or 58 (Code C, Annex B)

An officer of the rank of superintendent or above for s. 58 of the Police and Criminal Evidence Act 1984 and inspector or above for s. 56 of the 1984 Act can only authorise a delay if he/she has reasonable grounds for believing that exercising the s. 56 and s. 58 rights will:

- lead to interference with or cause harm to evidence connected with an indictable offence or lead to interference with or cause physical injury to other people; or
- lead to alerting other people suspected of having committed an indictable offence but not yet arrested for it; or
- hinder the recovery of property obtained as a consequence of the commission of such an offence.

The delay may also be authorised under s. 56 and/or s. 58 where the officer has reasonable grounds for believing that the person detained for an indictable offence has benefited from his/her criminal conduct and the recovery of the value of the property constituting the benefit will be hindered by telling the named person of the arrest or his/her right of access to legal advice.

For these purposes whether a person has benefited from his/her criminal conduct is to be decided in accordance with s. 76(1) and (4) of the Proceeds of Crime Act 2002. Briefly, criminal conduct is conduct which constitutes an offence in England and Wales, or would constitute such an offence if it occurred in England and Wales. A person benefits from conduct if he/she obtains property as a result of or in connection with the conduct.

In cases where the person is detained under the Terrorism Act 2000 an officer of the rank of superintendent or above may delay the exercise of either right or both if he/she has reasonable grounds for believing that the exercise of the right will lead to any of the consequences of:

- interference with, or harm to, evidence connected with an indictable offence;
- interference with, or physical harm to, other people;
- the alerting of other people suspected of having committed an indictable offence but not yet arrested for it;
- hinder the recovery of property obtained as a result of an indictable offence or in respect of which a forfeiture order could be made;
- interference with the gathering of information about the commission, preparation or instigation of acts of terrorism;
- the alerting of any person, making it more difficult to prevent an act of terrorism;
- by alerting any person, making it more difficult to prevent an act of terrorism or secure the apprehension, prosecution or conviction of any person in connection with the commission, preparation or instigation of an act of terrorism;
- the detained person has benefited from his/her criminal conduct, and the recovery of the value of the property constituting the benefit will be hindered by informing the named person of the detained person's detention or access to legal advice. For these purposes whether a person has benefited from his/her criminal conduct is to be decided in accordance with part 2 of the Proceeds of Crime Act 2002. Briefly, criminal conduct is conduct which constitutes an offence in England and Wales, or would constitute such an offence if it occurred in England and Wales. A person benefits from conduct if he/she obtains property as a result of or in connection with the conduct (Code C, Annex B, paras 8 and 9).

If the delay is authorised the detained person must be given the reason for the delay which must correspond to one of the above grounds and an entry must be made in the custody record.

Once the reason for authorising the delay has ceased, the detained person must be allowed to exercise his/her rights. Once this point has been reached, the detained person must as soon as practicable be asked if he/she wishes to exercise the right (or rights), the custody record must be noted accordingly, and the relevant action taken (Code C, Annex B, para. 6).

The fact that the grounds for delaying notification of arrest may be satisfied does not automatically mean that the grounds for delaying access to legal advice will also be satisfied (Code C, Annex B, para. 5).

When considering whether to deny access to a solicitor the fact that he/she might advise the person not to answer any questions or that the solicitor was initially asked to attend the police station by someone else, provided that the person himself/herself then wishes to see the solicitor, is not a reason for delaying access to a solicitor (Code C, Annex B, para. 4). When considering the delay of access to a solicitor the authorising officer must bear in mind that access to a solicitor is 'a fundamental right of a citizen' (*R* v *Samuel* [1988] 2 WLR 920). The authorising officer must actually believe that by allowing access to the solicitor he/she will intentionally or inadvertently alert other suspects. There must also be objective reasons upon which the officer authorising the delay can base his/her beliefs. If the reason for authorising the delay of access to a solicitor is because there are concerns with the particular solicitor who has been requested or is offering his/her services to the detained person the officer should offer the detained person access to a solicitor (who is not the specific solicitor referred to above) on the Duty Solicitor Scheme (Code C, Annex B, para. 3). Annex B, Note B3 suggests that occasions where this delay will be authorised in such circumstances will be rare and only when it can be shown that the suspect is capable of misleading that particular solicitor and there is more than a substantial risk that the suspect will succeed in causing information to be conveyed which will lead to one or more of the specified consequences. In deciding whether such an interview will be admissible the court will consider how reliable it is and will consider how the refusal to allow that particular detained person access to a solicitor affected their decision to make a confession. One such case where the confession was excluded is *R* v *Sanusi* [1992] Crim LR 43, where a person from another country was denied access to a solicitor and the court held that his right to advice was particularly significant due to his lack of familiarity with police procedures.

In terrorism cases a direction may be given by an officer of at least the rank of Commander or Assistant Chief Constable which may provide that a detained person who wishes to exercise the right to consult a solicitor may do so only in the sight and hearing of a qualified officer, this person being a uniform officer of at least the rank of inspector not connected with the investigation from the authorising officer's force.

2.11.6.8 Relevant Time

As discussed above, there are limits on how long a person can be detained. The Police and Criminal Evidence Act 1984 and the Codes of Practice talk of the 'relevant time'. This is the time from which the limits of detention are calculated. The relevant time of a person's detention starts in accordance with s. 41(2) to (5) of the 1984 Act. Section 41 states:

(2) The time from which the period of detention of a person is to be calculated (in this Act referred to as 'the relevant time')—
   (a) in the case of a person to whom this paragraph applies, shall be—
      (i) the time at which that person arrives at the relevant police station; or
      (ii) the time 24 hours after the time of that person's arrest,
      whichever is the earlier;
   (b) in the case of a person arrested outside England and Wales, shall be—
      (i) the time at which that person arrives at the first police station to which he is taken in the police area in England or Wales in which the offence for which he was arrested is being investigated; or
      (ii) the time 24 hours after the time of that person's entry into England and Wales,
      whichever is the earlier,
   (c) in the case of a person who—
      (i) attends voluntarily at a police station; or
      (ii) accompanies a constable to a police station without having been arrested, and is arrested at the police station, the time of his arrest;
   (ca) in the case of a person who attends a police station to answer to bail granted under section 30A, the time he arrives at the police station;
   (d) in any other case, except where subsection (5) below applies, shall be the time at which the person arrested arrives at the first police station to which he is taken after his arrest.
(3) Subsection (2)(a) above applies to a person if—
   (a) his arrest is sought in one police area in England and Wales;
   (b) he is arrested in another police area, and

(c) he is not questioned in the area in which he is arrested in order to obtain evidence in relation to an offence for which he is arrested;

and in sub-paragraph (i) of that paragraph 'the relevant police station' means the first police station to which he is taken in the police area in which his arrest was sought.

(4) Subsection (2) above shall have effect in relation to a person arrested under section 31 above as if every reference in it to his arrest or his being arrested were a reference to his arrest or his being arrested for the offence for which he was originally arrested.

(5) If—

   (a) a person is in police detention in a police area in England and Wales ('the first area'); and

   (b) his arrest for an offence is sought in some other police area in England and Wales ('the second area'); and

   (c) he is taken to the second area for the purposes of investigating that offence, without being questioned in the first area in order to obtain evidence in relation to it,

the relevant time shall be—

     (i) the time 24 hours after he leaves the place where he is detained in the first area; or

     (ii) the time at which he arrives at the first police station to which he is taken in the second area,

whichever is the earlier.

KEYNOTE

Note that under s. 41(5) the relevant time may vary depending on whether the detainee is interviewed in relation to the offence whilst still in the first police area.

For those detained under the Terrorism Act 2000 (**see para. 2.12.12**) the detention clock starts from the time the person is arrested, not the time they arrive at the police station.

The Criminal Justice Act 2003 inserted s. 41(2)(ca) into the Police and Criminal Evidence Act 1984. This allows for a person who has been arrested to be bailed before being taken to a police station. When the person attends the police station to which he/she has been bailed the relevant time starts when he/she arrives at the police station.

For the provisions of s. 31 of the 1984 Act relating to people who have been arrested for one offence and if released from the police station would be liable to arrest for some other offence, **see General Police Duties, chapter 4.4.**

Some situations occur where a person is arrested at one police station and has been circulated as wanted by another police station in the same force area. In these cases, where the person is not wanted on warrant, the detention clock for the second offence starts at the same time as for the original offence for which they were arrested. Consideration will need to be given as to how to protect the detention period for the second offence while officers are dealing with the first matter. Options that might be considered would include bailing the person for one of the offences or conducting both investigations at the same station Here there may be a risk of 'confusing' the suspect, which may allow him/her to retract or qualify any confession he/she might make.

In *Henderson* v *Chief Constable of Cleveland* [2001] 1 WLR 1103 the court considered the policy of not executing a court warrant until after other matters for which the person had been detained were completed. The court held that, once a warrant was executed, there was a requirement to follow the directions of the warrant. The police however had a discretion as to *when* to execute the warrant. This may be relevant where a person has been arrested for one offence and it is discovered that he/she is also wanted for another offence or where there are warrants in existence for that person at more than one court. In such cases, if the warrant is executed immediately, the direction on the warrant tells officers to take the person before the next available court, an action which could interfere with the investigation. If *Henderson* is followed there is no requirement to execute the warrant straight away and the other matters can be dealt with before the requirement to produce the person at court under the warrant applies.

2.11.6.9 Detention of People under Arrest

Section 37 of the 1984 Act states:

(1) Where—
    (a) a person is arrested for an offence—
       (i) without a warrant; or
      (ii) under a warrant not endorsed for bail,
    the custody officer at each police station where he is detained after his arrest shall determine whether he has before him sufficient evidence to charge that person with the offence for which he was arrested and may detain him at the police station for such period as is necessary to enable him to do so.

(2) If the custody officer determines that he does not have such evidence before him, the person arrested shall be released either on bail or without bail, unless the custody officer has reasonable grounds for believing that his detention without being charged is necessary to secure or preserve evidence relating to an offence for which he is under arrest or to obtain such evidence by questioning him.

(3) If the custody officer has reasonable grounds for so believing, he may authorise the person arrested to be kept in police detention.

(4) Where a custody officer authorises a person who has not been charged to be kept in police detention, he shall, as soon as is practicable, make a written record of the grounds for the detention.

(5) Subject to subsection (6) below, the written record shall be made in the presence of the person arrested who shall at that time be informed by the custody officer of the grounds for his detention.

People who have been arrested, returned on bail, or have voluntarily given themselves up at a police station, which includes a person who has attended the police station after having been given street bail (**see para. 2.4.2.1**), will be brought before a custody officer who must decide whether the person should be detained at the police station or released. People who attend police stations voluntarily to assist the police with their investigations are not subject to this procedure; their treatment is dealt with by s. 29 of the 1984 Act and PACE Code C, paras 3.21 and 22 (**see General Police Duties, chapter 4.4**). However if an officer forms a view that the person should be arrested at the police station for the purpose of interview and informs the custody officer of this view, the custody officer can authorise detention for the interview and is entitled to assume the arrest by the officer is lawful (*Fayed* v *Metropolitan Police Commissioner* [2004] EWCA Civ 1579).

The arresting officer informs the custody officer of the reasons for arrest; these grounds can be given remotely, e.g. by telephone or by a third party (Code C, para. 3.4). This will include *what* offence the person was arrested for and brief details of the *grounds* for the arrest, e.g. the arrest is for robbery and the accused was seen to punch the victim in the face and steal her holdall. As this information must be given to the person on arrest—in most cases—the details given to the custody officer should be fresh in the mind of the arresting officer; they should also accord with the reasons and grounds given to the person on arrest. If the grounds were not given at the time of arrest (on justifiable grounds) the custody officer should consider whether the arrested person is now in a position to be given the grounds for the arrest (as being the first practicable opportunity (s. 28(3) of the 1984 Act)). If the grounds for arrest were not given when they should have been, the arrest is unlawful regardless of what information is given later (*Wilson* v *Chief Constable of Lancashire* (2000) unreported).

Having heard the details of and grounds for the arrest, the custody officer must then decide whether or not there are reasons which justify authorising that person's detention

(s. 37 of the Police and Criminal Evidence Act 1984 deals with the procedures to be followed before a person is charged). Some commentators have suggested that it is also the role of the custody officer to establish that the arrest itself was lawful. While this would seem to be sensible and good practice, the custody officer's duty is confined to acting in accordance with the requirements set out in s. 37 of the 1984 Act. These duties do not appear to include considering whether the arrest was lawful unless this is relevant to the main question of whether there is sufficient evidence to charge the suspect. The view is supported by the decision of the Divisional Court in *DPP* v *L* [1999] Crim LR 752, where the court held that there was no express or implied requirement imposing a duty on a custody officer to inquire into the legality of an arrest and in that case the custody officer was therefore entitled to assume that it was lawful. A subsequent finding that the arrest was unlawful did not invalidate the decision of the custody officer to hold the person in custody. However, where the custody officer is aware that the arrest is unlawful, he/she will need to consider whether continued detention is justifiable, particularly in light of the Human Rights Act 1998.

If the person is arrested on a warrant (**see General Police Duties, chapter 4.4**), any directions given by the court in the warrant must be followed. Consideration can always be given to contacting the court to get a variation on the conditions of the warrant. (If the warrant was issued for the arrest of a person who has not yet been charged or summonsed for an offence, he/she should be dealt with as any other person arrested for an offence without warrant unless there are any additional directions on the warrant that must be followed.)

Where a person who has been bailed under s. 37(7)(a) in order that the Director of Public Prosecutions can make a case disposal decision answers his/her bail or is arrested for failing to return on bail, detention can only be authorised to allow him/her to be further bailed under s. 37D of the 1984 Act or in order that he/she can be charged or cautioned for offences connected with the original bail. If the person is not in a fit state to be dealt with he/she may be kept in police detention until he/she is (s. 37D of the Police and Criminal Evidence Act 1984).

2.11.6.10 Authorising a Person's Detention

A custody officer can authorise the detention of a person when there is sufficient evidence to charge and, more commonly, when there is *not* sufficient evidence to charge the suspect. If there is insufficient evidence to charge, the custody officer must decide if the detention is necessary to secure or preserve evidence relating to an offence for which the person is under arrest or to obtain such evidence by questioning him/her.

If a person representing the detained person does not feel the detention is lawful he/she can apply to the court for the detainee's release (*habeas corpus*). A detainee may also be able to make an application for release or damages following the incorporation of the European Convention on Human Rights. Article 5(4) states:

> Everyone who is deprived of his liberty by arrest or detention shall be entitled to take proceedings by which the lawfulness of his detention shall be decided speedily by a court and his release ordered if the detention is not lawful.

2.11.6.11 Sufficient Evidence to Charge

Here the custody officer is looking at the evidence in order to satisfy him/herself that no further investigation is needed before the person can be charged. If this is the case, detention may be authorised for the purpose of charging the detained person.

Where a custody officer decides that there is sufficient evidence to charge a suspect who is in police detention, he/she is to have regard to any guidance issued by the Director of Public Prosecutions in determining whether the suspect should be released without charge but on bail, released without charge and without bail, or charged. Where a case is referred to the Crown Prosecution Service to determine whether proceedings should be instituted (and if so on which charge), it was the case that if the decision to charge was not made at the time, the detained person had to be released on police bail with or without conditions. However, the Police and Justice Act 2006 has amended s. 37 of PACE and the person can now be kept in police detention pending the decision (subject to the normal time limits for detention applying). Once the CPS has made a decision the suspect is then to be charged, cautioned, or informed in writing that he/she is not to be prosecuted. For a discussion as to when a detained person should be charged or bailed when there is sufficient evidence **see para. 2.11.9.**

Where there is sufficient evidence to charge, a delay in bringing charges may be seen to be unreasonable under Article 6 of the European Convention on Human Rights (*D v HM Advocate* (2000) *The Times*, 14 April). In deciding whether there is sufficient evidence to charge for the purposes of authorising detention or when a person's detention is reviewed; where there is a conflict between the detained person's account and victims' or witnesses' accounts it is reasonable to be in possession of at least one witness statement in the English language before preferring charges (*R v Chief Constable of Hertfordshire, ex parte Wiles* [2002] EWHC Admin 387). There is no breach of the Police and Criminal Evidence Act 1984 in keeping the detained person in police detention while a statement is translated. It is suggested that the translation needs to be completed expeditiously.

Under s. 37(9) release can be delayed if the person is not in a fit state to be released (e.g. he/she is drunk), until he/she is fit. Where a person is detained for charge, the custody officer should record the grounds for detention in the custody record in the presence of the detained person if practicable (Code C, para. 3.23).

For the situation relating to drunk drivers, **see Road Policing, chapter 3.5.**

2.11.6.12 Insufficient Evidence to Charge

This creates two separate criteria for detention, that is to say, where detention is necessary to:

- secure and preserve evidence relating to an offence for which the person is arrested; or
- obtain such evidence by questioning the detained person.

If the custody officer has determined that there is not sufficient evidence to charge the person, the person must be released unless the custody officer has *reasonable grounds* for believing that the person's detention is necessary to preserve or to obtain such evidence by questioning the person. 'Reasonable grounds for believing' requires a greater amount of evidence than 'reasonable cause to suspect' (**see General Police Duties, chapter 4.4**) and the custody officer must be able to justify any decision not to release a person from detention.

When deciding if detention should be authorised in order to obtain evidence by questioning, the case of *R v McGuinness* [1999] Crim LR 318 should be considered. There the court held that the words 'sufficient evidence to prosecute' and 'sufficient evidence for a prosecution to succeed', in Code C, para. 16.1 (this was the wording under the previous PACE Code of Practice), had to involve some consideration of any explanation, or lack of one, from the suspect. While an interview may not be needed in all cases, questioning of detained people before they are charged may be necessary, particularly where intention or dishonesty (**see Crime, chapter 1.1**) is involved or where there may be a defence (**see Crime, chapter 1.4**). It may also be important to put questions to the person about the offence or his/her explanation, as this may be important to negate any defence the person raised at court (see s. 34 of the Criminal Justice and Public Order Act 1994).

Where initial suspicion rests on several people, it may be appropriate to hold all suspects until they all are interviewed before deciding whether there is enough evidence to warrant a charge against any of them. Detention for questioning where there are reasonable grounds for suspecting that an offence has been committed is lawful so long as the suspicion has not been dispelled in the interim and the questioning is not unnecessarily delayed (*Clarke* v *Chief Constable of North Wales* (2000) *The Independent*, 22 May).

Article 5 of the European Convention on Human Rights makes the decision to authorise detention even more crucial, as it states:

> (1) Everyone has the right to liberty and security of person. No one shall be deprived of his liberty save in the following cases and in accordance with a procedure prescribed by law:
>   (a) the lawful detention of a person after conviction by a competent court;
>   (b) the lawful arrest or detention of a person for non-compliance with the lawful order of a court or in order to secure the fulfilment of any obligation prescribed by law;
>   (c) the lawful arrest or detention of a person effected for the purpose of bringing him before the competent legal authority on reasonable suspicion of having committed an offence or when it is reasonably considered necessary to prevent his committing an offence or fleeing after having done so ...

For a full discussion of the Convention, **see General Police Duties, chapter 4.3**.

The custody officer can detain the person for such period as is necessary in order to make this decision (s. 37(1) of the 1984 Act). Clearly any such period must be 'reasonable' in all the circumstances. For instance, where there are several prisoners waiting to be dealt with it may be reasonable that the last prisoner is not dealt with for 30 minutes because the custody officer is busy with the other prisoners (Code C, para. 1.1A and Note 1H). For the custody officer to be able to make this decision, the arresting officer needs to give sufficient detail about the offence. The account given by the arresting officer should be made in the presence of the arrested person and any comment made by that person in response should be recorded in the custody record (Code C, para. 3.4) (unless the person is violent or it is impractical to do so for some other reason, in which case this fact should also be recorded). If the arresting officer is not available, his/her account must be made either remotely or by a third party.

The mere fact that a person needs to be interviewed about the offence is not of itself justification for authorising detention. The question that has to be asked is whether the person can be bailed prior to the interview or even bailed before being taken to the police station (s. 30A of the 1984 Act). Factors which might be relevant in making this decision include:

- whether the person may interfere with witnesses;
- whether he/she is likely to return if bailed;
- where there is more than one suspect,
- that they would have an opportunity to confer before their interviews;
- whether there is outstanding property;
- whether the person's name and address is verified.

The fact that the officers and any legal representative will be ready to start the interview shortly may also be relevant when making this decision.

Section 37(4) and (5) of the 1984 Act require the custody officer to make a written record of the grounds of detention and to make that record in the presence of the detained person, informing him/her at the same time of the grounds of his/her detention (unless s. 37(6) applies). It is suggested that the custody officer record all the reasons for authorising the person's detention. For example: 'To obtain statements from the victim and witnesses as this information will be needed before interview to fully put the allegation to the suspect and then to allow the suspect to be interviewed about the allegation. If bailed prior to interview he/she may interfere with the witnesses, who are known to the suspect.' It is suggested that detail of at least this minimal level should be included, as it may be necessary in any criminal or civil proceedings. Indeed, it will be difficult for the custody officer to explain his/her decision without such information.

Section 37(6) states:

Subsection (5) above shall not apply where the person arrested is, at the time when the written record is made—
(a) incapable of understanding what is said to him;
(b) violent or likely to become violent; or
(c) in urgent need of medical attention.

2.11.6.13 Additional Action to be Taken by the Custody Officer

The action to be taken by the custody officer when receiving detained people is set out in Code C, paras 3.1 to 3.11. For the action relating to special groups, **see paras 2.11.11** and **2.11.11.4**.

Paragraph 3.1 sets out the information the detained person is entitled to. These are *continuing* entitlements and can be requested at any time during the person's detention. See Code C, Note 3B for choice of language and audio versions of these rights.

Paragraph 3.2 deals with written notices which must be given to the detained person in relation to his/her rights. (Code C, para. 1.2 requires that a copy of the Codes of Practice must also be readily available to detained persons should they request it.) There should be versions of these rights in languages other than English available in the custody suite.

Paragraph 3.5 requires the custody officer to establish whether the detained person wishes to have a solicitor at this stage. If he/she declines, the custody officer should ask the person the reason why and, if any reasons are given, these should be recorded in the custody record (Code C, para. 6.5). The detained person must still be asked if they require a solicitor even if they are to be held *incommunicado*.

2.11.7 Limits on Detention and Review

Once detention has been authorised this does not mean that a person can be detained indefinitely. Section 34 of the Police and Criminal Evidence Act 1984 requires the custody officer to release a person if he/she becomes aware that the grounds for detention no longer apply and that no other grounds exist for the continuing detention (unless the person appears to be unlawfully at large when they were arrested). Failure to comply with this could also lead to a breach of Article 5 of the European Convention on Human Rights. If there are additional grounds, these should be recorded in the custody record and the person informed of these additional grounds in the same way as when a person is first detained. For example, this could be for new offences or it could be that it becomes necessary to preserve evidence by questioning the detained person.

It is only the custody officer who can authorise the release of a detained person (s. 34(3)). In addition to the requirement to release a person should the grounds for detention no longer exist, there are also maximum time limits for which a person can be detained without charge (**see para. 2.11.7.1**). Once this limit has been reached, it will be necessary to proceed by summons or by warrant. There are also limits on the time a person can be kept in custody after being charged, refused bail and appearing at court (see below).

2.11.7.1 Time Limits: Without Charge

While a person is in police detention there is a requirement that his/her continuing detention is reviewed. This is dealt with below. There are minimum time requirements for when these reviews must be conducted, with the timing of the first review being calculated from the time detention is authorised. This time can be considered as the 'review time'. The question of whether a person should be kept in custody is a continuous one and the review process is intended as an added protection to the detained person.

The maximum period that a person can be detained without charge (with the exception of suspected acts of terrorism, in which case it is 28 days) is 96 hours. The necessity for the continued detention of the person must be reviewed throughout this time. The period of detention is calculated from the 'relevant time' (**see para. 2.11.6.8**) which can be calculated from the chart below (**see para. 2.11.7.3**). (*Do not confuse the relevant time with the time from which reviews are due.*) The relevant time 'clock' will always start before, or at the same time as, the review 'clock'. This is because the review clock does not start until detention has been authorised which clearly cannot happen until the person is brought before the custody officer which, as can be seen from the chart below, is at the very latest, the time the prisoner walks into the custody suite (*with the exception of where the person has been under arrest for 24 hours but has not yet been taken to a police station*).

This relevant time period (that is, the maximum period a person can be detained for) relates to the actual time spent in custody and not a 24-hour period in time. This means that every time the person is bailed the clock stops and usually continues from the time that the person returns to custody for the offence(s) for which he/she was bailed.

Where a person has been released and re-arrested for an offence, it is possible that the relevant time will start again. This is covered by s. 47 of the 1984 Act:

> (7) Where a person who was released on bail under this Part subject to a duty to attend at a police station is re-arrested, the provisions of this Part of this Act shall apply to him as they apply to a person arrested for the first time but this subsection does not apply to a person who is arrested under section 46A above or has attended a police station in accordance with the grant of bail (and who accordingly is deemed by section 34(7) above to have been arrested for an offence).

KEYNOTE

In cases where this subsection applies, the relevant time starts again and a fresh clock starts. This will apply where the person has been re-arrested for the same offence because of some new evidence (except at such time as when he/she is returning on bail at the appointed time) under s. 30C(4), 41(9) or 47(2).

Section 41 states:

> (9) A person released under subsection (7) [i.e. where his/her relevant time period had expired] above shall not be re-arrested without a warrant for the offence for which he was previously arrested unless new evidence justifying a further arrest has come to light since his release; but this subsection does not prevent an arrest under section 46A below.

Section 47 states:

> (2) Nothing in the Bail Act 1976 shall prevent the re-arrest without warrant of a person released on bail subject to a duty to attend at a police station if new evidence justifying a further arrest has come to light since his release.

Section 30C states:

> (4) Nothing in section 30A or 30B or in this section prevents the re-arrest without warrant of a person released on bail under section 30A (bail by a constable elsewhere than a police station) if new evidence justifying a further arrest has come to light since his release

---

KEYNOTE

The issue will be whether new evidence has come to light since the grant of bail and it will be a question of fact as to what the new evidence is. It is suggested that this must be evidence which was not available at the time the person was last in detention or which would not have been available even if all reasonable inquiries had been conducted.

It will always be important to check how much time is left on the person's 'relevant time' and when his/her next review is due.

2.11.7.2 The Three Stages of Pre-charge Detention

After the custody officer has authorised detention but before a person has been charged there are three distinct stages of detention. These are distinguished by the level at which authorisation for continuing detention is required.

The three stages of detention under the 1984 Act are:

- The basic period of detention, which is the period of detention up to 24 hours, as first authorised by the custody officer.
- Those authorised by an officer of the rank of superintendent or above (s. 42) up to 36 hours (**see para. 2.11.7.4**) (indictable offences only).
- Those authorised by a magistrates' court (ss. 43 and 44) up to a maximum of 96 hours (**see para. 2.11.7.5**).

For offences under s. 41 of the Terrorism Act 2000, **see para. 2.11.7.5**. Each of these is examined in detail below.

2.11.7.3 The Basic Period of Detention

The majority of people detained by the police are detained for less than six hours; most other cases are dealt with within 24 hours. If a person's continued detention is not authorised beyond 24 hours and the person is not charged with an offence, he/she *must* be released (with or without bail) and cannot be re-arrested for the offence unless new evidence comes to light (s. 41(7) and (9) of the 1984 Act). New evidence is not defined by the 1984 Act but it is suggested that it covers evidence which was not available at the time the person was detained, or which would not have been available if the investigating officers had conducted reasonable inquiries.

During this period of detention the custody officer has a responsibility to monitor whether the grounds for detention still exist. An officer of at least the rank of inspector not involved in the investigation (s. 40(1)(b)) must review the person's detention *at least once in the first six hours* and then, after the first review, *within nine hours of that review*. Further reviews must then be conducted *no later than nine hours after the last review* was conducted, until the person is either charged or released. The detention of persons in police custody not subject to the statutory review requirement in Code C, para. 15.1 should still be reviewed periodically as a matter of good practice and they can be carried out by an officer of the rank of sergeant or above (Code C, Note 15B); **see also para. 2.11.7.6.**

If a detained person is taken to hospital for medical treatment, the time at hospital and the period spent travelling to and from the hospital does not count towards the relevant time unless the person is asked questions for the purpose of obtaining evidence about an offence. Where questioning takes place, this period would count towards the relevant time and therefore the custody officer must be informed of it (s. 41(6)).

2.11.7.4 Detention Authorised by an Officer of the Rank of Superintendent or above

Under s. 42(1) of the Police and Criminal Evidence Act 1984, detention can only be authorised beyond 24 hours and up to a maximum of 36 hours from the relevant time if:

- an offence being investigated is an 'indictable offence' (see s. 116 of the 1984 Act and **General Police Duties, chapter 4.4**); *and*
- an officer of the rank of superintendent or above who is responsible for the station at which the person is detained (referred to here as the authorising officer); *and*
- that that senior officer is satisfied that:
  - ♦ there is not sufficient evidence to charge; *and*
  - ♦ the investigation is being conducted diligently and expeditiously; *and*
  - ♦ that the person's detention is necessary to secure or preserve evidence relating to the offence or to obtain such evidence by questioning that person.

Where a person has been arrested under s. 41 of the Terrorism Act 2000 he/she can be kept in police detection (in this case this is generally from the time of their arrest) up to 48 hours without the court authorising an extension of time (for the grounds, **see para. 2.11.7.7**). At this stage if the authorising officer considers that there is sufficient evidence to charge, he/she cannot authorise further detention beyond 24 hours unless the detained person is in custody for another indictable offence for which further detention can be authorised (*R v Samuel* [1988] QB 615 and Code C, para. 16.1).

The grounds for this continuing detention are the same as those when the custody officer made the initial decision to detain, with the additional requirements that the case has been conducted diligently and expeditiously. It is suggested that Article 5 of the European Convention requires this to be a consideration at all times of detention as a person's right to freedom is one of his/her human rights and any unnecessary periods of detention might be considered actionable. To be able to satisfy the senior officer of this, it will be necessary for the custody record to be available for inspection and details of what inquiries have been made and evidence that the investigation has been moving at a pace that will satisfy the senior officer that the inquires should not already have been completed. Code C, para. 15.2A outlines issues to be considered before extending the period of juveniles and mentally vulnerable persons.

The authorising officer (which here must be an officer of the rank of superintendent or above who is responsible for the station at which the person is detained) can authorise detention up to a maximum of 36 hours from the 'relevant time' of detention. The period can be shorter than this and can then be further authorised by that officer or any other officer of the rank of superintendent or above who is responsible for the station at which the person is detained to allow the period to be further extended up to the maximum 36-hour period (s. 42(2)). Code C, Note 15E gives guidance as to which officers this would include.

Maximum Periods of Detention for Non Terrorism Act Offences

Arrest	Relevant time starts	Review clock relevant time	24 hours from detention	24 to 36 hours' detention	36 to 42 hours' detention	42 to 78 hours' detention	Up to 96 hours'
Arrested locally.	24 hours from arrest or arrival at police station whichever earliest.		All offences other than indictable offences.	Only indictable offences.	Only indictable offences.	Only indictable offences.	Only indictable offences.
Arrested outside England and Wales.	Time first arrives at police station in police area where matter being investigated or 24 hours after first entered England or Wales, whichever earliest.	Time custody officer authorises detention.	Release unless s. 41(1 applies.	Detention authorised by superintendent or above (s. 42).	Where delay in applying for warrant of further detention is reasonable (s. 43(5)).	First warrant for further detention issued by magistrates' court (s. 42).	Further warrants of detention issued by magistrates' court (s. 43).
Arrested for an offence in one police area in England or Wales then transferred to another police area for separate offence in that second police area which is also in England or Wales.	24 hours from time he/she leaves the police station in the first police area or the time he/she arrives at the first police station in second police area where the crime is being investigated provided not interviewed about the offence while detained in the first police area, whichever is the earliest.	This timing applies where the person was in detention for an offence in the first police area (s. 41(5)).			**See para. 2.11.7.5** for the dangers of not applying within the 36-hour period.	Remember the warrant can be applied for at any stage of detention.	
Arrested and bailed at a place other than a police station.	Time of arrival at the police station to which the notice of bail states he/she must attend.						

Arrest	Relevant time starts	Review clock relevant time	24 hours from detention	24 to 36 hours' detention	36 to 42 hours' detention	42 to 78 hours' detention	Up to 96 hours'
Voluntarily attends police station or accompanies constable to station but not under arrest.	Time of arrest.						
Arrested in one police area in England or Wales for an offence in another police area in England or Wales, there being no 'local' offence(s) for which he/she has been arrested.	From time the suspect arrives at the first police station in the area he/she is being sought or from 24 hours after the time he/she is arrested or if questioned about the offence while in the first police area the relevant time starts from the time he/she first arrived at a police station in the first police area, whichever is the earliest.						

The extension of a person's detention by a superintendent or above must be made within 24 hours of the relevant time and cannot be made before at least two reviews have been carried out by a review officer under s. 40 of the 1984 Act (i.e. those normally carried out by an inspector) (s. 42(4)) (Code C, para. 15.2).

If an extension to the period of detention is authorised, a record must be made and shall state the number of hours and minutes by which the detention period is extended or further extended (Code C, para. 15.16).

For the situation regarding 'acting' ranks, **see General Police Duties, chapter 4.4**.

Section 42(5) to (8) mirrors the responsibility on the authorising officer at this stage with those of the review officer during the 'general period' of detention with regard to allowing representations, informing the detained person of the decision to authorise further detention and the need to record the decision. The main difference here is that the authorising officer must look into how the case is being investigated and whether this is being done diligently and expeditiously. Consequently, the authorising officer must also consider any representations on these points and these points should also be covered in any record as to whether detention should continue. When considering whether to authorise further detention the authorising officer must check whether the detained person has exercised his/her right to have someone informed and to consult with a legal representative. If these options have not been taken, s. 42(9) requires the authorising officer to inform the detained person of these rights and also whether he/she will be allowed to exercise these rights if it is an indictable offence and the right has so far been delayed as per Code C, Annex B. The authorising officer should record the detainee's decision in the custody record and the grounds for denying the person those rights where appropriate.

If it is proposed to transfer a detained person from one police area to another for the purpose of investigating the offences for which he/she is detained, the authorising officer may take into consideration the period it will take to get to the other police area when deciding whether detention can go beyond 24 hours (s. 42(3)).

2.11.7.5 Detention Authorised by a Magistrates' Court

Once the 36-hour limit has been reached, a person's detention can only continue with the authority of the courts through the issuing of a warrant of further detention and this power only applies to indictable offences. If a person's continued detention is not authorised beyond 36 hours by a court and the person is not charged with an offence, he/she must be released with or without bail and cannot be re-arrested for the offence unless new evidence comes to light (as to new evidence, **see para. 2.11.7.1**).

Warrants of Further Detention

Applications for warrants of further detention are made at the magistrates' court. Initially, the magistrates can issue a warrant for further detention for a period of up to 36 hours. This can be extended by the courts on further applications by police up to a maximum total period of detention of 96 hours. The warrant will specify what period of further detention the court has authorised. If detention of the person is required for any longer period, further applications can be made to the court up to a maximum of 96 hours' detention. The grounds on which the court must decide whether to grant a warrant authorising further detention are the same as those that must be considered by a 'superintendent's review' (**see para. 2.11.7.4**).

Should it be necessary to apply for a warrant it is important that the time restraints are kept in mind at all times and the application procedure followed closely.

Procedure

The application is made in the magistrates' court and both the detained person and the police must be in attendance (s. 43(1) and (2) of the Police and Criminal Evidence Act 1984). The application is made by laying an information before the court. The officer making the application does so on oath and is subject to cross-examination (**see chapter 2.5**). Under s. 43(14) the information must set out:

- the nature of the offence (this must be an indictable offence);
- the general nature of the evidence on which the person was arrested;
- what inquiries have been made;
- what further inquiries are proposed; and
- the reasons for believing that continuing detention is necessary for the such further inquiries.

It will be important to be able to demonstrate why the person needs to remain in detention while additional inquiries are made, for instance, that further facts need to be verified before further questioning of the suspect can continue and that this cannot be done effectively if the person is released. The detained person must be provided with a copy of the information before the matter can be heard (s. 43(2)). He/she is also entitled to be legally represented. If the person is not legally represented but then requests legal representation at court, the case must be adjourned to allow representation (s. 43(3)). In cases where the person is not represented it may be prudent to remind the person of his/her right to legal representation prior to the court hearing and to make a record of this in the custody record. Should the detained person choose to be legally represented at court, and thereby try to delay the police investigation, s. 43(3)(b) allows the person to be taken back into police detention during the adjournment.

Timing of the application

If it appears likely that the investigation of the indictable offence requires the person's detention to go beyond 36 hours, then thought must be given as to when to make the application to the magistrates' court. Section 43(5) allows the application to be made before the expiry of the 36-hour period (calculated from the relevant time) or, where it has not been practicable for the court to sit within the 36-hour period, the application can be made within the next six hours. There are dangers in applying outside the 36-hour period in that if the court feels that it would have been reasonable to make the application within the 36-hour period then it must refuse the application for the warrant regardless of the merits of the case (s. 43(7)). If the court is not satisfied that there are reasonable grounds for believing that further detention is justified, the court may either refuse the application or adjourn the hearing until such time as it specifies up to the end of the 36-hour period of detention (s. 43(8)). If the application is refused, the person must be charged or released with or without bail at the expiry of the current permissible period of detention (s. 43(15)).

The application for the warrant can be made at any time, *even before a superintendent's review has been carried out*. If the application is made within the 36-hour period and it is refused, it does not mean the person must be released straight away. Section 43(16) allows the person to be detained until the end of the current detention period (24 hours or 36 hours). The benefit of an early application has to be set against the risk that, once the court has refused an application, it is not allowed to hear any further applications for a warrant of further detention unless new evidence has come to light since the application was refused (s. 43(17)). Code C, Note 15D gives guidance on when an application should be made to the court. Note 15D states:

An application to a magistrates' court under PACE, sections 43 or 44 for a warrant of further detention or its extension should be made between 10 am and 9 pm, and if possible during normal court hours. It will not usually be practicable to arrange for a court to sit specially outside the hours of 10 am to 9 pm. If it appears a special sitting may be needed outside normal court hours but between 10 am and 9 pm, the clerk to the justices should be given notice and informed of this possibility, while the court is sitting if possible.

In *R* v *Slough Justices, ex parte Stirling* [1987] Crim LR 576, the 36-hour period expired at 12.53 pm. The case was not heard by the justices until 2.45 pm. The Divisional Court held that the police should have made their application between 10.30 am and 11.30 am, even though this was before the 36-hour time limit had been reached.

In monitoring a person's detention, officers should be mindful of whether a warrant for further detention may be required and, if it is, consider whether a court will be available to hear the application. If a court will not be available then consideration should be given to making an earlier application. The process the magistrates go through in deciding the merits of the application also provides some safeguards in that the person's continued detention has been considered by the courts and therefore may reduce the likelihood of the defence suggesting that detention was not justified. If a warrant for further detention, or extension, is granted under s. 43 or 44, a record shall be made stating the detention period authorised by the warrant and the date and time it was granted (Code C, para. 15.16).

Applying to Extend Warrants of Further Detention

Under s. 44 of the 1984 Act, the process for applying to extend the warrant follows the same procedure as for the initial warrant, with the exception that the application *must be* made before the expiry of the extension given in the previous warrant. Once the period of detention that has been authorised has expired, and no other applications have been made, the detained person must be charged or released with or without bail.

Terrorism Cases

The court can extend the period of detention of a person up to a total of 28 days. In the case of those arrested under s. 41 this starts at the time of arrest or, if the person was being detained under sch. 7 when he was arrested under s. 41, with the time when his/her examination under that schedule began (Terrorism Act 2000, sch. 8, para. 36(3A)).

A person detained in these circumstances may only be held for a maximum of 48 hours without charge before an application must be made to a court to issue or extend a warrant of further detention. At the end of that period, the detained person must either be released or an application to a court for a warrant for an extension to that detention must have been made and granted prior to the expiry of the initial 48-hour period. Extensions by the court will normally be for a seven day period unless the application for a warrant of further detention requests a shorter period or the court is satisfied that it would be inappropriate for the period to be as long as seven days.

If detention is required beyond the first seven days, further applications are required to be made to the court as it is not possible for the court to issue a warrant authorising the full 28 days' detention on the first occasion that a warrant for detention is sought. For the grounds on which a warrant of further detention can be authorised see the review officer's grounds at **para. 2.11.7.7** (Code H, Note 14B).

The application to the court must be made by a superintendent or a crown prosecutor. Usually applications that cover a period of detention that does not extend beyond 14 days are heard by a District Judge in the magistrates' court (unless an application in that case has already been considered by a High Court Judge and those that cover the period beyond 14 days are heard by a High Court Judge. Section 37 of the Terrorism Act 2000 states that if at any time the police officer or person in charge of the case considers that the grounds on which the warrant of further detention authorised by the court no longer apply the detained person must be released. Paragraph 33 of sch. 8 to the Terrorism Act 2000 allows for these applications to be conducted by live television links. The person who makes the application may also apply to the court for an order that specified information upon which he/she intends to rely should be withheld from the person to whom the application relates and anyone representing him/her. The order to withhold information can only be made if one of the following applies:

- evidence of an offence under any of the provisions mentioned in s. 40(1)(a) of the Terrorism Act 2000 (**see para. 2.12.12**) would be interfered with or harmed;
- the recovery of property obtained as a result of an offence under any of those provisions would be hindered;
- the recovery of property in respect of which a forfeiture order could be made under s. 23 of the Terrorism Act 2000 would be hindered;
- the apprehension, prosecution or conviction of a person who is suspected of committing offences under the Terrorism Act 2000 would be made more difficult as a result of his/her being alerted;
- the prevention of an act of terrorism would be made more difficult as a result of the person being alerted;
- the gathering of information about the commission, preparation or instigation of an act of terrorism would be interfered with; or
- a person would be interfered with or physically injured;
- the detained person has benefited from his criminal conduct and the recovery of the value of the property constituting the benefit would be hindered if the information were disclosed (sch. 8, part III to the Terrorism Act 2000).

Where a warrant is issued which authorises detention beyond a period of 14 days from the time of arrest the detainee must be transferred from detention in a police station to detention in a designated prison as soon as it practicable, unless:

(a) the detainee specifically requests to remain in detention at a police station and that request can be accommodated, or

(b) there are reasonable grounds to believe that transferring a person to a prison would:
  (i) significantly hinder a terrorism investigation;
  (ii) delay charging of the detainee or his release from custody, or
  (iii) otherwise prevent the investigation from being conducted diligently and expeditiously.

If any of the grounds in (b)(i) to (iii) are relied upon, these must be presented to the judicial authority as part of the application for the warrant that would extend detention beyond a period of 14 days from the time of arrest. After grounds (b)(i) to (iii) cease to apply the person must be transferred to a prison as soon as practicable.

2.11.7.6 The Review

While a person is in police detention (**see para. 2.11.4.1**) before charge, his/her detention must be reviewed by an officer of the rank of inspector or above (inspector reviews). This review acts as another safeguard to protect the detained person's right to be detained for only such periods as are necessary to allow for the investigation of an offence. Reviews of police detention are covered by s. 40 of the Police and Criminal Evidence Act 1984.

Section 40 sets out the times when reviews must be conducted:

(3) Subject to subsection (4) . . .
    (a) the first review shall be not later than six hours after the detention was first authorised;
    (b) the second review shall be not later than nine hours after the first;
    (c) subsequent reviews shall be at intervals of not more than nine hours.

KEYNOTE

The periods set out in s. 40(3) are the *maximum* periods that a review can be left; should the review officer wish to review before this time for operational reasons etc., the review could be brought forward. The first review must be made within six hours of the custody officer authorising detention (this, it must be remembered, is not the time from which the 24-hour clock starts, i.e. the time the detainee came into the station, but the time at which the custody officer authorised detention). Thereafter, each review must be made within nine hours of the last review.

For the situation regarding 'acting' ranks, **see General Police Duties, chapter 4.4**. Section 40(4)(b) does allow reviews to be delayed if it is not practicable to carry out the review. Conducting late reviews should be avoided where at all possible (see *Roberts* v *Chief Constable of Cheshire Constabulary* [1999] 1 WLR 662). If delayed, the grounds for and extent of any delay must be recorded (Code C, para. 15.13).

Review officer for the purposes of ss. 40 and 40A of the 1984 Act means, in the case of a person arrested but not charged, an officer of at least inspector rank not directly involved in the investigation and, if a person has been arrested and charged, the custody officer. In cases under the Terrorism Act 2000, the review officer means an officer not directly involved in the investigation connected with the detention and of at least inspector rank, for reviews within 24 hours of the detainee's arrest or a superintendent for all other reviews.

It is suggested that even where a detainee is not in police detention as defined by s. 118 of the 1984 Act, consideration should be given to reviewing his/her detention; this can be conducted by the custody officer. A case that supports this view is *Chief Constable of Cleveland Police* v *McGrogan* [2002] 1 FLR 707 which involved a person detained at a police station overnight after having been arrested for breach of the peace. The Court of Appeal held that the need regularly to review the person's detention was required even though breach of the peace was not an 'offence' for the purpose of s. 118.

Section 40(4) provides two other occasions where it may be justified to delay the review if at that time:

• the person in detention is being questioned by a police officer and the review officer is satisfied that an interruption of the questioning for the purpose of carrying out the review would prejudice the investigation in connection with which he/she is being questioned (s. 40(4)(b)(i));

• no review officer is readily available (s. 40(4)(4)(b)(ii)).

It is suggested that it will be necessary to justify why no review officer was available and that where it is known that a review may fall during an interview, the review is conducted prior to the interview where appropriate. It is suggested that with the ability to undertake reviews by telephone or video link, a delay to a review is likely to need greater justification.

In *Roberts*, the defendant had his first review conducted eight hours, 20 minutes after his detention had been authorised. The Court of Appeal held that under s. 40(1)(b) of the 1984 Act a review of his detention should have been carried out by an officer of the rank of inspector or above six hours after detention was first authorised. Section 34(1) was mandatory and provided that a person must not be kept in police detention except in accordance with the relevant provisions of the Act. Therefore, the respondent's detention had been unlawful unless some event occurred to have made it lawful.

The court made it clear that the 1984 Act existed in order to ensure members of the public were not detained except in certain defined circumstances. In the absence of a review, the time spent in detention between 5.25 am, and 7.45 am meant that for that period the defendant's detention was unlawful and amounted to a false imprisonment.

Subject to the passing of regulations, s. 45A of the 1984 Act allows for pre-charge reviews to be conducted by a review officer who is not present in that police station if they have access to the use of video-conferencing facilities that enable him/her to communicate with persons in that station. Provision for video conferencing is included within Code C, however there are currently no regulations allowing such remote reviews.

Where a review is due under s. 40 and the detainee has not been charged, the review may be carried out by means of a discussion, conducted by telephone, with one or more persons at the police station where the arrested person is held. Code C, para. 15.3C provides guidance as to the style of review in terms of telephone, video-conferencing or in-person reviews. Review conducted by telephone or video-conferencing can be terminated by the review officer and then conducted in person.

Where this review is done by telephone, an officer at the station holding the detainee must fulfil the reviewing officer's obligations under the Police and Criminal Evidence Act 1984 (see Code C, para. 15.10). Code C, para. 15.11 identifies the methods that can be used to ensure that the rights of the detainee, appropriate adult and solicitor to make representations to the reviewing officer under Code C, para. 15.3 are satisfied: for example by fax, email message or orally by telephone. The use of telephones to conduct reviews does not include reviews to extend the period of detention beyond the 24-hour clock. Where the review is conducted by telephone, a record must be made of the following: the reason the review officer did not attend the station holding the detainee; the place the review officer was; and the method by which representations were made to the review officer (Code C, para. 15.14). Telephone reviews do not apply to reviews of detention after charge by the custody officer or to reviews under the Terrorism Act 2000, sch. 8, part II in terrorism cases (Code C, Note 15F). If the review is delayed then it must still be conducted as soon as practicable and the reason for the delay must be recorded in the custody record by the review officer. In these circumstances the nine-hour period until the next review is calculated from the latest time the review should have been carried out and not from the time it was actually carried out. For instance, if the review was due at 3.15 pm and was delayed until 4 pm, the next review would have to be conducted no later than 12.15 am and not 1 am. When the review is conducted the review officer does not have to authorise detention for the full nine-hour period; he/she could decide that the case should be reviewed again within a shorter period and the review decision would reflect this.

When reviewing the detention of a person the review officer goes through the same process as the custody officer did when detention was first authorised (ss. 40(8) and 37(1)–(6)), namely by asking:

- Is there sufficient evidence to charge? If 'yes', charge or release the person with or without bail. If 'no', then:
- Is detention necessary in order to secure or preserve evidence or is it necessary to detain the person in order to obtain such evidence by questioning him/her? If 'yes', authorise continued detention. If 'no', release the person with or without bail.

It is suggested that in order to consider whether there is sufficient evidence to charge, the review officer should have consideration for the Code for Crown Prosecutors and the

Threshold Test, **see para. 2.11.9**. The situation may arise where the review officer considers that there is sufficient evidence to charge and only authorises continued detention to charge even though the custody officer disagrees. In this case it is suggested that the custody officer must either charge or release the person with or without bail in line with s. 37B of the Police and Criminal Evidence Act 1984. Where bailed this may be in order to submit papers to the Crown Prosecution Service in order for a decision to be made as to whether to charge and for what offence. There may also be situations where the custody officer has concluded that there is sufficient evidence to charge but the review officer disagrees; in these cases the review officer cannot overrule the custody officer's decision under s. 37(7). In any case where the decision has been made that there is sufficient evidence to charge, the review officer should confirm that the referral has been made, note the custody record to this effect and, thereafter, check to ensure that the decision is made within a *reasonable time*.

It is suggested that the reviewing officer (or any other officer other than a superintendent or above) cannot tell the custody officer what they must do. The reviewing officer may wish to give advice but it will be for the custody officer to decide whether to take that advice. Clearly failure to do so could lead to internal criticism but legally there is no requirement to follow that advice.

If there is not sufficient evidence to charge, the review officer may want to consider the question: 'If this person is bailed, what evidence will be lost'? If the answer is none, continued detention would seem unlawful. As stated above, it is suggested that Article 5 of the European Convention or Human Rights requires that an investigation must be conducted diligently and expeditiously in order to minimise the time a person is deprived of his/her liberty (particularly where the case does not lead to a prosecution). In order to monitor the effectiveness of the investigation and the time spent in custody, the reviewing officer should consider the period of detention since the last review to ensure that any defect in the person's treatment is corrected, and where necessary, take steps to speed up the investigation.

In cases where it has been decided that a person should be charged but he/she has been detained because he/she is not in a fit state to be charged (s. 37(9)), the review officer must determine whether the person is yet in a fit state. If the detainee is in a fit state, the custody officer should be informed that the person should be charged or released. If the detainee is not in a fit state, detention can be authorised for a further period (s. 40(9)). In such cases, if the person is still unfit, it may be prudent to consider the welfare of the detained person.

During the process of reviewing a person's detention, the review officer must give the detained person (unless he/she is asleep) or any solicitor representing the detained person who is available at the time of the review, an opportunity to make representations about his/her continued detention (s. 40(12)). If the detained person is likely to be asleep at the time the review is to be carried out, the review should be brought forward to allow the detained person to be present at the time of the review (Code C, Note 15C). If the detainee is asleep when the reviewing officer authorises his/her continued detention, the detainee must be informed of the decision when he/she wakes (Code C, para. 15.7) and the details of the officer who informed the detainee of the decision should also be recorded (Code C, para. 15.16). It may be prudent for the review officer specifically to inform the custody officer of the need for this and record this fact, and details of the custody officer informed, in the custody record. If the detainee makes a comment it may be necessary to inform the reviewing officer (or his/her replacement) of the comment (Code C, para. 15.5). The review officer must also ensure that the detained person is reminded of his/her right to free legal advice and that this reminder is recorded in the custody record (Code C, para. 15.4). In the case of juveniles, the appropriate adult should also be allowed to make representations and the review officer has the discretion to allow other people having an interest in the welfare of the detained person to make representations (Code C, paras 15.3 and 15.3A). These representations may be in writing or oral (s. 40(13)). Where the review is conducted by telephone or video-conferencing, the written representations may be forwarded to the reviewing officer by fax, email or any other medium that ensures they are received. If made in writing, the document should be retained (Code C, para. 15.15). The review officer can refuse to hear oral representations from the detained person if the review officer considers that the person is unfit to make such representations, either because of his/her condition or behaviour (e.g. drunk or violent) (Code C, para. 15.3B). A detainee who is not asleep during the review must be present when the grounds for his/her continued detention are recorded and must at the same time be informed of those grounds unless the review officer considers the person is incapable of understanding what is said, is violent or likely to become violent or is in urgent need of medical attention (Code C, Note 15C); any comment made by the detainee should be recorded (Code C, para. 15.5). However, the review officer must not put any questions to the person about his/her comments (Code C, para. 15.6). Also, as the role of review officer is intended to be independent of the investigation, he/she should not put any questions to the person about his/her involvement in any offence; this mirrors the instruction to custody officers (Code C, para. 15.6).

If at any stage an officer of a rank higher than the review officer gives directions which are at variance with a decision made or action taken by the review officer, or which would have been made by the review officer but for the directions by the more senior officer, then s. 40(11) requires the matter to be referred *at once* to an officer of the rank of superintendent or above who is *responsible for the police station*.

It is important to understand the difference between the action of authorising an extension to the 'detention clock' and the role of the review officer. These are two distinct roles and both need to be carried out. When an officer of the rank of superintendent or above extends the 'relevant time' period, this is not automatically a review (although there is nothing to stop that officer from conducting the review). This means that the 'reviewing' officer may still have to conduct a review even though the relevant time has only recently been extended, unless the officer of the rank of superintendent or above extending the relevant time has shown the review as having been conducted in the custody record.

2.11.7.7 Terrorism Act Reviews

(See also General Police Duties, chapter 4.6.)

In cases where the person has been detained under the Terrorism Act 2000 the first review should be conducted as soon as reasonably practicable after his/her arrest and then at least every 12 hours; after 24 hours it must be conducted by an officer of the rank of superintendent or above. Once a warrant of further detention has been obtained there is no requirement to conduct further reviews. If an officer of higher rank than the review officer gives directions relating to the detained person, and those directions are at variance with the performance by the review officer of a duty imposed on him/her then he/she must refer the matter at once to an officer of at least the rank of superintendent.

A review officer may only authorise a person's continued detention if he/she is satisfied that it is necessary:

- in order to obtain relevant evidence whether by questioning the person or otherwise;
- to preserve relevant evidence;
- pending a decision whether to apply to the Secretary of State for a deportation notice to be served on the detained person;

- pending the making of an application to the Secretary of State for a deportation notice to be served on the detained person;
- pending consideration by the Secretary of State whether to serve a deportation notice on the detained person; or
- pending a decision whether the detained person should be charged with an offence;
- pending the result of an examination or analysis of any relevant evidence or an examination or analysis of anything that may result in relevant evidence being obtained. An examination or analysis would include a DNA test.

In all cases the review officer must be satisfied that the matter is being dealt with diligently and expeditiously. Where the detained person's rights to a solicitor have been withheld or he/she is being held *incommunicado* at the time of the review, the review officer must consider whether the reason or reasons for which the delay was authorised continue to exist. If in his/her opinion the reason or reasons no longer exist, he/she must inform the officer who authorised the delay of his/her opinion. When recording the grounds for the review the officer must also include his/her conclusion on whether there is a continuing need to withhold the detained person's rights.

In cases where the person is detained under the Terrorism Act 2000 and the review officer does not authorise continued detention, the person does not have to be released if an application for a warrant for further detention is going to be applied for or if an application has been made and the result is pending (s. 41 and sch. 8).

The Prevention of Terrorism Act 2005 allows a control order to be served against an individual that imposes obligations on him/her for purposes connected with protecting members of the public from a risk of terrorism. Section 5 of the 2005 Act allows a constable to arrest a person to ensure that the order can be served on that person. Section 5(2) requires the constable who has arrested an individual to take him/her to the designated place (which are the same as the Terrorism Act 2000) that the constable considers most appropriate as soon as practicable after the arrest.

An individual taken to a designated place under this section may be detained there until the end of 48 hours from the time of his arrest unless:

- he/she has become bound by a derogating control order made against him/her on the Secretary of State's application; or
- the court has dismissed the application.

If the court considers that it is necessary to do so to ensure that the individual in question is available to be given notice of any derogating control order that is made against him, it may, during the 48 hours following his arrest, extend the period for which the individual may be detained under this section by a period of no more than 48 hours (Prevention of Terrorism Act 2005, s. 5).

2.11.8 **Cautioning, Reprimands and Final Warnings, and Conditional Cautioning**

2.11.8.1 **Police Caution**

There are occasions where a person for whom there is sufficient evidence to charge may be cautioned as an alternative method of disposing with the case. *R v Chief Constable of Lancashire Constabulary, ex parte Atkinson* (1998) 162 JP 275 is a case which considered the level of evidence required before a caution can be considered. There the court said that, provided it was clear that there had been an admission of guilt, it was not necessary, for the purposes of administering a caution, to show that the admission had been obtained in circumstances which satisfied the Codes of Practice. That was not to say that police authorities would not be well advised to take precautions which would satisfy the Code, but it did not follow that in every case there had to be a formal interview. However, police officers would be well advised to take precautions that would satisfy Code C. It would be both fairer and more reliable for a formal interview to take place.

Before making a case disposal decision it is essential that the matter has been fully investigated in order to reach an informed decision. In *Omar* v *Chief Constable of Bedfordshire Constabulary* [2002] EWHC 3060, the Divisional Court quashed a caution that had been administered in order to allow a prosecution to be pursued. The court held that a number of reasonable lines of enquiry had not been made, for instance, the police had failed to take a statement from the victim's friend or obtained CCTV that was available or fully investigated the victim's injuries. Further, that the length of time in custody (17 hours) should not have been a relevant consideration and that the suspect's admission was ambiguous. Therefore it was in the public interest that a decision to caution rather than to change should not prevent the subsequent pursuit of the prosecution of the offender.

While there is no general obligation on the police to disclose material prior to charge, there may be a need to make some disclosure to a suspect's legal representative in order that he/she can advise on whether a caution should be accepted (*DPP* v *Ara* [2001] 4 All ER 559). In *Ara*, the suspect had been interviewed without a legal representative being present but the officers refused to disclose the terms of the interview.

Guidance as to the use of cautioning is provided by Home Office Circular 18/94, *The Cautioning of Offenders*. The guidelines should be considered carefully in all cases as any decision can be challenged by judicial review (**see para. 2.2.5.7**).

In cases where the case has been referred to the Crown Prosecution Service (CPS) under s. 37B of the 1984 Act and a decision has been made that the suspect should receive a caution, an officer involved in the investigation of the offence will be informed in writing. The notification will include the offence in respect of which a caution should be administered. If it is not possible to give the suspect such a caution then they must be charged with the offence (s. 37B(7)).

2.11.8.2 Reprimands and Warnings

Sections 65 and 66 of the Crime and Disorder Act 1998 made provisions for reprimands and warnings for children and young persons (**see chapter 2.6**) which the custody officer must take into account as alternatives to prosecution.

There is only one exception to the rule that reprimands and warnings replace cautions, and that is in respect of prostitutes' cautions. This approach to dealing with child prostitutes recognises that they are victims of abuse, and do not consent freely to prostitution. Joint guidance issued by the Home Office and the Department of Health sets out the appropriate way to deal with children in prostitution. That treatment aims to divert children away from prostitution, rather than to prosecute them (**see Crime, chapter 1.9**).

2.11.8.3 Conditional Cautioning

Sections 22 to 27 of the Criminal Justice Act 2003 introduced conditional cautioning, its aim being to deal with offenders without the involvement of the usual court processes.

2.11.9 **Charging**

2.11.9.1 **The Decision to Charge or Not**

Section 37 of the Police and Criminal Evidence Act 1984 states:

(1) Where—
  (a) a person is arrested for an offence—
    (i) without a warrant; or
    (ii) under a warrant not endorsed for bail, or
  (b) repealed,
  the custody officer at each police station where he is detained after his arrest shall determine whether he has before him sufficient evidence to charge that person with the offence for which he was arrested and may detain him at the police station for such period as is necessary to enable him to do so.
(2) If the custody officer determines that he does not have such evidence before him, the person arrested shall be released either on bail or without bail, unless the custody officer has reasonable grounds for believing that his detention without being charged is necessary to secure or preserve evidence relating to an offence for which he is under arrest or to obtain such evidence by questioning him.
  . . .
(7) Subject to section 41(7) below [expiry of 24 hours after the relevant time], if the custody officer determines that he has before him sufficient evidence to charge the person arrested with the offence for which he was arrested, the person arrested—
  (a) shall be—
    (i) released without charge and on bail, or
    (ii) kept in police detention,
    for the purpose of enabling the Director of Public Prosecutions to make a decision under section 37B below,
  (b) shall be released without charge and on bail but not for that purpose,
  (c) shall be released without charge and without bail, or
  (d) shall be charged.
(7A) The decision as to how a person is to be dealt with under subsection (7) above shall be that of the custody officer.
(7B) Where a person is released under subsection (7)(a) above, it shall be the duty of the custody officer to inform him that he is being released to enable the Director of Public Prosecutions to make a decision under section 37B below.
(8) Where—
  (a) a person is released under subsection (7)(b) or (c) above; and
  (b) at the time of his release a decision whether he should be prosecuted for the offence for which he was arrested has not been taken,
  it shall be the duty of the custody officer so to inform him.

Section 37A of the Police and Criminal Evidence Act 1984 states:

(1) The Director of Public Prosecutions may issue guidance—
  (a) for the purpose of enabling custody officers to decide how persons should be dealt with under section 37(7) above or 37(C)(2) below, and
  (b) as to the information to be sent to the Director of Public Prosecutions under section 37B(1) below.
  . . .
(3) Custody officers are to have regard to guidance under this section in deciding how persons should be dealt with under section 37(7) above or 37(C)(2) below.

The custody officer must decide whether there is sufficient evidence to charge a person when he/she is first brought to the police station (s. 37(1) of the 1984 Act) and when an officer in charge of the investigation informs the custody officer that he/she considers there is sufficient evidence to provide a realistic prospect of the detainee's conviction (Code C, para. 16.1). Unless officers are still investigating other offences for which the person is in police detention, s. 37(7) requires the custody officer to review the evidence in order to determine whether there is sufficient evidence to charge the detained person. When a person is arrested under the provisions of the Criminal Justice Act 2003 which allow a person to be retried after being acquitted of a serious offence (**see appendix 2.1**), provided a further prosecution has not been precluded by the Court of Appeal, an officer of the rank of superintendent or above who has not been directly involved in the investigation is responsible for determining whether the evidence is sufficient to charge (Code C, Note 16AA). If the custody officer decides that there is sufficient evidence to charge the detained person then that person must be charged or, if not charged, released in relation to that matter, in any of the following ways:

- without charge on bail for the purpose of enabling the Director of Public Prosecutions to make a decision under s. 37B (in this case the custody officer must inform the person that he/she is being released to enable the DPP to make a decision as to case disposal);
- without charge on bail but not for the case to be referred to the DPP; or
- without charge and without bail (in either of these last two bullet points if at the time of their release a decision whether they should be prosecuted has not been made it shall be the duty of the custody officer to inform the detained person of this).

Once the custody officer has determined that there is sufficient evidence to charge the detained person (this decision may be taken in consultation with the CPS), he/she can detain that detainee for no longer than is reasonably necessary to decide how that person is to be dealt with, otherwise it is likely that further detention will be unlawful. The detained person must then be released within a reasonable time (Code C, Note 16AB) unless the person is to be charged and bail refused (or they are wanted for another offence).

Under s. 37(A)(1) guidance has been issued to enable custody officers to decide whether there is sufficient evidence to charge, this Guidance is contained in the Code for Crown Prosecutors. Custody officers must comply with the Guidance of the DPP in deciding how a person should be dealt with under s. 37(7) as amended. The DPP has set out a list of those offences that require consultation with the CPS before charge, these are listed in Table A, below. Therefore those cases where there is a possibility that the person will be charged and kept in custody for court must be referred to the CPS prosecutor as soon as reasonably practicable; an out-of-hours CPS advice service will be available through the 'CPS Direct' telephone service.

Charging decisions in cases will be made following a review of evidence and in accordance with the Code for Crown Prosecutors. This requires that the custody officer or Crown Prosecutor making the decision is satisfied that there is enough evidence for there to be a realistic prospect of conviction and that it is in the public interest to prosecute (Full Code Test). In order to allow the matter to have full consideration, often the time needed to consider the matter will require the detained person to be bailed. However, there will clearly be occasions where it will not be desirable to bail the detained person but the evidence required to permit the Full Code Test to be applied is not available. In such a case the Threshold Test should be applied, which requires there to be reasonable suspicion that the suspect has committed an offence and it is in the public interest to charge that suspect. The evidential considerations include:

- the evidence available at the time;
- the likelihood and nature of further evidence being obtained;

Table A

Column A Police may decide on charge:	Column B Prosecutors must decide on charge:
All cases suitable for early disposal as a guilty plea in the magistrates' court. But not: • wounding or GBH—s. 20 of the Offences Against the Person Act 1861; • assault—s. 47 of the Offences Against the Person Act 1861 (ABH); • violent disorder—s. 2 of the Public Order Act 1986; • affray—s. 3 Public Order Act 1986; • handling stolen goods—s. 22 of the Theft Act 1968. **The police may also charge (whether an early guilty plea case or not):** • offences contrary to the Bail Act 1976; • offences contrary to s. 5 of the Public Order Act 1986; • Town Police Clauses Act 1847; • Metropolitan Police Act 1839; • Vagrancy Act 1824; • Street Offences Act 1959; • s. 91 of the Criminal Justice Act 1967; • s. 12 of the Licensing Act 1872; • any offence under any bye-law or any summary offence punishable on conviction with a term of imprisonment of three months or less. **All motoring cases EXCEPT:** • cases involving a death; • allegations of dangerous driving; • allegations of driving while disqualified where there has been no admission in a PACE interview to both driving and the disqualification; • offences of being in charge of a motor vehicle while unfit where the statutory defence may be raised; • allegations of the unlawful taking or aggravated taking of a motor vehicle (unless suitable for early disposal as a guilty plea in the magistrates' court).	• Any offence requiring the consent of the Attorney-General, Solicitor-General or Director of Public Prosecutions. • All offences triable on indictment only. • Any either way offence triable only on indictment due to the surrounding circumstances of the commission of the offence or the previous convictions of the person. • Offences under the Terrorism Act 2000 or Prevention of Terrorism Act 2005. • Offences under the Anti-terrorism, Crime and Security Act 2001. • Offences under the Explosive Substances Act 1883. • Offences under any of the Official Secrets Acts. • Any other offence linked with terrorist activity. • Any offence involving any racial, religious or homophobic aggravation. • Any offence classified as domestic violence. • Any offences under the Sexual Offences Act 2003 committed by or upon any person under the age of 18. • Offences involving persistent young offenders, unless chargeable by the police under para. 3.3. • Offences arising directly or indirectly out of activities associated with hunting wild mammals, whether constituting an offence under the Hunting Act 2004, or any other legislation. • Any either way offence not suitable for early disposal in the magistrates' court as a guilty plea (i.e. all contested Crown Court and magistrates' court cases initially listed for an early administrative hearing). • Those cases suitable for early disposal as a guilty plea in the magistrates' court but excluded from police charging. • Those motoring cases excluded from police charging. • Any summary offence not referred to under column A.

- the reasonableness for believing that evidence will become available;
- the time it will take to gather that evidence and the steps being taken to do so;
- the impact the expected evidence will have on the case;
- the charges that the evidence will support.

For the public interest factors to be considered see the Code of Practice for Crown Prosecutors, para. 5.9.

Where a decision is made to charge this will need to be reviewed when further evidence is available using the Full Code test.

It is the custody officer's responsibility to ensure that there is sufficient evidence to charge the person, albeit directions may be given as to case disposal by the CPS.

Where a detained person is not in a fit state to be charged or released in accordance with s. 34(7) (for instance because he/she is drunk), he/she may be kept in custody until fit (but medical care may have to be considered). (See also the provisions relating to drunk drivers in **Road Policing, chapter 3.5.**)

2.11.9.2   Cases where the Detained Person is Bailed to Allow Consultation with the CPS

Section 37B of the Police and Criminal Evidence Act 1984 states:

(1) Where a person is released on bail under section 37(7)(a) above, an officer involved in the investigation of the offence shall, as soon as is practicable, send to the Director of Public Prosecutions such information as may be specified in guidance under section 37A above.

(2) The Director of Public Prosecutions shall decide whether there is sufficient evidence to charge the person with an offence.

(3) If he decides that there is sufficient evidence to charge the person with an offence, he shall decide—

    (a) whether or not the person should be charged and, if so, the offence with which he should be charged, and

    (b) whether or not the person should be given a caution and, if so, the offence in respect of which he should be given a caution.

(4) The Director of Public Prosecutions shall give written notice of his decision to an officer involved in the investigation of the offence.

(5) If his decision is—

    (a) that there is not sufficient evidence to charge the person with an offence, or

    (b) that there is sufficient evidence to charge the person with an offence but that the person should not be charged with an offence or given a caution in respect of an offence,

    a custody officer shall give the person notice in writing that he is not to be prosecuted.

Where a person has been bailed under s. 37(7)(a) with or without bail conditions, the CPS must be consulted in order to determine what case disposal decision will be made (this may itself require further inquiries to gather further evidence). This referral should be made using forms MG3 (Report to Crown Prosecutor for a Charging Decision), and MG3A (Further Report to Crown Prosecutor for a Charging Decision). The pre-charge advice file can be a pre-charge expedited report (straight forward and guilty plea cases) or a pre-charge evidential report (contested/Crown Court cases) and must also include other relevant information including:

Pre-charge Expedited Report

- MG3
- MG11(s)—Witness statement or Index notes (if offence is witnessed by more than one officer and up to four, use the statement of one officer and summarise the others)
- MG15—Record of interview

- Phoenix print of suspect(s)' previous convictions/cautions/reprimands/final warnings. If there is any other information that may be relevant, include it on form MG6—Case File Information.

Pre-charge Evidential Report

- MG3
- MG5—Case summary (unless the statements cover all elements of the case)
- MG6—Case file information
- MG11—Key witness statement(s), or Index notes (if offence is witnessed by police use the statement of one officer and summarise the others)
- MG12—Exhibit list
- MG15—Interview record
- Crime Report and Incident Log
- Unused material likely to undermine the case
- Copies of key documentary exhibits
- Phoenix print of suspect(s) pre-cons/cautions/reprimands/final warnings.

The Prosecutor will decide whether there is sufficient evidence to charge or caution the person and shall give written notice of the decision to an officer involved in the investigation of the details of the offence. This decision must be followed (s. 37B(6)) if the decision was for the person to be cautioned (this includes conditional cautions) and if the person refuses or for some other reason a caution cannot be given they must be charged with the offence (s. 37B(7)).

In cases where the prosecutor decides that there is not sufficient evidence to charge the person with an offence, or that there is sufficient evidence to charge the person with an offence but that the person should not be charged with an offence or given a caution in respect of an offence, the custody officer must inform the person in writing of the decision. Similarly the person must be informed of those cases where there is insufficient evidence to charge them but if further evidence or information comes to light in the future the case may be reconsidered under the Code for Crown Prosecutors.

In cases where further time is needed to obtain evidence or for the prosecutor to make a case disposal decision, the person can be further bailed. In these cases the custody officer must give the person notice in writing. This does not affect any bail conditions that were included when the detained person was bailed (s. 37D(1) to (3)).

2.11.9.3   Bail to Allow Referral to the CPS

Section 47 of the Police and Criminal Evidence Act 1984 states:

> (1A) The normal powers to impose conditions of bail shall be available to him where a custody officer releases a person on bail under section 37(7)(a) above or section 38(1) above (including that subsection as applied by section 40(10) above) but not in any other cases. In this subsection, 'the normal powers to impose conditions of bail' has the meaning given in section 3(6) of the Bail Act 1976.

Where the person is bailed after charge or bailed without charge and on bail for the purpose of enabling the CPS to make a decision regarding case disposal, the custody officer may impose conditions on that bail (**see para. 2.4.7**) In cases where a person is bailed without being charged under s. 37(7)(b) or (c), the custody officer cannot impose conditions on that bail (s. 47(1A)).

2.11.9.4 Charging the Detained Person

If a decision is taken to charge the detained person, Code C, para. 16 sets out the procedures to be followed by the custody officer. When a detained person is charged with or informed that he/she may be prosecuted for an offence, para. 16.2 requires him/her to be cautioned. The caution varies slightly from that when arrested or interviewed (**see General Police Duties, chapter 4.4**) and is as follows:

> You do not have to say anything. But it may harm your defence if you do not mention now something which you later rely on in court. Anything you do say may be given in evidence.

The above caution should not be used in circumstances where the detained person has been denied access to a solicitor (**see para. 2.13.4**) in which case the following cautions should be used:

> You do not have to say anything, but anything you do say may be given in evidence.

At the time a person is charged, he/she shall be given a written notice as set out in Code C, para. 16.3 and a record shall be made of anything the person says when charged (para. 16.8). Where the person being charged is a juvenile or is mentally disordered or mentally vulnerable, the appropriate adult should be present and the notice given to him/her (paras 16.3 and 16.6).

Once the person has been charged with or informed that he/she may be prosecuted for an offence, fingerprints can be taken if it is a recordable offence and he/she has not had his/her fingerprints taken during the course of the investigation (s. 61(3) unless the fingerprints previously taken do not constitute a complete set or they are not of sufficient quality to allow satisfactory analysis, comparison or matching (s. 61(3A)) (**see chapter 2.12**). Photographs may also be taken and in some cases DNA samples may be taken (**see para. 2.12.7**).

If fingerprints are taken, the person must be informed of the reason why and that those prints may be used for a speculative search concerning other crimes (**see para. 2.12.5**). The reasons should also be recorded in the custody record, along with confirmation that the detained person has been given the required information. If the person's photograph is taken, this should also be recorded in the custody record.

Once a person has been charged or informed that he/she may be prosecuted for an offence (which does not include the service of the Notice of Intended Prosecution under ss. 1 and 2 of the Road Traffic Offenders Act 1988; **see Road Policing, chapter 3.3**), generally the person cannot be questioned or spoken to about the matter. Code C, paras 16.4 and 16.5 set out occasions where further investigation involving the person may be allowed and para. 16.9 sets out the procedure to be adopted. It should only be in these circumstances that the custody officer allows any further inquiries involving the detained person to be made. Paragraphs 16.4 and 16.5 deal with:

- written statements made by other people which the investigating officers may wish to show to another person charged;
- questions necessary for the purpose of preventing or minimising harm or loss to some other person or to the public or for clearing up an ambiguity in a previous answer or statement;
- where it is in the interests of justice that the person should have put to him/her—and have an opportunity to comment on—information concerning the offence which has come to light since he/she was charged or informed that he/she might be prosecuted.

2.11.10 Bail After Charge

If the person is charged then the custody officer has to decide whether the person is going to be bailed to appear at court or whether bail will be refused and the person kept in custody until the next available court. This is a review of the person's detention and therefore the person or his/her solicitor should be given an opportunity to make representations to the custody officer. The review should be conducted with regard to Code C, paras 15.1, 15.3 to 15.7.

Where bail has been refused this decision must be reviewed by the custody officer within nine hours of the last review (the first being the post-charge review). These reviews must continue until the person is taken to court in the same manner required by a review officer.

In addition to the grounds for refusing bail covered in **chapter 2.4**, the custody officer may also detain the person after charge if he/she has reasonable grounds for believing that the detention of the person is necessary to enable a sample to be taken from him/her under s. 63B of the Police and Criminal Evidence Act 1984 (**see para. 2.11.15**). The custody officer may authorise a person to be kept in police detention for a period not exceeding six hours beginning when the person was charged with the offence.

For occassions where the custody officer refuses bail of a juvenile after charge, see Code C, para. 16.7.

For a full discussion of bail, **see chapter 2.4**.

In *Williamson* v *Chief Constable of West Midlands* [2004] 1 WLR 14, the Court of Appeal clarified the point that breach of the peace is not a criminal offence. Consequently, as there is no power in the Bail Act 1976 to grant bail except in criminal proceedings, no power exists to grant bail for breach of the peace. This means that if the person is bailed, there is no power to arrest the person or obtain a warrant for his/her failure to appear at court under the Bail Act 1976.

2.11.11 Custody Officer's Checklist

The following provides a guide to be followed when a person is brought to the police station. The PACE Code of Practice, Code C applies throughout and custody officers should be conversant with its contents.

Throughout the period of detention of a person there are occasions where information must be given to that person. The Codes do allow these requirements to be delayed in certain circumstances, i.e. the detained person is violent or likely to become violent, or is incapable of understanding what is being said or is in need of urgent medical attention (Code C, para. 1.8). If the detained person is not informed at the time, he/she must be informed as soon as practicable. Where the person is incapable of understanding what is being said because of a language or hearing barrier, action must be taken to obtain an interpreter so that the information can be relayed to the detained person (Code C, para. 3.12).

2.11.11.1 Initial Action when Commencing Custody Officer's Duties

- Ensure a poster as set out in Code C, para. 6.3 and Note 6H is displayed in the charging area and copies of the Codes of Practice are readily available (para. 1.2).
- Ensure cells that might be used comply with paras 8.2 and 8.4.
- Ensure that suitable blankets etc. will be available (para. 8.3).

- If video cameras are installed in the custody areas, notices of such cameras must be prominently displayed showing cameras are in use (para. 3.11). (Any request to turn the cameras off shall be refused.) Any audio or video recording made in the custody area does not form part of the custody record (para. 2.1).

2.11.11.2 On Arrival of the Arrested Person (Including People Transferred from Other Police Stations)

- Begin custody record even if detention is not authorised (para. 2.1).
- Inform the arrested person of his/her rights (para. 3.1).
- If an appropriate adult is present or required, follow the guidance in paras 3.15 and 3.17.
- Provide the detained person with a written notice setting out his/her rights (para. 3.2 and Note 3A).
- Ask the person to sign the custody record to acknowledge receipt of the notice or note refusal to sign in the custody record (para. 3.2).
- Undertake a risk assessment for the detainee (para. 3.6).

When making records concerning a detained person, all entries must be made in the custody record unless otherwise specified (para. 2.1). Action taken by a person must be noted in the custody record with the person's name and rank, except for officers dealing with persons detained under the Terrorism Act 2000 (para. 2.2) or where para. 2.6A applies.

2.11.11.3 Risk Assessments

The Custody Officer is responsible for initiating a risk assessment to consider whether the detainee is likely to present specific risks to custody staff or themselves (Code C, para. 3.6). Although the risk assessment is the responsibility of the custody officer, he/she may need to consult with others such as the arresting officer or an appropriate health care professional. The risk assessment, which includes a check on the Police National Computer, should be carried out as soon as practicable and reasons for delaying the initiation or completion of the assessment must be recorded. (Code C, para. 3.6). This process is ongoing and further assessments must be undertaken if circumstances change (Code C, paras 3.9 and 3.10). The risk assessment must follow a structured process which clearly defines the categories of risk to be considered, guidance is given in Home Office Circular 32/2000, Annex A Detainee Risk Assessment and Revised Prisoner Escort (PER) Form. The result of the risk assessment must be included within the custody record and the custody officer is responsible for making sure that those responsible for the detainee's custody are appropriately briefed about the risks (Code C, para. 3.8). The custody officer is also responsible for ensuring action is taken to minimise any risks that are identified (Code C, para. 3.9). For this reason it is suggested that the risk assessment should be completed prior to the detainee being placed in a cell or detention room.

Where the custody officer consults an appropriate health care professional and he/she has any doubts or is in any way uncertain about any aspect of the clinical directions given, he/she must ask for clarification. It is particularly important that directions concerning the frequency of visits are clear, precise and capable of being implemented (Code C, para. 9.14).

2.11.11.4 Special Groups

- If the person is deaf or there is doubt over his/her hearing or speaking ability or ability to understand English refer to para. 3.12 Code C. The custody officer, or any other interviewing officer, must ensure that there is a proper mutual understanding between the detained person and the interpreter (or interpreters, if it is necessary to have more than one interpreter to allow the detained person to understand and be understood) (*R* v *West London Youth Court, ex parte J* [2000] 1 All ER 823).

- If the person is blind or seriously visually impaired or is unable to read, refer to para. 3.20.
- If the detained person could be a juvenile (para. 1.5), obtain the services of an appropriate adult.
- If the person is mentally disordered or vunerable (for people that fall in to this group, see Note 1G), obtain the services of an appropriate adult.

2.11.11.5 Decision to Authorise Detention

(See also para. 2.11.6.10)

- Arresting officer to give the reasons of arrest (in the presence of the arrested person) (Code C, para. 3.4).
- Record the offence(s) that the detainee has been arrested for and the reason(s) for the arrest on the custody record. (para. 3.4).
- If the custody officer authorises a person's detention, the detainee must be informed of the grounds as soon as practicable and before they are questioned about any offence.
- Note any comment made by the detained person (para. 3.4). If detention is authorised, record the reasons in the custody record and inform the detained person of the decision (paras 3.4 and 3.23). (If the detained person is violent, likely to become violent or incapable of understanding what is being said (but if due to hearing/language barriers consider para. 3.12), or is in need of urgent medical attention he/she *must* be informed as soon as practicable (para. 1.8 and s. 37(6) of the 1984 Act).)

If the person has already been in custody for the offence for which he/she has been arrested and a new detention clock has not started, it will be necessary to confirm that the person still has time left within his/her 'detention period'. (The review clock is also relevant in terms of when the next review is due.)

2.11.11.6 Ascertain whether Detained Person requires Legal Advice

- Ask the detained person if he/she wants legal advice (para. 3.5) and point out that legal advice is free (para. 6.1).
- Ask the detained person to sign the custody record to indicate whether he/she requires legal advice and ensure he/she signs it in the right place (para. 3.5).
- If legal advice is requested it must be given unless Annex B to Code C applies or delay would hinder the investigation (para. 6.6). If any delay occurs, record the reason (para. 1.1A).
- If delay is not authorised, the custody officer must act without delay to secure the provision of legal advice (para. 6.5).
- If the offer of legal advice is declined, point out the right to speak to a solicitor on the phone (para. 6.5).
- If legal advice is still declined, ask the detained person for reasons why and record any reasons given in the custody record (if during interview this can be recorded in the interview record) (para. 6.5). Once it is clear that the detained person does not wish

to have any contact with a legal adviser, the custody officer should cease to ask why (para. 6.5).

When complying with the need to provide legal advice the following should be considered:

- For the treatment of the detained person who is to be interviewed or continue to be interviewed once he/she has requested legal advice, see para. 6.6.
- Remember that this is a continuing right that can be exercised at any time during police detention (para. 6.1).
- Note 6B provides guidance on how much choice the detained person has in choosing a solicitor.
- For those persons who can provide legal advice under the Codes of Practice, see para. 6.12. Refer to paras 6.12A to 6.14 if refusing an adviser access.
- If a solicitor arrives to provide legal advice, inform the detained person unless Annex B applies (para. 6.15).
- If the detained person cannot understand the solicitor because of a language barrier or hearing or speech difficulties refer to para. 13.9 (people who can act as interpreters).
- Consultation with a solicitor must be in private (para. 6.1) with the exception of those detained on terrorism charges. See Note 6J.

2.11.11.7 Right to Inform Third Party

In addition to a request to have someone informed, the following action must be taken:

- Contact must be made with a juvenile's appropriate adult (para. 3.13).
- For detained persons who are citizens of independent commonwealth countries or foreign nationals, see paras 7.1 to 7.5.

Ascertain whether the detained person wants a third party informed of his/her detention. Should the detained person at any stage request that a person be informed of his/her arrest, consider whether this right should be delayed. This right can only be delayed in circumstances outlined in Annex B to Code C, otherwise paras 5.1 to 5.3 and 5.8 must be followed. If the detained person has no one to contact, see Note 5C for guidance.

The detained person has the right to send letters and make phone calls (paras 5.6 to 5.8) but this can be delayed or denied (para. 5.6).

If a person inquires about a detained person, refer to para. 5.5 and Note 5D. Consideration should also be given to the Data Protection Act 1998 when information is being given to third parties.

Visits are covered by para. 5.4 and Note 5B.

2.11.11.8 Searching

The proper searching of a detained person is very important, particularly with the introduction of the Human Rights Act 1998. It may lead to the discovery of new evidence, it may also avoid people being injured or even escaping from police detention. The law governing the searching of people on arrest and searches under warrant is discussed elsewhere (**see General Police Duties, chapter 4.4**).

Section 54 of the Police and Criminal Evidence Act 1984 details the duties and powers relating to the searching of detained persons:

(1) The custody officer at a police station shall ascertain everything which a person has with him when he is—

    (a) brought to the station after being arrested elsewhere or after being committed to custody by an order or sentence of a court; or

    (b) arrested at the station or detained there, as a person falling within section 34(7), under section 37 above.

(2) The custody officer may record or cause to be recorded all or any of the things which he ascertains under subsection (1).

(2A) In the case of an arrested person, any such record may be made as part of his custody record.

(3) Subject to subsection (4) below, a custody officer may seize and retain any such thing or cause any such thing to be seized and retained.

(4) Clothes and personal effects may only be seized if the custody officer—

    (a) believes that the person from whom they are seized may use them—

        (i) to cause physical injury to himself or any other person;

        (ii) to damage property;

        (iii) to interfere with evidence; or

        (iv) to assist him to escape; or

    (b) has reasonable grounds for believing that they may be evidence relating to an offence.

(5) Where anything is seized, the person from whom it is seized shall be told the reason for the seizure unless he is—

    (a) violent or likely to become violent; or

    (b) incapable of understanding what is said to him.

(6) Subject to subsection (7) below, a person maybe searched if the custody officer considers it necessary to enable him to carry out his duty under subsection (1) above and to the extent that the custody officer considers necessary for that purpose.

(6A) A person who is in custody at a police station or is in police detention otherwise than at a police station may at any time be searched in order to ascertain whether he has with him anything which he could use for any of the purposes specified in subsection(4)(a) above.

(6B) Subject to subsection (6C) below, a constable may seize and retain, or cause to be seized and retained, anything found on such a search.

(6C) A constable may only seize clothes and personal effects in the circumstances specified in subsection (4) above.

(7) An intimate search may not be conducted under this section.

(8) A search under this section shall be carried out by a constable.

(9) The constable carrying out a search shall be of the same sex as the person searched.

KEYNOTE

Section 54 places a duty on a custody officer to ascertain what property a person has with him/her when:

- arrested and brought to the station;
- committed to police custody by order or sentence of the court;
- arrested at the station;
- detained after surrendering to bail;
- arrested after failing to surrender to bail.

The custody officer must also consider what property the detained person might have in his/her possession for an unlawful or harmful purpose while in custody. The safekeeping of any property taken from the detained person and kept at the police station, is the responsibility of the custody officer.

The Criminal Justice Act 2003 has amended s. 54 of the 1984 Act in that it removes the requirement on the custody officer to record everything a detained person has with him/her. The custody officer will have a discretion as to the nature and detail of any recording and there is no longer any requirement for this to be recorded in the custody record. However, custody officers should be mindful of any force instructions as to what will need to be recorded and where. It is suggested that it will still be necessary to make records, not least to ensure against claims that property has been mishandled or removed. However, it will now be open to the custody officer to make judgements about how to balance the need for recording against the amount of administrative work involved.

2.11.11.9 The Search

While the custody officer has a duty to ascertain what property a person has with them (often by means of searching the person), there is also a need to consider the rights of that detained person. The custody officer may authorise a constable to search a detained person, or may search the detained person themselves in order to ascertain what property the detained person has with them (s. 54(6)). It should be noted that the custody officer must first authorise any search and the extent of the search; officers should not search a person until this authority has been given. Therefore the custody officer may only authorise a search to the extent that he/she considers necessary to comply with this duty. In order to safeguard the rights of the detained person there are three levels to which searches can be conducted:

- searches that do not involve the removal of more than the detained person's outer clothing (this includes shoes and socks (Code C, Annex A, para. 9));
- strip searches;
- intimate searches.

Each of these is examined below.

If the detained person is not going to be placed in a cell and is only going to be kept in detention for a short period, the custody officer has the option not to search (Code C, Note 4A). If no search is conducted the custody record should be endorsed 'not searched'. Under health and safety it may be appropriate for the custody officer to complete a risk assessment in order to consider whether to search the detained person and balance the risk of injury to staff—this is likely to form part of the risk assessment required by Code C, para. 3.6. The duty to ascertain what property a person has with them is a continuing duty and therefore the custody officer can have the person searched at a later time if he/she feels it is necessary to comply with his/her responsibility under the 1984 Act or the Codes.

The extent of the search is determined by the custody officer on the basis of what he/she honestly believes is necessary in order to comply with the above duties. Both the decision to search the detained person and the extent of the search must be decided on the facts of the case in question. It may be important to consider cultural issues that might affect the detained person, for instance would it be necessary and justifiable to search a Sikh's turban? Force standing orders are not an automatic right to search all detained persons (*Brazil* v *Chief Constable of Surrey* [1983] Crim LR 483). A custody officer can authorise a strip search but an intimate search can only be authorised by an officer of the rank of inspector or above (see below).

2.11.11.10 Searches that do not involve the Removal of More than the Detained Person's Outer Clothing

In effect this is any search that does not become a strip search or an intimate search. This type of search applies to almost every person coming before the custody officer unless Code

C, Note 4A applies. Typically this will involve emptying out all items that are in the person's pockets, removing jewellery and the searching of other areas that can be conducted without the need to remove more than outer garments such as coats and possibly items such as jumpers. This type of authorisation would also lend itself to a 'pat down' of the detained person. If there is any doubt as to whether the search goes beyond one that falls into this category, it is suggested that it should be treated as a strip search. Where metal detectors are used in custody suites an indication from the device may give the grounds for authorising a strip search.

2.11.11.11 Strip Searches

Strip searches are dealt with in Code C, Annex A, paras 9 to 12. A strip search is a search involving the removal of more than outer clothing. Although a person's mouth may be examined during a strip search, the examination of any other body orifice would amount to an intimate search. It must be remembered that a strip search is the search of any part of a person that requires the removal of more than that person's outer clothing. Where the custody officer authorises a strip search this does not automatically mean a search of the whole person and it will be for the custody officer to decide what parts of the detained person need to be searched.

A strip search may take place only if the custody officer reasonably considers that the detained person might have concealed an article which he/she would not be allowed to keep, such as those items which the detained person may use to:

- cause harm to him/herself or others;
- damage property;
- effect an escape; or
- which might be evidence of an offence; *and*

that if such an item were found it would be necessary to remove it.

Reasons for the search, the extent of the authorised search, details of the people present and the results of the search must be recorded in the custody record (Annex A, para. 12). The search must be conducted in accordance with Annex A, para. 11. The custody officer may be required to justify why he/she considered that a strip search was necessary. It is suggested that 'I authorise a strip search in case the person may have a weapon hidden' would not be sufficient!

2.11.11.12 Intimate Searches

Intimate searches are dealt with in Code C, Annex A. An intimate search is a search which consists of the physical examination of a person's body orifices other than the mouth. Such searches can only be carried out in two circumstances and then only if they are authorised by an officer of the rank of inspector or above.

The circumstances mentioned above are that the authorising officer has reasonable grounds for believing:

- that an article which could cause physical injury to the detained person or others at the police station has been concealed; or
- that the detained person has concealed a Class A drug which he/she intended to supply to another or to export.

Not only must the authorising officer have reasonable grounds for believing that one or both of the above grounds are satisfied but he/she must also believe that an intimate search is the only means of removing an item. Where the search relates to a drug offence the detainee's appropriate consent must be given in writing and the detainee must be warned as to the risk of not giving consent as set out in Code C, Annex A, para. 2B and note A6. Code C, Annex A, para. 2A sets out what the detained person must be told before the search is carried out. Before authorising the search the authorising officer needs to consider Code C, Annex A, Notes A1 and A2. In determining who should conduct the search the authorising officer should be mindful of the guidance provided by Notes A3 to A5.

The custody officer must record which parts of the person's body were searched (Annex A, para. 7), the authorisation for the search, who carried out the search, who was present, the grounds for the search, why the item could not be removed by some other means and the result of the search. In addition for drug searches the record must also include the fact that a warning was given in relation to the person's failure to consent, the fact that the appropriate consent was given or (as the case may be) refused, and if refused, the reason given for the refusal (if any). If the search is carried out by a police officer, the reason why it was impracticable for a registered medical practitioner or registered nurse to conduct it must be recorded.

2.11.11.13   Drug Search—X-rays and Ultrasound Scans

Section 55A of the 1984 Act allows a detained person to have an X-ray taken of them or an ultrasound scan to be carried out on them (or both) if an officer of inspector rank or above who has reasonable grounds for believing that the detained person:

- may have swallowed a Class A drug; and
- was in possession of that Class A drug with the intention of supplying it to another or to export;

authorises that X-ray and/or ultrasound scan and the detained person's appropriate consent has been given in writing (Code C, Annex K, para. 1). Code C, Annex K, para. 2 outlines the requirements for obtaining the person's consent.

An X-ray may be taken, or an ultrasound scan may be carried out, only by a registered medical practitioner or registered nurse, and only at a hospital, surgery or other medical premises (Code C, Annex K, para. 4). Code C, Annex K, para. 5 sets out what documentation must be completed.

2.11.11.14   Conduct of a Search

The manner in which a search must be conducted is set out in Code C, paras 4.1 to 4.5. Some relevant practical matters are set out below:

- Before the search begins the detained person should be informed of the reasons for the search, unless it is impracticable to do so (*Brazil* v *Chief Constable of Surrey* [1983] Crim LR 483).
- The search must be conducted by an officer or designated detention officer (s. 54(8) of the 1984 Act) of the same sex (s. 54(9) and Code C, para. 4.1).
- Reasonable force may be used (s. 117 of the 1984 Act).
- The custody officer should specify the level of the search to be conducted and must be recorded in the person's record.
- Reference to Code A, para. 3.1 may be useful when considering how to conduct the search: 'Every reasonable effort must be made to minimise the embarrassment that a person being searched may experience.'

- For cases where the intimate search has been authorised to search for a concealed Class A drug which the detained person intended to supply to another or to export:
  - ◆ The search may only be carried out by a registered medical practitioner or registered nurse unless Code C, Annex A, paras 3 and 3A apply.
  - ◆ The search must take place at a hospital, surgery or other medical premises.
  - ◆ No person of the opposite sex who is not a medical practitioner or nurse should be present.
  - ◆ A minimum of two people, other than the person searched, must be present during the search.

2.11.11.15 What Property can be Retained?

Once a person has been searched and the custody officer has ascertained what property the detained person has with him/her, a decision must be made as to what property will be returned to the detained person and what property will be retained by the police.

The basic position is that, with the exception of articles subject to legal privilege, all property in the possession of a detained person may be retained by the police. However, in the case of clothing and personal items (as defined by Code C, para. 4.3), these may only be retained if the custody officer believes that the item(s) may be used by the detained person to:

- cause harm to him/herself or others;
- damage to property;
- effect an escape; or
- that they might be evidence of an offence (Code C, para. 4.2 and s. 54(4) of the 1984 Act).

Where personal items are retained by the custody officer, he/she must inform the person of the reasons why they have been retained.

It is suggested that the custody officer may authorise the seizure of an article of clothing under s. 54(4)(b) of the 1984 Act, where he/she has reasonable grounds for believing that such clothing may be evidence relating to an offence. For instance, if the detained person is wearing a pair of trainers of the same type as those which are reasonably believed to have made impressions at the scene of a recent burglary and the detained person has a burglary record then, unless the custody officer knows of other facts clearly putting the suspect at some other place at the time of the offence, he/she is plainly justified in having those shoes forensically examined. However, it is submitted that this does not authorise the custody officer to seize footwear on the off-chance that some officer or some other police force may have obtained impressions at a burglary site which might match the trainers of the detained person.

Where it is necessary to retain items of clothing that the detained person is wearing, replacement clothing of a reasonable standard of comfort and cleanliness must be provided (Code C, para. 8.5). What is 'reasonable' clothing will be a question of fact. At the time of writing there is no available case law on this point but the dignity of the person will be a consideration the court might take into account if the detained person's detention is alleged to have breached his/her 'human rights'. It is also important to make a record of any offer of replacement clothing (Code C, para. 8.9). It may be appropriate to collect the detained person's own clothes or arrange to have some delivered.

Where the person is searched and a record of his/her property is made, the detained person should be allowed to check the property list and be invited to sign the list as correct. If he/she declines, this should be recorded in the custody record (Code C, para. 4.4).

Unless the property has been seized and retained as evidence under s. 22 of the 1984 Act, it must be returned to the detained person on his/her release. If property has been seized from a third party in the course of the investigation the property can only be retained for so long as it is necessary in accordance with s. 22(1) of the 1984 Act, even if it might be needed for another matter it should be returned to the third party unless there was an additional power to seize the item (*Settelen* v *Metropolitan Police Commissioner* [2004] EWHC 2171 (Ch)). If property is rightfully seized but retained unnecessarily this would be unlawful and could lead to a claim for damages (*Martin* v *Chief Constable of Nottinghamshire*, 1 May 1998, unreported). The seizure of a person's property is also protected by the European Convention on Human Rights, First Protocol, Article 1, which states:

> Every natural or legal person is entitled to the peaceful enjoyment of his possessions. No one shall be deprived of his possessions except in the public interest and subject to the conditions provided for by law and by the general principles of international law....

If property is retained the reasons for this should be recorded.

(**See also General Police Duties, chapter 4.4.**)

2.11.11.16   Juveniles

Juveniles are provided with the additional safeguard of an appropriate adult to look out for their interests while in police detention. The Codes of Practice state that where a juvenile or a mentally disordered/mentally vunerable person is the subject of a strip search or an intimate search, in most cases, an appropriate adult must be present (Code C, Annex A, paras 5 and 11). The Codes do not make any mention of this requirement for an ordinary search and therefore searches other than strip and intimate searches may be conducted without an appropriate adult being present. Where an appropriate adult is required:

- the appropriate adult may be of the opposite sex if the detainee specifically requests it and the adult is readily available;
- where there is a risk of serious harm to the detained person or to others the search may be conducted without the appropriate adult being present;
- a search of a juvenile may take place in the absence of the appropriate adult only if the juvenile signifies in the presence of the appropriate adult that he/she prefers the search to be done in his/her absence and the appropriate adult agrees. In such cases a record shall be made of the juvenile's decision and signed by the appropriate adult.

2.11.11.17   Well-being of Detained Person

The custody officer should be mindful at all times for the well-being of the detained person. Code C, para. 12.2 provides a requirement for a detained person to have a rest period:

> Except as below, in any period of 24 hours a detainee must be allowed a continuous period of at least 8 hours for rest, free from questioning, travel or any interruption in connection with the investigation concerned. This period should normally be at night or other appropriate time which takes account of when the detainee last slept or rested. If a detainee is arrested at a police station after going there voluntarily, the period of 24 hours runs from the time of their arrest and not the time of arrival at the police station. The period may not be interrupted or delayed, except:
>
> (a) when there are reasonable grounds for believing not delaying or interrupting the period would:
>   (i) involve a risk of harm to people or serious loss of, or damage to, property;
>   (ii) delay unnecessarily the person's release from custody;
>   (iii) otherwise prejudice the outcome of the investigation;
> (b) at the request of the detainee, their appropriate adult or legal representative;

    (c) when a delay or interruption is necessary in order to:
      (i) comply with the legal obligations and duties arising under section 15;
      (ii) to take action required under section 9 or in accordance with medical advice.

If the period is interrupted in accordance with (a), a fresh period must be allowed. Interruptions under (b) and (c), do not require a fresh period to be allowed.

At least two light meals and one main meal shall be offered in any period of 24 hours. Drinks should be provided at meal times and upon reasonable request between meal times (Code C, para. 8.6). Meals should so far as practicable be offered at recognised meal times (Code C, Note 8B) but consider any religious variations.

Detainees should be visited at least every hour. If no reasonably foreseeable risk was identified in a risk assessment, there is no need to wake a sleeping detainee. Those suspected of being intoxicated through drink or drugs or having swallowed drugs or whose level of consciousness causes concern must, subject to any clinical directions given by the appropriate health care professional, be visited and roused at least every half hour. When rousing the detainee, the checklist provided at Code C, Annex H should be used and clinical treatment arranged if appropriate.

Brief outdoor exercise must be given if practicable (Code C, para. 8.7).

Under Article 2 of the European Convention on Human Rights the State is under a duty to provide a plausible explanation of events that lead to a death in police custody where the person had originally been detained in good health (*Velikova* v *Bulgaria*, application no. 41488/98 (27 April 2000)). This is another good reason why all events that affect the detained person are recorded in the custody record.

If a complaint is made by or on behalf of the detained person, or the person is treated improperly, follow Code C, para. 9.2.

2.11.11.18 Medical Care of the Detained Person

When must a Health Care Professional be Called?

A health care professional is defined by Code C, Note 9A. When arrangements are made to secure clinical attention for a detainee, the custody officer must make sure all relevant information which might assist in the detainee's treatment is made available to the responsible health care professional. Any officer or police staff with relevant information must inform the custody officer of that information as soon as practicable.

The custody officer should call an appropriate health care professional in any of the following circumstances:

- If a complaint is made by, or on behalf of, a detainee concerning a possible assault or the possibility of the unnecessary or unreasonable use of force (Code C, para. 9.2).
- The detainee:
  - ♦ appears to be suffering from physical illness; or
  - ♦ is injured; or
  - ♦ appears to be suffering from a mental disorder (see Code C, para. 9.5);
  - ♦ appears to need clinical attention (Code C, para. 9.5).
- If it appears to the custody officer, or they are told, that a person brought to a station under arrest may be suffering from an infectious disease or condition, then advice must be sought from an appropriate health care professional (Code C, para. 9.7).
- The detainee requests a clinical examination (Code C, para. 9.8).

- If a detainee is required to take or apply any medication in compliance with clinical directions prescribed before their detention, the custody officer must consult the appropriate health care professional before the use of the medication (Code C, para. 9.9).
- Where the custody officer would like the advice of an appropriate health care professional to decide whether the detainee is fit for interview (Code C, para. 12.3).

The police surgeon or, if appropriate, some other health care professional should also be called if needed to examine a detainee for the purposes of obtaining evidence relating to any offence in which the detainee is suspected of being involved (Code C, para. 9.1).

Code C, para. 9.5 does not apply to minor ailments or injuries which do not need attention. However, all such ailments or injuries must be recorded in the custody record and any doubt must be resolved in favour of calling the appropriate health care professional. If a safe and appropriate care plan for the detainee cannot be provided, the police surgeon's advice must be sought (Code C, para. 9.8).

Any information that is available about the detained person should be considered in deciding whether to request a medical examination. In *R v HM Coroner for Coventry, ex parte Chief Constable of Staffordshire Police* (2000) 164 JP 665 the detained person had been drunk on arrest and was detained to be interviewed. The detained person made no complaint of his condition but his sister called the police to advise them that he would get the shakes. It was clear at interview and the following morning that he did have the shakes but no complaint was made and no doctor was called. A verdict of accidental death aggravated by neglect was an option in the case as the deceased had died while in police custody. The court considered the facts, such as the deceased's withdrawal and the warning as to his condition, from which a properly directed jury could have concluded that had certain steps been taken it was at least possible that the deceased would not have died. In this case a verdict of accidental death aggravated by neglect was left open to the jury, even though a doctor at the inquest gave evidence that he doubted whether calling a doctor would have made any difference to the eventual outcome.

Medical Record forming Part of the Custody Record

A record must be made in the custody record of the injury, ailment, condition or other reason which made it necessary to call an appropriate health care professional. Once the detainee has been seen by the health care professional any clinical directions and advice, including any further clarifications, given to police by the health care professional concerning the care and treatment of the detainee must be recorded in the custody record (Code C, para. 9.15). This does not, however, require the health care professional to record his/her clinical findings in the custody record, provided information which is necessary to custody staff to ensure the effective ongoing care and well-being of the detainee is openly recorded in the custody record (Code C, para. 9.16).

A solicitor or appropriate adult must be permitted to consult a detainee's custody record as soon as practicable after their arrival at the station and at any other time while the person is detained (Code C, para. 2.4). Therefore details required to be included in the custody record concerning the detainee's injuries and ailments will be accessible to both the solicitor and appropriate adult. It is therefore important to bear in mind the guidance of Code C, Note 9E with regard to not disclosing any more information than is required to be recorded in the custody record. Note 9E states:

> It is important to respect a person's right to privacy and information about their health must be kept confidential and only disclosed with their consent or in accordance with clinical advice when it is necessary to protect the detainee's health or that of others who come into contact with them.

As the Codes specify matters which must be included within the custody record, it is suggested that all other matters recorded by the appropriate health care professional do not form part of the custody record and therefore do not need to be made available to the solicitor or appropriate adult under Code C, para. 2.4, i.e. the notes made by the health care professional.

2.11.11.19 Independent Custody Visiting (Lay Visitors)

Section 51 of the Police Reform Act 2002 introduced independent custody visitors on a statutory basis. The arrangements may confer on independent custody visitors such powers as the police authority considers necessary to enable them to carry out their functions under the arrangements and may, in particular, confer on them powers to:

- require access to be given to each police station;
- examine records relating to the detention of persons;
- meet detainees for the purposes of a discussion about their treatment and conditions while detained; and
- inspect the facilities including, in particular, cell accommodation, washing and toilet facilities and the facilities for the provision of food.

A Code of Practice and National Standards has been published outlining the role of the independent visitor (this can be found at www.icva.org.uk).

2.11.11.20 Other Events involving the Detained Person

- Where the detained person is delivered to the custody of another officer, the fact must be recorded and the reason why. Any refusal to hand over the detained person must also be recorded with the reasons why (para. 12.10).
- When handing over the custody of a detained person to another police officer, the custody officer ceases to have responsibility for ensuring that the detained person is treated in accordance with the Codes of Practice and the responsibility passes to the person to whom the detained person is handed (s. 39(2)). However, the custody officer is responsible for deciding whether the detainee should be handed over (Code C, para. 12.1).
- When the detained person is returned to the care of the custody officer, the person returning the detained person must report to the custody officer as to the manner in which the Codes of Practice have been complied with (s. 39(3)). This information must be recorded in the custody record along with any reported breaches of the Codes.
- If a police officer wishes to interview, or conduct inquiries which require the presence of a detained person, the custody officer is responsible for deciding whether to deliver him/her into the officer's custody (Code C, para. 12.1). In considering this decision, the custody officer should bear in mind the following factors:
  - ◆ Whether the person is in need of a rest period (Code C, para. 12.2).
  - ◆ Whether the detained person is fit to be interviewed. This should be reviewed where necessary in consultation with the officer in the case and/or the appropriate health care professional (Code C, para. 12.3).
  - ◆ Whether the right of access to legal advice is being complied with as required by Code C, paras 6.1 to 6.17.
- If the detained person is to be interviewed, the custody officer should consider the following questions under Code C:
  - ◆ Will the interview room be adequately heated, lit and ventilated? (para. 12.4)

- ♦ Is seating available in the interview room? (para. 12.6)
- ♦ If an interpreter is required, will he/she be available for the interview? (paras 13.2, 13.5 and 13.6)
- ♦ The guidance contained in Code C, Annex G.
- Where the detained person is a juvenile or a person who is mentally disordered or vulnerable, whether suspected or not, do not hand over the detained person to the interviewing officer without an appropriate adult being present unless paras 11.1 and 11.18 to 11.20 apply (para. 11.15).

In *Butcher* v *DPP* [2003] EWHC 580 (Admin), the custody officer physically escorted the detainee's appropriate adult from the custody suite as she had entered the custody suite without being invited and had been verbally abusive and aggressive. The court held that the custody sergeant had not detained the appropriate adult, but had merely used reasonable force to remove her in order to maintain the operational effectiveness of the custody suite. The court held that the custody sergeant was entirely entitled to ask her to leave and use reasonable force when she failed to comply with that request.

- The PACE Codes of Practice do not specifically prevent placing more than one prisoner in a cell. However, Code C, para. 8.1 states that so far as practicable this should not be done. The Codes go on to say that in no circumstances must a juvenile be placed in a cell or detention room with an adult and that where detained people have to share a cell they must be of the same sex. A juvenile shall not be placed in a police cell unless no other secure accommodation is available and the custody officer considers it is not practicable to supervise them if they are not placed in a cell or that a cell provides more comfortable accommodation then other secure accommodation in the station. Where the custody officer is considering placing more than one person in a cell, he/she must be mindful of the following points:
  - ♦ that there must be sufficient bedding available for each person;
  - ♦ he/she is responsible for the safety of all the prisoners and there may be a risk of assault in the cells;
  - ♦ he/she is responsible for the safety of police staff and other visitors to the police station who could be over-powered by more than one prisoner;
  - ♦ the dignity of the prisoners (e.g. should they have to go to the toilet with someone else watching);
  - ♦ security of evidence.
- Allow private consultation with a legal adviser (para. 6.1).
- Allow visits (para. 5.4).
- Release either with or without bail.

It is suggested that the custody officer should undertake a further risk assessment which should be recorded in the custody record before more than one person is placed in a cell. Any steps taken to minimise the risk should also be included in the custody record. (Paragraph 2.3 requires the time of release to be recorded, this is relevant in calculating any period of detention which may still be remaining if the person has been bailed and periods in police detention also count towards the period a person serves in custody.)

Section 117 of the 1984 Act provides that where any provision of this Act confers a power on a constable and does not provide that the power may only be exercised with the consent of some person, other than a police officer, the officer may use reasonable force, if necessary, in the exercise of the power.

This is not a blanket power to use force. In *R* v *Jones* (1999) *The Times*, 21 April, the Court said that s. 117 should not be interpreted as giving a right to police to exercise force whenever the consent of a suspect was not required.

Code C, para. 8.2 recognises that in using force there may be occasions where additional restraints need to be used on a detainee whilst he/she is in a locked cell. Such restraints should only be used when absolutely necessary and then only restraint equipment approved for use in that force by the Chief Officer, which is reasonable and necessary in the circumstances having regard to the detainee's demeanour and with a view to ensuring their safety and the safety of others. When such restraints are used the reasons for it and, if appropriate, the arrangements for enhanced supervision of the detainee whilst restrained, must be recorded (Code C, para. 8.11).

A further important duty is placed upon a custody officer where a person is to be handed over to prison custody. The custody officer must complete a form in respect of every prisoner handed over for prison custody who is reasonably suspected of:

- being likely to try to escape;
- being associated with a dangerous gang who may attempt rescue;
- against whom other serious charges may be brought;
- being of a violent nature;
- any other reason which may help the governor in deciding whether this prisoner represents a special security risk, e.g. having suicidal tendencies, being ill, being liable to take drugs into prison, etc.

(See Home Office Circular 32/2000, Detainee Risk Assessment and Revised Prisoner Escort (PER) Form, Annexes B and C, which includes this form and fully describes how it should be completed.)

2.11.12 Taking Photographs of Detained Persons

Section 64A of the Police and Criminal Evidence Act 1984 has been amended by the Serious and Organised Crime and Police Act 2005. This means that a person who is detained at a police station or elsewhere than at a police station may be photographed with his/her consent; or if it is withheld or it is not practicable to obtain it, without his/her consent. Code D, para. 5.12 sets out the circumstances where a person who is not detained at a police station may be photographed. It is suggested that it would be necessary to ask the person for his/her consent before taking the photograph or justify why this was not possible (Code D, paras 5.12 and 5.14 and Note 5E). A photograph includes any process to produce a single, still or moving, visual image, and 'photographs', 'films', 'negatives' and 'copies' include relevant visual images recorded, stored, or reproduced through any medium (Code D, para. 2.16). A photograph may only be taken by a constable. For the purpose of obtaining a photograph, a person taking a photograph may require the removal of any item or substance worn on or over the whole or any part of the head or face of the person to be photographed. If the requirement is not complied with, the officer may remove the item or substance using powers of force under s. 117 of the 1984 Act. The use of reasonable force to take the photograph of a suspect elsewhere than at a police station must be carefully considered. Code D, Note 5F gives guidance as to how or when this should be done.

A photograph taken under s. 64A may be used by, or disclosed to, any person for any purpose related to the prevention or detection of crime, the investigation of an offence or the conduct of a prosecution or the enforcement of a sentence. Code D, Note 5B gives examples where such photographs may be of use. The use of the photograph is for any conduct which constitutes a criminal offence (whether under UK law or in another country). This therefore allows the photograph to be used in the preparation of any identification procedure that is being arranged involving the suspect (Code D, para. 3.30).

When there are reasonable grounds for suspecting the involvement of a person in a criminal offence, but that person is at a police station voluntarily and not detained, that person may be photographed subject to the modifications set out in Code D, paras 5.20 to 5.24.

2.11.12.1 Searches and Examination to Ascertain Identity

The Anti-terrorism, Crime and Security Act 2001 inserted s. 54A into the Police and Criminal Evidence Act 1984. This section is intended to assist officers in obtaining the true identity of a detained person and will allow officers to search the person for marks that may link him/her to the offence. Guidance is given in the Codes at Code D, paras 5.1 to 5.11.

If an officer of at least the rank of inspector authorises it, a detained person may be searched and/or examined, without his/her consent, in order to ascertain whether he/she has any mark that would tend to identify him/her as a person involved in the commission of an offence or to assist to identify him/her (this would include showing that he/she is not a particular person). Mark includes features and injuries; and a mark is an identifying mark for the purposes of s. 54A if it assists to identify the person or his/her involvement in the commission of an offence. Section 54A deals with cases where consent of the detained person has not been given; clearly if consent is given (in writing in the person's custody record) a search could be undertaken, and it is suggested that such a search should comply with the Codes. While the search may be detailed, the extent is likely to have to be justified and it does not permit officers to carry out an intimate search.

Where the search/examination is intended to establish a suspect's identity, grounds where authority may be given are:

- the person in question has refused to identify him/herself; or
- the authorising officer has reasonable grounds for suspecting that person is not who he/she claims to be; and
- consent to a search or examination has been withheld or it is not practicable to obtain such consent (as to meaning of appropriate consent, **see para. 2.12.5.2**) (Code D, para. 5.2).

In cases where the search/examination is intended to find marks the authorising officer may give authority where consent to a search or examination has been withheld or it is not practicable to obtain such consent (as to meaning of appropriate consent, **see para. 2.12.5.2**).

Authorisation may be given orally or in writing, but if given orally it must be confirmed in writing as soon as is practicable (Code D, para. 5.2).

All the procedures under s. 54A (except the authorisation) must be conducted by a person of the same sex (Code D, para. 5.5). Should it be necessary, the person carrying out any of these procedures may use powers of force under s. 117 of the 1984 Act. If it is established that a person is unwilling to co-operate sufficiently to enable a search and/or examination to take place or a suitable photograph to be taken, an officer may use reasonable force to search and/or examine a detainee without his/her consent and/or photograph any identifying marks without his/her consent (Code D, para. 5.9).

A person detained at a police station to be searched under a stop and search power is not a detainee for the purposes of these powers.

Where a mark is found, it may be photographed (or recorded by some other method). The person should first be asked if he/she consents to the photograph; if he/she declines the photograph can still be taken (Code D, para. 5.4).

A photograph taken under s. 54A may be used by, or disclosed to, any person for any purpose related to the prevention or detection of crime, the investigation of an offence or the conduct of a prosecution. The use of the photograph is for any conduct which constitutes a criminal offence (whether under UK law or in another country). Code D, Note 5B gives examples where such photographs may be of use.

For a similar provision to obtain a person's identity from fingerprints, **see para. 2.12.5.1**.

2.11.13   **Special Groups and Appropriate Adults**

In cases where the detained person is a juvenile or a person who is mentally vulnerable or appears to be suffering from mental disorder, the custody officer must inform an appropriate adult as soon as practicable (this must be done in the case of a juvenile regardless of whether he/she is held *incommunicado* (Code C, para. 3.15). In the case of a juvenile who is the subject of a supervision order, the person supervising the juvenile should also be informed. If the custody officer has any doubt as to the mental state or capacity of a person detained, an appropriate adult should be called (Code C, Note 1G).

A juvenile for the purpose of the 1984 Act is any person who is under the age of 17 or who appears to be under the age of 17 until it is established that he/she is 17 or over (Code C, para. 1.5).

Code C, Note 1G defines 'mentally vulnerable' as applying to any detainee who, because of their mental state or capacity, may not understand the significance of what is said, of questions or of their replies. 'Mental disorder' is defined in the Mental Health Act 1983, s. 1(2) as 'mental illness, arrested or incomplete development of mind, psychopathic disorder and any other disorder or disability of mind'. Code C, para. 1.4 also states:

If an officer has any suspicion, or is told in good faith, that a person of any age may be mentally disordered or otherwise mentally vulnerable, in the absence of clear evidence to dispel that suspicion, the person shall be treated as such for the purposes of this Code. See Note 1G.

An appropriate adult is defined by Code C, para. 1.7. Paragraph 1.7 states:

'The appropriate adult' means, in the case of a:
(a) juvenile:
    (i) the parent, guardian or, if the juvenile is in local authority or voluntary organisation care, or is otherwise being looked after under the Children Act 1989, a person representing that authority or organisation;
    (ii) a social worker of a local authority social services department;
    (iii) failing these, some other responsible adult aged 18 or over who is not a police officer or employed by the police.
(b) person who is mentally disordered or mentally vulnerable: See Note 1D:
    (i) a relative, guardian or other person responsible for their care or custody;
    (ii) someone experienced in dealing with mentally disordered or mentally vulnerable people but who is not a police officer or employed by the police;
    (iii) failing these, some other responsible adult aged 18 or over who is not a police officer or employed by the police.

KEYNOTE

The role of the appropriate adult is to assist and advise the detained person. Care should be taken when considering the suitability of an appropriate adult in relation to mentally disordered or mentally vulnerable persons. Code C, Note 1D gives guidance for choosing the appropriate adult. Evidence obtained while a person is in custody where the person called as an appropriate adult does not have that person's best interests in mind or is not capable of assisting them could be excluded.

An appropriate adult is not required for a 17 year old (*R* v *Stratford Youth Court, ex parte Harding* [2001] EWHC Admin 615).

In *R* v *Aspinall* [1999] 2 Cr App R 115, the Court of Appeal emphasised the importance of appropriate adults. There it was held that an appropriate adult played a significant role in respect of a vulnerable person whose condition rendered him/her liable to provide information which was unreliable, misleading or self-incriminating.

It is also important to consider the welfare of the appropriate adult. This is demonstrated by the case of *Leach* v *Chief Constable of Gloucestershire Constabulary* [1999] 1 All ER 215. Here L was asked by a police officer to attend police interviews of a murder suspect who was also thought to be mentally disordered, as an 'appropriate adult' per the requirement of the Codes. She was told only that the suspect was a 52-year-old male, and was not informed of the nature of the case. The suspect was in fact Frederick West, who was being questioned in connection with murders committed in particularly harrowing and traumatic circumstances. For many weeks L acted as an appropriate adult, accompanying the officer and suspect to murder scenes and on many occasions being left alone in a locked cell with the suspect. She claimed to be suffering from post-traumatic stress and psychological injury as well as a stroke as a result of her experiences. The Court of Appeal said that the Fred West case was notorious among modern crimes and it was forseeable that psychiatric harm might arise. While there was no requirement to pre-select or warn appropriate adults as to the nature of the case, however in some cases, counselling or trained help should be offered.

2.11.14 Interpreters

Where the detained person is unable to speak effectively in English, an interpreter must be called to safeguard the rights of the person and to allow him/her to communicate. The interpreter is there for the benefit of the detained person and should not be considered to be part of the prosecution team. The case of *Bozkurt* v *Thames Magistrates' Court* (2001) *The Times*, 26 June, demonstrates the importance of the interpreter's role. In *Bozkurt*, the police arranged for an interpreter to attend the custody suite and interpret for the drink-drive procedure at the police station. The police then arranged for the interpreter to attend court. The interpreter translated for the defendant while he took advice from the duty solicitor at court. The interpreter failed to inform the solicitor that he had translated for the drink-drive procedure at the police station. The court held that an interpreter was under an equal duty to that of the solicitor to keep confidential what he might hear during a conference. In these circumstances it would have been preferable for a different interpreter to be used, or at least for the interpreter to have obtain the permission of the solicitor to interpret for the conference.

Guidance as to the use of interpreters is provided by Code C, paras 13.2 to 13.11. Should there be any difficulty in obtaining an interpreter this should be brought to the attention of the Chief Officer who is responsible for arranging access to interpreters (Code C, para. 13.1).

2.11.15 **Testing for Presence of Class A Drugs**

Subject to regulations being passed by the Home Secretary (see below for police areas covered), s. 63(B) of the Police and Criminal Evidence Act 1984 provides that a sample of urine or a non-intimate sample may be taken from a person aged 14 or over in police detention for the purpose of ascertaining whether he/she has any specified Class A drug in his/her body (currently this is cocaine its salts and any preparation or other product containing cocaine or its salts; and diamorphine, its salts and any preparation or other product containing diamorphine or its salts). The taking of drugs tests is covered by Code C, paras 17.1 to 17.17.

The circumstances allowing a sample to be taken vary depending on the age of the detained person. If the detained person is over 18, a sample can be taken if the conditions set out below are met for any offence for which the detained person has been arrested or charged. Where the detained person is over 14 but under 18, a sample may only be taken where the conditions set out below are met for offences that he/she has been charged with (Code C, paras 17.3 and 17.4).

The relevant conditions that need to be met for a sample to be taken are as follows:

(1) that the person has been charged with one or more of the following trigger offences:
  - Offences under the following provisions of the Theft Act 1968
    - s. 1 (theft)
    - s. 8 (robbery)
    - s. 9 (burglary)
    - s. 10 (aggravated burglary)
    - s. 12 (taking motor vehicle or other conveyance without authority)
    - s. 12A (aggravated vehicle-taking)
    - s. 22 (handling stolen goods)
    - s. 25 (going equipped for stealing, etc.)
  - Offences under the following provisions of the Misuse of Drugs Act 1971, if committed in respect of a specified Class A drug:
    - s. 4 (restriction on production and supply of controlled drugs)
    - s. 5(2) (possession of controlled drug)
    - s. 5(3) (possession of controlled drug with intent to supply)
  - Offences under the following provisions of the Fraud Act 2006:
    - s. 1 (fraud)
    - s. 6 (possession etc. of articles for use in frauds)
    - s. 7 (making or supplying articles for use in frauds)
  - An offence under s. 1(1) of the Criminal Attempts Act 1981, if committed in respect of an offence under any of the following provisions of the Theft Act 1968:
    - s. 1 (theft)
    - s. 8 (robbery)
    - s. 9 (burglary)
    - s. 22 (handling stolen goods)
  - Offences under the following provisions of the Vagrancy Act 1824:
    - s. 3 (begging)
    - s. 4 (persistent begging)
  - a police officer of at least the rank of inspector, who has reasonable grounds for suspecting that the misuse by that person of any specified Class A drug caused or contributed to the offence, has authorised the sample to be taken. This authority may be given orally or in writing but, if given orally, the authorising officer must

confirm it in writing as soon as is practicable (Code C, para. 17.8). The detained person must also be informed that the authority has been given (and if the person has not attained the age of 17 this must have been done in the presence of an appropriate adult); and

(2) a police officer has requested the person concerned to give the sample as set out in Code C, para. 17.6 and warned the detained person that if, when so requested, he/she fails without good cause to do so he/she may be liable to prosecution (and if the person has not attained the age of 17 this must have been done in the presence of an appropriate adult). A form of words is provided at Code C, Note 17A. In cases where a sample has been obtained before charge a further sample cannot be taken after charge (Code C, para. 17.9). Where the sample is taken before charge it must be done within 24 hours of the arrest (Code C, para. 17.11).

Information obtained from a sample taken under this section may be used for the following purposes:

- for the purpose of informing any decision about the giving of a conditional caution;
- for the purpose of informing any decision about granting bail in criminal proceedings;
- where the person concerned is in police detention or is remanded in or committed to custody by an order of a court or has been granted such bail, for the purpose of informing any decision about his/her supervision;
- where the person concerned is convicted of an offence, for the purpose of informing any decision about the appropriate sentence to be passed by a court and any decision about his/her supervision or release;
- for the purpose of ensuring that appropriate advice and treatment is made available to the person concerned;
- for the purpose of an assessment which the person concerned is required to attend by virtue of s. 9(2) or 10(2) of the Drugs Act 2005;
- for the purpose of proceedings against the person concerned for an offence under s. 12(3) or 14(3) of that Act.

There is no power to use force to obtain a sample (Code C, para. 17.14), however a person who fails without good cause to give any sample which may be taken from him under this section shall be guilty of an offence (s. 63B(8)) (Code C, para. 17.13). The Secretary of State may authorise people other than police officers to take samples. For the purpose of drug testing under this section a custody officer may detain someone for up to six hours following charge (Code C, para. 17.10). Where a sample is taken it must be retained until the person concerned has made their first appearance before the court (Code C, para. 17.16). The documentation required for drug testing is set out in Code C, para. 17.12.

Currently, drug testing for those for those aged 14 to 17 applies only in the following police areas: Cleveland, Greater Manchester, Humberside, Merseyside, Metropolitan Police District, Nottinghamshire, and West Yorkshire. For those over 18 the police areas are: Avon and Somerset, Bedfordshire, Cambridgeshire, Cleveland, Devon and Cornwall, Greater Manchester, Gwent, Humberside, Lancashire, Leicestershire, Merseyside, Metropolitan Police District, Northumbria, North Wales, Nottinghamshire, South Wales, South Yorkshire, Staffordshire, Thames Valley, West Midlands, and West Yorkshire.

2.11.15.1   **Requirement to Attend an Initial Drug Misuse Assessment**

Under the provisions of part 3 of the Drugs Act 2005, where a detainee has tested positive for a specified Class A drug under s. 63B of the 1984 Act a police officer may, at any time before the person's release from the police station, impose a requirement for them to attend an initial assessment of their drug misuse by a suitably qualified person and to remain for its duration. The conditions of when this can be imposed are set out at Code C, paras 17.17 to 17.22.

2.12 | Identification

2.12.1 Introduction

A critical issue in the investigation and prosecution of offences is the identification of the offender and this, like all other facts in issue, must be proved beyond a reasonable doubt. Many different methods of identification exist but the main feature which must be considered in relation to each is its *reliability*.

2.12.2 Code D

Identification evidence is governed by Code D of the PACE Codes of Practice (**see appendix 2.2**). These Codes were amended on 31 December 2005 and have effect in relation to any identification procedure carried out after midnight on 31 December 2005.

Generally, the methods of identification covered by Code D can be divided into two:

- occasions where the identity of the suspect is known; and
- occasions where the identity of the suspect is not known.

Where the identity of the suspect is known this can be further divided into those cases where the suspect is available and those where he/she is not available.

Although a breach of Code D (or any of the other Codes of Practice) will not automatically result in the evidence being excluded (*R v Khan* [1997] Crim LR 584), the judge or magistrate(s) will consider the effects of any breach on the fairness of any subsequent proceedings. The Codes are intended to provide protection to suspects and, if it is felt that the breach of Code D has resulted in unfairness or other prejudicial effect on the defendant, the court may exclude the related evidence under s. 78 of the Police and Criminal Evidence Act 1984 (**see chapter 2.9**).

The Police Reform Act 2002 has introduced designated support staff who have some of the powers that police officers have (**see para. 2.11.3**).

2.12.3 Check 'This'

Conversely, even if Code D is followed, that is no guarantee that evidence obtained will be admissible. In each case the ultimate purpose of any identification procedure should be borne in mind and the 'this' list used elsewhere in the series (**see General Police Duties** and **Road Policing**) should be applied to any proposed procedure by asking:

> How reliable is *this* piece of evidence in proving, or disproving, *this* person's involvement in *this* offence?

This approach should be adopted even if the provisions of Code D are followed. A good example of a situation where such an approach may have helped is *R v Hickin* [1996] Crim LR 584. This case was decided under the old Codes of Practice before it was necessary to obtain a first description from a witness. In the case, a group of some 14 suspects were arrested following an attack on two men at night. Clearly it would have been impracticable to arrange identification parades or group identifications for each suspect at that time, thereby allowing for a direct confrontation (**see para. 2.12.4.2**). However, witnesses could have been asked to provide initial descriptions of suspects before being used in the confrontation. The witnesses' comments at the time of the confrontation could also have been noted and some witnesses might have been asked to remain behind to take part in some later identification parades. As these things were not done, the Court of Appeal held that the identification evidence obtained by the confrontation procedure was unfairly prejudicial, *even though the provisions of Code D had been followed*.

2.12.4 Methods of Identification

2.12.4.1 Visual

The visual identification of suspects by witnesses is one of the most common forms of identification; it is also one of the most unreliable. Even under research conditions, the recall of eye witnesses is inconsistent; where the witness sees or experiences the spontaneous commission of a crime, that reliability is reduced even further.

It was for these reasons that the *Turnbull* guidelines (**see chapter 2.7**) were set out, together with the provisions of Code D. If there is no identification evidence, the *Turnbull* guidelines will not apply. It should be remembered that a witness who does not identify the suspect may still be able to provide other valuable evidence to the case, for instance a description of the person who committed the offence, or a description of what they were wearing. Again it is not uncommon for witnesses to qualify their identification of the suspect by indicating that they 'cannot be quite certain'. While a defendant cannot be convicted on such a qualified identification alone, it may be admissible to support the case where other evidence is also available (*R v George* [2003] Crim LR 282).

Problems of reliability in identification can arise even where the person accused is known to the witness. See, for example, *R v Conway* (1990) 91 Cr App R 143 (**see para. 2.12.4.2**).

A lot will depend on the individual circumstances of each case but it is essential that these issues are covered in any interview or other evidence gathering process.

'Dock identifications', where the witness's first identification of the accused involves pointing out the person in the dock, are often dramatised by film makers but, in practice, are generally disallowed as being unreliable and unfair.

The rules for identification differ between cases where the suspect *is known* and those where suspect is *not known*. Code D, para. 3.4 defines the terms as:

> ... a suspect being 'known' mean there is sufficient information known to the police to justify the arrest of a particular person for suspected involvement in the offence. A suspect being 'available' means they are immediately available or will be within a reasonably short time and willing to take an effective part in at least one of the following which it is practicable to arrange;
> • video identification;
> • identification parade; or
> • group identification.

Code D requires that a first description provided of a person suspected of a crime (regardless of the time it was given) must be recorded (para. 3.1). This must also be disclosed to the defence in the pre-trial procedure in all cases and, in particular, before any identification procedures take place. This record must be made and kept in a form which enables details of that description to be accurately produced from it, in a visible and legible form (Code D, para. 3.1), which can be given to the suspect or the suspect's solicitor. Such a record could be made electronically or be paper based. The Code also makes provision for the disclosure of materials previously released to the media in relation to an inquiry and for witnesses to be asked if they saw such material before they took part in any identification procedure.

2.12.4.2 Identification where there is a Known Suspect

Where the suspect is known, there are four possible methods of identification provided for in Code D (paras 3.4 to 3.23). These are:

- video identification;
- identification parades;
- group identification; and
- confrontation (this is only of limited use and value).

Previous modifications to the PACE Codes of Practice altered the hierarchy of identification procedures in cases of disputed identification. Under the previous provisions, the preferred method of identification was the identification parade. Only in cases where an identification parade had been refused by the suspect, or was considered impracticable, could a group identification be considered. It was only if that form of identification was refused or impracticable, that a video identification could be considered, and, as a last resort, a confrontation could be held. Now the emphasis is placed on video identification with moving images or, if necessary, still images. Code D, paras 3.5 to 3.9 define the four types of identification procedure.

The Code draws a distinction between situations where the known suspect is available and where they are unavailable. The Code suggests that video identification, identification parades and group identification are appropriate where the suspect is known and available and that confrontation may be an added appropriate identification procedure where the suspect is known and unavailable.

It is crucial that once the person becomes a known suspect, any witnesses, *including police officers*, who might be used at an identification parade, are kept apart from the suspect, as any contact could jeopardise a conviction. In *R* v *Lennon*, 28 June 1999, unreported, a suspect was arrested for public order offences after his description was circulated by the police officers that witnessed the offence. The suspect was placed in a van and the officers accidentally went in the van and identified the suspect. The court held that the person was a known suspect and the identification evidence should have been excluded. Paragraph 3.4 gives guidance as to when a suspect will become 'known' or 'available'. Code D, Note 3D gives guidance where a person deliberately makes themselves unavailable.

The Code also makes provision for the disclosure of materials previously released to the media in relation to an inquiry and for witnesses to be asked if they saw such material before taking part in any identification procedure. When a witness has previously been shown photographs or computerised or artist's composite or similar likeness, the suspect and their solicitor must be informed of this fact before the identification procedure takes place. It is the responsibility of the officer in charge of the investigation to make the identification officer aware that this is the case (Code D, Annex E, para. 9).

The Codes recognise that the showing of films or photographs to the public through the national or local media, or to police officers for the purposes of recognition and tracing suspects, may be necessary. However, Code D, para. 3.28, provides that when such material is shown to potential witnesses, including police officers, to obtain identification evidence, it shall be shown on an individual basis to avoid any possibility of collusion, and, as far as possible, the showing shall follow the principles for video identification if the suspect is known, or identification by photographs if the suspect is not known (see Code D, paras 3.4 and 3.3.).

When a broadcast or publication is made, a copy of the relevant material released to the media for the purposes of recognising or tracing the suspect shall be kept. The suspect or their solicitor shall be allowed to view such material before any identification procedure is carried out provided that it is practicable and would not unreasonably delay the investigation. After they have taken part each witness involved in the procedure shall be asked whether they have seen any broadcast or published films or photographs relating to the offence or any description of the suspect and their replies shall be recorded. This paragraph does not affect any separate requirement under the Criminal Procedure and Investigations Act 1996 to retain material in connection with criminal investigations (Code D, para. 3.29).

Where it has been decided that an identification procedure is to be held (see Code D, para. 3.12), the identification officer and the officer in charge of the investigation must consult each other to determine which procedure is to be offered (Code D, para. 3.14). The suspect shall initially be offered a video identification unless:

- a video identification is not practicable; or
- an identification parade is both practicable and more suitable than a video identification; or
- the officer in charge of the investigation considers a group identification is more suitable than a video identification or an identification parade and the identification officer considers it practicable to arrange (Code D, para. 3.16).

A video identification would normally be more suitable if it could be arranged and completed sooner than an identification parade.

If a suspect refuses the identification procedure first offered, the suspect shall be asked to state their reason for refusing and may get advice from their solicitor and/or if present, their appropriate adult. The suspect, solicitor and/or appropriate adult shall be allowed to make representations about why another procedure should be used. A record should be made of the reasons for refusal and any representations made. After considering any reasons given, and representations made, the identification officer shall, if appropriate, arrange for the suspect to be offered an alternative which the officer considers suitable and practicable. If the officer decides it is not suitable and practicable to offer an alternative identification procedure, the reasons for that decision must be recorded (Code D, para. 3.15).

Where a suspect is identified by witnesses, other evidence should still be sought to strengthen the case (or to prove the person's innocence) as identification evidence is often challenged at court. Such supporting evidence may include admissions by the suspect that links him/her to the identification evidence; for example, that he/she owns the vehicle that was driven at the time of the offence (*R v Ward* [2001] Crim LR 316).

The photographing of a suspect is covered in **chapter 2.11** (at **para. 2.11.12**) and Code D, paras 5.1 to 5.24. Such photographs might prove useful for an identification procedure process.

2.12.4.3 When Must an Identification Procedure be Held?

Identification procedures should be held for the benefit of the defence as well as the prosecution (*R v Wait* [1998] Crim LR 68). The Codes give guidance on when an identification parade shall be held. Code D, paras 3.12 and 3.13 state:

> 3.12 Whenever:
>> (i) a witness has identified a suspect or purported to have identified them prior to any identification procedure set out in paragraphs 3.5 to 3.10 having been held; or
>> (ii) there is a witness available, who expresses an ability to identify the suspect, or where there is a reasonable chance of the witness being able to do so, and they have not been given an opportunity to identify the suspect in any of the procedures set out in paragraphs 3.5 to 3.10,
>
> and the suspect disputes being the person the witness claims to have seen, an identification procedure shall be held unless it is not practicable or it would serve no useful purpose in proving or disproving whether the suspect was involved in committing the offence. For example, when it is not disputed that the suspect is already well of known to the witness who claims to have seen them commit the crime.
>
> 3.13 Such a procedure may also be held if the officer in charge of the investigation considers it would be useful.

KEYNOTE

Code D, para. 3.12(ii) provides that there is no need to go through any of the identification procedures where it is not practicable or it would serve no useful purpose in proving or disproving whether the suspect was involved in committing the offence. This view is supported by the Court of Appeal decision *R v Chen* (2001) *The Times*, 17 April. The defence in that case was one of duress but the appeal was based on the failure of the police to hold identification parades. The Court of Appeal stated that this was not a case about identification as none of the defendants denied their presence at the scene. What they denied was their criminal participation in the activities that took place. It followed, therefore, that Code D did not apply. Other examples would be where it is not in dispute that the suspect is already well known to the witness who claims to have seen the suspect commit the crime or where there is no reasonable possibility that a witness would be able to make an identification.

There have been a number of Court of Appeal cases concerning the requirement to hold identification parades. It is suggested that these should be applied to the revised Code regardless of which form of identification procedure is used. The leading case is *R v Forbes* [2001] 2 WLR 1, which was based on earlier versions of the Code of Practice. The House of Lords held that if the police are in possession of sufficient evidence to justify the arrest of a suspect, and that suspect's identification depends on eye-witness identification evidence, even in part, then if the identification is disputed, the Code requires that an identification parade should be held with the suspect's consent, unless one of the exceptions applies. The exceptions are set out in Code D, para. 3.12. This is particularly so where the suspect disputes identification.

The House of Lords went on to say that this mandatory obligation to hold an identification parade ('parade' at the time of judgment was right but this applies equally to any indentification procedure) applies even if there has been a 'fully satisfactory', 'actual and complete' or 'unequivocal' identification of the suspect.

Despite the wording of Code D, it has been held that a suspect's right to have an identification [procedure] is not confined to cases where a dispute over identity has already arisen; that right also applies where such a dispute might reasonably be anticipated (*R v Rutherford and Palmer* (1994) 98 Cr App R 191). Similarly, a suspect's failure to request an identification [procedure] does not mean that the police may proceed without one (*R v Graham* [1994] Crim LR 212).

It is important to consider the distinction between identification of a suspect and the suspect's clothing or other features. In *D v DPP* (1998) *The Times*, 7 August, a witness had observed two youths for a continuous period of five to six minutes and then informed the police of what he had seen, describing the age of the youths and the clothes that they were wearing. The court held that there had not been an identification within the terms of the Codes of Practice because the witness had at no stage identified the defendant or the co-accused. He had described only their clothing and their approximate ages, and the police, acting on that information, had made the arrests. An identification parade could have served no useful purpose since the clothing would have been changed and those persons used for the parade would have been the same approximate age. This point was further supported in *R v Haynes* (2004) *The Times*, 27 February, where the Court of Appeal held that as a practical point the identification parade, whether or not the suspect was regarded as a known or unknown suspect, was of little value where the witness identified the suspect by clothing and not by recognition of the suspect's features. An identification parade would have provided little assistance.

The *key factor* to consider when deciding whether to hold an identification parade is whether *a failure to hold a parade could be a matter of genuine potential prejudice to the suspect*. If it is decided to hold an identification procedure, it should be held as soon as practicable (Code D, para. 3.11).

The question for the court will be whether it is fair to admit the identification evidence. When looking at this issue the court will consider how reliable that identification evidence is.

Any decision to proceed without an identification parade must be capable of justification later to the relevant court. The courts have taken different approaches to justification based on practical difficulties. In an early case, the submissions of the identification officer that it was impracticable to find enough people who sufficiently resembled the defendant were treated fairly dismissively by the trial judge (*R v Gaynor* [1988] Crim LR 242). In later cases, however, the courts have been more lenient, accepting that the time scales involved in arranging identification parades may render them 'impracticable' (see *R v Jamel* [1993] Crim LR 52 where the court refused an objection by the defence to a group identification). A group identification was used in *Jamel* because a parade using mixed-race volunteers would have taken too long to arrange. All reasonable steps must be taken to investigate the possibility of one identification option before moving on to an alternative, and an offer from a suspect's solicitor to find volunteers to stand on a parade is such a 'reasonable' step (*R v Britton and Richards* [1989] Crim LR 144).

2.12.4.4   Recognition Cases

Recognition cases, that is to say, those cases where the witness states that they know the person who committed the offence as opposed to only being able to give a description, need to be carefully considered. In *R v Ridley* (1999) *The Times*, 13 October, the Court of Appeal stated that there has never been a rule that an identification parade had to be held in all recognition cases and that it will be a question of fact in each case whether or not there is a need to do so. The view that an identification procedure is not required in these cases is supported by para. 3.12(ii).

The facts in *Ridley*, which it is suggested are not uncommon among patrolling officers, were that two police officers in a marked police vehicle noticed a car, which had been stolen earlier that day, drive past them. Both officers said that they recognised the defendant driving the car. The officers gave chase and gave evidence that the car was speeding and being driven dangerously. They decided that it was unsafe to continue pursuit, but arrested the suspect six days later. One of the officers claimed to have recognised the suspect because she had interviewed him for some 20 minutes five months previously and had seen him about town. She gave evidence that she had a view of the suspect in the car for about nine seconds. The other officer said that he recognised the suspect from a photograph but could not say when he had seen that photograph. He said that he had seen the suspect in the car for about two seconds. The Court found that the female police officer's identification had been complete and there was no requirement for her to have further identified the suspect.

Ridley can be contrasted with *R* v *Conway* (1990) 91 Cr App R 143, where the witnesses' evidence was not as strong. There the witnesses stated that they recognised the accused simply because they knew him. The defence argument was that the witnesses did not actually know the accused and so could not have recognised him at the time of the offence. His conviction was quashed because of the prejudice caused by the absence of a parade. In *R* v *Davies* [2004] EWHC 2242 a witness identified a masked attacker from his voice and eyes. The court in this case held that this identification evidence coupled with other circumstantial evidence was sufficient for a conviction.

A case can still amount to one of recognition even where the witness does not know the name of the suspect but later obtained those details from a third party, for example where the witness and the suspect went to the same school and the witness became aware of the suspect's full names from other pupils at the school (*R* v *C*; *R* v *B* (2003) 4 March 2003).

In *H* v *DPP* (2003) 24 January 2003, the court accepted that it was reasonable for the police not to undertake an identification procedure. In the circumstances of the case the police had every reason to believe that the claimant and the victim were well known to each other. The claimant had accepted that the victim knew her. There was no question of doubt as to the victim's ability to recognise the claimant and as such this was a case of pure recognition where it was futile to hold an identification parade.

Care must be taken in cases where it is believed that the case is one of recognition not requiring an identification procedure. In *R* v *Harris* [2002] EWCA Crim 174 the witness stated that he recognised the suspect as being someone he went to school with. The suspect gave a prepared statement in which he disputed the suggestion that he was well known to the witness. Here the court held that an identification procedure should have been undertaken, as the circumstances of the case did not fall within the general exception of the Code, that it would serve no useful purpose in proving or disproving whether the suspect had been involved in committing the offence.

When a suspect is filmed committing an offence, it is admissible to give evidence of identification by way of recognition from a witness not present at the scene but who knew the defendant and who, having seen the film, identified the suspect as being the defendant (*Attorney-General's Reference (No. 2 of 2002)* [2003] Crim LR 192).

2.12.4.5 Identification of Disqualified Drivers

Another common identification problem is that of disqualified drivers and being able to satisfy the court that the person charged with disqualified driving is the same person who was disqualified by the court. This is because s. 73 of the Police and Criminal Evidence Act 1984 requires proof that the person named in a certificate of conviction as having been convicted is the person whose conviction is to be proved. There has been some guidance from the courts as to how this can be achieved. In *R* v *Derwentside Justices, ex parte Heaviside* [1996] RTR 384, the court stated that this could be done by:

- fingerprints under s. 39 of the Criminal Justice Act 1948;
- the evidence of a person who was present in court when the disqualification order was made;
- admission of the defendant (preferably in interview) *DPP* v *Mooney* (1997) RTR 434;
- requiring the suspect's solicitor who was present when he/she was disqualified on the earlier occasion to give evidence (such a summons is a last resort when there was no other means of identifying whether an individual had been disqualified from driving) (*R (On the Application of Howe) and Law Society (Interested Party)* v *South Durham Magistrates' Court and CPS (Interested Party)* [2004] EWHC 362 (Admin)).

The methods outlined in *Ex parte Heaviside*, are not exhaustive, but just suggested methods (*DPP* v *Mansfield* [1997] RTR 96). A good example of where the police were able to satisfy s. 73 of the 1984 Act came in the case of *Olakunori* v *DPP* [1998] COD 443. In this case Olakunori was charged with driving while disqualified. He had been stopped by police officers and gave a false name and a false date of birth. At the police station, after he was arrested, he gave a different false name and false date of birth to the custody officer. When he was interviewed, he confirmed his surname was Olakunori. A man named Olatokubo Olakunori, born 20 July 1974, had previously been disqualified from holding and obtaining a driving licence for an offence of driving without a valid certificate of insurance. Olakunori denied all knowledge of the previous disqualification. The prosecution argued that Olakunori had given false names in order to avoid detection for the offence and there was sufficient evidence to establish that Olakunori was the person who had been previously disqualified. This included the court register of the previous convictions, Olakunori's birth certificate which was in the name of Olatunji Olatokunbo Adeola Olakunori, showing his date of birth as 20 July 1974, and his passport which was in the name of Olatokunbo Olakunori. The Court held that the justices had been entitled to find that the false names which the appellant had given were a deliberate attempt to avoid the charge, were relevant to the material issues and that there was no innocent explanation why they had been given. The lies supported the conclusion that the appellant was guilty and accordingly the justices had been entitled to take them into account. Such evidence would be useful to obtain from suspects being investigated for offences of disqualified driving. For the offence of disqualified driving, **see Road Policing, chapter 3.10**.

2.12.4.6 **Control of the Identification Process**

The arrangements for and conduct of identification procedures is the responsibility of an officer not below the rank of inspector who is not involved with the investigation ('the identification officer'). However, except where the Codes expressly state otherwise, the identification officer may allow another officer or police staff to make arrangements for, and to conduct, any of the identification procedures in paras 3.11, 3.19 (serving the notice of the identification process on the detained person) and 2.21. When the identification officer delegates these procedures, he/she must be able to supervise effectively and either intervene or be available to be contacted for advice.

It is important to note that no officer or any other person involved with the investigation of the case against the suspect, may take any part in these procedures or act as the identification officer. However, the identification officer may consult the officer in charge of the investigation in order to determine which procedure to use.

If the identification officer considers that it is not practicable to hold a video identification or identification parade, the reasons shall be recorded and explained to the suspect (para. 3.26). Should the suspect fail or refuse to co-operate in a video identification, identification parade or group identification, a record should be made including any reasons (paras 3.15 and 3.27).

Just because a suspect has an unusual physical feature it does not mean that a video identification procedure is impracticable. Code D, Annex A, paras 2A to 2C give guidance as to how to manage such situations which includes concealment of the unusual physical feature or replicating the feature on other people. Before a video identification, an identification parade or group identification is arranged, para. 3.17 outlines a number of matters that must be explained to the suspect and must be recorded in a written notice and handed to the suspect. Paragraph 3.17 must be completed by the identification officer or if it is proposed to hold an identification procedure at a later date and an inspector is not available to act as the identification police officer, it can be performed by the custody officer before the suspect leaves the station. When dealing with a witness who is or appears to be mentally disordered, otherwise mentally vulnerable or a juvenile, the procedure should take place in the presence of a pre-trial support person. However, the support person must not be allowed to prompt any identification of a suspect by a witness (Code D, para. 2.15A). (See also guidance at Code D, Note 2A as to how the appropriate adult should be dealt with.) Code D, Note 2AB explains the role of *a pre-trial support person*.

2.12.4.7 Which Identification Procedure should be Used?

Initially the choice should be that of a video identification or an identification parade (para. 3.14). However, a group identification could be used where the officer in charge of the investigation considers that in the particular circumstances it is more suitable and practicable to arrange (para. 3.16). The identification officer and the officer in charge of the investigation shall consult each other to determine which of these two options is the most suitable and practicable in the particular case. Paragraphs 3.14 to 3.16 give guidance as to factors to consider.

While the choice of procedure is for the police, the suspect, solicitor and/or appropriate adult shall be allowed to make representations as to why another procedure should be used (para. 3.15). If a suspect refuses the identification procedure which is first offered, he/she must be asked to state his/her reasons for refusing and may obtain advice from his/her solicitor and appropriate adult if present (para. 3.15).

Even where a person refuses to take part in an identification procedure, it is still possible to use covert video identification, covert group identification or confrontation (paras 3.21 to 3.24). If the identification officer and the officer in charge of the investigation have reasonable grounds to suspect that the person will take steps to avoid being seen by a witness in any identification procedure, the identification officer has a discretion to arrange for images of him/her to be obtained for use in a video identification procedure. If images of the suspect are obtained in these circumstances, the suspect may, for the purposes of a video identification procedure, co-operate in providing suitable images which shall be used in place of those previously taken (para. 3.20).

Section 64A of the Police and Criminal Evidence Act 1984 provides powers to take photographs and images of detained suspects and allows the photographs and images so taken to be used to assist with arranging the identification process (**see para. 2.11.12**). After being so used or disclosed, they may be retained but may not be used or disclosed for any purpose other than that related to the prevention or detection of crime, the investigation of offences or the conduct of prosecutions by, or on behalf of, police or other law enforcement and prosecuting authorities inside and outside the United Kingdom or the enforcement of a sentence. After being so used or disclosed, they may be retained but can be used or disclosed only for the same purposes (Code D, para. 3.30).

Code D, paras 3.31 to 3.33 provide further guidance on the destruction and retention of photographs taken for the purpose of or in connection with identification procedures.

Where a known suspect is not available (or has ceased to be available for any reason), the identification officer has a discretion to make arrangements for a video identification to be conducted. This must be done in accordance with the provisions applicable to covert video identification (para. 3.21 and Note 3D).

If necessary, the identification officer may follow the video identification procedures but using still images. Any suitable moving or still images may be used and these may be obtained covertly if necessary. Any covert activity should be strictly limited to that necessary to test the ability of the witness to identify the suspect. Alternatively, the identification officer may make arrangements for a group identification. These provisions may be applied to juveniles where the consent of their parent or guardian is either refused or reasonable efforts to obtain that consent have failed (Code D, paras 3.21 and 3.22).

It is only if none of the other options are practicable that the identification officer may arrange for the suspect to be confronted by the witness. A confrontation does not require the suspect's consent. In *R v McCullock*, 6 May 1999, unreported, the Court of Appeal made it clear that confrontations between suspects and witnesses should only be carried out if no other procedure is practicable (see below).

2.12.4.8 Conduct of Identification Parades

Identification evidence can be crucial to the success of a prosecution. There are clear guidelines that must be followed. Where such guidelines are not followed it is likely that the defence will strongly attempt to have the identification evidence excluded. In *R v Jones* (1999) *The Times*, 21 April, identification evidence was excluded as the officers told the suspect that if he did not comply with the procedure, force would be used against him.

The conduct of identification parades was criticised in the Stephen Lawrence Inquiry Report. The Report stated at paras 21.19 and 21.21 that the timing of any identification parade during an investigation must also be considered carefully:

> Where there are a number of suspects and witnesses and where identification evidence may be crucial this can only emphasise the extreme need for careful planning and foresight.... The ID parades were delayed until about the middle or end of May partly because of the delay in making the arrests of the suspects. If the arrests had been made earlier it can be said that there would have been more prospect of successful identification, since the passage of time inevitably blunts the memory of the features or look of somebody who has been seen committing a crime.

The need for the identification procedure to be conducted as soon as practicable is now recognised by the Codes (para. 3.11).

Annexes A to E of Code D set out in detail the procedures and requirements which must be followed in conducting identification procedures. There is also guidance concerning documentation and retention of material.

Although the courts are aware of the many practical difficulties involved in organising and running identification procedures (see e.g. *R v Jamel* [1993] Crim LR 52), any flaws in the procedure will be considered in the light of their potential impact on the defendant's trial. Serious or deliberate breaches (such as the showing of photographs to witnesses before the parade), will invariably lead to any evidence so gained being excluded (*R v Finley* [1993] Crim LR 50). The key question for the court will be whether the breach of the Codes is likely to have made the identification less reliable. Officers must therefore fully understand and follow the Codes of Practice and relevant Annex for the procedure being used.

Breaches which appear to impact on the safeguards imposed by Annexes A to E to separate the functions of investigation and identification (e.g. where the investigating officer becomes involved with the running of the parade in a way which allows him/her to talk to the witnesses (*R* v *Gall* (1989) 90 Cr App R 64)) will also be treated seriously by the court.

The case of *R* v *Marrin* (2002) *The Times*, 5 March provides some guidance as to methods that could be used to get a suitable pool of participants for an ID parade. The court held that there was nothing inherently unfair or objectionable in some colouring or dye being used on the facial stubble of some volunteers to make them look more like the suspect. However, care needed to be taken with such measures because the procedure would be undermined if it was obvious to the witness that make-up had been used. Another point raised was that it may sometimes be appropriate for those on parade to wear hats, but if possible the wearing of hats should be avoided if hats had not been worn during the offence because this would make it more difficult for a witness to make an identification. However, there could be circumstances where the wearing of hats could help to achieve a resemblance and might be desirable to minimise differences. Finally an identification of a suspect was not invalidated by the witness's request for the removal of a hat. There was nothing unfair in that taking place and there was no breach of any Code either. Under para. 18 of Annex B, a witness could ask for any parade member to adopt any specified posture or that he/she should move.

It is important to follow the guidance in the Codes regardless of what agreement is obtained from the suspect or his/her solicitor. In *R* v *Hutton* [1999] Crim LR 74, at the suggestion of the suspect's solicitor, all the participants in the identification parade wore back to front baseball caps and had the lower part of their faces obscured by material. That identification was the only evidence against the defendant on that count. The court excluded the evidence and did not accept the fact that the decision had been agreed by the defence.

It will be essential that any photographs, photofits or other such material is stored securely in a manner that restricts access so as to be able to demonstrate to the court that the material cannot have been viewed by any of the witnesses and that copies have not been made that have not been accounted for.

2.12.4.9 Identification where there is No Suspect

Where the police have no suspect, Code D provides for witnesses (including police officers) to be shown photographs (Annex E) or taken to a place where the suspect might be (paras 3.2 and 3.3).

If photographs are to be shown, the procedure set out at Annex E must be followed. Once a witness has made a positive identification from the photographs, computerised or artist's composite, no further witnesses should be shown photographs (para. 3.3) (unless the person identified is eliminated from the enquiry (Annex E, para. 6)).

Using photographs from police criminal records can affect the judgment of a jury and nothing should be done to draw their attention to the fact that the defendant's photograph was already held by the police (*R* v *Lamb* (1979) 71 Cr App R 198). This rule does not apply if the jury are already aware of the defendant's previous convictions (*R* v *Allen* [1996] Crim LR 426).

The showing of a CCTV film used for security purposes is addressed at para. 3.28 of Code D.

If a film which has been shown to a witness is later lost or unavailable, the witness may give evidence of what he/she saw on that film but the court will have to consider all the relevant circumstances in deciding whether to admit that evidence *and* what weight to attach to it. (For a discussion of those circumstances, see *Taylor* v *Chief Constable of Cheshire* [1986] 1 WLR 1479.) This is particularly so as the Codes require that the film is retained (Annex A, para. 15 and para. 3.29).

Videos or photographs can be shown to the public at large through the national or local media, or to police officers for the purposes of recognition and tracing suspects. However, when such material is shown to potential witnesses (including police officers) it should be shown on an individual basis so as to avoid any possibility of collusion, and the showing shall, as far as possible, follow the principles for video identification if the suspect is known (paras 3.28, 3.29 and Annex A) or identification by photographs if the suspect is not known (see paras 3.4, 3.3 and Annex E).

2.12.4.10 Identification at the Scene

There are occasions where the identification is made immediately after the alleged offence. This usually happens when the witness is taken round a particular area to try and find the suspect (in which case Code D, para. 3.2 must be complied with). The need for 'scene identifications' was recognised by Lord Lane CJ in *R* v *Oscar* [1991] Crim LR 778 and by the Court of Appeal in *R* v *Rogers* [1993] Crim LR 386.

In *Oscar*, the court held that there had been no requirement for an identity parade in that case and Lord Lane pointed out that, in any case, a later parade where the suspect was dressed differently would be of no value at all. In *Rogers*, the suspect was found near a crime scene and was confronted by a witness who positively identified him. The court held that the identification in that case was necessary for an arrest to be made, although the court felt a later parade could have been carried out.

In such cases, where the meeting of the suspect and the witness takes place soon after the event, wherever possible the officers should comply with para. 3.2. Matters to consider before doing a 'scene identification' include:

- where practicable, a record shall be made of any description of the suspect given by the witness as in para. 3.1(a);
- care must be taken not to direct the witness's attention to any individual unless, taking into account all the circumstances, this cannot be avoided;
- if there is more than one witness, try to keep them separate;
- once there is sufficient information to justify the arrest of a suspect, a formal identification procedure must be adopted;
- the officer or police staff accompanying the witness must make a record in his/her pocket book of the action taken as soon as practicable and in as much detail as possible.

The admissibility of identification evidence obtained when carrying out a 'scene identification' may be compromised if before a person is identified, the witness's attention is specifically drawn to that person.

Careful consideration must be given before a decision to identify a suspect in this manner is used. If there is sufficient evidence to arrest the suspect without using a witnesses identification, then it is likely the courts will find that an identification method outlined at **para. 2.12.4.2** should have been used and the evidence may be excluded. Confrontations between witnesses and suspects on the street can be useful at times, but where this takes place it defeats the formal identification process and needs to be carefully considered.

The reason for this is that, even if the suspect is picked out on the identification parade by that witness, the defence will be able to argue that the identification was from the confrontation after the incident and not at the time of the commission of the offence. If there is more than one witness available and a decision is taken to use a witness to try to identify a suspect at the scene, other witnesses should be moved away, so as to reduce the possibility of a chance encounter with the suspect. Where possible, these witnesses should be kept apart until the identification parade and ideally should not discuss the matter between themselves.

An example where a street identification was appropriate is *R v El-Hannachi* [1998] 2 Cr App R 226. Here an affray took place in the car park of a public house. A witness had seen the man earlier in the pub and she had had an unobstructed view in good light before the attack. The witness described the attacker's clothing to the police and then identified a group of men who had been stopped by other officers a short distance away. The court accepted that this was the correct approach. The defendants were not known suspects when they were stopped by the police prior to the witness's identification. The court also accepted that it had not been practicable for a record to have been made of the witness's description, as required by Code D, para. 3.1, prior to the identification. Where a record has been made prior to the identification this may support the identification itself. It should be remembered, however, that the description does not now have to be recorded in writing and could be recorded by some quicker method (e.g. tape recording) (para. 3.1).

A not uncommon situation is where police officers chase a suspect who is arrested by other officers on the description circulated by the chasing officer, who then attends the scene to confirm the person's identity. The case of *R v Nunes* [2001] EWCA Crim 2283, covers this point and points out the dangers of this practice. The facts of the case were that a police officer saw a man inside a house and circulated a description on his radio. A person fitting the description was seen and arrested. The first officer arrived on the scene and identified the arrested person as the man he had earlier seen in the house. The Court of Appeal held that on the particular facts of this case the identification amounted to a breach of the Code. By the time of the identification, the man had been arrested for suspected involvement in the offence and, on his arrest, the identity of the suspect was known to the police. Therefore, by the time the witnessing officer arrived on the scene, the case involved 'disputed identification evidence' because the suspect had said that he had not done anything while the police had told him he matched the description of a suspected burglar. That said, the court did go on to hold that the judge had the discretion to allow the identification evidence to be adduced notwithstanding the breach of the Codes but a full and carefull direction regarding the breaches, together with a warning about the shortcomings in the procedure would have been necessary.

2.12.4.11 Photographs, Image and Sound Reproduction Generally

The use of photographic and computer-generated images (such as E-Fit) to identify suspects has increased considerably over the last few years. Although the courts will exercise considerable caution when admitting such evidence (see *R v Blenkinsop* [1995] 1 Cr App R 7), these methods of identification are particularly useful. Expert evidence (**see chapter 2.7**) may be admitted to interpret images on film (see e.g. *R v Stockwell* (1993) 97 Cr App R 260) and police officers who are very familiar with a particular film clip (e.g. of crowd violence at a football match) may be allowed to assist the court in interpreting and explaining events shown within it (see *R v Clare* (1995) 159 JP 412).

Logically E-Fit and other witness-generated images would be treated as 'visual state-ments', in that they represent the witness's recollection of what he/she saw. However, the Court of Appeal has decided that they are not to be so treated (*R* v *Cook* (1987) 1 All ER 1049) and therefore the restrictions imposed by the rule against hearsay (**see chapter 2.7**) will not apply (see also *R* v *Constantinou* (1990) 91 Cr App R 74 where this ruling was fol-lowed in relation to a photofit image).

2.12.4.12 Voice Identification

Voice identification from what a suspect on an identification parade says, is dealt with un-der para. 18 of Annex B to Code D. The Codes do not preclude the police making use of aural identification procedures such as a 'voice identification parade', where they judge that appropriate.

Generally, a witness may give evidence identifying the defendant's voice (*R* v *Robb* (1991) 93 Cr App R 161), while expert testimony may be admitted in relation to tape recordings of a voice which is alleged to belong to the defendant. In the latter case, the jury should be allowed to hear the recording(s) so that they can draw their own conclusions (*R* v *Bentum* (1989) 153 JP 538).

Home Office Circular 57/2003, *Advice on the Use of Voice Identification Parades*, provides guidance on the use of voice identification parades which is based on procedures devised by DS McFarlane of the Metropolitan Police in the case of *R* v *Khan & Bains*.

2.12.5 Fingerprints

The Serious Organised Crime and Police Act 2005 has made several amendments to the law covered by this chapter which include photographing of suspects, fingerprints, impressions of footwear and intimate samples.

Identification by fingerprints applies when a person's fingerprints are taken to compare with fingerprints found at the scene of a crime, check and prove convictions, or help to ascertain a person's identitiy (Code D, para. 1.3).

A fingerprint is defined by Code D, para. 4.1 and s. 65(1) of the Police and Criminal Evidence Act 1984 as any record, produced by any method, of the skin pattern and other physical characteristics or features of a person's fingers or palms. Fingerprints can be taken electronically provided that they are taken using such devices as the Secretary of State has approved for the purposes of electronic fingerprinting (s. 61(8A) of the 1984 Act). Where a person's fingerprints are to be taken without their consent, under the powers set out in Code D, paras 4.3 and 4.4, reasonable force may be used if necessary.

Expert evidence on fingerprints is admissible from suitably qualified individuals who have at least five years' experience in that field.

Whether fingerprint evidence is admissible as evidence tending to prove guilt, depends on:

- the experience and expertise of the witness,
- the number of similar ridge characteristics (if there are fewer than eight ridge charac-teristics matching the fingerprints of the accused with those found by the police, it is unlikely that a judge would exercise his/her discretion to admit such evidence),
- whether there are dissimilar characteristics,
- the size of print relied on, and
- the quality and clarity of print relied on.

The jury should be warned that expert evidence is not conclusive in itself and that guilt has to be proved in the light of all evidence (*R* v *Buckley* (1999) 163 JP 403).

2.12.5.1 Before Conviction

The power to take fingerprints has been amended by the Criminal Justice Act 2003 which has amended s. 61 of the Police and Criminal Evidence Act 1984. This amendment to s. 61 of the 1984 Act is intended to prevent persons who come into police custody and who may be wanted on a warrant or for questioning on other matters, from avoiding detection by giving the police a false name and address. Using Livescan technology, which enables the police to take fingerprints electronically and which is linked to the national fingerprint database (NAFIS), the police will be able to confirm a person's identity while still in police detention if the person's fingerprints have been taken previously. It will also assist in enabling vulnerable or violent people to be identified more quickly and dealt with more effectively. The taking of finger and palm prints is governed by s. 61 of the Police and Criminal Evidence Act 1984.

Section 61 states:

(1) Except as provided by this section no person's fingerprints may be taken without the appropriate consent.

(2) Consent to the taking of a person's fingerprints must be in writing if it is given at a time when he is at a police station.

(3) The fingerprints of a person detained at a police station may be taken without the appropriate consent if—

    (a) he is detained in consequence of his arrest for a recordable offence; and

    (b) he has not had his fingerprints taken in the course of the investigation of the offence by the police.

(3A) Where a person mentioned in paragraph (a) of subsection (3) or (4) has already had his fingerprints taken in the course of the investigation of the offence by the police, that fact shall be disregarded for the purposes of that subsection if—

    (a) the fingerprints taken on the previous occasion do not constitute a complete set of his fingerprints; or

    (b) some or all of the fingerprints taken on the previous occasion are not of sufficient quality to allow satisfactory analysis, comparison or matching (whether in the case in question or generally).

(4) The fingerprints of a person detained at a police station may be taken without the appropriate consent if—

    (a) he has been charged with a recordable offence or informed that he will be reported for such an offence; and

    (b) he has not had his fingerprints taken in the course of the investigation of the offence by the police.

(4A) The fingerprints of a person who has answered to bail at a court or police station may be taken without the appropriate consent at the court or station if—

    (a) the court, or

    (b) an officer of at least the rank of inspector,

    authorises them to be taken.

KEYNOTE

Where fingerprints have been taken and they do not constitute a complete set of that person's fingerprints; or some or all of the fingerprints taken on the previous occasion are not of sufficient quality to allow satisfactory analysis, comparison or matching further fingerprints can be taken (Code D, para. 4.3(a), (b)).

An officer of at least the rank of inspector (or the court) may authorise the taking of a person's fingerprints who has answered to bail at a court or police station if the person who has answered to bail has answered to it for a person whose fingerprints were taken on a previous occasion and there are reasonable grounds for believing that he/she is not the same person or the person claims to be a different person from a person whose fingerprints were taken on a previous occasion (s. 61(4A) and (4B)). This authority may be given orally or in writing but, if he/she gives it orally, he/she shall confirm it in writing as soon as is practicable (s. 61(5) of the 1984 Act).

Where a person has been arrested on suspicion of being involved in a recordable offence or has been charged with such an offence or has been informed that he/she will be reported for such an offence, fingerprints taken from the person may be checked against:

(a) other fingerprints or samples to which the person seeking to check has access and which are held by or on behalf of any one or more relevant law enforcement authorities or which are held in connection with or as a result of an investigation of an offence. This speculative search of the fingerprint crime scene database may reveal if the person has been involved in other crimes.

(b) information derived from other samples if the information is contained in records to which the person seeking to check has access and which are held as mentioned in paragraph (a) above (s. 63A of the 1984 Act).

Before any fingerprints are taken the person must be informed of the reason their fingerprints are to be taken, if Code D, para. 4.3(c) applies the grounds on which the relevant authority has been given, that their fingerprints may be retained and may be the subject of a speculative search (unless destruction of the fingerprints is required in accordance with Annex F, Part (a)), and that if their fingerprints are required to be destroyed, they may witness their destruction as provided for in Annex F, Part (a), Code D, para. 4.7.

A record must be made when a person has been informed of the possibility that their fingerprints may be the subject of a speculative search (Code D, para. 4.9). A record must also be made, as soon as possible, of the reason for taking a person's fingerprints without consent and, if force is used, the circumstances and those present (Code D, para. 4.8). Where the person is detained at a police station these records must be made in their custody record.

Where the suspect does consent to their fingerprints being the subject of such a speculative search, the consent must be in writing. Note 6E provides an example of a basic form of words. Once the suspect has given consent for the sample to be retained and used, he/she cannot withdraw this consent. **See para. 2.12.11** and Code D, Annex F regarding the retention and use of fingerprints and samples taken with consent for elimination purposes. Note 4B explains what a speculative search means. Code D, paras 4.10 to 4.15 deal with the taking of fingerprints in connection with immigration inquiries and Annex F, para. 5 deals with their retention and destruction.

2.12.5.2 After Conviction, Reprimand or Caution

Fingerprints may be taken with the appropriate consent, where a person refuses to give that consent, fingerprints can only be taken if s. 61(6) of the 1984 Act applies, i.e. from a person who has been:

- convicted of a recordable offence;
- given a caution in respect of a recordable offence which, at the time of the caution, the person admitted; or
- warned or reprimanded under s. 65 of the Crime and Disorder Act 1998 for a recordable offence.

For the purposes of taking fingerprints, the meaning of appropriate consent is in relation to:

- a person 17 or over, his/her consent;
- a person 14 to 17, the consent of that person and his/her parent or guardian;
- a person under 14, the consent of his/her parent or guardian.

Section 27 of the 1984 Act provides that a person may be required to attend a police station to have his/her fingerprints taken if he/she:

- has been convicted of a recordable offence; given a caution in respect of a recordable offence which, at the time of the caution, the person admitted; or warned or reprimanded under s. 65 of the Crime and Disorder Act 1998, for a recordable offence; and
- the fingerprints taken on the previous occasion do not constitute a complete set of his/her fingerprints; or some or all of the fingerprints taken on the previous occasion are not of sufficient quality to allow satisfactory analysis, comparison or matching; or
- where a person has been convicted of a recordable offence and has already had his/her fingerprints taken but the fingerprints taken on the previous occasion did not constitute a complete set of his/her fingerprints or some or all of the fingerprints taken on the previous occasion are not of sufficient quality to allow satisfactory analysis, comparison or matching (s. 27(1A)).

The requirement must be made within one month of the date the person is convicted, cautioned, warned or reprimanded and the person must be given a period of at least seven days within which to attend. This seven-day period need not fall during the month allowed for making the requirement. If a person fails to comply with the requirement, he/she can be arrested without warrant (Code D, para. 4.4).

Before any fingerprints are taken with or without consent as above, the person must be informed of the reason his/her fingerprints are to be taken. Before any fingerprints are taken at the police station, the person must also be informed that his/her fingerprints may be retained and may be the subject of a speculative search against other fingerprints. Code D, Note 4B explains what a speculative search means (Code D, para. 4.7). A record must be made when a person has been informed of the possibility that his/her fingerprints may be the subject of a speculative search (Code D, para. 4.9). A record must also be made, as soon as possible, of the reason for taking a person's fingerprints without consent and, if force is used, a record must be made of the circumstances and those present (Code D, para. 4.8).

2.12.5.3 Retention of Fingerprints

In terms of the disposal of the case, cautioning a person for an offence is the equivalent of a conviction at court. Therefore if the person has been in police detention and has not had his/her fingerprints taken prior to the caution, there is no power to take that person's fingerprints under the 1984 Act (**see para. 2.12.5.1**). This is also the case where a person is released and subsequently summonsed.

It should be noted that s. 64 of the 1984 Act, as amended by the Criminal Justice and Police Act 2001, has removed the requirement to destroy fingerprints of suspects who are not convicted and custody officers should no longer inform detained persons of the right to destruction (see Code D, Annex F). The Act removes this obligation in relation to fingerprints and samples where the person is cleared of the offence for which they were taken or a decision is made not to prosecute (**see para. 2.12.11**). The obligation to destroy is replaced by a rule to the effect that any fingerprints or samples retained can only be used for the purposes related to the prevention and detection of crime, the investigation of any offence or the conduct of any prosecution. This means that if a match is established at a subsequent crime scene with an individual who has been cleared of an earlier offence, the police are able to use this information in the investigation of the crime. The system of retaining DNA samples and fingerprint evidence after a suspect had been cleared of the offence that gave rise to the collection of those items of evidence is compatible with both Article 8 and Article 14 of the European Convention on Human Rights (*R* v *Chief Constable of South Yorkshire, ex parte Marper* (2002) *The Times*, 4 April).

Fingerprints and samples taken from a person suspected of committing a recordable offence but not arrested, charged or informed they will be reported for it, may be subject to a speculative search only if the person consents in writing. Code D, Note 4B gives an example of the wording to be used for the consent. Once taken, the sample or fingerprints will be retained and used for purposes related to the prevention and detection of a crime, the investigation of an offence or the conduct of a prosecution either nationally or internationally. Once the person gives consent for the sample to be retained, it cannot be withdrawn.

Where a person, who is not a suspect, provides a sample or fingerprints voluntarily, e.g. for the purposes of elimination, there is no obligation for him/her to allow the samples or fingerprints to be retained or used other than for the purpose for which they were taken. Where consent is not given the fingerprints or samples must be destroyed and the information derived from them cannot be used in evidence against the person concerned or for the purposes of investigation of any offence. When seeking consent from a person for elimination samples and fingerprints the consents should be obtained separately and whether the person is consenting to their use and retention needs to be fully explained. Code D, Annex F, Note F1 should be followed when consent is being requested.

2.12.5.4   Criminal Record and Conviction Certificates

Under s. 118 of the Police Act 1997, in certain circumstances the Secretary of State issues certificates concerning an individual's previous convictions. In some cases the Secretary of State will not do this until he/she has been able to verify the person's identity, which can be done through the taking of their fingerprints. Where this is the case, the Secretary of State may require the police officer in charge of the specified police station, or any other police station he/she reasonably determines, to take the applicant's fingerprints at the specified station at such reasonable time as the officer may direct and notify to the applicant.

If fingerprints are taken in these circumstances they must be destroyed as soon as is practicable after the identity of the applicant is established to the satisfaction of the Secretary of State. The destruction can be witnessed by the person giving the fingerprints if he/she requests and/or the person can ask for a certificate stating the fingerprints have been destroyed. The certificate must be issued within three months of the request.

In the case of an individual under the age of 18 years the consent of the applicant's parent or guardian to the taking of the applicant's fingerprints is also required.

2.12.5.5   Footwear Impressions

The Serious Organised Crime and Police Act 2005 inserted a new s. 61A into the Police and Criminal Evidence Act 1984. The section provides power for a police officer to take a person's footwear impressions in connection with the investigation of an offence without consent from any person over the age of ten years who is detained at a police station (reasonable force may be used if necessary) and any other persons with their consent (if at a police station this must be in writing). Where the person does not consent he/she must be in police detention in consequence of being arrested for a recordable offence or must have been charged with a recordable offence, or informed that he/she will be reported for such an offence. Such a sample cannot be taken from a detained person without their consent unless he/she has not had an impression of his/her footwear taken in the course of the investigation of the offence unless the previously taken impression is not complete or is not of sufficient quality to allow satisfactory analysis, comparison or matching (Code D, paras 4.16 to 4.18). Code C, para. 4.19 sets out what the person must be told before the impression is taken and Code D, paras 4.20 and 4.21 set out what documentation is required.

2.12.6 Body Samples and Impressions

The taking of samples and impressions is governed by ss. 62 to 63A of the Police and Criminal Evidence Act 1984, together with Code D (paras 6.1 to 6.12) (see appendix 2.2).

Inferences from a defendant's refusal to consent to the taking of certain samples may be drawn by a court.

2.12.6.1 DNA Profiles

DNA stands for deoxyribo-nucleic acid. It is the chemical which is found in virtually every cell in our bodies and which carries genetic information from one generation to the next and determines our physical characteristics such as hair and eye colour. A number of techniques have been used to identify DNA:

- **SGM**—Second Generation Multiplex is a DNA profiling system which looks at seven areas (six areas plus a sex indicator area) to give a DNA profile. The average discrimination potential for an SGM profile is one in 50 million.
- **SGM Plus®**—The current technique, used since June 1999, for profiling DNA samples on the NDNAD. It looks at 11 areas (10 areas plus a sex indicator area) to give a DNA profile. The average discrimination potential for an SGM Plus is one in a billion.
- **DNA LCN**—DNA Low Copy Number is an extension of the SGM Plus profiling technique. It is more sensitive and enables scientists to produce DNA profiles from samples containing very few cells even if they are too small to be visible to the naked eye.

The purpose behind the taking of many samples is to enable the process of DNA profiling. Very basically, this involves an analysis of the sample taken from the suspect (the first sample), an analysis of samples taken from the crime scene or victim (the second sample) and then a comparison of the two. Both the process and the conclusions which might be drawn from the results are set out by Lord Taylor CJ in *R v Deen* (1994) *The Times*, 10 January.

The matching process involves creating 'bands' from each sample and then comparing the number of those bands which the two samples share. The more 'matches' that exist between the first and second samples, the less probability there is of that happening by pure chance. A 'good match' between the two samples does not of itself prove that the second sample came from the defendant. In using such samples to prove identification the prosecution will give evidence of:

- the *probability* of such a match happening by chance; and
- the *likelihood* that the person responsible was in fact the defendant.

When applying the 'this' rule (**see para. 2.12.3**) a jury must consider the second issue, that is, the likelihood of the defendant's being responsible.

The jury's task was set out by Phillips LJ in *R v Doheny* [1997] 1 Cr App R 369. In that case, involving a semen sample, his Lordship said:

> If you accept the scientific evidence called by the Crown, that indicates there are probably only four or five white males in the United Kingdom from whom that semen stain could have come. The defendant is one of them. The decision you have to reach, on all the evidence, is whether you are sure that it was the defendant who left that stain or whether it is possible that it is one of that other small group of men who share the same DNA characteristics.

(See also *Blackstone's Criminal Practice, 2008*, para. F18.31.)

In most cases there will be other evidence against the defendant, evidence which clearly increases the likelihood of his/her having committed the offence.

It will be for the prosecution to produce other facts to the court which reduces the 'chance' of the DNA sample belonging to someone other than the defendant. This may require further enquiries linking the suspect to the area or circumstances of the crime or may come from questions put to the suspect during interview. In *R v Lashley*, 25 February 2000, unreported, the sole evidence against the defendant for a robbery was DNA evidence from a half-smoked cigarette found behind the counter of the post office. The DNA matched a sample obtained from the suspect and would have matched the profile of seven to ten other males in the United Kingdom. The court held that the significance of DNA evidence depended critically upon what else was known about the suspect. Had there been evidence that the suspect was in the area, or normally lived there, or had connections there, at the material time, then the jury could have found that the case was compelling. This, the court said, would be because it may have been almost incredible that two out of seven men in the United Kingdom were in the vicinity at the relevant time. The courts are willing to allow the jury to consider partial or incomplete DNA profiles in some circumstances. In *R v Bates* [2006] EWCA Crim 1395, DNA evidence at the scene produced a partial profile that was interpreted as providing a 1 in 610,000 probability that Bates was the killer. The Court of Appeal held that there was no reason why partial profile DNA evidence should not be admissible provided that the jury are made aware of its inherent limitations and are given a sufficient explanation to enable them to evaluate it.

It is also important to ensure that there is no cross-contamination of DNA evidence between crime scenes, victims and suspects as was seen in the infamous American case of OJ Simpson's murder trial. It will be important to ensure that any allegations that officers may have contaminated evidence through handling/being present at several crime scenes can be successfully challenged. It is suggested that the best evidence here will be through records of crime scene logs and, where suspects have are being held in custody, records of who visited the custody suite. It will also be important that suspects and victims are kept apart. The integrity and continuity of DNA samples will be important evidence and likely to be challenged by the defence if not managed properly.

The Criminal Justice Act 2003 contains provisions that extend the circumstances in which a non-intimate sample may be taken without consent from a person in police detention. These provisions were implemented on 5 April 2005.

As a result, s. 23 of Home Office Circular 16/1995, *National DNA Database* which provides guidance regarding charging where DNA identification is involved, has been amended by Home Office Circular 58/2004, *Charges on Basis of Speculative Search Match on the National DNA Database*, and it states:

Speculative searches may be carried out of the National DNA Database and a suspect may now be charged on the basis of a match between a profile from DNA from the scene of the crime and a profile on the National DNA Database from an individual, *so long as there is further supporting evidence.*

It should also be noted that the databases can also now be used for the purpose of identifying a deceased person or a person from whom a body part came (s. 117(7) of SOCPA 2005 amending s. 64 of the 1984 Act).

However, there is a significant chance that matches involving partial DNA profiles (including SGM profiles) will not match if the profiles are upgraded to SGM Plus. Therefore, where any match is on the basis of a partial or SGM profile:

(a) strong consideration should be given to upgrading the partial or SGM profile to SGM Plus to ensure there is still a match before the matter comes to trial;

(b) if there is a decision to charge on the basis of such a match, the supporting evidence needs to be all the stronger. The amount of supporting evidence required will depend on the value of the DNA evidence in the context of the case. A scientist should be consulted where the value of the DNA evidence requires clarification.

2.12.7 Intimate and Non-intimate Samples

As discussed earlier, there are three key ways to prove a person's involvement in a criminal offence:

- witnesses
- confessions
- scientific evidence.

Given the inherent problems and weaknesses of the first two (**see chapters 2.5 and 2.9**), together with the advances being made in scientific procedures, the last of these is becoming more and more important in criminal evidence.

The analysis of intimate and non-intimate samples may provide essential evidence in showing or refuting a person's involvement in an offence. However, the courts have made it clear that DNA evidence alone will not be sufficient for a conviction and that there needs to be other supporting evidence to link the suspect to the crime. Such evidence may include confessions, that the suspect was near the crime scene at the time of the offence, that the suspect lived in the locality or had connections in the area.

The police powers to obtain intimate and non-intimate samples are provided by the Police and Criminal Evidence Act 1984 and were extended by amendments made by the Criminal Justice and Public Order Act 1994. Further guidance as to the exercise of these powers is contained within Code D of the PACE Codes of Practice.

2.12.7.1 Intimate and Non-intimate Samples Defined

Code D, para. 6 1 provides the definition of intimate and non-intimate samples:

(a) an 'intimate sample' means, a dental impression or sample of blood, semen or any other tissue fluid, urine, or pubic hair, or a swab taken from any part of a person's genitals or from a person's body orifice other than the mouth;

(b) a 'non-intimate sample' means:

(i) a sample of hair, other than pubic hair, which includes hair plucked with the root, see Note 6A;

(ii) a sample taken from a nail or from under a nail;
(iii) a swab taken from any part of a person's body other than a part from which a swab taken would be an intimate sample;
(iv) saliva;
(v) a skin impression which means any record, other than a fingerprint, which is a record, in any form and produced by any method, of the skin pattern and other physical characteristics or features of the whole, or any part of, a person's foot or of any other part of their body.

Code D, Note 6A sets out advice for taking non-intimate hair samples and states:

> When hair samples are taken for the purpose of DNA analysis (rather than for other purposes such as making a visual match), the suspect should be permitted a reasonable choice as to what part of the body the hairs are taken from. When hairs are plucked, they should be plucked individually, unless the suspect prefers otherwise and no more should be plucked than the person taking them reasonably considers necessary for a sufficient sample.

2.12.8 Intimate Samples

Section 62 of the Police and Criminal Evidence Act 1984 sets out police powers to take intimate samples. Code D of the PACE Codes of Practice provides additional guidance as to the exercise of the powers. The provisions of s. 62 together with Code D describe the circumstances and manner in which intimate samples can be taken. These can be understood by considering a number of key issues.

2.12.8.1 Consent

Before an intimate sample can be taken from a person in police detention, the consent of an officer of at least the rank of inspector is necessary, *together with the written consent of the person*. Without the consent of *both*, such a sample cannot be taken (Code D, para. 6.2).

Taking a sample without the relevant authority may amount to inhuman or degrading treatment under Article 3 of the European Convention on Human Rights (as to which, **see General Police Duties, chapter 4.3**). It may also amount to a criminal offence of assault (**see Crime**) and give rise to liability at civil law.

Where a person (who is a suspect) is not in police detention, an intimate sample may be taken where that person has already provided two (or more) non-intimate samples in the course of the investigation of the offence, which have proved insufficient for *the same means of analysis*. Should this pre-condition apply then the consent of both a police officer of at least the rank of inspector and the person concerned is necessary, as in the case of a person in police detention (Code D, para. 6.2).

Note 6C of Code D recognises that a sample may be taken from a person not in police detention, for the purposes of elimination, providing his/her consent is given.

In all cases where an intimate sample is to be taken from a young person aged over 14 but under 17, the consent of his/her parents or guardian is also necessary. If the person is a child under 14, the consent of his/her parents or guardian is necessary only.

2.12.8.2 Grounds for Authorisation

Regardless of whether the person is in police detention or not, a inspector may only give his/her authorisation if he/she has reasonable grounds:

- for suspecting the involvement of the person from whom the sample is to be taken in a recordable offence; *and*
- for believing that the sample will tend to confirm or disprove the person's involvement in the offence.

For further discussion on the meaning of 'reasonable grounds to suspect', **see General Police Duties, chapter 4.4**).

2.12.8.3 Information to be Given to the Suspect

Where an authorisation has been given and it is proposed to take a sample, an officer shall inform the suspect that the authorisation has been given *and* of the grounds for its being given. If the person has been arrested on suspicion of being involved in a recordable offence, charged or reported for a recordable offence then, in addition to the above, an officer must also inform the person, before the sample is taken, that the sample may be subject to a 'speculative search' (Code D, para. 6.8, Note 6E).

(A speculative search is a check made against other samples and information derived from other samples contained in records or held by or on behalf of the police or held in connection with or as a result of an investigation of an offence.)

Paragraph 6.3 of Code D also requires that, before the sample is given, the suspect must be warned that if he/she refuses without good cause, that refusal may harm his/her case if it comes to trial. Where the suspect is in police detention, or is at the police station voluntarily, the officer shall also explain the entitlement to legal advice (as to which, **see chapter 2.11**).

2.12.8.4 Recording the Authorisation

An inspector's authorisation may be given orally but, if so given, it must be confirmed in writing as soon as practicable. The consent from the suspect must be given in writing (s. 62(3) and (4) of the 1984 Act).

2.12.8.5 Other Information to be Recorded

Where an intimate sample is taken, certain information must be recorded. This information includes:

- the reasons for taking a sample or impression and if applicable, of its destruction must be made as soon as practicable;
- that the person gave written consent (and where that record can be found);
- if they are a suspect that they have been warned that if they refuse without good cause, their refusal may harm their case if it comes to trial (see para. 6.3);
- if they are in police detention or voluntarily at the police station that they have been reminded of their right to legal advice;
- that the person has been informed as in para. 6.8(c) that samples may be subject to a speculative search.

This information shall be recorded as soon as practicable after the sample has been taken. Where a suspect is in police detention the information shall be recorded in the custody record.

Refusal of a Suspect to Give Consent

Where a suspect refuses, without good cause, to provide an intimate sample, then, in proceedings against that person for an offence, the court may draw such inferences as appear proper. The court may use such an inference for the purposes of determining:

- guilt;
- whether there is a case to answer;
- whether to commit for trial;
- whether an application to dismiss charges should be granted (where a notice of transfer from a magistrates' court to a Crown Court for an indictable only offence and any other linked offences has been given earlier) (s. 62(10)).

2.12.8.7 **Taking an Intimate Sample**

Dental impressions may only be taken by a registered dentist. Intimate samples, other than urine, may only be taken by a registered medical practitioner or a registered nurse or a registered paramedic (Code D, para. 6.4).

Paragraph 6.9 of Code D sets out the provisions to be followed where clothing needs to removed in circumstances likely to cause embarrassment. These are:

- no person of the opposite sex may be present (other than a registered medical practitioner or registered health care professional);
- only people whose presence is necessary for the taking of the sample should in fact be present;
- in the case of a juvenile or mentally disordered or mentally vulnerable person, an appropriate adult of the opposite sex may be present *if specifically requested by the person and the person is readily available*;
- in the case of a juvenile, clothing may only be removed in the absence of an appropriate adult if the person signifies (in the presence of the appropriate adult) that he/she prefers his/her absence and the appropriate adult agrees.
- Clearly, as consent is needed to take a sample, the use of force would be inappropriate.

2.12.9 **Non-intimate Samples**

The taking by police of non-intimate samples is governed by s. 63 of the Police and Criminal Evidence Act 1984. Additional guidance in the exercise of the powers is provided by Code D. The key requirements of these provisions are:

2.12.9.1 **Consent**

A person may consent to the taking of a non-intimate sample. If he/she does so, the consent must be given in writing.

Code D, para. 6.6 sets out those occasions when non-intimate samples can be taken without consent; these circumstances vary as to whether the person is in police detention or not.

In police detention

A non-intimate sample may be taken from a person without the appropriate consent if the person is in police detention in consequence of his arrest for a recordable offence and he/she either:

- has not had a non-intimate sample of the same type and from the same part of the body taken in the course of the investigation of the offence by police; or
- he/she has had such a sample taken but it proved insufficient (s. 63(2A) to (2C)).

If the person is being held in custody by the police on the authority of a court an officer of at least the rank of inspector may authorise the taking of a non-intimate sample without the appropriate consent if he/she has reasonable grounds for believing the person's involvement in a recordable offence and believes that the sample will tend to confirm or disprove his/her involvement. Such an authority must not be given for a non-intimate sample consisting of a skin impression if a skin impression of the same part of the body has already been taken from that person in the course of the investigation of the offence and the impression previously taken is not one that has proved insufficient (s. 63(3), (4) and (5A)).

Whether or not in police detention

A non-intimate sample may be taken from a person (whether or not he/she is in police detention or is being held in custody by the police on the authority of a court) without the appropriate consent if he/she has been:

- charged with a recordable offence or informed that he/she will be reported for such an offence; and either he/she has not had a non-intimate sample taken from him/her in the course of the investigation of the offence by the police or he/she has had a non-intimate sample taken from him/her but either it was not suitable for the same means of analysis or, though so suitable, the sample proved insufficient (Code D, para. 6.6(b));
- detained following acquittal on grounds of insanity or finding of unfitness to plead;
- convicted of a recordable offence (s. 3(3A) to (3C)).

'Recordable offences' in relation to the PACE Codes relate to those offences for which convictions, cautions, reprimands or warnings may be recorded in national police records (see Code D, Note 4A). In order to close a gap in the legislation, the Criminal Evidence (Amendment) Act 1997 was passed, allowing the taking of non-intimate samples without consent in the case of people serving sentences for certain sexual, violent or other specified offences. The effect of ss. 1 and 2 of the 1997 Act is to allow the taking of such samples from people serving a sentence of imprisonment or being detained under a hospital order (under the Mental Health Act 1983) if they were convicted of a recordable offence listed at sch. 1 before 10 April 1995. The provisions also extend to people who were not convicted by reason of their insanity or their unfitness to plead but who were detained at the relevant time under the Mental Health Act 1983.

2.12.9.2 Information to be Given to the Suspect

Where an authorisation has been given by an officer of at least the rank of inspector and it is proposed to take a sample, an officer shall inform the suspect that the authorisation has been given *and* of the grounds for it being given (including the nature of the offence the person is suspected of committing).

Where a non-intimate sample is taken as a result of the suspect being charged, informed he/she is to be reported, following conviction for a recordable offence or while in police detention following his/her arrest for a recordable offence, he/she must be told of the reason why the sample is to be taken and the reason shall be recorded as soon as practicable after the sample is taken.

The person must be informed—before the sample is taken—that the sample may be subject to a 'speculative search' (Code D, para. 6.8) (**see para. 2.12.8**).

2.12.9.3 Recording the Authorisation

Where an authorisation is required from an officer of at least the rank of inspector this may be given orally, but if so given, must be confirmed in writing as soon as practicable. The consent from the suspect must be given in writing (Code D, para. 6.10).

2.12.9.4 Other Information to be Recorded

Where a non-intimate sample is taken as a result of an officer of at least the rank of inspector's authority, the following information should be recorded:

- the *authorisation* by virtue of which the sample was taken;
- the *grounds* for the authorisation;
- the fact that the person has been informed that the sample may be subject to a *speculative search*.

This information must be recorded *as soon as practicable* after the sample has been taken.

In other cases where a sample is taken without the person's consent, the reason shall be recorded as soon as practicable after the sample is taken.

Where a suspect is in police detention, the information shall be recorded in the custody record (s. 63(9) of the 1984 Act).

2.12.9.5 Use of Force

Paragraph 6.7 of Code D provides that reasonable force may be used if necessary to obtain non-intimate samples in the circumstances described. Where force is used, a record should be made of the circumstances and those present at the time.

2.12.9.6 Taking a Non-intimate Sample

Where clothing needs to be removed in order to take a non-intimate sample, para. 6.9 of Code D should be applied to prevent embarrassment.

Where a non-intimate sample consisting of a skin impression is taken electronically from a person, it must be taken only in such manner, and using such devices, as the Secretary of State has approved for the purpose of the electronic taking of such an impression (s. 63(9A)). No such devices are currently approved.

2.12.10 Power to Require Persons to Attend a Police Station to Provide Samples

In addition to the powers outlined, s. 63A of the Police and Criminal Evidence Act 1984 also provides for a constable to require a person to attend a police station for samples to be taken. The circumstances under which this requirement can be made are summarised as follows.

2.12.10.1 When Can the Requirement be Made?

A constable may make the requirement:

- where a person has been charged with a recordable offence or informed that he/she will be reported, or
- where the person has been convicted of a recordable offence

and, in either case, the person has not had a sample taken in the course of the investigation into the offence, or he/she has had a sample taken but it proved either unsuitable for the same means of analysis or the sample was insufficient.

2.12.10.2 The Period during which a Constable may Make the Requirement

The requirement to attend a police station must be made:

- within one month of the date of charge or of conviction or within one month of the date of reporting; or
- within one month of the appropriate officer being informed that the sample is not suitable or has proved insufficient for analysis.

In making the requirement the officer:

- shall give the person at least seven days within which the person must attend; and
- may direct the person to attend at a specified time of day or between specified times of day.

2.12.10.3 Failure to Comply with the Requirement

Should a person fail to comply with the requirement, a constable may arrest the person without a warrant.

An appropriate officer is:

- the officer investigating the offence in the case of a person charged or told he/she will be reported;
- the officer in charge of the police station from which the investigation was conducted in the case of a person convicted.

For the corresponding power to take finger and palm prints, **see para. 2.12.5.**

2.12.11 Destruction of Samples

Code D, Annex F deals with the destruction and the speculative searches of fingerprints and samples and speculative searches of footwear impressions. It is important that the Annex is followed particularly in relation to obtaining consent and explaining to volunteers what they are consenting to. Annex F, Note F1 provides suggested wordings that can be used when obtaining a person's consent to provide fingerprints footwear impressions or DNA samples for elimination purposes. It is important to use the correct wording depending on what the person has volunteered to, for example whether it is just to allow the fingerprint or sample to be used only for the purposes of a specific investigation; or for that investigation *and* retained by the police for future use. Such future use is limited to purposes related to the prevention or detection of crime, the investigation of an offence or the conduct of a prosecution in, as well as outside, the United Kingdom and may also be subject to a speculative search. This includes checking fingerprints and samples against other fingerprints or footwear impressions and DNA records held by, or on behalf of, the police and other law enforcement authorities in, as well as outside, the United Kingdom.

When fingerprints or footwear impressions or DNA samples are taken from a person in connection with an investigation and the person is not suspected of having committed the offence, the fingerprints or footwear impressions and/or sample must be destroyed as soon as they have fulfilled the purpose for which they were taken unless:

- they were taken for the purposes of an investigation of an offence for which a person has been convicted; and
- fingerprints or footwear impressions or samples were also taken from the convicted person for the purposes of that investigation.

The reason why fingerprints or footwear impressions and samples are retained is to allow for all fingerprints or footwear impressions and samples in a case to be available for any subsequent miscarriage of justice investigation. They may not be used in the investigation of any offence or in evidence against the person who is, or would be, entitled to the destruction of the fingerprints or footwear impressions and samples unless the person gives their written consent for their fingerprints or footwear impressions or sample to be retained and used after they have fulfilled the purpose for which they were taken.

Annex F, para. 3 details what must be done when a person's fingerprints or footwear impressions or sample are to be destroyed; this includes all copies of the fingerprints or footwear impressions.

Annex F, para. 5 deals with the retention and destruction of fingerprints or footwear impressions taken in connection with Immigration Service inquiries.

2.12.12 Terrorism Offences

There are additional powers and procedures for those suspects arrested in connection with terrorism which are contained in the Terrorism Act 2000 (as to which, **see General Police Duties, chapter 4.6**).

With the exception of fingerprints, non-intimate samples or intimate samples, a constable may take any steps which are reasonably necessary for:

- photographing the detained person;
- measuring him/her, or identifying him/her (sch. 8, para. 2 to the 2000 Act).

2.12.12.1 Fingerprints and Non-intimate Samples

Fingerprints and non-intimate samples may be taken from a person detained under s. 41 of or sch. 7 to the Terrorism Act 2000 only if they are taken by a constable either:

- with the consent of the detained person given in writing; or
- where he/she is detained at a police station and does not give constant, a police officer of at least the rank of superintendent authorises the fingerprints or sample to be taken; or

- where the person has been convicted of a recordable offence and does not give consent, where a non-intimate sample is to be taken, he/she was convicted of the offence on or after 10 April 1995 (sch. 8, para. 10(1) to (4) to the 2000 Act).

2.12.12.2 Intimate Samples

An intimate sample may be taken from a detained person only if:

- he/she is detained at a police station;
- the appropriate consent is given in writing;
- a police officer of at least the rank of superintendent authorises the sample to be taken (sch. 8, para. 10(5) to the 2000 Act).

The sample must be taken by a constable but an intimate sample, other than a sample of urine or a dental impression, may be taken only by a registered medical practitioner acting on the authority of a constable. An intimate sample which is a dental impression may be taken only by a registered dentist acting on the authority of a constable.

The grounds for which an authorisation may be given under the Terrorism Act 2000 are:

- the officer reasonably suspects that the person has been involved in an offence under any of the provisions mentioned in s. 40(1)(a) of the Terrorism Act 2000 and the officer reasonably believes that the fingerprints or sample will tend to confirm or disprove his/her involvement; or
- the officer is satisfied that the taking of the fingerprints or sample from the person is necessary in order to assist in determining whether he/she is or has been concerned in the commission, preparation or instigation of acts of terrorism (s. 40(1)(b) of the Terrorism Act 2000); or
- the officer is satisfied that the taking of fingerprints of the detained person will facilitate the ascertainment of that person's identity (or showing that he/she is not a particular person): and that person has refused to identify him/herself or the officer has reasonable grounds for suspecting that that person is not who he/she claims to be.

Section 40(1)(a) of the Terrorism Act 2000 refers to offences of:

- membership to a proscribed organisation;
- arranging, managing or assisting in arranging or managing a meeting to support a proscribed organisation or to further the activities of a proscribed organisation;
- addressing a meeting for the purpose of encouraging support for a proscribed organisation or to further its activities;
- fund-raising for the purposes of terrorism;
- using and possessing money or other property for the purposes of terrorism or making arrangements for its use;
- money laundering;
- providing instruction or training in the making or use of weapons;
- directing terrorist organisation;
- possession of articles for terrorist purposes;
- collection or possession of information of a kind likely to be useful to a person committing or preparing an act of terrorism;
- inciting terrorism overseas;
- funding arrangements.

Before fingerprints or a sample are taken from a person he/she must be informed that the authorisation has been given, the grounds upon which it has been given and, where relevant, of the nature of the offence in which it is suspected that he/she has been involved.

Where appropriate written consent to the taking of an intimate sample from a person is refused without good cause, in any proceedings against that person for an offence, the court, in determining whether to commit him for trial or whether there is a case to answer, may draw such inferences from the refusal as appear proper, and the court or jury, in determining whether that person is guilty of the offence charged, may draw such inferences from the refusal as appear proper.

It should be noted that s. 63A, as amended by the Criminal Justice and Police Act 2001 and SOCPA 2005, widens the extent that fingerprints, footwear impressions and DNA profiles can be cross-searched against those held by another UK or Island force. This has been extended to other police forces (for example, foreign police forces, the Ministry of Defence and the Armed Forces police forces) on the same basis that already exists between UK and Island forces. This also applies to fingerprints and samples obtained under the Terrorism Act 2000. Section 118 of SOCPA makes a number of consequential amendments to ss. 63A and 64 of PACE 1984 to allow footwear impressions to be retained and searched against the National Footwear Reference Collection and speculatively searched against the Mark Intelligence Index.

Where a sample proves to be insufficient there are provisions for obtaining further samples; this must be authorised by an officer of the rank of superintendent or above.

2.13 Interviews

2.13.1 Introduction

Much police time is spent interviewing witnesses and suspects. Confessions are often seen by the police to be an important part of the prosecution case but have frequently been a source of attack by the defence. The power imbalance between a detained person and his/her custodians has been an issue which has often brought into question the reliability of any confession, particularly as it had, until recently, been the right of an individual detainee to remain silent without any adverse inferences being drawn (**see chapter 2.7**). The PACE Codes of Practice C, E and F are intended to provide some protection to people being interviewed by police and lay down guidelines as to how interviews should be conducted. This protection means that confessions may be held to be inadmissible because of:

- the conduct of the interviewing officers (s. 76(2)(a) of the Police and Criminal Evidence Act 1984);
- the unreliability of the confession (s. 76(2)(b)); or
- unfairness in the proceedings (s. 78).

It may seem that the balance is in favour of the detained person. However, the position now is that, while a person may still remain silent and the rules remain to preserve this right, inferences may now be drawn from a person's silence in some circumstances (**see chapter 2.7**).

It is not unusual for it to be alleged that officers have fabricated evidence or obtained a confession through trickery or by some kind of oppression. In order to provide safeguards against the risk of such evidence from questioning being obtained by oppression or in circumstances rendering it unreliable or obtained in a manner that breaches an individual's remaining right to silence, there are restrictions and guidelines on police questioning. These rules can be found throughout Codes C and E of the PACE Codes of Practice, giving guidance on the questioning of persons by police officers. Failure to follow these rules may lead to evidence being excluded and/or disciplinary charges and ultimately could lead to civil claims for compensation. For conduct that might lead to the exclusion of evidence, **see para. 2.9.3**. For police disciplinary proceedings, **see General Police Duties, chapter 4.1**.

2.13.2 What is an Interview?

Not all discussions between the police and members of the public will be protected or governed by the PACE Codes of Practice. Code C, para. 11.1A defines an interview as follows:

> An interview is the questioning of a person regarding their involvement or suspected involvement in a criminal offence or offences which, under paragraph 10.1, must be carried out under caution.

Whenever a person is interviewed they must be informed of the nature of the offence, or further offence. Procedures under the Road Traffic Act 1988, section 7 or the Transport and Works Act 1992, section 31 do not constitute interviewing for the purpose of this Code.

KEYNOTE

Whether an interaction between a police officer and a member of the public is defined as an interview by the court can be crucial as to whether it will be admissible in evidence. It is therefore essential to understand the definition of an interview for the purposes of PACE and when a caution must be given and which caution must be given (for cautions, **see para. 2.13.4**).

If a person is asked questions for reasons *other than obtaining evidence about his/her involvement or suspected involvement in an offence*, this is not an interview (and a caution need not be given). (For the use of cautions, **see para. 2.13.4**.) This point is confirmed in the case of *R* v *McGuinness* [1999] Crim LR 318, where the court confirmed that it was only when a person was suspected of an offence that the caution must be administered before questioning. Consequently, in *R* v *Miller* [1998] Crim LR 209 the court held that asking a person the single question, 'Are these ecstasy tablets?' criminally implicated the person and therefore the conversation was an interview (i.e. it would not be necessary to ask such a question if there were no suspicion that the tablets were a controlled substance).

Guidance on when questions do not amount to an interview is given by Code C, para. 10.1:

... A person need not be cautioned if questions are for other necessary purposes, e.g.:
(a) solely to establish their identity or ownership of any vehicle;
(b) to obtain information in accordance with any relevant statutory requirement ...;
(c) in furtherance of the proper and effective conduct of a search, e.g. to determine the need to search in the exercise of powers of stop and search or to seek co-operation while carrying out a search;
(d) to seek verification of a written record as in paragraph 11.13;
(e) when examining a person in accordance with the Terrorism Act 2000, schedule 7 and the Code of Practice for Examining Officers issued under that Act, schedule 14, paragraph 6.

KEYNOTE

Code C, para. 10.1 is not an exhaustive list and officers may have other valid reasons to speak to a person before it becomes an interview.

Before a person can be interviewed about their involvement in an offence, that person must be cautioned. So it might be said that an interview is any questioning of a person after such time as a caution has been or should have been administered. Where a person is arrested for an offence, he/she must also be cautioned, as any questioning will amount to an interview (see General Police Duties, chapter 4.4).

Where the questions go beyond issues raised by Code C, para. 10.1 and go to the question of guilt, this is likely to be an interview for the purposes of the Police and Criminal Evidence Act 1984. In *Crown Prosecution Service* v *O'Shea*, 11 May 1998, unreported, police were called to a road traffic accident. O'Shea, the owner of the vehicle, was near the car, exhibiting signs of drunkenness and there was no one else in the vicinity who might have been driving the vehicle. The officer said to O'Shea the words, 'An accident has just happened that is alleged was your fault'. The court held that it was clear that when the officer had asked O'Shea whether he was driving his vehicle at the time of the accident, the officer had known that he was the owner of the vehicle and therefore the question was not solely to establish whether he was the owner. Accordingly, the thrust of the question was whether he had committed an offence. The defendant's subsequent answer was held to be inadmissible as the PACE Codes of Practice had not been complied with. *O'Shea* can be contrasted with *R* v *Maguire* [1989] Crim LR 815 where the court held that Code C does not prevent a police officer from asking questions at or near the scene of the crime to elicit an explanation which, if true or accepted, would clear the suspect.

Where a suspect makes any comment which is outside the context of an interview but which might be relevant to the offence, a written record must be made of these (Code C, para. 11.13)

2.13.3 When a Caution must be Given

Code C, para. 10.1 states:

A person whom there are grounds to suspect of an offence, see Note 10A, must be cautioned before any questions about an offence, or further questions if the answers provide the grounds for suspicion, are put to them if either the suspect's answers or silence, (i.e. failure or refusal to answer or answer satisfactorily) may be given in evidence to a court in a prosecution. . . .

KEYNOTE

A caution is required to be given to a person who has been arrested or before asking any further questions of a person where there are grounds to suspect that he/she has committed an offence. The courts have given some guidance as to when a caution should be administered. There must be real grounds for suspicion; a mere hunch is not sufficient. The grounds have to be such as to lead to suspicion that an offence has been committed by that person. This view is confirmed in *Batley* v *DPP* (1998) *The Times*, 5 March, where the court accepted that, in general terms, where police officers had nothing more than a hunch that an offence was being committed, there would not be enough to activate the Code. However, it was necessary to caution a person before asking questions which went to the very heart of the issue as to whether he/she might be committing an offence, especially since the suspect was being invited to incriminate him/herself.

In *Fox* v *United Kingdom* (1990) 13 EHRR 157, the court stated that reasonable suspicion arises from facts or information which would satisfy an objective observer that the person concerned may have committed the offence. Clearly there will be a need to record this information in detail to inform the court of the facts as known at the time of the decision to caution or not to caution.

Further guidance was provided in *R* v *Smith* [2001] 1 WLR 1031 where the court held that establishing a reasonable suspicion was an objective test and an honest belief by a police officer was not required. Suspicion could take into account evidence that could not be adduced, such as hearsay. Except where evidence had been obtained in blatant breach of a statute, improperly obtained information could still be relied on. A case where the court held that a caution was not necessary is *Ridehalgh* v *DPP* [2005] EWHC 1100 (Admin). Here the defendant was a police officer who had been called to a police station to deal with a detained person. Police officers at the station noticed a smell of alcohol on the defendant and the other officers asked if he had been drinking, and whether he had driven to the station. As a result of his answer he was breath tested and then arrested, cautioned and charged. The court held that a necessary precondition for the administration of a caution was that there had to be grounds for the suspicion of a criminal offence. All that the police officers had prior to the questions posed was a smell of alcohol on the defendant's breath; they had no indication as to how much alcohol R had consumed or whether he had driven.

Once a person has been cautioned, consideration of further cautions must be given. The need for additional cautions is provided for by the PACE Codes of Practice. In addition, in *R* v *Miller* [1998] Crim LR 209, the court said that one caution was not necessarily enough, and before other questions are asked of a suspect at a later stage, a further caution may be necessary.

In addition to the duty to caution a suspect, there will be occasions where a person arrested for an offence will have to be given a 'special warning' in interview. Special warnings are concerned with a person's right to silence (see ss. 34 to 37 of the Criminal Justice and Public Order Act 1994). As mentioned above, this will only apply where the detainee has had the opportunity to seek legal advice.

2.13.4 The Caution

Until 2003 there was effectively only one caution that police officers gave to a suspect before the suspect was interviewed or arrested. This caution had itself been amended by the Criminal Justice and Public Order Act 1994 which allowed for inferences to be drawn at court from a suspect's silence to questions put by the interviewing officer. The amended caution following the 1994 Act, along with the special warnings required by ss. 36 and 37 of that Act, were intended to provide the suspect with sufficient warning concerning his/her choice to remain silent. However this position was changed by the case of *Murray* v *United Kingdom* (1996) 22 EHRR 29 and there is now a requirement to consider which of two cautions is required and at what stage of the investigation.

In *Murray* it was held that adverse inferences may not be drawn from the silence of a person who wants legal advice if they have not been allowed an opportunity to receive it. As a result of this decision Code C, Annex C sets out the restriction on drawing adverse inferences from silence and the terms of the caution when the restriction applies. Adverse inferences from silence are restricted in some cases where the detainee has not had legal advice. In these cases the caution that must be given to the person has been amended in order to remove the infringement on the person's right to remain silent.

2.13.4.1 Which Caution Should be Given?

In all cases other than those where the restriction on drawing adverse inferences apply, the caution to be given is set out in Code C, para. 10.5:

> You do not have to say anything. But it may harm your defence if you do not mention when questioned something which you later rely on in Court. Anything you do say may be given in evidence.

The occasions where the alternative caution is required are set out in Code C, Annex C, para. 1, that is occasions where the restriction on drawing an adverse inference apply.
This restriction applies:

- to any detainee at a police station who has asked for legal advice and not been allowed an opportunity to consult a solicitor and has not changed their mind;
- to any detainee at a police station who has had their right to consult a solicitor suspended by an officer of the rank of superintendent or above (Code C, Annex B);
- where an officer of superintendent rank or above has authorised an interview without waiting for the detainee to consult with a solicitor as set out in Code C, para. 6.6(b)(ii);
- where the interview goes ahead without a solicitor, including a duty solicitor, because awaiting their arrival would cause unreasonable delay to the process of the investigation and the person has not changed their mind about wanting a solicitor (Code C, para. 6.6(b)(ii))

- where a person has been charged with, or informed they may be prosecuted for an offence and:
  - ◆ has had brought to their notice a written statement made by another person or the content of an interview with another person which relates to that offence,
  - ◆ is interviewed about that offence, or
  - ◆ makes a written statement about that offence.

Annex C, para. 2 sets out the alternative terms of the caution to be used when the restriction on drawing adverse inferences from silence applies:

> You do not have to say anything, but anything you do say may be given in evidence.

The situation is likely to occur during a detainee's detention where it will be necessary to administer both of these cautions at various times during his/her detention. As there is a significant difference between them in relation to the right to silence, it will be important to make it clear which caution applies to the detainee during any interview or charge procedure. Guidance as to what the detainee should be told, is provided by Code C, Annex C, Note C2, this paragraph gives sample explanations that need to be explained to the detainee before the change is caution is given.

Full caution already given (in most cases given when arrested)	→ Detainee's access to legal advice restricted as per Code C, Annex C, para. 1. Need to give alternative caution	→ Explain change in caution as set out at Code C, Annex C Note C2(a)(i)	→ Give caution as set out at Annex C, para. 2
Full caution already given	→ Detainee has been charged but is further interviewed (Code C, Annex C, para. 1). Need to give alternative caution	→ Explain change in caution as set out at Code C, Annex C, Note C2(a)(ii)	→ Give caution as set out at Annex C, para. 2
Caution as set out at Annex C, para. 2, given	→ Detainee has now had access to a solicitor or changed their mind. Need to give alternative caution	→ Explain change in caution as set out at Code C, Annex C, Note C2(b)	→ Give caution Code C, para. 10.5

Where Code C, Annex C, para. 1 applies (i.e. the detainee has not been given access to a solicitor) and the detainee is charged with an offence or informed they may be prosecuted, the caution at Annex C, para. 2 should be used, on all other occasions the caution at Code C, para. 16.2 should be used:

> You do not have to say anything. But it may harm your defence if you do not mention now something which you later rely on in court. Anything you do say may be given in evidence.

2.13.4.2 Consequences of Not Giving a Caution

If a person is questioned without being cautioned when a caution should have been given, any admissions made by that person are likely to be inadmissible in evidence. One of the main reasons for this is that a person has a right to remain silent and if the caution has not been given, the suspect has not been warned of this right nor of the risks of self-incrimination. Conversely, if a caution is not required and one is given, the person may not make admissions which he/she might otherwise have made. Consequently, it is important to be aware of when to administer a caution and, in cases of doubt, to err on the side of caution. Should an interview be excluded, this may have implications on other evidence obtained as a consequence of the confession (**see para. 2.9.2.6**).

2.13.4.3 Unsolicited Comments

There will be occasions where suspects make unsolicited comments implicating them in an offence before they are suspected of any involvement and therefore before they are cautioned (or further cautioned if already suspected). Such statements are likely to be admissible provided the PACE Codes of Practice are complied with. Code C, paras 11.13 and 11.14 state:

> 11.13 A written record shall be made of any comments made by a suspect, including unsolicited comments, which are outside the context of an interview but which might be relevant to the offence. Any such record must be timed and signed by the maker. When practicable the suspect shall be given the opportunity to read that record and to sign it as correct or to indicate how they consider it inaccurate. See Note 11E
>
> 11.14 Any refusal by a person to sign an interview record when asked in accordance with this Code must itself be recorded.

Note 11E states:

> When a suspect agrees to read records of interviews and other comments and sign them as correct, they should be asked to endorse the record with, e.g. 'I agree that this is a correct record of what was said' and add their signature. If the suspect does not agree with the record, the interviewer should record the details of any disagreement and ask the suspect to read these details and sign them to the effect that they accurately reflect their disagreement. Any refusal to sign should be recorded.

KEYNOTE

It is particularly important to record the comment and give the person an opportunity to see what has been recorded and to comment/endorse it. Where the person has had this opportunity and signs the record then it will strengthen the evidence and if he/she declines to sign it, this may assist in establishing what the defence case may be.

In *R v Miller* (above) the court held that Code C, para. 11.13 requires a written record, timed and signed by the suspect as correct or an opportunity for the suspect to indicate which parts were inaccurate.

While it is suggested that this should be done at an early opportunity, in *Batley* v *DPP* (1998) *The Times*, 5 March, where it was held that as the Code did not require an *immediate* endorsement and no time factor was laid down, there was nothing to constrain the police from returning the next day to get their endorsement.

2.13.5 Interview of Person not Under Arrest

If a person has not been arrested then he/she can be interviewed almost anywhere (but an officer intending to interview a person on private property must consider whether he/she is trespassing, **see General Police Duties, chapter 4.4**). If the interview with a person not under arrest takes place in a police station, Code C, para. 3.21 and Note 1A must be followed.

If the interview is to be with a juvenile, Code C, para. 11.16, gives guidance as to when interviews should take place at a juvenile's place of education. This should only be in exceptional circumstances and with the agreement of the principal or the principal's nominee. The juvenile's parent(s) or person(s) responsible for his/her welfare and the appropriate adult (if a different person) should be notified of the interview and be afforded reasonable time in which to attend. Code C, Note 1B outlines occasions when a person should not act as an appropriate adult). The principal or nominee can act as the appropriate adult where waiting for an appropriate adult would cause unreasonable delay. This is not the case where the juvenile is suspected of an offence against his/her educational establishment (Code C, para. 11.15). Where a juvenile is at a police station Code C, paras 11.18 to 11.20 and Note 11C outline the limited circumstances when a juvenile may be interviewed without an appropriate adult being present.

In cases where the person is not under arrest, certain information must be given to him/her. This is covered by Code C, para. 10.2 which states:

> Whenever a person not under arrest is initially cautioned, or reminded they are under caution, that person must at the same time be told they are not under arrest and are free to leave if they want to. See Note 10C

For the situation where a person is a police station voluntarily and not under arrest, see Code C, para. 3.21 (**see General Police Duties, chapter 4.4**).

When carrying out an interview, officers should be mindful of how they treat the person, this it is suggested, also applies to witnesses as well as suspects. For instance in *L* v *Reading Borough Council* [2001] 1 WLR 1575, the court stated that it was arguable that when interviewing a young child victim there was an assumption of responsibility and a special relationship was created. Part of the responsibility was to protect the child from future harm that could ensue from the manner of the investigation. Following this line, failure to protect the victims/witnesses could lead to a claim for damages if they suffer harm. If a child is a witness or victim they should be interviewed via visual recording in line with current procedures.

2.13.6 Interview of Person Under Arrest

Any interview of a person who is under arrest must take place at a police station (Code C, para. 11.1) or other authorised place of detention unless waiting until the interview can be conducted at such a place is likely to:

- lead to interference with or harm to evidence connected with an offence or interference with or physical harm to other people or serious loss of, or damage to property; or
- lead to the alerting of other people suspected of having committed an offence but not yet arrested for it; or
- hinder the recovery of property obtained in consequence of the commission of an offence.

Code C requires that interviewing in any of these circumstances shall cease once the relevant risk has been averted or the necessary questions have been put in order to attempt to avert that risk (para. 11.1). There is a danger in these cases of continuing the interview past the point where the risk has been averted, this could lead to the whole interview being excluded.

The courts have recognised that there may be times when a person who is under arrest will be asked questions other than when at the police station. One such example is where the arrested person is present while officers search his/her address (**see General Police Duties, chapter 4.4**). In *R* v *Hanchard*, 6 December 1999, unreported, the court recognised that searches of premises could not be conducted in complete silence. The court stated that it would be unfair and unreasonable not to put any questions to owners of premises undergoing a search; however, what questions can be asked will be a matter of fact and degree in each individual case. Where questions go beyond that needed for the immediate investigation it would be a breach of the Codes. In *Hanchard*, the questions which were admissible included whether cannabis at the address belonged to the suspect and where a large quantity of money had come from.

If a person has been arrested by one police force on behalf of another and the lawful period of detention in respect of that offence has not yet begun (in accordance with s. 41 of the Police and Criminal Evidence Act 1984 (**see para. 2.11.6.8**)), no questions may be put to him/her about the offence while he/she is in transit between the forces except in order to clarify any voluntary statement made by him/her (Code C, para. 14.1).

If a person is in police detention at a hospital, he/she may not be questioned without the agreement of a responsible doctor (Code C, para. 14.2). If an interview does take place, the interviewing officer must inform the custody officer as the period will count to the total time spent in custody (Note 14A).

If questioning does take place in any of these circumstances it will affect the suspect's 'detention clock' (**see chapter 2.11**). The custody officer must be informed of such an interview as it may affect the lawfulness of the suspect's detention (**see para. 2.11.7.1**).

It is essential to comply with the rules on interviewing after arrest, as a failure could jeopardise any future admissions made in interview. In *R* v *Webster*, 12 December 2000 unreported, the police evidence was that during the search of his house the defendant, having been arrested but not cautioned, had made admissions as to where the drugs were located in his house and as to the amount of drugs that he possessed. No contemporaneous note was taken of the search. The defendant was then interviewed on the same basis as his answers to the questions which had been asked during the search. The court held that the later interview at the police station did not cure the breaches of the Codes of Practice which had occurred during the search and both interviews were excluded.

2.13.7 Person Charged with an Offence

Once a person has been charged with an offence generally he/she cannot be interviewed about the offence unless it is necessary:

- to prevent or minimise harm or loss to some other person or to the public; or
- to clear up an ambiguity in a previous answer or statement; or
- in the interest of justice that the person should have questions put to him/her and have an opportunity to comment on information concerning the offence which has come to light since he/she was charged or informed that he/she might be prosecuted.

It should be noted that the service of the Notice of Intended Prosecution under ss. 1 and 2 of the Road Traffic Offenders Act 1988 (**see Road Policing, chapter 3.3**), does not amount to informing a person that he/she may be prosecuted for an offence and so does not preclude further questioning in relation to that offence (Code C, Note 16B).

If a person is interviewed for any other reason, the interview is likely to be inadmissible in evidence.

Where a person is interviewed after charge, Code C, para. 16.5 states:

> ... Before any such interview, the interviewer shall:
>   (a) caution the detainee, 'You do not have to say anything, but anything you do say may be given in evidence.';
>   (b) remind the detainee about their right to legal advice.
> See Note 16B

This caution does not restrict the right to silence. It is not unusual for a person who has been charged with offences (and therefore his/her detention is for other reasons, e.g. because bail has been refused) to be paid a 'social visit' or to be spoken to for debrief intelligence purposes. Clearly there is a risk that the person may provide additional evidence about the offences for which he/she has been detained on other matters. *R v Williams* (1992) *The Times*, 6 February, recognised that this practice did occur but gave some guidance. The court held that investigating officers should avoid paying 'social visits' to people in custody whose conduct was under investigation. If, after being charged with an offence, a suspect of his/her own volition said that he/she wished to make a statement admitting or giving details of the offence, after properly cautioning the person and complying with the rest of the Codes of Practice, investigating officers were not debarred from recording what he/she had to say. Prior to a person being visited in his/her cell, the custody officer must give his/her authority and the visit must be recorded in the detained person's custody record.

2.13.8   When must an Interview be Held?

Code C, para. 16.1 states:

> When the officer in charge of the investigation reasonably believes there is sufficient evidence to provide a realistic prospect of the detainee's conviction, see paragraph 11.6, they shall without delay, and subject to the following qualification, inform the custody officer who will be responsible for considering whether the detainee should be charged ...

KEYNOTE

It is suggested that, in a case where a suspect has not been interviewed about an offence, Code C, para. 16.1, requires that person to be asked if he/she has anything further to say about the matter, in which case this will be an interview.

This view is supported by the case of *R v Pointer* [1997] Crim LR 676 which held that giving a suspect the opportunity to say something more when the officer already has enough evidence to charge is an interview within the definition of Code C, para. 11.1A, and, therefore, an event which attracts the protection of a caution, legal representation and tape recording.

Interviews in these circumstances are conducted to allow the suspect to make any additional comments and for the interviewing officers to follow up on those responses. If the interview is held for any other reason it is likely to be inadmissible. This was the case in *Pointer* where the court held that there was sufficient evidence to charge prior to the interview and consequently Code C, para. 16.1 had not been complied with. Such an interview may assist the investigating officer to make reasonable lines of inquiry which support the defence.

2.13.9 Conducting and Recording Interviews

The conduct of officers and the proper treatment of the suspect during an interview are essential if an interview is to be admissible in evidence. If an interview is not conducted properly, confessions made during the interview may be excluded (**see chapter 2.9**). The PACE Codes of Practice are there to afford suspects proper protection from false confessions and treatment which may lead a court to the conclusion that the confession may not be reliable. It is essential, therefore, that officers are fully aware of the relevant Codes and comply with them. For occasions when evidence may be excluded, **see chapter 2.9**. For evidential purposes interviews need to be recorded contemporaneously. An accurate record must be made of each interview with a person suspected of an offence, whether or not the interview takes place at a police station (Code C, para. 11.7).

Interviews currently fall into two main groups:

- those that are audibly or visually recorded; and
- those where the only record will be made in writing.

While there is no statutory requirement on police officers to visually record interviews, the contents of Code F should be considered if an interviewing officer decides to make a visual recording, with sound, of an interview with a suspect.

Code F3.1 provides guidance to interviewing officers as to the occasion when it may be appropriate to visually record an interview; it is important to note that the Terrorism Act 2000 has a separate code of practice for the visual recording of interviews in a police station for those detained under sch. 7 or s.41 of the Act. See Note 3E for those occasions when it only becomes clear during the course of an interview that is being visually recorded that the interviewee may have committed an offence under the Terrorism Act 2000. Code F, para. F3.1 is not intended to preclude visual recordings of interviews at police stations with people cautioned in respect of other offences, or responses made by interviewees after they have been charged with, or informed they may be prosecuted for, an offence. Even a person who is voluntarily attending the police station should be visually interviewed.

While it is at the discretion of the interviewing officers as to when an interview should be visually recorded, a decision not to visually record an interview for any reason may be the subject of comment in court. The authorising officer should therefore be prepared to justify his/her decision in each case. The custody officer may authorise the interviewing officer not to record the interview visually in the circumstances laid out in Code F, para. 3.3.

The Criminal Justice and Police Act 2001 inserted s. 60A into the Police and Criminal Evidence Act 1984. This allows the Secretary of State to issue a code of practice for the visual recording of interviews held by police officers at police stations, and to make an order requiring the use of visual recording of interviews. An order issued by the Secretary of State may specify what offences or police stations or both the order applies to; currently there are no such requirements in place, although a code of practice has been issued (this is Code F of the PACE Codes of Practice, **see appendix 2.4**).

If a suspect makes unsolicited comments which are outside the context of an interview but which might be relevant to the offence, those comments should be recorded and Code C, para. 11.13 should be followed (**see chapter 2.9**). Code C, Note 11E gives guidance as to what must be included in the record and when the record should be made. As the relevance of the comment may not be obvious at the time it is made, it is suggested that all comments are recorded.

2.13.9.1 When Interviews must be Audio Recorded

The interviewing of suspects is governed by PACE Code of Practice E. Code E, paras 3.1 and 3.5 set out which interviews at a police station must be audio recorded. The most noticeable absence from this list is for interviews about matters which can only be tried summarily. These requirements do not *preclude* other interviews being audio recorded. Investigators may well be advised to audio record interviews concerning summarily only offences as it may be more difficult for the defence to suggest any confession was fabricated. If these interviews are recorded, they must follow the requirements of audio recorded interviews (see Code E, Note 3A).

The whole of each interview shall be recorded, including the taking and reading back of any statement (Code E, para. 3.5).

All interviews listed in Code E, para. 3.1 conducted at a police station must be audio recorded *unless* the custody officer authorises the interviewing officer not to audio record the interview. If the custody officer authorises the interview to go ahead without being audio recorded, the interview must be recorded in writing. A custody officer authorising this may have to justify the decision at court and the reasons for his/her decision should be recorded.

Code E, para. 3.3 allows the custody officer to make this decision where:

- It is not reasonably practicable to audio record the interview because of:
  - ◆ failure of the equipment; or
  - ◆ the non-availability of a suitable interview room or recorder; and
  - ◆ the custody officer considers on reasonable grounds that the interview should not be delayed until the failure has been rectified or a suitable room or recorder becomes available
- or it is clear from the outset that no prosecution will ensue
- where the custody officer has authorised that the detainee can be interviewed in his/her cell (Code E, para. 3.4).

Further, Code E, para. 3.1 does not apply to:

- certain interviews involving terrorism (Code E, para. 3.2).

For cases where a person objects to the interview being audio recorded, see Code E, para. 4.8.

2.13.9.2 Preparation before Interview at Police Station

Preparation is essential before any interview (indeed it is the first step in the PEACE interviewing model). This preparation should include the following points:

- Decide where the interview will be conducted. Consider the availability of a room and the timing of the interview.
- The location must have a seat for the person being interviewed (Code C, para. 12.6) and should be adequately lit, heated and ventilated (Code C, para. 12.4). The detained person must also have clothing of a reasonable standard of comfort and cleanliness (Code C, para. 8.5). (It will be a question of fact as to what amounts to adequate clothing and it is suggested that if the clothing is such as to degrade the detained person or make him/her uncomfortable, it may lead to the confession being held to be unreliable.)

- If the interview is being audio recorded, ensure that there are sufficient recording media for the anticipated length of the interview (or at least until the first break period). If the interview is being recorded in writing, ensure there are enough forms.
- If the interview is being audio recorded, ensure the notice as set out in Code E, para. 4.19 is available to be given at the end of the interview.
- In deciding the timing of the interview, consideration must be given to the detainee's rest period, which should not be interrupted or delayed unless Code C, para. 12.2 applies. Where the interview goes ahead during the rest period under Code C, para. 12.2(a), a fresh rest period must be allowed. Before a detainee is interviewed, the custody officer, in consultation with the officer in charge of the investigation and appropriate healthcare professionals as necessary, shall assess whether the detainee is fit enough to be interviewed (Code C, para. 12.3 and Annex G.)
- If legal advice has been requested you must arrange for the legal representative to be present at the interview unless Code C, para. 6.6 applies.
- If a person has asked for legal advice and an interview is initiated in the absence of a legal adviser (e.g. where the person has agreed to be interviewed without his/her legal adviser being present or because of the urgent need to interview under Code C, para. 11.1), a record must be made in the interview record (Code C, para. 6.17).
- If an appropriate adult should be present, arrange for his/her attendance. (For the definition of appropriate adult, see Code C, para. 1.7.)
- If an interpreter is needed for the interview, arrange for his/her attendance (**see para. 2.11.14**).

It is also important to draw up an interview plan and to include any relevant areas that may provide a general or specific defence (as to which, **see Crime, chapter 1.4**).

- Look at the evidence available and identify any significant statement or silence by the suspect in order that it can be put to him/her in interview (Code C, para. 11.4).

2.13.9.3 Starting Interviews

In order to interview a detained person, the interviewing officer must obtain permission from the custody officer. An entry must be made in the custody record to record that the interviewing officer accepts responsibility for the detained person. If the request to hand over the detained person is declined, the custody officer must record this fact and the reasons why on the custody record (Code C, para. 12.10). The responsibility for the detained person at this stage rests with the officer to whom the transfer is made and remains with this person until the detained person is returned to the custody officer (s. 39(2) of the Police and Criminal Evidence Act 1984). Section 39 of the 1984 Act states:

(2) If this custody officer, in accordance with any code of practice issued under this Act, transfers or permits the transfer of a person in police detention—
(a) to the custody of a police officer investigating an offence for which that person is in police detention; or
(b) to the custody of an officer who has charge of that person outside the police station, the custody officer shall cease in relation to that person to be subject to the duty imposed on him by subsection (1)(a) above; and it shall be the duty of the officer to whom the transfer is made to ensure that he is treated in accordance with the provisions of this Act and of any such codes of practice as are mentioned in subsection (1) above.

Before allowing a detainee to be interviewed the custody officer shall undertake a risk assessment in order to ensure that conducting the interview will not significantly harm the detainee's physical or mental state or that their physical or mental state might result in the them saying something in the interview about their involvement or suspected involvement in the offence being considered unreliable in subsequent court proceedings (Code C, Annex G, paras 1 and 2). The risk assessment should be done, where necessary, in consultation with the officer in charge of the investigation and appropriate health care professionals. Annex G, para. 3 sets out a number of factors that must be considered when conducting this risk assessment. Where risks are identified, the custody officer must determine what safeguards are needed to minimise those risks in order to allow the interview to take place. It should be remembered that vulnerable suspects listed at Code C, para. 11.18 must always be treated as if being at some risk during an interview and therefore may not be interviewed except in accordance with Code C, paras 11.18 to 11.20 (Code C, para. 12.3). Code C, Annex G provides guidance to help police officers and health care professionals assess whether a detainee might be at risk in an interview.

The risk assessment can be very important in terms of ensuring that any confession in an interview is admissible. In *R* v *Utip* [2003] EWCA Crim 1256, the court held that the law required that where there were grounds to suspect mental illness, a defendant should be examined by a doctor to establish whether he/she was fit for interview. Where a defendant had been assessed as fit to be interviewed by a psychiatrist and had his/her interests protected by an appropriate adult and solicitor, there was no unfairness in allowing evidence of the interview to go before the jury.

2.13.9.4 Preliminary Issues for Interviews not being Audio Recorded

Before an interview begins the following points must be dealt with:

- Immediately before the commencement of the interview remind the suspect of his/her right to legal advice (Code C, para. 11.2) and make a note of this reminder and any response in the interview record.
- For the interview record, identify all officers present in the interview as required by Code C, para. 12.7.
- If an appropriate adult is present, inform that person of his/her role (Code C, para. 11.17).
- Administer the relevant caution (Code C, para. 10.1) (and re-administer where appropriate, **see para. 2.13.4**).

2.13.9.5 Preliminary Issues for Interviews being Audio Recorded

Before an interview commences the following points must be dealt with:

- The recording media must be unwrapped or opened in the suspect's presence (Code E, para. 4.3).
- in the suspect's sight, load the recorder with new recording media and set it to record (Code E, para. 4.3).
- Inform the suspect about the recording process in accordance with Code E, para. 4.4.
- Verbally identify all persons present at the interview (Code E, para. 4.4).
- Administer the relevant caution (Code E, para. 4.5) (and re-administer where appropriate, **see para. 2.13.4**).
- Remind the suspect of his/her right to free legal advice (Code E, para. 4.5 and Code C, paras 6.1 and 6.5) and ensure that the response is recorded (for instance a nod of the head would not be picked up by the recording).

2.13.9.6 Additional Preliminary Issues for Interviews being Visually Recorded

- Estimate the likely length of the interview and ensure that an appropriate quantity of certified recording media and labels with which to seal the master copies are available in the interview room.
- If not fixed, camera(s) should be placed in the interview room so as to ensure coverage of as much of the room as is practicably possible while the interviews are taking place.
- When the camera is brought into the interview in sight of the suspect, load the recording equipment and set it to record. The recording media must be unwrapped or otherwise opened in the presence of the suspect (Code F, para. 4.3).
- Inform the suspect formally about the visual recording as set out in Code F, para. 4.4.
- The interviewer must caution the suspect, which should follow that set out in Code C (Code F, para. 4.5).
- Remind the suspect of his/her entitlement to free and independent legal advice and that he/she can speak to a solicitor on the telephone (Code F, para. 4.5).

2.13.9.7 What should be Disclosed to the Solicitor

It is important not to confuse the duty of disclosure to a person once charged with the need to disclose evidence to a suspect before interviewing them. After a person has been charged, and before trial, the rules of disclosure are clear (**see chapter 2.10**) and almost all material must be disclosed to the defence.

However, this is not necessarily the case at the interview stage of the investigation. There is no specific provision within the Police and Criminal Evidence Act 1984 for the disclosure of any information by the police at the police station, with the exception of the custody record and, in identification cases, the initial description given by the witnesses. Further, there is nothing within the Criminal Justice and Public Order Act 1994 that states that information must be disclosed before an inference from silence can be made. Indeed, in *R* v *Imran* [1997] Crim LR 754 the court held that it is totally wrong to submit that a defendant should be prevented from lying by being presented with the whole of the evidence against him/her prior to the interview.

In *R* v *Argent* [1997] Crim LR 346 the court dismissed the argument that an inference could not be drawn under s. 34 of the Criminal Justice and Public Order Act 1994 because there had not been full disclosure at the interview. However, the court did recognise that it may be a factor to take into account, but it would be for the jury to decide whether the failure to answer questions was reasonable.

In *R* v *Roble* [1997] Crim LR 449, the court suggested that an inference would not be drawn where a solicitor gave advice to remain silent where, for example, the interviewing officer had disclosed too little of the case for the solicitor usefully to advise his/her client, or where the nature of the offence, or the material in the hands of the police, was so complex or related to matters so long ago that no sensible immediate response was feasible.

It was not uncommon in the past for solicitors to advise on no comment interviews and this has been relied on by defendants to avoid adverse inferences being drawn from their silence. The courts and legal advisers are now very aware of the consequences of advising a suspect to offer no comment. In *R* v *Morgan* [2001] EWCA Crim 445, the Court of Appeal stated that a court was entitled to assume that a solicitor would advise his/her client about the adverse inferences rule. In *R* v *Ali* [2001] EWCA Crim 683, the court stated that the question was not whether the advice to remain silent was good advice but whether it provided an adequate reason for failing to answer questions.

In *R v Hoare* [2004] EWCA Crim 784 the Court of Appeal held that the purpose of s. 34 was to qualify a defendant's right to silence rather than to exclude a jury from drawing an adverse inference against a defendant merely because he/she had been advised by their solicitor to remain silent, whether or not he/she genuinely or reasonably relied on that advice. Where a defendant had an explanation to give that was consistent with his/her innocence it was not 'reasonable', within the meaning of s. 34(1), for him/her to fail to give that explanation in interview even where he/she had been advised by his/her solicitor to remain silent. Legal advice by itself could not preclude the drawing of an adverse inference.

There is a balance to be struck between providing the solicitor with enough information to understand the nature of the case against his/her client and keeping back material which, if disclosed, may allow the suspect the opportunity to avoid implicating him/herself. For instance in *R v Thirlwell* [2002] EWCA Crim 286, the Court of Appeal agreed that the solicitor had not been entitled to provisional medical evidence as to possible causes of death in a murder case. The disclosure of material may well be a factor which the defendant relies on in showing that the failure to mention possible defences was reasonable. If the officers are not hoping to draw inferences from silence then tactically they may decide not to disclose as much information—it will be a question of fact in each case.

2.13.9.8 Conduct During Interview

- Code C, para. 11.5 reiterates the fact that officers must not act oppressively.
- If a complaint is made by the suspect concerning the provisions of the codes the interviewing officer must inform the custody officer and follow Code C, para. 12.9. If the complaint is not concerning the codes, Code E, Note 4F applies.
- Officers should only indicate the possible effect of refusing to answer questions or of answering questions if he/she is asked about those possible effects by the suspect *unless this is done as part of a special warning* (see Code C, paras 10.10, 10.11 and 11.15).
- Code E, para. 4.8 provides guidance where the person objects to the interview being audio recorded.
- Code C, Note 11C reminds officers of the risks associated with the reliability of interviewing juveniles or people who are mentally disordered or otherwise mentally vulnerable.

At the start of the interview the investigating officer should put to the suspect any significant statement or silence which occurred before his/her arrival at the police station and ask the suspect whether he/she confirms the earlier statement or silence and whether he/she wishes to add anything. Code C, para. 11.4A defines a 'significant' statement or silence. This aspect of the interview is very important in terms of establishing whether the facts are disputed. If they are not disputed at this stage, it is unlikely that they will be challenged at any later court hearing and, if challenged, the defence will have to explain why this was not done at the time of the interview. The courts may also view this failure to put the statement to the suspect in a more sinister light. In *R v Allen*, 10 July 2001, unreported, the court were concerned that the police failed to put the admission to the suspect in interview, despite thorough questioning, which they felt clearly placed a question mark over its reliability. If the suspect remains silent in relation to a 'significant silence', that silence may give rise to an adverse inference being drawn under s. 34 of the Criminal Justice and Public Order Act 1994 if the person raises it in his/her defence at court. (As this is very important issue, it may be necessary to delay the interview until the arrest notes are completed or the officers witnessing the offence/arrest have been consulted to ensure that all matters are put to the suspect at this stage.) Consideration should be given to putting questions to a suspect who makes no comment, or even where the legal representative has stated that the suspect will make no comment, as this may allow the court to draw inferences against a defence that the suspect raises at court (**see para. 2.7.6.1**). The interviewer may wish to go through any significant statement or silence again if during earlier interviews adverse inferences could not be drawn.

2.13.9.9 Issues Specific to Audio Recorded Interviews

- If the equipment fails, rectify the fault quickly if possible. If this is not possible, look for an alternative recording machine or room. If none available, seek the authority of the custody officer to continue without the interview being audio recorded (see Code E, para. 4.15).
- If *the media or the recording equipment fails*, follow Code E, Note 4H.
- When recording media is removed from the recorder it must be retained (see Code E, para. 4.16) and the procedure at para. 4.18 followed.
- If you need to change recording media during interview, for instance when the recorder shows the recording media only has a short time left, follow Code E, para. 4.11.
- If a suspect objects to the interview being audio recorded at any stage of the interview, the procedure in Code E, para. 4.8 must be followed and Note 4D should be taken into account in deciding whether to continue to audio record the interview.
- If a suspect indicates that he/she wishes to tell the police about matters not connected with the offence(s) being investigated but does not wish this information to be audio recorded, Code E, para. 4.10 requires this to be dealt with at the conclusion of the formal interview. Any comment by the suspect would still need to be recorded in writing.

2.13.9.10 Issues Specific to Visually Recorded Interview

- If the equipment fails, rectify the fault if possible and follow the guidance set out in Code F, para. 4.12 (breaks in interviews) and para. 4.15. If, however, it is not possible to continue recording on that particular recorder and no alternative equipment is readily available, the interview may continue without being recorded visually.
- If a suspect raises objections to the interview being visually recorded at any stage, the procedures in Code F, para. 4.8 must be followed
- If in the course of an interview a complaint is made by the person being questioned, or on their behalf, concerning the provisions of Code F or of Code C, then the interviewer shall act in accordance with Code C, record it in the interview record and inform the custody officer (Code F, para. 4.9 and Notes 4B and 4C).
- If a suspect indicates that he/she wishes to tell the interviewer about matters not directly connected with the offence(s) of which they are suspected and that they are unwilling for these matters to be recorded, Code F, para. 4.10 requires this to be dealt with at the conclusion of the formal interview.
- If the interviewer needs to change the recording media during the interview, follow Code F, para. 4.11
- When the recording medium is removed from the recording machine it must be retained (see Code F, para. 4.16) and the procedure at para. 4.18 followed.

- In cases as set out in Code F, para. 2.5 where an officer's identity should not be disclosed, the officer will have their back to the camera and shall use their warrant or other identification number and the name of the police station to which they are attached. Such instances and the reasons for them shall be recorded in the custody record.

2.13.9.11 Breaks

Breaks from interviewing must be made at recognised meal times or at other times that take account of when the person last had a meal (Code C, para. 12.8). Short breaks for refreshment must also be provided at intervals of approximately two hours. Code C, Note 12B gives guidance on how long breaks should be. Code C, para. 12.8 sets out the exceptions to the requirement to provide breaks. These exceptions exist where to break the interview would:

- involve a risk of harm to people or serious loss of, or damage to property;
- delay unnecessarily the person's release from custody; or
- otherwise prejudice the outcome of the investigation.

Any decision to delay a break during an interview must be recorded, with grounds, in the interview record (either on the written record or on the recording media) (Code C, para. 12.12).

2.13.9.12 Breaks—Additional Issues for Visually Recorded Interviews

Whether the recording equipment will be left to run during a break will depend on the circumstances such as length of time of the break and whether the interview room will be vacated; guidance is provided by Code F, paras 4.12 to 4.14. On the re-commencement of an interview, the officer should consider summarising on the record the reason for the break and confirming this with the suspect (Code F, Note 4E).

2.13.9.13 Solicitors and Legal Advice

A 'solicitor' for the purposes of the Codes of Practice means:

- a solicitor holding a current practising certificate;
- a trainee solicitor;
- a duty solicitor representative or an accredited or probationary representative included on the register of representatives maintained by the Legal Services Commission (Code C, para. 6.12).

Where a solicitor is available at the time the interview begins or while it is in progress, the solicitor must be allowed to be present while the person in interviewed (Code C, para. 6.8). (This applies unless the suspect states that he/she does not want the solicitor to be present or where access is denied under s. 58 of the 1984 Act, see Code C, Annex B.)

If a solicitor arrives at the station to see a suspect, the suspect must be asked whether he/she would like to see the solicitor *regardless of what legal advice has already been received*. The solicitor's attendance and the suspect's decision must be recorded in the custody record (Code C, para. 6.15).

If the investigating officer considers that a solicitor is acting in such a way that he/she is unable properly to put questions to the suspect, he/she will stop the interview and consult an officer not below the rank of superintendent, if one is readily available, otherwise an officer not below the rank of inspector who is not connected with the investigation to decide whether that solicitor should be excluded from the interview. The interview may also have to be stopped in order to allow another solicitor to be instructed (Code C, para. 6.10). For the proper role of the legal representatives, see Code C, Note 6D. Code C, para. 6.6 sets out those occasions where a person can be interviewed without a solicitor being present even though he/she has requested a solicitor (**see para. 2.11.6.6**). Any authority to exclude a solicitor will need to be justified to the court if necessary (Code C, Note 6E).

With regard to the exclusion of probationer solicitor this has to be considered in relation to the specific investigation and whether that person is likely to interfere with the investigation. The decision can take into account the character of the person. Internal advice could also provide guidance as to what the decision should be but the decision has to be made in relation to each individual case. It is not permissible to have blanket bans on such persons (*R v Chief Constable of the Northumbria Constabulary, ex parte Thompson* [2001] 1 WLR 1342).

If a request for legal advice is made during an interview, the interviewing officer must stop the interview straightaway and arrange for legal advice to be provided. If the suspect changes his/her mind again, the interview can continue provided Code C, para. 6.6 is complied with.

It is important to remember that Code C, para. 6.4 reminds officers that they should *not* try to dissuade the detained person from obtaining legal advice. If an appropriate adult requests legal advice but the detained juvenile does not wish to consult with the solicitor, he/she cannot be forced to speak to the solicitor (Code C, para. 6.5A).

2.13.9.14 When must the Interview be Concluded?

Guidance is provided by Code C, para. 11.6 as to when an interview should be concluded. Paragraph 11.6 states that the interview shall cease if the investigating officer considers that:

- all the questions relevant to obtaining accurate and reliable information about the offence have been put to the suspect, this includes allowing the suspect an opportunity to give an innocent explanation and asking questions to test if the explanation is accurate and reliable;
- has taken account of any other available evidence; and
- there is sufficient evidence to provide a realistic prospect of conviction for that offence if the person was prosecuted for it.

The investigating officer shall then bring the detained person before the custody officer for charge.

The interview may continue until the above conditions are satisfied with regard to other offences being investigated (Code C, para. 16.1).

It is important to remember that the interview should not be concluded at the point when there is sufficient evidence to prosecute but when there is sufficient evidence to provide a realistic prospect of conviction. (In *Prouse* v *DPP* [1999] All ER (D) 748 the question was said to be not how much evidence there is but the quality of it.) Once there is enough evidence to prosecute, it may still be necessary to cover those other points in the interview that may be relevant to the defence case (**see Crime, chapter 1.4**). If these points are not covered in the interview, the defence may surprise the prosecution case with matters that the prosecution have not covered or with issues that may result in the loss of an inference being drawn from the suspect's silence. This was considered in *R v McGuinness* [1999] Crim LR 318 where the court held that the words 'sufficient evidence to prosecute' and 'sufficient evidence for a prosecution to succeed' in Code C, para. 11.6 must involve some consideration of any explanation, or lack of one, from the suspect. It would depend on the facts of a case whether the stage where a suspect ought to be charged has been reached. As a word of caution, the court also said that under Code C, paras 16.1 and 11.6 it was not open for a suspect to be questioned beyond the point when he/she ought to have been charged. If the suspect was questioned beyond that point, then the interview was liable to be ruled inadmissible and the content would not be available to support the prosecution case.

Paragraph 3.4 of the Code of Practice to the Criminal Procedure and Investigations Act 1996 says that in conducting an investigation, the investigator should pursue all reasonable lines of enquiry, whether these point towards or away from the suspect. What is reasonable will depend on the particular circumstances. Interviewers should keep this in mind when deciding what questions to ask in an interview.

2.13.9.15 Special Groups

As a confession can be very damning evidence against a defendant, it is important to provide safeguards that give all suspects the same level of protection. The PACE Codes of Practice recognise certain groups as being in need of additional protection. These groups include juveniles, people who do not speak English, those suffering from a mental impairment and those who are deaf. Such suspects must not be interviewed without the relevant person being present.

For juveniles and those suffering from a mental impairment (or who appear to be such), an appropriate adult must be present (Code C, para. 11.15).

Under Code C, para. 13.2, a person capable of acting as interpreter is required where:

- the suspect has difficulty in understanding English;
- the interviewing officer cannot speak the person's own language; and
- the suspect wishes an interpreter to be present.

If the suspect appears to be deaf or there is any doubt about his/her hearing or speaking ability, an interpreter should be found (unless he/she agrees *in writing* to proceed without an interpreter) (Code C, para. 13.5). This requirement also applies in the case of the appropriate adult who appears to be deaf or there is doubt about his/her hearing or speaking ability (Code C, para. 13.6).

There are limited circumstances where an interview may be conducted without an interpreter or appropriate adult being present. These are set out in Code C, paras 11.1 and 11.15. Once those conditions no longer apply, the interview must be suspended until the appropriate person is present. For it to be an 'interview' a police officer or a designated investigating officer must be present (Code C, para. 13.4).

Where interpreters are required, Code C, paras 13.3 to 13.11 are to be followed.

If an interpreter who can translate straight from the detained person's language to English cannot be found then more than one interpreter should be used to bridge the language gap. It is the *interviewer* who is responsible for ensuring that the detained person can understand and be understood (*R v West London Youth Court, ex parte J* [2000] 1 All ER 823).

Audio Recorded Interviews and Special Groups

If the suspect is deaf or there is doubt about his/her hearing ability, a contemporaneous written record should be made as well as the audio recording. This record should be the same as where there is no audio record of the interview (Code E, para. 4.7).

2.13.9.16 Special Warnings

Now that inferences can be drawn from a suspect's silence (albeit in limited circumstances), it is necessary to warn the person of the dangers of remaining silent. For this reason the 'special warning' was introduced (**see para. 2.7.6.3**) where there is potentially incriminating evidence relating to objects, marks or substances; or relating to the accused's presence at a particular place. If the special warning is not given, inferences from silence will not be allowed to boost the prosecution case but the potentially incriminating evidence may still be admissible. Code C, paras 10.10 to 10.11 must be followed if any questions are to be put to the arrested suspect about:

- any object, marks or substances found on the him/her, or
- in or on his/her clothing or footwear, or
- otherwise in his/her possession, or
- in the place where he/she was arrested

(see s. 36 of the Criminal Justice and Public Order Act 1994).

These provisions also apply to any questions about why the suspect was:

- at the scene of the offence,
- at or near the time of the offence for which the constable who saw the suspect there arrested him/her, and
- unable to account for his/her presence at or near the scene of the offence

(see s. 37 of the Criminal Justice and Public Order Act 1994).

It must be made clear to the suspect what matters he/she is being asked to answer and the consequences of remaining silent on each occasion.

See **para. 2.13.4** and Code C, Annex C for occasions when special warnings and adverse inferences do not apply.

2.13.9.17 Conclusion of Interview

Written Interviews

- The person interviewed (and the appropriate adult or the suspect's solicitor if present during the interview (Code C, para. 11.12)) must be given an opportunity to read the interview record and to sign it as correct or to indicate the respects in which he/she considers it inaccurate (Code C, para. 11.11). If the person concerned cannot read or refuses to read the record or to sign it, the senior police officer present shall read it to him/her (Code C, para. 11.11). If there is any delay in recording the interview, if practicable, the suspect should still be given an opportunity to read the statement.
- Any refusal to sign the record must be recorded (Code C, para. 11.14).
- If an interpreter has been present at the interview, he/she should be given an opportunity to read the record and certify its accuracy (Code C, para. 13.7).
- If the person is in police detention, return him/her to the custody officer, informing that officer whether the Codes have been complied with, if any incidents occurred and whether there were any breaches of the Codes (s. 39(3) of the Police and Criminal Evidence Act 1984).

2.13.9.18 Audio Recorded Interviews

- The person interviewed must be offered the opportunity to clarify anything he/she has said during the interview and to add anything he/she may wish (Code E, para. 4.17). This may be important when the case comes to court and the defence try to explain why certain things were said during the interview.

- Turn off the recording medium and seal it with a master recording label (Code E, para. 4.18). If the seal on the master recording needs to be broken for any reason, follow Code E, para. 6.2 or, if decision has been made not to institute criminal proceedings, follow Code E, para. 6.3.
- Sign the label and ask the suspect and any third party present to sign it also. If the suspect or third party refuses to sign it, an inspector, or if not available a custody officer, shall be called into the interview room and asked to sign it (Code E, para. 4.18).
- Hand the suspect the notice which explains the use which will be made of the audio recording and the arrangement for access to it (Code E, para. 4.19).
- Make a personal pocket book entry about the interview as required by Code E, para. 5.1 (see Code E, para. 1.10).
- Follow force standing orders or local procedures in relation to master recording security whether or not the person is charged (Code E, paras 6.1 and 5.2).

2.13.9.19 Conclusion of Interview—Additional Issues for Visually Recorded Interviews

- The person interviewed must be offered the opportunity to clarify anything he/she has said during the interview and to add anything he/she may wish (Code F, para. 4.17). This may be important when the case comes to court and the defence try to explain why certain things were said during the interview.
- Turn off the recording equipment and seal the master record with a master copy label and treat as an exhibit in accordance with the force standing orders (Code F, para. 4.18). In addition to the master copy, a second copy will be used as a working copy. If the seal on the master record needs to be broken for any reason, follow Code E, para. 6.2 or, if a decision has been made not to institute criminal proceedings, follow Code E, para. 6.3.
- Sign the label and ask the suspect and any third party present to sign it also. If the suspect or third party refuses to sign it, an inspector, or if not available a custody officer, must be called into the interview room and asked to sign it (Code F, para. 4.18).
- Hand the suspect the notice which explains the use which will be made of the recording and the arrangement for access to it (Code F, para. 4.19).
- Make a personal pocket book entry about the interview as required by Code F, para. 5.1.
- Follow force standing orders or local procedures in relation to master recording security whether or not the person is charged (Code F, para. 6.1).
- Once the master copy of the interview has been sealed it should only be broken in the circumstances set out in Code F, paras 6.2 to 6.7.

2.13.10 Statements from Suspects

Statements under caution, particularly of a detained person, are less common than interviews. If a person has been interviewed and it has been audio or visually recorded or an interview has been recorded contemporaneously in writing, a statement under caution should normally be conducted only at the person's express wish (Code C, Note 12A). A statement must not be elicited by the use of oppression (Code C, para. 11.5) and, if written at the police station, the statement must be on the correct forms (Code C, para. 12.13). Code C, Annex D sets out how the statement should be taken and matters that must be included in the statement whether it is written by the suspect or a police officer. See Code C,

Annex C for restrictions on drawing inferences and Annex D for the variable declarations the person must include in his/her statements.

When completing the statement, the person must always be invited to write down what he/she wants to say and should be allowed to do so without any prompting, except that a police officer may indicate which matters are material or question any ambiguity in the statement. In the case of a person making a statement in a language other than English, Code C, para. 13.4 states:

(a) the interpreter shall record the statement in the language it is made;
(b) the person shall be invited to sign it;
(c) an official English translation shall be made in due course

(in these cases, para. 13.4 means that the person will not be invited to write the statement themselves which is an exception to the guidance in Annex D).

A juvenile or a person who is mentally disordered or mentally vulnerable, *whether suspected or not*, must not be asked to provide or sign a written statement in the absence of the appropriate adult unless Code C, paras 11.1, 11.18 to 11.20 or Annex C applies (Code C, para. 11.15). Statements made by an accused under caution to the police are confidential. It is clearly implicit in the relationship between the police and the accused that the information, before being used in open court, is used only for the purposes for which it is provided and not for extraneous purposes, such as the media. However, the obligation of confidentiality (which is now included in the Police Code of Conduct; **see General Police Duties, chapter 4.1**) in respect of such a statement will be brought to an end where the contents of the statement are already in the public domain (*Bann* v *British Broadcasting Corporation and Another* (1998) 148 NLJ 979).

2.13.11 Statements from Defence Witnesses

The Criminal Justice Act 2003 introduces a code of practice for police officers interviewing a witness notified by the accused. While this is still at the consultation stages it is likely to be introduced within the next year.

2.13.12 Interviews on Behalf of Scottish Forces and Vice Versa

The Crown Prosecution Service, in consultation with the Scottish Crown Office, has produced guidelines in relation to the potential admissibility of interview evidence when officers from England and Wales conduct interviews on behalf of Scottish forces and vice versa. These interviews relate to people subject to cross-border arrest as provided by ss. 136 to 140 of the Criminal Justice and Public Order Act 1994 (**see General Police Duties, chapter 4.4**).

2.13.12.1 Suspects in Scotland: Interview Evidence Required for Prosecutions in England and Wales

Under the legislation governing prosecutions in Scotland, the suspect is not entitled to legal representation during an interview. Suspects are not warned that a failure to answer questions may harm their defence. Failure to answer questions cannot harm their defence. Interviews under caution are, however, subject to guidelines which incorporate judicial precedent fairness to the accused.

In investigations of any great seriousness, English/Welsh constables should attend in Scotland, arrest the suspect and bring him/her back to their jurisdiction for interview. If such an arrest is made, the arrested person must be taken either to the nearest designated police station in England or a designated police station in a police area in England and Wales in which the offence is being investigated (s. 137(1) and (7)(a) of the 1994 Act).

Scottish officers do not have any statutory or common law powers to detain or arrest a suspect without warrant who is believed to have committed an offence in England and Wales. If there is insufficient evidence for the issue of a warrant, and the case is not sufficiently serious to justify officers travelling to Scotland, Scottish officers can be requested to invite the suspect to attend a police station on a voluntary basis for interview under caution.

When it has not been practicable for an English/Welsh constable to make an arrest, but a constable has gone to Scotland to interview a suspect following arrest or detention by a Scottish constable for Scottish offences, or a person has voluntarily agreed to be interviewed, the English/Welsh constable should comply, insofar as it is practical, with the PACE Codes of Practice, in particular:

- A suspect not under arrest or detention should be told that he/she is not under arrest or detention and that he/she is free to leave.
- A suspect should be told that he/she may seek legal advice and that arrangements are made for legal representation when required. An appropriate adult should also be present when interviewing a youth or a mentally disordered or mentally handicapped person.
- Administer an English/Welsh law caution. When appropriate officers should warn arrested suspects of the consequences of failure or refusal to account for objects, substances or marks (s. 36 of the 1994 Act) and the failure or refusal to account for their presence in a particular place (s. 37).
- Audio record the interview if possible.
- If it is not possible to audio record the interview, a contemporaneous written record of the interview should be made. The suspect must be given the opportunity to read the record and to sign it.
- Also, fingerprints etc. and non-intimate samples may be taken from an arrested or detained person with the authority of an officer of a rank no lower than inspector (s. 18 of the Criminal Procedure (Scotland) Act 1995).

Scottish constables interviewing suspects in Scotland when they are aware that the interview is required for a prosecution in England and Wales, should comply with Scottish law. In addition, in so far as it is practical:

- A suspect should be told that he/she may seek legal advice and that arrangements are made for legal representation when required. A solicitor may be present during any subsequent interview if the suspect requires. An appropriate adult should also be present when interviewing a youth or a mentally disordered or mentally vulnerable person.
- When it is certain that the interview evidence will only be used in English/Welsh courts, the appropriate English/Welsh caution should be used.
- Audio record the interview if possible.
- If it is not possible to audio record the interview, a written contemporaneous record of the interview should be made. The suspect must be given the opportunity to read the record and to sign it.

English/Welsh officers should assist interviewing Scottish officers by providing a schedule of points to be covered in an interview. This could include a list of appropriate questions.

2.13.12.2 Suspects in England and Wales: Interview Evidence Required for Prosecutions in Scotland

- English officers do not have any statutory or common law powers to detain or arrest a suspect without warrant who is believed to have committed an offence in Scotland. If there is insufficient evidence for the issue of a warrant, and the case is not sufficiently serious to justify Scottish officers travelling to England or Wales to exercise their cross-border powers under the Act, English or Welsh officers can be requested to invite the suspect to attend an interview on a voluntary basis for interview under caution.
- Where a Scottish officer has attended to interview the suspect, the Scottish form of caution should be given.
- English and Welsh constables interviewing suspects in England/Wales when they are aware that the interview is required for a prosecution in Scotland, should comply with the PACE Codes of Practice, save that a Scottish caution should be used in the following terms: 'You are not obliged to say anything but anything you do say will be noted and may be used in evidence.'

The use of an English/Welsh caution may render the interview inadmissible in Scotland.

Scottish officers should assist the interviewing officers by providing a schedule of points to be covered in an interview and a possible list of appropriate questions.

In all circumstances officers should ensure that suspects fully understand the significance of a caution or warning.

Appendix 2.1

PACE Code of Practice for the Detention, Treatment and Questioning of Persons by Police Officers (Code C)

This Code applies to people in police detention after midnight on 24 July 2006, notwithstanding that their period of detention may have commenced before that time.

1 General

1.1 All persons in custody must be dealt with expeditiously, and released as soon as the need for detention no longer applies.

1.1A A custody officer must perform the functions in this Code as soon as practicable. A custody officer will not be in breach of this Code if delay is justifiable and reasonable steps are taken to prevent unnecessary delay. The custody record shall show when a delay has occurred and the reason. See *Note 1H*

1.2 This Code of Practice must be readily available at all police stations for consultation by:
- police officers
- police staff
- detained persons
- members of the public.

1.3 The provisions of this Code:
- include the *Annexes*
- do not include the *Notes for Guidance*.

1.4 If an officer has any suspicion, or is told in good faith, that a person of any age may be mentally disordered or otherwise mentally vulnerable, in the absence of clear evidence to dispel that suspicion, the person shall be treated as such for the purposes of this Code. *See Note 1G*

1.5 If anyone appears to be under 17, they shall be treated as a juvenile for the purposes of this Code in the absence of clear evidence that they are older.

1.6 If a person appears to be blind, seriously visually impaired, deaf, unable to read or speak or has difficulty orally because of a speech impediment, they shall be treated as such for the purposes of this Code in the absence of clear evidence to the contrary.

1.7 'The appropriate adult' means, in the case of a:
(a) juvenile:
  (i) the parent, guardian or, if the juvenile is in local authority or voluntary organisation care, or is otherwise being looked after under the Children Act 1989, a person representing that authority or organisation;
  (ii) a social worker of a local authority social services department;
  (iii) failing these, some other responsible adult aged 18 or over who is not a police officer or employed by the police.
(b) person who is mentally disordered or mentally vulnerable: See *Note 1D*
  (iv) a relative, guardian or other person responsible for their care or custody;

(v) someone experienced in dealing with mentally disordered or mentally vulnerable people but who is not a police officer or employed by the police;

(vi) failing these, some other responsible adult aged 18 or over who is not a police officer or employed by the police.

1.8 If this Code requires a person be given certain information, they do not have to be given it if at the time they are incapable of understanding what is said, are violent or may become violent or in urgent need of medical attention, but they must be given it as soon as practicable.

1.9 References to a custody officer include any:
- police officer; or
- designated staff custody officer acting in the exercise or performance of the powers and duties conferred or imposed on them by their designation,

performing the functions of a custody officer. See *Note 1J*.

1.9A When this Code requires the prior authority or agreement of an officer of at least inspector or superintendent rank, that authority may be given by a sergeant or chief inspector authorised to perform the functions of the higher rank under the Police and Criminal Evidence Act 1984 (PACE), section 107.

1.10 Subject to *paragraph 1.12*, this Code applies to people in custody at police stations in England and Wales, whether or not they have been arrested, and to those removed to a police station as a place of safety under the Mental Health Act 1983, sections 135 and 136. *Section 15* applies solely to people in police detention, e.g. those brought to a police station under arrest or arrested at a police station for an offence after going there voluntarily.

1.11 People detained under the Terrorism Act 2000, Schedule 8 and section 41 and other provisions of that Act are not subject to any part of this Code. Such persons are subject to the Code of Practice for detention, treatment and questioning of persons by police officers detained under that Act.

1.12 This Code's provisions do not apply to people in custody:

(i) arrested on warrants issued in Scotland by officers under the Criminal Justice and Public Order Act 1994, section 136(2), or arrested or detained without warrant by officers from a police force in Scotland under section 137(2). In these cases, police powers and duties and the person's rights and entitlements whilst at a police station in England or Wales are the same as those in Scotland;

(ii) arrested under the Immigration and Asylum Act 1999, section 142(3) in order to have their fingerprints taken;

(iii) whose detention is authorised by an immigration officer under the Immigration Act 1971;

(iv) who are convicted or remanded prisoners held in police cells on behalf of the Prison Service under the Imprisonment (Temporary Provisions) Act 1980;

(v) not used

(vi) detained for searches under stop and search powers except as required by Code A.

The provisions on conditions of detention and treatment in *sections 8* and *9* must be considered as the minimum standards of treatment for such detainees.

1.13 In this Code:

(a) 'designated person' means a person other than a police officer, designated under the Police Reform Act 2002, Part 4 who has specified powers and duties of police officers conferred or imposed on them;

(b) reference to a police officer includes a designated person acting in the exercise or performance of the powers and duties conferred or imposed on them by their designation.

1.14 Designated persons are entitled to use reasonable force as follows:-

(a) when exercising a power conferred on them which allows a police officer exercising that power to use reasonable force, a designated person has the same entitlement to use force; and

(b) at other times when carrying out duties conferred or imposed on them that also entitle them to use reasonable force, for example:

- when at a police station carrying out the duty to keep detainees for whom they are responsible under control and to assist any other police officer or designated person to keep any detainee under control and to prevent their escape.
- when securing, or assisting any other police officer or designated person in securing, the detention of a person at a police station.
- when escorting, or assisting any other police officer or designated person in escorting, a detainee within a police station.
- for the purpose of saving life or limb; or
- preventing serious damage to property.

1.15 Nothing in this Code prevents the custody officer, or other officer given custody of the detainee, from allowing police staff who are not designated persons to carry out individual procedures or tasks at the police station if the law allows. However, the officer remains responsible for making sure the procedures and tasks are carried out correctly in accordance with the Codes of Practice. Any such person must be:

(a) a person employed by a police authority maintaining a police force and under the control and direction of the Chief Officer of that force;

(b) employed by a person with whom a police authority has a contract for the provision of services relating to persons arrested or otherwise in custody.

1.16 Designated persons and other police staff must have regard to any relevant provisions of the Codes of Practice.

1.17 References to pocket books include any official report book issued to police officers or other police staff.

Notes for guidance

1A *Although certain sections of this Code apply specifically to people in custody at police stations, those there voluntarily to assist with an investigation should be treated with no less consideration, e.g. offered refreshments at appropriate times, and enjoy an absolute right to obtain legal advice or communicate with anyone outside the police station.*

1B *A person, including a parent or guardian, should not be an appropriate adult if they:*
- *are*
  - *suspected of involvement in the offence*
  - *the victim*
  - *a witness*
  - *involved in the investigation*
- *received admissions prior to attending to act as the appropriate adult.*

Note: If a juvenile's parent is estranged from the juvenile, they should not be asked to act as the appropriate adult if the juvenile expressly and specifically objects to their presence.

1C *If a juvenile admits an offence to, or in the presence of, a social worker or member of a youth offending team other than during the time that person is acting as the juvenile's appropriate adult, another appropriate adult should be appointed in the interest of fairness.*

1D *In the case of people who are mentally disordered or otherwise mentally vulnerable, it may be more satisfactory if the appropriate adult is someone experienced or trained in their care rather than a relative lacking such qualifications. But if the detainee prefers a relative to a better qualified stranger or objects to a particular person their wishes should, if practicable, be respected.*

1E *A detainee should always be given an opportunity, when an appropriate adult is called to the police station, to consult privately with a solicitor in the appropriate adult's absence if they want. An appropriate adult is not subject to legal privilege.*

1F *A solicitor or independent custody visitor (formerly a lay visitor) present at the police station in that capacity may not be the appropriate adult.*

1G *'Mentally vulnerable' applies to any detainee who, because of their mental state or capacity, may not understand the significance of what is said, of questions or of their replies. 'Mental disorder' is defined in the Mental Health Act 1983, section 1(2) as 'mental illness, arrested or incomplete development of mind, psychopathic disorder and any other disorder or disability of mind'. When the custody officer has any doubt about the mental state or capacity of a detainee, that detainee should be treated as mentally vulnerable and an appropriate adult called.*

1H Paragraph 1.1A is intended to cover delays which may occur in processing detainees e.g. if:
- *a large number of suspects are brought into the station simultaneously to be placed in custody;*
- *interview rooms are all being used;*
- *there are difficulties contacting an appropriate adult, solicitor or interpreter.*

1I The custody officer must remind the appropriate adult and detainee about the right to legal advice and record any reasons for waiving it in accordance with section 6.

1J The designation of police staff custody officers applies only in police areas where an order commencing the provisions of the Police Reform Act 2002, section 38 and Schedule 4A, for designating police staff custody officers is in effect.

1K This Code does not affect the principle that all citizens have a duty to help police officers to prevent crime and discover offenders. This is a civic rather than a legal duty; but when a police officer is trying to discover whether, or by whom, an offence has been committed he is entitled to question any person from whom he thinks useful information can be obtained, subject to the restrictions imposed by this Code. A person's declaration that he is unwilling to reply does not alter this entitlement.

2 Custody records

2.1A When a person is brought to a police station:
- under arrest
- is arrested at the police station having attended there voluntarily or
- attends a police station to answer bail

they should be brought before the custody officer as soon as practicable after their arrival at the station or, if appropriate, following arrest after attending the police station voluntarily. This applies to designated and non-designated police stations. A person is deemed to be "at a police station" for these purposes if they are within the boundary of any building or enclosed yard which forms part of that police station.

2.1 A separate custody record must be opened as soon as practicable for each person brought to a police station under arrest or arrested at the station having gone there voluntarily or attending a police station in answer to street bail. All information recorded under this Code must be recorded as soon as practicable in the custody record unless otherwise specified. Any audio or video recording made in the custody area is not part of the custody record.

2.2 If any action requires the authority of an officer of a specified rank, subject to *paragraph 2.6A*, their name and rank must be noted in the custody record.

2.3 The custody officer is responsible for the custody record's accuracy and completeness and for making sure the record or copy of the record accompanies a detainee if they are transferred to another police station. The record shall show the:
- time and reason for transfer;
- time a person is released from detention.

2.4 A solicitor or appropriate adult must be permitted to consult a detainee's custody record as soon as practicable after their arrival at the station and at any other time whilst the person is detained. Arrangements for this access must be agreed with the custody officer and may not unreasonably interfere with the custody officer's duties.

2.4A When a detainee leaves police detention or is taken before a court they, their legal representative or appropriate adult shall be given, on request, a copy of the custody record as soon as practicable. This entitlement lasts for 12 months after release.

2.5 The detainee, appropriate adult or legal representative shall be permitted to inspect the original custody record after the detainee has left police detention provided they give reasonable notice of their request. Any such inspection shall be noted in the custody record.

2.6 Subject to *paragraph 2.6A*, all entries in custody records must be timed and signed by the maker. Records entered on computer shall be timed and contain the operator's identification.

2.6A Nothing in this Code requires the identity of officers or other police staff to be recorded or disclosed:
(a) not used;

(b) if the officer or police staff reasonably believe recording or disclosing their name might put them in danger.

In these cases, they shall use their warrant or other identification numbers and the name of their police station. See *Note 2A*

2.7 The fact and time of any detainee's refusal to sign a custody record, when asked in accordance with this Code, must be recorded.

Note for guidance

2A *The purpose of paragraph 2.6A(b) is to protect those involved in serious organised crime investigations or arrests of particularly violent suspects when there is reliable information that those arrested or their associates may threaten or cause harm to those involved. In cases of doubt, an officer of inspector rank or above should be consulted.*

3 Initial action

(a) Detained persons—normal procedure

3.1 When a person is brought to a police station under arrest or arrested at the station having gone there voluntarily, the custody officer must make sure the person is told clearly about the following continuing rights which may be exercised at any stage during the period in custody:

(i) the right to have someone informed of their arrest as in *section 5*;

(ii) the right to consult privately with a solicitor and that free independent legal advice is available;

(iii) the right to consult these Codes of Practice. See *Note 3D*

3.2 The detainee must also be given:

- a written notice setting out:
  - the above three rights;
  - the arrangements for obtaining legal advice;
  - the right to a copy of the custody record as in *paragraph 2.4A*;
  - the caution in the terms prescribed in *section 10*.
- an additional written notice briefly setting out their entitlements while in custody, see *Notes 3A* and *3B*.

Note: The detainee shall be asked to sign the custody record to acknowledge receipt of these notices. Any refusal must be recorded on the custody record.

3.3 A citizen of an independent Commonwealth country or a national of a foreign country, including the Republic of Ireland, must be informed as soon as practicable about their rights of communication with their High Commission, Embassy or Consulate. See *section 7*

3.4 The custody officer shall:

- record the offence(s) that the detainee has been arrested for and the reason(s) for the arrest on the custody record. See *paragraph 10.3* and *Code G paragraphs 2.2 and 4.3*.
- note on the custody record any comment the detainee makes in relation to the arresting officer's account but shall not invite comment. If the arresting officer is not physically present when the detainee is brought to a police station, the arresting officer's account must be made available to the custody officer remotely or by a third party on the arresting officer's behalf. If the custody officer authorises a person's detention the detainee must be informed of the grounds as soon as practicable and before they are questioned about any offence;
- note any comment the detainee makes in respect of the decision to detain them but shall not invite comment;
- not put specific questions to the detainee regarding their involvement in any offence, nor in respect of any comments they may make in response to the arresting officer's account

or the decision to place them in detention. Such an exchange is likely to constitute an interview as in *paragraph 11.1A* and require the associated safeguards in *section 11*. See *paragraph 11.13* in respect of unsolicited comments.

3.5 The custody officer shall:

  (a) ask the detainee, whether at this time, they:

    (i) would like legal advice, see *paragraph 6.5*;

    (ii) want someone informed of their detention, see *section 5*;

  (b) ask the detainee to sign the custody record to confirm their decisions in respect of (a);

  (c) determine whether the detainee:

    (i) is, or might be, in need of medical treatment or attention, see *section 9*;

    (ii) requires:

- an appropriate adult;
- help to check documentation;
- an interpreter;

  (d) record the decision in respect of (c).

3.6 When determining these needs the custody officer is responsible for initiating an assessment to consider whether the detainee is likely to present specific risks to custody staff or themselves. Such assessments should always include a check on the Police National Computer, to be carried out as soon as practicable, to identify any risks highlighted in relation to the detainee. Although such assessments are primarily the custody officer's responsibility, it may be necessary for them to consult and involve others, e.g. the arresting officer or an appropriate health care professional, see *paragraph 9.13*. Reasons for delaying the initiation or completion of the assessment must be recorded.

3.7 Chief Officers should ensure that arrangements for proper and effective risk assessments required by *paragraph 3.6* are implemented in respect of all detainees at police stations in their area.

3.8 Risk assessments must follow a structured process which clearly defines the categories of risk to be considered and the results must be incorporated in the detainee's custody record. The custody officer is responsible for making sure those responsible for the detainee's custody are appropriately briefed about the risks. If no specific risks are identified by the assessment, that should be noted in the custody record. See *Note 3E* and *paragraph 9.14*

3.9 The custody officer is responsible for implementing the response to any specific risk assessment, e.g.:

- reducing opportunities for self harm;
- calling a health care professional;
- increasing levels of monitoring or observation.

3.10 Risk assessment is an ongoing process and assessments must always be subject to review if circumstances change.

3.11 If video cameras are installed in the custody area, notices shall be prominently displayed showing cameras are in use. Any request to have video cameras switched off shall be refused.

(b) Detained persons—special groups

3.12 If the detainee appears deaf or there is doubt about their hearing or speaking ability or ability to understand English, and the custody officer cannot establish effective communication, the custody officer must, as soon as practicable, call an interpreter for assistance in the action under *paragraphs 3.1–3.5*. See *section 13*

3.13 If the detainee is a juvenile, the custody officer must, if it is practicable, ascertain the identity of a person responsible for their welfare. That person:

- may be:
  - the parent or guardian;
  - if the juvenile is in local authority or voluntary organisation care, or is otherwise being looked after under the Children Act 1989, a person appointed by that authority or organisation to have responsibility for the juvenile's welfare;
  - any other person who has, for the time being, assumed responsibility for the juvenile's welfare.

- must be informed as soon as practicable that the juvenile has been arrested, why they have been arrested and where they are detained. This right is in addition to the juvenile's right in *section 5* not to be held incommunicado. See *Note 3C*

3.14 If a juvenile is known to be subject to a court order under which a person or organisation is given any degree of statutory responsibility to supervise or otherwise monitor them, reasonable steps must also be taken to notify that person or organisation (the 'responsible officer'). The responsible officer will normally be a member of a Youth Offending Team, except for a curfew order which involves electronic monitoring when the contractor providing the monitoring will normally be the responsible officer.

3.15 If the detainee is a juvenile, mentally disordered or otherwise mentally vulnerable, the custody officer must, as soon as practicable:
- inform the appropriate adult, who in the case of a juvenile may or may not be a person responsible for their welfare, as in *paragraph 3.13*, of:
  — the grounds for their detention;
  — their whereabouts.
- ask the adult to come to the police station to see the detainee.

3.16 It is imperative that a mentally disordered or otherwise mentally vulnerable person, detained under the Mental Health Act 1983, section 136, be assessed as soon as possible. If that assessment is to take place at the police station, an approved social worker and a registered medical practitioner shall be called to the station as soon as possible in order to interview and examine the detainee. Once the detainee has been interviewed, examined and suitable arrangements made for their treatment or care, they can no longer be detained under section 136. A detainee must be immediately discharged from detention under section 136 if a registered medical practitioner, having examined them, concludes they are not mentally disordered within the meaning of the Act.

3.17 If the appropriate adult is:
- already at the police station, the provisions of *paragraphs 3.1* to *3.5* must be complied with in the appropriate adult's presence;
- not at the station when these provisions are complied with, they must be complied with again in the presence of the appropriate adult when they arrive.

3.18 The detainee shall be advised that:
- the duties of the appropriate adult include giving advice and assistance;
- they can consult privately with the appropriate adult at any time.

3.19 If the detainee, or appropriate adult on the detainee's behalf, asks for a solicitor to be called to give legal advice, the provisions of *section 6* apply.

3.20 If the detainee is blind, seriously visually impaired or unable to read, the custody officer shall make sure their solicitor, relative, appropriate adult or some other person likely to take an interest in them and not involved in the investigation is available to help check any documentation. When this Code requires written consent or signing the person assisting may be asked to sign instead, if the detainee prefers. This paragraph does not require an appropriate adult to be called solely to assist in checking and signing documentation for a person who is not a juvenile, or mentally disordered or otherwise mentally vulnerable (see *paragraph 3.15*).

(c) Persons attending a police station voluntarily

3.21 Anybody attending a police station voluntarily to assist with an investigation may leave at will unless arrested. See *Note 1K*. If it is decided they shall not be allowed to leave, they must be informed at once that they are under arrest and brought before the custody officer, who is responsible for making sure they are notified of their rights in the same way as other detainees. If they are not arrested but are cautioned as in *section 10*, the person who gives the caution must, at the same time, inform them they are not under arrest, they are not obliged to remain at the station but if they remain at the station they may obtain free and independent legal advice if they want. They shall be told the right to legal advice includes the right to speak with a solicitor on the telephone and be asked if they want to do so.

3.22 If a person attending the police station voluntarily asks about their entitlement to legal advice, they shall be given a copy of the notice explaining the arrangements for obtaining legal advice. See *paragraph 3.2.*

(d) Documentation

3.23 The grounds for a person's detention shall be recorded, in the person's presence if practicable.

3.24 Action taken under *paragraphs 3.12* to *3.20* shall be recorded.

(e) Persons answering street bail

3.25 When a person is answering street bail, the custody officer should link any documentation held in relation to arrest with the custody record. Any further action shall be recorded on the custody record in accordance with paragraphs 3.23 and 3.24 above.

Notes for guidance

3A *The notice of entitlements should:*
- *list the entitlements in this Code, including:*
  - *visits and contact with outside parties, including special provisions for Commonwealth citizens and foreign nationals;*
  - *reasonable standards of physical comfort;*
  - *adequate food and drink;*
  - *access to toilets and washing facilities, clothing, medical attention, and exercise when practicable.*
- *mention the:*
  - *provisions relating to the conduct of interviews;*
  - *circumstances in which an appropriate adult should be available to assist the detainee and their statutory rights to make representation whenever the period of their detention is reviewed.*

3B *In addition to notices in English, translations should be available in Welsh, the main minority ethnic languages and the principal European languages, whenever they are likely to be helpful. Audio versions of the notice should also be made available.*

3C *If the juvenile is in local authority or voluntary organisation care but living with their parents or other adults responsible for their welfare, although there is no legal obligation to inform them, they should normally be contacted, as well as the authority or organisation unless suspected of involvement in the offence concerned. Even if the juvenile is not living with their parents, consideration should be given to informing them.*

3D *The right to consult the Codes of Practice does not entitle the person concerned to delay unreasonably any necessary investigative or administrative action whilst they do so. Examples of action which need not be delayed unreasonably include:*
- *procedures requiring the provision of breath, blood or urine specimens under the Road Traffic Act 1988 or the Transport and Works Act 1992;*
- *searching detainees at the police station;*
- *taking fingerprints, footwear impressions or non-intimate samples without consent for evidential purposes.*

3E *Home Office Circular 32/2000 provides more detailed guidance on risk assessments and identifies key risk areas which should always be considered.*

4 Detainee's property

(a) Action

4.1 The custody officer is responsible for:

(a) ascertaining what property a detainee:

       (i) has with them when they come to the police station, whether on:

- arrest or re-detention on answering to bail;
- commitment to prison custody on the order or sentence of a court;
- lodgement at the police station with a view to their production in court from prison custody;
- transfer from detention at another station or hospital;
- detention under the Mental Health Act 1983, section 135 or 136;
- remand into police custody on the authority of a court

      (ii) might have acquired for an unlawful or harmful purpose while in custody;

(b) the safekeeping of any property taken from a detainee which remains at the police station. The custody officer may search the detainee or authorise their being searched to the extent they consider necessary, provided a search of intimate parts of the body or involving the removal of more than outer clothing is only made as in *Annex A*. A search may only be carried out by an officer of the same sex as the detainee. See *Note 4A*

4.2 Detainees may retain clothing and personal effects at their own risk unless the custody officer considers they may use them to cause harm to themselves or others, interfere with evidence, damage property, effect an escape or they are needed as evidence. In this event the custody officer may withhold such articles as they consider necessary and must tell the detainee why.

4.3 Personal effects are those items a detainee may lawfully need, use or refer to while in detention but do not include cash and other items of value.

(b) Documentation

4.4 It is a matter for the custody officer to determine whether a record should be made of the property a detained person has with him or had taken from him on arrest. Any record made is not required to be kept as part of the custody record but the custody record should be noted as to where such a record exists. Whenever a record is made the detainee shall be allowed to check and sign the record of property as correct. Any refusal to sign shall be recorded.

4.5 If a detainee is not allowed to keep any article of clothing or personal effects, the reason must be recorded.

Notes for guidance

4A PACE, Section 54(1) and paragraph 4.1 require a detainee to be searched when it is clear the custody officer will have continuing duties in relation to that detainee or when that detainee's behaviour or offence makes an inventory appropriate. They do not require every detainee to be searched, e.g. if it is clear a person will only be detained for a short period and is not to be placed in a cell, the custody officer may decide not to search them. In such a case the custody record will be endorsed 'not searched', paragraph 4.4 will not apply, and the detainee will be invited to sign the entry. If the detainee refuses, the custody officer will be obliged to ascertain what property they have in accordance with paragraph 4.1.

4B Paragraph 4.4 does not require the custody officer to record on the custody record property in the detainee's possession on arrest if, by virtue of its nature, quantity or size, it is not practicable to remove it to the police station.

4C Paragraph 4.4 does not require items of clothing worn by the person be recorded unless withheld by the custody officer as in paragraph 4.2.

5 Right not to be held incommunicado

(a) Action

5.1 Any person arrested and held in custody at a police station or other premises may, on request, have one person known to them or likely to take an interest in their welfare informed at public expense of their whereabouts as soon as practicable. If the person cannot be contacted the detainee may choose up to two alternatives. If they cannot be contacted, the person in charge of detention or the investigation has discretion to allow further attempts until the information has been conveyed. See *Notes 5C* and *5D*

5.2 The exercise of the above right in respect of each person nominated may be delayed only in accordance with *Annex B*.

5.3 The above right may be exercised each time a detainee is taken to another police station.

5.4 The detainee may receive visits at the custody officer's discretion. See *Note 5B*

5.5 If a friend, relative or person with an interest in the detainee's welfare enquires about their whereabouts, this information shall be given if the suspect agrees and *Annex B* does not apply. See *Note 5D*

5.6 The detainee shall be given writing materials, on request, and allowed to telephone one person for a reasonable time, see *Notes 5A* and *5E*. Either or both these privileges may be denied or delayed if an officer of inspector rank or above considers sending a letter or making a telephone call may result in any of the consequences in:

(a) *Annex B paragraphs 1* and *2* and the person is detained in connection with an indictable offence;

(b) *Not used*

Nothing in this paragraph permits the restriction or denial of the rights in *paragraphs 5.1* and *6.1*.

5.7 Before any letter or message is sent, or telephone call made, the detainee shall be informed that what they say in any letter, call or message (other than in a communication to a solicitor) may be read or listened to and may be given in evidence. A telephone call may be terminated if it is being abused. The costs can be at public expense at the custody officer's discretion.

5.7A Any delay or denial of the rights in this section should be proportionate and should last no longer than necessary.

(b) Documentation

5.8 A record must be kept of any:

(a) request made under this section and the action taken;

(b) letters, messages or telephone calls made or received or visit received;

(c) refusal by the detainee to have information about them given to an outside enquirer. The detainee must be asked to countersign the record accordingly and any refusal recorded.

Notes for guidance

5A A person may request an interpreter to interpret a telephone call or translate a letter.

5B At the custody officer's discretion, visits should be allowed when possible, subject to having sufficient personnel to supervise a visit and any possible hindrance to the investigation.

5C If the detainee does not know anyone to contact for advice or support or cannot contact a friend or relative, the custody officer should bear in mind any local voluntary bodies or other organisations who might be able to help. Paragraph 6.1 applies if legal advice is required.

5D In some circumstances it may not be appropriate to use the telephone to disclose information under paragraphs 5.1 and 5.5.

5E The telephone call at paragraph 5.6 is in addition to any communication under paragraphs 5.1 and 6.1.

6 Right to legal advice

(a) Action

6.1 Unless *Annex B* applies, all detainees must be informed that they may at any time consult and communicate privately with a solicitor, whether in person, in writing or by telephone, and that free independent legal advice is available from the duty solicitor. See *paragraph 3.1, Note 6B* and *Note 6J*

6.2 Not Used

6.3 A poster advertising the right to legal advice must be prominently displayed in the charging area of every police station. See *Note 6H*

6.4 No police officer should, at any time, do or say anything with the intention of dissuading a detainee from obtaining legal advice.

6.5 The exercise of the right of access to legal advice may be delayed only as in *Annex B*. Whenever legal advice is requested, and unless *Annex B* applies, the custody officer must act without delay to secure the provision of such advice. If, on being informed or reminded of this right, the detainee declines to speak to a solicitor in person, the officer should point out that the right includes the right to speak with a solicitor on the telephone. If the detainee continues to waive this right the officer should ask them why and any reasons should be recorded on the custody record or the interview record as appropriate. Reminders of the right to legal advice must be given as in *paragraphs 3.5, 11.2, 15.4, 16.4, 2B of Annex A, 3 of Annex K* and *16.5* and Code D, *paragraphs 3.17(ii)* and *6.3*. Once it is clear a detainee does not want to speak to a solicitor in person or by telephone they should cease to be asked their reasons. See *Note 6K*

6.5A In the case of a juvenile, an appropriate adult should consider whether legal advice from a solicitor is required. If the juvenile indicates that they do not want legal advice, the appropriate adult has the right to ask for a solicitor to attend if this would be in the best interests of the person. However, the detained person cannot be forced to see the solicitor if he is adamant that he does not wish to do so.

6.6 A detainee who wants legal advice may not be interviewed or continue to be interviewed until they have received such advice unless:

(a) *Annex B* applies, when the restriction on drawing adverse inferences from silence in *Annex C* will apply because the detainee is not allowed an opportunity to consult a solicitor; or

(b) an officer of superintendent rank or above has reasonable grounds for believing that:
   (i) the consequent delay might:
   - lead to interference with, or harm to, evidence connected with an offence;
   - lead to interference with, or physical harm to, other people;
   - lead to serious loss of, or damage to, property;
   - lead to alerting other people suspected of having committed an offence but not yet arrested for it;
   - hinder the recovery of property obtained in consequence of the commission of an offence.
   (ii) when a solicitor, including a duty solicitor, has been contacted and has agreed to attend, awaiting their arrival would cause unreasonable delay to the process of investigation.
   Note: In these cases the restriction on drawing adverse inferences from silence in *Annex C* will apply because the detainee is not allowed an opportunity to consult a solicitor;

(c) the solicitor the detainee has nominated or selected from a list:
   (i) cannot be contacted;
   (ii) has previously indicated they do not wish to be contacted; or
   (iii) having been contacted, has declined to attend; and
   the detainee has been advised of the Duty Solicitor Scheme but has declined to ask for the duty solicitor.
   In these circumstances the interview may be started or continued without further delay provided an officer of inspector rank or above has agreed to the interview proceeding.
   Note: The restriction on drawing adverse inferences from silence in *Annex C* will not apply because the detainee is allowed an opportunity to consult the duty solicitor;

(d) the detainee changes their mind, about wanting legal advice.
   In these circumstances the interview may be started or continued without delay provided that:
   (i) the detainee agrees to do so, in writing or on the interview record made in accordance with Code E or F; and

(ii) an officer of inspector rank or above has inquired about the detainee's reasons for their change of mind and gives authority for the interview to proceed.

Confirmation of the detainee's agreement, their change of mind, the reasons for it if given and, subject to *paragraph 2.6A*, the name of the authorising officer shall be recorded in the written interview record or the interview record made in accordance with Code E or F. See *Note 6I*.

Note: In these circumstances the restriction on drawing adverse inferences from silence in *Annex C* will not apply because the detainee is allowed an opportunity to consult a solicitor if they wish.

6.7 If *paragraph 6.6(b)(i)* applies, once sufficient information has been obtained to avert the risk, questioning must cease until the detainee has received legal advice unless *paragraph 6.6(a), (b)(ii), (c) or (d)* applies.

6.8 A detainee who has been permitted to consult a solicitor shall be entitled on request to have the solicitor present when they are interviewed unless one of the exceptions in *paragraph 6.6* applies.

6.9 The solicitor may only be required to leave the interview if their conduct is such that the interviewer is unable properly to put questions to the suspect. See *Notes 6D and 6E*

6.10 If the interviewer considers a solicitor is acting in such a way, they will stop the interview and consult an officer not below superintendent rank, if one is readily available, and otherwise an officer not below inspector rank not connected with the investigation. After speaking to the solicitor, the officer consulted will decide if the interview should continue in the presence of that solicitor. If they decide it should not, the suspect will be given the opportunity to consult another solicitor before the interview continues and that solicitor given an opportunity to be present at the interview. See *Note 6E*

6.11 The removal of a solicitor from an interview is a serious step and, if it occurs, the officer of superintendent rank or above who took the decision will consider if the incident should be reported to the Law Society. If the decision to remove the solicitor has been taken by an officer below superintendent rank, the facts must be reported to an officer of superintendent rank or above who will similarly consider whether a report to the Law Society would be appropriate. When the solicitor concerned is a duty solicitor, the report should be both to the Law Society and to the Legal Services Commission.

6.12 'Solicitor' in this Code means:
- a solicitor who holds a current practising certificate
- an accredited or probationary representative included on the register of representatives maintained by the Legal Services Commission.

6.12A An accredited or probationary representative sent to provide advice by, and on behalf of, a solicitor shall be admitted to the police station for this purpose unless an officer of inspector rank or above considers such a visit will hinder the investigation and directs otherwise. Hindering the investigation does not include giving proper legal advice to a detainee as in *Note 6D*. Once admitted to the police station, *paragraphs 6.6 to 6.10* apply.

6.13 In exercising their discretion under *paragraph 6.12A*, the officer should take into account in particular:
- whether:
  - the identity and status of an accredited or probationary representative have been satisfactorily established;
  - they are of suitable character to provide legal advice, e.g. a person with a criminal record is unlikely to be suitable unless the conviction was for a minor offence and not recent.
- any other matters in any written letter of authorisation provided by the solicitor on whose behalf the person is attending the police station. See *Note 6F*

6.14 If the inspector refuses access to an accredited or probationary representative or a decision is taken that such a person should not be permitted to remain at an interview, the inspector must notify the solicitor on whose behalf the representative was acting and give them an opportunity to make alternative arrangements. The detainee must be informed and the custody record noted.

6.15   If a solicitor arrives at the station to see a particular person, that person must, unless *Annex B* applies, be so informed whether or not they are being interviewed and asked if they would like to see the solicitor. This applies even if the detainee has declined legal advice or, having requested it, subsequently agreed to be interviewed without receiving advice. The solicitor's attendance and the detainee's decision must be noted in the custody record.

(b) Documentation

6.16 Any request for legal advice and the action taken shall be recorded.

6.17 A record shall be made in the interview record if a detainee asks for legal advice and an interview is begun either in the absence of a solicitor or their representative, or they have been required to leave an interview.

Notes for guidance

6A *In considering if paragraph 6.6(b) applies, the officer should, if practicable, ask the solicitor for an estimate of how long it will take to come to the station and relate this to the time detention is permitted, the time of day (i.e. whether the rest period under paragraph 12.2 is imminent) and the requirements of other investigations. If the solicitor is on their way or is to set off immediately, it will not normally be appropriate to begin an interview before they arrive. If it appears necessary to begin an interview before the solicitor's arrival, they should be given an indication of how long the police would be able to wait before 6.6(b) applies so there is an opportunity to make arrangements for someone else to provide legal advice.*

6B *A detainee who asks for legal advice should be given an opportunity to consult a specific solicitor or another solicitor from that solicitor's firm or the duty solicitor. If advice is not available by these means, or they do not want to consult the duty solicitor, the detainee should be given an opportunity to choose a solicitor from a list of those willing to provide legal advice. If this solicitor is unavailable, they may choose up to two alternatives. If these attempts are unsuccessful, the custody officer has discretion to allow further attempts until a solicitor has been contacted and agrees to provide legal advice. Apart from carrying out these duties, an officer must not advise the suspect about any particular firm of solicitors.*

6C *Not Used*

6D *A detainee has a right to free legal advice and to be represented by a solicitor. The solicitor's only role in the police station is to protect and advance the legal rights of their client. On occasions this may require the solicitor to give advice which has the effect of the client avoiding giving evidence which strengthens a prosecution case. The solicitor may intervene in order to seek clarification, challenge an improper question to their client or the manner in which it is put, advise their client not to reply to particular questions, or if they wish to give their client further legal advice. Paragraph 6.9 only applies if the solicitor's approach or conduct prevents or unreasonably obstructs proper questions being put to the suspect or the suspect's response being recorded. Examples of unacceptable conduct include answering questions on a suspect's behalf or providing written replies for the suspect to quote.*

6E *An officer who takes the decision to exclude a solicitor must be in a position to satisfy the court the decision was properly made. In order to do this they may need to witness what is happening.*

6F *If an officer of at least inspector rank considers a particular solicitor or firm of solicitors is persistently sending probationary representatives who are unsuited to provide legal advice, they should inform an officer of at least superintendent rank, who may wish to take the matter up with the Law Society.*

6G *Subject to the constraints of Annex B, a solicitor may advise more than one client in an investigation if they wish. Any question of a conflict of interest is for the solicitor under their professional code of conduct. If, however, waiting for a solicitor to give advice to one client may lead to unreasonable delay to the interview with another, the provisions of paragraph 6.6(b) may apply.*

6H *In addition to a poster in English, a poster or posters containing translations into Welsh, the main minority ethnic languages and the principal European languages should be displayed wherever they are likely to be helpful and it is practicable to do so.*

6I *Paragraph 6.6(d) requires the authorisation of an officer of inspector rank or above to the continuation of an interview when a detainee who wanted legal advice changes their mind. It is permissible for such authorisation to be given over the telephone, if the authorising officer is able to satisfy themselves about the reason for the detainee's change of mind and is satisfied it is proper to continue the interview in those circumstances.*

6J *Whenever a detainee exercises their right to legal advice by consulting or communicating with a solicitor, they must be allowed to do so in private. This right to consult or communicate in private is fundamental. If the requirement for privacy is compromised because what is said or written by the detainee or solicitor for the purpose of giving and receiving legal advice is overheard, listened to, or read by others without the informed consent of the detainee, the right will effectively have been denied. When a detainee chooses to speak to a solicitor on the telephone, they should be allowed to do so in private unless this is impractical because of the design and layout of the custody area or the location of telephones. However, the normal expectation should be that facilities will be available, unless they are being used, at all police stations to enable detainees to speak in private to a solicitor either face to face or over the telephone.*

6K *A detainee is not obliged to give reasons for declining legal advice and should not be pressed to do so.*

7 Citizens of independent Commonwealth countries or foreign nationals

(a) Action

7.1 Any citizen of an independent Commonwealth country or a national of a foreign country, including the Republic of Ireland, may communicate at any time with the appropriate High Commission, Embassy or Consulate. The detainee must be informed as soon as practicable of:
- this right;
- their right, upon request, to have their High Commission, Embassy or Consulate told of their whereabouts and the grounds for their detention. Such a request should be acted upon as soon as practicable.

7.2 If a detainee is a citizen of a country with which a bilateral consular convention or agreement is in force requiring notification of arrest, the appropriate High Commission, Embassy or Consulate shall be informed as soon as practicable, subject to *paragraph 7.4*. The countries to which this applies as at 1 April 2003 are listed in *Annex F*.

7.3 Consular officers may visit one of their nationals in police detention to talk to them and, if required, to arrange for legal advice. Such visits shall take place out of the hearing of a police officer.

7.4 Notwithstanding the provisions of consular conventions, if the detainee is a political refugee whether for reasons of race, nationality, political opinion or religion, or is seeking political asylum, consular officers shall not be informed of the arrest of one of their nationals or given access or information about them except at the detainee's express request.

(b) Documentation

7.5 A record shall be made when a detainee is informed of their rights under this section and of any communications with a High Commission, Embassy or Consulate.

Note for guidance

7A *The exercise of the rights in this section may not be interfered with even though Annex B applies.*

8 Conditions of detention

(a) Action

8.1 So far as it is practicable, not more than one detainee should be detained in each cell.

8.2 Cells in use must be adequately heated, cleaned and ventilated. They must be adequately lit, subject to such dimming as is compatible with safety and security to allow people detained overnight to sleep. No additional restraints shall be used within a locked cell unless absolutely necessary and then only restraint equipment, approved for use in that force by the Chief Officer, which is reasonable and necessary in the circumstances having regard to the detainee's demeanour and with a view to ensuring their safety and the safety of others. If a detainee is deaf, mentally disordered or otherwise mentally vulnerable, particular care must be taken when deciding whether to use any form of approved restraints.

8.3 Blankets, mattresses, pillows and other bedding supplied shall be of a reasonable standard and in a clean and sanitary condition. See *Note 8A*

8.4 Access to toilet and washing facilities must be provided.

8.5 If it is necessary to remove a detainee's clothes for the purposes of investigation, for hygiene, health reasons or cleaning, replacement clothing of a reasonable standard of comfort and cleanliness shall be provided. A detainee may not be interviewed unless adequate clothing has been offered.

8.6 At least two light meals and one main meal should be offered in any 24 hour period. See *Note 8B*. Drinks should be provided at meal times and upon reasonable request between meals. Whenever necessary, advice shall be sought from the appropriate health care professional, see *Note 9A*, on medical and dietary matters. As far as practicable, meals provided shall offer a varied diet and meet any specific dietary needs or religious beliefs the detainee may have. The detainee may, at the custody officer's discretion, have meals supplied by their family or friends at their expense. See *Note 8A*

8.7 Brief outdoor exercise shall be offered daily if practicable.

8.8 A juvenile shall not be placed in a police cell unless no other secure accommodation is available and the custody officer considers it is not practicable to supervise them if they are not placed in a cell or that a cell provides more comfortable accommodation than other secure accommodation in the station. A juvenile may not be placed in a cell with a detained adult.

(b) Documentation

8.9 A record must be kept of replacement clothing and meals offered.

8.10 If a juvenile is placed in a cell, the reason must be recorded.

8.11 The use of any restraints on a detainee whilst in a cell, the reasons for it and, if appropriate, the arrangements for enhanced supervision of the detainee whilst so restrained, shall be recorded. See *paragraph 3.9*

Notes for guidance

8A *The provisions in paragraph 8.3 and 8.6 respectively are of particular importance in the case of a person likely to be detained for an extended period. In deciding whether to allow meals to be supplied by family or friends, the custody officer is entitled to take account of the risk of items being concealed in any food or package and the officer's duties and responsibilities under food handling legislation.*

8B *Meals should, so far as practicable, be offered at recognised meal times, or at other times that take account of when the detainee last had a meal.*

9 Care and treatment of detained persons

(a) General

9.1 Nothing in this section prevents the police from calling the police surgeon or, if appropriate, some other health care professional, to examine a detainee for the purposes of obtaining evidence relating to any offence in which the detainee is suspected of being involved. See *Note 9A*

9.2 If a complaint is made by, or on behalf of, a detainee about their treatment since their arrest, or it comes to notice that a detainee may have been treated improperly, a report must be made as soon as practicable to an officer of inspector rank or above not connected with the investigation. If the matter concerns a possible assault or the possibility of the unnecessary or unreasonable use of force, an appropriate health care professional must also be called as soon as practicable.

9.3 Detainees should be visited at least every hour. If no reasonably foreseeable risk was identified in a risk assessment, see *paragraphs 3.6–3.10*, there is no need to wake a sleeping detainee. Those suspected of being intoxicated through drink or drugs or having swallowed drugs, see *Note 9CA*, or whose level of consciousness causes concern must, subject to any clinical directions given by the appropriate health care professional, see *paragraph 9.13*:
- be visited and roused at least every half hour
- have their condition assessed as in *Annex H*
- and clinical treatment arranged if appropriate

See *Notes 9B, 9C* and *9H*

9.4 When arrangements are made to secure clinical attention for a detainee, the custody officer must make sure all relevant information which might assist in the treatment of the detainee's condition is made available to the responsible health care professional. This applies whether or not the health care professional asks for such information. Any officer or police staff with relevant information must inform the custody officer as soon as practicable.

(b) Clinical treatment and attention

9.5 The custody officer must make sure a detainee receives appropriate clinical attention as soon as reasonably practicable if the person:
(a) appears to be suffering from physical illness; or
(b) is injured; or
(c) appears to be suffering from a mental disorder;
(d) appears to need clinical attention.

9.5A This applies even if the detainee makes no request for clinical attention and whether or not they have already received clinical attention elsewhere. If the need for attention appears urgent, e.g. when indicated as in *Annex H*, the nearest available health care professional or an ambulance must be called immediately.

9.5B The custody officer must also consider the need for clinical attention as set out in Note for Guidance 9C in relation to those suffering the effects of alcohol or drugs.

9.6 *Paragraph 9.5* is not meant to prevent or delay the transfer to a hospital if necessary of a person detained under the Mental Health Act 1983, section 136. See *Note 9D*. When an assessment under that Act takes place at a police station, see *paragraph 3.16*, the custody officer must consider whether an appropriate health care professional should be called to conduct an initial clinical check on the detainee. This applies particularly when there is likely to be any significant delay in the arrival of a suitably qualified medical practitioner.

9.7 If it appears to the custody officer, or they are told, that a person brought to a station under arrest may be suffering from an infectious disease or condition, the custody officer must take reasonable steps to safeguard the health of the detainee and others at the station. In deciding what action to take, advice must be sought from an appropriate health care professional. See *Note 9E*. The custody officer has discretion to isolate the person and their property until clinical directions have been obtained.

9.8 If a detainee requests a clinical examination, an appropriate health care professional must be called as soon as practicable to assess the detainee's clinical needs. If a safe and appropriate care plan cannot be provided, the police surgeon's advice must be sought. The detainee may also be examined by a medical practitioner of their choice at their expense.

9.9 If a detainee is required to take or apply any medication in compliance with clinical directions prescribed before their detention, the custody officer must consult the appropriate health care professional before the use of the medication. Subject to the restrictions in *paragraph 9.10*, the custody officer is responsible for the safekeeping of any medication and for making sure the detainee is given the opportunity to take or apply prescribed or approved medication. Any such consultation and its outcome shall be noted in the custody record.

9.10 No police officer may administer or supervise the self-administration of medically prescribed controlled drugs of the types and forms listed in the Misuse of Drugs Regulations 2001, Schedule 2 or 3. A detainee may only self-administer such drugs under the personal supervision of the registered medical practitioner authorising their use. Drugs listed in Schedule 4 or 5 may be distributed by the custody officer for self-administration if they have consulted the registered medical practitioner authorising their use, this may be done by telephone, and both parties are satisfied self-administration will not expose the detainee, police officers or anyone else to the risk of harm or injury.

9.11 When appropriate health care professionals administer drugs or other medications, or supervise their self-administration, it must be within current medicines legislation and the scope of practice as determined by their relevant professional body.

9.12 If a detainee has in their possession, or claims to need, medication relating to a heart condition, diabetes, epilepsy or a condition of comparable potential seriousness then, even though *paragraph 9.5* may not apply, the advice of the appropriate health care professional must be obtained.

9.13 Whenever the appropriate health care professional is called in accordance with this section to examine or treat a detainee, the custody officer shall ask for their opinion about:
- any risks or problems which police need to take into account when making decisions about the detainee's continued detention;
- when to carry out an interview if applicable; and
- the need for safeguards.

9.14 When clinical directions are given by the appropriate health care professional, whether orally or in writing, and the custody officer has any doubts or is in any way uncertain about any aspect of the directions, the custody officer shall ask for clarification. It is particularly important that directions concerning the frequency of visits are clear, precise and capable of being implemented. See *Note 9F*.

(c) Documentation

9.15 A record must be made in the custody record of:
(a) the arrangements made for an examination by an appropriate health care professional under *paragraph 9.2* and of any complaint reported under that paragraph together with any relevant remarks by the custody officer;
(b) any arrangements made in accordance with *paragraph 9.5*;
(c) any request for a clinical examination under *paragraph 9.8* and any arrangements made in response;
(d) the injury, ailment, condition or other reason which made it necessary to make the arrangements in (a) to (c), see *Note 9G*;
(e) any clinical directions and advice, including any further clarifications, given to police by a health care professional concerning the care and treatment of the detainee in connection with any of the arrangements made in (a) to (c), see *Note 9F*;
(f) if applicable, the responses received when attempting to rouse a person using the procedure in *Annex H, see Note 9H*.

9.16 If a health care professional does not record their clinical findings in the custody record, the record must show where they are recorded. See *Note 9G*. However, information which is necessary to custody staff to ensure the effective ongoing care and well being of the detainee must be recorded openly in the custody record, see *paragraph 3.8* and *Annex G, paragraph 7*.

9.17 Subject to the requirements of *Section 4*, the custody record shall include:
- a record of all medication a detainee has in their possession on arrival at the police station;
- a note of any such medication they claim to need but do not have with them.

Notes for guidance

9A   *A 'health care professional' means a clinically qualified person working within the scope of practice as determined by their relevant professional body. Whether a health care professional is 'appropriate' depends on the circumstances of the duties they carry out at the time.*

9B   *Whenever possible juveniles and mentally vulnerable detainees should be visited more frequently.*

9C   *A detainee who appears drunk or behaves abnormally may be suffering from illness, the effects of drugs or may have sustained injury, particularly a head injury which is not apparent. A detainee needing or dependent on certain drugs, including alcohol, may experience harmful effects within a short time of being deprived of their supply. In these circumstances, when there is any doubt, police should always act urgently to call an appropriate health care professional or an ambulance. Paragraph 9.5 does not apply to minor ailments or injuries which do not need attention. However, all such ailments or injuries must be recorded in the custody record and any doubt must be resolved in favour of calling the appropriate health care professional.*

9CA *Paragraph 9.3 would apply to a person in police custody by order of a magistrates' court under the Criminal Justice Act 1988, section 152 (as amended by the Drugs Act 2005, section 8) to facilitate the recovery of evidence after being charged with drug possession or drug trafficking and suspected of having swallowed drugs. In the case of the healthcare needs of a person who has swallowed drugs, the custody officer subject to any clinical directions, should consider the necessity for rousing every half hour. This does not negate the need for regular visiting of the suspect in the cell.*

9D   *Whenever practicable, arrangements should be made for persons detained for assessment under the Mental Health Act 1983, section 136 to be taken to a hospital. There is no power under that Act to transfer a person detained under section 136 from one place of safety to another place of safety for assessment.*

9E   *It is important to respect a person's right to privacy and information about their health must be kept confidential and only disclosed with their consent or in accordance with clinical advice when it is necessary to protect the detainee's health or that of others who come into contact with them.*

9F   *The custody officer should always seek to clarify directions that the detainee requires constant observation or supervision and should ask the appropriate health care professional to explain precisely what action needs to be taken to implement such directions.*

9G   *Paragraphs 9.15 and 9.16 do not require any information about the cause of any injury, ailment or condition to be recorded on the custody record if it appears capable of providing evidence of an offence.*

9H   *The purpose of recording a person's responses when attempting to rouse them using the procedure in Annex H is to enable any change in the individual's consciousness level to be noted and clinical treatment arranged if appropriate.*

10 Cautions

(a) When a caution must be given

10.1 A person whom there are grounds to suspect of an offence, see *Note 10A*, must be cautioned before any questions about an offence, or further questions if the answers provide the grounds for suspicion, are put to them if either the suspect's answers or silence, (i.e. failure or refusal to answer or answer satisfactorily) may be given in evidence to a court in a prosecution. A person need not be cautioned if questions are for other necessary purposes, e.g.:

(a) solely to establish their identity or ownership of any vehicle;

(b) to obtain information in accordance with any relevant statutory requirement, see *paragraph 10.9*;

(c) in furtherance of the proper and effective conduct of a search, e.g. to determine the need to search in the exercise of powers of stop and search or to seek co-operation while carrying out a search;

(d) to seek verification of a written record as in *paragraph 11.13*;

(e) Not used

10.2 Whenever a person not under arrest is initially cautioned, or reminded they are under caution, that person must at the same time be told they are not under arrest and are free to leave if they want to. See *Note 10C*

10.3 A person who is arrested, or further arrested, must be informed at the time, or as soon as practicable thereafter, that they are under arrest and the grounds for their arrest, see *paragraph 3.4, Note 10B* and *Code G, paragraphs 2.2* and *4.3.*

10.4 As per *Code G, section 3*, a person who is arrested, or further arrested, must also be cautioned unless:

(a) it is impracticable to do so by reason of their condition or behaviour at the time;

(b) they have already been cautioned immediately prior to arrest as in *paragraph 10.1*.

(b) Terms of the cautions

10.5 The caution which must be given on:

(a) arrest;

(b) all other occasions before a person is charged or informed they may be prosecuted, see *section 16*,

should, unless the restriction on drawing adverse inferences from silence applies, see *Annex C*, be in the following terms:

"You do not have to say anything. But it may harm your defence if you do not mention when questioned something which you later rely on in Court. Anything you do say may be given in evidence."

See *Note 10G*

10.6 *Annex C, paragraph 2* sets out the alternative terms of the caution to be used when the restriction on drawing adverse inferences from silence applies.

10.7 Minor deviations from the words of any caution given in accordance with this Code do not constitute a breach of this Code, provided the sense of the relevant caution is preserved. See *Note 10D*

10.8 After any break in questioning under caution, the person being questioned must be made aware they remain under caution. If there is any doubt the relevant caution should be given again in full when the interview resumes. See *Note 10E*

10.9 When, despite being cautioned, a person fails to co-operate or to answer particular questions which may affect their immediate treatment, the person should be informed of any relevant consequences and that those consequences are not affected by the caution. Examples are when a person's refusal to provide:

• their name and address when charged may make them liable to detention;

• particulars and information in accordance with a statutory requirement, e.g. under the Road Traffic Act 1988, may amount to an offence or may make the person liable to a further arrest.

(c) Special warnings under the Criminal Justice and Public Order Act 1994, sections 36 and 37

10.10 When a suspect interviewed at a police station or authorised place of detention after arrest fails or refuses to answer certain questions, or to answer satisfactorily, after due warning, see *Note 10F*, a court or jury may draw such inferences as appear proper under the Criminal Justice and Public Order Act 1994, sections 36 and 37. Such inferences may only be drawn when:

(a) the restriction on drawing adverse inferences from silence, see *Annex C*, does not apply; and

(b) the suspect is arrested by a constable and fails or refuses to account for any objects, marks or substances, or marks on such objects found:
- on their person;
- in or on their clothing or footwear;
- otherwise in their possession; or
- in the place they were arrested;

(c) the arrested suspect was found by a constable at a place at or about the time the offence for which that officer has arrested them is alleged to have been committed, and the suspect fails or refuses to account for their presence there.

When the restriction on drawing adverse inferences from silence applies, the suspect may still be asked to account for any of the matters in (*b*) or (*c*) but the special warning described in *paragraph 10.11* will not apply and must not be given.

10.11 For an inference to be drawn when a suspect fails or refuses to answer a question about one of these matters or to answer it satisfactorily, the suspect must first be told in ordinary language:

(a) what offence is being investigated;

(b) what fact they are being asked to account for;

(c) this fact may be due to them taking part in the commission of the offence;

(d) a court may draw a proper inference if they fail or refuse to account for this fact;

(e) a record is being made of the interview and it may be given in evidence if they are brought to trial.

(d) Juveniles and persons who are mentally disordered or otherwise mentally vulnerable

10.12 If a juvenile or a person who is mentally disordered or otherwise mentally vulnerable is cautioned in the absence of the appropriate adult, the caution must be repeated in the adult's presence.

(e) Documentation

10.13 A record shall be made when a caution is given under this section, either in the interviewer's pocket book or in the interview record.

Notes for guidance

10A There must be some reasonable, objective grounds for the suspicion, based on known facts or information which are relevant to the likelihood the offence has been committed and the person to be questioned committed it.

10B An arrested person must be given sufficient information to enable them to understand that they have been deprived of their liberty and the reason they have been arrested, e.g. when a person is arrested on suspicion of committing an offence they must be informed of the suspected offence's nature, when and where it was committed. The suspect must also be informed of the reason or reasons why the arrest is considered necessary. Vague or technical language should be avoided.

10C The restriction on drawing inferences from silence, see Annex C, paragraph 1, does not apply to a person who has not been detained and who therefore cannot be prevented from seeking legal advice if they want, see paragraph 3.21.

10D If it appears a person does not understand the caution, the person giving it should explain it in their own words.

10E It may be necessary to show to the court that nothing occurred during an interview break or between interviews which influenced the suspect's recorded evidence. After a break in an interview or at the beginning of a subsequent interview, the interviewing officer should summarise the reason for the break and confirm this with the suspect.

10F *The Criminal Justice and Public Order Act 1994, sections 36 and 37 apply only to suspects who have been arrested by a constable or Customs and Excise officer and are given the relevant warning by the police or customs officer who made the arrest or who is investigating the offence. They do not apply to any interviews with suspects who have not been arrested.*

10G *Nothing in this Code requires a caution to be given or repeated when informing a person not under arrest they may be prosecuted for an offence. However, a court will not be able to draw any inferences under the Criminal Justice and Public Order Act 1994, section 34, if the person was not cautioned.*

11 Interviews—general

(a) Action

11.1A An interview is the questioning of a person regarding their involvement or suspected involvement in a criminal offence or offences which, under *paragraph 10.1*, must be carried out under caution. Whenever a person is interviewed they must be informed of the nature of the offence, or further offence. Procedures under the Road Traffic Act 1988, section 7 or the Transport and Works Act 1992, section 31 do not constitute interviewing for the purpose of this Code.

11.1 Following a decision to arrest a suspect, they must not be interviewed about the relevant offence except at a police station or other authorised place of detention, unless the consequent delay would be likely to:

(a) lead to:
  • interference with, or harm to, evidence connected with an offence;
  • interference with, or physical harm to, other people; or
  • serious loss of, or damage to, property;

(b) lead to alerting other people suspected of committing an offence but not yet arrested for it; or

(c) hinder the recovery of property obtained in consequence of the commission of an offence.

Interviewing in any of these circumstances shall cease once the relevant risk has been averted or the necessary questions have been put in order to attempt to avert that risk.

11.2 Immediately prior to the commencement or re-commencement of any interview at a police station or other authorised place of detention, the interviewer should remind the suspect of their entitlement to free legal advice and that the interview can be delayed for legal advice to be obtained, unless one of the exceptions in *paragraph 6.6* applies. It is the interviewer's responsibility to make sure all reminders are recorded in the interview record.

11.3 Not Used

11.4 At the beginning of an interview the interviewer, after cautioning the suspect, see *section 10*, shall put to them any significant statement or silence which occurred in the presence and hearing of a police officer or other police staff before the start of the interview and which have not been put to the suspect in the course of a previous interview. See *Note 11A*. The interviewer shall ask the suspect whether they confirm or deny that earlier statement or silence and if they want to add anything.

11.4A A significant statement is one which appears capable of being used in evidence against the suspect, in particular a direct admission of guilt. A significant silence is a failure or refusal to answer a question or answer satisfactorily when under caution, which might, allowing for the restriction on drawing adverse inferences from silence, see *Annex C*, give rise to an inference under the Criminal Justice and Public Order Act 1994, Part III.

11.5 No interviewer may try to obtain answers or elicit a statement by the use of oppression. Except as in *paragraph 10.9*, no interviewer shall indicate, except to answer a direct question, what action will be taken by the police if the person being questioned answers questions, makes a statement or refuses to do either. If the person asks directly what action will be taken if they answer questions, make a statement or refuse to do either, the interviewer may inform them what action the police propose to take provided that action is itself proper and warranted.

11.6 The interview or further interview of a person about an offence with which that person has not been charged or for which they have not been informed they may be prosecuted, must cease when:

(a) the officer in charge of the investigation is satisfied all the questions they consider relevant to obtaining accurate and reliable information about the offence have been put to the suspect, this includes allowing the suspect an opportunity to give an innocent explanation and asking questions to test if the explanation is accurate and reliable, e.g. to clear up ambiguities or clarify what the suspect said;

(b) the officer in charge of the investigation has taken account of any other available evidence; and

(c) the officer in charge of the investigation, or in the case of a detained suspect, the custody officer, see *paragraph 16.1*, reasonably believes there is sufficient evidence to provide a realistic prospect of conviction for that offence. See *Note 11B*

This paragraph does not prevent officers in revenue cases or acting under the confiscation provisions of the Criminal Justice Act 1988 or the Drug Trafficking Act 1994 from inviting suspects to complete a formal question and answer record after the interview is concluded.

(b) Interview records

11.7 (a) An accurate record must be made of each interview, whether or not the interview takes place at a police station

(b) The record must state the place of interview, the time it begins and ends, any interview breaks and, subject to *paragraph 2.6A*, the names of all those present; and must be made on the forms provided for this purpose or in the interviewer's pocket book or in accordance with the Codes of Practice E or F;

(c) Any written record must be made and completed during the interview, unless this would not be practicable or would interfere with the conduct of the interview, and must constitute either a verbatim record of what has been said or, failing this, an account of the interview which adequately and accurately summarises it.

11.8 If a written record is not made during the interview it must be made as soon as practicable after its completion.

11.9 Written interview records must be timed and signed by the maker.

11.10 If a written record is not completed during the interview the reason must be recorded in the interview record.

11.11 Unless it is impracticable, the person interviewed shall be given the opportunity to read the interview record and to sign it as correct or to indicate how they consider it inaccurate. If the person interviewed cannot read or refuses to read the record or sign it, the senior interviewer present shall read it to them and ask whether they would like to sign it as correct or make their mark or to indicate how they consider it inaccurate. The interviewer shall certify on the interview record itself what has occurred. See *Note 11E*

11.12 If the appropriate adult or the person's solicitor is present during the interview, they should also be given an opportunity to read and sign the interview record or any written statement taken down during the interview.

11.13 A written record shall be made of any comments made by a suspect, including unsolicited comments, which are outside the context of an interview but which might be relevant to the offence. Any such record must be timed and signed by the maker. When practicable the suspect shall be given the opportunity to read that record and to sign it as correct or to indicate how they consider it inaccurate. See *Note 11E*

11.14 Any refusal by a person to sign an interview record when asked in accordance with this Code must itself be recorded.

(c) Juveniles and mentally disordered or otherwise mentally vulnerable people

11.15 A juvenile or person who is mentally disordered or otherwise mentally vulnerable must not be interviewed regarding their involvement or suspected involvement in a criminal offence or offences, or asked to provide or sign a written statement under caution or record of interview, in the absence of the appropriate adult unless *paragraphs 11.1, 11.18 to 11.20* apply. See *Note 11C*

11.16 Juveniles may only be interviewed at their place of education in exceptional circumstances and only when the principal or their nominee agrees. Every effort should be made to notify the parent(s) or other person responsible for the juvenile's welfare and the appropriate adult, if this is a different person, that the police want to interview the juvenile and reasonable time should be allowed to enable the appropriate adult to be present at the interview. If awaiting the appropriate adult would cause unreasonable delay, and unless the juvenile is suspected of an offence against the educational establishment, the principal or their nominee can act as the appropriate adult for the purposes of the interview.

11.17 If an appropriate adult is present at an interview, they shall be informed:
- they are not expected to act simply as an observer; and
- the purpose of their presence is to:
  — advise the person being interviewed;
  — observe whether the interview is being conducted properly and fairly;
  — facilitate communication with the person being interviewed.

(d) Vulnerable suspects—urgent interviews at police stations

11.18 The following persons may not be interviewed unless an officer of superintendent rank or above considers delay will lead to the consequences in *paragraph 11.1(a) to (c)*, and is satisfied the interview would not significantly harm the person's physical or mental state (see Annex G):
(a) a juvenile or person who is mentally disordered or otherwise mentally vulnerable if at the time of the interview the appropriate adult is not present;
(b) anyone other than in (*a*) who at the time of the interview appears unable to:
  - appreciate the significance of questions and their answers; or
  - understand what is happening because of the effects of drink, drugs or any illness, ailment or condition;
(c) a person who has difficulty understanding English or has a hearing disability, if at the time of the interview an interpreter is not present.

11.19 These interviews may not continue once sufficient information has been obtained to avert the consequences in *paragraph 11.1(a) to (c)*.

11.20 A record shall be made of the grounds for any decision to interview a person under *paragraph 11.18*.

Notes for guidance

11A *Paragraph 11.4 does not prevent the interviewer from putting significant statements and silences to a suspect again at a later stage or a further interview.*

11B *The Criminal Procedure and Investigations Act 1996 Code of Practice, paragraph 3.4 states 'In conducting an investigation, the investigator should pursue all reasonable lines of enquiry, whether these point towards or away from the suspect. What is reasonable will depend on the particular circumstances.' Interviewers should keep this in mind when deciding what questions to ask in an interview.*

11C *Although juveniles or people who are mentally disordered or otherwise mentally vulnerable are often capable of providing reliable evidence, they may, without knowing or wishing to do so, be particularly prone in certain circumstances to provide information that may be unreliable, misleading or self-incriminating. Special care should always be taken when questioning such a person, and the appropriate adult should be involved if there is any doubt about a person's age, mental state or capacity. Because of the risk of unreliable evidence it is also important to obtain corroboration of any facts admitted whenever possible.*

11D *Juveniles should not be arrested at their place of education unless this is unavoidable. When a juvenile is arrested at their place of education, the principal or their nominee must be informed.*

11E *Significant statements described in paragraph 11.4 will always be relevant to the offence and must be recorded. When a suspect agrees to read records of interviews and other comments and sign them as correct, they should be asked to endorse the record with, e.g. 'I agree that this is a correct record of what was said' and add their signature. If the suspect does not agree with the record, the interviewer should record the details of any disagreement and ask the suspect to read these details and sign them to the effect that they accurately reflect their disagreement. Any refusal to sign should be recorded.*

12 Interviews in police stations

(a) Action

12.1 If a police officer wants to interview or conduct enquiries which require the presence of a detainee, the custody officer is responsible for deciding whether to deliver the detainee into the officer's custody.

12.2 Except as below, in any period of 24 hours a detainee must be allowed a continuous period of at least 8 hours for rest, free from questioning, travel or any interruption in connection with the investigation concerned. This period should normally be at night or other appropriate time which takes account of when the detainee last slept or rested. If a detainee is arrested at a police station after going there voluntarily, the period of 24 hours runs from the time of their arrest and not the time of arrival at the police station. The period may not be interrupted or delayed, except:

   (a) when there are reasonable grounds for believing not delaying or interrupting the period would:
      (i) involve a risk of harm to people or serious loss of, or damage to, property,
      (ii) delay unnecessarily the person's release from custody;
      (iii) otherwise prejudice the outcome of the investigation;
   (b) at the request of the detainee, their appropriate adult or legal representative;
   (c) when a delay or interruption is necessary in order to:
      (i) comply with the legal obligations and duties arising under *section 15*;
      (ii) to take action required under *section 9* or in accordance with medical advice.

   If the period is interrupted in accordance with *(a)*, a fresh period must be allowed. Interruptions under *(b)* and *(c)*, do not require a fresh period to be allowed.

12.3 Before a detainee is interviewed the custody officer, in consultation with the officer in charge of the investigation and appropriate health care professionals as necessary, shall assess whether the detainee is fit enough to be interviewed. This means determining and considering the risks to the detainee's physical and mental state if the interview took place and determining what safeguards are needed to allow the interview to take place. See *Annex G*. The custody officer shall not allow a detainee to be interviewed if the custody officer considers it would cause significant harm to the detainee's physical or mental state. Vulnerable suspects listed at *paragraph 11.18* shall be treated as always being at some risk during an interview and these persons may not be interviewed except in accordance with *paragraphs 11.18* to *11.20*.

12.4 As far as practicable interviews shall take place in interview rooms which are adequately heated, lit and ventilated.

12.5 A suspect whose detention without charge has been authorised under PACE, because the detention is necessary for an interview to obtain evidence of the offence for which they have been arrested, may choose not to answer questions but police do not require the suspect's consent or agreement to interview them for this purpose. If a suspect takes steps to prevent themselves being questioned or further questioned, e.g. by refusing to leave their cell to go to a suitable interview room or by trying to leave the interview room, they shall be advised their consent or agreement to interview is not required. The suspect shall be cautioned as in *section 10*, and informed if they fail or refuse to co-operate, the interview may take place in the cell and that their failure or refusal to co-operate may be given in evidence. The suspect shall then be invited to co-operate and go into the interview room.

12.6 People being questioned or making statements shall not be required to stand.

12.7 Before the interview commences each interviewer shall, subject to *paragraph 2.6A*, identify themselves and any other persons present to the interviewee.

12.8 Breaks from interviewing should be made at recognised meal times or at other times that take account of when an interviewee last had a meal. Short refreshment breaks shall be provided at approximately two hour intervals, subject to the interviewer's discretion to delay a break if there are reasonable grounds for believing it would:

(i) involve a:
- risk of harm to people;
- serious loss of, or damage to, property;

(ii) unnecessarily delay the detainee's release;

(iii) otherwise prejudice the outcome of the investigation.

See *Note 12B*

12.9 If during the interview a complaint is made by or on behalf of the interviewee concerning the provisions of this Code, the interviewer should:

(i) record it in the interview record;

(ii) inform the custody officer, who is then responsible for dealing with it as in *section 9*.

(b) Documentation

12.10 A record must be made of the:
- time a detainee is not in the custody of the custody officer, and why
- reason for any refusal to deliver the detainee out of that custody

12.11 A record shall be made of:

(a) the reasons it was not practicable to use an interview room; and

(b) any action taken as in *paragraph 12.5*.

The record shall be made on the custody record or in the interview record for action taken whilst an interview record is being kept, with a brief reference to this effect in the custody record.

12.12 Any decision to delay a break in an interview must be recorded, with reasons, in the interview record.

12.13 All written statements made at police stations under caution shall be written on forms provided for the purpose.

12.14 All written statements made under caution shall be taken in accordance with *Annex D*. Before a person makes a written statement under caution at a police station they shall be reminded about the right to legal advice. See *Note 12A*

Notes for guidance

12A It is not normally necessary to ask for a written statement if the interview was recorded in writing and the record signed in accordance with paragraph 11.11 or audibly or visually recorded in accordance with Code E or F. Statements under caution should normally be taken in these circumstances only at the person's express wish. A person may however be asked if they want to make such a statement.

12B Meal breaks should normally last at least 45 minutes and shorter breaks after two hours should last at least 15 minutes. If the interviewer delays a break in accordance with paragraph 12.8 and prolongs the interview, a longer break should be provided. If there is a short interview, and another short interview is contemplated, the length of the break may be reduced if there are reasonable grounds to believe this is necessary to avoid any of the consequences in paragraph 12.8(i) to (iii).

13 Interpreters

(a) General

13.1 Chief officers are responsible for making sure appropriate arrangements are in place for provision of suitably qualified interpreters for people who:
- are deaf;
- do not understand English.

Whenever possible, interpreters should be drawn from the National Register of Public Service Interpreters (NRPSI) or the Council for the Advancement of Communication with Deaf People (CADCP) Directory of British Sign Language/English Interpreters.

(b) Foreign languages

13.2 Unless *paragraphs 11.1, 11.18* to *11.20* apply, a person must not be interviewed in the absence of a person capable of interpreting if:
 (a) they have difficulty understanding English;
 (b) the interviewer cannot speak the person's own language;
 (c) the person wants an interpreter present.

13.3 The interviewer shall make sure the interpreter makes a note of the interview at the time in the person's language for use in the event of the interpreter being called to give evidence, and certifies its accuracy. The interviewer should allow sufficient time for the interpreter to note each question and answer after each is put, given and interpreted. The person should be allowed to read the record or have it read to them and sign it as correct or indicate the respects in which they consider it inaccurate. If the interview is audibly recorded or visually recorded, the arrangements in Code E or F apply.

13.4 In the case of a person making a statement to a police officer or other police staff other than in English:
 (a) the interpreter shall record the statement in the language it is made;
 (b) the person shall be invited to sign it;
 (c) an official English translation shall be made in due course.

(c) Deaf people and people with speech difficulties

13.5 If a person appears to be deaf or there is doubt about their hearing or speaking ability, they must not be interviewed in the absence of an interpreter unless they agree in writing to being interviewed without one or *paragraphs 11.1, 11.18* to *11.20* apply.

13.6 An interpreter should also be called if a juvenile is interviewed and the parent or guardian present as the appropriate adult appears to be deaf or there is doubt about their hearing or speaking ability, unless they agree in writing to the interview proceeding without one or *paragraphs 11.1, 11.18* to *11.20* apply.

13.7 The interviewer shall make sure the interpreter is allowed to read the interview record and certify its accuracy in the event of the interpreter being called to give evidence. If the interview is audibly recorded or visually recorded, the arrangements in Code E or F apply.

(d) Additional rules for detained persons

13.8 All reasonable attempts should be made to make the detainee understand that interpreters will be provided at public expense.

13.9 If *paragraph 6.1* applies and the detainee cannot communicate with the solicitor because of language, hearing or speech difficulties, an interpreter must be called. The interpreter may not be a police officer or any other police staff when interpretation is needed for the purposes of obtaining legal advice. In all other cases a police officer or other police staff may only interpret if the detainee and the appropriate adult, if applicable, give their agreement in writing or if the interview is audibly recorded or visually recorded as in Code E or F.

13.10 When the custody officer cannot establish effective communication with a person charged with an offence who appears deaf or there is doubt about their ability to hear, speak or to understand English, arrangements must be made as soon as practicable for an interpreter to explain the offence and any other information given by the custody officer.

(e) Documentation

13.11 Action taken to call an interpreter under this section and any agreement to be interviewed in the absence of an interpreter must be recorded.

14 Questioning—special restrictions

14.1 If a person is arrested by one police force on behalf of another and the lawful period of detention in respect of that offence has not yet commenced in accordance with PACE, section 41 no questions may be put to them about the offence while they are in transit between the forces except to clarify any voluntary statement they make.

14.2 If a person is in police detention at a hospital they may not be questioned without the agreement of a responsible doctor. See *Note 14A*

Note for guidance

14A *If questioning takes place at a hospital under paragraph 14.2, or on the way to or from a hospital, the period of questioning concerned counts towards the total period of detention permitted.*

15 Reviews and extensions of detention

(a) Persons detained under PACE

15.1 The review officer is responsible under PACE, section 40 for periodically determining if a person's detention, before or after charge, continues to be necessary. This requirement continues throughout the detention period and except as in *paragraph 15.10*, the review officer must be present at the police station holding the detainee. See *Notes 15A* and *15B*

15.2 Under PACE, section 42, an officer of superintendent rank or above who is responsible for the station holding the detainee may give authority any time after the second review to extend the maximum period the person may be detained without charge by up to 12 hours. Further detention without charge may be authorised only by a magistrates' court in accordance with PACE, sections 43 and 44. See *Notes 15C, 15D* and *15E*

15.2A Section 42(1) of PACE as amended extends the maximum period of detention for indictable offences from 24 hours to 36 hours. Detaining a juvenile or mentally vulnerable person for longer than 24 hours will be dependent on the circumstances of the case and with regard to the person's:

(a) special vulnerability;

(b) the legal obligation to provide an opportunity for representations to be made prior to a decision about extending detention;

(c) the need to consult and consider the views of any appropriate adult; and

(d) any alternatives to police custody.

15.3 Before deciding whether to authorise continued detention the officer responsible under *paragraphs 15.1* or *15.2* shall give an opportunity to make representations about the detention to:

(a) the detainee, unless in the case of a review as in *paragraph 15.1*, the detainee is asleep;

(b) the detainee's solicitor if available at the time; and

(c) the appropriate adult if available at the time.

15.3A Other people having an interest in the detainee's welfare may also make representations at the authorising officer's discretion.

15.3B Subject to *paragraph 15.10*, the representations may be made orally in person or by telephone or in writing. The authorising officer may, however, refuse to hear oral representations from the detainee if the officer considers them unfit to make representations because of their condition or behaviour. See *Note 15C*

15.3C The decision on whether the review takes place in person or by telephone or by video conferencing (see Note 15G) is a matter for the review officer. In determining the form the review may take, the review officer must always take full account of the needs of the person in custody. The benefits of carrying out a review in person should always be considered, based on the individual circumstances of each case with specific additional consideration if the person is:

(a) a juvenile (and the age of the juvenile); or

(b) mentally vulnerable; or

(c) has been subject to medical attention for other than routine minor ailments; or

(d) there are presentational or community issues around the person's detention.

15.4 Before conducting a review or determining whether to extend the maximum period of detention without charge, the officer responsible must make sure the detainee is reminded of their entitlement to free legal advice, see *paragraph 6.5*, unless in the case of a review the person is asleep.

15.5 If, after considering any representations, the officer decides to keep the detainee in detention or extend the maximum period they may be detained without charge, any comment made by the detainee shall be recorded. If applicable, the officer responsible under *paragraph 15.1* or *15.2* shall be informed of the comment as soon as practicable. See also *paragraphs 11.4* and *11.13*

15.6 No officer shall put specific questions to the detainee:

• regarding their involvement in any offence; or

• in respect of any comments they may make:

— when given the opportunity to make representations; or

— in response to a decision to keep them in detention or extend the maximum period of detention.

Such an exchange could constitute an interview as in *paragraph 11.1A* and would be subject to the associated safeguards in *section 11* and, in respect of a person who has been charged, *paragraph 16.5*. See also *paragraph 11.13*

15.7 A detainee who is asleep at a review, see *paragraph 15.1*, and whose continued detention is authorised must be informed about the decision and reason as soon as practicable after waking.

15.8 Not used

(b) Telephone review of detention

15.9 PACE, section 40A provides that the officer responsible under section 40 for reviewing the detention of a person who has not been charged, need not attend the police station holding the detainee and may carry out the review by telephone.

15.9A PACE, section 45A(2) provides that the officer responsible under section 40 for reviewing the detention of a person who has not been charged, need not attend the police station holding the detainee and may carry out the review by video conferencing facilities (See *Note 15G*).

15.9B A telephone review is not permitted where facilities for review by video conferencing exist and it is practicable to use them.

15.9C The review officer can decide at any stage that a telephone review or review by video conferencing should be terminated and that the review will be conducted in person. The reasons for doing so should be noted in the custody record.

See *Note 15F*

15.10 When a telephone review is carried out, an officer at the station holding the detainee shall be required by the review officer to fulfil that officer's obligations under PACE section 40 or this Code by:

(a) making any record connected with the review in the detainee's custody record;

(b) if applicable, making a record in (a) in the presence of the detainee; and

(c) giving the detainee information about the review.

15.11 When a telephone review is carried out, the requirement in *paragraph 15.3* will be satisfied:

(a) if facilities exist for the immediate transmission of written representations to the review officer, e.g. fax or email message, by giving the detainee an opportunity to make representations:

(i) orally by telephone; or

(ii) in writing using those facilities; and

(b) in all other cases, by giving the detainee an opportunity to make their representations orally by telephone.

(c) Documentation

15.12 It is the officer's responsibility to make sure all reminders given under *paragraph 15.4* are noted in the custody record.

15.13 The grounds for, and extent of, any delay in conducting a review shall be recorded.

15.14 When a telephone review is carried out, a record shall be made of:

(a) the reason the review officer did not attend the station holding the detainee;

(b) the place the review officer was;

(c) the method representations, oral or written, were made to the review officer, see *paragraph 15.11*.

15.15 Any written representations shall be retained.

15.16 A record shall be made as soon as practicable about the outcome of each review or determination whether to extend the maximum detention period without charge or an application for a warrant of further detention or its extension. If *paragraph 15.7* applies, a record shall also be made of when the person was informed and by whom. If an authorisation is given under PACE, section 42, the record shall state the number of hours and minutes by which the detention period is extended or further extended. If a warrant for further detention, or extension, is granted under section 43 or 44, the record shall state the detention period authorised by the warrant and the date and time it was granted.

Notes for guidance

15A *Review officer for the purposes of:*
- PACE, sections 40 and 40A means, in the case of a person arrested but not charged, an officer of at least inspector rank not directly involved in the investigation and, if a person has been arrested and charged, the custody officer;

15B *The detention of persons in police custody not subject to the statutory review requirement in paragraph 15.1 should still be reviewed periodically as a matter of good practice. Such reviews can be carried out by an officer of the rank of sergeant or above. The purpose of such reviews is to check the particular power under which a detainee is held continues to apply, any associated conditions are complied with and to make sure appropriate action is taken to deal with any changes. This includes the detainee's prompt release when the power no longer applies, or their transfer if the power requires the detainee be taken elsewhere as soon as the necessary arrangements are made. Examples include persons:*

(a) *arrested on warrant because they failed to answer bail to appear at court;*

(b) *arrested under the Bail Act 1976, section 7(3) for breaching a condition of bail granted after charge;*

(c) *in police custody for specific purposes and periods under the Crime (Sentences) Act 1997, Schedule 1;*

(d) *convicted, or remand prisoners, held in police stations on behalf of the Prison Service under the Imprisonment (Temporary Provisions) Act 1980, section 6;*

(e) *being detained to prevent them causing a breach of the peace;*

(f) *detained at police stations on behalf of the Immigration Service.*

(g) *detained by order of a magistrates' court under the Criminal Justice Act 1988, section 152 (as amended by the Drugs Act 2005, section 8) to facilitate the recovery of evidence after being charged with drug possession or drug trafficking and suspected of having swallowed drugs.*

The detention of persons remanded into police detention by order of a court under the Magistrates' Courts Act 1980, section 128 is subject to a statutory requirement to review that detention. This is to make sure the detainee is taken back to court no later than the end of the period authorised by the court or when the need for their detention by police ceases, whichever is the sooner.

15C *In the case of a review of detention, but not an extension, the detainee need not be woken for the review. However, if the detainee is likely to be asleep, e.g. during a period of rest allowed as in paragraph 12.2, at the latest time a review or authorisation to extend detention may take place, the officer should, if the legal obligations and time constraints permit, bring forward the procedure to allow the detainee to make representations. A detainee not asleep during the review must be present when the grounds for their continued detention are recorded and must at the same time be informed of those grounds unless the review officer considers the person is incapable of understanding what is said, violent or likely to become violent or in urgent need of medical attention.*

15D *An application to a Magistrates' Court under PACE, sections 43 or 44 for a warrant of further detention or its extension should be made between 10am and 9pm, and if possible during normal court hours. It will not usually be practicable to arrange for a court to sit specially outside the hours of 10am to 9pm. If it appears a special sitting may be needed outside normal court hours but between 10am and 9pm, the clerk to the justices should be given notice and informed of this possibility, while the court is sitting if possible.*

15E *In paragraph 15.2, the officer responsible for the station holding the detainee includes a superintendent or above who, in accordance with their force operational policy or police regulations, is given that responsibility on a temporary basis whilst the appointed long-term holder is off duty or otherwise unavailable.*

15F *The provisions of PACE, section 40A allowing telephone reviews do not apply to reviews of detention after charge by the custody officer. When video conferencing is not required, they allow the use of a telephone to carry out a review of detention before charge. The procedure under PACE, section 42 must be done in person.*

15G *The use of video conferencing facilities for decisions about detention under section 45A of PACE is subject to the introduction of regulations by the Secretary of State.*

16 Charging detained persons

(a) Action

16.1 When the officer in charge of the investigation reasonably believes there is sufficient evidence to provide a realistic prospect of conviction for the offence (see *paragraph 11.6*), they shall without delay, and subject to the following qualification, inform the custody officer who will be responsible for considering whether the detainee should be charged. See *Notes 11B and 16A*. When a person is detained in respect of more than one offence it is permissible to delay informing the custody officer until the above conditions are satisfied in respect of all the offences, but see *paragraph 11.6*. If the detainee is a juvenile, mentally disordered or otherwise mentally vulnerable, any resulting action shall be taken in the presence of the appropriate adult if they are present at the time. See *Notes 16B and 16C*

16.1A Where guidance issued by the Director of Public Prosecutions under section 37A is in force the custody officer must comply with that Guidance in deciding how to act in dealing with the detainee. See *Notes 16AA and 16AB*.

16.1B Where in compliance with the DPP's Guidance the custody officer decides that the case should be immediately referred to the CPS to make the charging decision, consultation should take place with a Crown Prosecutor as soon as is reasonably practicable. Where the Crown Prosecutor is unable to make the charging decision on the information available at that time, the detainee may be released without charge and on bail (with conditions if necessary) under section 37(7)(a). In such circumstances, the detainee should be informed that they are being released to enable the Director of Public Prosecutions to make a decision under section 37B.

16.2 When a detainee is charged with or informed they may be prosecuted for an offence, see *Note 16B*, they shall, unless the restriction on drawing adverse inferences from silence applies, see *Annex C*, be cautioned as follows:

'You do not have to say anything. But it may harm your defence if you do not mention now something which you later rely on in court. Anything you do say may be given in evidence.'

Annex C, paragraph 2 sets out the alternative terms of the caution to be used when the restriction on drawing adverse inferences from silence applies.

16.3 When a detainee is charged they shall be given a written notice showing particulars of the offence and, subject to *paragraph 2.6A*, the officer's name and the case reference number. As far as possible the particulars of the charge shall be stated in simple terms, but they shall also show the precise offence in law with which the detainee is charged. The notice shall begin:

'You are charged with the offence(s) shown below.' Followed by the caution.

If the detainee is a juvenile, mentally disordered or otherwise mentally vulnerable, the notice should be given to the appropriate adult.

16.4 If, after a detainee has been charged with or informed they may be prosecuted for an offence, an officer wants to tell them about any written statement or interview with another person relating to such an offence, the detainee shall either be handed a true copy of the written statement or the content of the interview record brought to their attention. Nothing shall be done to invite any reply or comment except to:

(a) caution the detainee, *'You do not have to say anything, but anything you do say may be given in evidence.'*; and

(b) remind the detainee about their right to legal advice.

16.4A If the detainee:

• cannot read, the document may be read to them

• is a juvenile, mentally disordered or otherwise mentally vulnerable, the appropriate adult shall also be given a copy, or the interview record shall be brought to their attention

16.5 A detainee may not be interviewed about an offence after they have been charged with, or informed they may be prosecuted for it, unless the interview is necessary:

• to prevent or minimise harm or loss to some other person, or the public

• to clear up an ambiguity in a previous answer or statement

• in the interests of justice for the detainee to have put to them, and have an opportunity to comment on, information concerning the offence which has come to light since they were charged or informed they might be prosecuted

Before any such interview, the interviewer shall:

(a) caution the detainee, *'You do not have to say anything, but anything you do say may be given in evidence.'*;

(b) remind the detainee about their right to legal advice.

See *Note 16B*

16.6 The provisions of *paragraphs 16.2* to *16.5* must be complied with in the appropriate adult's presence if they are already at the police station. If they are not at the police station then these provisions must be complied with again in their presence when they arrive unless the detainee has been released.

See *Note 16C*

16.7 When a juvenile is charged with an offence and the custody officer authorises their continued detention after charge, the custody officer must try to make arrangements for the juvenile to be taken into the care of a local authority to be detained pending appearance in court unless the custody officer certifies it is impracticable to do so or, in the case of a juvenile of at least 12 years old, no secure accommodation is available and there is a risk to the public of serious harm from that juvenile, in accordance with PACE, section 38(6). See *Note 16D*

(b) Documentation

16.8 A record shall be made of anything a detainee says when charged.

16.9 Any questions put in an interview after charge and answers given relating to the offence shall be recorded in full during the interview on forms for that purpose and the record signed by the detainee or, if they refuse, by the interviewer and any third parties present. If the questions are audibly recorded or visually recorded the arrangements in Code E or F apply.

16.10 If it is not practicable to make arrangements for a juvenile's transfer into local authority care as in *paragraph 16.7*, the custody officer must record the reasons and complete a certificate to be produced before the court with the juvenile. See *Note 16D*

Notes for guidance

16A *The custody officer must take into account alternatives to prosecution under the Crime and Disorder Act 1998, reprimands and warning applicable to persons under 18, and in national guidance on the cautioning of offenders, for persons aged 18 and over.*

16AA *When a person is arrested under the provisions of the Criminal Justice Act 2003 which allow a person to be re-tried after being acquitted of a serious offence which is a qualifying offence specified in Schedule 5 to that Act and not precluded from further prosecution by virtue of section 75(3) of that Act the detention provisions of PACE are modified and make an officer of the rank of superintendent or above who has not been directly involved in the investigation responsible for determining whether the evidence is sufficient to charge.*

16AB *Where Guidance issued by the Director of Public Prosecutions under section 37B is in force, a custody officer who determines in accordance with that Guidance that there is sufficient evidence to charge the detainee, may detain that person for no longer than is reasonably necessary to decide how that person is to be dealt with under PACE, section 37(7)(a) to (d), including, where appropriate, consultation with the Duty Prosecutor. The period is subject to the maximum period of detention before charge determined by PACE, sections 41 to 44. Where in accordance with the Guidance the case is referred to the CPS for decision, the custody officer should ensure that an officer involved in the investigation sends to the CPS such information as is specified in the Guidance.*

16B *The giving of a warning or the service of the Notice of Intended Prosecution required by the Road Traffic Offenders Act 1988, section 1 does not amount to informing a detainee they may be prosecuted for an offence and so does not preclude further questioning in relation to that offence.*

16C *There is no power under PACE to detain a person and delay action under paragraphs 16.2 to 16.5 solely to await the arrival of the appropriate adult. After charge, bail cannot be refused, or release on bail delayed, simply because an appropriate adult is not available, unless the absence of that adult provides the custody officer with the necessary grounds to authorise detention after charge under PACE, section 38.*

16D *Except as in paragraph 16.7, neither a juvenile's behaviour nor the nature of the offence provides grounds for the custody officer to decide it is impracticable to arrange the juvenile's transfer to local authority care. Similarly, the lack of secure local authority accommodation does not make it impracticable to transfer the juvenile. The availability of secure accommodation is only a factor in relation to a juvenile aged 12 or over when the local authority accommodation would not be adequate to protect the public from serious harm from them. The obligation to transfer a juvenile to local authority accommodation applies as much to a juvenile charged during the daytime as to a juvenile to be held overnight, subject to a requirement to bring the juvenile before a court under PACE, section 46.*

17 Testing persons for the presence of specified Class A drugs

(a) Action

17.1 This section of Code C applies only in selected police stations in police areas where the provisions for drug testing under section 63B of PACE (as amended by section 5 of the Criminal Justice Act 2003 and section 7 of the Drugs Act 2005) are in force and in respect of which the Secretary of State has given a notification to the relevant chief officer of police that arrangements for the taking of samples have been made. Such a notification will cover either a police area as a whole or particular stations within a police area. The notification indicates whether the testing applies to those arrested or charged or under the age of 18 as the case may be and testing can only take place in respect of the persons so indicated in the notification. Testing cannot be carried out unless the relevant notification has been given and has not been withdrawn. See *Note 17F*

17.2 A sample of urine or a non-intimate sample may be taken from a person in police detention for the purpose of ascertaining whether he has any specified Class A drug in his body only where they have been brought before the custody officer and:

(a) either the arrest condition, see *paragraph 17.3*, or the charge condition, see *paragraph 17.4* is met;

(b) the age condition see *paragraph 17.5*, is met;

(c) the notification condition is met in relation to the arrest condition, the charge condition, or the age condition, as the case may be. (Testing on charge and/or arrest must be specifically provided for in the notification for the power to apply. In addition, the fact that testing of under 18s is authorised must be expressly provided for in the notification before the power to test such persons applies.). See *paragraph 17.1*; and

(d) a police officer has requested the person concerned to give the sample (the request condition).

17.3 The arrest condition is met where the detainee:

(a) has been arrested for a trigger offence, see *Note 17E*, but not charged with that offence; or

(b) has been arrested for any other offence but not charged with that offence and a police officer of inspector rank or above, who has reasonable grounds for suspecting that their misuse of any specified Class A drug caused or contributed to the offence, has authorised the sample to be taken.

17.4 The charge condition is met where the detainee:

(a) has been charged with a trigger offence, or

(b) has been charged with any other offence and a police officer of inspector rank or above, who has reasonable grounds for suspecting that the detainee's misuse of any specified Class A drug caused or contributed to the offence, has authorised the sample to be taken.

17.5 The age condition is met where:

(a) in the case of a detainee who has been arrested but not charged as in *paragraph 17.3*, they are aged 18 or over;

(b) in the case of a detainee who has been charged as in *paragraph 17.4*, they are aged 14 or over.

17.6 Before requesting a sample from the person concerned, an officer must:

(a) inform them that the purpose of taking the sample is for drug testing under PACE. This is to ascertain whether they have a specified Class A drug present in their body;

(b) warn them that if, when so requested, they fail without good cause to provide a sample they may be liable to prosecution;

(c) where the taking of the sample has been authorised by an inspector or above in accordance with *paragraph 17.3(b)* or *17.4(b)* above, inform them that the authorisation has been given and the grounds for giving it;

      (d) remind them of the following rights, which may be exercised at any stage during the period in custody:

        (i) the right to have someone informed of their arrest [see section 5];

        (ii) the right to consult privately with a solicitor and that free independent legal advice is available [see section 6]; and

        (iii) the right to consult these Codes of Practice [see section 3].

17.7 In the case of a person who has not attained the age of 17—

    (a) the making of the request for a sample under *paragraph 17.2(d)* above;

    (b) the giving of the warning and the information under *paragraph 17.6* above; and

    (c) the taking of the sample,

may not take place except in the presence of an appropriate adult. (see Note 17G)

17.8 Authorisation by an officer of the rank of inspector or above within *paragraph 17.3(b)* or *17.4(b)* may be given orally or in writing but, if it is given orally, it must be confirmed in writing as soon as practicable.

17.9 If a sample is taken from a detainee who has been arrested for an offence but not charged with that offence as in *paragraph 17.3*, no further sample may be taken during the same continuous period of detention. If during that same period the charge condition is also met in respect of that detainee, the sample which has been taken shall be treated as being taken by virtue of the charge condition, see *paragraph 17.4*, being met.

17.10 A detainee from whom a sample may be taken may be detained for up to six hours from the time of charge if the custody officer reasonably believes the detention is necessary to enable a sample to be taken. Where the arrest condition is met, a detainee whom the custody officer has decided to release on bail without charge may continue to be detained, but not beyond 24 hours from the relevant time (as defined in section 41(2) of PACE), to enable a sample to be taken.

17.11 A detainee in respect of whom the arrest condition is met, but not the charge condition, see *paragraphs 17.3* and *17.4*, and whose release would be required before a sample can be taken had they not continued to be detained as a result of being arrested for a further offence which does not satisfy the arrest condition, may have a sample taken at any time within 24 hours after the arrest for the offence that satisfies the arrest condition.

(b) Documentation

17.12 The following must be recorded in the custody record:

    (a) if a sample is taken following authorisation by an officer of the rank of inspector or above, the authorisation and the grounds for suspicion;

    (b) the giving of a warning of the consequences of failure to provide a sample;

    (c) the time at which the sample was given; and

    (d) the time of charge or, where the arrest condition is being relied upon, the time of arrest and, where applicable, the fact that a sample taken after arrest but before charge is to be treated as being taken by virtue of the charge condition, where that is met in the same period of continuous detention. See *paragraph 17.9*

(c) General

17.13 A sample may only be taken by a prescribed person. See *Note 17C*.

17.14 Force may not be used to take any sample for the purpose of drug testing.

17.15 The terms "Class A drug" and "misuse" have the same meanings as in the Misuse of Drugs Act 1971. "Specified" (in relation to a Class A drug) and "trigger offence" have the same meanings as in Part III of the Criminal Justice and Court Services Act 2000.

17.16 Any sample taken:

    (a) may not be used for any purpose other than to ascertain whether the person concerned has a specified Class A drug present in his body; and

(b) must be retained until the person concerned has made their first appearance before the court.

(d) Assessment of misuse of drugs

17.17 Under the provisions of Part 3 of the Drugs Act 2005, where a detainee has tested positive for a specified Class A drug under section 63B of PACE a police officer may, at any time before the person's release from the police station, impose a requirement for them to attend an initial assessment of their drug misuse by a suitably qualified person and to remain for its duration. The requirement may only be imposed on a person if:

(a) they have reached the age of 18

(b) notification has been given by the Secretary of State to the relevant chief officer of police that arrangements for conducting initial assessments have been made for those from whom samples for testing have been taken at the police station where the detainee is in custody.

17.18 When imposing a requirement to attend an initial assessment the police officer must:

(a) inform the person of the time and place at which the initial assessment is to take place;

(b) explain that this information will be confirmed in writing; and

(c) warn the person that he may be liable to prosecution if he fails without good cause to attend the initial assessment and remain for it's [sic] duration

17.19 Where a police officer has imposed a requirement to attend an initial assessment in accordance with *paragraph 17.17*, he must, before the person is released from detention, give the person notice in writing which:

(a) confirms that he is required to attend and remain for the duration of an initial assessment; and

(b) confirms the information and repeats the warning referred to in *paragraph 17.18*.

17.20 The following must be recorded in the custody record:

(a) that the requirement to attend an initial assessment has been imposed; and

(b) the information, explanation, warning and notice given in accordance with *paragraphs 17.17* and *17.19*.

17.21 Where a notice is given in accordance with *paragraph 17.19*, a police officer can give the person a further notice in writing which informs the person of any change to the time or place at which the initial assessment is to take place and which repeats the warning referred to in *paragraph 17.18(c)*.

17.22 Part 3 of the Drugs Act 2005 also requires police officers to have regard to any guidance issued by the Secretary of State in respect of the assessment provisions.

Notes for guidance

17A *When warning a person who is asked to provide a urine or non-intimate sample in accordance with paragraph 17.6(b), the following form of words may be used:*

"You do not have to provide a sample, but I must warn you that if you fail or refuse without good cause to do so, you will commit an offence for which you may be imprisoned, or fined, or both".

17B *A sample has to be sufficient and suitable. A sufficient sample is sufficient in quantity and quality to enable drug-testing analysis to take place. A suitable sample is one which by its nature, is suitable for a particular form of drug analysis.*

17C *A prescribed person in paragraph 17.13 is one who is prescribed in regulations made by the Secretary of State under section 63B(6) of the Police and Criminal Evidence Act 1984. [The regulations are currently contained in regulation SI 2001 No. 2645, the Police and Criminal Evidence Act 1984 (Drug Testing Persons in Police Detention) (Prescribed Persons) Regulations 2001.]*

17D *The retention of the sample in paragraph 17.16(b) allows for the sample to be sent for confirmatory testing and analysis if the detainee disputes the test. But such samples, and the information derived from them, may not be subsequently used in the investigation of any offence or in evidence against the persons from whom they were taken.*

17E *Trigger offences are:*

   1. *Offences under the following provisions of the Theft Act 1968:*

section 1	*(theft)*
section 8	*(robbery)*
section 9	*(burglary)*
section 10	*(aggravated burglary)*
section 12	*(taking a motor vehicle or other conveyance without authority)*
section 12A	*(aggravated vehicle-taking)*
section 15	*(obtaining property by deception)*
section 22	*(handling stolen goods)*
section 25	*(going equipped for stealing etc.)*

   2. *Offences under the following provisions of the Misuse of Drugs Act 1971, if committed in respect of a specified Class A drug:—*

section 4	*(restriction on production and supply of controlled drugs)*
section 5(2)	*(possession of a controlled drug)*
section 5(3)	*(possession of a controlled drug with intent to supply)*

   3. *An offence under section 1(1) of the Criminal Attempts Act 1981 if committed in respect of an offence under any of the following provisions of the Theft Act 1968:*

section 1	*(theft)*
section 8	*(robbery)*
section 9	*(burglary)*
section 15	*(obtaining property by deception)*
section 22	*(handling stolen goods)*

   4. *Offences under the following provisions of the Vagrancy Act 1824:*

section 3	*(begging)*
section 4	*(persistent begging)*

17F *The power to take samples is subject to notification by the Secretary of State that appropriate arrangements for the taking of samples have been made for the police area as a whole or for the particular police station concerned for whichever of the following is specified in the notification:*

   (a) *persons in respect of whom the arrest condition is met;*

   (b) *persons in respect of whom the charge condition is met;*

   (c) *persons who have not attained the age of 18.*

Note: Notification is treated as having been given for the purposes of the charge condition in relation to a police area, if testing (on charge) under section 63B(2) of PACE was in force immediately before section 7 of the Drugs Act 2005 was brought into force; and for the purposes of the age condition, in relation to a police area or police station, if immediately before that day, notification that arrangements had been made for the taking of samples from persons under the age of 18 (those aged 14–17) had been given and had not been withdrawn.

17G *Appropriate adult in paragraph 17.7 means the person's—*

   (a) *parent or guardian or, if they are in the care of a local authority or voluntary organisation, a person representing that authority or organisation; or*

   (b) *a social worker of, in England, a local authority or, in Wales, a local authority social services department; or*

   (c) *if no person falling within (a) or (b) above is available, any responsible person aged 18 or over who is not a police officer or a person employed by the police.*

ANNEX A—INTIMATE AND STRIP SEARCHES

A Intimate search

1. An intimate search consists of the physical examination of a person's body orifices other than the mouth. The intrusive nature of such searches means the actual and potential risks associated with intimate searches must never be underestimated.

(a) Action

2. Body orifices other than the mouth may be searched only:
    (a) if authorised by an officer of inspector rank or above who has reasonable grounds for believing that the person may have concealed on themselves:
        (i) anything which they could and might use to cause physical injury to themselves or others at the station; or
        (ii) a Class A drug which they intended to supply to another or to export;
        and the officer has reasonable grounds for believing that an intimate search is the only means of removing those items; and
    (b) if the search is under *paragraph 2(a)(ii)* (a drug offence search), the detainee's appropriate consent has been given in writing.

2A. Before the search begins, a police officer, designated detention officer or staff custody officer, must tell the detainee:
    (a) that the authority to carry out the search has been given;
    (b) the grounds for giving the authorisation and for believing that the article cannot be removed without an intimate search.

2B Before a detainee is asked to give appropriate consent to a search under *paragraph 2(a)(ii)* (a drug offence search) they must be warned that if they refuse without good cause their refusal may harm their case if it comes to trial, see *Note A6*. This warning may be given by a police officer or member of police staff. A detainee who is not legally represented must be reminded of their entitlement to have free legal advice, see Code C, *paragraph 6.5*, and the reminder noted in the custody record.

3. An intimate search may only be carried out by a registered medical practitioner or registered nurse, unless an officer of at least inspector rank considers this is not practicable and the search is to take place under *paragraph 2(a)(i)*, in which case a police officer may carry out the search. See *Notes A1 to A5*

3A. Any proposal for a search under *paragraph 2(a)(i)* to be carried out by someone other than a registered medical practitioner or registered nurse must only be considered as a last resort and when the authorising officer is satisfied the risks associated with allowing the item to remain with the detainee outweigh the risks associated with removing it. See *Notes A1 to A5*

4. An intimate search under:
    * *paragraph 2(a)(i)* may take place only at a hospital, surgery, other medical premises or police station
    * *paragraph 2(a)(ii)* may take place only at a hospital, surgery or other medical premises and must be carried out by a registered medical practitioner or a registered nurse

5. An intimate search at a police station of a juvenile or mentally disordered or otherwise mentally vulnerable person may take place only in the presence of an appropriate adult of the same sex, unless the detainee specifically requests a particular adult of the opposite sex who is readily available. In the case of a juvenile the search may take place in the absence of the appropriate adult only if the juvenile signifies in the presence of the appropriate adult they do not want the adult present during the search and the adult agrees. A record shall be made of the juvenile's decision and signed by the appropriate adult.

6. When an intimate search under *paragraph 2(a)(i)* is carried out by a police officer, the officer must be of the same sex as the detainee. A minimum of two people, other than the detainee, must be present during the search. Subject to *paragraph 5*, no person of the opposite sex who is

not a medical practitioner or nurse shall be present, nor shall anyone whose presence is unnecessary. The search shall be conducted with proper regard to the sensitivity and vulnerability of the detainee.

(b) Documentation

7. In the case of an intimate search, the following shall be recorded as soon as practicable, in the detainee's custody record:
   (a) for searches under *paragraphs 2(a)(i)* and *(ii)*;
      - the authorisation to carry out the search;
      - the grounds for giving the authorisation;
      - the grounds for believing the article could not be removed without an intimate search
      - which parts of the detainee's body were searched
      - who carried out the search
      - who was present
      - the result.
   (b) for searches under paragraph 2(a)(ii):
      - the giving of the warning required by *paragraph 2B*;
      - the fact that the appropriate consent was given or (as the case may be) refused, and if refused, the reason given for the refusal (if any).
8. If an intimate search is carried out by a police officer, the reason why it was impracticable for a registered medical practitioner or registered nurse to conduct it must be recorded.

B Strip search

9. A strip search is a search involving the removal of more than outer clothing. In this Code, outer clothing includes shoes and socks.

(a) Action

10. A strip search may take place only if it is considered necessary to remove an article which a detainee would not be allowed to keep, and the officer reasonably considers the detainee might have concealed such an article. Strip searches shall not be routinely carried out if there is no reason to consider that articles are concealed.

The conduct of strip searches

11. When strip searches are conducted:
    (a) a police officer carrying out a strip search must be the same sex as the detainee;
    (b) the search shall take place in an area where the detainee cannot be seen by anyone who does not need to be present, nor by a member of the opposite sex except an appropriate adult who has been specifically requested by the detainee;
    (c) except in cases of urgency, where there is risk of serious harm to the detainee or to others, whenever a strip search involves exposure of intimate body parts, there must be at least two people present other than the detainee, and if the search is of a juvenile or mentally disordered or otherwise mentally vulnerable person, one of the people must be the appropriate adult. Except in urgent cases as above, a search of a juvenile may take place in the absence of the appropriate adult only if the juvenile signifies in the presence of the appropriate adult that they do not want the adult to be present during the search and the adult agrees. A record shall be made of the juvenile's decision and signed by the appropriate adult. The presence of more than two people, other than an appropriate adult, shall be permitted only in the most exceptional circumstances;

(d) the search shall be conducted with proper regard to the sensitivity and vulnerability of the detainee in these circumstances and every reasonable effort shall be made to secure the detainee's co-operation and minimise embarrassment. Detainees who are searched shall not normally be required to remove all their clothes at the same time, e.g. a person should be allowed to remove clothing above the waist and redress before removing further clothing;

(e) if necessary to assist the search, the detainee may be required to hold their arms in the air or to stand with their legs apart and bend forward so a visual examination may be made of the genital and anal areas provided no physical contact is made with any body orifice;

(f) if articles are found, the detainee shall be asked to hand them over. If articles are found within any body orifice other than the mouth, and the detainee refuses to hand them over, their removal would constitute an intimate search, which must be carried out as in *Part A*;

(g) a strip search shall be conducted as quickly as possible, and the detainee allowed to dress as soon as the procedure is complete.

(b) Documentation

12. A record shall be made on the custody record of a strip search including the reason it was considered necessary, those present and any result.

Notes for guidance

A1 Before authorising any intimate search, the authorising officer must make every reasonable effort to persuade the detainee to hand the article over without a search. If the detainee agrees, a registered medical practitioner or registered nurse should whenever possible be asked to assess the risks involved and, if necessary, attend to assist the detainee.

A2 If the detainee does not agree to hand the article over without a search, the authorising officer must carefully review all the relevant factors before authorising an intimate search. In particular, the officer must consider whether the grounds for believing an article may be concealed are reasonable.

A3 If authority is given for a search under paragraph 2(a)(i), a registered medical practitioner or registered nurse shall be consulted whenever possible. The presumption should be that the search will be conducted by the registered medical practitioner or registered nurse and the authorising officer must make every reasonable effort to persuade the detainee to allow the medical practitioner or nurse to conduct the search.

A4 A constable should only be authorised to carry out a search as a last resort and when all other approaches have failed. In these circumstances, the authorising officer must be satisfied the detainee might use the article for one or more of the purposes in paragraph 2(a)(i) and the physical injury likely to be caused is sufficiently severe to justify authorising a constable to carry out the search.

A5 If an officer has any doubts whether to authorise an intimate search by a constable, the officer should seek advice from an officer of superintendent rank or above.

A6 In warning a detainee who is asked to consent to an intimate drug offence search, as in paragraph 2B, the following form of words may be used:

> *"You do not have to allow yourself to be searched, but I must warn you that if you refuse without good cause, your refusal may harm your case if it comes to trial."*

ANNEX B—DELAY IN NOTIFYING ARREST OR ALLOWING ACCESS TO LEGAL ADVICE

A Persons detained under PACE

1. The exercise of the rights in *Section 5* or *Section 6*, or both, may be delayed if the person is in police detention, as in PACE, section 118(2), in connection with an indictable offence, has not yet been charged with an offence and an officer of superintendent rank or above, or inspector rank

or above only for the rights in Section 5, has reasonable grounds for believing their exercise will:

    (i) lead to:
- interference with, or harm to, evidence connected with an indictable offence; or
- interference with, or physical harm to, other people; or

    (ii) lead to alerting other people suspected of having committed an indictable offence but not yet arrested for it; or

    (iii) hinder the recovery of property obtained in consequence of the commission of such an offence.

2. These rights may also be delayed if the officer has reasonable grounds to believe that:

    (i) the person detained for an indictable offence has benefited from their criminal conduct (decided in accordance with Part 2 of the Proceeds of Crime Act 2002); and

    (ii) the recovery of the value of the property constituting that benefit will be hindered by the exercise of either right.

3. Authority to delay a detainee's right to consult privately with a solicitor may be given only if the authorising officer has reasonable grounds to believe the solicitor the detainee wants to consult will, inadvertently or otherwise, pass on a message from the detainee or act in some other way which will have any of the consequences specified under *paragraphs 1 or 2*. In these circumstances the detainee must be allowed to choose another solicitor. See *Note B3*

4. If the detainee wishes to see a solicitor, access to that solicitor may not be delayed on the grounds they might advise the detainee not to answer questions or the solicitor was initially asked to attend the police station by someone else. In the latter case the detainee must be told the solicitor has come to the police station at another person's request, and must be asked to sign the custody record to signify whether they want to see the solicitor.

5. The fact the grounds for delaying notification of arrest may be satisfied does not automatically mean the grounds for delaying access to legal advice will also be satisfied.

6. These rights may be delayed only for as long as grounds exist and in no case beyond 36 hours after the relevant time as in PACE, section 41. If the grounds cease to apply within this time, the detainee must, as soon as practicable, be asked if they want to exercise either right, the custody record must be noted accordingly, and action taken in accordance with the relevant section of the Code.

7. A detained person must be permitted to consult a solicitor for a reasonable time before any court hearing.

B Not used

C Documentation

13. The grounds for action under this Annex shall be recorded and the detainee informed of them as soon as practicable.

14. Any reply given by a detainee under *paragraphs 6 or 11* must be recorded and the detainee asked to endorse the record in relation to whether they want to receive legal advice at this point.

D Cautions and special warnings

15. When a suspect detained at a police station is interviewed during any period for which access to legal advice has been delayed under this Annex, the court or jury may not draw adverse inferences from their silence.

Notes for guidance

B1 Even if Annex B applies in the case of a juvenile, or a person who is mentally disordered or otherwise mentally vulnerable, action to inform the appropriate adult and the person responsible for a juvenile's welfare if that is a different person, must nevertheless be taken as in paragraph 3.13 and 3.15.

B2 In the case of Commonwealth citizens and foreign nationals, see Note 7A.

B3 A decision to delay access to a specific solicitor is likely to be a rare occurrence and only when it can be shown the suspect is capable of misleading that particular solicitor and there is more than a substantial risk that the suspect will succeed in causing information to be conveyed which will lead to one or more of the specified consequences.

ANNEX C—RESTRICTION ON DRAWING ADVERSE INFERENCES FROM SILENCE AND TERMS OF THE CAUTION WHEN THE RESTRICTION APPLIES

(a) The restriction on drawing adverse inferences from silence

1. The Criminal Justice and Public Order Act 1994, sections 34, 36 and 37 as amended by the Youth Justice and Criminal Evidence Act 1999, section 58 describe the conditions under which adverse inferences may be drawn from a person's failure or refusal to say anything about their involvement in the offence when interviewed, after being charged or informed they may be prosecuted. These provisions are subject to an overriding restriction on the ability of a court or jury to draw adverse inferences from a person's silence. This restriction applies:
   (a) to any detainee at a police station, see *Note 10C* who, before being interviewed, see *section 11* or being charged or informed they may be prosecuted, see *section 16*, has:
      (i) asked for legal advice, see *section 6, paragraph 6.1*;
      (ii) not been allowed an opportunity to consult a solicitor, including the duty solicitor, as in this Code; and
      (iii) not changed their mind about wanting legal advice, see *section 6, paragraph 6.6(d)*
      Note the condition in (ii) will
      — apply when a detainee who has asked for legal advice is interviewed before speaking to a solicitor as in *section 6, paragraph 6.6(a)* or *(b)*.
      — not apply if the detained person declines to ask for the duty solicitor, see *section 6, paragraphs 6.6(c)* and *(d)*.
   (b) to any person charged with, or informed they may be prosecuted for, an offence who:
      (i) has had brought to their notice a written statement made by another person or the content of an interview with another person which relates to that offence, see *section 16, paragraph 16.4*;
      (ii) is interviewed about that offence, see *section 16, paragraph 16.5*; or
      (iii) makes a written statement about that offence, see *Annex D paragraphs 4* and *9*.

(b) Terms of the caution when the restriction applies

2. When a requirement to caution arises at a time when the restriction on drawing adverse inferences from silence applies, the caution shall be:
   'You do not have to say anything, but anything you do say may be given in evidence.'

3. Whenever the restriction either begins to apply or ceases to apply after a caution has already been given, the person shall be re-cautioned in the appropriate terms. The changed position on drawing inferences and that the previous caution no longer applies shall also be explained to the detainee in ordinary language. See *Note C2*

Notes for guidance

C1 The restriction on drawing inferences from silence does not apply to a person who has not been detained and who therefore cannot be prevented from seeking legal advice if they want to, see paragraphs 10.2 and 3.15.

C2 *The following is suggested as a framework to help explain changes in the position on drawing adverse inferences if the restriction on drawing adverse inferences from silence:*

(a) *begins to apply:*

'The caution you were previously given no longer applies. This is because after that caution:

(i) *you asked to speak to a solicitor but have not yet been allowed an opportunity to speak to a solicitor. See paragraph 1(a); or*

(ii) *you have been charged with/informed you may be prosecuted.' See paragraph 1(b).*

'This means that from now on, adverse inferences cannot be drawn at court and your defence will not be harmed just because you choose to say nothing. Please listen carefully to the caution I am about to give you because it will apply from now on. You will see that it does not say anything about your defence being harmed.'

(b) *ceases to apply before or at the time the person is charged or informed they may be prosecuted, see paragraph 1(a);*

'The caution you were previously given no longer applies. This is because after that caution you have been allowed an opportunity to speak to a solicitor. Please listen carefully to the caution I am about to give you because it will apply from now on. It explains how your defence at court may be affected if you choose to say nothing.'

ANNEX D—WRITTEN STATEMENTS UNDER CAUTION

(a) Written by a person under caution

1. A person shall always be invited to write down what they want to say.

2. A person who has not been charged with, or informed they may be prosecuted for, any offence to which the statement they want to write relates, shall:

   (a) unless the statement is made at a time when the restriction on drawing adverse inferences from silence applies, see Annex C, be asked to write out and sign the following before writing what they want to say:

   '*I make this statement of my own free will. I understand that I do not have to say anything but that it may harm my defence if I do not mention when questioned something which I later rely on in court. This statement may be given in evidence.*';

   (b) if the statement is made at a time when the restriction on drawing adverse inferences from silence applies, be asked to write out and sign the following before writing what they want to say;

   '*I make this statement of my own free will. I understand that I do not have to say anything. This statement may be given in evidence.*'

3. When a person, on the occasion of being charged with or informed they may be prosecuted for any offence, asks to make a statement which relates to any such offence and wants to write it they shall:

   (a) unless the restriction on drawing adverse inferences from silence, see *Annex C*, applied when they were so charged or informed they may be prosecuted, be asked to write out and sign the following before writing what they want to say:

   '*I make this statement of my own free will. I understand that I do not have to say anything but that it may harm my defence if I do not mention when questioned something which I later rely on in court. This statement may be given in evidence.*';

   (b) if the restriction on drawing adverse inferences from silence applied when they were so charged or informed they may be prosecuted, be asked to write out and sign the following before writing what they want to say:

   '*I make this statement of my own free will. I understand that I do not have to say anything. This statement may be given in evidence.*'

4. When a person, who has already been charged with or informed they may be prosecuted for any offence, asks to make a statement which relates to any such offence and wants to write it they shall be asked to write out and sign the following before writing what they want to say:

'I make this statement of my own free will. I understand that I do not have to say anything. This statement may be given in evidence.';

5. Any person writing their own statement shall be allowed to do so without any prompting except a police officer or other police staff may indicate to them which matters are material or question any ambiguity in the statement.

(b) Written by a police officer or other police staff

6. If a person says they would like someone to write the statement for them, a police officer, or other police staff shall write the statement.

7. If the person has not been charged with, or informed they may be prosecuted for, any offence to which the statement they want to make relates they shall, before starting, be asked to sign, or make their mark, to the following:

   (a) unless the statement is made at a time when the restriction on drawing adverse inferences from silence applies, see Annex C:

   'I, ..., wish to make a statement. I want someone to write down what I say. I understand that I do not have to say anything but that it may harm my defence if I do not mention when questioned something which I later rely on in court. This statement may be given in evidence.';

   (b) if the statement is made at a time when the restriction on drawing adverse inferences from silence applies:

   'I, ..., wish to make a statement. I want someone to write down what I say. I understand that I do not have to say anything. This statement may be given in evidence.'

8. If, on the occasion of being charged with or informed they may be prosecuted for any offence, the person asks to make a statement which relates to any such offence they shall before starting be asked to sign, or make their mark to, the following:

   (a) unless the restriction on drawing adverse inferences from silence applied, see Annex C, when they were so charged or informed they may be prosecuted:

   'I, ..., wish to make a statement. I want someone to write down what I say. I understand that I do not have to say anything but that it may harm my defence if I do not mention when questioned something which I later rely on in court. This statement may be given in evidence.';

   (b) if the restriction on drawing adverse inferences from silence applied when they were so charged or informed they may be prosecuted:

   'I, ..., wish to make a statement. I want someone to write down what I say. I understand that I do not have to say anything. This statement may be given in evidence.'

9. If, having already been charged with or informed they may be prosecuted for any offence, a person asks to make a statement which relates to any such offence they shall before starting, be asked to sign, or make their mark to:

   'I, ..., wish to make a statement. I want someone to write down what I say. I understand that I do not have to say anything. This statement may be given in evidence.'

10. The person writing the statement must take down the exact words spoken by the person making it and must not edit or paraphrase it. Any questions that are necessary, e.g. to make it more intelligible, and the answers given must be recorded at the same time on the statement form.

11. When the writing of a statement is finished the person making it shall be asked to read it and to make any corrections, alterations or additions they want. When they have finished reading they shall be asked to write and sign or make their mark on the following certificate at the end of the statement:

   'I have read the above statement, and I have been able to correct, alter or add anything I wish. This statement is true. I have made it of my own free will.'

12. If the person making the statement cannot read, or refuses to read it, or to write the above mentioned certificate at the end of it or to sign it, the person taking the statement shall read it to them and ask them if they would like to correct, alter or add anything and to put their

signature or make their mark at the end. The person taking the statement shall certify on the statement itself what has occurred.

ANNEX E—SUMMARY OF PROVISIONS RELATING TO MENTALLY DISORDERED AND OTHERWISE MENTALLY VULNERABLE PEOPLE

1. If an officer has any suspicion, or is told in good faith, that a person of any age may be mentally disordered or otherwise mentally vulnerable, or mentally incapable of understanding the significance of questions or their replies that person shall be treated as mentally disordered or otherwise mentally vulnerable for the purposes of this Code. See *paragraph 1.4*

2. In the case of a person who is mentally disordered or otherwise mentally vulnerable, 'the appropriate adult' means:
   (a) a relative, guardian or other person responsible for their care or custody;
   (b) someone experienced in dealing with mentally disordered or mentally vulnerable people but who is not a police officer or employed by the police;
   (c) failing these, some other responsible adult aged 18 or over who is not a police officer or employed by the police.
   See *paragraph 1.7(b) and Note 1D*

3. If the custody officer authorises the detention of a person who is mentally vulnerable or appears to be suffering from a mental disorder, the custody officer must as soon as practicable inform the appropriate adult of the grounds for detention and the person's whereabouts, and ask the adult to come to the police station to see them. If the appropriate adult:
   • is already at the station when information is given as in *paragraphs 3.1* to *3.5* the information must be given in their presence
   • is not at the station when the provisions of *paragraph 3.1* to *3.5* are complied with these provisions must be complied with again in their presence once they arrive.
   See *paragraphs 3.15* to *3.17*

4. If the appropriate adult, having been informed of the right to legal advice, considers legal advice should be taken, the provisions of *section 6* apply as if the mentally disordered or otherwise mentally vulnerable person had requested access to legal advice. See *paragraph 3.19* and *Note E1*

5. The custody officer must make sure a person receives appropriate clinical attention as soon as reasonably practicable if the person appears to be suffering from a mental disorder or in urgent cases immediately call the nearest health care professional or an ambulance. It is not intended these provisions delay the transfer of a detainee to a place of safety under the Mental Health Act 1983, section 136 if that is applicable. If an assessment under that Act is to take place at a police station, the custody officer must consider whether an appropriate health care professional should be called to conduct an initial clinical check on the detainee. See *paragraph 9.5* and *9.6*

6. It is imperative a mentally disordered or otherwise mentally vulnerable person detained under the Mental Health Act 1983, section 136 be assessed as soon as possible. If that assessment is to take place at the police station, an approved social worker and registered medical practitioner shall be called to the station as soon as possible in order to interview and examine the detainee. Once the detainee has been interviewed, examined and suitable arrangements been made for their treatment or care, they can no longer be detained under section 136. A detainee should be immediately discharged from detention if a registered medical practitioner having examined them, concludes they are not mentally disordered within the meaning of the Act. See *paragraph 3.16*

7. If a mentally disordered or otherwise mentally vulnerable person is cautioned in the absence of the appropriate adult, the caution must be repeated in the appropriate adult's presence. See *paragraph 10.12*

8. A mentally disordered or otherwise mentally vulnerable person must not be interviewed or asked to provide or sign a written statement in the absence of the appropriate adult unless the provisions of *paragraphs 11.1* or *11.18* to *11.20* apply. Questioning in these circumstances may not continue in the absence of the appropriate adult once sufficient information to avert the risk has been obtained. A record shall be made of the grounds for any decision to begin an interview in these circumstances. See *paragraphs 11.1, 11.15* and *11.18* to *11.20*

9. If the appropriate adult is present at an interview, they shall be informed they are not expected to act simply as an observer and the purposes of their presence are to:
   - advise the interviewee
   - observe whether or not the interview is being conducted properly and fairly
   - facilitate communication with the interviewee
   See *paragraph 11.17*

10. If the detention of a mentally disordered or otherwise mentally vulnerable person is reviewed by a review officer or a superintendent, the appropriate adult must, if available at the time, be given an opportunity to make representations to the officer about the need for continuing detention. See *paragraph 15.3*

11. If the custody officer charges a mentally disordered or otherwise mentally vulnerable person with an offence or takes such other action as is appropriate when there is sufficient evidence for a prosecution this must be done in the presence of the appropriate adult. The written notice embodying any charge must be given to the appropriate adult. See *paragraphs 16.1* to *16.4A*

12. An intimate or strip search of a mentally disordered or otherwise mentally vulnerable person may take place only in the presence of the appropriate adult of the same sex, unless the detainee specifically requests the presence of a particular adult of the opposite sex. A strip search may take place in the absence of an appropriate adult only in cases of urgency when there is a risk of serious harm to the detainee or others. See *Annex A, paragraphs 5* and *11(c)*

13. Particular care must be taken when deciding whether to use any form of approved restraints on a mentally disordered or otherwise mentally vulnerable person in a locked cell. See *paragraph 8.2*

Notes for guidance

E1 *The purpose of the provision at paragraph 3.19 is to protect the rights of a mentally disordered or otherwise mentally vulnerable detained person who does not understand the significance of what is said to them. If the detained person wants to exercise the right to legal advice, the appropriate action should be taken and not delayed until the appropriate adult arrives. A mentally disordered or otherwise mentally vulnerable detained person should always be given an opportunity, when an appropriate adult is called to the police station, to consult privately with a solicitor in the absence of the appropriate adult if they want.*

E2 *Although people who are mentally disordered or otherwise mentally vulnerable are often capable of providing reliable evidence, they may, without knowing or wanting to do so, be particularly prone in certain circumstances to provide information that may be unreliable, misleading or self-incriminating. Special care should always be taken when questioning such a person, and the appropriate adult should be involved if there is any doubt about a person's mental state or capacity. Because of the risk of unreliable evidence, it is important to obtain corroboration of any facts admitted whenever possible.*

E3 *Because of the risks referred to in Note E2, which the presence of the appropriate adult is intended to minimise, officers of superintendent rank or above should exercise their discretion to authorise the commencement of an interview in the appropriate adult's absence only in exceptional cases, if it is necessary to avert an immediate risk of serious harm. See paragraphs 11.1, 11.18 to 11.20*

ANNEX F—COUNTRIES WITH WHICH BILATERAL CONSULAR CONVENTIONS OR AGREEMENTS REQUIRING NOTIFICATION OF THE ARREST AND DETENTION OF THEIR NATIONALS ARE IN FORCE AS AT 1 APRIL 2003

Armenia	Kazakhstan
Austria	Macedonia
Azerbaijan	Mexico
Belarus	Moldova
Belgium	Mongolia
Bosnia-Herzegovina	Norway
Bulgaria	Poland
China*	Romania
Croatia	Russia
Cuba	Slovak Republic
Czech Republic	Slovenia
Denmark	Spain
Egypt	Sweden
France	Tajikistan
Georgia	Turkmenistan
German Federal Republic	Ukraine
Greece	USA
Hungary	Uzbekistan
Italy	Yugoslavia
Japan	

* Police are required to inform Chinese officials of arrest/detention in the Manchester consular district only. This comprises Derbyshire, Durham, Greater Manchester, Lancashire, Merseyside, North South and West Yorkshire, and Tyne and Wear.

ANNEX G—FITNESS TO BE INTERVIEWED

1. This Annex contains general guidance to help police officers and health care professionals assess whether a detainee might be at risk in an interview.
2. A detainee may be at risk in an interview if it is considered that:
   (a) conducting the interview could significantly harm the detainee's physical or mental state;
   (b) anything the detainee says in the interview about their involvement or suspected involvement in the offence about which they are being interviewed **might** be considered unreliable in subsequent court proceedings because of their physical or mental state.
3. In assessing whether the detainee should be interviewed, the following must be considered:
   (a) how the detainee's physical or mental state might affect their ability to understand the nature and purpose of the interview, to comprehend what is being asked and to appreciate the significance of any answers given and make rational decisions about whether they want to say anything;
   (b) the extent to which the detainee's replies may be affected by their physical or mental condition rather than representing a rational and accurate explanation of their involvement in the offence;
   (c) how the nature of the interview, which could include particularly probing questions, might affect the detainee.
4. It is essential health care professionals who are consulted consider the functional ability of the detainee rather than simply relying on a medical diagnosis, e.g. it is possible for a person with severe mental illness to be fit for interview.

5. Health care professionals should advise on the need for an appropriate adult to be present, whether reassessment of the person's fitness for interview may be necessary if the interview lasts beyond a specified time, and whether a further specialist opinion may be required.

6. When health care professionals identify risks they should be asked to quantify the risks. They should inform the custody officer:
   - whether the person's condition:
     — is likely to improve
     — will require or be amenable to treatment; and
   - indicate how long it may take for such improvement to take effect

7. The role of the health care professional is to consider the risks and advise the custody officer of the outcome of that consideration. The health care professional's determination and any advice or recommendations should be made in writing and form part of the custody record.

8. Once the health care professional has provided that information, it is a matter for the custody officer to decide whether or not to allow the interview to go ahead and if the interview is to proceed, to determine what safeguards are needed. Nothing prevents safeguards being provided in addition to those required under the Code. An example might be to have an appropriate health care professional present during the interview, in addition to an appropriate adult, in order constantly to monitor the person's condition and how it is being affected by the interview.

ANNEX H—DETAINED PERSON: OBSERVATION LIST

1. If any detainee fails to meet any of the following criteria, an appropriate health care professional or an ambulance must be called.

2. When assessing the level of rousability, consider:
   Rousability—can they be woken?
   - go into the cell
   - call their name
   - shake gently
   Response to questions—can they give appropriate answers to questions such as:
   - What's your name?
   - Where do you live?
   - Where do you think you are?
   Response to commands—can they respond appropriately to commands such as:
   - Open your eyes!
   - Lift one arm, now the other arm!

3. Remember to take into account the possibility or presence of other illnesses, injury, or mental condition, a person who is drowsy and smells of alcohol may also have the following:
   - Diabetes
   - Epilepsy
   - Head injury
   - Drug intoxication or overdose
   - Stroke

ANNEX I—NOT USED

ANNEX J—NOT USED

ANNEX K—X-RAYS AND ULTRASOUND SCANS

(a) Action

1. PACE, section 55A allows a person who has been arrested and is in police detention to have an X-ray taken of them or an ultrasound scan to be carried out on them (or both) if:

    (a) authorised by an officer of inspector rank or above who has reasonable grounds for believing that the detainee:

      (i) may have swallowed a Class A drug; and

      (ii) was in possession of that Class A drug with the intention of supplying it to another or to export; and

    (b) the detainee's appropriate consent has been given in writing.

2. Before an x-ray is taken or an ultrasound scan carried out, a police officer, designated detention officer or staff custody officer must tell the detainee:

    (a) that the authority has been given; and

    (b) the grounds for giving the authorisation.

3. Before a detainee is asked to give appropriate consent to an x-ray or an ultrasound scan, they must be warned that if they refuse without good cause their refusal may harm their case if it comes to trial, see *Notes K1* and *K2*. This warning may be given by a police officer or member of police staff. A detainee who is not legally represented must be reminded of their entitlement to have free legal advice, see *Code C, paragraph 6.5*, and the reminder noted in the custody record.

4. An x-ray may be taken, or an ultrasound scan may be carried out, only by a registered medical practitioner or registered nurse, and only at a hospital, surgery or other medical premises.

(b) Documentation

5. The following shall be recorded as soon as practicable in the detainee's custody record:

    (a) the authorisation to take the x-ray or carry out the ultrasound scan (or both);

    (b) the grounds for giving the authorisation;

    (c) the giving of the warning required by *paragraph 3*; and

    (d) the fact that the appropriate consent was given or (as the case may be) refused, and if refused, the reason given for the refusal (if any); and

    (e) if an x-ray is taken or an ultrasound scan carried out:

      • where it was taken or carried out

      • who took it or carried it out

      • who was present

      • the result

6. Paragraphs 1.4–1.7 of this Code apply and an appropriate adult should be present when consent is sought to any procedure under this Annex.

Notes for guidance

K1 If authority is given for an x-ray to be taken or an ultrasound scan to be carried out (or both), consideration should be given to asking a registered medical practitioner or registered nurse to explain to the detainee what is involved and to allay any concerns the detainee might have about the effect which taking an x-ray or carrying out an ultrasound scan might have on them. If appropriate consent is not given, evidence of the explanation may, if the case comes to trial, be relevant to determining whether the detainee had a good cause for refusing.

K2 In warning a detainee who is asked to consent to an X-ray being taken or an ultrasound scan being carried out (or both), as in paragraph 3, the following form of words may be used:

    "You do not have to allow an x-ray of you to be taken or an ultrasound scan to be carried out on you, but I must warn you that if you refuse without good cause, your refusal may harm your case if it comes to trial."

Appendix 2.2

PACE Code of Practice for the Identification of Persons by Police Officers (Code D)

This code has effect in relation to any identification procedure carried out after midnight on 31 December 2005

1 Introduction

1.1 This Code of Practice concerns the principal methods used by police to identify people in connection with the investigation of offences and the keeping of accurate and reliable criminal records.

1.2 Identification by witnesses arises, e.g., if the offender is seen committing the crime and a witness is given an opportunity to identify the suspect in a video identification, identification parade or similar procedure. The procedures are designed to:

- test the witness' ability to identify the person they saw on a previous occasion
- provide safeguards against mistaken identification.

While this Code concentrates on visual identification procedures, it does not preclude the police making use of aural identification procedures such as a "voice identification parade", where they judge that appropriate.

1.3 Identification by fingerprints applies when a person's fingerprints are taken to:

- compare with fingerprints found at the scene of a crime
- check and prove convictions
- help to ascertain a person's identity.

1.3A Identification using footwear impressions applies when a person's footwear impressions are taken to compare with impressions found at the scene of a crime.

1.4 Identification by body samples and impressions includes taking samples such as blood or hair to generate a DNA profile for comparison with material obtained from the scene of a crime, or a victim.

1.5 Taking photographs of arrested people applies to recording and checking identity and locating and tracing persons who:

- are wanted for offences
- fail to answer their bail.

1.6 Another method of identification involves searching and examining detained suspects to find, e.g., marks such as tattoos or scars which may help establish their identity or whether they have been involved in committing an offence.

1.7 The provisions of the Police and Criminal Evidence Act 1984 (PACE) and this Code are designed to make sure fingerprints, samples, impressions and photographs are taken, used and retained, and identification procedures carried out, only when justified and necessary for preventing, detecting or investigating crime. If these provisions are not observed, the application of the relevant procedures in particular cases may be open to question.

2 General

2.1   This Code must be readily available at all police stations for consultation by:
- police officers and police staff
- detained persons
- members of the public

2.2   The provisions of this Code:
- include the *Annexes*
- do not include the *Notes for guidance.*

2.3   Code C, paragraph 1.4, regarding a person who may be mentally disordered or otherwise mentally vulnerable and the *Notes for guidance* applicable to those provisions apply to this Code.

2.4   Code C, paragraph 1.5, regarding a person who appears to be under the age of 17 applies to this Code.

2.5   Code C, paragraph 1.6, regarding a person who appears blind, seriously visually impaired, deaf, unable to read or speak or has difficulty orally because of a speech impediment applies to this Code.

2.6   In this Code:
- 'appropriate adult' means the same as in Code C, paragraph 1.7,
- 'solicitor' means the same as in Code C, paragraph 6.12 and the *Notes for guidance* applicable to those provisions apply to this Code.

2.7   References to custody officers include those performing the functions of custody officer, see *paragraph 1.9* of Code C.

2.8   When a record of any action requiring the authority of an officer of a specified rank is made under this Code, subject to *paragraph 2.18,* the officer's name and rank must be recorded.

2.9   When this Code requires the prior authority or agreement of an officer of at least inspector or superintendent rank, that authority may be given by a sergeant or chief inspector who has been authorised to perform the functions of the higher rank under PACE, section 107.

2.10   Subject to *paragraph 2.18*, all records must be timed and signed by the maker.

2.11   Records must be made in the custody record, unless otherwise specified. References to 'pocket book' include any official report book issued to police officers or police staff.

2.12   If any procedure in this Code requires a person's consent, the consent of a:
- mentally disordered or otherwise mentally vulnerable person is only valid if given in the presence of the appropriate adult
- juvenile, is only valid if their parent's or guardian's consent is also obtained unless the juvenile is under 14, when their parent's or guardian's consent is sufficient in its own right. If the only obstacle to an identification procedure in *section 3* is that a juvenile's parent or guardian refuses consent or reasonable efforts to obtain it have failed, the identification officer may apply the provisions of *paragraph 3.21*. See *Note 2A*.

2.13   If a person is blind, seriously visually impaired or unable to read, the custody officer or identification officer shall make sure their solicitor, relative, appropriate adult or some other person likely to take an interest in them and not involved in the investigation is available to help check any documentation. When this Code requires written consent or signing, the person assisting may be asked to sign instead, if the detainee prefers. This paragraph does not require an appropriate adult to be called solely to assist in checking and signing documentation for a person who is not a juvenile, or mentally disordered or otherwise mentally vulnerable (see Note 2B and Code C *paragraph 3.15*).

2.14   If any procedure in this Code requires information to be given to or sought from a suspect, it must be given or sought in the appropriate adult's presence if the suspect is mentally disordered, otherwise mentally vulnerable or a juvenile. If the appropriate adult is not present when the information is first given or sought, the procedure must be repeated in the presence of the appropriate adult when they arrive. If the suspect appears deaf or there is doubt about their hearing or speaking ability or ability to understand English, and effective communication cannot be established, the information must be given or sought through an interpreter.

2.15 Any procedure in this Code involving the participation of a suspect who is mentally disordered, otherwise mentally vulnerable or a juvenile must take place in the presence of the appropriate adult. See *Code C paragraph 1.4.*

2.15A Any procedure in this Code involving the participation of a witness who is or appears to be mentally disordered, otherwise mentally vulnerable or a juvenile should take place in the presence of a pre-trial support person. However, the support-person must not be allowed to prompt any identification of a suspect by a witness. See *Note 2AB.*

2.16 References to:

- 'taking a photograph', include the use of any process to produce a single, still or moving, visual image
- 'photographing a person', should be construed accordingly
- 'photographs', 'films', 'negatives' and 'copies' include relevant visual images recorded, stored, or reproduced through any medium
- 'destruction' includes the deletion of computer data relating to such images or making access to that data impossible.

2.17 Except as described, nothing in this Code affects the powers and procedures:

(i) for requiring and taking samples of breath, blood and urine in relation to driving offences, etc, when under the influence of drink, drugs or excess alcohol under the:
- Road Traffic Act 1988, sections 4 to 11
- Road Traffic Offenders Act 1988, sections 15 and 16
- Transport and Works Act 1992, sections 26 to 38;

(ii) under the Immigration Act 1971, Schedule 2, paragraph 18, for taking photographs and fingerprints from persons detained under that Act, Schedule 2, paragraph 16 (Administrative Controls as to Control on Entry etc.); for taking fingerprints in accordance with the Immigration and Asylum Act 1999; sections 141 and 142(3), or other methods for collecting information about a person's external physical characteristics provided for by regulations made under that Act, section 144;

(iii) under the Terrorism Act 2000, Schedule 8, for taking photographs, fingerprints, skin impressions, body samples or impressions from people:
- arrested under that Act, section 41,
- detained for the purposes of examination under that Act, Schedule 7, and to whom the Code of Practice issued under that Act, Schedule 14, paragraph 6, applies ('the terrorism provisions')
See *Note 2C*;

(iv) for taking photographs, fingerprints, skin impressions, body samples or impressions from people who have been:
- arrested on warrants issued in Scotland, by officers exercising powers under the Criminal Justice and Public Order Act 1994, section 136(2)
- arrested or detained without warrant by officers from a police force in Scotland exercising their powers of arrest or detention under the Criminal Justice and Public Order Act 1994, section 137(2), (Cross Border powers of arrest etc.).

Note: In these cases, police powers and duties and the person's rights and entitlements whilst at a police station in England and Wales are the same as if the person had been arrested in Scotland by a Scottish police officer.

2.18 Nothing in this Code requires the identity of officers or police staff to be recorded or disclosed:

(a) in the case of enquiries linked to the investigation of terrorism;

(b) if the officers or police staff reasonably believe recording or disclosing their names might put them in danger.

In these cases, they shall use warrant or other identification numbers and the name of their police station. See *Note 2D*

2.19 In this Code:

(a) 'designated person' means a person other than a police officer, designated under the Police Reform Act 2002, Part 4, who has specified powers and duties of police officers conferred or imposed on them;

(b) any reference to a police officer includes a designated person acting in the exercise or performance of the powers and duties conferred or imposed on them by their designation.

2.20 If a power conferred on a designated person:

(a) allows reasonable force to be used when exercised by a police officer, a designated person exercising that power has the same entitlement to use force;

(b) includes power to use force to enter any premises, that power is not exercisable by that designated person except:

(i) in the company, and under the supervision, of a police officer; or

(ii) for the purpose of:

• saving life or limb; or

• preventing serious damage to property.

2.21 Nothing in this Code prevents the custody officer, or other officer given custody of the detainee, from allowing police staff who are not designated persons to carry out individual procedures or tasks at the police station if the law allows. However, the officer remains responsible for making sure the procedures and tasks are carried out correctly in accordance with the Codes of Practice. Any such person must be:

(a) a person employed by a police authority maintaining a police force and under the control and direction of the Chief Officer of that force;

(b) employed by a person with whom a police authority has a contract for the provision of services relating to persons arrested or otherwise in custody.

2.22 Designated persons and other police staff must have regard to any relevant provisions of the Codes of Practice.

Notes for guidance

2A For the purposes of paragraph 2.12, the consent required from a parent or guardian may, for a juvenile in the care of a local authority or voluntary organisation, be given by that authority or organisation. In the case of a juvenile, nothing in paragraph 2.12 requires the parent, guardian or representative of a local authority or voluntary organisation to be present to give their consent, unless they are acting as the appropriate adult under paragraphs 2.14 or 2.15. However, it is important that a parent or guardian not present is fully informed before being asked to consent. They must be given the same information about the procedure and the juvenile's suspected involvement in the offence as the juvenile and appropriate adult. The parent or guardian must also be allowed to speak to the juvenile and the appropriate adult if they wish. Provided the consent is fully informed and is not withdrawn, it may be obtained at any time before the procedure takes place.

2AB The Youth Justice and Criminal Evidence Act 1999 guidance "Achieving Best Evidence in Criminal Proceedings" indicates that a pre-trial support person should accompany a vulnerable witness during any identification procedure. It states that this support person should not be (or not be likely to be) a witness in the investigation.

2B People who are seriously visually impaired or unable to read may be unwilling to sign police documents. The alternative, i.e. their representative signing on their behalf, seeks to protect the interests of both police and suspects.

2C Photographs, fingerprints, samples and impressions may be taken from a person detained under the terrorism provisions to help determine whether they are, or have been, involved in terrorism, as well as when there are reasonable grounds for suspecting their involvement in a particular offence.

2D The purpose of paragraph 2.18(b) is to protect those involved in serious organised crime investigations or arrests of particularly violent suspects when there is reliable information that those arrested or their associates may threaten or cause harm to the officers. In cases of doubt, an officer of inspector rank or above should be consulted.

3 Identification by witnesses

3.1 A record shall be made of the suspect's description as first given by a potential witness. This record must:

(a) be made and kept in a form which enables details of that description to be accurately produced from it, in a visible and legible form, which can be given to the suspect or the suspect's solicitor in accordance with this Code; and

(b) unless otherwise specified, be made before the witness takes part in any identification procedures under *paragraphs 3.5* to *3.10, 3.21* or *3.23*.

A copy of the record shall where practicable, be given to the suspect or their solicitor before any procedures under *paragraphs 3.5* to *3.10, 3.21* or *3.23* are carried out. See *Note 3E*

(a) Cases when the suspect's identity is not known

3.2 In cases when the suspect's identity is not known, a witness may be taken to a particular neighbourhood or place to see whether they can identify the person they saw. Although the number, age, sex, race, general description and style of clothing of other people present at the location and the way in which any identification is made cannot be controlled, the principles applicable to the formal procedures under *paragraphs 3.5* to *3.10* shall be followed as far as practicable. For example:

(a) where it is practicable to do so, a record should be made of the witness' description of the suspect, as in paragraph 3.1(a), before asking the witness to make an identification;

(b) care must be taken not to direct the witness' attention to any individual unless, taking into account all the circumstances, this cannot be avoided. However, this does not prevent a witness being asked to look carefully at the people around at the time or to look towards a group or in a particular direction, if this appears necessary to make sure that the witness does not overlook a possible suspect simply because the witness is looking in the opposite direction and also to enable the witness to make comparisons between any suspect and others who are in the area; See *Note 3F*

(c) where there is more than one witness, every effort should be made to keep them separate and witnesses should be taken to see whether they can identify a person independently;

(d) once there is sufficient information to justify the arrest of a particular individual for suspected involvement in the offence, e.g., after a witness makes a positive identification, the provisions set out from paragraph 3.4 onwards shall apply for any other witnesses in relation to that individual. Subject to *paragraphs 3.12* and *3.13*, it is not necessary for the witness who makes such a positive identification to take part in a further procedure;

(e) the officer or police staff accompanying the witness must record, in their pocket book, the action taken as soon as, and in as much detail, as possible. The record should include: the date, time and place of the relevant occasion the witness claims to have previously seen the suspect; where any identification was made; how it was made and the conditions at the time (e.g., the distance the witness was from the suspect, the weather and light); if the witness's attention was drawn to the suspect; the reason for this; and anything said by the witness or the suspect about the identification or the conduct of the procedure.

3.3 A witness must not be shown photographs, computerised or artist's composite likenesses or similar likenesses or pictures (including 'E-fit' images) if the identity of the suspect is known to the police and the suspect is available to take part in a video identification, an identification parade or a group identification. If the suspect's identity is not known, the showing of such images to a witness to obtain identification evidence must be done in accordance with *Annex E*.

(b) Cases when the suspect is known and available

3.4 If the suspect's identity is known to the police and they are available, the identification procedures set out in paragraphs 3.5 to 3.10 may be used. References in this section to a suspect being 'known' mean there is sufficient information known to the police to justify the arrest of a particular person for suspected involvement in the offence. A suspect being 'available' means they are immediately available or will be within a reasonably short time and willing to take an effective part in at least one of the following which it is practicable to arrange:

- video identification;
- identification parade; or
- group identification.

Video identification

3.5 Change to: 'A 'video identification' is when the witness is shown moving images of a known suspect, together with similar images of others who resemble the suspect. Moving images must be used unless:

- the suspect is known but not available (see *paragraph 3.21* of this Code); or
- in accordance with *paragraph 2A of Annex A* of this Code, the identification officer does not consider that replication of a physical feature can be achieved or that it is not possible to conceal the location of the feature on the image of the suspect.

The identification officer may then decide to make use of video identification but using still images.

3.6 Video identifications must be carried out in accordance with *Annex A*.

Identification parade

3.7 An 'identification parade' is when the witness sees the suspect in a line of others who resemble the suspect.

3.8 Identification parades must be carried out in accordance with *Annex B*.

Group identification

3.9 A 'group identification' is when the witness sees the suspect in an informal group of people.

3.10 Group identifications must be carried out in accordance with *Annex C*.

Arranging identification procedures

3.11 Except for the provisions in *paragraph 3.19*, the arrangements for, and conduct of, the identification procedures in paragraphs 3.5 to 3.10 and circumstances in which an identification procedure must be held shall be the responsibility of an officer not below inspector rank who is not involved with the investigation, 'the identification officer'. Unless otherwise specified, the identification officer may allow another officer or police staff, see *paragraph 2.21*, to make arrangements for, and conduct, any of these identification procedures. In delegating these procedures, the identification officer must be able to supervise effectively and either intervene or be contacted for advice. No officer or any other person involved with the investigation of the case against the suspect, beyond the extent required by these procedures, may take any part in these procedures or act as the identification officer. This does not prevent the identification officer from consulting the officer in charge of the investigation to determine which procedure to use. When an identification procedure is required, in the interest of fairness to suspects and witnesses, it must be held as soon as practicable.

Circumstances in which an identification procedure must be held

3.12 Whenever:

(i) a witness has identified a suspect or purported to have identified them prior to any identification procedure set out in paragraphs 3.5 to 3.10 having been held; or

(ii) there is a witness available, who expresses an ability to identify the suspect, or where there is a reasonable chance of the witness being able to do so, and they have not been given an opportunity to identify the suspect in any of the procedures set out in paragraphs 3.5 to 3.10, and the suspect disputes being the person the witness claims to have seen, an identification procedure shall be held unless it is not practicable or it would serve no useful purpose in proving or disproving whether the suspect was involved in committing the offence. For example, when it is not disputed that the suspect is already well known to the witness who claims to have seen them commit the crime.

3.13 Such a procedure may also be held if the officer in charge of the investigation considers it would be useful.

Selecting an identification procedure

3.14 If, because of paragraph 3.12, an identification procedure is to be held, the suspect shall initially be offered a video identification unless:

(a) a video identification is not practicable; or

(b) an identification parade is both practicable and more suitable than a video identification; or

(c) paragraph 3.16 applies.

The identification officer and the officer in charge of the investigation shall consult each other to determine which option is to be offered. An identification parade may not be practicable because of factors relating to the witnesses, such as their number, state of health, availability and travelling requirements. A video identification would normally be more suitable if it could be arranged and completed sooner than an identification parade.

3.15 A suspect who refuses the identification procedure first offered shall be asked to state their reason for refusing and may get advice from their solicitor and/or if present, their appropriate adult. The suspect, solicitor and/or appropriate adult shall be allowed to make representations about why another procedure should be used. A record should be made of the reasons for refusal and any representations made. After considering any reasons given, and representations made, the identification officer shall, if appropriate, arrange for the suspect to be offered an alternative which the officer considers suitable and practicable. If the officer decides it is not suitable and practicable to offer an alternative identification procedure, the reasons for that decision shall be recorded.

3.16 A group identification may initially be offered if the officer in charge of the investigation considers it is more suitable than a video identification or an identification parade and the identification officer considers it practicable to arrange.

Notice to suspect

3.17 Unless *paragraph 3.20* applies, before a video identification, an identification parade or group identification is arranged, the following shall be explained to the suspect:

(i) the purposes of the video identification, identification parade or group identification;

(ii) their entitlement to free legal advice; see Code C, paragraph 6.5;

(iii) the procedures for holding it, including their right to have a solicitor or friend present;

(iv) that they do not have to consent to or co-operate in a video identification, identification parade or group identification;

(v) that if they do not consent to, and co-operate in, a video identification, identification parade or group identification, their refusal may be given in evidence in any subsequent trial and police may proceed covertly without their consent or make other arrangements to test whether a witness can identify them, see *paragraph 3.21;*

(vi) whether, for the purposes of the video identification procedure, images of them have previously been obtained, see *paragraph 3.20*, and if so, that they may co-operate in providing further, suitable images to be used instead;

(vii) if appropriate, the special arrangements for juveniles;

(viii) if appropriate, the special arrangements for mentally disordered or otherwise mentally vulnerable people;

(ix) that if they significantly alter their appearance between being offered an identification procedure and any attempt to hold an identification procedure, this may be given in evidence if the case comes to trial, and the identification officer may then consider other forms of identification, see *paragraph 3.21* and *Note 3C*;

  (x) that a moving image or photograph may be taken of them when they attend for any identification procedure;

 (xi) whether, before their identity became known, the witness was shown photographs, a computerised or artist's composite likeness or similar likeness or image by the police, see *Note 3B;*

(xii) that if they change their appearance before an identification parade, it may not be practicable to arrange one on the day or subsequently and, because of the appearance change, the identification officer may consider alternative methods of identification, see *Note 3C;*

(xiii) that they or their solicitor will be provided with details of the description of the suspect as first given by any witnesses who are to attend the video identification, identification parade, group identification or confrontation, see *paragraph 3.1.*

3.18 This information must also be recorded in a written notice handed to the suspect. The suspect must be given a reasonable opportunity to read the notice, after which, they should be asked to sign a second copy to indicate if they are willing to co-operate with the making of a video or take part in the identification parade or group identification. The signed copy shall be retained by the identification officer.

3.19 The duties of the identification officer under *paragraphs 3.17* and *3.18* may be performed by the custody officer or other officer not involved in the investigation if:

(a) it is proposed to release the suspect in order that an identification procedure can be arranged and carried out and an inspector is not available to act as the identification officer, see *paragraph 3.11*, before the suspect leaves the station; or

(b) it is proposed to keep the suspect in police detention whilst the procedure is arranged and carried out and waiting for an inspector to act as the identification officer, see *paragraph 3.11*, would cause unreasonable delay to the investigation.

The officer concerned shall inform the identification officer of the action taken and give them the signed copy of the notice. See *Note 3C*

3.20 If the identification officer and officer in charge of the investigation suspect, on reasonable grounds that if the suspect was given the information and notice as in *paragraphs 3.17* and *3.18*, they would then take steps to avoid being seen by a witness in any identification procedure, the identification officer may arrange for images of the suspect suitable for use in a video identification procedure to be obtained before giving the information and notice. If suspect's images are obtained in these circumstances, the suspect may, for the purposes of a video identification procedure, co-operate in providing new images which if suitable, would be used instead, see *paragraph 3.17(vi).*

(c) Cases when the suspect is known but not available

3.21 When a known suspect is not available or has ceased to be available, see *paragraph 3.4*, the identification officer may make arrangements for a video identification (see Annex A). If necessary, the identification officer may follow the video identification procedures but using **still** images. Any suitable moving or still images may be used and these may be obtained covertly if necessary. Alternatively, the identification officer may make arrangements for a group identification. See *Note 3D*. These provisions may also be applied to juveniles where the consent of their parent or guardian is either refused or reasonable efforts to obtain that consent have failed (see *paragraph 2.12*).

3.22 Any covert activity should be strictly limited to that necessary to test the ability of the witness to identify the suspect.

3.23 The identification officer may arrange for the suspect to be confronted by the witness if none of the options referred to in paragraphs 3.5 to 3.10 or 3.21 are practicable. A "confrontation" is when the suspect is directly confronted by the witness. A confrontation does not require the suspect's consent. Confrontations must be carried out in accordance with Annex D.

3.24 Requirements for information to be given to, or sought from, a suspect or for the suspect to be given an opportunity to view images before they are shown to a witness, do not apply if the suspect's lack of co-operation prevents the necessary action.

(d) Documentation

3.25 A record shall be made of the video identification, identification parade, group identification or confrontation on forms provided for the purpose.

3.26 If the identification officer considers it is not practicable to hold a video identification or identification parade requested by the suspect, the reasons shall be recorded and explained to the suspect.

3.27 A record shall be made of a person's failure or refusal to co-operate in a video identification, identification parade or group identification and, if applicable, of the grounds for obtaining images in accordance with *paragraph 3.20*.

(e) Showing films and photographs of incidents and information released to the media

3.28 Nothing in this Code inhibits showing films or photographs to the public through the national or local media, or to police officers for the purposes of recognition and tracing suspects. However, when such material is shown to potential witnesses, including police officers, see *Note 3A*, to obtain identification evidence, it shall be shown on an individual basis to avoid any possibility of collusion, and, as far as possible, the showing shall follow the principles for video identification if the suspect is known, see *Annex A*, or identification by photographs if the suspect is not known, see *Annex E*.

3.29 When a broadcast or publication is made, see *paragraph 3.28*, a copy of the relevant material released to the media for the purposes of recognising or tracing the suspect, shall be kept. The suspect or their solicitor shall be allowed to view such material before any procedures under *paragraphs 3.5 to 3.10, 3.21 or 3.23* are carried out, provided it is practicable and would not unreasonably delay the investigation. Each witness involved in the procedure shall be asked, after they have taken part, whether they have seen any broadcast or published films or photographs relating to the offence or any description of the suspect and their replies shall be recorded. This paragraph does not affect any separate requirement under the Criminal Procedure and Investigations Act 1996 to retain material in connection with criminal investigations.

(f) Destruction and retention of photographs taken or used in identification procedures

3.30 PACE, section 64A, see *paragraph 5.12*, provides powers to take photographs of suspects and allows these photographs to be used or disclosed only for purposes related to the prevention or detection of crime, the investigation of offences or the conduct of prosecutions by, or on behalf of, police or other law enforcement and prosecuting authorities inside and outside the United Kingdom or the enforcement of a sentence. After being so used or disclosed, they may be retained but can only be used or disclosed for the same purposes.

3.31 Subject to *paragraph 3.33*, the photographs (and all negatives and copies), of suspects not taken in accordance with the provisions in *paragraph 5.12* which are taken for the purposes of, or in connection with, the identification procedures in *paragraphs 3.5 to 3.10, 3.21 or 3.23* must be destroyed unless the suspect:

(a) is charged with, or informed they may be prosecuted for, a recordable offence;

(b) is prosecuted for a recordable offence;

(c) is cautioned for a recordable offence or given a warning or reprimand in accordance with the Crime and Disorder Act 1998 for a recordable offence; or

(d) gives informed consent, in writing, for the photograph or images to be retained for purposes described in *paragraph 3.30*.

3.32 When *paragraph 3.31* requires the destruction of any photograph, the person must be given an opportunity to witness the destruction or to have a certificate confirming the destruction if they request one within five days of being informed that the destruction is required.

3.33 Nothing in *paragraph 3.31* affects any separate requirement under the Criminal Procedure and Investigations Act 1996 to retain material in connection with criminal investigations.

Notes for guidance

3A   *Except for the provisions of Annex E, paragraph 1, a police officer who is a witness for the purposes of this part of the Code is subject to the same principles and procedures as a civilian witness.*

3B   *When a witness attending an identification procedure has previously been shown photographs, or been shown or provided with computerised or artist's composite likenesses, or similar likenesses or pictures, it is the officer in charge of the investigation's responsibility to make the identification officer aware of this.*

3C   *The purpose of paragraph 3.19 is to avoid or reduce delay in arranging identification procedures by enabling the required information and warnings, see sub-paragraphs 3.17(ix) and 3.17(xii), to be given at the earliest opportunity.*

3D   *Paragraph 3.21 would apply when a known suspect deliberately makes themself 'unavailable' in order to delay or frustrate arrangements for obtaining identification evidence. It also applies when a suspect refuses or fails to take part in a video identification, an identification parade or a group identification, or refuses or fails to take part in the only practicable options from that list. It enables any suitable images of the suspect, moving or still, which are available or can be obtained, to be used in an identification procedure. Examples include images from custody and other CCTV systems and from visually recorded interview records, see Code F Note for Guidance 2D.*

3E   *When it is proposed to show photographs to a witness in accordance with Annex E, it is the responsibility of the officer in charge of the investigation to confirm to the officer responsible for supervising and directing the showing, that the first description of the suspect given by that witness has been recorded. If this description has not been recorded, the procedure under Annex E must be postponed. See Annex E paragraph 2*

3F   *The admissibility and value of identification evidence obtained when carrying out the procedure under paragraph 3.2 may be compromised if:*

    (a) before a person is identified, the witness' attention is specifically drawn to that person; or

    (b) the suspect's identity becomes known before the procedure.

4 Identification by fingerprints and footwear impressions

(A) Taking fingerprints in connection with a criminal investigation

(a) General

4.1 References to 'fingerprints' means any record, produced by any method, of the skin pattern and other physical characteristics or features of a person's:

(i) fingers; or

(ii) palms.

(b) Action

4.2 A person's fingerprints may be taken in connection with the investigation of an offence only with their consent or if *paragraph 4.3* applies. If the person is at a police station consent must be in writing.

4.3 PACE, section 61, provides powers to take fingerprints without consent from any person over the age of ten years:

(a) under section 61(3), from a person detained at a police station in consequence of being arrested for a recordable offence, see Note 4A, if they have not had their fingerprints taken in the course of the investigation of the offence unless those previously taken fingerprints are not a complete set or some or all of those fingerprints are not of sufficient quality to allow satisfactory analysis, comparison or matching.

(b) under section 61(4), from a person detained at a police station who has been charged with a recordable offence, see Note 4A, or informed they will be reported for such an offence if they have not had their fingerprints taken in the course of the investigation of the offence unless those previously taken fingerprints are not a complete set or some or all of those fingerprints are not of sufficient quality to allow satisfactory analysis, comparison or matching.

(c) under section 61(4A), from a person who has been bailed to appear at a court or police station if the person:

    (i) has answered to bail for a person whose fingerprints were taken previously and there are reasonable grounds for believing they are not the same person; or

    (ii) who has answered to bail claims to be a different person from a person whose fingerprints were previously taken;

and in either case, the court or an officer of inspector rank or above, authorises the fingerprints to be taken at the court or police station;

(d) under section 61(6), from a person who has been:

    (i) convicted of a recordable offence;

    (ii) given a caution in respect of a recordable offence which, at the time of the caution, the person admitted; or

    (iii) warned or reprimanded under the Crime and Disorder Act 1998, section 65, for a recordable offence.

4.4 PACE, section 27, provides power to:

(a) require the person as in *paragraph 4.3(d)* to attend a police station to have their fingerprints taken if the:

    (i) person has not been in police detention for the offence and has not had their fingerprints taken in the course of the investigation of that offence; or

    (ii) fingerprints that were taken from the person in the course of the investigation of that offence, do not constitute a complete set or some, or all, of the fingerprints are not of sufficient quality to allow satisfactory analysis, comparison or matching; and

(b) arrest, without warrant, a person who fails to comply with the requirement.

Note: The requirement must be made within one month of the date the person is convicted, cautioned, warned or reprimanded and the person must be given a period of at least 7 days within which to attend. This 7 day period need not fall during the month allowed for making the requirement.

4.5 A person's fingerprints may be taken, as above, electronically.

4.6 Reasonable force may be used, if necessary, to take a person's fingerprints without their consent under the powers as in *paragraphs 4.3* and *4.4*.

4.7 Before any fingerprints are taken with, or without, consent as above, the person must be informed:

(a) of the reason their fingerprints are to be taken;

(b) of the grounds on which the relevant authority has been given if the power mentioned in *paragraph 4.3 (c) applies;*

(c) that their fingerprints may be retained and may be subject of a speculative search against other fingerprints, see *Note 4B*, unless destruction of the fingerprints is required in accordance with *Annex F, Part (a)*; and

(d) that if their fingerprints are required to be destroyed, they may witness their destruction as provided for in *Annex F, Part (a)*.

(c) Documentation

4.8 A record must be made as soon as possible, of the reason for taking a person's fingerprints without consent. If force is used, a record shall be made of the circumstances and those present.

4.9 A record shall be made when a person has been informed under the terms of *paragraph 4.7(c)*, of the possibility that their fingerprints may be subject of a speculative search.

(B) Taking fingerprints in connection with immigration enquiries

Action

4.10 A person's fingerprints may be taken for the purposes of Immigration Service enquiries in accordance with powers and procedures other than under PACE and for which the Immigration Service (not the police) are responsible, only with the person's consent in writing or if *paragraph 4.11* applies.

4.11 Powers to take fingerprints for these purposes without consent are given to police and immigration officers under the:

(a) Immigration Act 1971, Schedule 2, paragraph 18(2), when it is reasonably necessary for the purposes of identifying a person detained under the Immigration Act 1971, Schedule 2, paragraph 16 (Detention of person liable to examination or removal);

(b) Immigration and Asylum Act 1999, section 141(7)(a), from a person who fails to produce, on arrival, a valid passport with a photograph or some other document satisfactorily establishing their identity and nationality if an immigration officer does not consider the person has a reasonable excuse for the failure;

(c) Immigration and Asylum Act 1999, section 141(7)(b), from a person who has been refused entry to the UK but has been temporarily admitted if an immigration officer reasonably suspects the person might break a condition imposed on them relating to residence or reporting to a police or immigration officer, and their decision is confirmed by a chief immigration officer;

(d) Immigration and Asylum Act 1999, section 141(7)(c), when directions are given to remove a person:

- as an illegal entrant,
- liable to removal under the Immigration and Asylum Act 1999, section 10,
- who is the subject of a deportation order from the UK;

(e) Immigration and Asylum Act 1999, section 141(7)(d), from a person arrested under UK immigration laws under the Immigration Act 1971, Schedule 2, paragraph 17;

(f) Immigration and Asylum Act 1999, section 141(7)(e), from a person who has made a claim:

- for asylum
- under Article 3 of the European Convention on Human Rights; or

(g) Immigration and Asylum Act 1999, section 141(7)(f), from a person who is a dependant of someone who falls into (b) to (f) above.

4.12 The Immigration and Asylum Act 1999, section 142(3), gives a police and immigration officer power to arrest, without warrant, a person who fails to comply with a requirement imposed by the Secretary of State to attend a specified place for fingerprinting.

4.13 Before any fingerprints are taken, with or without consent, the person must be informed:

(a) of the reason their fingerprints are to be taken;

(b) the fingerprints, and all copies of them, will be destroyed in accordance with *Annex F, Part B.*

4.14 Reasonable force may be used, if necessary, to take a person's fingerprints without their consent under powers as in *paragraph 4.11.*

4.15 *Paragraphs 4.1* and *4.8* apply.

(C) Taking footwear impressions in connection with a criminal investigation

(a) Action

4.16 Impressions of a person's footwear may be taken in connection with the investigation of an offence only with their consent or if *paragraph 4.17* applies. If the person is at a police station consent must be in writing.

4.17 PACE, section 61A, provides power for a police officer to take footwear impressions without consent from any person over the age of ten years who is detained at a police station:

(a) in consequence of being arrested for a recordable offence, see *Note 4A*; or if the detainee has been charged with a recordable offence, or informed they will be reported for such an offence; and

(b) the detainee has not had an impression of their footwear taken in the course of the investigation of the offence unless the previously taken impression is not complete or is not of sufficient quality to allow satisfactory analysis, comparison or matching (whether in the case in question or generally).

4.18 Reasonable force may be used, if necessary, to take a footwear impression from a detainee without consent under the power in *paragraph 4.17*.

4.19 Before any footwear impression is taken with, or without, consent as above, the person must be informed:

(a) of the reason the impression is to be taken;

(b) that the impression may be retained and may be subject of a speculative search against other impressions, see *Note 4B*, unless destruction of the impression is required in accordance with *Annex F, Part (a)*; and

(c) that if their footwear impressions are required to be destroyed, they may witness their destruction as provided for in *Annex F, Part (a)*.

(b) Documentation

4.20 A record must be made as soon as possible, of the reason for taking a person's footwear impressions without consent. If force is used, a record shall be made of the circumstances and those present.

4.21 A record shall be made when a person has been informed under the terms of *paragraph 4.19(b)*, of the possibility that their footwear impressions may be subject of a speculative search.

Notes for guidance

4A *References to 'recordable offences' in this Code relate to those offences for which convictions, cautions, reprimands and warnings may be recorded in national police records. See PACE, section 27(4). The recordable offences current at the time when this Code was prepared, are any offences which carry a sentence of imprisonment on conviction (irrespective of the period, or the age of the offender or actual sentence passed) as well as the non-imprisonable offences under the Vagrancy Act 1824 sections 3 and 4 (begging and persistent begging), the Street Offences Act 1959, section 1 (loitering or soliciting for purposes of prostitution), the Road Traffic Act 1988, section 25 (tampering with motor vehicles), the Criminal Justice and Public Order Act 1994, section 167 (touting for hire car services) and others listed in the National Police Records (Recordable Offences) Regulations 2000 as amended.*

4B *Fingerprints, footwear impressions or a DNA sample (and the information derived from it) taken from a person arrested on suspicion of being involved in a recordable offence, or charged with such an offence, or informed they will be reported for such an offence, may be subject of a speculative search. This means the fingerprints, footwear impressions or DNA sample may be checked against other fingerprints, footwear impressions and DNA records held by, or on behalf of, the police and other law enforcement authorities in, or outside, the UK, or held in connection with, or as a result of, an investigation of an offence inside or outside the UK. Fingerprints, footwear impressions and samples taken from a person suspected of committing a recordable offence but not arrested, charged or informed they will be reported for it, may be subject to a speculative search only if the person consents in writing. The following is an example of a basic form of words:*

> *"I consent to my fingerprints, footwear impressions and DNA sample and information derived from it being retained and used only for purposes related to the prevention and detection of a crime, the investigation of an offence or the conduct of a prosecution either nationally or internationally.*

> *I understand that my fingerprints, footwear impressions or DNA sample may be checked against other fingerprint, footwear impressions and DNA records held by or on behalf of relevant law enforcement authorities, either nationally or internationally.*
>
> *I understand that once I have given my consent for my fingerprints, footwear impressions or DNA sample to be retained and used I cannot withdraw this consent."*

See *Annex F* regarding the retention and use of fingerprints and footwear impressions taken with consent for elimination purposes.

5 Examinations to establish identity and the taking of photographs

(A) Detainees at police stations

(a) Searching or examination of detainees at police stations

5.1 PACE, section 54A (1), allows a detainee at a police station to be searched or examined or both, to establish:

(a) whether they have any marks, features or injuries that would tend to identify them as a person involved in the commission of an offence and to photograph any identifying marks, see *paragraph 5.5*; or

(b) their identity, see *Note 5A*.

A person detained at a police station to be searched under a stop and search power, see Code A, is not a detainee for the purposes of these powers.

5.2 A search and/or examination to find marks under section 54A (1) (a) may be carried out without the detainee's consent, see *paragraph 2.12*, only if authorised by an officer of at least inspector rank when consent has been withheld or it is not practicable to obtain consent, see *Note 5D*.

5.3 A search or examination to establish a suspect's identity under section 54A (1) (b) may be carried out without the detainee's consent, see *paragraph 2.12*, only if authorised by an officer of at least inspector rank when the detainee has refused to identify themselves or the authorising officer has reasonable grounds for suspecting the person is not who they claim to be.

5.4 Any marks that assist in establishing the detainee's identity, or their identification as a person involved in the commission of an offence, are identifying marks. Such marks may be photographed with the detainee's consent, see *paragraph 2.12*; or without their consent if it is withheld or it is not practicable to obtain it, see *Note 5D*.

5.5 A detainee may only be searched, examined and photographed under section 54A, by a police officer of the same sex.

5.6 Any photographs of identifying marks, taken under section 54A, may be used or disclosed only for purposes related to the prevention or detection of crime, the investigation of offences or the conduct of prosecutions by, or on behalf of, police or other law enforcement and prosecuting authorities inside, and outside, the UK. After being so used or disclosed, the photograph may be retained but must not be used or disclosed except for these purposes, see *Note 5B*.

5.7 The powers, as in *paragraph 5.1*, do not affect any separate requirement under the Criminal Procedure and Investigations Act 1996 to retain material in connection with criminal investigations.

5.8 Authority for the search and/or examination for the purposes of *paragraphs 5.2* and *5.3* may be given orally or in writing. If given orally, the authorising officer must confirm it in writing as soon as practicable. A separate authority is required for each purpose which applies.

5.9 If it is established a person is unwilling to co-operate sufficiently to enable a search and/or examination to take place or a suitable photograph to be taken, an officer may use reasonable force to:

(a) search and/or examine a detainee without their consent; and

(b) photograph any identifying marks without their consent.

5.10 The thoroughness and extent of any search or examination carried out in accordance with the powers in section 54A must be no more than the officer considers necessary to achieve the required purpose. Any search or examination which involves the removal of more than the person's outer clothing shall be conducted in accordance with Code C, Annex A, paragraph 11.

5.11 An intimate search may not be carried out under the powers in section 54A.

(b) Photographing detainees at police stations and other persons elsewhere than at a police station

5.12 Under PACE, section 64A, an officer may photograph:

(a) any person whilst they are detained at a police station; and

(b) any person who is elsewhere than at a police station and who has been:-

(i) arrested by a constable for an offence;

(ii) taken into custody by a constable after being arrested for an offence by a person other than a constable;

(iii) made subject to a requirement to wait with a community support officer under *paragraph 2(3) or (3B)* of Schedule 4 to the Police Reform Act 2002;

(iv) given a penalty notice by a constable in uniform under Chapter 1 of Part 1 of the Criminal Justice and Police Act 2001, a penalty notice by a constable under section 444A of the Education Act 1996, or a fixed penalty notice by a constable in uniform under section 54 of the Road Traffic Offenders Act 1988;

(v) given a notice in relation to a relevant fixed penalty offence (within the meaning of paragraph 1 of Schedule 4 to the Police Reform Act 2002) by a community support officer by virtue of a designation applying that paragraph to him; or

(vi) given a notice in relation to a relevant fixed penalty offence (within the meaning of paragraph 1 of Schedule 5 to the Police Reform Act 2002) by an accredited person by virtue of accreditation specifying that that paragraph applies to him.

5.12A Photographs taken under PACE, section 64A:

(a) may be taken with the person's consent, or without their consent if consent is withheld or it is not practicable to obtain their consent, see *Note 5E*; and

(b) may be used or disclosed only for purposes related to the prevention or detection of crime, the investigation of offences or the conduct of prosecutions by, or on behalf of, police or other law enforcement and prosecuting authorities inside and outside the United Kingdom or the enforcement of any sentence or order made by a court when dealing with an offence. After being so used or disclosed, they may be retained but can only be used or disclosed for the same purposes. see *Note 5B*.

5.13 The officer proposing to take a detainee's photograph may, for this purpose, require the person to remove any item or substance worn on, or over, all, or any part of, their head or face. If they do not comply with such a requirement, the officer may remove the item or substance.

5.14 If it is established the detainee is unwilling to co-operate sufficiently to enable a suitable photograph to be taken and it is not reasonably practicable to take the photograph covertly, an officer may use reasonable force, see *Note 5F*.

(a) to take their photograph without their consent; and

(b) for the purpose of taking the photograph, remove any item or substance worn on, or over, all, or any part of, the person's head or face which they have failed to remove when asked.

5.15 For the purposes of this Code, a photograph may be obtained without the person's consent by making a copy of an image of them taken at any time on a camera system installed anywhere in the police station.

(c) Information to be given

5.16 When a person is searched, examined or photographed under the provisions as in *paragraph 5.1* and *5.12*, or their photograph obtained as in *paragraph 5.15*, they must be informed of the:

(a) purpose of the search, examination or photograph;

(b) grounds on which the relevant authority, if applicable, has been given; and

(c) purposes for which the photograph may be used, disclosed or retained.

This information must be given before the search or examination commences or the photograph is taken, except if the photograph is:

(i) to be taken covertly;

(ii) obtained as in *paragraph 5.15*, in which case the person must be informed as soon as practicable after the photograph is taken or obtained.

(d) Documentation

5.17 A record must be made when a detainee is searched, examined, or a photograph of the person, or any identifying marks found on them, are taken. The record must include the:

(a) identity, subject to paragraph 2.18, of the officer carrying out the search, examination or taking the photograph;

(b) purpose of the search, examination or photograph and the outcome;

(c) detainee's consent to the search, examination or photograph, or the reason the person was searched, examined or photographed without consent;

(d) giving of any authority as in *paragraphs 5.2* and *5.3*, the grounds for giving it and the authorising officer.

5.18 If force is used when searching, examining or taking a photograph in accordance with this section, a record shall be made of the circumstances and those present.

(B) Persons at police stations not detained

5.19 When there are reasonable grounds for suspecting the involvement of a person in a criminal offence, but that person is at a police station **voluntarily** and not detained, the provisions of *paragraphs 5.1* to *5.18* should apply, subject to the modifications in the following paragraphs.

5.20 References to the 'person being detained' and to the powers mentioned in *paragraph 5.1* which apply only to detainees at police stations shall be omitted.

5.21 Force may not be used to:

(a) search and/or examine the person to:

(i) discover whether they have any marks that would tend to identify them as a person involved in the commission of an offence; or

(ii) establish their identity, see *Note 5A*;

(b) take photographs of any identifying marks, see *paragraph 5.4*; or

(c) take a photograph of the person.

5.22 Subject to *paragraph 5.24*, the photographs of persons or of their identifying marks which are not taken in accordance with the provisions mentioned in *paragraphs 5.1* or *5.12*, must be destroyed (together with any negatives and copies) unless the person:

(a) is charged with, or informed they may be prosecuted for, a recordable offence;

(b) is prosecuted for a recordable offence;

(c) is cautioned for a recordable offence or given a warning or reprimand in accordance with the Crime and Disorder Act 1998 for a recordable offence; or

(d) gives informed consent, in writing, for the photograph or image to be retained as in *paragraph 5.6*.

5.23　When *paragraph 5.22* requires the destruction of any photograph, the person must be given an opportunity to witness the destruction or to have a certificate confirming the destruction provided they so request the certificate within five days of being informed the destruction is required.

5.24　Nothing in *paragraph 5.22* affects any separate requirement under the Criminal Procedure and Investigations Act 1996 to retain material in connection with criminal investigations.

Notes for guidance

5A　*The conditions under which fingerprints may be taken to assist in establishing a person's identity, are described in Section 4.*

5B　*Examples of purposes related to the prevention or detection of crime, the investigation of offences or the conduct of prosecutions include:*

(a)　*checking the photograph against other photographs held in records or in connection with, or as a result of, an investigation of an offence to establish whether the person is liable to arrest for other offences;*

(b)　*when the person is arrested at the same time as other people, or at a time when it is likely that other people will be arrested, using the photograph to help establish who was arrested, at what time and where;*

(c)　*when the real identity of the person is not known and cannot be readily ascertained or there are reasonable grounds for doubting a name and other personal details given by the person, are their real name and personal details. In these circumstances, using or disclosing the photograph to help to establish or verify their real identity or determine whether they are liable to arrest for some other offence, e.g. by checking it against other photographs held in records or in connection with, or as a result of, an investigation of an offence;*

(d)　*when it appears any identification procedure in section 3 may need to be arranged for which the person's photograph would assist;*

(e)　*when the person's release without charge may be required, and if the release is:*

(i)　*on bail to appear at a police station, using the photograph to help verify the person's identity when they answer their bail and if the person does not answer their bail, to assist in arresting them; or*

(ii)　*without bail, using the photograph to help verify their identity or assist in locating them for the purposes of serving them with a summons to appear at court in criminal proceedings;*

(f)　*when the person has answered to bail at a police station and there are reasonable grounds for doubting they are the person who was previously granted bail, using the photograph to help establish or verify their identity;*

(g)　*when the person arrested on a warrant claims to be a different person from the person named on the warrant and a photograph would help to confirm or disprove their claim;*

(h)　*when the person has been charged with, reported for, or convicted of, a recordable offence and their photograph is not already on record as a result of (a) to (f) or their photograph is on record but their appearance has changed since it was taken and the person has not yet been released or brought before a court.*

5C　*There is no power to arrest a person convicted of a recordable offence solely to take their photograph. The power to take photographs in this section applies only where the person is in custody as a result of the exercise of another power, e.g. arrest for fingerprinting under PACE, section 27.*

5D　*Examples of when it would not be practicable to obtain a detainee's consent, see paragraph 2.12, to a search, examination or the taking of a photograph of an identifying mark include:*

(a)　*when the person is drunk or otherwise unfit to give consent;*

(b)　*when there are reasonable grounds to suspect that if the person became aware a search or examination was to take place or an identifying mark was to be photographed, they would take steps to prevent this happening, e.g. by violently resisting, covering or concealing the mark etc and it would not otherwise be possible to carry out the search or examination or to photograph any identifying mark;*

(c) in the case of a juvenile, if the parent or guardian cannot be contacted in sufficient time to allow the search or examination to be carried out or the photograph to be taken.

5E *Examples of when it would not be practicable to obtain the person's consent, see paragraph 2.12, to a photograph being taken include:*

(a) when the person is drunk or otherwise unfit to give consent;

(b) when there are reasonable grounds to suspect that if the person became aware a photograph, suitable to be used or disclosed for the use and disclosure described in paragraph 5.6, was to be taken, they would take steps to prevent it being taken, e.g. by violently resisting, covering or distorting their face etc, and it would not otherwise be possible to take a suitable photograph;

(c) when, in order to obtain a suitable photograph, it is necessary to take it covertly; and

(d) in the case of a juvenile, if the parent or guardian cannot be contacted in sufficient time to allow the photograph to be taken.

5F *The use of reasonable force to take the photograph of a suspect elsewhere than at a police station must be carefully considered. In order to obtain a suspect's consent and co-operation to remove an item of religious headwear to take their photograph, a constable should consider whether in the circumstances of the situation the removal of the headwear and the taking of the photograph should be by an officer of the same sex as the person. It would be appropriate for these actions to be conducted out of public view.*

6 Identification by body samples and impressions

(A) General

6.1 References to:

(a) an 'intimate sample' mean a dental impression or sample of blood, semen or any other tissue fluid, urine, or pubic hair, or a swab taken from any part of a person's genitals or from a person's body orifice other than the mouth;

(b) a 'non-intimate sample' means:

(i) a sample of hair, other than pubic hair, which includes hair plucked with the root, see *Note 6A*;

(ii) a sample taken from a nail or from under a nail;

(iii) a swab taken from any part of a person's body other than a part from which a swab taken would be an intimate sample;

(iv) saliva;

(v) a skin impression which means any record, other than a fingerprint, which is a record, in any form and produced by any method, of the skin pattern and other physical characteristics or features of the whole, or any part of, a person's foot or of any other part of their body.

(B) Action

(a) Intimate samples

6.2 PACE, section 62, provides that intimate samples may be taken under:

(a) section 62(1), from a person in police detention only:

(i) if a police officer of inspector rank or above has reasonable grounds to believe such an impression or sample will tend to confirm or disprove the suspect's involvement in a recordable offence, see *Note 4A*, and gives authorisation for a sample to be taken; and

(ii) with the suspect's written consent;

(b) section 62(1A), from a person not in police detention but from whom two or more non-intimate samples have been taken in the course of an investigation of an offence and the samples, though suitable, have proved insufficient if:

(i) a police officer of inspector rank or above authorises it to be taken; and

(ii) the person concerned gives their written consent. See *Notes 6B* and *6C*

6.3 Before a suspect is asked to provide an intimate sample, they must be warned that if they refuse without good cause, their refusal may harm their case if it comes to trial, see *Note 6D*. If the suspect is in police detention and not legally represented, they must also be reminded of their entitlement to have free legal advice, see Code C, *paragraph 6.5*, and the reminder noted in the custody record. If *paragraph 6.2(b)* applies and the person is attending a station voluntarily, their entitlement to free legal advice as in Code C, *paragraph 3.21* shall be explained to them.

6.4 Dental impressions may only be taken by a registered dentist. Other intimate samples, except for samples of urine, may only be taken by a registered medical practitioner or registered nurse or registered paramedic.

(b) Non-intimate samples

6.5 A non-intimate sample may be taken from a detainee only with their written consent or if *paragraph 6.6* applies.

6.6 (a) under section 63, a non-intimate sample may not be taken from a person without consent and the consent must be in writing

(aa) A non-intimate sample may be taken from a person without the appropriate consent in the following circumstances:

(i) under section 63(2A) where the person is in police detention as a consequence of his arrest for a recordable offence and he has not had a non-intimate sample of the same type and from the same part of the body taken in the course of the investigation of the offence by the police or he has had such a sample taken but it proved insufficient.

(ii) Under section 63(3) (a) where he is being held in custody by the police on the authority of a court and an officer of at least the rank of Inspector authorises it to be taken.

(b) under section 63(3A), from a person charged with a recordable offence or informed they will be reported for such an offence: and

(i) that person has not had a non-intimate sample taken from them in the course of the investigation; or

(ii) if they have had a sample taken, it proved unsuitable or insufficient for the same form of analysis, see *Note 6B*; or

(c) under section 63(3B), from a person convicted of a recordable offence after the date on which that provision came into effect. PACE, section 63A, describes the circumstances in which a police officer may require a person convicted of a recordable offence to attend a police station for a non-intimate sample to be taken.

6.7 Reasonable force may be used, if necessary, to take a non-intimate sample from a person without their consent under the powers mentioned in *paragraph 6.6*.

6.8 Before any intimate sample is taken with consent or non-intimate sample is taken with, or without, consent, the person must be informed:

(a) of the reason for taking the sample;

(b) of the grounds on which the relevant authority has been given;

(c) that the sample or information derived from the sample may be retained and subject of a speculative search, see *Note 6E*, unless their destruction is required as in *Annex F*, Part A.

6.9 When clothing needs to be removed in circumstances likely to cause embarrassment to the person, no person of the opposite sex who is not a registered medical practitioner or registered health care professional shall be present, (unless in the case of a juvenile, mentally disordered or mentally vulnerable person, that person specifically requests the presence of an appropriate adult of the opposite sex who is readily available) nor shall anyone whose presence is unnecessary. However, in the case of a juvenile, this is subject to the overriding proviso that such a removal of clothing may take place in the absence of the appropriate adult only if the juvenile signifies, in their presence, that they prefer the adult's absence and they agree.

(c) Documentation

6.10 A record of the reasons for taking a sample or impression and, if applicable, of its destruction must be made as soon as practicable. If force is used, a record shall be made of the circumstances and those present. If written consent is given to the taking of a sample or impression, the fact must be recorded in writing.

6.11 A record must be made of a warning given as required by *paragraph 6.3.*

6.12 A record shall be made of the fact that a person has been informed as in *paragraph 6.8(c)* that samples may be subject of a speculative search.

Notes for guidance

6A *When hair samples are taken for the purpose of DNA analysis (rather than for other purposes such as making a visual match), the suspect should be permitted a reasonable choice as to what part of the body the hairs are taken from. When hairs are plucked, they should be plucked individually, unless the suspect prefers otherwise and no more should be plucked than the person taking them reasonably considers necessary for a sufficient sample.*

6B *(a) An insufficient sample is one which is not sufficient either in quantity or quality to provide information for a particular form of analysis, such as DNA analysis. A sample may also be insufficient if enough information cannot be obtained from it by analysis because of loss, destruction, damage or contamination of the sample or as a result of an earlier, unsuccessful attempt at analysis.*

(b) An unsuitable sample is one which, by its nature, is not suitable for a particular form of analysis.

6C *Nothing in paragraph 6.2 prevents intimate samples being taken for elimination purposes with the consent of the person concerned but the provisions of paragraph 2.12 relating to the role of the appropriate adult, should be applied. Paragraph 6.2(b) does not, however, apply where the non-intimate samples were previously taken under the Terrorism Act 2000, Schedule 8, paragraph 10.*

6D *In warning a person who is asked to provide an intimate sample as in paragraph 6.3, the following form of words may be used:*

> *"You do not have to provide this sample/allow this swab or impression to be taken, but I must warn you that if you refuse without good cause, your refusal may harm your case if it comes to trial."*

6E *Fingerprints or a DNA sample and the information derived from it taken from a person arrested on suspicion of being involved in a recordable offence, or charged with such an offence, or informed they will be reported for such an offence, may be subject of a speculative search. This means they may be checked against other fingerprints and DNA records held by, or on behalf of, the police and other law enforcement authorities in or outside the UK or held in connection with, or as a result of, an investigation of an offence inside or outside the UK. Fingerprints and samples taken from any other person, e.g. a person suspected of committing a recordable offence but who has not been arrested, charged or informed they will be reported for it, may be subject to a speculative search only if the person consents in writing to their fingerprints being subject of such a search. The following is an example of a basic form of words:*

> *"I consent to my fingerprints/DNA sample and information derived from it being retained and used only for purposes related to the prevention and detection of a crime, the investigation of an offence or the conduct of a prosecution either nationally or internationally.*
>
> *I understand that this sample may be checked against other fingerprint/DNA records held by or on behalf of relevant law enforcement authorities, either nationally or internationally.*
>
> *I understand that once I have given my consent for the sample to be retained and used I cannot withdraw this consent."*

See Annex F regarding the retention and use of fingerprints and samples taken with consent for elimination purposes.

6F *Samples of urine and non-intimate samples taken in accordance with sections 63B and 63C of PACE may not be used for identification purposes in accordance with this Code. See Code C note for guidance 17D.*

ANNEX A—VIDEO IDENTIFICATION

(a) General

1. The arrangements for obtaining and ensuring the availability of a suitable set of images to be used in a video identification must be the responsibility of an identification officer, who has no direct involvement with the case.

2. The set of images must include the suspect and at least eight other people who, so far as possible, resemble the suspect in age, general appearance and position in life. Only one suspect shall appear in any set unless there are two suspects of roughly similar appearance, in which case they may be shown together with at least twelve other people.

2A If the suspect has an unusual physical feature, e.g., a facial scar, tattoo or distinctive hairstyle or hair colour which does not appear on the images of the other people that are available to be used, steps may be taken to:

   (a) conceal the location of the feature on the images of the suspect and the other people; or

   (b) replicate that feature on the images of the other people.

   For these purposes, the feature may be concealed or replicated electronically or by any other method which it is practicable to use to ensure that the images of the suspect and other people resemble each other. The identification officer has discretion to choose whether to conceal or replicate the feature and the method to be used. If an unusual physical feature has been described by the witness, the identification officer should, if practicable, have that feature replicated. If it has not been described, concealment may be more appropriate.

2B If the identification officer decides that a feature should be concealed or replicated, the reason for the decision and whether the feature was concealed or replicated in the images shown to any witness shall be recorded.

2C If the witness requests to view an image where an unusual physical feature has been concealed or replicated without the feature being concealed or replicated, the witness may be allowed to do so.

3. The images used to conduct a video identification shall, as far as possible, show the suspect and other people in the same positions or carrying out the same sequence of movements. They shall also show the suspect and other people under identical conditions unless the identification officer reasonably believes:

   (a) because of the suspect's failure or refusal to co-operate or other reasons, it is not practicable for the conditions to be identical; and

   (b) any difference in the conditions would not direct a witness' attention to any individual image.

4. The reasons identical conditions are not practicable shall be recorded on forms provided for the purpose.

5. Provision must be made for each person shown to be identified by number.

6. If police officers are shown, any numerals or other identifying badges must be concealed. If a prison inmate is shown, either as a suspect or not, then either all, or none of, the people shown should be in prison clothing.

7. The suspect or their solicitor, friend, or appropriate adult must be given a reasonable opportunity to see the complete set of images before it is shown to any witness. If the suspect has a reasonable objection to the set of images or any of the participants, the suspect shall be asked to state the reasons for the objection. Steps shall, if practicable, be taken to remove the grounds for objection. If this is not practicable, the suspect and/or their representative shall be told why their objections cannot be met and the objection, the reason given for it and why it cannot be met shall be recorded on forms provided for the purpose.

8. Before the images are shown in accordance with *paragraph 7*, the suspect or their solicitor shall be provided with details of the first description of the suspect by any witnesses who are to attend the video identification. When a broadcast or publication is made, as in *paragraph 3.28*, the suspect or their solicitor must also be allowed to view any material released to the media by the police for the purpose of recognising or tracing the suspect, provided it is practicable and would not unreasonably delay the investigation.

9. The suspect's solicitor, if practicable, shall be given reasonable notification of the time and place the video identification is to be conducted so a representative may attend on behalf of the suspect. If a solicitor has not been instructed, this information shall be given to the suspect. The suspect may not be present when the images are shown to the witness(es). In the absence of the suspect's representative, the viewing itself shall be recorded on video. No unauthorised people may be present.

(b) Conducting the video identification

10. The identification officer is responsible for making the appropriate arrangements to make sure, before they see the set of images, witnesses are not able to communicate with each other about the case, see any of the images which are to be shown, see, or be reminded of, any photograph or description of the suspect or be given any other indication as to the suspect's identity, or overhear a witness who has already seen the material. There must be no discussion with the witness about the composition of the set of images and they must not be told whether a previous witness has made any identification.

11. Only one witness may see the set of images at a time. Immediately before the images are shown, the witness shall be told that the person they saw on a specified earlier occasion may, or may not, appear in the images they are shown and that if they cannot make a positive identification, they should say so. The witness shall be advised that at any point, they may ask to see a particular part of the set of images or to have a particular image frozen for them to study. Furthermore, it should be pointed out to the witness that there is no limit on how many times they can view the whole set of images or any part of them. However, they should be asked not to make any decision as to whether the person they saw is on the set of images until they have seen the whole set at least twice.

12. Once the witness has seen the whole set of images at least twice and has indicated that they do not want to view the images, or any part of them, again, the witness shall be asked to say whether the individual they saw in person on a specified earlier occasion has been shown and, if so, to identify them by number of the image. The witness will then be shown that image to confirm the identification, see *paragraph 17*.

13. Care must be taken not to direct the witness' attention to any one individual image or give any indication of the suspect's identity. Where a witness has previously made an identification by photographs, or a computerised or artist's composite or similar likeness, the witness must not be reminded of such a photograph or composite likeness once a suspect is available for identification by other means in accordance with this Code. Nor must the witness be reminded of any description of the suspect.

14. After the procedure, each witness shall be asked whether they have seen any broadcast or published films or photographs, or any descriptions of suspects relating to the offence and their reply shall be recorded.

(c) Image security and destruction

15. Arrangements shall be made for all relevant material containing sets of images used for specific identification procedures to be kept securely and their movements accounted for. In particular, no-one involved in the investigation shall be permitted to view the material prior to it being shown to any witness.

16. As appropriate, *paragraph 3.30* or *3.31* applies to the destruction or retention of relevant sets of images.

(d) Documentation

17. A record must be made of all those participating in, or seeing, the set of images whose names are known to the police.

18. A record of the conduct of the video identification must be made on forms provided for the purpose. This shall include anything said by the witness about any identifications or the conduct of the procedure and any reasons it was not practicable to comply with any of the provisions of this Code governing the conduct of video identifications.

ANNEX B—IDENTIFICATION PARADES

(a) General

1. A suspect must be given a reasonable opportunity to have a solicitor or friend present, and the suspect shall be asked to indicate on a second copy of the notice whether or not they wish to do so.

2. An identification parade may take place either in a normal room or one equipped with a screen permitting witnesses to see members of the identification parade without being seen. The procedures for the composition and conduct of the identification parade are the same in both cases, subject to *paragraph 8* (except that an identification parade involving a screen may take place only when the suspect's solicitor, friend or appropriate adult is present or the identification parade is recorded on video).

3. Before the identification parade takes place, the suspect or their solicitor shall be provided with details of the first description of the suspect by any witnesses who are attending the identification parade. When a broadcast or publication is made as in *paragraph 3.28*, the suspect or their solicitor should also be allowed to view any material released to the media by the police for the purpose of recognising or tracing the suspect, provided it is practicable to do so and would not unreasonably delay the investigation.

(b) Identification parades involving prison inmates

4. If a prison inmate is required for identification, and there are no security problems about the person leaving the establishment, they may be asked to participate in an identification parade or video identification.

5. An identification parade may be held in a Prison Department establishment but shall be conducted, as far as practicable under normal identification parade rules. Members of the public shall make up the identification parade unless there are serious security, or control, objections to their admission to the establishment. In such cases, or if a group or video identification is arranged within the establishment, other inmates may participate. If an inmate is the suspect, they are not required to wear prison clothing for the identification parade unless the other people taking part are other inmates in similar clothing, or are members of the public who are prepared to wear prison clothing for the occasion.

(c) Conduct of the identification parade

6. Immediately before the identification parade, the suspect must be reminded of the procedures governing its conduct and cautioned in the terms of Code C, paragraphs 10.5 or 10.6, as appropriate.

7. All unauthorised people must be excluded from the place where the identification parade is held.

8. Once the identification parade has been formed, everything afterwards, in respect of it, shall take place in the presence and hearing of the suspect and any interpreter, solicitor, friend or appropriate adult who is present (unless the identification parade involves a screen, in which case everything said to, or by, any witness at the place where the identification parade is held, must be said in the hearing and presence of the suspect's solicitor, friend or appropriate adult or be recorded on video).

9. The identification parade shall consist of at least eight people (in addition to the suspect) who, so far as possible, resemble the suspect in age, height, general appearance and position in life. Only one suspect shall be included in an identification parade unless there are two suspects of roughly similar appearance, in which case they may be paraded together with at least twelve other people. In no circumstances shall more than two suspects be included in one identification parade and where there are separate identification parades, they shall be made up of different people.

10. If the suspect has an unusual physical feature, e.g., a facial scar, tattoo or distinctive hairstyle or hair colour which cannot be replicated on other members of the identification parade, steps may be taken to conceal the location of that feature on the suspect and the other members

of the identification parade if the suspect and their solicitor, or appropriate adult, agree. For example, by use of a plaster or a hat, so that all members of the identification parade resemble each other in general appearance.

11. When all members of a similar group are possible suspects, separate identification parades shall be held for each unless there are two suspects of similar appearance when they may appear on the same identification parade with at least twelve other members of the group who are not suspects. When police officers in uniform form an identification parade any numerals or other identifying badges shall be concealed.

12. When the suspect is brought to the place where the identification parade is to be held, they shall be asked if they have any objection to the arrangements for the identification parade or to any of the other participants in it and to state the reasons for the objection. The suspect may obtain advice from their solicitor or friend, if present, before the identification parade proceeds. If the suspect has a reasonable objection to the arrangements or any of the participants, steps shall, if practicable, be taken to remove the grounds for objection. When it is not practicable to do so, the suspect shall be told why their objections cannot be met and the objection, the reason given for it and why it cannot be met, shall be recorded on forms provided for the purpose.

13. The suspect may select their own position in the line, but may not otherwise interfere with the order of the people forming the line. When there is more than one witness, the suspect must be told, after each witness has left the room, that they can, if they wish, change position in the line. Each position in the line must be clearly numbered, whether by means of a number laid on the floor in front of each identification parade member or by other means.

14. Appropriate arrangements must be made to make sure, before witnesses attend the identification parade, they are not able to:
    (i) communicate with each other about the case or overhear a witness who has already seen the identification parade;
    (ii) see any member of the identification parade;
    (iii) see, or be reminded of, any photograph or description of the suspect or be given any other indication as to the suspect's identity; or
    (iv) see the suspect before or after the identification parade.

15. The person conducting a witness to an identification parade must not discuss with them the composition of the identification parade and, in particular, must not disclose whether a previous witness has made any identification.

16. Witnesses shall be brought in one at a time. Immediately before the witness inspects the identification parade, they shall be told the person they saw on a specified earlier occasion may, or may not, be present and if they cannot make a positive identification, they should say so. The witness must also be told they should not make any decision about whether the person they saw is on the identification parade until they have looked at each member at least twice.

17. When the officer or police staff (see paragraph 3.11) conducting the identification procedure is satisfied the witness has properly looked at each member of the identification parade, they shall ask the witness whether the person they saw on a specified earlier occasion is on the identification parade and, if so, to indicate the number of the person concerned, see *paragraph 28*.

18. If the witness wishes to hear any identification parade member speak, adopt any specified posture or move, they shall first be asked whether they can identify any person(s) on the identification parade on the basis of appearance only. When the request is to hear members of the identification parade speak, the witness shall be reminded that the participants in the identification parade have been chosen on the basis of physical appearance only. Members of the identification parade may then be asked to comply with the witness' request to hear them speak, see them move or adopt any specified posture.

19. If the witness requests that the person they have indicated remove anything used for the purposes of *paragraph 10* to conceal the location of an unusual physical feature, that person may be asked to remove it.

20. If the witness makes an identification after the identification parade has ended, the suspect and, if present, their solicitor, interpreter or friend shall be informed. When this occurs, consideration should be given to allowing the witness a second opportunity to identify the suspect.

21. After the procedure, each witness shall be asked whether they have seen any broadcast or published films or photographs or any descriptions of suspects relating to the offence and their reply shall be recorded.

22. When the last witness has left, the suspect shall be asked whether they wish to make any comments on the conduct of the identification parade.

(d) Documentation

23. A video recording must normally be taken of the identification parade. If that is impracticable, a colour photograph must be taken. A copy of the video recording or photograph shall be supplied, on request, to the suspect or their solicitor within a reasonable time.

24. As appropriate, *paragraph 3.30* or *3.31*, should apply to any photograph or video taken as in *paragraph 23*.

25. If any person is asked to leave an identification parade because they are interfering with its conduct, the circumstances shall be recorded.

26. A record must be made of all those present at an identification parade whose names are known to the police.

27. If prison inmates make up an identification parade, the circumstances must be recorded.

28. A record of the conduct of any identification parade must be made on forms provided for the purpose. This shall include anything said by the witness or the suspect about any identifications or the conduct of the procedure, and any reasons it was not practicable to comply with any of this Code's provisions.

ANNEX C—GROUP IDENTIFICATION

(a) General

1. The purpose of this Annex is to make sure, as far as possible, group identifications follow the principles and procedures for identification parades so the conditions are fair to the suspect in the way they test the witness' ability to make an identification.

2. Group identifications may take place either with the suspect's consent and cooperation or covertly without their consent.

3. The location of the group identification is a matter for the identification officer, although the officer may take into account any representations made by the suspect, appropriate adult, their solicitor or friend.

4. The place where the group identification is held should be one where other people are either passing by or waiting around informally, in groups such that the suspect is able to join them and be capable of being seen by the witness at the same time as others in the group. For example people leaving an escalator, pedestrians walking through a shopping centre, passengers on railway and bus stations, waiting in queues or groups or where people are standing or sitting in groups in other public places.

5. If the group identification is to be held covertly, the choice of locations will be limited by the places where the suspect can be found and the number of other people present at that time. In these cases, suitable locations might be along regular routes travelled by the suspect, including buses or trains or public places frequented by the suspect.

6. Although the number, age, sex, race and general description and style of clothing of other people present at the location cannot be controlled by the identification officer, in selecting the location the officer must consider the general appearance and numbers of people likely to be present. In particular, the officer must reasonably expect that over the period the witness observes the group, they will be able to see, from time to time, a number of others whose appearance is broadly similar to that of the suspect.

7. A group identification need not be held if the identification officer believes, because of the unusual appearance of the suspect, none of the locations it would be practicable to use satisfy the requirements of *paragraph 6* necessary to make the identification fair.

8. Immediately after a group identification procedure has taken place (with or without the suspect's consent), a colour photograph or video should be taken of the general scene, if practicable, to give a general impression of the scene and the number of people present. Alternatively, if it is practicable, the group identification may be video recorded.

9. If it is not practicable to take the photograph or video in accordance with *paragraph 8*, a photograph or film of the scene should be taken later at a time determined by the identification officer if the officer considers it practicable to do so.

10. An identification carried out in accordance with this Code remains a group identification even though, at the time of being seen by the witness, the suspect was on their own rather than in a group.

11. Before the group identification takes place, the suspect or their solicitor shall be provided with details of the first description of the suspect by any witnesses who are to attend the identification. When a broadcast or publication is made, as in *paragraph 3.28*, the suspect or their solicitor should also be allowed to view any material released by the police to the media for the purposes of recognising or tracing the suspect, provided that it is practicable and would not unreasonably delay the investigation.

12. After the procedure, each witness shall be asked whether they have seen any broadcast or published films or photographs or any descriptions of suspects relating to the offence and their reply recorded.

(b) Identification with the consent of the suspect

13. A suspect must be given a reasonable opportunity to have a solicitor or friend present. They shall be asked to indicate on a second copy of the notice whether or not they wish to do so.

14. The witness, the person carrying out the procedure and the suspect's solicitor, appropriate adult, friend or any interpreter for the witness, may be concealed from the sight of the individuals in the group they are observing, if the person carrying out the procedure considers this assists the conduct of the identification.

15. The person conducting a witness to a group identification must not discuss with them the forthcoming group identification and, in particular, must not disclose whether a previous witness has made any identification.

16. Anything said to, or by, the witness during the procedure about the identification should be said in the presence and hearing of those present at the procedure.

17. Appropriate arrangements must be made to make sure, before witnesses attend the group identification, they are not able to:
    (i) communicate with each other about the case or overhear a witness who has already been given an opportunity to see the suspect in the group;
    (ii) see the suspect; or
    (iii) see, or be reminded of, any photographs or description of the suspect or be given any other indication of the suspect's identity.

18. Witnesses shall be brought one at a time to the place where they are to observe the group. Immediately before the witness is asked to look at the group, the person conducting the procedure shall tell them that the person they saw may, or may not, be in the group and that if they cannot make a positive identification, they should say so. The witness shall be asked to observe the group in which the suspect is to appear. The way in which the witness should do this will depend on whether the group is moving or stationary.

Moving group

19. When the group in which the suspect is to appear is moving, e.g. leaving an escalator, the provisions of *paragraphs 20* to *24* should be followed.

20. If two or more suspects consent to a group identification, each should be the subject of separate identification procedures. These may be conducted consecutively on the same occasion.

21. The person conducting the procedure shall tell the witness to observe the group and ask them to point out any person they think they saw on the specified earlier occasion.

22. Once the witness has been informed as in *paragraph 21* the suspect should be allowed to take whatever position in the group they wish.

23. When the witness points out a person as in *paragraph 21* they shall, if practicable, be asked to take a closer look at the person to confirm the identification. If this is not practicable, or they cannot confirm the identification, they shall be asked how sure they are that the person they have indicated is the relevant person.

24. The witness should continue to observe the group for the period which the person conducting the procedure reasonably believes is necessary in the circumstances for them to be able to make comparisons between the suspect and other individuals of broadly similar appearance to the suspect as in *paragraph 6.*

Stationary groups

25. When the group in which the suspect is to appear is stationary, e.g. people waiting in a queue, the provisions of *paragraphs 26* to *29* should be followed.

26. If two or more suspects consent to a group identification, each should be subject to separate identification procedures unless they are of broadly similar appearance when they may appear in the same group. When separate group identifications are held, the groups must be made up of different people.

27. The suspect may take whatever position in the group they wish. If there is more than one witness, the suspect must be told, out of the sight and hearing of any witness, that they can, if they wish, change their position in the group.

28. The witness shall be asked to pass along, or amongst, the group and to look at each person in the group at least twice, taking as much care and time as possible according to the circumstances, before making an identification. Once the witness has done this, they shall be asked whether the person they saw on the specified earlier occasion is in the group and to indicate any such person by whatever means the person conducting the procedure considers appropriate in the circumstances. If this is not practicable, the witness shall be asked to point out any person they think they saw on the earlier occasion.

29. When the witness makes an indication as in *paragraph 28,* arrangements shall be made, if practicable, for the witness to take a closer look at the person to confirm the identification. If this is not practicable, or the witness is unable to confirm the identification, they shall be asked how sure they are that the person they have indicated is the relevant person.

All cases

30. If the suspect unreasonably delays joining the group, or having joined the group, deliberately conceals themselves from the sight of the witness, this may be treated as a refusal to co-operate in a group identification.

31. If the witness identifies a person other than the suspect, that person should be informed what has happened and asked if they are prepared to give their name and address. There is no obligation upon any member of the public to give these details. There shall be no duty to record any details of any other member of the public present in the group or at the place where the procedure is conducted.

32. When the group identification has been completed, the suspect shall be asked whether they wish to make any comments on the conduct of the procedure.

33. If the suspect has not been previously informed, they shall be told of any identifications made by the witnesses.

(c) Identification without the suspect's consent

34. Group identifications held covertly without the suspect's consent should, as far as practicable, follow the rules for conduct of group identification by consent.

35. A suspect has no right to have a solicitor, appropriate adult or friend present as the identification will take place without the knowledge of the suspect.

36. Any number of suspects may be identified at the same time.

(d) Identifications in police stations

37. Group identifications should only take place in police stations for reasons of safety, security or because it is not practicable to hold them elsewhere.
38. The group identification may take place either in a room equipped with a screen permitting witnesses to see members of the group without being seen, or anywhere else in the police station that the identification officer considers appropriate.
39. Any of the additional safeguards applicable to identification parades should be followed if the identification officer considers it is practicable to do so in the circumstances.

(e) Identifications involving prison inmates

40. A group identification involving a prison inmate may only be arranged in the prison or at a police station.
41. When a group identification takes place involving a prison inmate, whether in a prison or in a police station, the arrangements should follow those in *paragraphs 37* to *39*.If a group identification takes place within a prison, other inmates may participate. If an inmate is the suspect, they do not have to wear prison clothing for the group identification unless the other participants are wearing the same clothing.

(f) Documentation

42. When a photograph or video is taken as in *paragraph 8 or 9,* a copy of the photograph or video shall be supplied on request to the suspect or their solicitor within a reasonable time.
43. *Paragraph 3.30* or *3.31*, as appropriate, shall apply when the photograph or film taken in accordance with *paragraph 8* or *9* includes the suspect.
44. A record of the conduct of any group identification must be made on forms provided for the purpose. This shall include anything said by the witness or suspect about any identifications or the conduct of the procedure and any reasons why it was not practicable to comply with any of the provisions of this Code governing the conduct of group identifications.

ANNEX D—CONFRONTATION BY A WITNESS

1. Before the confrontation takes place, the witness must be told that the person they saw may, or may not, be the person they are to confront and that if they are not that person, then the witness should say so.
2. Before the confrontation takes place the suspect or their solicitor shall be provided with details of the first description of the suspect given by any witness who is to attend. When a broadcast or publication is made, as in *paragraph 3.28*, the suspect or their solicitor should also be allowed to view any material released to the media for the purposes of recognising or tracing the suspect, provided it is practicable to do so and would not unreasonably delay the investigation.
3. Force may not be used to make the suspect's face visible to the witness.
4. Confrontation must take place in the presence of the suspect's solicitor, interpreter or friend unless this would cause unreasonable delay.
5. The suspect shall be confronted independently by each witness, who shall be asked "Is this the person?". If the witness identifies the person but is unable to confirm the identification, they shall be asked how sure they are that the person is the one they saw on the earlier occasion.
6. The confrontation should normally take place in the police station, either in a normal room or one equipped with a screen permitting a witness to see the suspect without being seen. In both cases, the procedures are the same except that a room equipped with a screen may be used only when the suspect's solicitor, friend or appropriate adult is present or the confrontation is recorded on video.

7. After the procedure, each witness shall be asked whether they have seen any broadcast or published films or photographs or any descriptions of suspects relating to the offence and their reply shall be recorded.

ANNEX E—SHOWING PHOTOGRAPHS

(a) Action

1. An officer of sergeant rank or above shall be responsible for supervising and directing the showing of photographs. The actual showing may be done by another officer or police staff, see *paragraph 3.11*.

2. The supervising officer must confirm the first description of the suspect given by the witness has been recorded before they are shown the photographs. If the supervising officer is unable to confirm the description has been recorded they shall postpone showing the photographs.

3. Only one witness shall be shown photographs at any one time. Each witness shall be given as much privacy as practicable and shall not be allowed to communicate with any other witness in the case.

4. The witness shall be shown not less than twelve photographs at a time, which shall, as far as possible, all be of a similar type.

5. When the witness is shown the photographs, they shall be told the photograph of the person they saw may, or may not, be amongst them and if they cannot make a positive identification, they should say so. The witness shall also be told they should not make a decision until they have viewed at least twelve photographs. The witness shall not be prompted or guided in any way but shall be left to make any selection without help.

6. If a witness makes a positive identification from photographs, unless the person identified is otherwise eliminated from enquiries or is not available, other witnesses shall not be shown photographs. But both they, and the witness who has made the identification, shall be asked to attend a video identification, an identification parade or group identification unless there is no dispute about the suspect's identification.

7. If the witness makes a selection but is unable to confirm the identification, the person showing the photographs shall ask them how sure they are that the photograph they have indicated is the person they saw on the specified earlier occasion.

8. When the use of a computerised or artist's composite or similar likeness has led to there being a known suspect who can be asked to participate in a video identification, appear on an identification parade or participate in a group identification, that likeness shall not be shown to other potential witnesses.

9. When a witness attending a video identification, an identification parade or group identification has previously been shown photographs or computerised or artist's composite or similar likeness (and it is the responsibility of the officer in charge of the investigation to make the identification officer aware that this is the case), the suspect and their solicitor must be informed of this fact before the identification procedure takes place.

10. None of the photographs shown shall be destroyed, whether or not an identification is made, since they may be required for production in court. The photographs shall be numbered and a separate photograph taken of the frame or part of the album from which the witness made an identification as an aid to reconstituting it.

(b) Documentation

11. Whether or not an identification is made, a record shall be kept of the showing of photographs on forms provided for the purpose. This shall include anything said by the witness about any identification or the conduct of the procedure, any reasons it was not practicable to comply with any of the provisions of this Code governing the showing of photographs and the name and rank of the supervising officer.

12. The supervising officer shall inspect and sign the record as soon as practicable.

ANNEX F—FINGERPRINTS, FOOTWEAR IMPRESSIONS AND SAMPLES—DESTRUCTION AND SPECULATIVE SEARCHES

(a) Fingerprints, footwear impressions and samples taken in connection with a criminal investigation

1. When fingerprints, footwear impressions or DNA samples are taken from a person in connection with an investigation and the person is not suspected of having committed the offence, see *Note F1*, they must be destroyed as soon as they have fulfilled the purpose for which they were taken unless:

   (a) they were taken for the purposes of an investigation of an offence for which a person has been convicted; and

   (b) fingerprints, footwear impressions or samples were also taken from the convicted person for the purposes of that investigation.

   However, subject to *paragraph 2*, the fingerprints, footwear impressions and samples, and the information derived from samples, may not be used in the investigation of any offence or in evidence against the person who is, or would be, entitled to the destruction of the fingerprints, footwear impressions and samples, see *Note F2*.

2. The requirement to destroy fingerprints, footwear impressions and DNA samples, and information derived from samples, and restrictions on their retention and use in paragraph 1 do not apply if the person gives their written consent for their fingerprints, footwear impressions or sample to be retained and used after they have fulfilled the purpose for which they were taken, see *Note F1*.

3. When a person's fingerprints, footwear impressions or sample are to be destroyed:

   (a) any copies of the fingerprints and footwear impressions must also be destroyed;

   (b) the person may witness the destruction of their fingerprints, footwear impressions or copies if they ask to do so within five days of being informed destruction is required;

   (c) access to relevant computer fingerprint data shall be made impossible as soon as it is practicable to do so and the person shall be given a certificate to this effect within three months of asking; and

   (d) neither the fingerprints, footwear impressions, the sample, or any information derived from the sample, may be used in the investigation of any offence or in evidence against the person who is, or would be, entitled to its destruction.

4. Fingerprints, footwear impressions or samples, and the information derived from samples, taken in connection with the investigation of an offence which are not required to be destroyed, may be retained after they have fulfilled the purposes for which they were taken but may be used only for purposes related to the prevention or detection of crime, the investigation of an offence or the conduct of a prosecution in, as well as outside, the UK and may also be subject to a speculative search. This includes checking them against other fingerprints, footwear impressions and DNA records held by, or on behalf of, the police and other law enforcement authorities in, as well as outside, the UK.

(b) Fingerprints taken in connection with Immigration Service enquiries

5. Fingerprints taken for Immigration Service enquiries in accordance with powers and procedures other than under PACE and for which the Immigration Service, not the police, are responsible, must be destroyed as follows:

   (a) fingerprints and all copies must be destroyed as soon as practicable if the person from whom they were taken proves they are a British or Commonwealth citizen who has the right of abode in the UK under the Immigration Act 1971, section 2(1)(b);

   (b) fingerprints taken under the power as in *paragraph 4.11(g)* from a dependant of a person in *4.11 (b)* to *(f)* must be destroyed when that person's fingerprints are to be destroyed;

   (c) fingerprints taken from a person under any power as in *paragraph 4.11* or with the person's consent which have not already been destroyed as above, must be destroyed within ten years of being taken or within such period specified by the Secretary of State under the Immigration and Asylum Act 1999, section 143(5).

Notes for guidance

F1 *Fingerprints, footwear impressions and samples given voluntarily for the purposes of elimination play an important part in many police investigations. It is, therefore, important to make sure innocent volunteers are not deterred from participating and their consent to their fingerprints, footwear impressions and DNA being used for the purposes of a specific investigation is fully informed and voluntary. If the police or volunteer seek to have the fingerprints, footwear impressions or samples retained for use after the specific investigation ends, it is important the volunteer's consent to this is also fully informed and voluntary.*

Examples of consent for:

- *DNA/fingerprints/footwear impressions - to be used only for the purposes of a specific investigation;*
- *DNA/fingerprints/footwear impressions - to be used in the specific investigation **and**retained by the police for future use.*

*To minimise the risk of confusion, each consent should be physically separate and the volunteer should be asked to sign **each consent**.*

(a) DNA:

(i) DNA sample taken for the purposes of elimination or as part of an intelligence-led screening and to be used only for the purposes of that investigation and destroyed afterwards:

"I consent to my DNA/mouth swab being taken for forensic analysis. I understand that the sample will be destroyed at the end of the case and that my profile will only be compared to the crime stain profile from this enquiry. I have been advised that the person taking the sample may be required to give evidence and/or provide a written statement to the police in relation to the taking of it"

(ii) DNA sample to be retained on the National DNA database and used in the future:

"I consent to my DNA sample and information derived from it being retained and used only for purposes related to the prevention and detection of a crime, the investigation of an offence or the conduct of a prosecution either nationally or internationally."

"I understand that this sample may be checked against other DNA records held by, or on behalf of, relevant law enforcement authorities, either nationally or internationally".

"I understand that once I have given my consent for the sample to be retained and used I cannot withdraw this consent."

(b) Fingerprints:

(i) Fingerprints taken for the purposes of elimination or as part of an intelligence-led screening and to be used only for the purposes of that investigation and destroyed afterwards:

"I consent to my fingerprints being taken for elimination purposes. I understand that the fingerprints will be destroyed at the end of the case and that my fingerprints will only be compared to the fingerprints from this enquiry. I have been advised that the person taking the fingerprints may be required to give evidence and/or provide a written statement to the police in relation to the taking of it."

(ii) Fingerprints to be retained for future use:

"I consent to my fingerprints being retained and used only for purposes related to the prevention and detection of a crime, the investigation of an offence or the conduct of a prosecution either nationally or internationally".

"I understand that my fingerprints may be checked against other records held by, or on behalf of, relevant law enforcement authorities, either nationally or internationally."

"I understand that once I have given my consent for my fingerprints to be retained and used I cannot withdraw this consent."

(c) *Footwear impressions:*

(i) *Footwear impressions taken for the purposes of elimination or as part of an intelligence-led screening and to be used only for the purposes of that investigation and destroyed afterwards:*

"I consent to my footwear impressions being taken for elimination purposes. I understand that the footwear impressions will be destroyed at the end of the case and that my footwear impressions will only be compared to the footwear impressions from this enquiry. I have been advised that the person taking the footwear impressions may be required to give evidence and/or provide a written statement to the police in relation to the taking of it."

(ii) *Footwear impressions to be retained for future use:*

"I consent to my footwear impressions being retained and used only for purposes related to the prevention and detection of a crime, the investigation of an offence or the conduct of a prosecution, either nationally or internationally".

"I understand that my footwear impressions may be checked against other records held by, or on behalf of, relevant law enforcement authorities, either nationally or internationally."

"I understand that once I have given my consent for my footwear impressions to be retained and used I cannot withdraw this consent."

F2 *The provisions for the retention of fingerprints, footwear impressions and samples in paragraph 1 allow for all fingerprints, footwear impressions and samples in a case to be available for any subsequent miscarriage of justice investigation.*

Appendix 2.3

PACE Code of Practice on Audio Recording Interviews with Suspects (Code E)

This code applies to interviews carried out after midnight on 31 December 2005, notwithstanding that the interview may have commenced before that time.

1 General

1.1 This Code of Practice must be readily available for consultation by:
- police officers
- police staff
- detained persons
- members of the public.

1.2 The *Notes for Guidance* included are not provisions of this Code.

1.3 Nothing in this Code shall detract from the requirements of Code C, the Code of Practice for the detention, treatment and questioning of persons by police officers.

1.4 This Code does not apply to those people listed in Code C, *paragraph 1.12*.

1.5 The term:
- 'appropriate adult' has the same meaning as in Code C, *paragraph 1.7*
- 'solicitor' has the same meaning as in Code C, *paragraph 6.12*.

1.6 In this Code:
- (a) 'recording media' means any removable, physical audio recording medium (such as magnetic type, optical disc or solid state memory) which can be played and copied.
- (b) 'designated person' means a person other than a police officer, designated under the Police Reform Act 2002, Part 4 who has specified powers and duties of police officers conferred or imposed on them;
- (c) any reference to a police officer includes a designated person acting in the exercise or performance of the powers and duties conferred or imposed on them by their designation.

1.7 If a power conferred on a designated person:
- (a) allows reasonable force to be used when exercised by a police officer, a designated person exercising that power has the same entitlement to use force;
- (b) includes power to use force to enter any premises, that power is not exercisable by that designated person except:
  - (i) in the company, and under the supervision, of a police officer; or
  - (ii) for the purpose of:
    - saving life or limb; or
    - preventing serious damage to property.

1.8 Nothing in this Code prevents the custody officer, or other officer given custody of the detainee, from allowing police staff who are not designated persons to carry out individual procedures or tasks at the police station if the law allows. However, the officer remains responsible for making sure the procedures and tasks are carried out correctly in accordance with these Codes. Any such police staff must be:

(a) a person employed by a police authority maintaining a police force and under the control and direction of the Chief Officer of that force; or

(b) employed by a person with whom a police authority has a contract for the provision of services relating to persons arrested or otherwise in custody.

1.9 Designated persons and other police staff must have regard to any relevant provisions of the Codes of Practice.

1.10 References to pocket book include any official report book issued to police officers or police staff.

1.11 References to a custody officer include those performing the functions of a custody officer as in *paragraph 1.9* of Code C.

2 Recording and sealing master recordings

2.1 Recording of interviews shall be carried out openly to instil confidence in its reliability as an impartial and accurate record of the interview.

2.2 One recording, the master recording, will be sealed in the suspect's presence. A second recording will be used as a working copy. The master recording is either of the two recordings used in a twin deck/drive machine or the only recording in a single deck/drive machine. The working copy is either the second/third recording used in a twin/triple deck/drive machine or a copy of the master recording made by a single deck/drive machine. See *Notes 2A* and *2B*

2.3 Nothing in this Code requires the identity of officers or police staff conducting interviews to be recorded or disclosed:

(a) in the case of enquiries linked to the investigation of terrorism; or

(b) if the interviewer reasonably believes recording or disclosing their name might put them in danger.

In these cases interviewers should use warrant or other identification numbers and the name of their police station. See Note 2C

Notes for guidance

2A *The purpose of sealing the master recording in the suspect's presence is to show the recording's integrity is preserved. If a single deck/drive machine is used the working copy of the master recording must be made in the suspect's presence and without the master recording leaving their sight. The working copy shall be used for making further copies if needed.*

2B *Not used.*

2C *The purpose of paragraph 2.3(b) is to protect those involved in serious organised crime investigations or arrests of particularly violent suspects when there is reliable information that those arrested or their associates may threaten or cause harm to those involved. In cases of doubt, an officer of inspector rank or above should be consulted.*

3 Interviews to be audio recorded

3.1 Subject to *paragraphs 3.3* and *3.4*, audio recording shall be used at police stations for any interview:

(a) with a person cautioned under Code C, *section 10* in respect of any indictable offence, including an offence triable either way; see *Note 3A*

(b) which takes place as a result of an interviewer exceptionally putting further questions to a suspect about an offence described in *paragraph 3.1(a)* after they have been charged with, or told they may be prosecuted for, that offence, see Code C, *paragraph 16.5*

(c) when an interviewer wants to tell a person, after they have been charged with, or informed they may be prosecuted for, an offence described in *paragraph 3.1(a)*, about any written statement or interview with another person, see Code C, *paragraph 16.4.*

3.2 The Terrorism Act 2000 makes separate provision for a Code of Practice for the audio recording of interviews of those arrested under Section 41 or detained under Schedule 7 of the Act. The provisions of this Code do not apply to such interviews.

3.3 The custody officer may authorise the interviewer not to audio record the interview when it is:

(a) not reasonably practicable because of equipment failure or the unavailability of a suitable interview room or recorder and the authorising officer considers, on reasonable grounds, that the interview should not be delayed; or

(b) clear from the outset there will not be a prosecution.

Note: In these cases the interview should be recorded in writing in accordance with Code C, *section 11*. In all cases the custody officer shall record the specific reasons for not audio recording. See *Note 3B*

3.4 If a person refuses to go into or remain in a suitable interview room, see Code C *paragraph 12.5*, and the custody officer considers, on reasonable grounds, that the interview should not be delayed the interview may, at the custody officer's discretion, be conducted in a cell using portable recording equipment or, if none is available, recorded in writing as in Code C, *section 11*. The reasons for this shall be recorded.

3.5 The whole of each interview shall be audio recorded, including the taking and reading back of any statement.

Notes for guidance

3A *Nothing in this Code is intended to preclude audio recording at police discretion of interviews at police stations with people cautioned in respect of offences not covered by paragraph 3.1, or responses made by persons after they have been charged with, or told they may be prosecuted for, an offence, provided this Code is complied with.*

3B *A decision not to audio record an interview for any reason may be the subject of comment in court. The authorising officer should be prepared to justify that decision.*

4 The interview

(a) General

4.1 The provisions of Code C: 4
- *sections 10 and 11*, and the applicable *Notes for Guidance* apply to the conduct of interviews to which this Code applies
- *paragraphs 11.7 to 11.14* apply only when a written record is needed.

4.2 Code C, *paragraphs 10.10, 10.11* and Annex C describe the restriction on drawing adverse inferences from a suspect's failure or refusal to say anything about their involvement in the offence when interviewed or after being charged or informed they may be prosecuted, and how it affects the terms of the caution and determines if and by whom a special warning under sections 36 and 37 can be given.

(b) Commencement of interviews

4.3 When the suspect is brought into the interview room the interviewer shall, without delay but in the suspect's sight, load the recorder with new recording media and set it to record. The recording media must be unwrapped or opened in the suspect's presence.

4.4 The interviewer should tell the suspect about the recording process. The interviewer shall:
(a) say the interview is being audibly recorded
(b) subject to *paragraph 2.3*, give their name and rank and that of any other interviewer present
(c) ask the suspect and any other party present, e.g. a solicitor, to identify themselves

(d) state the date, time of commencement and place of the interview

(e) state the suspect will be given a notice about what will happen to the copies of the re‑
cording.

See *Note 4A*

4.5 The interviewer shall:
- caution the suspect, see Code C, *section 10*
- remind the suspect of their entitlement to free legal advice, see Code C, *paragraph 11.2.*

4.6 The interviewer shall put to the suspect any significant statement or silence; see Code C, *para‑
graph 11.4.*

(c) Interviews with deaf persons

4.7 If the suspect is deaf or is suspected of having impaired hearing, the interviewer shall make a
written note of the interview in accordance with Code C, at the same time as audio recording
it in accordance with this Code. See *Notes 4B* and *4C*

(d) Objections and complaints by the suspect

4.8 If the suspect objects to the interview being audibly recorded at the outset, during the in‑
terview or during a break, the interviewer shall explain that the interview is being audibly
recorded and that this Code requires the suspect's objections to be recorded on the audio
recording. When any objections have been audibly recorded or the suspect has refused to
have their objections recorded, the interviewer shall say they are turning off the recorder,
give their reasons and turn it off. The interviewer shall then make a written record of the
interview as in Code C, *section 11*. If, however, the interviewer reasonably considers they
may proceed to question the suspect with the audio recording still on, the interviewer may
do so. This procedure also applies in cases where the suspect has previously objected to the
interview being visually recorded, see *Code F 4.8*, and the investigating officer has decided to
audibly record the interview. See *Note 4D*

4.9 If in the course of an interview a complaint is made by or on behalf of the person being
questioned concerning the provisions of this Code or Code C, the interviewer shall act as in
Code C, *paragraph 12.9*. See *Notes 4E* and *4F*

4.10 If the suspect indicates they want to tell the interviewer about matters not directly connected
with the offence and they are unwilling for these matters to be audio recorded, the suspect
should be given the opportunity to tell the interviewer at the end of the formal interview.

(e) Changing recording media

4.11 When the recorder shows the recording media only has a short time left, the interviewer
shall tell the suspect the recording media are coming to an end and round off that part of
the interview. If the interviewer leaves the room for a second set of recording media, the sus‑
pect shall not be left unattended. The interviewer will remove the recording media from the
recorder and insert the new recording media which shall be unwrapped or opened in the sus‑
pect's presence. The recorder should be set to record on the new media. To avoid confusion
between the recording media, the interviewer shall mark the media with an identification
number immediately after they are removed from the recorder.

(f) Taking a break during interview

4.12 When a break is taken, the fact that a break is to be taken, the reason for it and the time
shall be recorded on the audio recording.

4.12A When the break is taken and the interview room vacated by the suspect, the recording
media shall be removed from the recorder and the procedures for the conclusion of an
interview followed, see *paragraph 4.18.*

4.13 When a break is a short one and both the suspect and an interviewer remain in the inter‑
view room, the recording may be stopped. There is no need to remove the recording media

and when the interview recommences the recording should continue on the same recording media. The time the interview recommences shall be recorded on the audio recording.

4.14 After any break in the interview the interviewer must, before resuming the interview, remind the person being questioned that they remain under caution or, if there is any doubt, give the caution in full again. See *Note 4G*

(g) Failure of recording equipment

4.15 If there is an equipment failure which can be rectified quickly, e.g. by inserting new recording media, the interviewer shall follow the appropriate procedures as in *paragraph 4.11*. When the recording is resumed the interviewer shall explain what happened and record the time the interview recommences. If, however, it will not be possible to continue recording on that recorder and no replacement recorder is readily available, the interview may continue without being audibly recorded. If this happens, the interviewer shall seek the custody officer's authority as in *paragraph 3.3*. See *Note 4H*

(h) Removing recording media from the recorder

4.16 When recording media is removed from the recorder during the interview, they shall be retained and the procedures in *paragraph 4.18* followed.

(i) Conclusion of interview

4.17 At the conclusion of the interview, the suspect shall be offered the opportunity to clarify anything he or she has said and asked if there is anything they want to add.

4.18 At the conclusion of the interview, including the taking and reading back of any written statement, the time shall be recorded and the recording shall be stopped. The interviewer shall seal the master recording with a master recording label and treat it as an exhibit in accordance with force standing orders. The interviewer shall sign the label and ask the suspect and any third party present during the interview to sign it. If the suspect or third party refuse to sign the label an officer of at least inspector rank, or if not available the custody officer, shall be called into the interview room and asked, subject to *paragraph 2.3*, to sign it.

4.19 The suspect shall be handed a notice which explains:

- how the audio recording will be used
- the arrangements for access to it
- that if the person is charged or informed they will be prosecuted, a copy of the audio recording will be supplied as soon as practicable or as otherwise agreed between the suspect and the police.

Notes for guidance

4A For the purpose of voice identification the interviewer should ask the suspect and any other people present to identify themselves.

4B This provision is to give a person who is deaf or has impaired hearing equivalent rights of access to the full interview record as far as this is possible using audio recording.

4C The provisions of Code C, section 13 on interpreters for deaf persons or for interviews with suspects who have difficulty understanding English continue to apply. However, in an audibly recorded interview the requirement on the interviewer to make sure the interpreter makes a separate note of the interview applies only to paragraph 4.7 (interviews with deaf persons).

4D The interviewer should remember that a decision to continue recording against the wishes of the suspect may be the subject of comment in court.

4E If the custody officer is called to deal with the complaint, the recorder should, if possible, be left on until the custody officer has entered the room and spoken to the person being interviewed. Continuation or termination of the interview should be at the interviewer's discretion pending action by an inspector under Code C, paragraph 9.2.

4F If the complaint is about a matter not connected with this Code or Code C, the decision to continue is at the interviewer's discretion. When the interviewer decides to continue the interview, they shall tell the suspect the complaint will be brought to the custody officer's attention at the conclusion of the interview. When the interview is concluded the interviewer must, as soon as practicable, inform the custody officer about the existence and nature of the complaint made.

4G *The interviewer should remember that it may be necessary to show to the court that nothing occurred during a break or between interviews which influenced the suspect's recorded evidence. After a break or at the beginning of a subsequent interview, the interviewer should consider summarising on the record the reason for the break and confirming this with the suspect.*

4H *Where the interview is being recorded and the media or the recording equipment fails the officer conducting the interview should stop the interview immediately. Where part of the interview is unaffected by the error and is still accessible on the media, that media shall be copied and sealed in the suspect's presence and the interview recommenced using new equipment/media as required. Where the content of the interview has been lost in its entirety the media should be sealed in the suspect's presence and the interview begun again. If the recording equipment cannot be fixed or no replacement is immediately available the interview should be recorded in accordance with Code C, section 11.*

5 After the interview

5.1 The interviewer shall make a note in their pocket book that the interview has taken place, was audibly recorded, its time, duration and date and the master recording's identification number.

5.2 If no proceedings follow in respect of the person whose interview was recorded, the recording media must be kept securely as in *paragraph 6.1* and *Note 6A*.

Note for guidance

5A *Any written record of an audibly recorded interview should be made in accordance with national guidelines approved by the Secretary of State.*

6 Media security

6.1 The officer in charge of each police station at which interviews with suspects are recorded shall make arrangements for master recordings to be kept securely and their movements accounted for on the same basis as material which may be used for evidential purposes, in accordance with force standing orders. See *Note 6A*

6.2 A police officer has no authority to break the seal on a master recording required for criminal trial or appeal proceedings. If it is necessary to gain access to the master recording, the police officer shall arrange for its seal to be broken in the presence of a representative of the Crown Prosecution Service. The defendant or their legal adviser should be informed and given a reasonable opportunity to be present. If the defendant or their legal representative is present they shall be invited to reseal and sign the master recording. If either refuses or neither is present this should be done by the representative of the Crown Prosecution Service. See *Notes 6B* and *6C*

6.3 If no criminal proceedings result or the criminal trial and, if applicable, appeal proceedings to which the interview relates have been concluded, the chief officer of police is responsible for establishing arrangements for breaking the seal on the master recording, if necessary.

6.4 When the master recording seal is broken, a record must be made of the procedure followed, including the date, time, place and persons present.

Notes for guidance

6A *This section is concerned with the security of the master recording sealed at the conclusion of the interview. Care must be taken of working copies of recordings because their loss or destruction may lead to the need to access master recordings.*

6B *If the recording has been delivered to the crown court for their keeping after committal for trial the crown prosecutor will apply to the chief clerk of the crown court centre for the release of the recording for unsealing by the crown prosecutor.*

6C *Reference to the Crown Prosecution Service or to the crown prosecutor in this part of the Code should be taken to include any other body or person with a statutory responsibility for prosecution for whom the police conduct any audibly recorded interviews.*

Appendix 2.4

PACE Code of Practice on Visual Recording with Sound of Interviews with Suspects (Code F)

The contents of this code should be considered if an interviewing officer decides to make a visual recording with sound of an interview with a suspect after midnight on 31 December 2005.

There is no statutory requirement to visually record interviews

1 General

1.1 This code of practice must be readily available for consultation by police officers and other police staff, detained persons and members of the public.

1.2 The notes for guidance included are not provisions of this code. They form guidance to police officers and others about its application and interpretation.

1.3 Nothing in this code shall be taken as detracting in any way from the requirements of the Code of Practice for the Detention, Treatment and Questioning of Persons by Police Officers (Code C). [See Note 1A].

1.4 The interviews to which this Code applies are set out in paragraphs 3.1–3.3.

1.5 In this code, the term "appropriate adult", "solicitor" and "interview" have the same meaning as those set out in Code C. The corresponding provisions and Notes for Guidance in Code C applicable to those terms shall also apply where appropriate.

1.6 Any reference in this code to visual recording shall be taken to mean visual recording with sound.

1.7 References to "pocket book" in this Code include any official report book issued to police officers.

Note for Guidance

1A As in paragraph 1.9 of Code C, references to custody officers include those carrying out the functions of a custody officer.

2 Recording and sealing of master tapes

2.1 The visual recording of interviews shall be carried out openly to instil confidence in its reliability as an impartial and accurate record of the interview. [See *Note 2A*].

2.2 The camera(s) shall be placed in the interview room so as to ensure coverage of as much of the room as is practicably possible whilst the interviews are taking place.

2.3 The certified recording medium will be of a high quality, new and previously unused. When the certified recording medium is placed in the recorder and switched on to record, the correct date and time, in hours, minutes and seconds, will be superimposed automatically, second by second, during the whole recording. [See *Note 2B*].

2.4 One copy of the certified recording medium, referred to in this code as the master copy, will be sealed before it leaves the presence of the suspect. A second copy will be used as a working copy. [See *Note 2C and 2D*].

2.5 Nothing in this code requires the identity of an officer to be recorded or disclosed if:

(a) the interview or record relates to a person detained under the Terrorism Act 2000; or

(b) otherwise where the officer reasonably believes that recording or disclosing their name might put them in danger.

In these cases, the officer will have their back to the camera and shall use their warrant or other identification number and the name of the police station to which they are attached. Such instances and the reasons for them shall be recorded in the custody record. [See *Note 2E*]

Notes for Guidance

2A *Interviewing officers will wish to arrange that, as far as possible, visual recording arrangements are unobtrusive. It must be clear to the suspect, however, that there is no opportunity to interfere with the recording equipment or the recording media.*

2B *In this context, the certified recording media will be of either a VHS or digital CD format and should be capable of having an image of the date and time superimposed upon them as they record the interview.*

2C *The purpose of sealing the master copy before it leaves the presence of the suspect is to establish their confidence that the integrity of the copy is preserved.*

2D *The recording of the interview may be used for identification procedures in accordance with paragraph 3.21 or Annex E of Code D.*

2E *The purpose of the paragraph 2.5 is to protect police officers and others involved in the investigation of serious organised crime or the arrest of particularly violent suspects when there is reliable information that those arrested or their associates may threaten or cause harm to the officers, their families or their personal property.*

3 Interviews to be visually recorded

3.1 Subject to paragraph 3.2 below, if an interviewing officer decides to make a visual recording these are the areas where it might be appropriate:

(a) with a suspect in respect of an indictable offence (including an offence triable either way) [see *Notes 3A and 3B*];

(b) which takes place as a result of an interviewer exceptionally putting further questions to a suspect about an offence described in sub-paragraph (a) above after they have been charged with, or informed they may be prosecuted for, that offence [see *Note 3C*];

(c) in which an interviewer wishes to bring to the notice of a person, after that person has been charged with, or informed they may be prosecuted for an offence described in sub-paragraph (a) above, any written statement made by another person, or the content of an interview with another person [see *Note 3D*]

(d) with, or in the presence of, a deaf or deaf/blind or speech impaired person who uses sign language to communicate;

(e) with, or in the presence of anyone who requires an "appropriate adult"; or

(f) in any case where the suspect or their representative requests that the interview be recorded visually.

3.2 The Terrorism Act 2000 makes separate provision for a code of practice for the video recording of interviews in a police station of those detained under Schedule 7 or section 41 of the Act. The provisions of this code do not therefore apply to such interviews [see *Note 3E*].

3.3 The custody officer may authorise the interviewing officer not to record the interview visually:

(a) where it is not reasonably practicable to do so because of failure of the equipment, or the non-availability of a suitable interview room, or recorder, and the authorising officer considers on reasonable grounds that the interview should not be delayed until the failure has been rectified or a suitable room or recorder becomes available. In such cases the custody officer may authorise the interviewing officer to audio record the interview in accordance with the guidance set out in Code E;

(b) where it is clear from the outset that no prosecution will ensue; or

(c) where it is not practicable to do so because at the time the person resists being taken to a suitable interview room or other location which would enable the interview to be recorded, or otherwise fails or refuses to go into such a room or location, and the authorising officer considers on reasonable grounds that the interview should not be delayed until these conditions cease to apply.

3.4 When a person who is voluntarily attending the police station is required to be cautioned in accordance with Code C prior to being interviewed, the subsequent interview shall be recorded, unless the custody officer gives authority in accordance with the provisions of paragraph 3.3 above for the interview not to be so recorded.

3.5 The whole of each interview shall be recorded visually, including the taking and reading back of any statement.

3.6 A visible illuminated sign or indicator will light and remain on at all times when the recording equipment is activated or capable of recording or transmitting any signal or information

Notes for Guidance

3A Nothing in the code is intended to preclude visual recording at police discretion of interviews at police stations with people cautioned in respect of offences not covered by paragraph 3.1, or responses made by interviewees after they have been charged with, or informed they may be prosecuted for, an offence, provided that this code is complied with.

3B Attention is drawn to the provisions set out in Code C about the matters to be considered when deciding whether a detained person is fit to be interviewed.

3C Code C sets out the circumstances in which a suspect may be questioned about an offence after being charged with it.

3D Code C sets out the procedures to be followed when a person's attention is drawn after charge, to a statement made by another person. One method of bringing the content of an interview with another person to the notice of a suspect may be to play him a recording of that interview.

3E When it only becomes clear during the course of an interview which is being visually recorded that the interviewee may have committed an offence to which paragraph 3.2 applies, the interviewing officer should turn off the recording equipment and the interview should continue in accordance with the provisions of the Terrorism Act 2000.

3F A decision not to record an interview visually for any reason may be the subject of comment in court. The authorising officer should therefore be prepared to justify their decision in each case.

4 The Interview

(a) General

4.1 The provisions of Code C in relation to cautions and interviews and the Notes for Guidance applicable to those provisions shall apply to the conduct of interviews to which this Code applies.

4.2 Particular attention is drawn to those parts of Code C that describe the restrictions on drawing adverse inferences from a suspect's failure or refusal to say anything about their involvement in the offence when interviewed, or after being charged or informed they may be prosecuted and how those restrictions affect the terms of the caution and determine whether a special warning under Sections 36 and 37 of the Criminal Justice and Public Order Act 1994 can be given.

(b) Commencement of interviews

4.3   When the suspect is brought into the interview room the interviewer shall without delay, but in sight of the suspect, load the recording equipment and set it to record. The recording media must be unwrapped or otherwise opened in the presence of the suspect. [See *Note 4A*]

4.4   The interviewer shall then tell the suspect formally about the visual recording. The interviewer shall:

(a) explain the interview is being visually recorded;

(b) subject to paragraph 2.5, give his or her name and rank, and that of any other interviewer present;

(c) ask the suspect and any other party present (e.g. his solicitor) to identify themselves.

(d) state the date, time of commencement and place of the interview; and

(e) state that the suspect will be given a notice about what will happen to the recording.

4.5   The interviewer shall then caution the suspect, which should follow that set out in Code C, and remind the suspect of their entitlement to free and independent legal advice and that they can speak to a solicitor on the telephone.

4.6   The interviewer shall then put to the suspect any significant statement or silence (i.e. failure or refusal to answer a question or to answer it satisfactorily) which occurred before the start of the interview, and shall ask the suspect whether they wish to confirm or deny that earlier statement or silence or whether they wish to add anything. The definition of a "significant" statement or silence is the same as that set out in Code C.

(c) Interviews with the deaf

4.7   If the suspect is deaf or there is doubt about their hearing ability, the provisions of Code C on interpreters for the deaf or for interviews with suspects who have difficulty in understanding English continue to apply.

(d) Objections and complaints by the suspect

4.8   If the suspect raises objections to the interview being visually recorded either at the outset or during the interview or during a break in the interview, the interviewer shall explain the fact that the interview is being visually recorded and that the provisions of this code require that the suspect's objections shall be recorded on the visual recording. When any objections have been visually recorded or the suspect has refused to have their objections recorded, the interviewer shall say that they are turning off the recording equipment, give their reasons and turn it off. If a separate audio recording is being maintained, the officer shall ask the person to record the reasons for refusing to agree to visual recording of the interview. Paragraph 4.8 of Code E will apply if the person objects to audio recording of the interview. The officer shall then make a written record of the interview. If the interviewer reasonably considers they may proceed to question the suspect with the visual recording still on, the interviewer may do so. See *Note 4G*.

4.9   If in the course of an interview a complaint is made by the person being questioned, or on their behalf, concerning the provisions of this code or of Code C, then the interviewer shall act in accordance with Code C, record it in the interview record and inform the custody officer. [See *4B and 4C*].

4.10 If the suspect indicates that they wish to tell the interviewer about matters not directly connected with the offence of which they are suspected and that they are unwilling for these matters to be recorded, the suspect shall be given the opportunity to tell the interviewer about these matters after the conclusion of the formal interview.

(e) Changing the recording media

4.11 In instances where the recording medium is not of sufficient length to record all of the interview with the suspect, further certified recording medium will be used. When the recording equipment indicates that the recording medium has only a short time left to run, the interviewer shall advise the suspect and round off that part of the interview. If the interviewer wishes to continue the interview but does not already have further certified recording media with him, they shall obtain a set. The suspect should not be left unattended in the interview room. The interviewer will remove the recording media from the recording equipment and insert the new ones which have been unwrapped or otherwise opened in the suspect's presence. The recording equipment shall then be set to record. Care must be taken, particularly when a number of sets of recording media have been used, to ensure that there is no confusion between them. This could be achieved by marking the sets of recording media with consecutive identification numbers.

(f) Taking a break during the interview

4.12 When a break is to be taken during the course of an interview and the interview room is to be vacated by the suspect, the fact that a break is to be taken, the reason for it and the time shall be recorded. The recording equipment must be turned off and the recording media removed. The procedures for the conclusion of an interview set out in paragraph 4.19, below, should be followed.

4.13 When a break is to be a short one, and both the suspect and a police officer are to remain in the interview room, the fact that a break is to be taken, the reasons for it and the time shall be recorded on the recording media. The recording equipment may be turned off, but there is no need to remove the recording media. When the interview is recommenced the recording shall continue on the same recording media and the time at which the interview recommences shall be recorded.

4.14 When there is a break in questioning under caution, the interviewing officer must ensure that the person being questioned is aware that they remain under caution. If there is any doubt, the caution must be given again in full when the interview resumes. [See *Notes 4D and 4E*].

(g) Failure of recording equipment

4.15 If there is a failure of equipment which can be rectified quickly, the appropriate procedures set out in paragraph 4.12 shall be followed. When the recording is resumed the interviewer shall explain what has happened and record the time the interview recommences. If, however, it is not possible to continue recording on that particular recorder and no alternative equipment is readily available, the interview may continue without being recorded visually. In such circumstances, the procedures set out in paragraph 3.3 of this code for seeking the authority of the custody officer will be followed. [See *Note 4F*].

(h) Removing used recording media from recording equipment

4.16 Where used recording media are removed from the recording equipment during the course of an interview, they shall be retained and the procedures set out in paragraph 4.18 below followed.

(i) Conclusion of interview

4.17 Before the conclusion of the interview, the suspect shall be offered the opportunity to clarify anything he or she has said and asked if there is anything that they wish to add.

4.18 At the conclusion of the interview, including the taking and reading back of any written statement, the time shall be recorded and the recording equipment switched off. The master tape or CD shall be removed from the recording equipment, sealed with a master copy label and treated as an exhibit in accordance with the force standing orders. The interviewer shall sign the label and also ask the suspect and any appropriate adults or other third party present during the interview to sign it. If the suspect or third party refuses to sign the label, an officer of at least the rank of inspector, or if one is not available, the custody officer, shall be called into the interview room and asked to sign it.

4.19 The suspect shall be handed a notice which explains the use which will be made of the recording and the arrangements for access to it. The notice will also advise the suspect that a copy of the tape shall be supplied as soon as practicable if the person is charged or informed that he will be prosecuted.

Notes for Guidance

4A *The interviewer should attempt to estimate the likely length of the interview and ensure that an appropriate quantity of certified recording media and labels with which to seal the master copies are available in the interview room.*

4B *Where the custody officer is called immediately to deal with the complaint, wherever possible the recording equipment should be left to run until the custody officer has entered the interview room and spoken to the person being interviewed. Continuation or termination of the interview should be at the discretion of the interviewing officer pending action by an inspector as set out in Code C.*

4C *Where the complaint is about a matter not connected with this code of practice or Code C, the decision to continue with the interview is at the discretion of the interviewing officer. Where the interviewing officer decides to continue with the interview, the person being interviewed shall be told that the complaint will be brought to the attention of the custody officer at the conclusion of the interview. When the interview is concluded, the interviewing officer must, as soon as practicable, inform the custody officer of the existence and nature of the complaint made.*

4D *In considering whether to caution again after a break, the officer should bear in mind that he may have to satisfy a court that the person understood that he was still under caution when the interview resumed.*

4E *The officer should bear in mind that it may be necessary to satisfy the court that nothing occurred during a break in an interview or between interviews which influenced the suspect's recorded evidence. On the re-commencement of an interview, the officer should consider summarising on the tape or CD the reason for the break and confirming this with the suspect.*

4F *If any part of the recording media breaks or is otherwise damaged during the interview, it should be sealed as a master copy in the presence of the suspect and the interview resumed where it left off. The undamaged part should be copied and the original sealed as a master tape in the suspect's presence, if necessary after the interview. If equipment for copying is not readily available, both parts should be sealed in the suspect's presence and the interview begun again.*

4G *The interviewer should be aware that a decision to continue recording against the wishes of the suspect may be the subject of comment in court.*

5 After the Interview

5.1 The interviewer shall make a note in his or her pocket book of the fact that the interview has taken place and has been recorded, its time, duration and date and the identification number of the master copy of the recording media.

5.2 Where no proceedings follow in respect of the person whose interview was recorded, the recording media must nevertheless be kept securely in accordance with paragraph 6.1 and Note 6A.

Note for Guidance

5A *Any written record of a recorded interview shall be made in accordance with national guidelines approved by the Secretary of State, and with regard to the advice contained in the Manual of Guidance for the preparation, processing and submission of files.*

6 Master copy security

(a) General

6.1 The officer in charge of the police station at which interviews with suspects are recorded shall make arrangements for the master copies to be kept securely and their movements accounted for on the same basis as other material which may be used for evidential purposes, in accordance with force standing orders [See *Note 6A*].

(b) Breaking master copy seal for criminal proceedings

6.2 A police officer has no authority to break the seal on a master copy which is required for criminal trial or appeal proceedings. If it is necessary to gain access to the master copy, the police officer shall arrange for its seal to be broken in the presence of a representative of the Crown Prosecution Service. The defendant or their legal adviser shall be informed and given a reasonable opportunity to be present. If the defendant or their legal representative is present they shall be invited to reseal and sign the master copy. If either refuses or neither is present, this shall be done by the representative of the Crown Prosecution Service. [See Notes 6B and 6C].

(c) Breaking master copy seal: other cases

6.3 The chief officer of police is responsible for establishing arrangements for breaking the seal of the master copy where no criminal proceedings result, or the criminal proceedings, to which the interview relates, have been concluded and it becomes necessary to break the seal. These arrangements should be those which the chief officer considers are reasonably necessary to demonstrate to the person interviewed and any other party who may wish to use or refer to the interview record that the master copy has not been tampered with and that the interview record remains accurate. [See *Note 6D*]

6.4 Subject to paragraph 6.6, a representative of each party must be given a reasonable opportunity to be present when the seal is broken, the master copy copied and re-sealed.

6.5 If one or more of the parties is not present when the master copy seal is broken because they cannot be contacted or refuse to attend or paragraph 6.6 applies, arrangements should be made for an independent person such as a custody visitor, to be present. Alternatively, or as an additional safeguard, arrangement should be made for a film or photographs to be taken of the procedure.

6.6 Paragraph 6.5 does not require a person to be given an opportunity to be present when:
- (a) it is necessary to break the master copy seal for the proper and effective further investigation of the original offence or the investigation of some other offence; and
- (b) the officer in charge of the investigation has reasonable grounds to suspect that allowing an opportunity might prejudice any such an investigation or criminal proceedings which may be brought as a result or endanger any person. [See *Note 6E*]

(d) Documentation

6.7 When the master copy seal is broken, copied and re-sealed, a record must be made of the procedure followed, including the date time and place and persons present.

Notes for Guidance

6A   This section is concerned with the security of the master copy which will have been sealed at the conclusion of the interview. Care should, however, be taken of working copies since their loss or destruction may lead unnecessarily to the need to have access to master copies.

6B   If the master copy has been delivered to the Crown Court for their keeping after committal for trial the Crown Prosecutor will apply to the Chief Clerk of the Crown Court Centre for its release for unsealing by the Crown Prosecutor.

6C *Reference to the Crown Prosecution Service or to the Crown Prosecutor in this part of the code shall be taken to include any other body or person with a statutory responsibility for prosecution for whom the police conduct any recorded interviews.*

6D *The most common reasons for needing access to master copies that are not required for criminal proceedings arise from civil actions and complaints against police and civil actions between individuals arising out of allegations of crime investigated by police.*

6E *Paragraph 6.6 could apply, for example, when one or more of the outcomes or likely outcomes of the investigation might be: (i) the prosecution of one or more of the original suspects, (ii) the prosecution of someone previously not suspected, including someone who was originally a witness; and (iii) any original suspect being treated as a prosecution witness and when premature disclosure of any police action, particularly through contact with any parties involved, could lead to a real risk of compromising the investigation and endangering witnesses.*

Appendix 2.5

Summary of PACE Code of Practice for the Detention, Treatment and Questioning of Persons under s. 41 of, and sch. 8 to, the Terrorism Act 2000 (Code H)

As stated at the start of chapter 11, Code H has been introduced and applies to people in police detention following their arrest under the Terrorism Act 2000, s. 41; it has effect from midnight on 24 July 2006 notwithstanding that the person has been arrested before that time. This has led to a number of revisions to Code C which include the following paragraphs:

- 1.11 making reference to Code H
- 1.12(v)—not used
- 2.6A(a)—not used
- 5.6(b)—amended to remove references to terrorism detainees
- 8A—amended to remove references to terrorism detainees
- 10.1(e)—not used
- 15.8—not used
- 15A—amended to remove references to terrorism detainees
- Annex B para B—not used

Code H is not reproduced within the manual but should be available in cusitdy suites and at police stations. Generally Code H mirrors much of Code C; however in relation to reviews and extensions of detention there are significant changes from the equivalent provisions in PACE Code C owing to the changes made to maximum detention times by the Terrorism Act 2006. These can be found in Code H in section 14.

Section 1—General

This section covers the scope and applicability of the Code (which are, by definition, different from the equivalent provisions of Code C); it also covers the availability of the Code, definitions, applicability to the deaf, blind and speech impaired and the use of reasonable force, and in these respects follows Code C.

Section 2—Custody Records

This section follows Code C. It covers general requirements for making custody records, including the exemption for counter terrorism officers from disclosing their identities on custody records and provisions as to access to custody records by detainees' solicitors and disclosure of those records to them.

Section 3—Initial Action in respect of arrested individuals

Code H broadly follows Code C in respect of detainees' rights and arrangements for exercising them but differs in a number of respects:

(a) the record will indicate that the arrest was under s. 41 as opposed to indicating the offence in respect of which the arrest was made—Note 3G indicates that, where an arrest is made on grounds of sensitive information which cannot be disclosed, the recorded grounds 'may be given in terms of the interpretation of "terrorist"' set out in s. 40(1)(a) or 40(1)(b);

(b) there is a specific provision to the effect that risk assessments do not form part of the custody record and should not be shown to the detainee or their legal representative;

(c) there are provisions relating to the initial steps that may be taken in connection with the identification of suspects.

Section 4—Detainees' Property

This section of Code H includes a simplification of the circumstances in which a custody officer should search a detainee to ascertain what they have in their possession but there is no material change in comparison with Code C.

Section 5—Right not to be Held Incommunicado

The detainee's right to have someone informed of his whereabouts closely follows the equivalent section of Code C but there is much more detailed guidance on visiting rights. A requirement is imposed for custody officers to liaise with the investigation team to ascertain the risks presented by visits. Where visits from relatives etc. present a risk, consideration of more frequent visits from independent visitor schemes is suggested. Visits from official visitors ('official visitors' may include accredited faith representatives and MPs) may be allowed subject to consultation with the officer in charge of the investigation. Note 5B indicates that custody officers should bear in mind the effects of prolonged detention under the Act and consider the health and welfare benefits that visits bring to the health and welfare of detainees who are held for extended periods. However, Note 5G reminds officers that the nature of terrorist investigations means that they need to have 'particular regard to the possibility of suspects attempting to pass information which may be detrimental to public safety, or to an investigation'.

Section 6—Right to Legal Advice

The principal difference from Code C is that there is provision for an authorisation to be given whereby a detainee may only consult a solicitor within sight and hearing of a qualified officer (a uniformed officer of at least the rank of inspector who has no connection with the investigation).

Section 7—Citizens of Independent Commonwealth Countries or Foreign Nationals

Section 7 shows no material change from the equivalent Code C provisions.

Section 8—Conditions of Detention

The main differences from Code C are that there is specific reference to allowing detainees to practise religious observance and to the provision of reading material, including religious texts. Police should consult with representatives of religious communities on provision of facilities for religious observance and handling of religious texts and other articles. The benefits of exercise for detainees, particularly in the cases of prolonged detention, are emphasised. If facilities exist, indoor exercise is to be offered if requested or if outdoor exercise is not practicable. Although the same restrictions on putting a juvenile in a cell apply as under Code C, there is no requirement to include occasions when a juvenile is so confined on the custody record.

Section 9—Care and Treatment of Detained Persons

Section 9 of Code H begins by requiring that, notwithstanding other requirements for medical attention, 'detainees who are held for more than 96 hours must be visited by a healthcare professional at least once every 24 hours'. In all other material respects, the provisions are the same as under Code C.

Section 10—Cautions

Insofar as relevant, the provisions on cautions closely follow those of Code C.

Section 11—Interviews (General)

There are no material differences from Code C under this section. The Code H equivalent is however much shorter, reflecting the fact that not all instances covered by the Code C equivalent are relevant to detention of terrorist suspects

Section 12—Interviews in Police Stations

The only material difference here is set out at para. 12.9:

12.9 During extended periods where no interviews take place, because of the need to gather further evidence or analyse existing evidence, detainees and their legal representative shall be informed that the investigation into the relevant offence remains ongoing. If practicable, the detainee and legal representative should also be made aware in general terms of any reasons for long gaps between interviews. Consideration should be given to allowing visits, more frequent exercise, or for reading or writing materials to be offered. *See paragraph 5.4, section 8* and *Note 12C.*

Note 12C indicates that consideration should be given to the matters referred to in para. 12.9 after a period of over 24 hours without questioning.

Section 13—Interpreters

The requirements for accredited interpreters to be provided for deaf or non-English speakers, for both general custody procedures and interviews are the same as under Code C.

Section 14—Reviews and extensions of detention

This section contains significant changes from the equivalent provisions in PACE Code C (PACE Code C, section 15), owing to the changes made to maximum detention times by the Terrorism Act 2006. It is set out in full below.

14 Reviews and Extensions of Detention

(a) Reviews and Extensions of Detention

14.1   The powers and duties of the review officer are in the Terrorism Act 2000, Schedule 8, Part II. See *Notes 14A* and *14B*. A review officer should carry out his duties at the police station where the detainee is held, and be allowed such access to the detainee as is necessary for him to exercise those duties.

14.2   For the purposes of reviewing a person's detention, no officer shall put specific questions to the detainee:
   • regarding their involvement in any offence; or
   • in respect of any comments they may make:
      — when given the opportunity to make representations; or
      — in response to a decision to keep them in detention or extend the maximum period of detention.

   Such an exchange could constitute an interview as in *paragraph 11.1* and would be subject to the associated safeguards in *section 11* and, in respect of a person who has been charged. See *PACE Code C Section 16.8.*

14.3   If detention is necessary for longer than 48 hours, a police officer of at least superintendent rank, or a Crown Prosecutor may apply for warrants of further detention under the Terrorism Act 2000, Schedule 8, Part III.

14.4   When an application for a warrant of further or extended detention is sought under Paragraph 29 or 36 of Schedule 8, the detained person and their representative must be informed of their rights in respect of the application. These include:
   (a) the right to a written or oral notice of the warrant. See *Note 14G.*
   (b) the right to make oral or written representations to the judicial authority about the application.
   (c) the right to be present and legally represented at the hearing of the application, unless specifically excluded by the judicial authority.
   (d) their right to free legal advice (see section 6 of this Code).

(b) Transfer of Detained Persons to Prison

14.5   Where a warrant is issued which authorises detention beyond a period of 14 days from the time of arrest (or if a person was being detained under TACT Schedule 7, from the time at which the examination under Schedule 7 began), the detainee must be transferred from detention in a police station to detention in a designated prison as soon as is practicable, unless:
   (a) the detainee specifically requests to remain in detention at a police station and that request can be accommodated, or
   (b) there are reasonable grounds to believe that transferring a person to a prison would:
      (i) significantly hinder a terrorism investigation;
      (ii) delay charging of the detainee or his release from custody, or
      (iii) otherwise prevent the investigation from being conducted diligently and expeditiously.

   If any of the grounds in (b)(i) to (iii) above are relied upon, these must be presented to the judicial authority as part of the application for the warrant that would extend detention beyond a period of 14 days from the time of arrest (or if a person was being detained under

TACT Schedule 7, from the time at which the examination under Schedule 7 began). *See Note 14J.*

14.6 If a person remains in detention at a police station under a warrant of further detention as described at section 14.5, they must be transferred to a prison as soon as practicable after the grounds at (b)(i) to (iii) of that section cease to apply.

14.7 Police should maintain an agreement with the National Offender Management Service (NOMS) that stipulates named prisons to which individuals may be transferred under this section. This should be made with regard to ensuring detainees are moved to the most suitable prison for the purposes of the investigation and their welfare, and should include provision for the transfer of male, female and juvenile detainees. Police should ensure that the Governor of a prison to which they intend to transfer a detainee is given reasonable notice of this. Where practicable, this should be no later than the point at which a warrant is applied for that would take the period of detention beyond 14 days.

14.8 Following a detained person's transfer to a designated prison, their detention will be governed by the terms of Schedule 8 and Prison Rules, and this Code of Practice will not apply during any period that the person remains in prison detention. The Code will once more apply if a detained person is transferred back from prison detention to police detention. In order to enable the Governor to arrange for the production of the detainee back into police custody, police should give notice to the governor of the relevant prison as soon as possible of any decision to transfer a detainee from prison back to a police station. Any transfer between a prison and a police station should be conducted by police, and this Code will be applicable during the period of transit. See *Note 14K.* A detainee should only remain in police custody having been transferred back from a prison, for as long as is necessary for the purpose of the investigation.

14.9 The investigating team and custody officer should provide as much information as necessary to enable the relevant prison authorities to provide appropriate facilities to detain an individual. This should include, but not be limited to:

(i) medical assessments
(ii) security and risk assessments
(iii) details of the detained person's legal representatives
(iv) details of any individuals from whom the detained person has requested visits, or who have requested to visit the detained person.

14.10 Where a detainee is to be transferred to prison, the custody officer should inform the detainee's legal adviser beforehand that the transfer is to take place (including the name of the prison). The custody officer should also make all reasonable attempts to inform:

• family or friends who have been informed previously of the detainee's detention; and
• the person who was initially informed of the detainee's detention as at *paragraph 5.1.*

(c) Documentation

14.11 It is the responsibility of the officer who gives any reminders as at *paragraph 14.4*, to ensure that these are noted in the custody record, as well any comments made by the detained person upon being told of those rights.

14.12 The grounds for, and extent of, any delay in conducting a review shall be recorded.

14.13 Any written representations shall be retained.

14.14 A record shall be made as soon as practicable about the outcome of each review or determination whether to extend the maximum detention period without charge or an application for a warrant of further detention or its extension.

14.15 Any decision not to transfer a detained person to a designated prison under paragraph *14.5,* must be recorded, along with the reasons for this decision. If a request under paragraph *14.5(a)* is not accommodated, the reasons for this should also be recorded.

Notes for guidance

14A TACT Schedule 8 Part II sets out the procedures for review of detention up to 48 hours from the time of arrest under TACT section 41 (or if a person was being detained under TACT Schedule 7, from the time at which the examination under Schedule 7 began). These include provisions for the requirement to review detention, postponing a review, grounds for continued detention, designating a review officer, representations, rights of the detained person and keeping a record. The review officer's role ends after a warrant has been issued for extension of detention under Part III of Schedule 8.

14B *Section 24(1) of the Terrorism Act 2006, amended the grounds contained within the 2000 Act on which a review officer may authorise continued detention. Continued detention may be authorised if it is necessary—*

 (a) to obtain relevant evidence whether by questioning him or otherwise

 (b) to preserve relevant evidence

 (c) while awaiting the result of an examination or analysis of relevant evidence

 (d) for the examination or analysis of anything with a view to obtaining relevant evidence

 (e) pending a decision to apply to the Secretary of State for a deportation notice to be served on the detainee, the making of any such application, or the consideration of any such application by the Secretary of State

 (f) pending a decision to charge the detainee with an offence.

14C *Applications for warrants to extend detention beyond 48 hours, may be made for periods of 7 days at a time (initially under TACT Schedule 8 paragraph 29, and extensions thereafter under TACT Schedule 8, paragraph 36), up to a maximum period of 28 days from the time of arrest (or if a person was being detained under TACT Schedule 7, from the time at which the examination under Schedule 7 began). Applications may be made for shorter periods than 7 days, which must be specified. The judicial authority may also substitute a shorter period if he feels a period of 7 days is inappropriate.*

14D *Unless Note 14F applies, applications for warrants that would take the total period of detention up to 14 days or less should be made to a judicial authority, meaning a District Judge (Magistrates' Court) designated by the Lord Chancellor to hear such applications.*

14E *Any application for a warrant which would take the period of detention beyond 14 days from the time of arrest (or if a person was being detained under TACT Schedule 7, from the time at which the examination under Schedule 7 began), must be made to a High Court Judge.*

14F *If an application has been made to a High Court Judge for a warrant which would take detention beyond 14 days, and the High Court Judge instead issues a warrant for a period of time which would not take detention beyond 14 days, further applications for extension of detention must also be made to a High Court Judge, regardless of the period of time to which they refer.*

14G *TACT Schedule 8 paragraph 31 requires a notice to be given to the detained person if a warrant is sought for further detention. This must be provided before the judicial hearing of the application for that warrant and must include:*

 (a) notification that the application for a warrant has been made

 (b) the time at which the application was made

 (c) the time at which the application is to be heard

 (d) the grounds on which further detention is sought.

A notice must also be provided each time an application is made to extend an existing warrant.

14H *An officer applying for an order under TACT Schedule 8 paragraph 34 to withhold specified information on which he intends to rely when applying for a warrant of further detention, may make the application for the order orally or in writing. The most appropriate method of application will depend on the circumstances of the case and the need to ensure fairness to the detainee.*

14I *Where facilities exist, hearings relating to extension of detention under Part III of Schedule 8 may take place using video conferencing facilities provided that the requirements set out in Schedule 8 are still met. However, if the judicial authority requires the detained person to be physically present at any hearing, this should be complied with as soon as practicable. Paragraphs 33(4) to 33(9) of TACT Schedule 8 govern the relevant conduct of hearings.*

14J *Transfer to prison is intended to ensure that individuals who are detained for extended periods of time are held in a place designed for longer periods of detention than police stations. Prison will provide detainees with a greater range of facilities more appropriate to longer detention periods.*

14K *The Code will only apply as is appropriate to the conditions of detention during the period of transit. There is obviously no requirement to provide such things as bed linen or reading materials for the journey between prison and police station.*

General

There are no equivalents to PACE Code C, sections 16 and 17, which cannot apply in the context of a terrorist investigation. The annexes to Code H are in terms which closely follow Code C—changes are only to remove or amend references that are not applicable to terrorism detention.

Index

A